Date: 9/2/21

780.9 MUS V.2
Music around the world.
a global encyclopedia /

PALM BEACH COUNTY
LIBRARY SYSTEM
3650 SUMMIT BLVD.
WEST PALM BEACH, FL 33406

Music around the World

Music around the World

A Global Encyclopedia

VOLUME 2: H–P

Andrew R. Martin and
Matthew Mihalka, Editors

ABC-CLIO®

An Imprint of ABC-CLIO, LLC
Santa Barbara, California • Denver, Colorado

Copyright © 2020 by ABC-CLIO, LLC

All rights reserved. No part of this publication may be reproduced, stored in a retrieval system, or transmitted, in any form or by any means, electronic, mechanical, photocopying, recording, or otherwise, except for the inclusion of brief quotations in a review, without prior permission in writing from the publisher.

Library of Congress Cataloging-in-Publication Data

Names: Martin, Andrew R., editor. | Mihalka, Matthew, editor.
Title: Music around the world : a global encyclopedia / Andrew R. Martin and Matthew Mihalka, editors.
Description: 1st edition. | Santa Barbara : ABC-CLIO, 2020. | Includes bibliographical references and index.
Identifiers: LCCN 2019042635 (print) | LCCN 2019042636 (ebook) | ISBN 9781440846366 (v. 1 ; cloth) | ISBN 9781440846373 (v. 2 ; cloth) | ISBN 9781440846380 (v. 3 ; cloth) | ISBN 9781610694988 (cloth) | ISBN 9781610694995 (ebook)
Subjects: LCSH: World music—Encyclopedias.
Classification: LCC ML100 .M894 2020 (print) | LCC ML100 (ebook) | DDC 780.9—dc23
LC record available at https://lccn.loc.gov/2019042635
LC ebook record available at https://lccn.loc.gov/2019042636

ISBN: 978-1-61069-498-8 (set)
    978-1-4408-4636-6 (vol. 1)
    978-1-4408-4637-3 (vol. 2)
    978-1-4408-4638-0 (vol. 3)
    978-1-61069-499-5 (ebook)

24 23 22 21 20   1 2 3 4 5

This book is also available as an eBook.

ABC-CLIO
An Imprint of ABC-CLIO, LLC

ABC-CLIO, LLC
147 Castilian Drive
Santa Barbara, California 93117
www.abc-clio.com

This book is printed on acid-free paper ∞

Manufactured in the United States of America

Contents

Alphabetical List of Entries   vii

Preface   xiii

Introduction   xv

Entries: A–Z   1

About the Editors   965

Contributors   967

Index   973

Alphabetical List of Entries

VOLUME ONE
Acadian Music
Accordion (Americas)
Accordion, Types of
Adé, "King" Sunny
African Spirituals
Afrobeat (Afropop)
Afro-Cuban Jazz
Ahmad, Fadzil
Amadinda
Amish Hymns (*Ausbund*, *Gesangbuch*)
Andalusian Music
Andean Region, Music of the
Arab Classical Music
Armenian Music
Armstrong, Louis
Ashkenazi Jews, Music of
Astatke, Mulatu
Austro-German Dances
Bağlama
Bagpipes
Bandoneón
Banjo
Bariu, Laver
Bartók, Béla
Bashir Brothers (Munir and Jamil)
Basque, Music of the
Batá Drums
Beatles, The
Bebop
Bedouin Music
Bélé
Belly Dance
Berimbau
Björk
Bluegrass
Blues
Bol
Bolivia, Music of
Bollywood Music
Bomba, Ecuador
Bomba, Puerto Rico
Bones (Britain and Ireland)
Brazil, Music of
Buena Vista Social Club
Bunraku
Cajun Music
Calypso
Candomblé
Cantopop
Caribbean Art Music
Carmody, Kevin Daniel "Kev"
Carnival, Music of
Carter Family, The

Čechomor
Celtic Music
Chamarrita
Chanson (Urban/Modern)
Chinese Pop
Chopi People, Music of the
Chutney
Chutney Soca
Classical Music, European
Claves and Clave Rhythm
Cohan, George M.
Colometry/Colometric
Coltrane, John
Concerto
Congo Square
Conjunto
Conjunto (Norteños)
Corrido
Cossacks, Music of
Country Music
Cretan Lyra
Cruz, Celia
Cuatro
Cumbia
Dancehall
Darbuka
Dastgah
Davis, Miles (Dewey, III)
Densmore, Frances
Dhol
Dhrupad
Didgeridoo
Dixieland
Djembe
Dmitri Pokrovsky Ensemble
Dorsey, Thomas A.
Duduk
Dulcimer
Dylan, Bob
Eastern Woodland Native American Music
Emmett, Dan (Daniel Decatur)
Enka Music
Erhu
Eurovision Song Contest
Fado
Fairuz
Fiddle
Field Hollers
Flamenco Music
Folkways Records
Foster, Stephen Collins
French Folk Dances
Fujara
Funk
Gagaku
Gamelan Orchestra (Balinese)
Gamelan Orchestra (Javanese)
Ganga
Ganga Singing
Gender Wayang
Gimbri
Gospel Music
Greek Popular Music
Gregorian Chant
Griot
Guitarrón Mexicano
Gumba
Guoyue
Guthrie, Woody
Guzheng
Gyil

Alphabetical List of Entries

VOLUME TWO

Handy, W. C.
Harana and Kundiman
Hardanger Fiddle (Hardingfele)
Harmonium
Hawaii, Music of
Highlife
Hōgaku
Hornbostel, Erich Moritz von
Huayno
Huqin
Icelandic Ballads
Indian Folk Songs
Indonesian Pop Music
Iranian Classical Music
Irish American Vocal Music
Irish Dance Music
Irish Step Dancing
Italian Folk Music (Various Regions)
Jackson, Mahalia
Jali
Janggu
Japan, Music of
Jazz
Jehan, Noor
Jingju (Beijing Opera)
Johnson, Robert
Joik
Joplin, Scott
J-Pop
Kabuki
Kalthoum, Umm
Kamancheh
Karnatic Music
Kayokyoku
Kebyar
Kecak
Kendang
Khaled, Cheb
Khan, Nusrat Fateh Ali
Khayal
Khene
Kidjo, Angelique
Klezmer
Kodály, Zoltán
Kora
Koto
K-Pop (Korean Pop)
Kulintang
Kuti, Fela
Ladysmith Black Mambazo
Ländler
Launeddas
Lead Belly
Lenya, Lotte
Lithuanian Music
Lomax, Alan and John
Madrigal
Makam
Makeba, Miriam
Malay Music
Malhūn
Malouf
Mambo
Mande Music
Manu Chao
Mariachi
Marimba
Marley, Bob
Marshall Islands, Music of
Masakela, Hugh
Mbalax
Mbila
Mbube

Alphabetical List of Entries

McPhee, Colin
Medieval Secular Song
Mento
Merengue
Mestizo Music
Mexican Regional Music
Mikagura
Min'yô
Moravian Music
Morin Khuur
Mridangam
Musafir
Musicals
Native American Church Music
Native American Flute
Native American Music
Native American Popular Music
Navajo, Music of
Ney
Nisiotika
Nô Theater
Nongak
Nordic Jazz
North Korea, Music of
Norwegian Folk Music
Nueva Canción
Nyckelharpa
Olatunji, Babatunde
Opera
Original Dixieland Jazz Band
Ottoman Classical Music
Oud
Owiyo, Suzanna
Pakistan, Music of
Pansori (P'ansori)
Parker, Charlie
Pashto Music

Philippines, Music of the
Piazzolla, Astor
Pimba
Pipa
Piphat
Polish National Dances
Polka
Polynesia, Music of
Polynesian Hymns
Presley, Elvis
Psaltery
Puente, Tito

VOLUME THREE

Qānūn
Qin (Guqin)
Qraqeb
Quadrille
Quelbe
Race Records
Raga
Ragtime
Rai
Rainey, Ma
Rakha, Alla
Rancho Folclórico
Rap/Hip-Hop
Rap/Hip-Hop in Africa and the Middle East
Rara
Rebab
Redzepova, Esma
Reggae
Reggaetón
Rímur
Riq
Rock and Roll

Alphabetical List of Entries

Rodgers, Jimmie
Rodrigues, Amália
Romani Music
Rumba
Runo Song
Russian Orthodox Church Music
Salsa
Samba Instruments
Samba Music
Sanjo
Schlager
Schottische
Schrammelmusik
Scotch Snap
Seeger, Peter
Sephardic Music
Shajarian, Mohammed-Reza
Shakuhachi
Shamanic Music in Mongolia and Inner Asia
Shamisen
Shankar, Ravi
Shape-Note Singing
Shômyô
Singspiel
Sitar
Ska
Smith, Bessie
Soca
Soul
Steel Guitar
Steelpan
Sufism, Music of
Swing
Symphonic Poem
Symphony
Tabla
Tagore, Rabindranath
Taiko
Taiwanese Opera
Taiwanese Traditional and Popular Music
Tala
Tamboo Bamboo
Tango
Taqsīm
Tar
Tassa Drumming
Tejano Music
Thumri
Tibetan Buddhist Chant
Tibetan Singing Bowls
Tin Pan Alley
Tin/Pennywhistle
Tombak
Touré, Ali Farka
Turbo-Folk
Tuvan Popular Bands
Tuvan Throat Singing
Ukulele
Vaudeville
Veena
Villa-Lobos, Heitor
Virginia Minstrels
Vocables
Waltz
Wayang Kulit
Xalam
Yodeling
Yuman Music
Zajal
Ziegfeld, Florenz, Jr.
Zither
Zouk
Zydeco

H

Handy, W. C. (1873–1958)

Widely hailed as the "Father of the Blues"—to the disdain of many musicologists and African American scholars—William Christopher Handy rose to prominence from the post-Reconstruction American South as a musician, bandleader, composer, author, and publisher, securing for blues music a position of lasting significance in the American mainstream and throughout the world today. Born in Florence, Alabama, on November 17, 1873, in a log cabin built by his grandfather, an African Methodist Episcopal (AME) preacher, Handy became musically inclined during his formative years, but received no encouragement from his parents. Upon acquiring a guitar with money he had dutifully saved, Handy was rebuked by his father, who considered musical instruments tools of the devil. Forced to return the guitar, Handy was instead enrolled in organ lessons, which were soon abandoned. Taking up the cornet, Handy played in a band as a teenager unbeknownst to his parents.

Various experiences prefaced and influenced Handy's career. Having earned a degree in 1892 from present-day Alabama Agricultural & Mechanical University, Handy was unable to earn a living teaching in Birmingham schools and turned temporarily to industrial work in Bessemer. During this time, he organized a string orchestra and taught musicians how to read shape notes before forming the Lauzetta Quartet. With lofty ambitions, the group traveled to Chicago and later to St. Louis, but never achieved notable success. Upon the group's disbandment, Handy left Alabama for Evansville, Indiana, where he joined a popular regional band. In 1893, Handy played cornet at the World's Columbian Exposition (Chicago World's Fair), an event to which the Lauzetta Quartet had traveled the year before only to discover that it had been postponed.

Though Handy experienced the woes of a struggling musician, he stubbornly persisted. As news of his musical prowess spread, Handy was invited to Henderson, Kentucky, where he was transformed "from a hobo and a member of a road gang to a professional musician" (Handy, 1941, p. 32). While performing at a barbecue in Henderson, Handy met Elizabeth Virginia Price, who would eventually become his first wife and bear his six children. Learning from the director of a local German singing society, Handy immersed himself in music and honed his skills.

Relocating to Chicago in 1896 to join Mahara's Minstrels proved to be crucial for Handy, who described the move as "the big moment that was presently to shape my course in life" (Handy, 1941, p. 32). Handy toured with the Minstrels from 1896 to 1900, performing in Chicago as well as Texas, Oklahoma, several southeastern states, and as far south as Cuba, earning a salary of six dollars per week. Upon their return from Havana, the group performed in northeast Alabama, where

Musician and composer W. C. Handy was an important figure in the popularization of blues music. (Michael Ochs Archives/Getty Images)

Handy's father, once adamantly opposed to show business vocations, embraced his son's performing for the first time. The road-weary Handy and his wife decided to remain with relatives in his hometown of Florence. Alabama A&M President William Hooper Councill soon offered Handy a music teaching position, and Handy taught at the college from 1900 to 1902. Feeling underpaid and disenchanted with the college's emphasis on European classical music, Handy rejoined Mahara's Minstrels and began directing a band organized by Clarksdale, Mississippi's "colored" Knights of Pythias.

In 1903, the nine-hour delay of a train in Tutwiler, Mississippi, proved to be a blessing in disguise for Handy, whose epiphany on the station platform was triggered by the song of an itinerant singer. Handy later recounted: "A lean, loose-jointed Negro had commenced plunking a guitar beside me while I slept. His clothes were rags; his feet peeped out of his shoes. His face had on it some of the sadness of the ages. As he played, he pressed a knife on the strings of the guitar in a manner popularized by Hawaiian guitarists who used steel bars. The effect was unforgettable. His song, too, struck me instantly" (Handy, 1941, p. 74).

The profound impact of his encounter with the bluesman prompted Handy to examine this distinct but variable music, which was rooted in enduring folk songs, field hollers, and spirituals, and encompassed the ethos of a people whose centuries of sacrifice, hardship, and heartbreak had found expression in song. Interestingly, when Handy received that first exposure to blues, "it may well have been in existence in a recognizable form for as long as 30 years." With widespread distribution throughout the American South, various forms of blues were well-established by the early 1870s. Exploring the songs from the vantage point of a developing songwriter, Handy discovered that blues "consisted of simple declarations expressed usually in three lines and set to a kind of earth-born music that was familiar throughout the Southland" (Handy, 1941, p. 75).

A move to Memphis in 1909 further contributed to Handy's creative output. Amid the vibrancy of the Beale Avenue nightclubs, Handy performed and composed in earnest. Asked to write a campaign song to elect E. H. "Boss" Crump mayor of Memphis, Handy accepted, but later rewrote the song, which he named "Memphis Blues." Published in 1912, it was his first big hit. While it is arguably not a true blues song, Handy's success with "Memphis Blues" precipitated the era in the 1920s during which female blues pioneers—largely former vaudeville performers such as Bessie Smith, Ma Rainey, and Ida Cox, and their respective piano accompanists—would precede the commercial success of the Delta guitarists with whom blues is primarily associated today. Though its structure and lyrical content can be debated by blues purists, "Memphis Blues" most certainly "inspired other composers to pen 'blues' songs, including Perry Bradford, who wrote 'Crazy Blues' for singer Mamie Smith" (Santelli, 2001, p. 191).

In partnership with businessman Harry H. Pace (1884–1943), Handy began his music publishing venture in 1912. Eager to advance in the world of music publishing, Pace and Handy moved their office in 1917 to the Gaiety Building on New York's Times Square, where "Beale Street Blues" (which would prompt the renaming of Memphis's Beale Avenue) and the smash hit "St. Louis Blues" were published by the year's end. Irked at the initial lack of interest in his music by black performers, Handy found that white artists, including the Original Dixieland Jazz Band, were among his earliest constituency. In addition to his own compositions, Pace and Handy published songs by other writers, including "Shake, Rattle and Roll." Although Mamie Smith recorded "That Thing Called Love" and "You Can't Keep a Good Man Down" from the Handy catalogue in 1920, it was her release of Bradford's "Crazy Blues," the first blues recording, that ably demonstrated the marketability of "race" records (phonographic recordings by African American performers). As sound recordings replaced sheet music as the primary means through which blues was marketed, Handy and other publishers could either face inevitable decline or adapt to the changing times. Handy saw his sheet music sales plummet, and his partnership with Pace ended amicably in 1920. Continuing with his music publishing, Handy started a record company in response to the reception of "Crazy Blues" and other blues recordings, but his record label proved unprofitable.

While Handy can neither be credited as the inventor of blues nor overlooked for his pivotal role in giving blues its commercially viable, contemporary form, historians and critics have been "justifiably annoyed at the way he was billed as 'the father of the blues.'" Still, his "success with 'St. Louis Blues' and other hits made his sheet music company on Broadway perhaps the largest black-owned business throughout the 1920s and early 1930s in New York City, and he was the foremost African American competitor there among the prolific and mostly white song composers and sheet music marketers whose offices were known collectively as Tin Pan Alley" (Robertson, 2009, p. 15).

On March 28, 1958, Handy succumbed to pneumonia in a New York hospital. Reportedly, some 25,000 mourners attended his funeral at Harlem's historic Abyssinian Baptist Church, and an additional 150,000 people congregated along the street to pay homage. It was also in 1958 that *St. Louis Blues*, the motion picture chronicling his life, was released. The film starred Nat "King" Cole, Pearl Bailey, Mahalia Jackson, Ruby Dee, Cab Calloway, Ella Fitzgerald, and Eartha Kitt.

The songs of W. C. Handy have been recorded by numerous artists, including Bessie Smith, Louis Armstrong, Bing Crosby, Jelly Roll Morton, Billie Holiday, Fletcher Henderson, Alberta Hunter, Ella Fitzgerald, Etta James, Lena Horne, Les Paul, Doc Watson, Chuck Berry, Bob Wills, Chet Atkins, and Guy Lombardo. His songs continue to be recorded today by artists from a variety of genres. In addition to performing, writing, and publishing music, Handy authored or edited five books.

Greg Freeman

See also: African Spirituals; Armstrong, Louis; Blues; Field Hollers; Jackson, Mahalia; Jazz; Original Dixieland Jazz Band; Race Records; Rainey, Ma; Smith, Bessie; Tin Pan Alley; Vaudeville

Further Reading

Cook, Bruce. 1973. *Listen to the Blues.* New York: Charles Scribner's Sons.

Handy, W. C. 1941. *Father of the Blues: An Autobiography.* New York: Collier Books.

Robertson, David. 2009. *W. C. Handy: The Life and Times of the Man Who Made the Blues.* New York: Alfred A. Knopf.

Santelli, Robert. 2001. *The Big Book of Blues: A Biographical Encyclopedia.* New York: Penguin Books.

Wyman, Bill. 2001. *Bill Wyman's Blues Odyssey: A Journey to Music's Heart & Soul.* New York: Dorling Kindersley.

Harana and Kundiman

Comprising a large repertoire in the Philippines, *harana* (from the Spanish *jarana*, "serenade") is the umbrella term for Tagalog courtship serenades. A full harana consists of a series of courtship songs, accompanied by acoustic guitar. The *pananapatan* (also *pagtawag* or *pagpapakilala*) is sung at a young lady's closed window (this same term is also used at Christmas to refer to caroling in groups). After a second song, she opens the window and invites the serenaders into the house. They sing a *pasasalamat* (song of thanks), then a *pagtumbok* and *paghiling*, which request that the young lady respond with a song. Then a series of songs is exchanged between the young lady and the serenaders. When the serenaders leave, they sing a *pamamaalam*. The texts of these songs follow the structure of traditional Tagalog poetry (*plosa*), consisting of quatrains of seven-syllable lines.

Kundiman, lyrical triple-meter love songs popular in the late 1800s, evolved from pre-Christian courtship songs (*komintang*) of the Tagalog into concert songs with smoothly flowing melodies, accompanied by piano. They usually begin in a minor key, with the second half (answering the first) shifting to major. Both sections are usually repeated, and the melody of the second part may be sung or played instrumentally. The lyrics usually portray the pleadings of a lover willing to sacrifice all on behalf of his beloved.

Early kundiman were a staple of Tagalog folk *haranistas* in the early Spanish colonial period. The Spanish *zarzuela* promoted the harana and the development of the indigenous Kundiman in the Tagalog provinces. Kundiman has also served as a vehicle to disguise patriotic sentiments: in their long struggle against an oppressive Spanish regime, Filipinos saw it as a tool that would ultimately unite revolutionaries to wage war during the Spanish-American War. "Jocelynang Baliwag" (1896), though dedicated to a real woman, incited patriotic fervor. "Bayan Ko" (My Homeland) is a 1928 kundiman with lyrics by Jose Corazon de Jesus and music by Constancio de Guzman, composed to protest American colonial rule in the mid-century and repurposed by rock singer Freddie Aguilar for Cory Aquino's 1986 campaign. It was sung during every protest during the martial law. Aguilar's "Katarungang" (Justice) became an anti-Marcos protest song.

Tagalog *sarswela* (zarzuela) composer Bonifacio Abdon (1876–1944) first combined native tunes with European elements. His most famous piece is "Magandang Diwata" (Beautiful maiden), a patriotic song that quotes from the folk kundiman "Awit Ng Pulubi" and "Jocelynang Baliwag." Dr. Francisco Santiago (1889–1938) brought the kundiman to the concert stage: his "Pakiusap" and "Anak-Dalita" became favorites of the celebrated Italian soprano Amelia Galli-Curci, who sang them on international recital tours.

The Spanish monarch King Alfonso XIII (1886–1941) requested visiting sopranos to perform kundiman in the royal court throughout the 1920s. Composer Nicanor Abelardo (1893–1934), on returning from his studies at the Chicago Musical College (United States) in 1931, expanded the form's harmonic vocabulary beyond tonic-dominant relationships ("Nasaan Ka, Irog?") and combined the old komintang form ("Mutya ng Pasig") with narrative poetry. He taught composition at the University of the Philippines Conservatory of Music, advocating for the composition of indigenous art songs.

Kundiman with modern instrumentation (*rondalla* [plucked string ensemble] consisting of Spanish guitar, acoustic bass, and sometimes violin) have featured in the repertoire of many Filipino entertainers, including Diomedes Naturan's "Three Dahlias" (1930s), opera singer Silvia La Torre (1933, nicknamed "Reyna ng Kundiman/Queen of Kundiman"), Pilita Corrales ("Asia's Queen of Songs"), rock singer Freddie Aguilar ("Anak" and the political anthem "Bayan Ko"), and Ruben Tagalog (1922–1989, nicknamed "Hari ng Kundiman/King of kundiman").

Laura Stanfield Prichard

See also: Philippines, Music of the

Further Reading

Maceda, José. 1971. "Means of Preservation and Diffusion of Traditional Music: The Philippine Situation." *Asian Music* 2(1), 14–17.

Montano de la Cruz, Edna. 2003. "Unit 3, Lesson 2: The Fascinating World of Music." In *The New Dimensions in Learning English*, 232–243. Manila, The Philippines: Rex Book Store Press.

Rodell, Paul. 2002. *Culture and Customs of the Philippines*. Westport, CT: Greenwood Press.

Santiago, Francisco. 1957. *The Development of Music in the Philippines*. Quezon City: University of the Philippines.

Hardanger Fiddle (Hardingfele)

The Hardanger fiddle is an iconic folk string instrument from Norway. As a member of the string family, it closely resembles the construction of a traditional European violin in size and construction, but its additional layer of sympathetic (freely vibrating) strings give the Hardanger fiddle a distinct timbre (sound color), the sound of which has become synonymous with Norwegian musical identity. Since its creation, a wide array of composers has been drawn to the Hardanger fiddle's vibrant resonance, as well as the folklore that surrounds this unique instrument.

The earliest known form of the Hardanger fiddle dates back to the mid-17th century. Its name is most likely derived from the Hardanger fjord (a steep cut in the mountainous terrain formed by moving glaciers) of Norway. Its construction includes a wood frame, similar to a violin, with a hollow resonating chamber. Very often, the wood case is ornately decorated with paintings, pen-and-ink drawings, or even gemstones. Yet the most unique aspect of the fiddle is its double set of strings, something entirely foreign to other instruments in the violin family. This sympathetic set vibrates below the four upper strings, which the player activates by bowing or plucking with the fingers. Unlike the common European violin, the Hardanger fiddle neck is comparatively wider and shorter to accommodate the extra group of pegs to which these sympathetic strings are attached. As a result of the natural vibrations that occur when the performer bows or plucks the upper strings, the lower set of strings resonates with sounding pitches of an interval of a fourth or fifth lower (often referred to as "drones"). Whereas early versions varied between three and six primary strings, modern fiddles now use the standard set of four. These qualities allow the performer to play polyphonic melodies (simultaneous melodic lines)—a hallmark of the instrument and its music.

The unique construction of the Hardanger fiddle also allows for multiple tunings and playing techniques that are not associated with other forms of the fiddle. Depending on the particular mode or scale of the folk song that is being played, the Hardanger fiddle can adopt a great variety of different tunings of its four strings. In addition, both sets of strings can be tuned to different intervals, thereby producing a wider variety of sounds than standard violins. Variations in tuning systems are also contingent upon the particular region from which the performers originate, as folk music differs greatly according to the specific subcultures that traditionally inhabited Norway.

Taken together, the features created by the combination of strings and tunings provide for an equally unique technique of playing. The relatively flat bridge allows players to bow on two or more strings at once (known as "double stops"), thus producing a percussive sound that is favorable for certain folk songs and dances. In addition, performers may use special ornaments to decorate melodies that can be executed through frequent bow changes, which highlight the complex rhythms of Norwegian folk music.

The uses of the Hardanger fiddle vary widely and range from the performance of folk songs/dances to more modern orchestral scores. It has also been employed in a variety of venues, from public competitions and festivals to more private fiddle clubs and domestic settings. It is within the category of folk songs and dances, however, for which the instrument was first employed in the history of Norway. Regions primarily in the Southern and Western parts of the country, such as Telemark, Hallingdal, and Valdres, all exhibit different cultures and customs. These distinctive regions have thereby given birth to an equally vibrant and eclectic body of folk music. This instrumental dance music is referred to as *slåtter*, and includes categories such as the *springar* (a couple's dance in 3/4 time), *halling* (a lively dance in duple meter), and the *gangar* (a walking dance often in duple meter).

Differences in tempo, mood, and rhythmic accents all contribute to the diversity of the folk music for which the instrument has traditionally been employed.

The popularity of the Hardanger fiddle expanded throughout the course of the 19th century as many prominent musicians began to employ it within different musical styles, thus bridging the spheres of folk and high art. Ole Bull (1810–1880) was among the first Norwegian figures to spread the iconic sounds of the Hardanger fiddle across the Western hemisphere. His career as a virtuoso string player, coupled with his love of folk music, fueled the appeal of Norwegian nationalism throughout the Scandinavian peninsula. Bull's frequent concert tours, which stretched from Germany to the United States, helped to cement the Hardanger fiddle as a unique symbol of Norway. In addition, Norwegian composers such as Edvard Grieg (1843–1907) turned to the Hardanger fiddle as a source of artistic inspiration. Grieg famously transcribed the sounds of the fiddle into arrangements for the piano, thus helping to bring its unique sound into more genres. For instance, his famous *Slåtter*, op. 72, for solo piano is based upon traditional fiddle tunes from the Telemark region of Norway. Grieg's arrangement is particularly notable not simply for its ability to bring the traits of the fiddle to new audiences, but also for its potential to engage that sound in a modern style marked by harmonic complexity.

Today, the Hardanger fiddle is frequently used in folk music competitions, as it has been since the 17th century. Its role as an important part of Norwegian folklore has been extended to the modern medium of the motion picture, as evidenced in soundtracks of films such as *The Lord of the Rings* and *Fargo*. Most importantly, the ongoing traditions and transformations of Norwegian folk music draw a distinct parallel to the Norwegian cultures they represent. The Hardanger fiddle thereby stands apart from other folk instruments for its distinctive and wide-ranging expressive capabilities, linking communities that contribute to the diverse cultural landscape of Norway, both past and present.

Ryan R. Weber

See also: Fiddle; Nordic Jazz; Norwegian Folk Music

Further Reading

Cai, Camilla, and Einar Haugen. 1992. *Ole Bull: Norway's Romantic Musician and Cosmopolitan Patriot*. Madison: University of Wisconsin Press.

Goertzen, Chris. 1997. *Fiddling for Norway: Revival and Identity*. Chicago: The University of Chicago Press.

Grimley, Daniel. 2006. *Edvard Grieg: Music, Landscape, and Norwegian Identity*. Woodbridge, UK: Boydell Press.

Hardanger Fiddle Association of America. 2011. "What Is a Hardanger Fiddle?" http://www.hfaa.org/Home/about-the-hardanger-fiddle.

Hopkins, Pandora. 1986. *Aural Thinking in Norway: Performance and Communication with the Hardingfele*. New York: Human Sciences Press.

Harmonium

The harmonium is a portable organ-like keyboard instrument with bellows that are pumped using the hands or feet. The hand-pumped harmonium is used widely throughout South Asia in most genres, with the exception of South Indian *karnataka* classical music. Unlike most instruments of South Asia, its scale is tempered and no microtones are possible. This instrument was brought to India by Christian missionaries. Although the harmonium had its origins in the medieval period and fell out of favor in Europe and the United States after its popularity peaked in the late 19th century, it has found a new home in the musical world of the Indian subcontinent, albeit with some controversy.

Danish professor Christian Gottlieb Kratzenstein (1723–1795) created the first free-reed organ in 1780. It was improved by French inventor Alexandre Debain (1809–1877). He named it "harmoni" and patented it in 1842. French reed organs, both foot-pump and hand-pumped types, were brought to colonies throughout the world in the mid-19th through early 20th centuries. They were preferred over the piano because they were more portable and less susceptible to the weather. Missionaries used the instrument to accompany hymn singing. Although the instruments were initially bought by mail order, by 1875 Dwarknath Ghose of Kolkatta was manufacturing harmoniums. He made the instrument more durable, with a simpler mechanism than the French models, and he added drone stops for use in Hindustani classical music.

The harmonium with the hand pump has become popular throughout the Indian subcontinent, and it is used in nearly every type of music in North India. During the nationalistic period in India from 1940–1971, the harmonium was banned from the national radio, because of its associations with the British colonizers. However, when the ban was lifted, musicians continued to play this practical and rewarding instrument.

There two kinds of harmonium—single reed and double reed—and most span three to three and one-half octaves in range. There are 22 microtones called *sruti* in Indian music theory, and most solo instruments in the Indian subcontinent are capable of creating ornaments with subtle microtones. However, the harmonium is usually limited to Western-tempered tuning with no microtones (though there have been some attempts to create harmoniums that play quarter-tones). The lack of microtones and the tempered tuning are the main reasons that people criticize use of the harmonium in classical Indian musical performance.

Despite these limitations, there are several reasons for its popularity. The instrument is relatively inexpensive, portable, and easy to play. Singers can accompany themselves and the instrument provides a melodic guide. The drone can replace the *tampura* of Indian performance practice and it provides the drone in a practice setting. Some additional benefits of the instrument, according to harmonium performer Kedar Naphade, are: sustained sound, support for vocalists to place scale degrees (*swara*), and the ability to play crisp *taans* (quick runs as part of improvisation). Many composers use the harmonium when composing original songs. The harmonium is the instrument most commonly found in Indian homes. Educators also find it convenient when teaching group vocal classes.

Harmoniums were first made on a small scale in India starting in 1925, and by the 1940s were being made on a large scale. One of the early harmonium makers in the 1940s was Sri S. P. Bhagat of Mumbai, whose harmoniums were played by the major performers. The principal cities for harmonium production are Mumbai,

Delhi, and Kolkatta. Kolkatta specializes in manufacturing scale-change transposing harmoniums, which feature a switch that transposes all pitches. This allows the player to transpose quickly to suit a singer's vocal range. The sruti harmonium adds quarter tones, attempting to emulate the ancient 22-note sruti scales. Harmoniums are manufactured widely in South Asia using a variety of types of wood. Most of the reeds are made in Palitana in Gujarat, but imported German reeds are used for high-end instruments.

Most performers play with the dominant hand while pumping the bellows with the opposite hand. Because South Asian music is generally monophonic, the melodies can be played with one hand. Foot-pump organs are more popular in Europe because they free both hands for playing harmony; in addition, European musicians tend to sit in a chair and pump with the feet. The foot pump is not practical in South Asia, as performers almost always perform while sitting on the floor, with the harmonium directly in front. However, in Qawwali Islamic devotional chanting style and some folk styles, one side of the instrument rests on one leg with the rest of the instrument resting on the floor. Street musicians or demonstrators sometimes use a strap or scarf around the shoulders to play the instrument while standing and walking on the street.

The main parts of the harmonium are: the bellows, which force air through the instrument; the reeds, which adjust the sound and dynamic level; drone stops (which create a constant sound of a single note); and coupler (on a double harmonium, the same key one octave lower will be played), along with one or two handles to carry the instrument. The reed area is covered by a piece of wood that is carved into a filigree pattern to allow lower frequencies to pass, while muting the higher frequencies. Harmoniums can take the form of a box with a handle on each side for carrying, or a suitcase-style portable version with one handle.

Harmonium notation uses Indian solfége syllables called *sargam*. In ascending order, they are: *sa-re-ga-ma-pa-dha-ni-sa*. There are 12 chromatic notes indicated with sharps, *bikrito suwara*, and flats, *komol*. Octaves are differentiated by the following terms: *udara* is the name for the lower octave, *mudara* is the middle, and *tara* is high. Fingering is notated with special symbols.

Harmonium is extremely versatile as an accompanying instrument for vocalists. Some prominent harmonium players in India who perform as accompanists are Pandit P. Madhukar, Pandit R. K. Bijapure, Pandit Manohar Chimote, Pandit Tulsidas Borkar, Dr. Sudhanshu Kulkarni, Dr. Ravindra Katoti, Ajay Joglekar, and Vyasmurthy Katti; in Bangladesh, Nakul Kumar Biswas is well known. Solo harmoniumists include Pandit Muneshwar Dayal, Pandit Montu Banerjee, and Pandit Pamabhusan Jnan Prakash. One of the most important pioneers of the solo style is Pandit Tulsidas Borkar of Mumbai. More recently, Dr. Arawind Thatte from Pune has sought to create a separate identity for the harmonium as a solo instrument, and the practice of solo performance is increasing.

The harmonium was banned from All India Radio from 1940 to 1971 because of its associations with British colonialism. When the instrument was banned, a large group of harmonium players staged a "funeral" for the instrument in front of the radio headquarters at Delhi, where they buried 11 instruments in a pre-made "grave." Although other instruments accompanied singers on the radio during this time, the harmonium was still widely used in live performances. Starting in 1971, the ban was partially lifted; singers now may accompany themselves with the harmonium, but it is not allowed as a solo instrument, with the exception of use in children's programming. Furthermore, there are no full-time harmonium players on staff at All Indian Radio. Despite these restrictions, it is played in a wide range of musical styles in live performance and on broadcasts.

Modern Indian musical educational institutions adopted the harmonium to teach singing and music to large classes of students. The harmonium is convenient for teaching tunes, and students learn with written notation in sargam. This is in marked contrast to the traditional aural transmission methods. Overall, the harmonium has had a strong democratizing effect on Indian music, overturning many of the traditional social class and caste associations with various instruments in classical music. The instrument has become a staple in the homes of music lovers in the Indian subcontinent, and it is likely to maintain its popularity into the future.

Abdur Rahman

See also: Dhrupad; Rakha, Alla; Sitar; Tabla

Further Reading

Courtney, David. 2016. "Harmonium." http://www.chandrakantha.com/articles/indian_music/harmonium.html.

Dastidar, Nitya Priya Ghosh. 1979. *Stepping Stone to Indian Music.* Calcutta: Sri J.B. Ghosh Dastidar.

Naphade, Kedar. 2008. "A Perspective on the Indian Harmonium." November 27. http://www.kedarnaphade.com/thanksgivingday.html.

Rahaim, Matt. 2011. "That Ban(e) of Indian Music: Hearing Politics in the Harmonium." *The Journal of Asian Studies* 70(3) (August), 657–682.

Hawaii, Music of

The Hawaiian archipelago (formerly called the Sandwich Islands) became an American state in 1959. Now known for its cultural pluralism, Hawaii was the northernmost group of islands settled by Polynesians and had a flourishing Polynesian culture when discovered by Captain Cook in 1778. There has been a strong revival of interest in traditional Hawaiian styles of music and dance, and these now flourish alongside Western-influenced art and popular music.

There is no word in the Hawaiian language that translates generally as *music*, but a diverse vocabulary exists to describe rhythms, instruments, styles, and elements of voice production. Traditional Hawaiian music and dance were functional, used to express praise; communicate genealogy and mythology; and accompany games, festivals, and other secular events.

Hawaiian folk music includes several varieties of chanting (*mele*) and music meant for highly ritualized dance (*hula*). Mele is traditionally accompanied by an *ipu* (a double gourd, struck with the hand or on a mat) and/or a *pahu* (sharkskin-covered drum). The term "mele" originally referred to any kind of poetic expression, but now is usually translated as "song." Two elements required for excellence in chanting are prolonged vowel fluctuation and the admired technique of *'i'i* (rapid chest-tone tremor).

When *a cappella* religious chants for solo voice (*mele'oli*) are accompanied by dancing, additional chanters, and percussion, the form is called *mele hula pahu*. Group chanters or singers (*haku mele*) are highly trained composers and performers, expected to extend song forms through improvisation. There are prescribed rhythmic structures for the accompaniment of all *mele hula*. Contrasting formulæ are assigned to the introduction, each stanza, the interludes between stanzas, and the cadence. The poetry that accompanies mimetic dance is highly nuanced and complex, and many subtleties of vocal styles survive today (such as the rapid *kepakepa* and the carefully enunciated *koihonua*). Specific types include *mele inoa* (naming chants), *mele pule* (prayers), *mele he'e nalu* (surfing themes) and *mele koihonua* (recitations of genealogies).

Of the 18 traditional categories of musical instruments, 10 are primarily associated with mele hula. In sitting dances (*hula noho i lalo*), the dancers usually accompany themselves on instruments or with body percussion. Standing dances (*hula ku i luna*) are usually accompanied by one or more seated chanter-drummers. The older, more traditional type of hula is called *kahiko*, while modern varieties are called *'auana*.

Accompaniment may be provided by the *pahu* (allegedly adapted from a Tahitian temple drum called *pahu 'heiau*); *ipu* (gourd); *'ili 'ili* (lava stone castanets worn by water action); *'ulī 'ulī* (paired gourd rattles, filled with seeds or stones, and feathered with colors representing fire or lava); *pu'ili* (paired bamboo stick rattles, slit multiple times longitudinally and struck together or on a palm); and *kala'au* (wooden rods). Pu'ili are traditionally played sitting, and accompany love or naming chants, whereas kala'au sticks provide a steady rhythm supporting a longer hula story chant. Male dancers wore *kupe'e niho 'ilio* (dog-teeth anklets), and *ka 'eke'eke* (bamboo pipes) were struck vertically on a hard surface.

The *'ohe hano ihu* (*'ohe* = bamboo; *hā* = breath, *ihu* = nose) is an indigenous nose-blown flute made from a bamboo tube that has two or three finger holes. *Kumu hula* (dance masters) were said to be able either to make the flute sound as though it were chanting, or to chant as they played. In the early 20th century, young men still used the 'ohe hano ihu as a way to win the affection and love of a woman. Two different oral traditions explain the use of the nose for playing the 'ohe hano ihu. According to one, the 'ohe hano ihu is played with air from the nose rather than from the mouth because a person's hā (breath) is expressive of the person's inner being. Another alleges that as the hā travels from the *na'ao* (gut) through the mouth, the hā can be used to lie. When the hā travels through the nose, it cannot lie. Therefore, if a young man loves a woman, that love should be expressed in the music he plays with his 'ohe hano ihu.

The *'ulili* (a spinning rattle of three gourds), the *ipu hokiokio* (gourd flute), and *'ukeke* (stringed mouth bow) are all "solo" instruments, and other sound-making objects include the *pu la'i* (leaf trumpet), the *oeoe* (bullroarer), the *ni'au kani* (coconut-shell jaw harp), and the *pu kani* (triton- or helmet-shell signal trumpet).

From 1778 onward, Hawaii began a period of acculturation with the introduction of numerous styles of European music, including Protestant missionary music.

Traditional Hawaiian musicians, sisters Nalani (left) and Pualani Kanaka'ole, chant and play *ipu hekes* (double gourds). (Jack Vartoogian/Getty Images)

The collection *Na himeni Hawaii* was published in 1823, and the first Western singing school opened the following year. Sailors and *vaqueros* (Spanish-speaking Mexican cowboys) imported by King Kamehameha III (1813–1854) beginning in 1832 introduced the guitar and *falsetto* singing to Hawaiian cowboys (*paniolos*).

The first full-scale concert oratorio was presented in 1860, and operas by Verdi, Donizetti, and Bellini were presented by traveling Italian troupes in 1862. Many generations of the Hawaiian royal family studied under Henri Berger (1844–1929), who was sent from Prussia in 1872 at the request of King Kamehameha V (1830–1872). Berger founded "The King's Own Band," now called the Royal Hawaiian Band (the oldest municipal band in the United States) and became fascinated by Hawaiian folk music. He first published many types of traditional music and instructed Hawaiian musicians and composers in European styles. With the arrival of the ship *Ravenscrag* in 1879, Portuguese immigrants brought the *braguinha* and *machête da braça*—small, four-stringed variants of the *cavaquinho*—from Madeira and began to call them *'ukulele*. The etymology of this word is disputed, as *uku* ("flea" or "gift")], *ukeke* (an indigenous three-string mouth bow), and *lele* (jumping, dancing, or coming) may all have contributed to the appellation. The virtuosic playing of Portuguese field worker João Fernandes was described as "like a jumpy flea." King Kalākaua (1874–1891, the last reigning king of Hawaii) enjoyed the playing of some of his English officers and requested that ukulele be featured in performances for royal gatherings. Called "the Merrie Monarch," he collaborated with Henri Berger on "Hawaii pono'i"—the national anthem and, later, state song. German singing societies (1880s–1890s) and small orchestras (1881–1884 and 1895–1902) were also active in Hawaii during this period.

Queen Lili'uokalani (1838–1917, the last monarch and only queen regnant of Hawaii, 1891–1895) was an accomplished songwriter and published author. She sang; played keyboard instruments such as piano and organ; and performed on guitar, zither, and ukulele. Her notable musical contributions include translating the Hawaiian creation chant (*Kumulipo*), combining traditional Hawaiian poetic forms with missionary harmonies, and composing the nationalist lament "Aloha 'Oe."

Steel-string guitars also arrived with the Portuguese in the 1860s, and *kī ho'alu* (slack-key fingerpicked style) had spread across the chain by 1889, when Joseph Kekuku claimed to have invented the *kila kila* (steel guitar). Modern slack-key guitar, in which all strings are tuned to a major chord, has become entirely instrumental. There are currently four sizes of ukulele: concert (smaller size developed in the 1920s), soprano or "standard" (the original size), tenor (1930s–), and baritone (1940s–). Less common are the sopranino (also called piccolo, bambino, and pocket uke), the bass (invented in 2009), and the taropatch ukulele, with six to eight strings in four courses. The most popular four-string ukulele tuning is a C6 chord (G4, C4, E4, A4, which in that order is called the "My dog has fleas" tuning by traditional players).

The Chicago World Columbian Exposition of 1893 was the earliest mainland presentation of Hawaiian music. At the beginning of the 20th century, Hawaiian dance bands (usually guitar quartets) played *hapa haole* (half-white songs) combining ragtime, popular song, and superficial elements of Hawaiian music. Victor made the first Hawaiian song recordings in 1906, and the 1912 show *Bird of Paradise* introduced elements of Hawaiian music and dance to Broadway.

During the Panama-Pacific Exposition in San Francisco of 1915, Hawaiian vocalists, dancers, and bands were featured in the Hawaiian Pavilion, visited by 18 million people. Both the ukulele and the lap steel guitar were featured daily throughout the nine-month-long international fair, and thousands of ukuleles were sold to tourists. This created nationwide enthusiasm for Hawaiian music: ukuleles were quickly incorporated into Tin Pan Alley songs, jazz combos, and even country/"old-timey" bands.

The swift and intricate rhythms of Tahitian and Samoan music influenced Hawaiian music in the 1920s. A uniquely Hawaiian style of jazz developed at the Moana and Royal Hawaiian hotels, and Hawaiian music/dance shows became an integral part of local tourism. Among the earliest and most popular musical attractions was the *Kodak Hula Show* (1937–2002) in which tourists purchased Kodak film to photograph dancers and musicians. The 1930s–1950s were the "Golden Age of Hawaiian music," due to a synthesis of folk and popular styles and the prominence of stars such as Lani Lani McIntire, John Kameaaloha Almeida, and Sol Hoopii.

The Hawaiian Renaissance of the 1960s marked a resurgence in interest in traditional music, especially slack-key, among ethnic Hawaiians. Long-standing performers such as Gabby Pahinui found their careers revitalized and inspired a legion of followers who played a mix of slack-key, country, rock, and other hybrid styles such as Hawaiian-language hip-hop (*na mele paleoleo*) and Jawaian (a local style of reggae music pioneered by the band Simplicity).

Major music festivals include the Merrie Monarch Hula Festival (1964) and several slack-key, steel guitar, and jazz events. Several large hotels and the new LDS Polynesian Cultural Center on Oahu feature pageants of traditional music and dance music in the afternoon or evening. The Honolulu Symphony Orchestra, founded in 1900, is the oldest such ensemble in the United States west of the Rockies. The

University of Hawaii (1907–), Hawaii Opera (1960–), and Honolulu Symphony Chorus (1978–) have inspired many similar groups throughout the islands.

Laura Stanfield Prichard

See also: Polynesia, Music of; Polynesian Hymns

Further Reading

Kanahele, George S. 1979. *Hawaiian Music and Musicians*. Honolulu: University of Hawaii Press.

Roberts, Helen H. 1926/1977. *Ancient Hawaiian Music*. Honolulu: Peter Smith.

Highlife

A style of popular music that first emerged along the Gold Coast of West Africa, highlife blended distinctive African rhythms with Western instrumentation to claim a mantle as the most influential and ubiquitous form of dance music in Ghana during the early and middle decades of the 20th century. Though its popularity waned thereafter, by the beginning of the 21st century, highlife's influence could be detected throughout the West African musical landscape, in such genres as Afrobeat, gospel highlife, and hiplife. Highlife's chief practitioners include some of the most popular musical acts in modern African history, such as E.T. Mensah, Fela Kuti, Ebo Taylor, and Victor Olaiya.

Deploying a triple offbeat rhythmic pattern native to the traditional music of the Akan people of present-day Ghana, highlife was nonetheless a manifestation of the dramatic social, cultural, and political changes occurring in the region due to the onset of European colonial rule. Then known as the Gold Coast, present-day Ghana was occupied by the British in 1867. As the new colonial power effected an economic transformation of the territory, more and more Africans began migrating to the coastal city of Accra, taking up work as colonial functionaries, domestic servants, and manual laborers. Though they carried their indigenous musical styles with them, they also were attracted to the Western instruments associated with European culture, including guitars and the brass instruments of British military drum and fife bands. It is from this marriage of African and Western musical conceptions that highlife was born, around the beginning of the 20th century, and popularized by such prominent acts as Kwame Asare, Lions Heart, and the Excelsior Orchestra. Such music proved especially popular with the small but emerging black middle classes of the largest cities—men and women who had leisure time and fashioned themselves as modern and upwardly mobile—and it is from this association that the music gained its name. As the highlife musician Kwadwo Donkoh once explained, "This particular fusion with three successive beats became the favorite of the people of the 'high life,' the high living people; you might say the relatively well-to-do" (Plageman, 2013, pp. 61–62).

As highlife music gained in popularity in the early decades of the 20th century, it did not take long to spread from Ghana to neighboring West African countries such as Nigeria, Sierra Leone, and Liberia. Wherever highlife traveled, it drew its inspiration from any and every musical style, from Nigerian *juju* to palmwine guitar music; at the same time, the music also evolved as West African musicians were exposed to other popular musical styles, including Afro-Caribbean calypso music and American jazz. Highlife music underwent an especially dramatic transformation during World War II, when American soldiers stationed in West Africa introduced swing music to local musicians, who eagerly picked up on the new sounds and adapted them to highlife's distinctive rhythmic palette. As E. T. Mensah later remembered, the Americans "usually came to town with a fat load of money, count so much and buy say two or three bottles of beer. . . . Bars began to spring up during the war so that any small corner there was a kiosk. They didn't mind sitting down at these bars from six at night to twelve midnight, drinking, talking, and listening to jazz and swing on the gramophone" (Mensah, 1986, pp. 13–14).

It was to entertain such troops, as well as to find new sources of musical inspiration, that highlife musicians began appropriating American and Afro-Caribbean musical styles for their own purposes, in the process creating new variations of highlife that would catapult the music to greater heights of popularity. After the end of World War II, the Tempos Band, led by Mensah, emerged as the predominant dance band in Ghana, and its upbeat and infectious rhythms became the soundtrack to the postwar optimism of the 1950s, which would witness Ghana's national independence as the first sub-Saharan African nation to free itself from European colonial rule. In particular, Mensah's hit 1957 song, "Ghana Freedom," celebrated national independence and the leadership of its first prime minister, Kwame Nkrumah. As Nkrumah and Ghana became symbols of the new African renaissance, Mensah's highlife music had an enormous impact on other West African musicians, including Bobby Benson and Victor Olaiya in Nigeria, and the Ticklers Dance Band of Sierra Leone.

No longer was the music associated only with the well-to-do in African society; highlife then became a music closely aligned with efforts to transform Ghana and neighboring countries into unified nations. In fact, during the 1950s and 1960s, political elites in Ghana and elsewhere attempted to appropriate highlife as the music of what Nkrumah called the "African Personality," an effort to eradicate the last vestiges of European cultural imperialism on the African continent. Yet, as the new political elite largely failed to deliver on the promises of national liberation, many West Africans began rebelling against government attempts to define their culture, and abandoned highlife as a music hopelessly compromised by its connections to a corrupted political elite. Emblematic of this shift was the legendary Nigerian musician Fela Kuti, who began his musical career playing highlife with his band the Koola Lobitos before forming the Africa '70 band that would launch the Afrobeat musical style. As Fela explained, "Highlife is a loose term which has no reference to any concrete happening in actual life" (Veal, 2000, p. 23). In part thanks to such pronouncements, as well as a general economic downturn that led to the shuttering of many West African nightclubs in the 1960s and 1970s, highlife music declined in popularity during the last decades of the 20th century.

Nonetheless, highlife's imprint can still be found throughout the West African musical landscape, not only in the Afrobeat styles popularized by Fela, but also in numerous musical styles popular throughout West Africa, from reggae highlife to gospel highlife and hiplife. Like American jazz, highlife has consistently resisted the attempts of elites and cultural power brokers to define the boundaries of the music, thereby remaining a vital musical force that speaks both to the enduring power of precolonial African culture and its capacity to incorporate outside influences without betraying the aesthetic integrity of the music.

David Crawford Jones

See also: Afrobeat (Afropop); Kuti, Fela; Masakela, Hugh

Further Reading

Collins, John. 1989. "The Early History of West African Highlife Music." *Popular Music* 8(3), 221–230.
Mensah, E. T. 1986. *The King of Highlife*. London: Off the Record Press.
Oti, Sonny. 2009. *Highlife Music in West Africa*. Lagos, Nigeria: Malthouse Press.
Plageman, Nate. 2013. *Highlife Saturday Night: Popular Music and Social Change in Urban Ghana*. Bloomington: Indiana University Press.
Veal, Michael E. 2000. *Fela: The Life and Times of an African Musical Icon*. Philadelphia, PA: Temple University Press.

Hōgaku

A general term for Japanese music, *hōgaku* is defined as Japanese traditional classical and theater music. Hōgaku music incorporates everything from imperial court music, *shômyô*, *gagaku*, and folk songs, to popular tunes, arrangements of J. S. Bach's works, avant-garde composers' music such as works by Cage and Stockhausen, and improvisational works. It does not typically include Ainu or Okinawan music. Hōgaku also describes any music that is made with traditional Japanese instruments, including the *shamisen* (a three-string banjo-like instrument), *shakuhachi* (five- and seven-hole bamboo flutes), *biwa* (four-string lute), *sho* (mouth organ), *hichiriki* (double-reed aerophone), *koto* (zither), and traditional drums.

Hōgaku developed during the time from the 17th to 19th centuries known as the Edo, or Tokugawa, period (1615–1868). This was a period of isolation from outside contact that enabled Japan to develop its own artistic resources without excessive foreign influence. It was further influenced by the Meiji Restoration of 1868. The blind koto master Miyagi Michio (1894–1956) is known as the father of modern Japanese music (*shin hōgaku*) that blended Western musical ideas with indigenous Japanese music. Michio's music was the bridge between old and new during Japan's period of change from the Meiji era to the Taishō period (1912–1968), then onward to the Shōwa period (1926–1989). Michio's "*Haru no iemi*" (Spring Sea), written for koto and shakuhachi, is one of the most famous hōgaku works and still enjoys popularity today.

Like Michio, other composers of the early 20th century often worked in three areas: Western-style compositions (albeit with Japanese lyrics); "new folk songs" in near-traditional style; and a hybrid that draws on the pentatonic major and minor scales. After World War II, a hybrid form of traditional Japanese and Western classical music emerged and became known as "contemporary traditional music." The genre enjoyed popularity during the mid-1960s, along with a revival of *enka*. Tôru Takemitsu's "November Steps" is a fine example of contemporary traditional music. Commissioned by the New York Philharmonic Orchestra in celebration of the ensemble's 125th anniversary, the work is written for shakuhachi and biwa with orchestra. Seiji Ozawa conducted the November 1967 premiere of the work, which endeavors to highlight musical elements of both Japanese and Western traditions. "November Steps" does not follow traditional Western musical form, but instead considers each sound individually.

During the past 30 years, hōgaku has benefited from its role in Japan's cultural renaissance. This rekindled interest in traditional music is concomitant with Japan's escalating global economic power, which has fostered a new sense of national pride, combined with an increased foreign interest in traditional cultural elements. Hōgaku concerts regularly occur in Japan's larger cities, as evidenced by the July 1996 edition of the monthly *Hōgaku Journal*, which listed 98 live performances in and around Tokyo, as well as performances abroad including concerts in the Middle East, Europe, and Southeast Asia. Hōgaku listings range from classical and contemporary to improvisational and folk styles, including a variety of traditional instrumentation.

The 1990s witnessed a second occurrence of interest in hōgaku precipitated by the global music trend in popular music with bands incorporating instrumental techniques. While performance groups such as the *Nihon Ongaku Shūdan* (Ensemble Nipponia, also known as Pro Musica Nipponia), established in 1964, continue to be active today, the past 10 years have witnessed the formation of new ensembles comprised of talented musicians; in addition, the demand for public performance in addition to guild performances has fostered hōgaku's growth. Performance practice takes many guises, ranging from concerts where only *kimono* are worn and the performers kneel on the floor; to ones where Western orchestral attire is worn, the performers sit on chairs, and follow a conductor; and ones where casual dress is worn and the performers move freely about the stage.

The new generation of hōgaku musicians is also making use of technological advances for audio recordings, videos, electronic instruments and the Internet. The more adventurous among recent pop musicians reflect globalization by mixing Western, Japanese and other elements with hōgaku in the best post-modern tradition. Recent years have brought forth arrangements by commercial musicians of shômyô with other instruments and musical styles (e.g., synthesizer, shamisen) or for the concert stage.

One successful example is the Wagakki Band, consisting of seven instrumentalists and singer Yuko Suzuhana. The group combines traditional instruments (koto, shakuhachi, shamisen, and *taiko* drum) with standard rock-band instrumentation to create a new genre of music that fuses vocaloid songs (digitally produced) with *wagakki* and Western rock. Wagakki Band's first music video, "Tsuki Kage Mai Ka" (Moon Shadow Dance Flower), which is a cover of the Hatsune Miku song, employs electronic dance music combined with distorted guitar riffs and traditional Japanese instruments. Groups such as Wagakki Band promote *wayou secchuu*, a blending of styles which is one very important way of keeping hōgaku in the hearts and minds of future generations of musicians and music aficionados.

Eldonna L. May

See also: Gagaku; Japan, Music of; Koto; Shamisen; Taiko; Wayang Kulit

Further Reading

Berger, Donald P. 1995. *Shōka and Dōyō: Songs of an Educational Policy and a Children's Song Movement of Japan, 1910–1926*. Ann Arbor: University of Michigan Press.

Eppstein, Ury. 1994. *The Beginnings of Western Music in Meiji Era Japan*. Lewiston, NY: Edwin Mellin Press.

Ohtake, Noriko. 1993. *Creative Sources for the Music of Toru Takemitsu*. Aldershot, UK: Scolar Press.

Toyotaka, Komiya, ed. 1956. *Japanese Music and Drama in the Meiji Era*. Tokyo: Obunsha Press Tokyo.

Hornbostel, Erich Moritz von (1877–1935)

Erich Moritz von Hornbostel was an Austrian interdisciplinary scholar who contributed substantially to the world of ethnomusicology and organology. Along with Curt Sachs, Hornbostel developed a classification system that is still utilized for musical instruments in the possession of museums and libraries. During the first three decades of the 20th century, Hornbostel's and Sachs's research and theory on organology and classification of musical instruments dominated the ethnomusicological world. Hornbostel is also considered one of the founders of comparative musicology.

Erich Moritz von Hornbostel was born in Vienna, Austria, on February 25, 1877, into an environment that developed musical culture. Although he studied several subjects, music was integral to his education. His mother, Helene Magnus, was a Jewish singer who enjoyed the songs and lieder of Johannes Brahms. Young Hornbostel studied harmony and counterpoint with noted musicologist Eusebius Mandyczewski (1857–1929).

Hornbostel studied philosophy at the University of Vienna and the University of Heidelberg, and earned a PhD in chemistry from the University of Vienna (1900). In 1905, he became an assistant to Carl Stumpf (1848–1936) at the University of Berlin. The following year (1906), Hornbostel went to the United States to research the music of the Pawnee tribe. From 1906 to 1933 he was director of the Phonogramm-Archiv in Berlin, and concurrently a professor at the University of Berlin (1917–1933).

A few years after his appointment as professor at the University of Berlin, Hornbostel taught music psychology, comparative musicology, and music as it related to ethnology. Although himself apolitical, he left Germany (due to his mother's Judaism) only months after the National Socialists attained power in 1933. Initially Hornbostel went to Switzerland, then to the New School for Social Research in New York. However, ill health forced him to spend his final years in London.

Hornbostel's major contribution to ethnomusicology was *Classification of Musical Instruments*, authored with Curt Sachs, and originally published as "*Systematik der Musikinstrumente: Ein Versuch*" in *Zeitschrift für Ethnologie*. His classification is seen as a systematic arrangement of musical instruments for use by musicologists, ethnologists, museum curators, and other collectors. Hornbostel and Sachs based their four-class system of instrumental music upon a system devised in 1875 by Sourindro Mohun Tagore (1840–1914). In 1880, Victor Charles Mahillon (1841–1924) developed Hornbostel's ideas further, basing his classifications upon the earlier work in zoology, with terms such as *classe, branche, section,* and *sous-section*. In their publications on musical instrument classification, Hornbostel and Sachs noted the pitfalls that the ancient Chinese experienced when they classified instruments based on material, to distinguish those made of stone, metal, wood, bamboo, or other substances. Hornbostel thus chose the means of sound production as the basis for his system. Hornbostel and Sachs chose a numerical system, rather than a lexical system, with terms free of linguistic inferences. They believed that nicknames and "popular etymology" would mislead those new to organology. Their classification scheme covered the complete universe of instruments, in a manner similar to that developed for books by Melvil Dewey (1851–1931), in his *Decimal Classification and Relative Index*, originally proposed in 1876. Hornbostel and Sachs expressed their admiration for Dewey's numerical system.

Hornbostel and Sachs devised four categories, based on the method of sound production:

1. Idiophones, in which sound is produced by striking, plucking, or by friction;
2. Membranophones, whose sound is produced by striking, plucking, or applying friction to tightly stretched membranes;
3. Chordophones, comprising one or more strings stretched between fixed points; and
4. Aerophones, that utilize air as the vibrating mechanism, either as free aerophones, or wind instruments proper that send the air through the instrument; the latter is further divided into those instruments in which the musician employs single or double reeds, or lips, to produce sound.

The categories are further subdivided utilizing suffixes with several digits. Hornbostel and Sachs also stated that any system must leave room for further divisions. Museologists and musicologists, including Francis W. Galpin (1858–1945), added categories to this classification system (such as electrophones, for example).

Those who explored new ideas and theories were often criticized by contemporary scholars of the day. One such case was Hornbostel's "Theory of Blown Fifths," in which he divided the sound spectrum into cents. Hornbostel hypothesized that overblowing a bamboo pipe would render a "blown fifth" equal to 678 cents, smaller than the pure fifth (702 cents) or the tempered fifth (700 cents). He called the composite scale, often more than seven tones, a *material* scale (*Materialleiter*), and those basic to specific songs the *use* scale (*Gebrauchsleiter*). Chief among the objectors to this theory was Manfred F. Bukofzer (1910–1955), who discovered that the intervals were dependent upon a wider number of variables than Hornbostel has assigned; thus there was no consistent intervallic deviation.

As one who pioneered the field of comparative musicology, Hornbostel wrote not just of musical instruments, but also of the differing uses of melody, harmony, and rhythm by various cultures. He analyzed the ethnic musics of Europe, Asia, Africa, and the Americas, and studied what was called at that time "exotic" music. In 1906, anthropologist Franz Boas submitted recordings to Hornbostel and Otto Abraham, who transcribed songs of British Columbia's indigenous populations. Hornbostel used this same transcription technique for music from other regions of the world, including Japan, Oceania, Asia, and Africa.

Music in the Orient was originally issued with a Parlaphone-Odeon recording in 1931 as *Musik des Orients: ein Schallplattenfolge orientalischer Musik von Japan bis Tunis*. Reissued by Decca (1951) and subsequently by Smithsonian Folkways (1992), Hornbostel sought a collection that had both high sound quality and a representation of various ethnological groups. He used the term "Orient" in a broad sense, including music from Japan, China, Indonesia, Siam, India, Persia, and Tunisia.

In his capacity at the Institute of Psychology, which became known as the Berlin Phonogramm-Archiv, Hornbostel contributed to the literature that related psychology, acoustics, and sound. In his research into experimental science, Hornbostel developed concepts derived from the junction of *gestalt* theory, musical perception, and acoustics. His articles appeared not only in musicological journals, but also in those for disciplines such as anthropology, physiology, psychology, and pharmacology. Hornbostel also collaborated with physician Otto Abraham on problems of tone distance, and with gestalt psychologist Max Wertheimer on how people detect the location of physical sound sources.

The Phonogramm-Archiv became a repository for sound recordings of music. The invention of the phonograph, with its dual carriers of the time (Emil Berliner's gramophone discs or Thomas Edison's wax cylinders), proved crucial in the early years of comparative musicology. In his capacity as director, Hornbostel provided wax cylinder recording machines to fieldworkers, and developed meticulous guidelines for the collection and preservation of field recordings. Hornbostel also tested approximately 200 musical instruments, and made meticulous notes about their characteristics; his transcriptions also illustrate the extent to which he carefully recorded each musical note. "Hornbostel's Black Box" includes detailed descriptions of these instruments, and resides in the Archives of Traditional Music, founded in Bloomington, Indiana, by George Herzog (1901–1983), who had served as an assistant to Hornbostel at the Phonogramm-Archiv during the 1920s.

From 1922 until his death, Hornbostel and Stumpf edited *Sammelbände für vergleichende Musikwissenschaft* (Collected Volumes for Comparative Musicology). In this journal Hornbostel published several of his ethnomusicological articles on the indigenous music of Native Americans, Africans, Asians, translations of others' musicological research, and his collaborations with Otto Abraham, Carl Stumpf, and Jaap Kunst.

Hornbostel had hoped to become part of the faculty of Cambridge University, but died before the opportunity came to fruition.

Ralph Hartsock

See also: Densmore, Frances

Further Reading

Hornbostel, Erich Moritz von. 2007. *The Demonstration Collection of E.M. von Hornbostel and the Berlin Phonogramm-Archiv*. Washington, DC: Smithsonian Folkways Recordings [CD].

Hornbostel, Erich Moritz von, and Curt Sachs. 1914. "Systematik der Musikinstrumente: Ein Versuch." *Zeitschrift für Ethnologie* 46, 553–590.

Hornbostel, Erich Moritz von, and Curt Sachs. 1992. "Classification of Musical Instruments." In Helen Myers (ed.), *Ethnomusicology: An Introduction*, 444–461. New York: W. W. Norton.

Jairazbhoy, Nazir Ali. 1990. "An Explication of the Hornbostel-Sachs Instrumental Classification System." In Sue Carole DeVale (ed.), *Selected Reports in Ethnomusicology; Vol. 8: Issues in Organology*, 283–314. Los Angeles: University of California.

Kartomi, Margaret. 2001. "The Classification of Musical Instruments: Changing Trends in Research from the Late Nineteenth Century, with Special Reference to the 1990s." *Ethnomusicology* 45(2), 283–314. http://www.jstor.org/stable/852676.

Koch, Lars-Christian. 2013. "Images of Sound: Erich M. von Hornbostel and the Berlin Phonogram Archive." In Philip V. Bohlman (ed.), *The Cambridge History of World Music*, 475–497. Cambridge: Cambridge University Press.

Nettl, Bruno, and Philip Vilas Bohlman. 1991. *Comparative Musicology and Anthropology of Music: Essays on the History of Ethnomusicology*. Chicago: University of Chicago Press.

Stumpf, Carl, and Erich Moritz von Hornbostel. 1975. *Sammelbände für vergleichende Musikwissenschaft* [Anthologies for comparative musicology]. Hildesheim, Germany: Olms.

Huayno

Huayno is a genre of music and dance from the Andean region; it is especially common in Bolivia and Peru, but also present in Ecuador, northern Chile, and northern Argentina. Due to regional variants, like other words in Quechua (language family from the Andes region), *huayno* has different spellings, such as *wayno*, *wayñu*, and *huaino*, among others.

Huayno dates back to precolonial times, and appears to have Incan origins. Its first historical record is from around 400 years ago. Given that written records of Andean culture began with the arrival of European colonizers, it is only logical that no previous mention of huayno is found. This, however, does not tell us how long before that the style emerged. Huayno is widely considered an unchanged music, present in our day exactly as it was in precolonial times. Thus, to many it represents an untouched legacy, a direct link to the past. Such was the case of Peruvian novelist, poet, and anthropologist José María Arguedas (1911–1969), who suggested that the music of huayno had suffered little change, although the lyrics have evolved rapidly and have taken infinitely diverse forms, almost one form for every person. The indigenous and the mestizo from today, as did those of a hundred years ago, still find in this music the entire expression of their spirit and all of their emotions. The same ancient huaynos are sung by mestizos today, and even though there are only traces of the old lyrics, the music has changed little from the ancient music. New huaynos, which have started to appear as the work of renowned popular composers, are really variations on the classical themes.

The idea of music unchanged through time is not particular to huayno, and is in fact very common in comparative musicology. It is important to point out, however, that although the result of both lines of thought was practically the same, the intentions were notoriously opposite. Whereas comparative musicology saw dynamism only in Western classical music, the idea of an untouched huayno comes from the idea of the music's power to survive against outside impositions or influences. It is, however, very difficult to measure what of the ancient huayno remains today. Scholars suggest that the "conquistadors" and the colonial authorities could not or did not want to understand the music of the Andean ancestors, and chose to ignore it or even condemn it. This did not change much with the Republic (after independence from Spain). Thus, there are almost no records of this music in either period, making it very difficult to measure the volatility of huayno through history.

Although today it retains some of its ancient musical, choreographic, cultural, and social characteristics, it is very likely that huayno has also undergone some changes through time. It is also important to point out that huayno has, and probably always has had, significant regional variants in its music, dance, and social meaning. Huayno is usually danced in pairs, but can also be danced in big rounds of both men and women, or just men, or just women; there is no rule, and the important thing is the *muyu muyu*, the circling and twirling made to the happy rhythm of the music.

Originally performed with panpipes and *quenas* (Andean flutes), and perhaps some percussion, huayno incorporated postcolonial instruments such as the charango, guitar, violin, and harp. Another substantial change was in its scale and harmony. Although many experts agree that it was originally constructed in a pentatonic structure (a very common scale in the Andes), it is now found with other melodic structures, and thus has adopted European harmony into its musical structure; later on it incorporated the melodic minor scale that "corrected" the augmented second between the sixth and seventh grades of the harmonic scale.

The form of huayno is classified as having a binary structure, composed of four phrases with a variation in the last one: A A B B'. Today, however, many new forms are found in huaynos, and again, the form changes according to the geographical region. Language has also had an important influence in the musical form. Originally in Quechua and Aymara, huaynos sung in Spanish had to adapt the phrases to a new metric.

The rhythmic base of the huayno is basically a 2/4 time, with each beat having an eighth note followed by two 16th notes. Some experts, however, claim that the pattern that best represents the rhythm of huayno are sequences of eighth-note triplets, where, depending on the lyrics, the accent may fall on any one of the eighth notes, thus prolonging it and shortening the other two. The prolongation of one of the notes in a triplet, and the resultant shortening of the other two, could also be interpreted as an eighth note and two 16th notes relationship. Although the 2/4 time, with the different variants presented, is a good approach to understanding huayno rhythm, it is important to know that huayno cannot be written precisely. The stressing and prolonging of different notes in an apparently imprecise or even random manner is not an embellishment, but rather an intrinsic part of the music. The fact that each region has its own and very particular way to interpret huayno shows us that there is nothing random about the nuances of each huayno.

Felix Eid

See also: Andean Region, Music of the; Bolivia, Music of

Further Reading

Arguedas, José María. 1977. *Nuestra música popular y sus intérpretes* [Our popular music and its performers]. Lima, Peru: Mosca Azul/Horizonte Editores.

Auza, Atiliano L. 1996. *Historia de la música boliviana* [History of Bolivian music]. La Paz/Cochabamba: Los Amigos del Libro.

Bravo, Antonio G. 1948. "Música, instrumentos y danzas indígenas [Indigenous music, instruments, and dances]." In Comité pro IV Centenario de la Fundación de La Paz (ed.), *La Paz en su IV Centenario, 1548–1948*, 403–423. La Paz, Bolivia.

Brinton, Daniel. 1892. "Studies in South American Native Languages." *Journal of the American Philosophical Society* 30(137) (January), 45–105.

Candia, Antonio Paredes. 1991. *La danza folclórica en Bolivia* [Folkloric dances in Bolivia]. La Paz, Bolivia: Librería Editorial Popular.

Mendívil, Julio. 2004. "Huaynos híbridos: Estrategias para entrar y salir de la tradición [Hybrid huaynos: Beginning and advanced strategies of the tradition]." *Lienzo* 25, 27–64.

Sachs, Curt. 1929. *Geist und Werden der Musikinstrumente* [Spirit and creation of musical instruments]. Berlín: Verlag von Dietrich Reimer.

Sigl, Eveline, and David S. Mendoza. 2012. *No se baila así no más . . . Danzas de Bolivia* [Do not dance like this anymore. . . . Bolivian dances], vol. 2. La Paz, Bolivia: Self-published.

Stevenson, Robert. 1968. *Music in Aztec & Inca Territory*. Berkeley: University of California Press.

Vásquez, Chalena, and Abilio F. Vergara. 1990. *Ranulfo, el hombre* [Ranulfo, the man]. Lima, Peru: Centro de Desarrollo Agropecuario.

Vega, Carlos. 1956. *El origen de las danzas folklóricas* [The origin of folkloric dances]. Buenos Aires, Argentina: Ricordi Americana.

Huqin

Huqin (*hu*: "barbarian"; *qin*: "string instrument") is a general term for Chinese bowed string instruments. The name indicates the origin of the instruments, which came from the "barbarian" tribes of northwestern China. Over the course of a thousand years, the huqin has evolved and developed into numerous variations. Huqins are usually played vertically. The resonators can be made of wood, bamboo, coconut shells, gourds, horns, and/or brass; normally are hexagonal, tubular, round, or octagonal in shape; and are covered with animal skins or wooden boards. Most have two strings, though some have three and four strings. The strings are traditionally silk or sheep gut, though today metal or nylon strings are commonly used. The bow is typically a lightly bent bamboo stick with horsehair stretched along it, and the bow is often threaded between the strings of the instrument. Huqins were never court instruments, but rather folk instruments that closely related to people's everyday musical lives. They have been used to accompany everything from folk singing to opera performances, and by street musicians and beggars to professional performers. It was not until the early 20th century that the *erhu* (*er* meaning "two," or second) was elevated as a solo instrument, described as the "Chinese violin," and came to represent the sonic signature of Chinese music.

The Chinese bowed instruments are believed to have developed from plucked string instruments. Written records of huqin predecessors as lutes plucked with the fingers date back as far as the Tang dynasty (618–907 CE). The early ancestor of the bowed lute was known as *xiqin*, named after a northern nomadic tribe. During the Song dynasty (960–1279 CE), xiqin was described as a foreign instrument by the music theorist Chen Yang (1064–1128) in his *Book of Music*. It had a bamboo neck and a wooden soundboard, and was sounded by rubbing a strip of bamboo against the strings.

From the late 11th century onward, bows with horsehair were employed on the huqin, and were assimilated throughout the Yuan dynasty (1279–1368 CE). During the Ming dynasty (1368–1644 CE), names of instruments were as fluid as their designs. Musicians would give new names to all kinds of huqin when they adopted them and modified the general design of the instruments to increase suitability for the local styles of opera. By the end of the Qing dynasty (1644–1911 CE), varied kinds of horsehair huqin were in use throughout China, employed for ensembles and accompaniment and popular among street musicians and beggars.

In the 20th century, the huqin was dominated by the influences of Western music and Chinese politics, as evidenced by changes in performance technique, aesthetics, instrument construction, and the organization and composition of music. Today, there are numerous instruments in the huqin family; among them, the erhu is probably the most popular and can be regarded as representative. Each of the huqin instruments is specific to cultures and regions and is played in distinctive styles. The following are just a few examples.

Starting around the rise of the *bangziqiang* opera forms in the late Ming/early Qing dynasty, the huqin developed its first important musical roles in Chinese dramas. The *banhu* ("board"-*hu*) was popular in northern China by the 18th century, used primarily for *bangzi* opera as well as various local operas. It has a coconut-shell resonator with one side covered with wooden board. Similarly, the *yehu* ("coconut"-*hu*) also has a coconut-shell resonator, though it is covered with a piece of coconut wood. It is important in Cantonese, Hakka, and Chaozhou musical traditions in southeastern China and Taiwan. A kind of yehu used in Taiwanese opera is called *kezaixian*. Another huqin popular in southern China and Taiwan is the *erxian* ("two-string"), which is an earlier name for two-string bowed instruments. There are two variants which are used in Cantonese, Chaozhou, and Nanguan music.

The *jinghu* ("capital"-*hu*) is the principal melodic instrument in Peking opera, which was developed in the late 18th century. Both the neck and the small tubular, snakeskin-faced body of the jinghu are made of bamboo. It is the smallest and highest pitched instrument in the huqin family. The *zhuihu* (also *zhuiqin* or *zhuizixian*) is significant in local operas and storytelling in Henan and Shandong provinces. It has a fretless fingerboard against which the strings are pressed while playing.

From the 1920s onward, several instruments were invented using the erhu as a model, in order to increase the range of the bowed string family used in the modern Chinese orchestra. The *gaohu* ("high"-*hu*) was introduced by the Cantonese composer Lu Wencheng (1898–1981) in the late 1920s as a higher-pitched adaptation of the erhu. It is a leading instrument of Cantonese ensembles, in which it is held with the resonator between the knees. In the modern Chinese orchestra, it serves as a high-range instrument in the bowed string section. The *zhonghu* ("middle"-*hu*) is a larger erhu tuned a fifth lower. It was developed in the 1930s to act as the alto huqin in the orchestra. The *gehu* ("reformed"-*hu*) and *diyin gehu* ("bass"-*gehu*) are large bass huqin developed in the 1950s. They are a fusion of the huqin and the cello/bass. They have four strings, and the tuning, bowing, and many playing techniques are similar to those for the cello and bass; however, the instrument's volume and timbre are influenced by the giant snakeskin attached to the resonator.

Huqins are also popular among China's many ethnic groups. To give some examples, the *matouqin* (horsehead fiddle, *morin khuur* in Mongolian) is an important instrument of the Mongolian ethnic group. The wooden body is typically shaped like a trapezoid with two strings made from nylon or horsetail. It is held nearly upright, with the instrument body either in the musician's lap or between the musician's legs. The bow is held in front of the strings instead of being threaded between them.

The *sanhu* ("three-(string)"-*hu*) is used by several ethnic groups in Yunnan, southwest of China, to accompany dance. It has three strings, and the resonator is covered by sheepskin or frogskin. The *maguhu* ("horse-bone"-*hu*) is used primarily by the Zhuang and Buyei ethnic groups of the southern Chinese province of Guangxi. It has two strings, and the resonator is made from the femur bone of a horse, cow, or mule, with the front end covered with snakeskin. The *aijieke* is a traditional four-stringed instrument of the Uyghur and Uzbek ethnic groups, popular in the Xinjiang province of western China. The resonator, shaped like a hemisphere, is made of peachwood, covered on the front with hide or board. The bow is separated from the strings. It is used to play folk tunes and traditional *mukamu*-style music.

Chia-Yu Joy Lu

See also: Erhu; Guoyue; Guzheng

Further Reading

Liu, Terence. 2002. "Instruments: Erhu." In Robert C. Provine, Yosihiko Tokumaru, and J. Lawrence Witzleben (eds.), *The Garland Encyclopedia of World Music; Vol. 7: East Asia: China, Japan, and Korea*, 175–178. New York: Routledge.

Picken, Laurence. 1965. "Early Chinese Friction-Chordophones." *The Galpin Society Journal* 18 (March), 82–89.

Stock, Jonathan. 1993. "A Historical Account of the Chinese Two-Stringed Fiddle Erhu." *The Galpin Society Journal* 46 (March), 83–113.

Tan Yong, Bihai Xu, and Xiaoli Sun. 2011. *Xibu Minzu Yunei Huqin Yanbian Ronghelu* [An integrated record of the Huqin's transformation among China's Western ethnic groups]. Beijing: Minzu Chubanshe.

Thrasher, Alan R. 2000. *Chinese Musical Instruments.* New York: Oxford University Press.

Thrasher, Alan R., and Gloria N. Wong. 2011. *Yueqi: Chinese Musical Instruments in Performance*. Vancouver, Canada: BC Chinese Music Association.

Wu Ben. 2002. "Archaeology and History of Musical Instruments in China." In Robert C. Provine, Yosihiko Tokumaru, and J. Lawrence Witzleben (eds.), *The Garland Encyclopedia of World Music; Vol. 7: East Asia: China, Japan, and Korea*, 105–114. New York: Routledge.

Yang Mu. 1993. *Chinese Musical Instruments: An Introduction*. Canberra: Coralie Rockwell Foundation, Australian National University.

Zhang Shao. 1989. *Erhu Guangbo Jiaoxue Jiangzuo* [A compiled lesson for erhu in broadcasting teaching program]. Shanghai: Shanghai Yinyue Chubanshe.

Icelandic Ballads

Icelandic ballads, of which there are many categories, have their roots in medieval Iceland. These ballads, known traditionally as *fornkvæði* (old poem) but later adopting the name *sagnadans* (narrative dance) (Hughes, 2005, p. 212), are typically based on knightly tales and folklore—material similar to that of the Icelandic *rímur* literary style. They differentiate from rímur in that themes of chivalry, legend, and the supernatural (such as elves and other mythological creatures) prevail over themes of heroism, as in rímur; also, themes of passionate love and hatred are overarching concepts, stemming from subjects of unrequited love, frustration, or lust (Ólason, 1993, p. 32). From the 17th through the 19th centuries, a thorough collection and categorization of all ballads took place. In the middle 20th century, Jón Helgason categorized all *sagnadansar* (1986), discovering roughly 110 ballads; this number is debatable, as other scholars have argued that some of these works are in fact not ballads at all, but other works of similar literary form (Hughes, 2005, pp. 213–214).

It is believed that the first international ballads made their way into Iceland some time before 1500 CE through Norway; most likely through the contacts with the archiepiscopal see at Trondheim or the Hanseatic trading post of Bergen (Hughes, 2005, p. 212). The latter was an important trading post, or *kontor* (office), as it established strong trade relations along the coastal regions bordering the North and Baltic Seas. Traded goods consisted of furs, cloth, timber, honey, and grains such as wheat or rye. With material goods came the trade of cultural heritage; as a trade post commonly serves as a center of cosmopolitan growth and worldliness, these trade posts exchanged British, Germanic, and Scandinavian cultural artifacts. It can be assumed that literary styles and genres were one of the many things exchanged at these trade posts.

The term "ballad" itself is part of a European literary tradition, referring to popular or traditional song beginning around the 13th century CE (Porter, n.d.). The term "ballad," from the Latin *ballare* (literally, "to dance") is a reference to a narrative song-and-dance form. In Iceland, the ballad (known at this time as the *fornkvæði*) was a form of oral literature that used music as a means to transmit the story. Icelandic ballads, much like other Nordic or Scandinavian ballads, share many similarities in their construction with ballads of other nearby countries such as Great Britain (Ólason, 2006, p. 60). Ballads of Great Britain, and of Scandinavian regions, at this time featured an excessive amount of dialogue, broken into couplets or quatrains (smaller, self-contained stanzas of two or four lines) with the interpolation of a refrain.

An example of a quatrain, consisting of two couplets, is the English nursery rhyme "Hickory Dickory Dock":

Hickory, dickory, dock,
The mouse ran up the clock,
The clock struck one,
The mouse ran down,
Hickory, dickory, dock.

The fifth stanza acts as a refrain, and bears little to no effect on the story itself; this is the same in Icelandic balladry. Early ballad stanzas did not feature alliteration as a literary tool, and rhyme schemes for stanzas were constructed in an A A X X form, with "X X" comprising the refrain material to be repeated in each subsequent stanza. Many of these ballads are not in fact Icelandic by place of composition; rather, many were imported from Norway, the Færoe Islands, or Denmark. Because these ballads were imported, rather than composed or written in Iceland, many original cultural artifacts—names, places, and in some cases, whole sentences—remained unaffected by the translation from their native tongues into Icelandic. Additionally, syntactical errors—grammatical mistakes, poorly constructed sentences, and odd diction—are frequent in Icelandic ballads, due to the attempted translation and homogenization of foreign materials (Hughes, 2005, p. 214). Ólason claims that this might have caused these ballads to take on a "poetic air" (Ólason, 1982, p. 98). This translation of foreign languages also reinforced the Icelanders' collective articulacy of the Icelandic language.

The development of ballads has been anything but evolutionary: Ólason states that "seldom is anything of significance added" (Ólason, 2006, p. 62), but things have been lost or simplified. The tales of knights and courtly love dominated the ballad genre—but the Icelandic rímur seemingly covered all of the jocular stories, or tales of heroes or holy men.

Joseph Harris alludes to the striking inverse relationship between a ballad's popularity and the quality of ballad writing: the earliest ballads—such as the *Tristrams kvæði*, which draws from the Tristram and Isolde tale—were composed during the golden age of balladry. By the 17th century, when *Gunnars kvæði* was composed, the ballad had become a dated literary and musical style, and "was no longer creative nor recreative" (Ólason, 1991, p. 122); much like the fugue in academe today, it became a regimented, compartmentalized literary genre that was more (or less) studied than compositionally practiced. Thus, these later ballads suffered greatly in their stylistic depth, perhaps due to the lack of a productive climate for the ballad genre. Inversely, the popularity of these late ballads greatly outweighs the popularity of earlier ones; Ólason attributes this to the lack of authority of earlier ballads, due to their age, the singer's conscious limitations of the text, and the lack of respect given to earlier ballads.

Today, the ballad has become a more academic genre than has its counterpart rímur. This discrepancy in Icelandic popularity may be due to rímur being a uniquely Icelandic literary genre, whereas the ballad was an exposition of international folklore. Rímur has seen a considerable rebirth in popular Icelandic culture, mostly through the collaborative efforts of popular musicians and folklorists such as Steindór Anderssen and Sigur Rós. There is still a considerable amount of research left to be done on the Icelandic ballad, although its similarities to other Nordic ballads indicates that much could be gained from comparative analyses.

John Forrestal

See also: Medieval Secular Song; Rímur

Further Reading

Helgason, Jón. 1986. *Kvæðabók* [Cashback poetry]. Reykjavík, Iceland: Mál og Menning.

Hughes, Shaun. 2005. "Late Secular Poetry." In Rory McTurk (ed.), *A Companion to Old Norse-Icelandic Literature and Culture*, 136–154. Malden, MA: Blackwell.

Ólason, Vésteinn. 1982. *The Traditional Ballads of Iceland: Historical Studies*. Reykjavík, Iceland: Stofun Árna Magnússonar.

Ólason, Vésteinn. 1991. "Literary Backgrounds of the Scandinavian Ballad." In Joseph Harris (ed.), *The Ballad and Oral Literature*, 116–138. Cambridge, MA: Harvard University Press.

Ólason, Vésteinn. 1993. "Fslendingasogur." In Phillip Pulsiano and Kirsten Wolf (eds.), *Medieval Scandinavia: An Encyclopedia*, 271–298. New York: Garland.

Ólason, Vésteinn. 2006. "Old Icelandic Poetry." In Daisy Neijmann (ed.), *A History of Icelandic Literature*, 1–63. Lincoln: University of Nebraska Press.

Porter, James. n.d. "Ballad." *Grove Music Online*. https://www.oxfordmusiconline.com.

Indian Folk Songs

Folk songs embody the raw emotions of almost every aspect of human life. Although in the current phase of globalization a vast impact of bourgeois and elite cultures is visible on folk songs, and under the postmodern conditions it has been difficult to extricate folk from elite culture, folk songs are still quite popular in India and have a motivating force. In elite culture, we see that trends and fashions are coming closer to many folk artifacts, and the intelligentsia is fascinated by (or forced to listen to) the folk under the pressures of alternative modernity. Folk songs are closer to folk spirit, in comparison to other folk genres such as folk tales, folk sayings, folk drama, and so on. The reason is nothing but the poignant appeal of folk songs due to their rhymes and content. Folk literature, handed down through the generations, consists of a rich body of creation myths, folk tales, animal stories, rhymes, songs, riddles, and proverbs in which the spoken word is closely connected with specific images, dance enactment, song cycles, symbolic acts, and plays.

Folk songs are often found in agrarian societies. For a country like India, where agriculture is the main occupation of the people, folk songs become exceedingly significant. The rich cultural traditions also add value to them. The folk songs in the Indian milieu are no longer considered negative or backward artistic expression. We find a discourse of the marginalized people in them. They are unique in their capacity to help us look at the patterns of life from an alternative perspective. They have also shown a mild criticism of authority, hegemony, and torture, but have never shown the destructionist motif. Folk songs reflect on traditional knowledge, wisdom, convention, practices, and ways of the people as collected and continued through oral tradition. These songs are always fresh, raw, noncanonical, agrarian, and popular in their locality and especially in folk subculture, having a unique mass culture.

Indian folk songs can be divided into folk lyrics and folk ballads. Folk ballads may be divided further into three categories: (1) the traditional secular ballads or incidental ballads, (2) the traditional mythological and religious ballads, and (3) the minstrel ballads (both traditional and contemporary). Among these, traditional mythological ballads have prime importance. The traditional secular ballads elucidate the cult of the Indian ethos and lofty human values. The incidental ballads highlight many events of national importance in Indian history—national, contemporary, and mythological. The *Alha* and other genres of songs, especially in the *Raso grantha*, fall into this category. The traditional mythological and religious ballads present the tradition of Hinduism, focusing especially on its practical aspects. They sing the glory of religious personalities, saints, gods, and goddesses. They also present the rich composite culture of India in Sufi, or Muslim mystic, songs. The minstrel ballads became popular in the middle ages of Indian sociopolitical history. The court poets started creating these ballads, and the tradition continues even today. In political rallies, supporters of a political leader are often found singing the glory of the leader or the political party in a hyperbolic way with quite visible conceits and imagery.

Folk lyrics may be broadly categorized as *samskara* lyrics, age lyrics, season lyrics, *vrata* (fasting) lyrics, deity lyrics, labor lyrics, and caste-based lyrics. Because India is a country of numerous dialects and traditions, it is neither appropriate nor possible to discuss in detail a particular folk song or lyric; rather, this article focuses on providing genre-based characteristics of the folk songs. The thoughts and emotions in the various lyrics are largely similar; the only perceptible difference is that of language.

The Sanskrit word *samskara* means to prepare or to make perfect, and it generally refers to a major ritual in one's life, such as a purification ritual. The samskara lyrics provide the foundation of Indian folk belief and religion. These lyrics enshrine popular culture of one Indian holistic view of life. In general, the subdivisions are birth samskara lyrics (sung at the time of child birth); *mundana samskara* lyrics (sung at the time of first shaving of the hair on the child's head); *yagyopaveeta samskara* lyrics (sung on the occasion of offering the sacred thread of Hinduism to a child, traditionally the beginning of education); marriage samskara lyrics (called marriage *sangeet* in popular usage, sung before and after the marriage ceremony); *gamana samskara* lyrics (sung as the bride moves from the parental home to the home of the husband); and the lyrics of last ritual. Indian philosophy recognizes four *ashrama* in human life: the *brahmacharya*, the *grahastha*, the *vanaprastha*, and the *sanyas*. When a person dies after completing a long and perfect life, in some cases songs are sung. Indian Hindu tradition marks 16 samskaras beginning from the time of conception to the last day of life in the world. In the life of householders (the grahastha), these samskara-based lyrics have great importance. They prevent human life from becoming monotonous and relate to the philosophy of life as a complete whole and to seeing it not in fragments but in unity and coherence.

In a traditional Indian way of life, there are also popular lyrics suitable for different life stages. From early childhood until old age, there are cradle lyrics, childhood lyrics, youth lyrics, and devotional lyrics (*bhajan*). India is a miniature world in itself, and the Indian way of life reflects a keen environmental awareness. The tropical climate of the country holds rich fascination with its changing seasons, and that has given rise to a set of season lyrics. The season lyrics include *Kajali, Hindola, Faag, Holi, Charakhi, Bindiaya*, and others, and they add to the festivities of the seasons. Among the season-based folk lyrics, *baramasa* is popular in almost every part of India. Its theme revolves around the separation of the lover from his or her beloved and its effect on the personalities and actions of the characters concerned. In Indian literature, seasons are depicted normally in two forms: *rituvarnana* and *baramasa*. The condition of togetherness and union of the lover and the beloved is depicted in rituvarnana and that of separation in the baramasa. In the rituvarnana, the poet divides the year into three or six time periods as different *ritus*, and in baramasa, the year is analyzed in 12 months. The correlation of season and psyche is reflected through the narrative of baramasa. In baramasa the characteristics of a season work as the catalyst in affecting the psyche of the beloved, and in associating herself with nature, she translates her anxiety, separation, and the good past days spent in union. The narration of baramasa depicts the circularity of the Indian concept of time.

The vrata lyrics are another significant branch of folk lyrics. For many, the Indian lifestyle is grounded in spirituality. For purging the soul from a spiritual and religious point of view and for keeping the metabolism at peace from a medical point of view, vrata (fasting) has been prescribed for different days of the year. Different days meant for vratas have certain stories and songs associated with them that are performed mostly in the evening. Deity lyrics are sung in the eulogy of the gods. In large part they are addressed to Shiva Ji, Sri Rama, Sri Krishna, goddess Durga Ji and her different forms, goddess Parvati Ji, Hanuman Ji, and others. Labor lyrics are meant for easing stress and fatigue while performing different kinds of work in farms, fields, and production houses. The caste-based lyrics are almost obsolete today, as the division of caste and creed is discouraged, but we cannot ignore the existence of *kahar* (the palanquin-bearer) songs, *mallah* (rover) songs, *aheer* (deer) songs, *lodhis* (Lodhi caste) songs, and others that are reminiscent of these social divisions.

Folk lyrics are quite relevant in the contemporary context because they carry the tradition, glory, and prosperity of folk wisdom to readers and listeners who may be unaware of their value. They are also useful in establishing healthy cultural relationships among different groups within the nation and beyond national boundaries, because ultimately they speak the language of love and equality. The studies of folk lyrics provide a storehouse of information and value to other disciplines of knowledge, including sociolinguistics, social anthropology, demography, literature, and philosophy.

Ravindra Pratap Singh

See also: Bol; Dhrupad; Harmonium; Rakha, Alla; Sitar; Tabla

Further Reading

Borrow, George. 1982. *The Ballads of All Nations*. London: Alston Rivers.

Singh, R. P. 2012. "Representative Folk Literature of Hindi Speaking North India." *Spark International Online Journal* 4(8) (August), 34–45.

Indonesian Pop Music

Both cosmopolitan and eclectic in nature, Indonesia's popular music consists of four principal genres: *gambus*, *dangdut*, *kroncong*, and *jaipongan*, all of which have shaped the cultural identity of the nation. Of these, only jaipongan is indigenous to the culture; the remaining genres carry cultural influences from a widely diverse universe that includes Western rock music, Arabic music, Bollywood films, and popular song.

The name *gambus* originally derived from an Arabic stringed instrument (the modern *oud*) that denotes its relationship with Islam. The instruments of gambus can include *qanum* (zither) and *dombak* (drum), and its music features short, sequential phrases with simple danceable rhythms. The vocal style is more Middle Eastern than Indonesian. Performers dress in *kaffiyeh* and *agal* (the latter an Arab headdress worn by men). Gambus lyrics feature Islamic subject matter, but also are valued for their musical qualities. Some conservative Muslims disapprove of the music because it is primitive and sensual in performance practice, and thus is not seen as consistent with proper Islamic values. Modern gambus recordings are primarily sung in Arabic, but instead of being praise songs instead feature arrangements of Arabic pop songs. Gambus performers are typically young men, with Orkes Gambus El Bass admirably representing this musical style.

Dangdut musically represents the urban poor; it arose initially in Jakarta, before spreading to other cities. Initially, the music was a combination of Indian and Malaysian film songs, reflecting social situations such as poverty and misfortune, as well as flirtation. It is disseminated to the public through recordings, films, and social and broadcast media. Tabla-like drumming style is a significant feature of the music, with a pattern that incorporates a low pitch before a strong beat then followed by a heavier, higher-pitched sound on the strong beat. The rhythmic pattern can be imitated using the syllables "dang-DUT," possibly the origin of the genre's name.

Gong Size

The Indonesian and Balinese *gamelan* ensembles are known for their gongs of various sizes, the largest of which are called the *gong ageng*. Made of bronze, these gongs range in size, usually from around 60–70 centimeters (26–30 inches) across, but can reach in excess of 100 centimeters (40 inches) in diameter and weight in excess of several hundred pounds. Bronze gong ageng are very expensive and sometimes less expensive iron copies are substituted—though this comes at the cost of a change in sound. Contrary to popular belief, the gong ageng is made of three interlocking pieces of metal riveted together, with the central knob formed by hand via intense hammering. The hammering and contouring are necessary to achieve a definite pitch, which is the hallmark of the gong ageng's sound.

Dangdut enjoyed success under the aegis of the pop star Rhoma Irama (1947–), who dominated the genre until the mid-1990s. Irama revolutionized dangdut in several respects, first by incorporating Middle Eastern musical inflections and reducing the Indian and Malaysian elements, which appealed to Indonesia's Muslim youth culture. He also added elements of American rock music (electric guitar riffs, synthesizers, and back-beat rhythmic patterns) and enhanced the lyrics to incorporate elements of social protest, poverty, and political corruption (e.g., "the rich get richer and the poor get poorer") instead of the laments of early dangdut songs. These innovations brought both acclaim and disdain: Irama was banned from state-controlled television and radio for the radical, incendiary comments in his music. Irama later began to incorporate more Islamic religious messages in his lyrics, even though dangdut is primarily secular. While Rhoma Irama represents one trend in dangdut, singers such as Mansyur S. remain true to the Indian film music element in the genre.

Indonesian dangdut singer Rhoma Irama and his band Soneta performing in 2019. (Adek Berry/AFP/Getty Images)

Kroncong, dating from the 1920s, is a form of popular dance music incorporating elements inherent in polka and waltz. Typical instrumentation features violins, guitars, ukulele, and indigenous drums; the incorporation of European musical instruments distinguishes it from other popular music forms. It derives its name from a stringed instrument of the same name that is similar to a ukulele. In performance, it features lyric melodic lines, *cantabile* vocal style, and simple harmonies punctuated by the pizzicato rhythmic patterns and the kroncong's backbeat strumming. Its rise in popularity can be traced to the adaptation of four- and eight-bar Tin Pan Alley song forms (A A B A) and the incorporation of the note bending and "blue notes" inherent in jazz. As a result, kroncong became an international commercial music while remaining true to its Javanese roots, which made it a music of popular appeal. This popularity galvanized public opinion during World War II when it became an outlet for nationalist sentiment against Japanese invading forces. Modern kroncong is more rock-inflected; however, there is still a strong market for the older forms.

The other category of Indonesian popular music is derived from Western youth culture's popular music, sung in the vernacular. This music, known as *pop*

Indonesia and based in Jakarta, has followed the trends of American popular music in form, style, and content. Likewise, its audience gains access to the music through social and broadcast media, rather than live performance. Its lyrics are noncontroversial (often love songs), and appeal to well-educated, affluent consumers. Indonesia's answer to Christian pop music, known as *pop rohani* (spiritual pop) is a subgenre of pop Indonesia and exhibits a more robust ensemble, including a female lead singer; female back-up singers who provide call-and-response patterns; and a "band" of guitars, violins, keyboards, and percussion including tambourines and the tabla-esque drums associated with dangdut. Subject matter for these songs focus on morality and behavior. Similar to the origins of rap and hip-hop in the United States, both dangdut and pop Indonesia's grassroots origins fostered a cottage industry in music that enabled amateur musicians across the island to write their own songs in local dialects, record their work economically, and disseminate the songs to consumers absent government support.

Jaipongan is a form of pop music that bears the distinction of being derived from folk entertainments of West Java (Sunda); unlike gambus, dangdut, and kroncong, it does not incorporate foreign musical influences. It features a female singer/dancer and a small group of musicians playing *rebab*, gong, three *kethuk* (horizontal gongs common in Javanese gamelan ensembles), *saron* (a bronze, seven-bar mini-xylophone used in gamelan ensembles), and drums. Jaipongan also imbues the spirit of community music-making in a type of audience participation performance where male audience members join in the performance. The word "jaipongan" itself was derived from syllables imitating drum sounds; and, like all Indonesian music, drumming and rhythmic patterns are the foundation of the genre. The musician Gugum Gumbira (1945–) is cited as the progenitor of the discipline, as he introduced the compilation of various Sudanese musical components that initiated the jaipongan phenomenon in the mid-1970s, beginning with his group's first public performance in 1974. Eclipsed by other musical genres in the 1980s, Gumbira created staged performances of jaipongan, transforming it into an accepted national stage dance. Although its international popularity was short-lived, jaipongan has remained popular as a regional popular music among the Sudanese in West Java.

Eldonna L. May

See also: Gamelan Orchestra (Javanese); Kebyar; Wayang Kulit

Further Reading

Frederick, W.H. 1982. "Rhoma Irama and the Dangdut Style: Aspects of Contemporary Indonesian Popular Culture." *Indonesia* (34), 103–130.

Harnish, David, and Ann Rasmussen, eds. 2011. *Divine Inspiration: Music and Islam in Indonesia.* New York: Oxford University Press.

Kornhauser, Bronia. 1978. "In Defence of Kroncong." In M. J. Kartomi (ed.), *Studies in Indonesian Music (Monash Papers on Southeast Asia No. 7)*, 104–105. Victoria, Australia: University of Monash.

Lockard, Craig A. 1998. *Dance of Life: Popular Music and Politics in Southeast Asia.* Honolulu: University of Hawaii Press.

Iranian Classical Music

Iranian classical music (also known as Persian classical music, or Persian art music) has its roots in both urban and court music traditions dating back to the Sassanian dynasty (224–651 CE) of the Persian Empire. In the mid- to late 19th century, Iranian classical music fully developed into the standardized practice that is known today, under the guidance of prominent court musicians. Since this period, classical music has been centered on the *radif*, a complex musical system of modes and melodies that dictates the structure and also guides the improvisation of a solo or group performance. Today, Iranian classical music continues as a rich cultural tradition in Iran as well as in the Iranian diaspora.

HISTORY

Throughout the Sassanid period, music culture was developed primarily in the court, where musicians were highly respected and held prominent positions. The Sassanids saw the use of various instruments, including harps, lutes, flutes, and bagpipes. Under Sassanian Emperor Khosrow II, who ruled from 591–628 CE, the musician Barbad is credited with creating the earliest known musical system. This system was based on the Zoroastrian calendar: seven modes, known as *khosrovani*, for the seven days of the week; 30 derivative modes, known as *lahn*, for the days in a month; and 360 melodies, for the days in a year.

Beginning in 642 CE, the Arab invasion resulted in a wider spread of Persian cultural influences across the Muslim world, as Persian musicians and scholars became increasingly well-known and sought after. During this time, music scholar Al-Farabi wrote *Kitab al-musiqi al-kabir* (*The great book on music*), a famous work compiling information on musical instruments and musical theory. One of Barbad's disciples, Ibn Sina, also documented concepts of music theory, including notions of consonance and dissonance, as well as the effects of music on people. Today, 12 main musical modes, known as *dastgah*, are named following some of the modal names used in Ibn Sina's writings. In the late 13th century, the scholar Safi al-din wrote highly influential works that helped in the development of a foundation for urban musical tradition: *Kitab all-adwar* (*Book of cycles*) and *Risala al-sharaffiyya fi al-nisab al-ta'lifiyyaa* (*Sharafian treatise on intervallic relations*).

From the 16th to the mid-19th centuries, there was a decline in music scholarship due to the strict Islamic—specifically Shi'a—attitude toward music. Many religious leaders believed that music exerted an immoral influence upon its listeners and was not suitable for Muslims who should be focusing more on achieving closeness to Allah. During this period, music was relegated to private performance, focusing on solo art music. Master *setar* player Mirza Abdollah (1845–1918) began to standardize the *radif*, a system of modes which were sectioned into groups known as *dastgah*. The consequential system of 12 dastgah became the foundation for all musical improvisation within this newly developed classical music.

From the mid to late 19th century, as music began to re-enter court life, the shahs of Iran employed French music scholars to lead their court musicians and further develop and modernize Persian music traditions. Bousquet organized a military band for royal ceremonies at the court, and Rouillon and Lemair established a school of music, which introduced Western instruments and the idea of fixed Western notation.

TRADITION OF THE RADIF

The radif is a hierarchical, highly detailed modal system of Persian art music, which was loosely standardized in the late 19th century. Throughout the early 20th century, the radif remained dependent upon local music traditions and was taught orally from musician to musician. It wasn't until the mid-20th century that the system of modes became fully standardized, as they were increasingly available in printed Western notation and annotated to include notes and practices specific to Persian tuning and performance traditions. With the introduction of new technology, sound recordings of the radif also became available.

The radif is composed of 12 distinct dastgahs, which in turn, consist of individual *gushehs*, or melodic pieces, which provide a modal framework for improvisatory performance. The dastgahs are defined by a set of pitches, or *maqam*, and a specific melodic character, or *mayeh*. Within the dastgah groups, the individual gushehs may be manipulated and improvised upon. Each gusheh carries its own specific name, as it represents a different genre within the radif tradition, and serves a specific function within a performance (whether it is introductory, conclusive, or transitory) to introduce dance-like sections or new modulations. The number of gushehs varies between dastgahs; some contain a large number and others only a few.

Traditionally, the art of Iranian classical music has been taught orally through private instruction from master to student. Students focus on the mastery of one instrument, including singers who learn to sing while playing a specific instrument. Because performance is entwined with improvisation, learning the radif is essential. Each dastgah is learned and gradually its respective gushehs are also learned—a process that may take years to fully master. Once the foundation and basic structures for improvisation are mastered, students may experiment with form and length of pieces.

COMPOSED CLASSICAL PIECES

In the late 19th and early 20th centuries, the tradition of performing the radif became influenced by Western traditions, such as Western instrumentation (tuned to Persian standards) and Western notation. The introduction of Western orchestral music influenced instrumental ensemble performance and contrasted with Persian solo playing. This gave rise to more composed, as opposed to improvised, pieces, particularly in the early 20th century. There are three types of instrumental composed music: *pishdaramad*, *reng*, and *chaharmezrab*. In addition, there is another form of composed music known as *tasnif*, or *taraneh*, which is reserved for vocal performance.

Composed pieces utilize the dastgahs along with their respective gushehs, but are rooted in set meters, unlike the radif which are rhythmically free or nonrhythmic. A variety of rhythms are employed, such as compound duple, simple duple, triple, and quadruple meters. Pieces begin with a theme indicative of the maqam and the mayeh, followed by sections referencing a specific gusheh. Only the chaharmezrab, which is intended for a solo instrument, is monothematic and does not follow this sequence.

Pishdaramad, credited to the tar master Darvish Khan (1872–1926), is known as an introduction to the other pieces to follow. It is usually composed for ensemble playing, but can sometimes be performed by a solo instrument. It is a short piece, usually between two and five minutes in length, and is most commonly performed in duple time in a moderate tempo, although sometimes a triple or quadruple meter is also used.

Reng is a traditional dance piece, which draws upon the gushehs but is performed at a much faster tempo in a 6/8 dance meter. Reng is most commonly the finale of a dastgah solo performance, but may also sometimes be played by an ensemble. Chaharmezrab is composed as a solo instrumental piece, demonstrating virtuosic mastery of an instrument. It is the least fixed of the composed types of pieces. Melodically, chaharmezrab is simple, with some rhythmic syncopation and melodic improvisation allowed, including some modular shifts. This piece may precede the pishdaramad, follow the chosen dastgah, or be placed before or after the gushehs, elaborating upon their particular modes. Sometimes it can be found at the end of a performance, instead of the reng, or it may precede the reng. The chaharmezrab has gradually become more popular as interest in virtuosic displays has increased.

Tasnif involves a vocal solo with an instrumental accompaniment played either by the soloist or by an ensemble. It is similar to pishdaramad in structure, but is typically performed toward the end of a performance, before the reng. Tasnifs are often set to classical poetry from Persian poets such as Rumi, Hafez, or Sa'di. More contemporary tasnifs are set on poetry that contains social messages or nationalistic sentiment. Alternatively, taraneh (sometimes used synonymously with tasnif) can be performed, which takes the form of a love ballad that has been influenced by Western melody and harmony.

IRANIAN CLASSICAL INSTRUMENTS

A wide array of instruments is used in Iranian classical music, although some, such as the *chang* and the *ud*, are no longer popularly used. Today, the most commonly used classical instruments are the *setar, tar, santur, kamancheh, ney*, and *tombak*. These instruments are native to Iran, but can often be found in similar or related forms across the Mediterranean, the Middle East, North Africa, and the Subcontinent.

The setar is perhaps the most central to Iranian classical performance. Although similar in name to the North Indian *sitar*, their construction differs. Originally known as the *tanbur* (a name which is still used in some native folk music), the instrument became known as the "setar" in the 16th century. The setar is a long-necked lute with a teardrop-shaped soundbox. Traditionally, it has three strings, usually strummed with the fingernail, spanning in range across two octaves and a fifth. In the 20th century, a fourth string was added to act as a drone. The tar does not share the ancient history of the setar, but is similar in construction, with the same range but in three courses of doubled strings. The first two courses are used for the melody, while the third course provides a drone. The tar is plucked with a metal plectrum, which creates a rich sonority.

The santur is a Persian hammered dulcimer, the form of which is very similar to forms found in North India and Greece. The kamancheh is a three- or four-stringed spike fiddle that is held upright and played with a blow. "Ney" is a generic name for all types of wind-blown flutes or pipes that can be found across the Middle East and North Africa. In the classical tradition, the *ney-e haftband* is commonly used; it is a wooden, rim-blown flute held obliquely, with six finger holes and one thumb hole. A range of percussive instruments are also used in Iranian classical music, including the *tombak, tabla*, and *daf*. The tombak (sometimes called *tonbak* or *dombak*) is perhaps the most prevalent form: a goblet drum held horizontally or at an angle and played with the fingers and palms of the hands. The tombak adds the rhythmic element to ensemble playing, but can also be used in solo, virtuosic performance.

Some Western instruments have made their way into Iranian classical performance as well, particularly in small ensembles. The violin often replaces the kamancheh, though modified to Persian tuning, and the ney is sometimes replaced by the clarinet, flute, or trumpet. The piano, despite its fixed tuning that clashes with Persian interval tuning, has also been used in contemporary Iranian classical performance as both an ensemble and solo instrument, and can sometimes undergo minor tuning changes to conform to Persian tuning standards.

When a performance requires a singer, the role of the vocalist is extremely significant. Often the decision as to the overall mood of a piece and the selection of dastgah, as well as the selection of poetry to be sung, falls to the singer. The singer may be accompanied by either a wind or a stringed instrument in combination with a percussive instrument, or a larger ensemble of instruments. Vocalists add to melodic phrases by the use of *tahrir*, an ornamental effect of a quavering voice and melodic embellishment. Occasionally, ensemble musicians may accompany the singer with back-up vocals on some of the verses. Prominent Persian music ensembles today that tour across the globe include the Kamkars, National Music Ensemble, Dastan Ensemble, Shakila's Group, and Naghmeh Ensemble.

PERFORMANCE IN THE 20TH CENTURY

Because religious officials often frowned upon public performance, classical music performance remained an elite tradition relegated to private performance in homes and in the court. Only after the early 20th century was Persian classical music opened up to public performance, as radio, television, and film helped bring Persian music traditions (including musical instruction) into the public domain. Following the death of the master tar player Darvish Khan in 1926, one of his former students, Morteza Neydavoud, founded the School of Darvish, where he taught about Iranian traditional music and culture. Neydavoud also documented the radif through a series of audio cassette recordings of 297 gushehs spanning all the dastgahs, for the benefit of future Iranian classical musicians. In 1923, Ali-Naqi Vaziri (1887–1979) founded the Academy of Music of Iran after spending five years studying music in Paris and Berlin. In addition to music lessons, Vaziri delivered lectures, organized Persian music concerts, and encouraged the integration of some European musical concepts he had learned while abroad. He went on to become the director of the Tehran Conservatory in 1941. Meanwhile, Adolhasan Saba, who became the director of the Conservatory of Rasht in 1927, collected regional folk melodies, which he later incorporated into his own classical compositions. Influenced by these melodies, Saba introduced new time signatures such as 5/4 and 7/4 into the Iranian classical repertoire.

Under Pahlavi rule (1925–1979), music was promoted heavily as an important aspect of national culture. Reza Shah Pahlavi established a conservatory of music in Tehran in the 1930s, under the Ministry of Culture and Arts. His son, Mohammad-Reza Shah Pahlavi, also encouraged the pursuit of music education, as a department of music was created in the University of Tehran in 1965, modeled after the American system and including subjects such as theory, composition, and the study of Western instruments, in addition to the study of Persian music traditions.

As Mohammad-Reza Shah sought to modernize the country, the face of Iranian music changed rapidly. Many master musicians of the Persian classical repertoire felt that Westernized music and music theory were encroaching upon Persian tradition and threatening to take over. At the same time, both Western and Iranian popular music were also growing and, in turn, influencing Iranian music as new forms of hybridized Western/Iranian styles surfaced. Some musicians entered under contract into the Tehran Symphony Orchestra which had been founded in the late 1930s. They regularly performed works commissioned by Western and Iranian composers. Many new composers, pianists, violinists, and singers of Western popular and classical music emerged. An opera company was formed in the late 1960s and the Rudaki Hall in Tehran was built to accommodate increasingly larger productions and the growing size and number of orchestras. The Shiraz Festival, held annually near the ancient city of Persepolis, which ran from 1967 to 1977, showcased the latest musical talent within Iran as well as from the international music community. This included new avant-garde works from Iranian and international composers under the baton of prominent European conductors and their orchestras.

After 1979, the Iranian Revolution brought with it a cultural revolution under the Ayatollah Khomeini, which temporarily brought all music to a halt. There were no musical broadcasts on radio or television; many music schools were forced to close and musical groups disbanded. After the initial years of the new Islamic Republic, music was gradually reintroduced, first in the form of revolutionary songs, after which some folk and traditional music, including classical music, re-entered the public domain. The Tehran Symphony Orchestra re-formed and music programs were slowly reinstated in schools and universities across Iran. However, fluctuating political preferences and laws regarding music continue to put music education and performance under great strain. As a result, many classical musicians have either emigrated to the West, or as in the case of Mohammad-Reza Shajarian, have turned toward touring internationally to sustain their careers.

Theresa Steward

See also: Dastgah; Kamancheh; Shajarian, Mohammed-Reza; Tar; Tombak

Further Reading

Farhat, Hormoz. 1973. *The Traditional Art Music of Iran.* Tehran, Iran: High Council of Culture and Art, Centre for Research and Cultural Co-ordination.

Farmer, Henry G. 1938. "An Outline History of Music and Musical Theory." In A. U. Pope and P. Ackerman (eds.), *A Survey of Persian Art*, 2783–2804. London: Oxford University Press.

Miller, Lloyd. 1999. *Music and Song in Persia: The Art of Avaz.* Salt Lake City: University of Utah Press.

Nettl, Bruno. 1987. *The Radif of Persian Music: Studies of Structure and Cultural Context.* Champaign, IL: Elephant & Cat.

Zonis, Ella. 1973. *Classical Persian Music: An Introduction.* Cambridge, MA: Harvard University Press.

Irish American Vocal Music

When the Irish came to America, they brought with them their tunes and songs. Many of those melodies have been transformed and subsumed into a new genre of mixed cultural identity: Irish American vocal music. This music took two distinct paths. The first was the music rooted in Ireland, which changed through emigration, and then developed in new communities. It would later serve as an important creative influence in the development of such genuinely American styles of music as bluegrass, country, and rock and roll. The second path was taken by a portion of this music that adhered to and maintained the traditions and musical styles from the Irish homeland, while other tunes changed and adapted to life in the new country.

For centuries, Ireland existed on the outskirts of Europe. Though geographically very close to the mainland, this tiny island nation had one foot in the First World and one in the Third; it was not fully industrialized and remained predominantly rural. In addition, its more than 800 years of colonization and oppression under the British removed almost all evidence of Gaelic life, culture, and language from Ireland. The Great Famine of 1845 changed everything. Entire villages uprooted themselves and left hopeful for the promise of America: opportunity, religious freedom, and prosperity. Throughout the mid-19th century, a flood of songs entered the United States with the emigrants who sought that new life. Nevertheless, the feeling of cultural isolation they experienced caused them to hold strongly to traditions and communities of their homeland.

Many of these Irish immigrants, mostly Scots-Irish (people from Northern Ireland of Scottish ancestry), settled in the Appalachian mountain regions. The music of this area underwent a transformation over time and became Appalachian old-time music, bluegrass music, or hillbilly music. That sound would later serve as a primary influence on early rock and roll. These emigrants were very involved in the landscape of Ireland and they mourned the land they left. Songs about the green hills and low valleys gave them comfort in America. For these people, the music and songs were a means for them to remain connected to their homeland and to share with younger generations visual descriptions of the homeland they had never seen. In many cases, the songs or tunes remained very similar, throughout several generations, to those that came with the first settlers. Over time, the lyrics changed to adapt to the new surroundings (O'Conner, 2001, p. 17).

By the turn of the 20th century, Irish music and Irish musicians had made a significant impact on the modern American entertainment and musical industries. Songs like *My Uncle Dan McCann* were popular standards. Many of these songs depicted the political upheaval still underway in Ireland, while at the same time offering support to those both in American and in the homeland. Other Irish songs and personalities had made their way onto the minstrel and vaudeville stages across the United States. Stephen Foster (1826–1864), often considered one of the most American of these early songwriters, was an Irish American. Foster wrote many of his songs, including *O! Susanna, Gentle Annie,* and *My Old Kentucky Home,* for the vaudeville or minstrel stage. Additionally, Irish fight Songs, such as *Tim Finegan's Wake,* were hugely popular (Moloney, 2002, pp. 24–30).

Throughout the early 1900s, Tin Pan Alley songwriters continued to popularize and romanticize the idealized vision of Ireland through music. According to Moloney, "By the turn of the century, many were the aging children or grandchildren of survivors of the great famine. . . . Images of an invented homeland that were harmless and positive tapped into an Irish-American need for affirmation" (Moloney, 2006, p. 394). Songs such as *Has Anybody Here Seen Kelly* (made popular by Bing Crosby) and *Who Threw the Overalls in Mrs. Murphy's Chowder?* were incredibly popular.

After the romance with Tin Pan Alley songs had waned, groups like the Clancy Brothers in the 1960s once again sparked an interest in Irish songs and singing. The Clancy Brothers strongly influenced the American folk revival that took place during the latter half of the 20th century, making Irish American vocal music a primary influence on all American popular music.

Stacie Lee Rossow

See also: Bluegrass; Celtic Music; Shape-Note Singing

Further Reading

Moloney, Mick. 2002. *Far From the Shamrock Shore: The Story of Irish-American Immigration Through Song.* New York: Crown.

Moloney, Mick. 2006. "Irish-American Popular Music." In J. J. Lee and Marion Casey (eds.), *Making the Irish American,* 381–405. New York: New York University Press.

O'Connor, Nuala. 2001. *Bringing It All Back Home: The Influence of Irish Music.* Dublin, Ireland: Merlin Publishing.

Irish Dance Music

Although there is no record in ancient Irish literature of the development of dance music, Celts and Norsemen contributed to the sung and danced heritage of Ireland. The Irish words *cor* and *port,* which are used to describe reels and jigs, do not properly signify these dances, but rather indicate lively pieces on the harp meant to accompany them. *Jigeánnai* comes through English (*jig*) from the Italian *giga* and *rileánna* through English (*reel*) from the Anglo-Saxon *ragla,* meaning to sway, walk, or stagger from side to side. The two Irish words used to describe dancing (*damhsa* and *rince*) are borrowed from France (*danse*) and England (skating *rink*), respectively.

After the Anglo-Norman invasion (1169–1172 CE), round dances from continental Europe became popular. Records from the 15th century indicate that caroling accompanied events such as the 1413 visit of the mayor of Waterford to O'Driscoll of Baltimore, and nearly 3,000 people attended the first great Festival of Arts at Killeigh in 1443.

Many references to Irish dances and dance music begin to appear in 16th-century Anglo-Irish and English literature, including roundelays, heys, trenchmores, jigs, and *rince fada* (field dance). Sir Henry Sidney wrote to Queen Elizabeth I in 1569 about the ladies of Galway dancing (group) Irish jigs in magnificent dress; Fynes Moryson was the first to describe the sword and withy dances to her in 1600. The earliest reference to *rince*—"*Rainge timcheall teinne as buibhin tseibhir treinneartmhuir*" (A dance around fires by a slender swift young group)—dates from 1588. Some country dances remained in vogue and were preserved in Ireland even after they were superseded in England by French dances.

Seventeenth-century sources include caustic remarks by Dr. Talbot, Archbishop of Dublin, about the followers of Friar Peter Walsh "dancing jigs and country dances" (1674) and descriptions of the *rince fada* long dance from Dineley's *Voyage through the Kingdom of Ireland* (1681). Dineley heard the bagpipe, Irish harp, and "Jewes Harpe" in addition to solo fiddle playing. When King James II traveled to Ireland in 1689, he was welcomed with a *rinceadh-fada*, performed by three persons moving abreast, each of whom held the end of a white handkerchief. They advanced to slow music, and were followed by the other dancers in pairs, each holding a white handkerchief between them. In Richard Head's *The Western Wonder* (1674), he observed "in every field a fiddle and the lasses footing it till they are all of a foam" (Dowling, 2016, p. 77). Other dances mentioned during this period include the withy dance, the sword dance, the war dance, and the long dance.

Eighteenth-century dancing masters were traveling bachelors who dressed elaborately, often in swallow-tailed coats and Caroline hats; they stayed for a "quarter" of one to six weeks in each location and were usually accompanied by a single piper or fiddler. The first steps taught were the rising step of the jig and the side step of the reel, although each master was also expected to compose new steps of his own (such as "Kelly's Number 5" or "Murphy's Reel Number 1"). Dancing masters fixed sugar and straw to their pupils' feet to enable them to distinguish the left from the right, and used jingles to impart the rhythm of the jig step: "Rise upon sugar, sit upon straw." In 1779, Arthur Young, noted English agriculturalist and traveler, wrote, "Dancing is very general among the poor people. Almost universal in every cabin. Dancing masters of their own rank travel throughout the country from cabin to cabin. Weddings are always celebrated with much dancing" (Foley, 2013, p. 13). Although the main 18th-century innovations in Irish dance were the introduction of reel and hornpipe measures, the 19th century was dominated by the arrival of the quadrille and other square-eight dances for four couples. After the quadrille was introduced to Dublin in 1816, a typical suite or "set" of dances comprised *Le pantalon* (in 6/8 time), *L'été* (in 6/8 time), *La poule* (in 2/4 time), *La pastourelle* (in 2/4 time), and *La finale* (in 6/8 time).

In Clare, the Caledonian set was popular; Kerry and Cork favored the Jenny Lind (Ginny Ling), the Victoria, and the Talavara. The Set of Erin and the Orange and Green were danced in the south and southwest. In the counties of Monahan and Fermanagh, and the Aran Islands, the usual pattern of five or six "figures" with a break between each figure were combined into a single sequence. The mazurka was danced to reels and called the *mazolka* (in Monaghan), the *mazorka* (Donegal), the *myserks* (Clare), and the *mesarts* (Kerry).

Aristocratic dancing masters around 1800 also taught deportment, continental court dances, and fencing for sixpence. In Wexford in 1816, pupils paid masters a "13" (there were 13 Irish pence in a British shilling) and paid a "tester" (sixpence-halfpenny) to musicians for a "quarter" of nine nights. By mid-century, the charge was 10 shillings for the master and five shillings for the musician for a "quarter" or up to six weeks. A dance master named O'Kearin from Castleisland in Kerry was the most widely traveled around 1820; he standardized many jig and reel steps. Several of his dances were recorded in O'Keeffe and O'Brian's *A Hand Book of Irish Dances* (1902), including his *rince fada*, four- and eight-hand reels, the High Caul Step, and the St. Patrick's Day eight-hand jig.

Tadgh Sean O'Sullivan (from County Kerry) defined the 12- and 16-hand reels, the half chain eight-hand reel, the Glenbeigh Bridge eight-hand jig, and the Humors of Bandon four-hand jig. John O'Reilly (of Killorglin, County Kerry) invented the Cross Reel and the full chain eight-hand reels, and Thomas Danaher (of Moonegay, Country Limerick) created a long progressive dance now called The Walls of Limerick. Three unusual *ceili* dances were collected in Northern Ireland: "The Three Tunes" is the only ceili dance to feature a change in tempo and tunes; it and "The Sweets of May" are the only Irish traditional dances to involve extensive pantomimed actions; and "The Trip to the Cottage" differs in construction, avoiding the initial "leap around" typical of ceili dances.

The reel began as a medieval dance and seems to be related to the French *haye* of the early 1500s. It was brought from Scotland to Ireland in the late 18th century, where it had been danced as the *reill* since 1590. Reels are lively dances for two or more couples, common in both Scotland and Ireland (the Highland Fling is a Scottish variant). They are the most popular tune type in Irish traditional music, performed in 4/4 or cut time with accents on the first and third beats of each bar. Most reels consist largely of eighth-note and triplet movement, and follow a standard AABB form, called a 32-bar "round." A round is repeated before a new reel is introduced, and tunes are usually grouped together.

The jig, first mentioned in Ireland in 1674, has many steps and turns, all of which are performed with difficult jumps. There is a distinction between "regular" jigs, consisting of two eight-measure phrases, and "irregular" ones, varying in length. Musical jigs are mostly native to Ireland. They are played in 6/8 or 9/8 and sometimes accompany Morris dances. The single and slip jig are associated with specific soft-shoe solo dancing still performed in competitions today, usually by female dancers. Fast versions of single jig (and sometimes double jig) tunes are called "slides" and usually end with two dotted quarter notes; slides are used in the dancing of sets.

The history of the British jig, hornpipe, and reel is complex and interwoven. The hornpipe, named after a medieval double-reed instrument, developed in the early 17th century in British maritime settings, as ship companies carried a resident fiddler for dance music. John Playford's *English Dancing Master* (1651) contained music and illustrations for country-dance hornpipes, although the Irish form has a different profile than the British. Early 18th-century English hornpipes featured supreme displays of heavy footwork and were performed between acts of a play by professional male dancers. The later, common-time hornpipe with constant eighth-note movement (or a dotted eighth/16th note pairs) was adopted by Irish dancing masters after 1760 and replaced an earlier 3/2 figured dance. By the end of the 18th century, the stage or "sailor's" hornpipe included light hopping and skipping movements akin to Scottish stepping. It can be danced as a solo dance, a couples' dance, or a ring dance.

At the end of the 19th century, *Conradh ne Gaelige* (the Gaelic League) was established to revive interest in the Irish language and reinvigorate a perceived decay of traditional culture. Conventions featured traditional dance and music—but in discerning "authentic" from "imported" forms, the League deliberately excised some sets from the repertoire. In the 1920s and 1930s, traditional music and dance suffered the ravages of emigration and condemnation by the church. *An Coimisiún Le Rinncí Gaelacha* (The Commission for Irish Dance) was founded in 1929 to sift "alien" from "native" dance: they only registered Irish-speaking teachers (which ironically excluded some of the older experts who had attended school before Irish was on the curriculum), and published handbooks of dances that were acceptably Irish (*Ár Rincí Foirne*). The Public Dance Hall Act of 1935 forbade the informal house dances and "crossroads dances" that had been the primary sites of rural social dancing. The act put pressure on dancers to attend formally organized dances in the newly built halls, most of which were run by local clergy. This time revival came in the form of radio and the gramophone. In 1951, *Comhaltas Ceoltóirí Éireann* (Society of the Musicians of Ireland) was established to promote traditional music and dance; radio programs for specialized audiences by archivist Ciarán MacMathúna and piper/folklorist Séamus Ennis promoted traditional music.

In the 1960s, two phenomena brought the traditional arts to the attention of the general public. In 1960, Séan Ó Riada formed the first traditional ensemble that was not a ceili band: Ceoltóirí Chualann, which boasted two fiddlers (one of whom doubled on concertina), flute, pipes, button accordion, singer, *bodhrán* (not a traditional instrument until Ó Riada adopted it), and metal-strung harpsichord (unlike the gut-strung Celtic harps of folk revivalists around 1900, the bardic harp was metal-strung). Ó Riada created new social contexts and formal performance practices for traditional music, partly through his written-out arrangements. Ceoltóirí Chualann spawned other groups, first of which was the Chieftains, with overlapping membership between the two ensembles. Folk ballad groups like the Clancy Brothers with Tommy Makem introduced the new concept of singing Irish songs in harmony. By the 1970s, groups proliferated, led by Planxty, the Bothy Band,

and De Dannan. According to Nicholas Carolan, director of the Irish Traditional Music Archive, the tension between cultural "purists" and innovators in Irish traditional music and dance has been everpresent in Irish culture, but has intensified in the past two decades. Pub sessions, the *bouzouki*, the bodhrán, keyboard accordions replacing button *bosca ceoil*, and harmonic accompaniment for dancing were unusual before the 1970s.

In Irish traditional music for dancing, rhythms are usually swung, with pairs of eighth notes receiving unequal weight. Dynamics constantly fluctuate, and players employ slides and both finger and breath vibrato. Most elements of articulation derive from the bellows-blown *uilleann* pipes, which in turn developed from the older pastoral bagpipe and *piob mór* (Great Irish warpipes) traditions. When playing C as a quick passing tone, Irish flute and whistle players prefer C-sharp, due to its easier fingering (most Irish flutes are set up best for playing in D major). Flute ornamentation both for repeated notes and in scalar passages includes "cuts" (achieved by lifting a finger briefly from a closed hole) and "strikes" (also called a tip, tap, slap, or pat, achieved by bouncing a finger over an open hole). Fiddle cuts and strikes are produced similarly, by rapid lifting or striking movements of the left-hand fingers. The cut and strike gave rise to the multi-note ornaments called *rolls* (three repeated tones, the second decorated from above, and the third from below [e.g., G-A-G-F-G, where the note G falls on the beat]) and *crans* (staccato low D played on the chanter of uilleann pipes with descending scalar grace notes [e.g., A-D-G-D-F-D, where the note D falls on the beat]).

Laura Stanfield Prichard

See also: Bones (Britain and Ireland); Irish American Vocal Music; Irish Step Dancing

Further Reading

Brannan, Helen. 2001. *The Story of Irish Dance.* Lanham, MD: Rowman.

Breathnach, Breandan. 1996. *Folk Music and Dances of Ireland: A Comprehensive Study Examining the Basic Elements of Irish Folk Music and Dance Traditions.* Dublin: Ossian.

Dowling, Martin. 2016. *Traditional Music and Irish Society: Historical Perspectives.* London: Routledge.

Foley, Catherine E. 2013. *Step Dancing in Ireland: Culture and History.* London: Routledge.

Vallely, Fintan. 1999. *The Companion to Irish Traditional Music.* New York: NYU Press.

Irish Step Dancing

Irish step dancing has become increasingly popular in all parts of the world, thanks in large part to the international success of *Riverdance* and Michael Flatley's *Lord of the Dance.* But step dancing has been part of the Irish culture for several hundred years. References to certain dances, such as the *rince fada*, the Irish Hey (dancing in the round), and jigs, date from the mid-1500s when travelers and statesmen compared them to similar dances in Scotland. There was even a letter to Queen Elizabeth from Sir Henry Sidney, dated 1569, that referenced the "Irish jigs danced by the ladies in Galway," though the reference is most likely to a group version of

> **Céili**
>
> In the United States, two of the most popular forms of participatory dance music are salsa and *céili* step dancing. Although the two styles are very different in their origins (salsa has Latin roots and céili hails from Ireland), the modern versions of both styles developed primarily in the United States as part of remade cultural traditions by Irish American and Latin American people and supporters. Céili step dancing has roots that more directly connect to the style's homeland; however, the way in which it is danced in bars, clubs, and heritage organizations through the United States is different than in Ireland. Céili is, in this regard, a remade tradition that has roots in the past but that lives and is evolving in the present. This is due in no small part to the participatory nature of céili dancing which, unlike *Lord of the Dance*-type Irish dance performances, encourages audience members to become participants regardless of age or skill level.

the dance (Cullinane, 1987, p. 8). In fact, many of these group or *céili* dances are still taught in dance schools around the world. The rince fada (long dance) is a progressive line dance to a double jig, which can have any number of dance pairs.

The modern concept of step dancing dates back to around 1750, with the rise in popularity of the county dance masters. The dance masters would travel from town to town and teach their steps to the residents. Arthur Young noted in the late 1700s, "Dancing . . . is almost universal in every [cabin]. Dancing masters . . . travel the country from [cabin to cabin] with a piper or blind fiddler: and the pay is sixpence a quarter. It is an absolute system of education" (Breathnach 1971, p. 49). A primary feature of Irish step dance, which may have historic significance regarding the evolution of the dance, is the limited movement of the body above the hips, though the rigidity of the arms is a relatively recent development. This posture can be viewed as a staple stylistic component since its earliest times and relates to the weight of the steps. Breathnach describes it as trapping each note of music on the floor. Often a solo dancer would perform dances on a single wooden plank, a door taken off the hinges, or (as related in several anecdotes) on a kitchen table. By keeping the upper body still, the dancers were able to focus on the intricacies of the steps rather than the style of the arms (Breathnach, 1971, p. 53). Ó Canainn perfectly describes the relationship of the dance style to other artistic ventures in Ireland: "Irish dancers are often criticized for their lack of exuberance and, in particular, for the non-involvement in the dance of any other part of their bodies except their feet. Those who expect the traditional Irish dancer to throw his arms about and shout in the style of another country just do not understand that the normal Irish artistic restraint combined with a minute attention to intricate patterns is exhibited in the dance just as surely as in the *sean-nós* style of singing" (Ó Canainn, 1978, p. 75).

Three standard dances, and their multiple versions, exist in the modern repertoire of Irish dance: the jig, the reel, and the hornpipe. These dances are defined by the musical structure of the tunes. Most dance tunes are in a binary form (AB) and consist of eight-measure "steps" which are typically repeated (A A B B). One time through this cycle is referred to as "turning the tune" or a single round. The A section, or *tune*, is repeated and followed by the B section, or *turn*, which is then repeated. The standard rhythms and meter of each tune define the step used.

The jig, a compound meter tune in which the beat is divided into three equal parts, has four variations: the single jig, the double jig (also referred to as the treble or heavy jig), the slip or hop jig, and the slide. The single and double jigs are both in 6/8 meter but have different rhythmic patterns. The single jig employs two groups of three equal eighth notes, whereas the double jig uses a repeated quarter-note/eighth-note pattern. The slip or hop jig is in a 9/8 meter with three sets of three equal eighth notes. The slide is written in 12/8 with a lilting quarter-eighth pattern. Regardless of the formal origin of the jig and the debate as to whether it is of native or Italian creation, it should be noted that the tunes were native to Ireland, possibly derived from ancient clan marches or songs, or at the least, borrowed from England or Scotland (Breathnach, 1971, pp. 56–60).

Irish step dancing typically involves quick movements of the feet while maintaining a stiff and still upper body. (Patrick Dugan/Moment Mobile/Getty Images)

The reel and the hornpipe are both written in duple meters where each beat is equally divided into two parts. The reel is typically notated in 4/4 time, but has the feel of two larger beats (cut time) with relatively equal beat stress. It is believed to be of Scottish origin and to have come to Ireland in the mid-1700s. The hornpipe, while still in duple meter, usually employs dotted rhythms and a lilt often associated with sailors' songs of the late 18th century. Until recently, the hornpipe was exclusively for male dancers due to the heaviness of the steps.

The dance masters of the 1700s, who traveled from village to village, would enter festivals and compete for titles against other masters. Winners could often lay claim to additional villages of the masters over whom they triumphed. Dance masters were judged according to the speed, intricacy, and number of steps in their repertoire. A "step" is a single part of the tune (eight-measure phrase). The steps, and the resulting dances, are learned in a genealogical fashion; they are passed from teacher to student, which enabled some dances to survive the diaspora of the 19th century (Casey, 2006, p. 420).

By the mid-1800s, references to dances from local festivals, rural fairs, sporting events, and wedding festivities were plentiful (Hast and Scott, 2004, pp. 26–27). In 1893 the *Conradh na Gaelige* (Gaelic League) formed and began to encourage the revival of the Irish culture that had been limited throughout almost 800 years of British occupation and colonization. Irish dance had become so popular that by 1929 the League, which had been primarily concerned with the promotion of the Irish language (*An Gaelige*), formed *An Coimisiún le Ricni' Gaelacha* (The Irish Dancing Commission) to establish and oversee the rules of teaching, judging, and competition within the newly standardized realm of competitive Irish dance.

Irish step dancing, as defined by An Coimisiún le Ricni' Gaelacha, is focused primarily on the footwork, although timing and rhythm are deemed incredibly important. It is also this focus on competition that eventually required the hands to become rigid and fixed. Various writings and anecdotes prior to 1920 describe small movements of the hands, though not wild and raucous, or the placement of them on the hips by both men and women. Today, the competitive standard is to have the hands and arms still and straight to the body. Competition occurs at all levels from beginner and local *feisianna* (festivals which included language, singing, and dance competitions) to *Oireachtas Rince na cruinne* (World Irish Dance Championships).

Costuming has also become a definitive feature of Irish step dancing. Traditionally, men or women in a *feis* competition might have worn their Sunday-best attire adorned with ribbons. There are references to both women and men wearing a specially made *brath* (traditional shawl) during dancing festivities. These garments were typically rectangular, full-length, hoodless, and sleeveless and attached at the shoulder or breast with a brooch. Around 1920 the length became considered too cumbersome for dancing, so they were shortened and attached at the hip (Cullinane, 1987, pp. 63–64). It was also during this time that ornate embroidery on dresses and vests became commonplace. Many of the designs were based upon the ancient Celtic illuminations seen in *The Book of Kells*.

While the phenomena of *Riverdance* and *Lord of the Dance* both emanated from Ireland, they reflected skills honed by American-born dancers fluent in traditional step dancing. Although Irish dance has been in the United States for more than 200 years, arriving with immigrants during the diaspora soon after its development in the countryside of Ireland, it has been the overwhelming success of these two shows over the past two decades that has brought Irish step dancing to more people worldwide then previously seen in the past 200 years.

Stacie Lee Rossow

See also: Celtic Music; Irish Dance Music

Further Reading

Breathnach, Brendán. 1971. *Folk Music and Dances of Ireland.* Cork, Ireland: Ossian Publications.

Casey, Marion R. 2006. "Before Riverdance: A Brief History of Irish Step Dancing in America." In *Making the Irish American: History and Heritage of the Irish in the United States*, 417–425. New York: New York University Press.

Cullinane, John P. 1987. *Aspects of the History of Irish Dancing.* Cork City, Ireland: J.P. Cullinane.

Hast, Dorothea, and Stanley Scott. 2004. *Music in Ireland.* Oxford: Oxford University Press.

Ó Canainn, Thomás. 1978. *Traditional Music in Ireland.* Cork, Ireland: Ossian Publications.

Italian Folk Music (Various Regions)

Italian folk music is a heterogeneous set of musical traditions with roots in several Mediterranean and central European cultures. Even after more than 150 years since the unification of Italy, such a repertoire still includes numerous local musical traditions, affected by different dialects and social environments.

On an ethnomusicological level, we can distinguish four main areas: Mediterranean (most of southern Italy and Sicily); central (with both northern and southern influences); northern; and Sardinian, which is characterized by remarkable autonomy. Some subregions can be identified within these four main areas, usually corresponding to the predominant Italian minorities, such as Albanian in the south; French and Provençal in Piedmont and Valle d'Aosta; and German, Slovenian, and Ladin in the northeast.

MEDITERRANEAN AREA

The first main area, the Mediterranean, must be put into the broader and heterogeneous context of the Mediterranean basin, from the Persian Gulf to Gibraltar, from Northern Africa to the Balkan and Greek coasts. Musically, southern Italian culture is mainly melodic, based on an oriental-style modal theory; where any tonal influence is perceivable, minor tonalities are predominant. Melodies tend to be melismatic, and are usually played (or sung) by a soloist. The vocal emission is often loud. Rhythm is generally free, and the music does not rely on strophic forms. Texts are mostly "lyrical" (as the antithesis of narrative), with lines of 11 syllables (hendecasyllables) using paroxytonic rhyme and assonance. Interesting examples of this style come from the regions of Sicily and Calabria, where subject matters of the songs are related to professions and craftsmanship. For instance, the repertoires *Canti di carrettiere* (Carter songs) and *Vicariote* (prison songs, so called after the name of the old prison in Palermo, *Vicaria*) are usually in the *canzuna* form, made of six or eight hendecasyllables.

A more narrative style, however, is not entirely absent from the southern corpus. Usually Mediterranean "stories" are extended in length, and commonly require a moralizing ending. The most popular of them, which has spread all over the area, is probably *La Baronessa di Carini* (The Baroness of Carini), inspired by a murder which happened in the Carini Castle near Palermo, in 1563 (the lord of the fortress murdered his daughter to punish her for her incestuous love affair with her cousin). In addition to solo songs, there are also polyphonic songs, although these are generally less harmonically complex than some from other areas' traditions. The polyphonic corpus features mainly processional or working songs. Processional songs use a drone, which is added to the final cadence of a solo section (e.g., the song for the Passion *Santa Crucida*, Ribera, Agrigento, Sicily). In working songs, the polyphony is very simple and mostly heterophonic. The rhythm of some of these songs is designed to correspond to the action of sailors lifting a sail, and can be compared with the English tradition of the *shanties*. Others accompany fishing, or loading and unloading vessels and vans.

NORTHERN AREA

The northern area includes Liguria, Piedmont, Lombardy, Emilia, and Veneto. Similar to the Mediterranean, this area has been culturally affected by several foreign influences, including southern French and Provençal, Austro-German, and Slovenian. The musical folklore is characterized by a focus on melody, rather than rhythm or harmony, and is based on northern European modal traditions. Where any tonal influence is perceivable, major tonalities are predominant. Melodies are strongly embellished but rarely completely melismatic; choral songs are fairly common.

Rhythmic structures are often quite rigid, and texts are strophic, sometimes presenting a refrain. Contrary to the southern tradition, texts are generally narrative rather than lyrical. Lines can be composed of seven, eight, or nine syllables with oxytone or paroxytonic rhymes, and assonance. Hendecasyllabic lines, likely imported from the south, are used only in the lyrical repertoire.

In the polyphonic corpus, the songs consist of a monodic introduction of the tune, followed by a harmonization of thirds. The polyphonic repertory includes both ballads and functional chants, such as the Christmas carol *"Vo girand per gli osterie"* (Wandering around taverns; Ripalta Nuova, Cremona, Lombardy), and *"La rondine importuna"* (The obtrusive swallow; Ripalta Nuova, Cremona, Lombardy). The "solo ballad" can be considered similarly archaic, using a modal-based melody and intervals such as the fourth and the fifth. This form is still present in Piedmont, for instance with *"Moran dell'Inghilterra"* (Moran from England; Castelnuovo Nigra, Turin), *"Prinsi Raimund/Gli anelli"* (Prince Raimond/The rings; Asti); and *"L'infanticida"* (The infanticide; Melle, Cuneo). *"Moran"* presents strong formal and topical relationships with the Spanish, Catalan, and Anglo-Scottish archaic ballads (e.g., "Young Beicham"). The topic of *"Prinsi"* represents a remarkable source for the study of an ancient European feudal society. *"L'infanticida,"* in contrast, is instead a cruel story about a woman who decides to drown her illegitimate child to wash away the sin of her forbidden love. The song is known outside Piedmont as well, in less violent and brutal versions.

The lyrical traditions still exist in northern Italy, but they must be distinguished from the ones found in the Mediterranean areas. This is especially true in terms of prosody, although such songs can have hendecasyllablic texts (for example, *"Lingua serpentina"* (a sequence of *stornelli* from Ceriana, Imperia, Liguria) and *"Il muratore"* (The bricklayer; Vimodrone, Milan, Lombardy). The nonsense refrain *liolela* appears frequently, likely replacing a lost instrumental refrain, as in the songs *"El me muruś el sta de la del sere"* (My partner is on the other side of the river Serio; Ripalta Nuova, Cremona, Lombardy) and *"Polesane"* (Songs from the Polese; Bagolino, Brescia, Lombardy).

Songs with instrumental refrains were likely used for dancing. Archaic texts and music are still present in magic spells, orations, lullabies (e.g., *"El vegnarà 'l papa* [Dad will come]"; Mésero, Milan, Lombardy; *"Nana cuncheta* [Little baby Cuncheta]"; Chiusa di Pesio, Cuneo, Piedmont), and working songs (e.g., *"Ritmo dei battipali* [pile driver rhythm]"; Venice, Veneto; and *"Ritmo dell'argano* [capstan rhythm]"; Pellestrina, Venice, Veneto). The ritual chant has early origins, although it often presents more recent musical features. In *Viva viva san martino*

(Hurrah for Saint Martin), for his celebration on November 11th; Chioggia, Venice, Veneto), a polyphonic and rather melismatic choir responds to the syllabic section sung by the soloist. Songs for Saint Martin have traditionally been associated with the topic of the *vino novello*, an early wine which is usually ready to drink in November. The Christmas carol "*San Giüśep e la Madona*" (Saint Joseph and the Virgin Mary; Cassago, Como, Lombardy) is popular all over Europe, and is even found in the United States. It is based on chapter 20 of the apocryphal gospel known as pseudo-Matthew. A further song, "*Canto di Capodanno*" (Song for the new year; Mezzogoro, Ferrara, Emilia) is dedicated to the celebration of the New Year; the practice of celebrating the New Year with folk songs survived in this area only.

CENTRAL AREA

The central area is not easily definable, not only in musical but also in geographical and cultural terms, yet some well-demarked traits can be recognized. Some of these can be traced back to southern traditions, although the central regions have been affected more by northern characteristics, such as the use of thirds in polyphony in Abruzzi, and the ballade corpus which significantly enriched the Tuscan repertoire. The central territory is demarked by an imaginary line which goes horizontally from La Spezia to Ravenna, and vertically from Rome to Pescara (thus including Tuscany, Lazio, Romagna, Marche, Umbria, and Abruzzi).

The central-area repertoire is mainly melodic, with lots of decoration and melismatic virtuosity. It is largely monodic, although polyphony is common over the Adriatic coasts and the Tuscan Apennines. The vocal style is varied and presents both northern and southern characteristics. In terms of prosody, hendecasyllabic verse is most common; topically, the repertory is predominantly lyrical. This is heard in *stornelli* from Tuscany, Abruzzi, Marche, and Lazio; *ritornelli* and *sonetti* from Lazio; and *rispetti* from Tuscany. The ballad, which does not use hendecasyllables, probably has northern influences. "*Il marinaio*" (The sailor; Cesacastina, Teramo, Abruzzi) is a song that has spread over Emilia, Lazio, Tuscany, and even Corsica, probably coming from Tuscany itself. "*La pesca dell'anello*" (Fishing the ring; Vico Canavese, Turin, Piedmont) is one of the most widely disseminated and popular Italian ballads, probably due to its early local origins (it was partially quoted by the music theorist Gioseffo Zarlino, 1517–1590). "*I falciatori*" (The reaper) is a ballad found in the mountains around Pistoia (Tuscany), as well as in Umbria.

Some central-Italian songs present a more narrative style. Mostly hendecasyllabic, they can be either fictional, or based on epic and heroic romances, such as *Orlando furioso* (*The Frenzy of Orlando*, by Ludovico Ariosto, 1516) or *La Gerusalemme liberata* (*Jerusalem Delivered*, by Torquato Tasso, 1559).

SARDINIA

Sardinian music is characterized by a clear regional style due to its organic culture. The formal bases of this musical tradition are the *mutu* (pl. *mutos*) and the *mutettu* (pl. *mutettos*). Mutu and mutettu are monodic songs, sung by both men and women and accompanied by the guitar. They have lyrical texts and lines most often of seven syllables, more rarely eight or 11.

The mutu generally starts with the *istérria* (introduction), composed of a variable number of lines (usually three or four, and no more than 11). Musical material is then developed in the *torrada*, composed of the same amount of lines as the istérria, as in the song "*Anninni' anninnia*" (Anninni' anninnia; Orgosolo, Nuoro). Other musical forms exist in Sardinia, such as *gozos* (hymns), or musical games for children (e.g., "*Su duru duru* [The Duru Duru]"; Nulvi, Sassari). Among the most common forms of polyphony are *tenores* and *tasgia*, popular in Barbagia, a northern area of the island. *Tenores* are ensembles of four singers: *sa boghe* (voice), *sa mesa boghe* (half voice), *sa contra* (counter-voice), and *su bassu* (bass). Sa boghe plays the role of soloist: it opens the song with the exposition of the tune. The other voices follow, singing meaningless syllables, harmonizing through intervals such as thirds, fifths, fourths, and sixths. An example of this form is the Christmas carol "*Su pizzineddu*" (The infant; Orgosolo, Nuoro), often used as a lullaby as well. The tasgia features five voices: *tipli, tinora* (tenor), *contra* (counter-voice), *basciu* (bass), and *falsittu* (falsetto). All the voices sing the text, and the role of the highest (falsittu) is to embellish the other four main parts.

Jacopo Mazzeo

See also: Bagpipes; Launeddas

Further Reading

Belloni, Alessandra Gottlieb Gordon. 2007. *Rhythm Is the Cure: Southern Italian Tambourine: Dedicated to the Healing Powers of the Tarantella Rhythm*. Pacific, MO: Mel Bay Publications.

Busk, Rachel Harriette. 1977. *The Folk-Songs of Italy*. New York: Arno Press.

Calabria. 1999. Rounder Records (USA).

Daboo, Jerri. 2010. *Ritual, Rapture and Remorse: A Study of Tarantism and Pizzica in Salento*. New York: Peter Lang.

Emilia Romagna. 2001. Rounder Records (USA).

Folk Music and Song of Italy. 1999. Rounder Records (USA).

Guizzi, Febo. 2002. *Gli strumenti della musica popolare in Italia, Guida alla musica popolare in Italia* [The instruments of popular music in Italy: Guide to popular music in Italy]. Lucca: Libreria Musicale Italiana.

Gurzau, Elba Farabegoli. 1969. *Folk Dances, Costumes, and Customs of Italy*. Newark, NJ: Folkraft.

Leydi, Roberto. 1996. *Guida alla musica popolare in Italia* [Guide to popular music in Italy]. Lucca: Libreria Musicale Italiana.

Lombardia. 2005. Rounder Records (USA).

Melis, Franco. 2002. *Launeddas, la musica della tradizione Sarda registrata nei luoghi di origine* [Launeddas, the music of the Sardinian tradition recorded in their places of origin]. Cagliari, Sardinia: Iscandula.

The Trallalleri of Genoa. 1999. Rounder Records (USA).

J

Jackson, Mahalia (1911–1972)

Once touted as the "World's Greatest Gospel Singer" by her record company, Mahalia Jackson enjoyed an illustrious career of unprecedented proportions, garnering fans and awards from around the globe. Introducing old-time spirituals to new audiences, becoming a mainstream sensation without abandoning gospel, and using her celebrity status to influence social change, Jackson was a force to be reckoned with.

Born Mahala Jackson on October 26, 1911, in a working-class section of uptown New Orleans, Louisiana, the future gospel star was reared by her aunt, Mahala Clark-Paul ("Aunt Duke"), following the death of her mother in 1917. From a very young age, Jackson possessed a big voice, and news of it reached her paternal cousin Jeanette Jackson and her husband, Josie Burnette, who performed with vaudeville singer Ma Rainey. Jackson's stern and strictly religious Aunt Duke would not permit her to join the tent-show circuit and Jackson remained at home, where she worked from sunup to sundown like all the other members of the household. Sunday morning church services, both a source of musical inspiration and an outlet for creative expression, profoundly affected her, as did the recordings of pioneering blues singer Bessie Smith.

In 1927, Jackson moved to Chicago, where she was soon invited to become a member of the Greater Salem Baptist Church Choir. It was during this time that Thomas A. Dorsey (1899–1993), a writer and performer rooted in both the gospel firmament and the down-and-dirty blues, became acquainted with Jackson, who by then had added the "i" to her name. Their working relationship proved mutually beneficial: many of Dorsey's compositions, including "Precious Lord, Take My Hand," would become some of Jackson's biggest hits. Having worked with singers such as Sallie Martin (1895–1988), Dorsey was always in search of developing singers.

Through her association with Dorsey, Jackson secured a contract with Decca Records, but the four sides, recorded in 1937, received little fanfare. Sister Rosetta Tharpe (1915–1973) would dominate the gospel music scene during the 1940s, while controversially straddling the line between gospel and blues/jazz. Meanwhile, years spent working with Dorsey would profit Jackson immensely. Her reputation as a soloist with the National Baptist Convention gained her a wide following, and with her 1947 recording of W. Herbert Brewster's "Move On Up a Little Higher," she was catapulted into the limelight as a gospel star and was named the queen of gospel singers by 1950. The Apollo release sold more than a million copies, a number unheard of in the gospel realm. "Move On Up" was followed by a number of other hits with Apollo, including "Amazing Grace," "How I Got Over" (1951), and "Didn't

It Rain" (1953). Such was her ability to stir listeners with her interpretation of a song that more than 20,000 callers flooded Danish national radio upon hearing Jackson perform the Christmas classic, "Silent Night."

In 1954, Columbia Records signed Jackson, and she began a short-lived CBS radio show, eventually appearing on American national television programs such as *The Ed Sullivan Show* and *The Flip Wilson Show*. Her Columbia debut album, *The World's Greatest Gospel Singer*, included arrangements of traditional songs as well as rousing renditions of Dorsey's compositions, "I'm Going to Live the Life I Sing About in My Song" and "Walk over God's Heaven." Through the years, Jackson's repertoire would include Richard Rodgers's and Oscar Hammerstein's "You'll Never Walk Alone," Dorsey's "Highway to Heaven," and H. L. Burke's "Somebody Bigger Than You and I," as well as "Lord, Don't Move That Mountain," a song she wrote with fellow gospel legend Doris Akers.

Inspired by great blues artists and black church music, Mahalia Jackson's majestic contralto, commanding presence, and deep emotion drew the world's attention and helped establish gospel music as a distinct genre. (Library of Congress)

With an ever-expanding audience, Jackson was frequently pressured to tone down her performance, but she was often "terrifically spirited" and prone to dancing. A testament to her sense of creative independence, Jackson was not easily constrained by formalities, as evidenced by a disclaimer printed on the handbill of her December 1957 concert at New York's Town Hall: "Because of the spontaneous nature of Miss Jackson's performance, the order of her selections as well as the selections themselves are subject to change." As the popularity of her music soared, propelling her into the mainstream, she shrugged off inevitable questions uttered among conservative church ranks: "Why play Carnegie Hall when she could be saving the flock?" Jackson took her music to the world, touring Europe on multiple occasions and performing at venues and events as varied as the Newport Jazz Festival (1957), President John F. Kennedy's inauguration (1961), and the New York World's Fair (1964).

Amid the strife of the civil rights movement of the late 1960s, Jackson trampled racial barriers by performing with the Sons of Song, a white gospel trio, at East

Tennessee State University in Johnson City in possibly the American South's first integrated gospel concert. In her autobiography, Jackson insisted, "When you come to hear religious music, you're not supposed to feel bigger than anybody else, and white people and Negroes applaud just as hard" (Jackson, 1966, p. 10). Though living comfortably in a stylish home in Chicago, far from the racial tensions and prevailing social injustices of the South, Jackson felt drawn to assist the emerging civil rights movement after meeting Martin Luther King Jr. and Ralph Abernathy at the National Baptist Convention in 1956. She wound up singing at a rally to benefit the Montgomery, Alabama, bus boycott, and performances at fundraisers for the Southern Christian Leadership Conference soon followed. As Jackson became immersed in the movement, becoming a friend of King, she was asked to sing at the historic March on Washington in 1963 where, at King's request, she performed "I Been 'Buked and I Been Scorned." As King delivered a prepared speech void of his typical emotional, oratorical fervor, Jackson prodded, "Tell them about the dream, Martin!" Improvising, King's famous *I Have a Dream* speech poured out, reverberating across the nation and into the American consciousness. Upon King's assassination in 1968, Jackson sang his favorite song, "Precious Lord, Take My Hand," at his funeral in Atlanta. Four years later, when Jackson passed away, R & B/soul singer Aretha Franklin sang the same song at her funeral.

From the National Academy of Recording Arts and Sciences, Jackson won Grammy awards with *Everytime I Feel the Spirit* (1961) and *Great Songs of Love and Faith* (1962). Posthumously, she was awarded the Grammy Lifetime Achievement Award (1972) and a final Grammy for *How I Got Over* (1976). In 1978, the Nashville, Tennessee-based Gospel Music Association inducted her into the Gospel Music Hall of Fame. Considered an influence on many modern-day rock-and-roll performers, Jackson was inducted into the Rock and Roll Hall of Fame in 1997. In addition to her phenomenal recording career and successful entrepreneurial endeavors, Jackson appeared in the films *St. Louis Blues* (1958), *Imitation of Life* (1959), *Jazz on a Summer's Day* (1960), and *The Best Man* (1964).

Greg Freeman

See also: African Spirituals; Blues; Dorsey, Thomas A.; Gospel Music; Jazz; Rainey, "Ma"; Smith, Bessie; Vaudeville

Further Reading

Cook, Bruce. 1973. *Listen to the Blues*. New York: Charles Scribner's Sons.

Darden, Robert. 2004. *People Get Ready!: A New History of Black Gospel Music*. New York: Continuum.

Harris, Michael W. 1992. *The Rise of Gospel Blues: The Music of Thomas Andrew Dorsey in the Urban Church*. New York: Oxford University Press.

Jackson, Mahalia, with Evan McLeod Wylie. 1966. *Movin' On Up*. New York: Hawthorn Books.

Santelli, Robert, Holly George-Warren, and Jim Brown, eds. 2001. *American Roots Music*. New York: Harry N. Abrams.

Wilson, Charles Reagan, and William Ferris, eds. 1989. *Encyclopedia of Southern Culture*. Chapel Hill: The University of North Carolina Press.

Jali

Jali (or *jeli*) is the term for a professional musician, oral historian, and storyteller among Mande cultures in the West African countries of Mali, Guinea, Senegal, Gambia, and Guinea-Bissau. Jali are known for their expertise with the instruments *kora*, *ngoni*, *balafon*, and *tama* as well as their mastery of powerful singing styles, epic historical narratives, folk tales, and genealogy. The jali position is hereditary, meaning that only properly trained members of certain families are allowed to fulfill the duties. The social status of the jali is complex, as they work in the service of wealthy patrons but also exert some power over those patrons. Jali are the most prominent of the *griots*, an umbrella term that refers to analogous social positions in several cultures of the West African Sahel, such as the Wolof *gewel*, Fula *gaulo*, Arabic and Moorish *iggio*, and Soninke *gesere*.

The position of a hereditary praise-singer in West Africa probably dates back to at least the ancient Ghanaian empire (800–1235 CE), which was centered in what is now Mali and Mauritania. The Islamic prophet Mohammed (ca. 570–632 CE) is also said to have traveled with a praise-singer named Surakata, a cultural role that may have contributed to the legacy of praise-singing when Islam gained popularity in West Africa beginning in the 10th century. Emerging from these existing traditions, the first true jali is usually considered to be Bala Faseke Kouyate (or his father, Gnankoman Duwa), who served as a praise-singer and advisor to the founder of the Mande (or Mali) empire, Sundiata Keita (ca. 1217–1255 CE). Present-day members of the Kouyate family trace their lineage and skills back through the centuries to this historical figure, and for this reason they are considered the purest jali family. Other important jali families include the Camara, Diabaté, Sissoko, and Suso lineages, among others. The notion of family lineage, called *jamu*, is central to the identity of a jali.

Mande social structure is based on two major groupings of people: professional artisans (*nyamakala*) and freeborn or noble farmers, warriors, and leaders (*horon*). A third social division of serfs or slaves (*jon*) existed historically but has largely faded away. Jali are part of the nyamakala artisan group, which also includes blacksmiths/sculptors (*numu*), leatherworkers (*garanke*), and religious speakers and teachers (*fina*). By performing their professional occupations, the artisan groups may unleash potentially dangerous spiritual forces called *nyama*. Only properly trained people from certain families possess a birthright and protective power called *dalilu*, which allows them to safely confront specific types of nyama. For that reason, certain instruments and songs can only be performed by people born into jali families. In addition to their primary responsibilities, jali also often serve as advisors, conflict mediators, and matchmakers.

The social status of jalis is complex. They are important keepers of cultural knowledge, and their dalilu gives them the sole right and power to perform certain types of music. Jalis can also influence political leaders through their power of speech and advising, and they can severely damage a leader's reputation if they feel disrespected. At the same time, though, jalis must work in the service of horon patrons or other wealthy clients, who sometimes negatively perceive them as shameless money-grubbers. Because most West African countries have shifted to a more egalitarian model of democracy in the decades since gaining independence, jalis are sometimes also thought of as relics of the past who supported oppressive hierarchical social structures. Nonetheless, jalis continue to dominate musical production in the Mande world, and they may become highly visible cultural ambassadors if they achieve international popularity.

The professional skillset of the jali is called *jaliya*. It is divided into three primary fields: speech (*kuma*), song (*dònkili*), and instrumental music (*kosiri*). Speech includes the performative recitation of epic historical narratives, genealogies, folk tales, and proverbs. Song includes knowledge of a repertoire or lyrics and poems as well as the skills to sing them forcefully. Instrumental music includes mastery of one of the jali instruments: kora, ngoni, balafon, or tama. While a jali is usually competent in at least two of these fields, they typically specialize in only one. Male jalis (called *jalike*) may specialize in any of the three fields, whereas female jalis (called *jalimuso*) most often specialize in song or speech.

Although there is increasing flexibility, traditionally only jali were allowed to play jali instruments, and jali would not play other Mande instruments (such as the harps and drums used by blacksmiths and hunter's guilds). The most iconic jali instrument is the kora, a large harp-lute with 21 strings that is unique to Mande cultures. The ngoni (or *koni*) is a plucked lute with four or five strings that is closely related to the large family of West African plucked lutes as well as the American banjo. The final melodic instrument played by jali is the balafon, a wooden xylophone with 16 to 20 keys. Jali also play the tama, an hourglass-shaped pressure drum that beats out sequences of tones and rhythms that correspond to Mande words and proverbs. Increasingly, jali musicians have taken up other traditional instruments, such as the *dundun* and *djembe* drums. The guitar is also popular among jalis, with playing techniques and repertoire translated from the kora and ngoni.

Jali perform music for life-cycle ceremonies (such as naming ceremonies and marriages), political events, and stage concerts. The audience typically sits and listens attentively, though they may dance if drums are involved or if the setting is appropriate. A small number of jali musicians have achieved international popularity and tour at festivals and large venues around the world. Traditionally, jali would perform solo or in small ensembles, with musical instruments used to accompany speech and song. Today, jali have developed purely instrumental repertoire to meet the expectations of their changing audiences, and they may play in large ensembles for national and international events. Some of the internationally known jali include Toumani Diabaté, Bassekou Kouyate, and Foday Musa Suso. Salif Keita, Ali Farka Touré, and Baaba Maal are often considered jalis even though they do not come from jali families, and the popular Malian groups Les Ambassadeurs and The Rail Band draw inspiration from jali music.

The jali song repertoire consists of a large number of compositions that are each associated with specific events and historical lineages. Each of the jali instruments has a closely associated set of compositions, though they may borrow from the repertoire of other jali instruments as well. Compositions typically consist of one or more relatively fixed melodic and rhythmic cycles, which are embellished during performances through variation and virtuosic accompanying passages. Because the compositions are cyclical, they may be as brief or long as the performers decide. Contemporary jalis may compose new pieces that reflect their personal beliefs and experiences while remaining grounded in the jali tradition, and they may draw from popular musics in the United States, Europe, the Caribbean, Latin America, North Africa, and the Middle East.

Scott V. Linford

See also: Griot; Mande Music; Xalam

Further Reading

Austen, Ralph, ed. 1999. *In Search of Sunjata: The Mande Oral Epic as History, Literature, and Performance.* Bloomington: Indiana University Press.

Conrad, David, and Barbara Frank, eds. 1995. *Status and Identity in West Africa: Nyamakalaw.* Bloomington: Indiana University Press.

Diawara, Manthia. 1997. "The Song of the Griot." *Transition* 74, 16–30.

Durán, Lucy. 1995. "Jelimusow: The Superwomen of Malian Music." In Graham Furniss and Liz Gunner (eds.), *Power, Marginality, and African Oral Literature*, 197–207. Cambridge: Cambridge University Press.

Eyre, Banning. 2000. *In Griot Time: An American Guitarist in Mali.* Philadelphia: Temple University Press.

Hale, Thomas. 2007. *Griots and Griottes: Masters of Words and Music* (African Expressive Cultures). Bloomington: Indiana University Press.

Schaffer, Matt. 2005. "Bound to Africa: The Mandinka Legacy in the New World." *History in Africa* 32, 321–369.

Suso, Foday Musa. 1996. "Jali Kunda: A Memoir." In Matthew Kopka and Iris Brooks (eds.), *Jali Kunda: Griots of West Africa and Beyond*, 17–72. Roslyn, NY: Ellipsis Arts.

Zemp, Hugo. 1966. "La légende des griots malinké [The legend of the Malinke griots]." *Cahiers d'études africaines* 6, 611–642.

Janggu

The Korean *janggu* or *changgo* (*jang* "stick" + *gu/go* "drum") is a large double-headed hourglass drum found in most genres of traditional music. Other regional names for the instrument include *changgu* (in central Korean folk music), *sol-changgo* (smaller drums with dogskin heads used in *nongak* farmer's percussion bands), and *seyogo* ("slim waist drum," a Chinese historical term). Although considered an accompanying instrument, players may demonstrate virtuosity through complex rhythms, dynamic contrast, and experimentation with timbre and pitch. The janggu plays a central role in contemporary *samul nori* percussion ensembles and has developed a solo repertoire.

Two animal-skin drum heads are mounted over metal hoops which extend 2.5 to 3 inches over the body of the hollow wood drum. The neck of the hourglass shape, called the *jorongmuk*, varies in diameter and affects the tone of the instrument. Poplar and paulownia woods are preferred, and surfaces may be decorated. Rope laces run from metal hooks on the hoops; these may be tightened to vary the head tension around the asymmetrical hourglass shape of the drum. The drum is usually placed horizontally on the floor in front of a seated performer for traditional *sanjo* music, but is suspended from the shoulder for parades. The left (*book*) face is struck with the open left hand, producing a deep, resonant bass sound. The right (*chae*, "stick") face, or the protruding edge of the metal hoop, is struck with a slender stick of bamboo (*yeolchae*) for a drier, higher, and more penetrating sound. *Nongat* musicians add a left-hand bamboo mallet with a ball to strike the left head, and suspend the drum to increase the volume and enhance the virtuosity of the rhythmic patterns. This knobbed mallet is called a *gungchae* (bridge), and is made from plastic or from a straightened (boiled) bamboo root with a hardwood knob. Dancers sometimes strap the janggu to their waists and play the instrument while dancing.

Early images of the janggu date from Koguryo murals (37 BCE–668 CE) and carved metal reliefs on bells from the Silla period (57 BCE–935 CE). The name of the instrument, *janggu-opsa* (one who plays the janggu), first dates to 1076, and it has remained a crucial part of Korean music throughout a millennium of changes in notation and music style. The *History of Goryeo* (1451) describes 20 janggu drums given by the Song Emperor Huizong to the Goryeo Court in Kaesong in 1114 for use in royal banquet music. The instrument may have evolved from the smaller *yogo* or the south Indian *idakka* in the early Silla period. According to the *Akhak kwebom* (1493), both heads were originally of horsehide, thick on the left to represent the masculine (now cowhide, and more rarely horsehide or deerskin) and thin on the right to represent the feminine (now sheepskin, horsehide, or more rarely dogskin). Related hourglass drums include the Korean *galgo*, the Japanese *tzuzumi*, and the Chinese *tanggu* (called *zhanggu* in the Qing dynasty).

Laura Stanfield Prichard

See also: North Korea, Music of; Sanjo

Further Reading

Howard, K. 1988. *Korean Musical Instruments: A Practical Guide.* Seoul: Se-Kwang Music Publishing.

Killick, Andrew P. 2002. "Musical Instruments of Korea." In Robert C. Provine, Yosihiko Tokumaru, and J. Lawrence Witzleben (eds.), *The Garland Encyclopedia of World Music; Vol. 7: East Asia: China, Japan, and Korea,* 821–831. New York: Routledge.

Provine, Robert. 2014. "Changgo." *Grove Music Online.* https://www.oxfordmusiconline.com.

Japan, Music of

Although music relics have been found from prehistoric times, the music of Japan developed largely from borrowed mainland Chinese instruments and art music (beginning ca. 250 CE–700 CE). Additionally, the prevalence of Buddhist religious principles and the indigenous Shintō spirituality helped to shape its musical form and aesthetic. A concerted political effort in the Nara and Heian periods (700–1200 CE) focused on the national ownership of foreign musical influences, leading to the codification of styles such as Japanese court music (*gagaku*), Buddhist chant (*shōmyō*), and Shintō dance (*kagura*). In the medieval era (1200–1600 CE), in addition to the transmission of earlier styles, genres such as narrated *biwa* (a four-stringed lute) music, *nō* theater, and *kyōgen* (a less formal version of nō) began to emerge. The country's lengthy period of global isolation in the Edo period (ca. 1600–1868) allowed national styles such as music for *kabuki* theater, *buyō* (a form of Japanese dance), and *bunraku* puppetry to evolve that separated the Japanese soundscape from its incipient musical heritages.

The introduction of Western classical art music and popular music in the late 19th century greatly shaped both the art music and popular music scenes in Japan. In particular, a strong tradition of Western orchestral and solo instrumental music developed over the 20th century and has greatly influenced Japanese music education. Also, the 20th century saw a great diversity of popular music stemming from the *ryūkōka* (fashionable song) of the early 1900s, which launched the tradition of the *min'yō* (folk song), the *kayōkyoku* (popular song), and the longer-lasting tradition of *enka* (country song or ballad). American popular music styles (jazz, rock, pop, metal, hip-hop) and other styles (reggae/ska) have contributed significantly to contemporary Japanese popular music, in particular, *kumi-daiko*, Visual *kei*, J-pop, and J-Core.

Certain characteristics of Japanese aesthetics, philosophy, and society are essential to the understanding of traditional and Western-influenced music in Japan. Many of these principles can be traced to the transmission of religious and philosophical ideas from China via Buddhism and Confucianism, whereas others exist as a byproduct of *shintō* philosophy or Japanese societal norms. The concept of *yin* and *yang* (developed in ancient China) implies a balance of opposites (night/day, etc.). The application of this concept to music manifests itself in various modes and scales as well as in the balance of sound versus silence or musical performance (the act of playing an instrument) versus mindful intention (cognitive awareness of performance), inducing an overall sense of complementarity and restraint. *Shin-gyō-sō* emphasizes the important qualities and distinctions between formal (*shin*), semi-formal (*gyō*), and informal (*sō*). Another tripartite hallmark of traditional music is *jyo-ha-kyū*, which implies a gradual transition in both tempo (from slow to fast) and texture (from simple to complex). The concept of *ma*, or space, places an emphasis on both musical silence as well as the performer's sense of stillness or concentration during moments of silence.

Elements of nature are often infused in both traditional and modern Japanese music. Additionally, respect for one's teacher, ancestry, heritage, community, musical instrument, and self influences many aspects of Japanese performance, practice, and pedagogy. The Japanese people have a long tradition of enthusiastically accepting foreign cultural markers into the fabric of their society. This process of acculturation is often attributed to the high level of literacy and mandatory education required of a Japanese citizen by law. This education includes music; in particular, Western classical art music is highly valued and appreciated and has influenced the performance and composition styles of many Japanese music traditions. Due to the fact that oral tradition (as opposed to written notation) predominated the dissemination of music before the late 19th century, *shōga* (a system of syllables used to aid in the memorization of music) continues to be used in the transmission and teaching of traditional Japanese music. Due to the strong sense of community in Japanese society, one will notice unique relationships between urban and rural music traditions as well as between performer and audience member. This Japanese societal trait also manifests itself in the complex relationships between music, theater, dance, text, and performance (intertextuality).

Traditional Japanese scales differ from modern Western diatonic scales. Many various scales exist, some with half-steps (or semi-tones) and others without them. For example, the *in* scale used often in *koto* and *shamisen* music contains semi-tones (such as D-E♭-G-A-B♭) whereas the *yo* scale does not contain half-steps (D-E-G-A-B). The scale more often than not sound pentatonic in nature. The notation system is often dependent on syllabic symbols and much traditional music continues to be imparted to students via oral tradition.

Most traditional Japanese instruments evolved from Chinese counterparts. The instruments used for gagaku (Imperial court music and dance) derived from Chinese musical performance of the T'ang period (eighth century), which migrated to Japan and flourished in the ninth through 11th centuries. This style of music exhibits many ancient musical styles other than Chinese: Indian, Korean, Persian, and so on. Various percussion instruments (mainly drums) such as *da-daiko, ninai-daiko, tsuri-daiko, san-no-tsuzumi,* and *kakko* are used to maintain rhythmic units (different from modern Western rhythm styles). The *shōko,* or gong, punctuates musical phrases and heightens the overall tone of the ensemble. Wind instruments such as the *hacki-kiri* (a short, double-reed woodwind), *ryūteki* (a seven-holed flute), the *koma-bue* (a six-holed flute), and the *shō* (a mouth-pipe with 17 vertically placed reeds) provide color and melodic interest. The *gaku-so* (predecessor of the *koto*) and the four-stringed *gaku-biwa* (or biwa) are used mainly to solidify melodic mode and to provide specific cadential structure.

The biwa is a short-necked, plucked instrument (similar to a lute), typically with four or five strings and played with a plectrum. The instrument derives from the Chinese *pipa* and came to Japan in the seventh century. Biwa playing over the centuries has extended to all socio-economic strata (from courtier to commoner) and is often associated with a specific style of singing, which originates from *shōmyō* (Buddhist chanting/singing). Shōmyō migrated to Japan via Buddhism, flourished during the eighth century, and continues to be used ceremonially. This singing style predominately focuses on the intonation of text and allows for a fair amount of ornamentation. A host of instruments are associated with the performance of this genre, notably *taku* (or clapper), *kane* (a small, suspended bronze bowl played with a mallet), *hatu* (hand cymbals), and *shakujō* (Buddhist priest's rattle). These instruments have infiltrated other styles of music throughout the centuries such as *nagauta* (music for *kabuki*), *gidayū bushi* (music for *bunraku*), and *kumi-daiko*.

Some traditional Japanese instruments are still in wide usage today. The *koto* is a 13-stringed zither (a long, relatively thin, and flat string instrument). The performer plucks the strings with the right hand and alters the pitch of the strings with the left. The koto can be used for accompaniment of the voice or other instruments as well as played in a solo, virtuosic style. The koto can also be found in ensembles. The *shakuhachi* is a wooden, cylindrical wind instrument. The name derives from its original length: one *shaku* and eight *sun* (one shaku equals approximately one foot and can be divided into 10 *sun*), although lengths have varied throughout the centuries. The bulk of the original repertory was composed by itinerate Zen priests of the Edo period. The Living National Treasure, Gorō Yamaguchi, is acclaimed as one of the foremost masters of shakuhachi music. The *shamisen* is a three-stringed plucked instrument with a rather long neck (held against the body and played with a plectrum like a guitar). The shamisen is mainly utilized in five different capacities: 1) *katarimono/tegotomono* (solo voice with shamisen accompaniment); 2) *gidayū-bushi* (narrative-driven music for bunraku theater); 3) *utaimono* (accompaniment for short solo song); 4) *nagauta* (music for *kabuki* theater); and 5) *jiuta/kumiuta* (mainly instrumental music). A popular ensemble for traditional music is the *sankyoku* (three instruments), consisting of the koto, shamisen, and shakuhachi. Finally, a host of various *taiko* (drums) are also used in theater music, festivals (*matsuri*), and for *kumi-daiko* (a modern version of ensemble taiko performance).

In the Muromachi period (1338–1573 CE), two important theater genres emerged. *Nō* theater consists of narrative-driven plays with stylized dance, accompanied by a chorus and sparse instrumental ensemble. The style was originated by drama troupes, who performed outside Buddhist and Shintō shrines; eventually, performance traditions were canonized and documented by several masters (one of the most important being Zeami). In nō, the narrative and chorus parts are mostly chanted. The instrumental ensemble consists of a *nōkan* (seven-holed wooden flute), two *tsuzumi* (handheld drums), and a taiko (a larger drum, typically on a stand). Nō typically utilizes the jyo-ha-kyū concept on a formal scale where *jo* acts as the introduction, *ha* the exposition, and *kyū* the denouement. *Kyōgen* is the farcical/comic version of nō. In kyōgen, not all of the music is chanted; folk songs (*min'yō*) and vocal pieces from kabuki are used instead.

In the Edo period (1603–1868), two additional theater genres developed and flourished, which remain very popular today. *Kabuki* theater originated in Kyōto as a new dance/theater genre by female prostitutes in the red-light district. The style quickly garnered popularity and began to be formalized by all-male troupes at the Imperial court and in genre-specific theaters. Kabuki utilizes three different styles of music: *gidayū-bushi* (narrative-style singing accompanied by shamisen), *nagauta* (vocal and instrumental ensemble music, predominantly featuring the shamisen), and *hayashi* (wind instruments with percussion). Gidayū-bushi, which can also be found in bunraku puppet theater, propels the story and is most often sung by a soloist and accompanied by a single shamisen and a percussionist. *Nagauta* (long song) consists of more poetic lyrics and melodic music sung by separate soloists, a chorus, shamisen soloist/s and ensemble, and a team of percussionists. Nagauta has two functions: 1) setting the mood for a play and developing the plot (*danmono*); and 2) accompanying dances (*hamono*). Nagauta music exemplifies several forms. The jyo-ha-kyū aesthetic pervades many of these forms. The *kumiuta* form stems from the shamisen song tradition and consists of an instrumental introduction (*maebiki*), first song (*maeuta*), instrumental interlude (*tegoto*), and a final song (*atouta*). The *jōruri* form is akin to the aforementioned gidayū-bushi. The form consists of eight parts: the *oki* or *okiuta* (introductory song, which sets the dramatic and sonic tone), *michiyuki* (introduces the characters), *kudoki* (a tender section), *monogatari* (the story), *uta* (song), the *odori* (dance), the *miarawashi* (climax of the plot), and *chirashi* (finale/denouement). The *hayashi* ensemble, which is a broader term that applies to similar accompanying ensembles in nō theater and other performances, in kabuki theater consists mainly of drums, flutes, and perhaps a gong. The last musical element of the kabuki performance is the *geza* ensemble that plays offstage, which comprises a variety of instruments depending on the production. Typically, the *tsuzumi* and taiko drums of the hayashi are represented; however, some instruments are atypical for kabuki music, such as the koto and the shakuhachi.

The music for *bunraku* puppet theater follows the *gidayū-bushi* or narrative form (similar to the jōruri form outlined earlier). The term *gidayu* originates from the acclaimed puppet master, Takemoto Gidayu, who significantly developed the narrative form of bunraku. The music consists of a vocalist/storyteller, the shamisen, and occasionally the koto or *kokyū* (a general term used for a bowed stringed instrument similar to the shamisen). Bunraku is still very popular in Japan today.

After the door to the West opened in 1868 (at the beginning of the Meiji period), Western art music flooded the professional, educational, and domestic sectors of Japanese music life (this phenomenon is often referred to as *yōgaku*). A special Music Investigation Committee was appointed by the Ministry of Education to develop a music curriculum based on Western art music for Japanese public education. This decision by the Meiji regime was more than likely an attempt at modernization, yet has somewhat complicated the formation of a national music identity for Japan. Particularly in the 20th century, intentional returns to traditional sounds and aesthetics (*hōgaku*) began to emerge in both art music and popular music. It is important to note that a synthesis of styles can be heard in many newly composed popular and art musics in Japan today.

An essential point to bear in mind concerning the traditional music of Japan is that while the more canonized versions of music were developing (gagaku, shomyō, nō, nagauta, gidayū-bushi, etc.), other musics existed simultaneously. Music of the Ainu people (a clan of native islanders from Northern Honshū and Hōkkaidō) consists of ritual and festival songs. A host of native instruments also accompany their music. Music of the Okinawa and Ryūkyū Islands have their own peculiar rhythms, scales, and social functions. Much of this music is accompanied on the *sanshin*, a derivative of the mainland shamisen. On the main island of Honshū, the people had their own songs (*uta*), which eventually took on the Germanic-influenced title *min'yō* (or folk song). These songs depict daily life and are accompanied by the shamisen, koto, or other solo instrument. Min'yō can also apply to a folk melody or song that is played by a solo instrument or instrumental ensemble. This popular form of music helped to influence the development of 20th-century popular music such as ryūkōka, kayōkyoku, enka, and eventually J-pop.

The adoption of Western popular styles into Japanese min'yō has a rather muddled history. Terminology was appropriated and repurposed so often that definitive styles cannot be easily detected. In the 1910s, a new version of min'yō began to develop that relied less on traditional Japanese scales and migrated toward Western diatonic harmonies. The new min'yō (or *shin min'yō*) also had another name: ryūkōka (popular or fashionable song). Because records were slow to find their way into homes, street musicians known as *enka-shi* would perform these songs. Later, when record players and radios became more prevalent, certain singers began to predominate the scene. Ichiro Fujiyama is acclaimed as one of the most influential singers of the ryūkōka style. Although much slippage can be found in regard to the terminology, after the World Wars, shin min'yō/ryūkōka split into three separate strains: 1) kayōkyoku exhibited a pronounced jazz influence; 2) enka predominantly maintained the pentatonic scale in the melody with effusively emotional lyrical content; and 3) *poppusu* drew directly from current Western styles such as boogie-woogie, rock and roll, and pop music. Since the 1980s, kayōkyoku has become less and less popular due to the influence of more modern popular rock styles. However, ballads of this ilk (as well as its predecessor, ryūkōka) continue to appear, especially in film or *anime* music. Enka has become quite widely appreciated and a specific consumer culture has developed around it. The genre appears to be reclaiming traditional Japanese roots; singers have begun to incorporate *kobushi* (a pronounced nasality and widening of the vibrato) and often wear more traditional costumes when performing. A good example of how these styles have intermeshed over the 20th century is the music of Hibari Misora, who began her career singing kayōkyoku and poppusu in the 1950s but since her death in 1989 is often remembered as an enka singer.

"J-pop" now seems to be the term of choice when referring to Western-influenced, contemporary rock or pop music. Much of this music can be easily identified with contemporary Western popular music trends such as hip-hop, rap, reggae, and so on; nevertheless, elements of traditional Japanese music do tend to manifest themselves occasionally (particularly in regard to singing style). J-pop musical trends gravitate toward the bubble-gum pop genre (catchy melodies, simple harmonies, up-tempo beats, targeted toward teenagers), especially in regard to female girl groups. Male boy bands often project a more suave, hard-edged image; however, both styles tend to interject English words and phrases into the lyrics. The phenomenon of girl groups and boy bands began in the early 2000s on the heels of the U.S. boy-band craze (Backstreet Boys, N'Sync, etc.) in addition to the Korean Wave bands, who often produce songs with Japanese lyrics specifically for the Japanese market (the group DBSK exemplifies this phenomenon). Other fascinating aspects of the Japanese rock scene are the hardcore (J-core) and Japanoise underground scenes that continue to perpetuate in Japan's multilayered music world.

Two final intriguing aspects of the music of Japan are the phenomena of *karaoke* and film or *anime* music. The word "*karaoke*" literally translates to "empty orchestra," meaning that the orchestrated music on the track does not have a singer. Although dispute exists concerning the originator of the karaoke machine and concept, many people claim that in the 1970s Daisuke Inoue of Kobe, Japan, was the first to use a machine of this type to entertain. Since this time, karaoke has spread all over the world. In Asia, karaoke mainly consists of single compartments, rooms, or boxes, where singers go to perform privately or semi-privately. In the West, however, karaoke bars, lounges, or even nightclubs tend to be more popular. Karaoke has become so popular that now singers can compete in an annual international karaoke contest.

Music for film and anime has become an entirely separate genre of music in Japan. The songs in particular often become exceedingly popular and ones that every Japanese person knows. The influence of Studio Ghibli director Hayao Miyazaki (*My Neighbor Totoro, Princess Mononoke*, etc.) has made the music of his movies and their composers, such as Joe Hisaishi (among others), household entities.

Bradley Fugate

See also: Bunraku; Enka Music; Gagaku; Hōgaku; J-Pop; Kabuki; Kayokyoku; Koto; Min'yô; Shakuhachi; Shômyô; Taiko

Further Reading

Adriaansz, Willem. 1973. *The "Kumiuta" and "Danmono" Traditions of Japanese Koto Music.* Berkeley: University of California Press.

Ando, Tsuruo. 1970. *Bunraku: The Puppet Theater.* New York: Walker/Weatherhill.

Condry, Ian. 2006. *Hip-Hop Japan: Rap and the Paths of Cultural Globalization.* Durham, NC: Duke University Press.

Eppstein, Ury. 1994. *The Beginnings of Western Music in Meiji Era Japan.* Lewiston, NY: Edwin Mellen Press.

Galliano, Luciana. 2002. *Yōgaku: Japanese Music in the Twentieth Century.* Lanham, MD: Scarecrow Press.

Garfias, Robert. 1959. *Gagaku: The Music and Dances of the Japanese Imperial Household.* New York: Theater Arts Books.

Gillan, Matthew. 2012. *Songs from the Edge of Japan: Music-Making in Yaeyama and Okinawa.* Burlington, VT: Ashgate.

Harick-Schneider, Eta. 1973. *A History of Japanese Music.* London: Oxford University Press.

Keene, Donald. 1965. *Bunraku: The Art of the Japanese Puppet Theatre.* New York: Harper & Row.

Kimura, Atsuko. 1991. "Japanese Corporations and Popular Music." *Popular Music* 10(1), 317–326.

Koizumi, Fumio. 1977. "Musical Scales in Japanese Music." In F. Koizumi, Y. Tokumaru, O. Yamaguchi, and R. Emmert (eds.), *Asian Musics from an Asian Perspective*, 135–141 Tokyo: Heibonsha.

Johnson, Henry. 2004. *The "Koto": A Traditional Instrument in Contemporary Japan.* Tokyo: Hotei.

Malm, William P. 1959. *Japanese Music and Musical Instruments.* Rutland, VT: Charles E. Tuttle.

Malm, William P. 1963. *Nagauta: The Heart of Kabuki Music.* Rutland, VT: Charles E. Tuttle.

Malm, William P. 2000. *Traditional Japanese Music and Musical Instruments* (rev. ed.). New York: Kodansha International.

Matsue, Jennifer Milioto. 2009. *Making Music in Japan's Underground: The Tokyo Hardcore Scene.* New York: Routledge.

Novak, David. 2013. *Japanoise: Music at the Edge of Circulation.* Durham, NC: Duke University Press.

Piggot, Francis. 1971. *The Music and Musical Instruments of Japan.* New York: Da Capo Press.

Roberson, James. 2010. "Okinawan Songs of Home, Departure, and Return." *Identities* 17(4), 430–53.

Sterling, Marvin. 2010. *Babylon East: Performing, Dancehall, Roots Reggae, and Rastafari in Japan.* Durham, NC: Duke University Press.

Tokita, Alison McQueen, and David W. Hughes, eds. 2008. *The Ashgate Research Companion to Japanese Music.* Burlington, VT: Ashgate.

Tokumaru, Yoshihiko, ed. 2002. "Japan." In Robert C. Provine, Yosihiko Tokumaru, and J. Lawrence Witzleben (eds.), *The Garland Encyclopedia of World Music; Vol. 7: East Asia: China, Japan, and Korea,* 530–798. New York: Routledge.

Wade, Bonnie C. 1976. *Tegotomono: Music for the Japanese Koto.* Westport, CT: Greenwood Press.

Wade, Bonnie C. 2005. *Music in Japan.* New York: Oxford University Press.

Jazz

Jazz is a musical genre that originated around the beginning of the 20th century in New Orleans, Louisiana. It is considered the quintessential form of American music because it can be described as a sort of musical melting pot. While the label "jazz" covers a wide array of musical styles and sounds, there are three basic characteristics that serve as a foundation: improvisation (the simultaneous act of composition and performance), syncopation (placement of rhythmic stresses where they would not ordinarily occur), and "swing" (the rhythmic feel of the music that drives it forward).

ORIGINS

There is not a definitive creation story for jazz; all indications are that the music just evolved over time as a result of a number of factors coming together. The musical climate of New Orleans was quite diverse. There was a flourishing European classical music scene, public brass band concerts in the parks, barbershop singing groups on the streets, and numerous saloons and speakeasies where blues and ragtime musicians could find work. The name "jazz" itself does not even have a single, defining genesis or spelling. "Jazz," "jass," "jaz," and "jas" were all in common use during the early years, but by 1918, "jazz" had become the standard spelling. The term and this particular spelling were used in sports journalism at the time to refer to players playing with a lot of energy or excitement, so some historians theorize that it was carried over to describe musicians with the same quality. Other

---

Vaudeville

Perhaps the one of the most lasting legacies from the vaudeville era was the proliferations of small theaters in the centers of small towns across the United States. Vaudeville theaters often featured seating capacities of 300 or less. Despite the fact that many have since been converted to movie theaters or repurposed for other needs, these small theaters were an important resource for small towns far from the major cities where theaters in excess of 2,000 seats were commonplace. Vaudeville theaters also provided much-needed opportunities for black, Jewish, and female performers to share the stage with their white counterparts. The format of the shows allowed for diverse show complexion and many important black and minority performing acts got their start on the vaudeville circuit.

theories include a connection to a musician named Jasbo Brown and a reference to the jasmine scents that were common in New Orleans brothels of the time, where many early jazz musicians found work as parlor entertainers. It was this seedy connection that led many performers in the New Orleans era, including pianist Jelly Roll Morton (1890–1941) and clarinetist Sidney Bechet (1897–1959), to refer to their music as "ragtime" rather than "jazz."

The first band described as playing in a syncopated jazz style was led by cornetist Buddy Bolden (1877–1931). His distinctive, syncopated sound was created by incorporating the habanera rhythm, or "Spanish tinge," into the last half of the drum pattern. Before long, many of the bands in New Orleans were incorporating syncopated Latin dance rhythms into their music, giving birth to jazz as it is now known. Bolden was diagnosed with dementia praecox in 1907 and was unable to continue performing, ending his career 10 years before the first jazz recordings appeared.

Early jazz groups tended to be connected to two main types of ensembles: parade bands and dance bands. The instrumentation was largely based on that of parade bands of the time and featured a "front line" of a cornet, clarinet, and trombone, along with a rhythm section that typically included a drum and piano. The front-line melody instruments used a style of playing known as *collective improvisation* in which the cornet played an embellished-but-recognizable version of the melody while the other two instruments improvised countermelodies around it. The music, however, was decidedly rooted in the dance-band tradition and was most often associated with dancing, as is evidenced by songs like "Dixie Jass Band One Step."

While Bolden's band was the first group to be identified as playing in a "jazz style," it was the Original Dixieland Jass Band (ODJB) that made the first recordings of jazz. In 1917, ODJB released "Livery Stable Blues" on the Victor label. The group's leader, cornetist Nick LaRocca (1889–1961), began promoting the group as the creators of jazz and claimed authorship of many songs that were jazz standards of the time.

BEYOND NEW ORLEANS

By the mid-1910s, many jazz musicians were touring with vaudeville troupes and minstrel shows, exposing audiences around the country to this new music. The increased interest in jazz in places like Chicago and New York, as well as easier access to recording studios, led many musicians to leave New Orleans for these other cities. In Chicago, jazz began to evolve into an earthier music. The banjo and saxophone became more common, and the New Orleans style of collective improvisation began to give way to a greater emphasis on solo improvisation. One of the musicians responsible for this transition was pianist Jelly Roll Morton. Morton began his career playing in Storyville, a section of New Orleans created to regulate prostitution. Morton was a significant figure in the transition from ragtime to jazz and actually claimed to have invented jazz in 1902. (In fact, in a series of interviews with folklorist Alan Lomax, Morton claimed to have been born in 1885 in order to make this claim more plausible.) Morton's piano style was a combination of later ragtime and shout styles with barrelhouse blues. In 1915, his "Jelly Roll

Blues" became the first published jazz arrangement and earned him the title of first jazz composer.

Another New Orleans-born emigrant to the North was cornetist/trumpeter Louis Armstrong (1901–1971). Armstrong was instrumental in the further development of the jazz style, primarily by abandoning the stiff rhythmic feel of ragtime in favor of the swinging jazz style. He also moved away from an improvisatory style focused on the melodic embellishment and toward one that was focused more on creating new melodies over the chord progression. In 1925, Armstrong formed the Hot Five and Hot Seven, groups that would set the standard for small-group jazz for many years.

In New York, an alternative to ragtime developed and served as the musical basis for indigenous jazz of that area. This new "stride" piano style was developed by James P. Johnson, most famous for his song "Charleston" that sparked a dance craze in the 1920s. The style is characterized by an alternating bass note/chord pattern in the left hand with a syncopated melody in the right hand. The jazz groups in New York also tended to be larger in order to compete with the established dance orchestras. Among the significant New York band leaders of the 1920 were Fletcher Henderson (1897–1952) and Edward Kennedy "Duke" Ellington (1899–1974). It was Henderson who established the formula for big-band arrangements from the late 1920s through the early 1940s. Henderson viewed his band as four interrelated sections (saxophones, trumpets, trombones, rhythm), and he wrote for each section as a unit. Sometimes all sections would play together, sometimes one section would be featured, and sometimes they would alternate with each other in a call-and-response pattern. He also interspersed ensemble sections with sections for individual soloists. Ellington largely patterned his arrangements after the Henderson model, but he was also famous for viewing his bands as a collection of individual players with their own unique sounds. The work of these two leaders helped to launch the most popular jazz style—swing.

THE SWING ERA

The 1930s are known as the Swing Era because of the popularity of this style of big-band jazz, which ranged from upbeat dance tunes to lyrical ballads. The Swing Era also marked the first time jazz drew a significant white audience. The racial segregation that was commonplace in society had an impact on jazz, as both bands and audiences were almost always divided along racial lines. Black bands, such as Henderson's and Ellington's, played primarily in nightclubs, whereas white bands, such as those led by Benny Goodman (1909–1986) and Tommy Dorsey (1905–1956), played more frequently in concert halls, theaters, and high-society events. Before long, stylistic differences began to emerge between the two types of bands. Many of the white bands moved closer toward a fully composed type of music, whereas many of the black bands retained more improvisation. The more relaxed, composed music was known as "sweet jazz" and the music that was more upbeat and improvisation-based came to be known as "hot jazz."

As the Depression worsened, many of the "hot" bands began to adopt some characteristics of the "sweet" bands, such as lush orchestrations and ballads, in order to survive. Some bands, both sweet and hot, added a vocalist to the group in order to increase their popularity. Many well-known singers, including Billie Holiday, Ella Fitzgerald, Bing Crosby, Rosemary Clooney, and Frank Sinatra, launched their careers in this way. Still, by the late 1930s, swing bands were struggling to survive and by the early 1940s, most of the well-known bands could no longer support themselves and disbanded.

The Northeast was the focal point for jazz in the 1930s, but there were two other locations that developed strong and distinctive jazz scenes during that time as well: Kansas City, which was famous for a blues-based "jump" style popularized by the Count Basie Orchestra; and Paris, France. Several American jazz musicians had toured in France, but it was not until the mid-1930s that a distinctive European style of jazz developed with the Quintette du Hot Club de France. The Quintette featured Belgian guitarist Django Reinhardt (1910–1953) and French violinist Stéphane Grappelli (1908–1997), along with a bassist and two rhythm guitarists.

BEBOP

The Swing Era came to a close with the Great Depression, World War II, and a recording ban by ASCAP. Additionally, many nightclub owners began to believe there was more money in drink sales than in dancing, so they added more tables and eliminated their dance floors. As a result, smaller groups were much more in demand. The new style of jazz that emerged—bebop—was considerably different from orchestrated swing music. Bebop was more musically challenging, with extremely fast tempos, irregular chord progressions, and melodies that were more technical than tuneful. The typical ensemble consisted of a saxophone, trumpet, piano, bass, and drums. Bebop songs were most commonly based on either the blues or chord progressions borrowed from pre-existing songs. The term *bebop* comes from a common onomatopoeic descending long-short melodic figure. Among the main proponents of this new musical style were saxophonist Charlie Parker (1920–1955), trumpeters John Birks "Dizzy" Gillespie (1917–1993) and Miles Davis (1926–1991), pianist Earl "Bud" Powell (1924–1966), and drummer Max Roach (1924–2007). Unlike the jazz that came before, bebop was not intended as dance music, which made it well-suited for the crowded nightclubs.

Bebop was popular among many musicians, but there was also widespread criticism of the style, mainly centered on the claim that it sacrificed musicality for technique. Many critics, Louis Armstrong among them, claimed that bebop musicians may have been able to play scales and arpeggios faster than other performers, but they lacked any sense of melody. In response to these criticisms, two styles emerged from bebop in the 1950s.

THE BIRTH OF THE COOL

"Cool jazz" developed in the late 1940s as a more relaxed alternative to the frenetic sound of bebop. Its roots in jazz can be traced back to the melody-oriented music of cornetist Bix Beiderbecke and saxophonists Frankie Trumbauer and

Lester Young in the 1920s and 1930s. In 1948, Miles Davis formed a nonet that included pianist/arranger Gil Evans, baritone saxophonist Gerry Mulligan, alto saxophonist Lee Konitz, pianist John Lewis, and others for the purpose of experimenting with a more relaxed and expressive sound within the bebop framework. Some of the 12 recordings made by this group were released in pairs on six separate 78-rpm records beginning in 1949. It was not until 1957 that the label, Capitol Records, compiled 11 of the tracks on one LP and released it as *The Birth of the Cool*. While the nonet was short-lived, it led to successful careers for some of its members in the new cool style. Mulligan and trumpeter Chet Baker formed a pianoless quartet and further explored the relaxed style. Lewis joined with vibraphonist Milt Jackson, bassist Percy Heath, and drummer Connie Kay to form the Modern Jazz Quartet. The Quartet not only continued the cool sound, it also incorporated a number of elements from classical music in what Gunther Schuller called "third stream" music.

Because of Mulligan's influence and his location in southern California, some journalists began to refer to cool jazz as "West Coast jazz." Perhaps the most enduring legacy of West Coast jazz is the work of pianist Dave Brubeck and alto saxophonist Paul Desmond and their 1959 album *Time Out*, which features the songs "Take Five," written in 5/4, and "Blue Rondo a la Turka," which is based loosely on the classical rondo form with 9/8 ensemble sections alternating with 4/4 sections for the solos.

HARD BOP

Emerging in the mid-1950s was hard bop, a more mainstream version of bebop with influences from rhythm and blues and gospel music. This style originated with a group called The Jazz Messengers led by pianist Horace Silver and drummer Art Blakey. Hard bop maintains the rhythmic drive and energy of bebop while also incorporating the compositional, or "pre-planned," aspects of cool jazz and swing. Hard bop is sometimes called "funky jazz" because of its strong rhythmic character, and sometimes referred to as "soul jazz" because of its connection to the sound of gospel music and rhythm and blues. Other musicians who contributed to the development of hard bop include bassist Charles Mingus; trumpeter Clifford Brown; saxophonists John Coltrane, Sonny Rollins, and Dexter Gordon; and pianist Thelonious Monk. In the 1980s, many of these artists saw a resurgence in their careers when British DJs used hard bop recordings over electronic dance beats to create "acid jazz."

MODAL JAZZ

In the late 1950s, Miles Davis began to experiment with an approach to jazz composition that was based on scales rather than chord progressions, which came to be known as modal jazz. In bebop, chords commonly change every two beats, but in modal jazz, the harmonies stay constant for extended periods of time, requiring musicians to conceive of their improvisations in terms of a linear melody rather than simply playing patterns over a set of chords. The first jazz recordings to really showcase this modal approach came from Miles Davis's 1959 album *Kind of Blue*. The first track, "So What" is based around 16 measures of D Dorian, eight measures of E♭ Dorian, and eight measures of D Dorian. Although Davis used this modal approach only sporadically in the 1960s, John Coltrane, who performed on *Kind of Blue*, made extensive use of modal jazz in his music, which is particularly evident in "Crescent," "Impressions," and his version of the Rodgers and Hammerstein classic "My Favorite Things." Pianist Herbie Hancock's "Maiden Voyage" is another classic modal jazz work.

"THE NEW THING"

In the 1960s, a number of jazz musicians sought to create music that was not limited by traditional musical structures such as harmony, tonality, form, and rhythm. Although it is now commonly called "free jazz," musicians at the time simply called it "the new thing." The label *free jazz* comes from saxophonist Ornette Coleman's 1960 album *Free Jazz: A Collective Improvisation*. The album was recorded by a double quartet with one quartet on each stereo channel playing simultaneously to produce a nearly 40-minute group improvisation. John Coltrane's contributions to this movement were connected to his further explorations of modal jazz and his spiritual quest to become one with "Om," the universal and first vibration in Hinduism. Bassist Charles Mingus and keyboardist Sun Ra attempted to integrate the principles of collective improvisation within the framework of big band jazz. Saxophonists Pharoah Sanders and Archie Shepp were among a group of free jazz musicians who sought to include non-Western musical ideas, particularly the music of North Africa, into their performances. Pianist Cecil Taylor incorporated many elements of the classical avant garde into his approach, including tone clusters and serialism. The one common thread uniting these disparate approaches to jazz was a desire to create music outside the strictures of earlier forms of jazz.

FUSION

In the late 1960s, Miles Davis experimented with combining the melodic and harmonic language of jazz with the instrumentation and rhythms of rock. He began using with electric piano and bass on the 1968 album *Miles Ahead*, but it was the 1969 *In a Silent Way* that was the first real step toward a jazz-rock fusion with an all-electric approach and the abandonment of the characteristic swing feel of jazz. Davis's follow-up album, *Bitches Brew* (1970), demonstrates the fullness of his integration of rock elements, the most dominant of which is the central role he gives the expanded rhythm section of two bassists, two or three drummers, two or three electric pianists, and a percussionist.

If the albums themselves were not enough to lay the foundation for jazz fusion, many of the musicians that played on them were active in ensembles that established the mature fusion style of the 1970s. Herbie Hancock created a funk-oriented fusion style on albums such as *Head Hunters*, and saxophonist Wayne Shorter and keyboardist Joe Zawinul founded perhaps the highest-profile fusion group of the 1970s, Weather Report. Later fusion innovations have included blending jazz with rap and hip-hop and even punk and heavy metal.

BEYOND FUSION

Jazz since the 1970s has been dominated by two strains. One, championed by trumpeter Wynton Marsalis, has been a resurgence of more traditional jazz styles from the 1930s through 1950s. This return to more "straight-ahead" jazz has been followed by many fusion and free jazz artists who have reverted to acoustic performances in more traditional styles.

The second major current of jazz since the 1980s has been *smooth jazz*, a type of fusion that is moderately paced with a solo instrument, usually a saxophone, layered over a bass-heavy electronic accompaniment. Smooth jazz artists such as saxophonists David Sanborn and Kenny G are heavily criticized for what critics perceive as bland, mediocre, formulaic music that lacks vitality and creativity. Some critics have even coined the term "fuzak" to describe this style of jazz—a pejorative that is given weight by the frequency with which smooth jazz songs are used as background music for other entertainments and activities. Despite these criticisms, however, smooth jazz was the fastest growing radio format in the United States in the late 1980s through the mid-1990s.

Eric S. Strother

See also: Afro-Cuban Jazz; Armstrong, Louis; Bebop; Blues; Coltrane, John; Congo Square; Davis, Miles; Dixieland; Gospel Music; Handy, W. C.; Joplin, Scott; Original Dixieland Jazz Band; Parker, Charlie; Ragtime; Smith, Bessie

Further Reading

Giddens, Gary, and Scott DeVeaux. 2009. *Jazz*. New York: W. W. Norton.

Giola, Ted. 2011. *The History of Jazz*. New York: Oxford University Press.

Porter, Lewis. 1992. *Jazz: From Its Origins to the Present*. Upper Saddle River, NJ: Prentice Hall.

Schuller, Gunther. 1986. *Early Jazz: Its Roots and Musical Development*. New York: Oxford University Press.

Schuller, Gunther. 1989. *The Swing Era*. New York: Oxford University Press.

Jehan, Noor (1925–2000)

Noor Jehan was an influential singer and film actress of the Indian subcontinent whose career spanned six decades. Also known by her honorific title "The Queen of Melody" (Urdu: *Malika-e-Tarannum*), she was one of the most prolific South Asian performers, recording more than 18,000 songs in various Indian and Pakistani languages including Urdu, Punjabi, Pashto, Sindhi, and Persian.

Born Allah Rakhi Wasai into a musical Punjabi Muslim family in British India, she trained in Hindustani classical and devotional music under Bade Ghulam Ali

Khan (1902–1968), focusing on *dhrupad, kahyaal*, and *thumri*. She first appeared on stage in Calcutta at age six, and by age nine, Punjabi composer Ghulam Ahmed Chishti (1905–1994) began to write *ghazals, na`ats*, and folk songs for her to perform. They both pursued careers in Lahore, with Wasai and her sisters performing live before film screenings. In the 1930s, her whole family moved to Calcutta in hopes of encouraging movie careers for her and her older sisters, Eiden Bai and Haider Bandi Wasai. She appeared under the stage name Baby Noor Jehan (Light of the World) until 1939, and her sisters were featured in Indira Movietone films as the *Punjab Mail*. Throughout the late 1930s, they sang child roles in Punjabi movies and became the first female singing stars of the Indian cinema.

In 1942, Noor Jehan played her first adult leading role (opposite Pran in *Khandaan*), shifted her career to Bombay, and married actor/director Shaukat Hussain Rizvi (1914–1999). In 1947, when the British partitioned India into India and Pakistan, they immigrated to Pakistan, working and raising three children in Lahore and Karachi. She became Pakistan's first female film director (co-directing *Chanway* in 1951) and made films with her husband until their divorce in 1954. She was remarkable for her embodied, emotional singing presentations, incorporating dance and movement with the *mehfil* style of song.

In 1959, she married a younger Pakistani film star, Ejaz Durrani (1935–), who pressured her to give up acting to concentrate on singing. She had three further children with Durrani, from whom she was divorced in 1971. One of her daughters was Pakistani singer and television performer Zil-e-Huma (1944–2014), and film actress Sonya Jehan (Sonya Rizvi, 1980–) is her granddaughter.

She had a very short career in Bollywood before the Partition (her last film was *Mirza Ghalib,* in 1961), but she became known as the Elizabeth Taylor of the Pakistani film industry due to her multiple marriages, alleged affairs, and sexualized, "queenly" presentation of the female body. She was invited back to New Delhi and Bombay to celebrate the golden jubilee of Indian talking films in 1982.

From 1960 to 1993, Jehan focused on playback singing, receiving accolades such as the Pride of Performance (1965), 13 Nigar Awards for Best Female Playback Singer, and the third and fourth highest civilian awards from Pakistan. She had a very wide range, with a distinctive, passionate delivery and even, melodious technique with a pure, nasal tone in all ranges, but she described singing well as emotionally and physically draining. Through her thousands of song recordings, she helped to evolve playback singing in the same ways Mehdi Hassan did for ghazal and Nusrat Fateh Ali Khan did for *qawwali*.

Her popularity was boosted by recordings and live performances of patriotic songs during the 1965 war between India and Pakistan. She was the *grande dame* of the Pakistani film industry, inspiring three generations of singers, including Lata Mangeshkar (1929–). The rise of television gave her the opportunity to reinvent herself as "the Melody Queen" in a series of musical programs: she re-recorded her earlier hits for a new generation and displayed her talents as a singer of ghazals and traditional songs.

Acknowledged by the great poet Faiz Ahmed Faiz (1911–1984) as his favorite singer, Noor Jehan proved that her renditions of his ghazals and nazms were unique. Notable duet partners included Ahmed Rushdi, Mehdi Hassan, Nusrat Fateh Ali

Khan, and Mujeeb Aalam. Pakistan Television named her "Voice of the Century" in 2000.

Laura Stanfield Prichard

See also: Dhrupad; Gimbri

Further Reading

Aziz, Ashraf. 2003. *Light of the Universe: Essays on Hindustani Film Music*, 2nd ed. New Delhi: Three Essays Collective.

Chugtahi, Tukir. 2004. *Noor Jehan*. Chandigarh, India: Unistar Books.

Hussein, Amir. 2017. "Noor Jehan: The Queen of Millions of Hearts across Generations." *Herald Magazine, Dawn* (September 21), 45–46.

Ramzi, Shanaz. 2002. "The Melody Queen Lives On." *Dawn.com*. February 10.

Jingju (Beijing Opera)

Jingju, or Peking Opera (a/k/a Beijing Opera), is a combination of acrobatics, dance, pantomime, martial art, song, dialogue, and incidental music. It was mainly developed in Beijing, the capital of the Qing dynasty (1636–1912 CE), in the 19th century and soon became popular in the Imperial court as well as in the marketplace and teahouse. Its name, "Jingju," also reflects the place where it was born: the capital, which is *Jing* in Chinese.

The librettos used in the court were primarily based on history or classical mythology, which carried the message of virtues that the Chinese admire, such as loyalty, integrity, filial piety, and purity. The stories told in the teahouses or marketplace mostly derived from folklore or everyday life, including romantic stories, chivalrous tales, and fairy tales. Peking opera has four primary stock characters: Sheng, which is an elegant and refined male character; Dan, the female ones; Jing, a bold and straightforward male character with painted face; and Chou, a male clown role. These characters are the focal point of Peking opera and they have elaborate costumes, which create a high contrast to the sparse, symbolic, "one-table-two-chairs" stage. The primary styles of vocal music that Peking opera applies are *Xipi* and *Erhuang* and in early times Peking opera was also called *Pihuang*, which designates a mixture of these two vocal styles.

ORIGINS AND DEVELOPMENT

The most important precursor of Peking opera is Hui opera (*Huiju*), a regional genre primarily developed from Huizhou, Anhui, originated during the Ming dynasty (1368–1644 CE). Hui opera was introduced to Beijing during the celebration of the 80th birthday of the Qianlong Emperor (1711–1799 [reigned 1735–1796]) in 1790. The Sanqing troupe first came to Beijing from Anhui to celebrate Qianlong's birthday. During the celebration, many different troupes, not limited to Hui opera, set up their stages from Xihua Gate to Xizhi Gate; therefore, different genres influenced each other. Before Hui opera, *Kunqu* and *Qingqiang* were two of the most popular vernacular genres in Beijing. However, Hui opera had more various and interesting librettos and performance styles, which took over the popularity of Kunqu and Qingqiang. After Qianlong's birthday celebration, more renowned Hui opera troupes came to Beijing, such as Sixi, Chuntai, and Hechun. Many actors of these two genres joined Hui opera troupes and brought their own styles to add to the variety of Hui opera.

During the reign of the Daoguang Emperor (1782–1850 CE [reigned 1820–1850]), Han opera (*Hanju*) actors came to Beijing from Hubei. Because they also used Xipi, it was convenient for them to join Hui opera troupes to perform. Hui opera gradually developed into a new form, incorporating elements from Kunqu, Qingqiang, Han opera, and Beijing accent. Because it used Xipi and Erhuang, it was first called *Pihuang* or *Pihuangxi*. Later people from Shanghai named it *Jingxi* or *Jingju*, meaning operas with Beijing flavor.

During the second half of the Qing dynasty, Peking opera rapidly developed in Beijing, first in the teahouses and marketplaces, later in the palace. During the reign of Xianfeng Emperor (1831–1861 CE [reigned 1850–1861]), Sanqing and Sixi troupes were invited to perform in the court. Empress Dowager Cixi (1835–1908) was a fan of Peking opera and on her 50th birthday, many famed Peking opera actors were invited to perform and teach eunuchs in the palace.

After the founding of the Republic of China (Taiwan) in 1911, Peking opera became more and more popular and was introduced abroad by Mei Lanfang (1894–1961). During the 1920s, Mei took Peking opera to Japan and then on a tour to New York City in 1930, which won such success that the tour was extended from two weeks to five weeks. Mei traveled across the United States and received two honorary degrees from Pomona College and the University of Southern California. He also visited the Soviet Union in 1935.

After the Chinese Civil War in 1949, Peking opera played a focal role of national identity for both involved parties. In Taiwan (the Republic of China), the Kuomintang government acknowledged Peking opera as "National opera" and encouraged this art form over other genres, such as the traditional Taiwanese opera, in an attempt to acquire a place as the sole representative of Chinese culture. Meanwhile, in China (People's Republic of China), the Communist Party of China used Peking opera as its vehicle for propaganda and transformed it into "model play" or "revolutionary opera," which gradually put the traditional, elaborate costumes aside and used modern clothes instead, especially during the Cultural Revolution (1966–1976).

Peking opera gradually lost its audience in the second half of the 20th century. The rise of television, film, pop music, and other entertainment reduced its importance, and to the younger generation its singing style sounded strange and esoteric. In the late 20th and early 21st centuries, some in the Chinese government led a movement to revitalize Peking opera. It was selected for the UNESCO Intangible Cultural Heritage List in 2010.

SYMBOLISM

Traditionally, the Peking opera stage is a square platform visible from three sides. The stage is spare, with few props, simple and basic drapes as background, and one table and two chairs for actors to use. A typical Peking opera stage is built

Jingju, also referred to as Beijing or Peking opera, is a Chinese theatrical tradition that combines music, singing, dialogue, dance, martial arts, and acrobatics. (Zhaohui/Dreamstime.com)

above the line of sight of the audience, and theatergoers are always seated south of the stage. Performers enter from the east and exit from the west. Through the actor's skill and the audience's imagination, one table and two chairs fulfill the needs of scene changes. The table and chairs covered with yellow satin embroidered clothes represent the palace; beige or pink could represent a young lady's bedroom. Yellow satin without decorations means in the temple, and adding a military curtain behind the table represents the army. According to the libretto, the table could be a hill, a tower, a bridge, a boat, a wall, a well, or a bed. An actor with a horsewhip means riding a horse, holding a paddle represents rowing a boat, and two vehicle flags designates a carriage. It requires great acting skill by the performers to make the audience understand what they are doing, such as opening a door, when the door does not exist on stage; or sewing a shoe sole, when one cannot see the needle and thread.

CHARACTERS

There were four stock characters—Sheng, Dan, Jing, and Chou—in Peking opera. The Sheng designates all the male roles in Peking opera. Young male characters are known as *Xiaosheng*, who are usually handsome, attractive, beardless, and sing in high, sharp voices. Older ones are *Laosheng*, who have a more gentle and cultivated personality and very often have a beard. *Wusheng* are highly trained in acrobatics, perform mostly martial arts, wear an elaborate military outfit, and have a natural voice when singing. *Hongsheng*, a red-faced older male character, is a subtype of laosheng. Guan Yu and Zhao Kuang-yin are two famous hongsheng characters.

Dan refers to all female roles, which were played by male performers during the Qing dynasty. In the first half of the 20th century, there were so-called "four famous Dans": Mei Lanfang, Cheng Yanqiu, Shang Xiaoyun, and Xun Huisheng, who were all men. Each of these four famous Dans led a school of acting and influenced many actors after them. Similar to Sheng, there are a couple of subtypes of Dan: *Qingyi* designates an elite, elegant female character; young female warriors were *Daomadan*; a vivacious and unmarried woman was *Huadan*; and *Laodan* means an old lady.

The *Jing* refers to a painted-face male role. This type of role generally embodies a forceful character, which requires a strong voice and exaggerated gestures. Peking opera claims that there are 15 basic facial patterns with more than 1,000 specific variations. The patterns and especially the coloring are derived from traditional Chinese color symbolism. Three basic colors include red, white, and black. Red represents honorableness and loyalty, such as the Guan Yu character. White denotes a wicked or crafty, deceitful character; one of the most famous roles of this type is Cao Cao. Black designates characteristics of trustworthiness and honesty; for instance, Bao Zheng. There are three essential subtypes of Jing: *Dahualian* (a/k/a *Tongchui*) is usually a prudent, wise, and modest character heavily involved in singing. *Erhualian* (a/k/a *Jiazihualian*) is usually bold and forthright, but could also represent a complicated role (for example, Cao Cao, a typical wicked, crafty character, is performed by Erhualian). *Wujing* usually denotes a martial and acrobatic character.

The *Chou* is a clown, a comedian, and nearly always plays an amusing secondary role. Those playing this role usually wear a small patch of white chalk around the nose, and therefore are also named *xiaohualian*. The Chou can be subdivided into *Wenchou*, a civilian role such as a merchant, a playboy, or a jailer; and *Wuchou*, a military character. The Wuchou is one of the most demanding characters in Peking opera, because it requires a balanced combination between comic acting, acrobatics, and singing.

MUSIC

The orchestra of the Peking opera, *Wenwuchang*, can be divided into two parts: the percussion section, which is called *Wuchang* and heavily used for scenes of combat; and an ensemble, called *Wenchang*, which consists of melodic instruments as well as some percussions and is used to accompany *Wenxi* (focus on singing).

Wenchang can be subdivided into two groups. The first group mainly involves string instruments, including *jinghu, erhu, yueqin,* and *sanxian*. This group predominantly accompanies the singing styles of Xipi, Erhuang, Sipingdiao, and Nanbangzi. The other group is primarily made up of wind instruments, comprising *dizi, sheng, suona,* and *haidizi*. This group chiefly accompanies Kunqu, Chuiqiang, Zaqiangxiaodiao, and Xichuiqupai.

The percussion instruments in Wuchang include *tanban, danpigu, tanggu, daluo, nao,* and *bo*. Combat scenes have been closely bonded with percussion for centuries. The strong, vivid, and clear rhythm helps the actors to perform and also builds tension. Traditionally there is no conductor for Wenwuchang; Gulao, the one who plays *guban* (tanban and danpigu), is the leader of the whole ensemble. In Peking opera, unlike Italian opera which uses fixed, composed music, the music is flexible. The whole ensemble will repeat a musical section, listen carefully to Gulao, and wait for his specific percussive pattern to continue or end the music, very much like the cadenza section in the Western classical music concerto; hence, the performers have more freedom to act so as to build up feelings.

IMPORTANT REPERTOIRES

In the convention of Peking opera, it is common to perform only a scene or an act instead of the whole opera, which is called *Zhezixi*. The famed actor is the center of the Peking opera and the audiences usually go to the theater for their favorite actors. Therefore, it is natural that the actor will choose those scenes that particularly showcase his acting, singing, and/or martial-arts skill.

Many of the repertoires of the Peking opera are derived from librettos of Kunqu, Hui opera, and other theatrical genres. *The Hegemon-King Bids His Concubine Farewell* (a/k/a *Farewell My Concubine*) is a well-known Peking opera, which was derived from Kunqu and initially performed by Yang Xiaolou and Shang Xiaoyun in 1918 in Beijing. In 1922, Yang Xiaolou and Mei Lanfang worked together to renew it, and their recreation became a classic repertoire for Mei Lanfang. The story tells that Xiang Yu (performed by Yang Xiaolou), the Hegemon-King of Western Chu, is losing the war and is surrounded by his opponent, Liu Bang's forces. Xiang Yu calls forth his horse and asks it to run away for the sake of its own safety, but the horse is very loyal and refuses to leave. He then calls for the company of his favorite concubine, Consort Yu (performed by Mei Lanfang). Realizing that they are losing the war, she begs to die alongside Xiang Yu, but he strongly rejects her wish. Thereafter, when he is distracted, Yu commits suicide with Xiang Yu's sword.

Another scene in Mei Lanfang's classic repertoire is *The Drunken Noble Consort*. In this story, Emperor Tang Minghuang asks his noble consort Yang Yuhuan to meet him at the Pavilion of Hundreds Flowers. After waiting for the Emperor for a long time and then learning that he has gone to another consort's palace, Yang Yuhuan feels extremely angry and disappointed and asks eunuchs to give her liquor to drink until she is quite drunk.

Huarong Boulevard is also an important repertoire piece of the Peking opera. The story happens during the Three Kingdoms (220–280), right after the Battle of Red Cliffs. Cao Cao is defeated by Zhuge Liang and Zhou Yu in Chibi. He flees and meets Guan Yu at Huarong Boulevard. Zhuge Liang has warned Guan Yu in advance that he is very likely to let Cao Cao run away, but Guan Yu rebukes him and requests that he be allowed to arrest Cao Cao. Cao Cao is afraid when he meets Guan Yu and begs Guan to remember how he honored and respected Guan before and let him escape. Guan has a soft heart. He ultimately gives in to Cao's begging and lets him go.

LEADING SCHOOLS

The most well-known schools of the Peking opera focus on the performance styles of Dan and Laosheng. Each of the four famous Dans leads his own school. Mei Lanfang (1894–1961) was known as the Queen of Peking Opera, especially for his performance of Qingyi. Mei was born into a family of Peking opera and Kunqu and made his debut in 1905. Throughout his whole career, he kept polishing his techniques and working on new practices, which were the basis of the Mei school style. There is no fancy vibrato or portamento in the Mei school, and the performance style is calm and peaceful. It seems to be plain at first, but its deep and subtle expression touches the audience. Mei built many classic standards, such as *The Drunken Noble Consort*, *The Hegemon-King Bids His Concubine Farewell*, *Mulan Enlisted*, and *The Phoenix Returns to Its Nest*, which was the first Peking opera to be translated into English in 1985.

Cheng Yanqiu (1904–1958) was Mei's student and also learned from Wang Yaoqing (1881–1954), and later created his own school. Cheng was good at portraying tragic female characters, who were outwardly weak and delicate but actually strong and tough. He was also known for using water sleeves, an extension to the cuff of garment sleeves. The Cheng school uses vibrato that helps intensify the grief and indignation of the female roles. Some classics in his repertoire include *Lady Wen Returned to Han*, *Tears of the Abandoned Mountain*, and *Assassin Nie Yinniang*.

Shang Xiaoyun (1900–1976) learned from both Wang Yaoqing and Sun Yiyun (1880–1944). Shang first studied Wusheng and later changed to Dan. He was celebrated for his performances of Daomadan as well as Qingyi. Shang's voice was bright and strong with a wide range, which became known as "metal voice." The Shang school created many dances and carried on his outstanding interpretations of Daomadan and Qingyi. His important repertoire includes *Reunion at Wujia Slope* and *Lady Zhaojun Departs for the Frontier*.

Xun Huisheng (1900–1968) learned from Li Shoushan (1866–1932) and Wang Yaoqing. He was good at acting an innocent, lively, and enthusiastic young lady. Xun's school incorporated Hebei Bangzi and added many fine and exquisite movements. *The Story of Su San*, *Romance of Mistakes in the Flower Field*, and *Meilong Garrison* are Xun's classic standards.

Ma Lianliang (1901–1966) was best known for his Laosheng and was considered one of the "Four Great Beards" (the Laosheng character usually wears a beard). He formed Fufeng Troupe when he was only 23 and established the Ma school. One of the most famous characters he performed was Zhuge Liang, a celebrated politician and military strategist in the Three Kingdoms.

Chloe Hsun Lin

See also: Opera; Taiwanese Opera

Further Reading

Bonds, Alexandra B. 2019. *Beijing Opera Costumes: The Visual Communication of Character and Culture*. New York: Routledge.

Guy, Nancy. 2005. *Peking Opera and Politics in Taiwan*. Urbana: University of Illinois Press.

Li, Ruru. 2010. *The Soul of Beijing Opera: Theatrical Creativity and Continuity in the Changing World.* Hong Kong: Hong Kong University Press.

Tian, Min. 2012. *Mei Lanfang and the Twentieth-Century International Stage: Chinese Theatre Placed and Displaced.* New York: Palgrave Macmillan.

Wichmann, Elizabeth. 1991. *Listening to Theatre: The Aural Dimension of Beijing Opera.* Honolulu: University of Hawaii Press.

Johnson, Robert (1911–1938)

Robert Johnson was an American blues singer and guitarist. He recorded 29 songs, in 1936 and 1937, whose influence and eventual commercial success established his reputation as a leading representative of the Delta blues style. When his recordings were reissued, beginning in 1959, he had a major impact on such rock musicians as the Rolling Stones, Eric Clapton, and Bob Dylan, among many others. Generations after Johnson died, dramatic accounts of his early death and an often-repeated legend that he sold his soul to the devil in exchange for his musical prowess have kept him alive and active in many imaginations.

Despite considerable research, many details of his life remain conjecture, because sources either contradict one another or do not exist. There is no known birth certificate; extant documents suggest that he was born in 1907, 1909, 1910, or 1912, although he was not included in the census of 1910, making the dates before that year unlikely. His half-sister Carrie Thompson, who also provided some of the only known photographs of him, reported his birth date as May 8, 1911, in Hazlehurst, Mississippi. The place and date of his death—August 16, 1938, in Greenwood, Mississippi—comes from his death certificate, a controversial and much-studied document. It describes him as a banjo player, instead of as a singer or guitarist, and suggests that the cause of death might have been syphilis, a claim that is not supported by any known medical evidence and perhaps reflects racial prejudice. According to dubious reports, he may have been stabbed, shot, or poisoned by a jealous husband. No doctor examined the body. Most vexing of all, a few of Johnson's acquaintances told researcher Robert "Mack" McCormick that Johnson remained alive years after 1938, suggesting that the death certificate—and how many anecdotes?—may refer to some other Robert Johnson. Gravestones in at least three Mississippi towns purport to mark his burial place.

Johnson was born out of wedlock to mother Julia Majors and father Noah Johnson. He was raised intermittently by a combination of Julia and her first husband, Charles Dodds (also known as Charles Spencer or C.D. Spencer and with whom Julia produced 10 children before Robert was born), and her second husband, Willie "Dusty" Willis. Because of the changing situations during his upbringing, Robert's contemporaries may have believed his last name to be Dodds, Spencer, or Willis at various points in his youth. He used Robert, Robert Leroy, R.L., and "Little Robert Dusty" (after "Dusty" Willis) as first names. During these early years, he lived in such places as Hazlehurst, Mississippi; Lucas, Arkansas; and Memphis, Tennessee. He attended Indian Creek School in Tunica, Mississippi, in the mid- and late 1920s, although the precise level of his education is unknown. On February 17,

1929, he married Virginia Travis, who died in childbirth the following year, along with the baby. In May 1931, he married Calletta "Callie" Craft, but left her a year later. About the same time, Robert also had a relationship with Virgie Mae Smith, which, on December 16, 1931, led to the birth of Claud Johnson, Robert's only known heir. From the early 1930s until his death in 1938, he travelled and performed in Mississippi, Arkansas, and Texas and perhaps as far away as Canada.

Judging from the few known photos of Robert Johnson, he was a slim black man who kept his hair trimmed short and his face clean-shaven. His left eye was slightly smaller than his right, and his left eyelid drooped somewhat, possibly due to a cataract or a lazy eye. The most distinguishing characteristics of his appearance were his extraordinarily long, slender fingers, which enabled his left hand to cover an unusually large area on the guitar fretboard. He was particularly adept at playing different patterns on the high strings and low strings at the same time. Because of his eye condition and slender fingers, some have speculated that he suffered from Marfan syndrome, and that this may have been a contributing factor in his death; these claims have not been medically tested or substantiated.

Some of Johnson's early acquaintances indicate that as a boy he played the diddley bow, a homemade instrument consisting of a single wire strung between two nails and secured against a resonating surface, such as the side of a barn. Similar anecdotes suggest that he also played the jaw harp in his youth. Eddie "Son" House (1902–1988) described him as an accomplished harmonica player and reported seeing him play a seven-string guitar as well. All of his recordings feature him singing and playing a six-string guitar but no other instruments. He may have learned some basic guitar skills from one of his half-brothers, and House, Willie Brown (1900–1952), and Isaiah "Ike" Zimmerman (1907–1967) were evidently influences on his early guitar playing. Further musical influences included Charley Patton, Tommy Johnson (no relation), James "Kokomo" Arnold, and Leroy Carr, among others. Johnson maintained a relationship with Estella Coleman; her son, Robert Lockwood, Jr., was his only known guitar student.

Johnson's entire musical reputation rests on two recording sessions, spread over five days in a period of about seven months. H. C. Speir, a record store owner and talent scout in Jackson, Mississippi, recommended him to Ernie Oertle, who worked for the American Record Company. Art Satherley and Don Law produced the recordings. The first session took place in the Gunter Hotel in San Antonio, Texas, on November 23, 26, and 27, 1936. The results were evidently successful enough to warrant a second session, which took place in the Vitagraph building in Dallas, Texas, on June 19 and 20, 1937. Recordings of 29 songs survive, including multiple takes of most—a rarity for the time. A few of these songs were released as singles on so-called race records in the 1930s, with "Terraplane Blues" (Vocalion, 1937) being the first and best selling (the B-side was "Kind Hearted Woman"). He achieved limited, regional success during his lifetime, was mostly forgotten for about 20 years after his death, and then achieved international fame and cachet.

In 1938, John H. Hammond organized a concert called "From Spirituals to Swing" at Carnegie Hall in New York, and he intended to invite Johnson as a representative of the Delta blues style. Johnson was not able to perform at the concert because he had died a few months earlier. As a result, Hammond filled his place on the program, along with Big Bill Broonzy, and played two of Johnson's recordings during the concert. Then Samuel Charters included Johnson's song "Preachin' Blues (Up Jumped the Devil)" on the recording that accompanied *The Country Blues* (1959), Charters's influential book on the blues, and Columbia began reissuing Johnson's recordings in 1961 (*King of the Delta Blues Singers*, 1961; *King of the Delta Blues Singers, Vol. II*, 1970; and finally *The Complete Recordings*, 1990). Beginning in the 1960s, Johnson's music became much more widely known than it ever had been during his lifetime, owing to performances by such artists as the Rolling Stones ("Walkin' Blues," "Love in Vain," "Stop Breakin' Down Blues"), Eric Clapton ("Crossroads," an arrangement of "Cross Road Blues"; *Me and Mr. Johnson*, an album of 14 of Johnson's songs), and Led Zeppelin ("Travelling Riverside Blues"). Among his numerous honors, in 1994, Johnson was selected to appear on a commemorative U.S. postage stamp, and in 2003, his recordings were selected for inclusion in the National Recording Registry of the Library of Congress.

Johnson's recordings demonstrate versatility and diversity in musical style. Some of his lyrics included expertly crafted double entendres ("Terraplane Blues") or hellish nightmares ("Hellhound on My Trail"), although others seem unplanned. Some of his musical arrangements include such remarkable rhythmic layering ("I Believe I'll Dust My Broom") that later listeners assumed they must have been played by multiple performers, instead of just one, or that the recordings were sped up. (Johnson is the lone performer, and none of his contemporaries thought the recordings sounded any faster than his live performances.) As a singer, he could croon ("From Four until Late"), moan ("Come On in My Kitchen"), or growl ("They're Red Hot"). He generally sang in the middle of his register, but occasionally he used falsetto or a high, strained vocal timbre (especially on "Cross Road Blues"). As a guitarist, he used a thumb pick and employed a bottleneck slide in creative ways ("Ramblin' on My Mind"). His playing is especially remarkable for playing two musical parts at once, as in his combination of piano and guitar parts in "Kind Hearted Woman," an answer song to Leroy Carr's "Mean Mistreated Mama" (1934). Playing like this eventually caused guitar to replace piano in many ensembles.

Joseph R. Matson

See also: Blues; Race Records; Smith, Bessie

Further Reading

Gioia, Ted. 2008. *Delta Blues: The Life and Times of the Mississippi Masters Who Revolutionized American Music*. New York: W. W. Norton.

Graves, Tom. 2008. *Crossroads: The Life and Afterlife of Blues Legend Robert Johnson*. Spokane, WA: Demers Books.

Greenberg, Alan. 1983. *Love in Vain: The Life and Times of Robert Johnson*. Garden City, NY: Doubleday. [Reprinted 1994 and 2012 as *Love in Vain: A Vision of Robert Johnson*]

Guralnick, Peter. 1989. *Searching for Robert Johnson*. New York: Dutton.

Johnson, Robert. 1990. *The Complete Recordings*. Liner notes by Stephen LaVere. Recorded 1936 and 1937. Sony Columbia C2K 46222 [CD].

Pearson, Barry Lee, and Bill McCullough. 2003. *Robert Johnson: Lost and Found*. Urbana: University of Illinois Press.

Wald, Elijah. 2004. *Escaping the Delta: Robert Johnson and the Invention of the Blues*. New York: HarperCollins.

Joik

The *joik* is a unique form of cultural expression for the Saami people of northern Scandinavia. The melody of this type of unaccompanied song is closely connected to a referential object, and uniquely expresses the identity of a person or thing. Linguistically, this is expressed by saying one "joiks" someone or something, rather than joiking *about* them, and the *subject* of the joik is considered to be the owner (not the performer of the joik). This mirrors the traditional role of art in Saami culture, as its central focus is on collectivity.

Traditional joiks were not intended to be performed as art. They fulfill social functions such as calming/herding reindeer, sharing memories, building community (both within a family and within society as a whole), self-expression, frightening wolves, and transporting a *noaidi*—the *siida's* resident shaman—between worlds, often to the accompaniment of a ceremonial drum.

Many joiks use vocables instead of words. A singer can use melody, rhythm, expressive articulation, and physical gestures in addition to text as forms of narrative. Traditional joikers employ extensive glissandi and build intensity through the gradual sharping of pitch; these aspects make joiks difficult to accompany. In 1799, Italian explorer Giuseppe Acerbi provided one of the earliest descriptions of joiking, describing it as "hideous cries . . . not connected with harmony . . . straining their throats." Although he was comparing traditional Saami singing to Italian operatic style, he was correct in identifying a compressed, nasal vocal tone achieved through careful breath control: "The Laplanders, after exhausting their breath, persevered in uttering the same cry in a kind of fainting or fading voice" (Acerbi, 1802, p. 68).

Saami joiks do not employ the linear organizing principles (phrases of equal lengths, clear beginning and end) found in most European folk song. They follow the Saami worldview of "No beginning, no end," and mimic the recirculating patterns of nature. Acerbi noticed that the rhythmic structure of joiks is unique, "without regard to time or measure . . . because there was nothing but a continued repetition of the same notes." His 1802 attempt to transcribe a joik included the following text:

"A good journey, my good gentleman—gentlemen—gentlemen—gentlemen,
a good journey—journey—journey—my good gentlemen—gentlemen,
a good journey—journey—journey—journey, etc.
and so on as long as they were able to fetch any breath: when this was exhausted, the song was ended."

Almost 90 years later, Sophus Tromholt observed similar traits in his 1885 book *Under the Rays of the Sun*, noting a "variation of two to three, at the most four tones to five tones to a melody," and melodies that were "most often improvisations, which, during incessant repetitions, express the mood, the character of nature or people, and so one of the person joiking" (Tromholt, 1885, p. 58).

Joiking can be divided into three distinct regional types, which roughly correspond to the dialectical areas of Saami language.

1. The North Saami form (called *luohti* in Saami) is the most common, as three-fourths of the native population lives in the North. The luohti is characterized by the use of leaps between elements of a pentatonic scale. A luohti always has a specific subject, usually a person, described in an intense voice. This form makes use of a marked rhythm with syncopations, shifting accents and vocal timbres, and the addition of glissandos and ornamental figures (such as vibrato). Different breathing styles are used to produce sound effects.

2. The *vuolle* is the South Saami form of the joik. Its characteristics include the use of just two or three notes close together and varying melodic spans consisting of several long sounds interspersed with quick glissandi and ornamental falsetto notes.

3. The Eastern Saami form of the joik, the *leu'dd*, is sometimes described as a rare "epic" form of joik, consisting of a long, personal narrative or village history in a more poetic and symbolic form. Improvisation and vocables play a key role in the leu'dd, and joikers incorporate elements of the vuolle and the luohti, make sudden changes to the melody, and touch upon a wide range of subjects (including political issues).

The role of the yoik in shamanism proved to be the basis for its systematic suppression by Christian missionaries in the 1600s and the governments of Scandinavia in the 1700s. As the result of research undertaken after World War II, the joik was found to be remarkably tenacious in both Norway and Sweden. In the late 1960s, Nils Aslak Valkeapää incorporated joiks, folk tunes, and instruments into a new form called "joik-song" (beginning with his 1968 album *Joikuja*). This new performative approach contrasts with the communal origins of the joik, and a tune inspired by South Saami joiking (combined with the Danish hymn "*Dejlig er jorden*/fairest Lord Jesus" by B. S. Ingemann) has even appeared in a 2014 choral version on the opening track for Disney's *Frozen* ("*Eatnemen Vuelie*" by Frode Fjellheim).

Laura Stanfield Prichard

See also: Norwegian Folk Music

Further Reading

Acerbi, Giuseppe. 1802. *Travels through Sweden, Finland, and Lapland, to the North Cape, in the Years 1798 and 1799.* Berkeley: University of California Libraries.

Jones-Bamman, Richard. 1993. "Negotiating Identity and the Performance of Culture: The Saami Joik." PhD diss., University of Washington.

Krumhansl, Carol L. 2000. "Cross-Cultural Music Cognition: Cognitive Methodology Applied to North Saami Yoiks." *Cognition* 76, 13–58.

Laitinen, Heikki. 1994. "The Many Faces of the Yoik." *Finnish Music Quarterly* 4, 2–15.

Länsman, Ursula. 1999. "Saami Culture and the Yoik." *FolkWorld* 9, 8–9.

Tromholt, Sophus. 1885. *Under the Rays of the Aurora Borealis*. London: Self-published.

Joplin, Scott (1867–1917)

Known as the "King of Ragtime Writers," Scott Joplin came to prominence following the publication of his "Maple Leaf Rag" in 1899—the most popular rag ever, which sold more than 1 million sheet-music copies. Joplin published more than 40 piano rags (a style of solo piano playing that coexisted with early New Orleans Dixieland jazz) between 1900 and 1906, including "The Entertainer" (1902) and wrote stage works such as "The Ragtime Dance" (1902), "A Guest of Honor" (1903), and the opera "Treemonisha" (1911), which was not performed in complete form during his lifetime. A posthumous Pulitzer Prize was awarded to Joplin in 1976 for his contribution to American music.

Much of Scott Joplin's early life is subject to speculation. The often-cited date of his birth, November 24, 1868, is incorrect. He was born sometime between July 19, 1867, and mid-January 1868, to Florence Givens, a free-born African American woman, and Giles Joplin, a former slave. He grew up in the town of Texarkana on the Texas–Arkansas border. Joplin's mother was a singer, and fostered her son's interest in music. Anecdotal evidence suggests that Julius Weiss, a local pianist, provided lessons to Joplin and served as a mentor by exposing the young Joplin to European art musical forms, including opera. Tom Turpin, the St. Louis saloon keeper and the first African American composer to publish instrumental ragtime ("Harlem Rag," 1897), was equally influential. Turpin's saloon and the Rosebud Bar became a gathering place and incubator for ragtime players in St. Louis and Joplin profited from his association with Turpin, composing "The Rosebud March" in 1905 and dedicating it to Turpin.

After leaving home as a teenager in the 1890s, Joplin traveled to Texas, Louisiana, Mississippi, and various towns in Arkansas. The earliest documentation of Joplin's musical activities consists of newspaper reports from the summer of 1891, when he was part of a traveling minstrel troupe. In 1893, Joplin was present at the Chicago World's Fair, leading a band and playing cornet. Making his way to Sedalia by way of St. Louis, he participated in the all-night ragtime piano competitions at Tom Turpin's Silver Dollar Saloon and played first cornet in the Queen City Cornet Band, a group of African American instrumentalists. Shortly thereafter, he

---

Sidebar-Ragtime Royalties

Ragtime composer Scott Joplin's "Maple Leaf Rag" (1899) was a major success, selling more than a million copies, and earning Joplin a place as the most successful African American composer of his day. This success was all but unique among composers of the day and was made possible by Joplin's shrewd business sense. Rather than selling the composition outright for a few hundred dollars, which was standard practice for the day—especially for African American composers—Joplin negotiated a royalty scheme with his publisher. Though standard practice today, this was uncommon during Joplin's time. Functioning as an annuity of sorts, "Maple Leaf Rag" earned Joplin hundreds of thousands of dollars. Joplin spent the rest of his career trying, largely unsuccessfully, to duplicate the success of the "Maple Leaf Rag," but he did so with a steady stream of royalties earned from sale of the composition.

formed his own ensemble, performing at dances and other engagements. Joplin still led the life of a freelance musician, "riding the rails," and traveling as far as Syracuse, New York, with his Texas Medley Quartette, a vocal group. His stellar performances garnered the attention of several business men in Syracuse who agreed to publish two of Joplin's songs—"Please Say You Will" and "A Picture of Her Face"—representing his first published musical works.

In 1894, Joplin settled in Sedalia, Missouri, and matriculated at George R. Smith College, an all-African American college. Also at this time, Joplin performed in the Williams Brothers Maple Leaf Club. Joplin was billed as "the entertainer" in club promotional materials and this later became the title of one of his famous classic rags. While working as a teacher, he also mentored other ragtime musicians, including James Scott, Artie Matthews, Paul Pratt, J. Russel Robinson, and Joseph F. Lamb. Joplin published "Original Rags," his first piano rag, in 1899, but was compelled to share the credit with Charles N. Daniels, an arranger, and received a flat fee of $25 for his efforts. Displeased with this standard music publishing industry practice, Joplin then secured the legal services of Robert Higdon to ensure that he would receive a one-cent royalty per sheet-music copy sold of his next composition, "The Maple Leaf Rag." In 1899, Joplin collaborated with music publisher John Stark to promote his compositions, defining them as "classic rags" and comparing their quality to that of European art music. As a result, Joplin retained the term for his work when negotiating with other music publishers in order to delineate his artistic agenda. The success of and attendant royalty fees from "The Maple Leaf Rag" provided Joplin with a small but consistent income, enabling him to compose at relative leisure in addition to earning him the title "King of Ragtime Writers."

Not content with merely being a ragtime composer, Joplin aspired to write for the theater. Written shortly after the success of "The Maple Leaf Rag," his initial composition in this arena was "The Ragtime Dance" (1902), a folk ballet with singer-narrator depicting social dancing activities and the Black American Ball held at Sedalia's Black 400 Club. Joplin relocated to St. Louis in 1901 with his new wife Belle Jones (1875–[death year unknown]), turning his attention more to composition and teaching, and less to performance. Belle Jones Joplin was Scott Hayden's sister-in-law and widow of his older brother. After the death of the family's infant daughter in 1903, the couple drifted apart and later divorced. It was during this time that he wrote an exemplary collection of rags, including "Sunflower Slow Drag" (1901, with Scott Hayden), "The Easy Winners" (1901), "The Entertainer" (1902), and "The Strenuous Life" (1902), dedicated to President Theodore Roosevelt. In 1904, Joplin married 19-year-old Freddie Alexander (1884–1904) and celebrated his success with the writing of "The Cascades" rag that he performed at the St. Louis World's Fair. Another piece composed at this time was "The Chrysanthemum," which Joplin dedicated to Freddie and subtitled "an Afro-American Intermezzo" in order to raise the profile of the classic rag. Sadly, Freddie developed pneumonia and died on September 10, 1904, at the age of 20—a mere 10 weeks following their marriage.

Joplin focused his energies on opera, writing "A Guest of Honor," based upon African American leader Booker T. Washington's 1902 White House dinner with President Theodore Roosevelt. Ever the entrepreneur, Joplin submitted a copyright application for the work in early 1903 and indicated that Stark would publish the opera in the forms. For some reason, copies of the music were never provided to the Library of Congress and the music remains lost. Newspaper commentary from the time indicates that Washington's White House dinner was a fractious event that divided the nation, with African Americans taking pride in the achievement and Joplin's seeking to commemorate it with music.

In 1907, Joplin began working on the opera "Treemonisha" and moved to New York, where he believed better professional opportunities awaited him. Joplin dissolved his business relationship with Stark and eventually entered into a contract with Seminary Music, which published his "Wall Street Rag," "Paragon Rag," "Solace," and "Pine Apple Rag." Seminary Music was loosely affiliated with Ted Snyder Music, Irving Berlin's employer, and it was through this relationship that Joplin asserted that Berlin had access to the "Treemonisha" score from which Berlin allegedly stole a theme for use in "Alexander's Ragtime Band." Joplin completed and self-published the lengthy score for "Treemonisha" in 1910, dedicating it to Freddie. The June 1911 issue of *American Musician and Art Journal* applauded the work and Joplin publicized several stagings, but none occurred. The only known performances during Joplin's life were an unstaged rehearsal without scenery or orchestra, in 1911; a staging of the finale, "A Real Slow Drag," in Bayonne, New Jersey, in 1913; and an orchestral concert in 1915 of the Act 2 ballet scene, "Frolic of the Bears," in 1915 at the Martin-Smith Music School in Harlem.

In 1913, Joplin and his new wife, Lottie Stokes Joplin (1878–1953), formed his own publishing company, and they issued "Magnetic Rag" in 1914. He also wrote several rags and songs, a musical, a symphony, a piano concerto, and a vaudeville act, but none were published and the manuscripts have been lost. By 1916, Joplin felt the effects of tertiary syphilis, a disease he had likely contracted some 20 years earlier. By mid-January 1917, he was hospitalized and then transferred to a mental institution, where he died on April 1, 1917. At the time of his death, Joplin was nearly forgotten. Interest in ragtime was fading as jazz captured audiences' attention. Even so, Joplin's "The Maple Leaf Rag" continued to influence the next generation of musicians and music lovers.

In the 1970s, new recordings of Joplin's music, now produced on classical record labels, set new sales records. Simultaneously, sheet music became available courtesy of a reprinted, two-volume set issued by the New York Public Library; and "Treemonisha" was successfully staged by the Houston Grand Opera—and finally reached Broadway. This presence inspired the incorporation of Joplin's music in George Roy Hill's film *The Sting*, whose popularity catapulted Joplin's music into Top 40 radio station playlists. Ushered in with music that Joplin had written some 50 years earlier, ragtime was transformed into a universally loved style of American music crossing all boundaries—from piano recitals to discos, to capacity-crowd stadiums to rock fans. Now a crossover phenomenon, Joplin recordings reached the top of the charts in both classical and popular categories. In recognition of his significant achievements, the Pulitzer Committee issued a posthumous award in 1976 to Scott Joplin for his contribution to American music.

Eldonna L. May

See also: Jazz; Race Records; Ragtime; Vaudeville

Further Reading

Albrecht, T. 1979. "Julius Weiss: Scott Joplin's First Piano Teacher." *College Music Symposium* 19(2), 89–105.

Berlin, Edward A. 1980. *Ragtime: A Musical and Cultural History*. (Revised 1984 with addenda). Berkeley: University of California Press.

Berlin, Edward A. 1994. *King of Ragtime: Scott Joplin and His Era*. New York: Oxford University Press.

Haskings, James, and Kathleen Benson. 1978. *Scott Joplin*. Garden City, NY: Doubleday.

J-Pop

J-pop is a term that evolved during the 20th century to denote Japanese pop music and its many correlative musical genres. Although Japanese "popular" music existed prior to 1945, many scholars choose to examine J-pop as an outgrowth of music after World War II due to the Western jazz and rock-and-roll styles that were permeating Japan's soundscape at the time. Through the years, Japanese pop music has continued to transform itself while simultaneously reflecting a strong connection to Japanese society. Although J-pop often stylistically resembles Western popular music, one should not assume that J-pop is essentially imitative or derivative in nature; rather, it is a synthesis of Western popular music and Japanese musico-cultural aesthetics. J-pop is an all-encompassing term for many subgenres, forcing practitioners, listeners, and researchers to continually consider what J-pop is *not*.

Popular song (*minyō*) has existed in Japan for centuries; however, due to an inculcation of Western art music in the late 19th century, these popular melodies and harmonies began—little by little—to exhibit Western diatonic harmonies and scales rather than the traditional Japanese ones. In the 1910s, this hybrid form of song (*shin minyō*) adopted a new name, *ryūkōka*. For example, in Namiki Michiko's "Ringo no uta" (Apple song) of 1945, one can hear a very European-sounding introduction with a more traditional Japanese-sounding melody sung during the verses and chorus. Three offshoots of ryūkōka developed: *kayōkyoku*, *enka*, and *poppusu*. *Kayōkyoku* drew on the Western pop ballad. *Enka* tended to use more traditional scales and harmonies as well as effusive emotional content. *Poppusu* exhibited traits of Western popular music such as blues and boogie-woogie. For example, Hattori Ryōichi's "*Wakare no burūsu*" (Farewell blues) (1937) duplicates with striking accuracy the Tin Pan Alley song style from the United States. The singer Kasagi Shizuko's "Tokyo Boogie Woogie" (1946) is another example of the major influence that U.S. music had on this genre after World War II. In fact, the similarity of poppusu songs to American popular music at the time created a short-lived flow of musical exchange between the countries, as evidenced by "*Gomen nasai*" (I'm sorry), co-written by Hattori in 1946 and distributed in the United States. This song was sung in English by a U.S. Army soldier and reached the Top 10 on American pop charts.

By the late 1950s, American rockabilly and rock and roll began to influence Japanese pop music. The 1958 Nichigeki Western Carnival was a public entrée for Japanese rockabilly musicians, who had theretofore been making music on the margins of Japanese music society. The full-blown expansion of rockabilly in Japan was to be short-lived; however, one of its stars, Sakamoto Kyū, was able to cross national borders musically by singing his kayōkyoku ballad *"Ue wo muite arukō"* (Walking with my head up) in 1961. This song, which later became the hit single "Sukiyaki" in the United States is an amalgamation of styles. The composer of the melody (Nakamura Hachidai) utilizes a quintessentially pentatonic scale, which sounds very Asian; however, Sakamoto (being a rockabilly singer) renders the melody with a style reminiscent of early rock-and-roll singers such as Buddy Holly or Jerry Lee Lewis. The walking bass line reminds one of a 1950s country and western song, and the brass obligato sections sound like a swing band. This unique sound made an impression on American audiences; the song spent three weeks at No. 1 on the *Billboard* charts in the summer of 1963 (the only Japanese song to ever do so well) and sold more than 13 million copies internationally.

Late 1960s pop music in Japan featured bands such as the Tigers. Their song, *"Hana no kubikazari"* (Flower necklace), in 1968, was reminiscent of British or American boy bands fashioned after the Beatles. Although the title of the song suggests a "flower power" message, which would suggest a musical knock-off, the lyrics actually align more closely with a Japanese poetry aesthetic. Also, the musical obligato parts swelling in the background of the song are characteristically pentatonic, allowing for a more synthetic rendering of the overall presentation. Also prominent in the late 1960s were more hard-edged rock bands such as the Spiders. Their song "Dynamite" starts with iterations of guitar noise and then fluctuates between sounds that remind one of the Doors but also Chuck Berry. The Jacks, a psychedelic/folk rock band whose lead singer Hayakawa Yoshio invoked Jim Morrison, also explored noise as a philosophical antipode to music. In fact, the current subcultural phenomenon of JapanNoise could possibly stem from these types of bands (in conjunction with electronic music discussed later in this article). The early 1970s band Happy End, although sounding derivative of U.S. folk rock and protest music, created some very unique sounds and quite melodic music. Arai Yumi (later known by her married name, Matsutoya) became popular with her album, *"Hikōki gumo"* (Airplane cloud). Matsutoya's style is very reminiscent of singer-songwriters such as Carole King, and she has released more than 36 albums and recorded many very popular and well-loved songs for film.

The group Yellow Magic Orchestra (YMO) helped to bring Japanese pop into the technological age of the 1980s. Coincidentally, one of the founding members of YMO, Hosono Haruomi, was the bassist for the group Happy End, and also played with the bands Caramel Mama and Tin Pan Alley, which accompanied Matsutoya on her first albums. Hosono collaborated with Sakamoto Ryūichi (a classically trained keyboardist and electronic music enthusiast) and the drummer Takahashi Yukihiro. YMO's techno-pop sound and development of computer game music have influenced electronica, ambient, house, trance, hip-hop, and video game musicians for decades. Concurrently in the 1980s, a pop-art/rock movement called *Visual kei* (literally, "visual style") began to develop. This movement features fashion and makeup as important aspects of performance and utilizes punk, glam rock, or heavy metal styles of music. Visual kei as a genre still continues today as a vital subgenre of J-pop. Many other 1980s and early 1990s bands in Japan found

Japanese all-girl pop group AKB48 performing in 2011. J-pop emerged as a genre in the 1990s and is now a term applied to most Japanese popular music. (Yoshikazu Tsuno/AFP/Getty Images)

success by exemplifying American and British sounds of the same time period, such as Anzen Shitai, Southern All Stars, Chage & Aska, B'z, and Mr. Children.

The term "J-pop" originated in 1988 as the title of a radio segment on the channel J-WAVE and over the years has become the ubiquitous term for pop, kayōkyoku, rock, electronica, punk, hip-hop, and many other similar music styles by Japanese artists. Basically, this term indicates music that is not enka, J-core (hard core), or other ethnic musics. In fact, many groups since the 1990s have explored a variety of genres under the J-pop umbrella. For example, the groups Spitz, Glay, and Luna Sea regularly draw upon a variety of different styles for each of their albums.

Since the 1990s, J-pop has been significantly influenced not only by American and British artists but also by K-pop, or Korean Wave pop music. This music features boy and girl bands singing in upbeat and "bubble gum" pop styles. These groups market and appeal heavily to younger teens. Many bands are now classified as "Japanese Idol Groups," such as Arashi (male), AKB48 (female).

Another important set of artists that began to become popular in the 1990s and 2000s were solo female artists. For example, Utada Hikaru is a singer-songwriter who has recorded not only in Japanese but also in English since her debut in 1999. Hamasaki Ayumi and Misia, both singer-songwriters, have enjoyed great success since their debuts in 2007.

Bradley Fugate

See also: Enka Music; Japan, Music of; Kayokyoku; Min'yô

Further Reading

Bourdaghs, Michael K. 2012. *Sayonara Amerika, Sayonara Nippon: A Geopolitical History of J-Pop*. New York: Columbia University Press.

Condry, Ian. 2006. *Hip-Hop Japan: Rap and the Paths of Cultural Globalization*. Durham, NC: Duke University Press.

Novak, David. 2013. *Japanoise: Music at the Edge of Circulation*. Durham, NC: Duke University Press.

Sterling, Marvin. 2005. *Music in Japan*. New York: Oxford University Press.

Sterling, Marvin. 2010. *Babylon East: Performing, Dancehall, Roots Reggae, and Rastafari in Japan*. Durham, NC: Duke University Press.

K

Kabuki

Kabuki is a popular theater genre known for its elaborate costumes, extreme makeup, and often satirical stories based on daily life of the Edo Period (1603–1868 CE, also known as the Tokugawa Period). Kabuki incorporates elements from two other important Japanese theater forms, *nô* and *bunraku*. All three flourished during the Edo Period and developed uniquely Japanese qualities because of a xenophobic closure of the country by the military ruling government known as the *shogunate*. This time of inward reflection allowed these theater forms to develop a truly Japanese sensibility, uninfluenced by outside sources.

Kabuki developed around 1600 CE as a type of entertainment theater in the pleasure districts of Kyoto, Osaka, and Edo (Tokyo). Initially, kabuki was a women's dance form rather than a dramatic presentation or setting. Women were banned from kabuki in 1629 CE and replaced by adolescent male dancers. These adolescents were in turn banned in 1652 CE, which initiated the adult male-only performance tradition. The female roles, which are played by men, are known as *onnagata* or *oyama*, "woman roles." It is commonly believed among actors, and indeed audiences today, that a woman cannot capture the nuances of the female form and that only a man can truly portray the elegance and grace of a woman on stage. The most beloved onnagata actor of the 20th century is Bandô Tamasaburô V (1950–). Born Shinichi Morita, he was given his stage name by his adopted father and mentor in 1964, and has a much-praised career and still performs today.

Kabuki has over time incorporated elements from other Japanese art forms, especially nô and bunraku theater. Nô theater developed in the 14th century CE, but during the Edo Period became the ceremonial art form of the shogunate. Bunraku, a puppet theater, developed in the late 16th century CE and features stories of the merchant class. Both theater forms have greatly influenced the style and performance practice of kabuki. The stories presented in kabuki and bunraku often center on daily Edo Period life but also draw upon Japanese mythology.

The *hayashi* instrumental ensemble from nô drama was adopted into kabuki in the early 1700s and is still used today. Narrative singing found in bunraku, based on the *jôruri* narrative style, was incorporated around 1714 CE (Motegi, 2001, p. 657). *Nagauta*, lyrical singing, developed in kabuki with the incorporation of the *shamisen*, a three-string long-neck lute. Additionally, kabuki has integrated other instruments and elements as the form progressed through the years to create a theatrical form that remains fresh in Japan today.

The sonic experience of kabuki can be bombastic and intense, and sometimes confusing for a first-time audience member. Often, when the setting calls for it, one style of music is heard from one ensemble placed on one area of the stage, while another ensemble may play a completely different style from a separate area of the stage. This cacophony of sound is meant to imitate a typical setting in the pleasure districts of the Edo Period. Generally, kabuki music is divided into two types—onstage and offstage—both led by shamisen and voice, most often in the nagauta form. The onstage music serves as the direct accompaniment for kabuki dance and drama. Other song and narrative forms are used in kabuki, but the predominant form is nagauta, which is a cosmopolitan genre that incorporates styles from many other forms of shamisen music.

The shamisen is an indigenized form of the *sanshin* from the Ryukyu Islands (Okinawa) and the Chinese *sanxian*. It was incorporated into many folk musics of Japan late in the 16th century CE. It became an important element of *gidayû bushi* in bunraku and later (in the 1650s) was brought into the kabuki tradition. There are several forms of shamisen, but the instrument used for nagauta is referred to as a narrow-neck, or *hosozao* shamisen, which allows for more virtuosity and nimble performance practice. Nagauta is considered a lyric song form, rather than a narrative form common in other theater genres. It is based on an earlier song form called *kouta* (short song) popular in the Edo Period, but with the influence of gidayû bushi and the jôruri narrative forms of bunraku, nagauta incorporates sections of narrative sequences within the song setting.

The onstage ensemble, called *debayashi*, is made up of nagauta performers and the hayashi ensemble borrowed from nô. Typically there are three nagauta singers and three shamisen players on stage, but this number can fluctuate. The hayashi is mostly identical to the nô ensemble: *kotsuzumi* (shoulder hourglass drum), *ôtsuzumi* (hip hourglass drum), *shimedaiko* (barrel drum), and a flute. However, the kabuki hayashi flute player will often use the more melodic bamboo flute known as *takebue* (or *shinobue*) in addition to the *nôkan* from nô. Depending on the size of the nagauta ensemble, additional kotsuzumi musicians can be used. The hayashi usually sits just in front and below the nagauta musicians at the rear of the stage facing the audience.

An important element of kabuki is the offstage ensemble that provides a sonic backdrop for drama and dance, as well as numerous symbolic sound effects that add audible texture to the performance. Known by many names, *geza ongaku* (lower-place music, named for its position offstage) is used here, but *narimono*, *kagebayashi*, and *kuromisu* are also common (Tokita, 2008, p. 231). Though technically on the stage, the ensemble is screened from audience view, making it a heard, but not seen, musical element, much like a sound track to a motion picture. This "sound track" is meant to add atmosphere to the performance, and actors rarely interact with it directly. The repertory, which is estimated at more than 800 pieces (Tokita, 2008, p. 232), ranges from full songs and instrumental music to sound effects produced by a varying array of instruments. The songs included are from the nagauta tradition. Gongs, bells, drums, and clappers, as well as other instruments for special occasions, produce the sound effects for the play through stereotypical melodic and rhythmic patterns. "*Geza* patterns can indicate setting (mountain, seaside, valley, riverside), climatic conditions (rain, snow, echo), social environment (court, manor, licensed [pleasure] district), the status of the character, the dramatic mood, and so forth" (Tokita, 2008, p. 234). For example, the *ôdaiko*, a large barrel drum, through a variety of stick slaps, taps, and strikes creates sounds that can evoke trickling rain, shutters being slammed by the wind, and the crashing of waves in the harbor, to name but a few.

Like its music, the kabuki stage has evolved over the years. Early settings for kabuki would have been simple outdoor stages with little thought given to aesthetics or the floor plan. The first major standardization occurred as kabuki moved into proper theater venues. The Tokugawa shogunate licensed nine official theaters, three each in Edo, Kyoto, and Osaka. These theaters were allowed to standardize their staging and productions and could thus distinguish themselves from the small, unlicensed theaters in surrounding areas. One element (allowed with government approval) was the incorporation of the *hanamichi* (flower path). The hanamichi is a characteristic piece of the kabuki stage that brings actors on and off via its elongated pathway running directly through the audience. Actors also use the hanamichi to deliver key speeches and to bring the action closer to the audience. A mid–18th-century development was the use of a revolving floor on the main stage, something Europe would not see for another hundred years. This movable floor allowed for quick scenery changes and other staging devices such as trap doors, hanging wires, and piped-in water (Brandon, 1997, p. 175). Though these elements are hundreds of years old, they have been an inspiration for many theatrical productions around the world, and are still considered state of the art.

As kabuki developed from a predominately dance form into a dramatic one, various acting styles developed. Five general acting styles survive, and each can be used in a play regardless of the play's overall type. These acting styles developed over time, the first being the *danmari*, or "wordless" style. Probably related to kabuki's origins of dance, this style, not often seen today, includes simple pantomime with no vocalization. The *aragoto*, or "rough style," developed in the Edo theaters and is meant to reflect the masculine vigor of the *samurai*. This acting style is characteristically overexaggerated. The character's costuming, gestures, dance style, and makeup are all larger than life. This style is often used for warriors and other superhuman characters. Their fierceness is reflected in intense makeup known as *kumadori*, "following the shadow," which consists of bold lines of red, blue, black, or grey (Brandon, Malm, and Shively, 1987, p. 69). The direct opposite of the aragoto style is the *wagoto*, or "soft style," developed in the Kyoto and Osaka area and known for its imperial refinement. This style is considered to be both comedic and sexually driven. It characteristically portrayed the youthful beauty of men as well as an immature bravado that was read as pitiful, almost effeminate, though these characters would often be featured in love scenes. However, this acting style is now tamed and the sexual nature of the characters is downplayed.

The *maruhon*, or "puppet style" (also known as *ningyô buri*), was adapted from bunraku. This style mimics the motions and intentions of the puppets in bunraku. Often, the actors will imitate the actions exactly to match the set texts used from the bunraku jôruri narrative form. In this style, the actor does not deliver his own dialogue; rather, he uses prescribed pantomime to express the words and emotion of the fixed text.

The *shosagoto*, or "dance style," is a highly developed solo dance that is considered to be the most complex of acting styles. Shosagoto can further be divided into three forms: *odori, mai,* and *furi*. Odori is known for its lively dance style that may include leaping in the air and other animated displays. Mai is based on the dance style of the nô drama. It characteristically uses deliberate movements and often will use poses reminiscent of nô: evenly spaced feet, a fan extended out overhead, and fingers grasping the actor's outstretched *kimono* sleeve (Brandon et al., 1987, pp. 78–79). Furi is a type of pantomime dance derived from bunraku. This form is less realistic and considered more abstract than the others.

Each style is characterized by stereotypical performance techniques, or *kata*. Wagoto characters are known for soft gestures and elegant mannerisms, whereas aragoto characters use exaggerated movements of rigid and quick motion. A unique element of kabuki is known as *mie*. This kata can be used by any actor style, but is very common with aragoto characters. Mie are dramatic poses that the actor uses to elevate the tension and emotion of a scene, while creating a "snapshot" of the character. The scene is frozen as the actor performs the mie, sometimes for several seconds. These mie resemble Edo Period woodblock paintings with fierce expressions and vivid makeup. Another important kata is the *roppô*, a stylized swaggering walk (Brandon et al., 1987, p. 86). There are different types, but the roppô is often seen as actors leave the main stage and exit on the hanamichi.

Justin R. Hunter

See also: Bunraku; Nô Theater

Further Reading

Brandon, James R. 1997. *The Cambridge Guide to Asian Theatre*. Cambridge: Cambridge University Press.

Brandon, James R., William P. Malm, and Donald H Shively. 1987. *Studies in Kabuki: Its Acting, Music, and Historical Context*. Honolulu: University of Hawaii Press.

Malm, William P. 1963. *Nagauta: The Heart of Kabuki Music*. Rutland, VT: Tuttle.

Malm, William P. 2000. *Traditional Japanese Music and Musical Instruments (The New Edition)*. Tokyo: Kodansha International.

Motegi, Kiyoko. 2001. "Theatrical Genres: Kabuki." In Robert Provine, Yosihiko Yokumaru, and J. Lawrence Witzleben (eds.), *The Garland Encyclopedia of World Music; Vol. 7: China, Japan, and Korea*, 657–661. New York: Routledge.

Okuyama, Keiko. 2001. "Theatrical Genres: Hayasi." In Robert Provine, Yosihiko Yokumaru, and J. Lawrence Witzleben (eds.), *The Garland Encyclopedia of World Music; Vol. 7: China, Japan, and Korea*, 683–685. New York: Routledge.

Okuyama, Keiko, and Reese Heinz-Dieter. 2001. "Theatrical Genres: Overview." In Robert Provine, Yosihiko Yokumaru, and J. Lawrence Witzleben (eds.), *The Garland Encyclopedia of World Music; Vol. 7: China, Japan, and Korea*, 653–655. New York: Routledge.

Otsuka, Haiko. 2001. "Theatrical Genres: Nagauta." In Robert Provine, Yosihiko Yokumaru, and J. Lawrence Witzleben (eds.), *The Garland Encyclopedia of World Music; Vol. 7: China, Japan, and Korea*, 671–674. New York: Routledge.

Tokita, Allison McQueen. 2008. "Music in *Kabuki*: More Than Meets the Eye." In Alison McQueen Tokita and David W. Hughes (eds.), *The Ashgate Research Companion to Japanese Music*, 229–260. Surrey, UK: Ashgate.

Kalthoum, Umm (1898–1975)

Umm Kalthoum, the beloved and charismatic Egyptian singer, captured world attention with her beautiful gift for singing and performing. She was born Fatma el-Zahraa Ibrahim, but as a professional singer took the stage name of Umm Kalthoum and was called "Star of the East" ("Kawkab al-Sharq"). Other variations of her name include Oum Kalsoum, Umm Kulthum, Umm Thulum, and Um Kalthoum. The name "Umm" or "Oum" is the Arabic for "mother," and Muhammad the Prophet's daughter was named Umm Kulthum.

Kalthoum was born on December 20, 1898, in the peasant village of Tamay al-Zahirah, Egypt. Some sources list her date of birth as May 4, 1904. This discrepancy is due to the fact that at the time, births in Egypt were often recorded years after the actual birth. The date on Umm Kalthoum's official birth certificate, May 4, 1904, was the date when her birth was recorded, although she was actually born in 1898. The youngest of three children, Umm Kalthoum had an older sister, Sayidda, who was born 10 years earlier, and a brother, Khalid, who was a year older.

Umm Kalthoum grew up in poverty. Her father, al-Shaykh Ibrahim al-Sayyid al-Baltiji (d. 1932), was a singer and leader of the mosque and her mother, Fatmah al-Maliji (d. 1947), was a stay-at-home mom. To help support the family, her father sang religious and folk songs at weddings and other social events. Her brother, Khalid, was also a singer. Umm Kalthoum attended the village school and was drawn to singing. She learned to sing by listening to her father teaching her brother. Much to her father's surprise, Umm Kalthoum learned and memorized the songs that she heard. She emulated the singing of her brother and father, who often took her along with him to sing. She began singing traditional religious Arabic songs when she was quite young.

Impressing those in her village with her exceptional musical voice, she was even paid to perform as a youngster. However, a young Muslim girl singing in public for men was not considered proper; therefore, her father dressed her as a boy. In the documentary film, *Umm Kulthum, a Voice Like Egypt*, she states: "My father was uneasy. The idea that his daughter should sing in front of men he didn't know was difficult for him to accept, but my singing helped support the family. So he dressed me in boy's clothes, and I sang this way for several years. I realize now that he wanted to convince himself, and the audience too, that the singer was a young boy, and not a young woman" (Goldman and Danielson, 1996/2006).

As a teenager, Umm Kalthoum continued to shine and appeal to the people in her village and nearby towns. Many invitations poured in for her to sing at various venues. She and her family relocated to Cairo around 1922 and her professional career began to bloom with the help of the singer Zakariyya Ahmad. Young Egyptian women were allowed to sing in public, and Umm Kalthoum often dressed in modern attire of the upper-class Egyptian society such as a long evening gown. Providing guidance and instruction, the poet Ahmad Rami and composer al-Shaykh Abu al-ila Muhammad were also instrumental in developing her career and helping her perfect her art. Rami provided instruction in Arabic poetry and literature and al-Shaykh Abu al-ila Muhammad provided music lessons, including singing instruction.

By this time, Umm Kalthoum was earning as much as $50 per performance, and created her own accompanying ensemble or *takht* (*nay* flute, *oud* lute, *qānūn* zither, *riq* drum, and violin). Her father and brother were members of this takht. Besides performing in public theaters and music halls, she also sang in the homes of noted Egyptians in Cairo. She had a gift for musical improvisation and composition which she extemporized to poetry. She performed not only religious music, but also classical and popular Arabic songs. Umm Kalthoum was unique compared to most Egyptian or Arabic women of the time, who tended to be traditional in appearance and attire. She let her long flowing black hair down, adopted modern Western attire, and often used a red silk scarf that became part of her performance. In Cairo, Umm Kalthoum continued her rise to fame as she amazed and attracted her audiences with her exquisite style of singing and performance. People from North Africa and the Middle East flocked to her concerts in Cairo.

Throughout her life and career, Umm Kalthoum sang the poetry of numerous poets. These included Ahmad Rami, whom she met in 1924 and with whom she had a romantic relationship, and Muḥammad ʿAbd al-Wahhāb. She also included the poetry of Bayram al-Tunsi in her songs. Umm Kalthoum's path took her into the upper crust in Egyptian society, and she became a close associate of King Farouk beginning in the 1920s. She was romantically involved with his uncle, Sharif Sabri Pasha, and they were engaged to be married; however, because they could not gain the approval of the royal family, the marriage was called off. Umm Kalthoum then hastily married an oud player, Mahmud Sharif, who was president of the Musicians Union, but the marriage was a short-lived failure.

Her first recording was in 1924 for Odeon. She also signed with Sono Cairo and Gramophone Records. By this time, she was earning quite a large salary of $10,000 annually and $500 for each recording. During her lifetime, she made almost 300 recordings. Umm Kalthoum was frequently heard on radio broadcasts and by 1928 she had achieved both fame and notoriety in Egypt. She also added orchestral accompaniment to her performances. Her "signature" song, "Al-Atlal," was composed by Riyad al-Sunbati. This song was heard in almost all of her concerts. She also performed in Lebanon, Libya, Paris, and Syria. Her first radio performance was in 1934 on Egyptian National Radio; these live radio broadcasts of her concerts included interviews and became quite popular. Millions tuned in to hear her on the first Thursday evening of every month. By the 1930s, she had developed fine virtuosic and artistic style, and modern romantic songs dominated her performances. She also enlarged her accompanying ensemble to the size of a small orchestra.

During the 1930s, Umm Kalthoum ventured into cinema and television. Her first film, *Widad 1936*, was of the typical Hollywood romantic type: A young female slave sings for her owner and falls in love with him. Losing all of his wealth, he has to sell her, and now the songs she sings to her new master are very sad. Among her other noted films are *Nashid al-amal* (1937), *Dananir* (1940), *Ayda* (1942), *Salamah* (1945), and *Fatma* (1947). Between 1940 and 1969, the noted director of Egyptian cinema, Ahmad Badrakhan (1909–1969), produced numerous melodramatic films starring Umm Kalthoum and Farid al-Atrash.

Appearing throughout the Arab world and in Europe during the 1940s, Umm Kalthoum had attracted quite a large following and achieved international stardom and prominence. But many medical and personal problems crept into her life beginning in the late 1930s, and became especially troublesome during the 1940s and 1950s. During the 1940s she was plagued by respiratory and thyroid problems, and eye inflammation. The latter was linked in later years to the stage lights and contributed to her having to wear dark glasses during performances. Depression also took hold of her and intensified with the death of her mother in 1947, the death of her brother shortly thereafter, and a romantic breakup. These episodes caused her much grief and eventually limited her performances. By 1949 a severe episode of depression led to her hospitalization at Maryland's Bethesda Naval Hospital.

In 1954, she married Dr. Hasan al-Hafnawi, a dermatologist. This was also the year in which the Voice of America began to broadcast her performances, which allowed her to reach an even larger audience. After the overthrow of King Farouk in 1952 by the coup led by Gamal Abdel Nasser, Umm Kalthoum became a close acquaintance of this new Egyptian president. She became more involved in politics and held a position in Nasser's regime. She even sang numerous songs on his behalf. This included the song "Wallāhi Zamān, Yā Silāḥī (By God, it's time, O my weapon)," which became so popular that it was selected as the national anthem of Egypt (1960–1979).

She sang the works of numerous Arab composers, including Muḥammad 'Abd al-Wahhāb and Mohammad al-Qasabji; the latter frequently accompanied her on the oud throughout her career and may have been romantically involved with her. Muḥammad 'Abd al-Wahhāb was a very popular Egyptian composer. Current political and social themes, including the liberation of Palestine and the unification of the Arab world, were often the focus al-Wahhāb's songs. His works called for full orchestral accompaniment.

Speaking out on various issues, by the 1960s Kalthoum's generosity to the Arab world intensified. For example, she began donating the profits from her performances to the Egyptian government and Arab issues. She also donated money to the poor in Egypt and channeled her political and revolutionary philosophy through the words of the songs that she sang. For example, Massad notes that in a 1969 song, "*Asbaha al-Ana 'indi Bunduqiyyah* (I now have a rifle)" (by al-Wahhāb, a setting of poetry by the Syrian Nizar Qabbani), Umm Kalthoum made known her dedication to the liberation of Palestine, indicating that she was willing to unite and fight with the revolutionaries.

During the early 1970s, Umm Kalthoum's health deteriorated and she suffered from kidney disease, but she continued her concerts on the first Thursday evening of each month. For her last performance, in 1973, she earned as much as $50,000. She died from a cerebral hemorrhage on February 3, 1975, in Zamalik, Egypt. So beloved was Umm Kalthoum that thousands of grief-stricken fans joined her funeral procession in Cairo's Tahrir Square on February 5, 1975. From the president of Egypt to heads of state, ambassadors, actors, singers, and ordinary citizens mourned her passing. She had one of the largest funerals in the history of Egypt and was mourned worldwide by millions.

Highly decorated, Umm Kalthoum received numerous awards from the government of Egypt, including knighthood and the al-Kamal medal from King Farouk in 1944. She had mass appeal and was truly the "Star of the East." Her vocal range was over two octaves and her voice was rich, dark, and strong. Her style of performance was usually in the classical and popular Muslim and Arabic style. It was characterized by deeply emotional singing mainly on topics of love, though she also sang religious, patriotic, and political songs. She could spend the entire evening repeating and improvising on a few lines or a stanza of one to three songs. The powerful emotions and rich tone of her voice captivated and moved her audiences to tears. One line of poetry could have so many subtle shadings and improvisations that she mesmerized her audiences with that one alone. Nevertheless, her repertoire was huge.

Even after her death, the voice and charisma of this legendary star continued. Thousands of her recordings are still sold and several documentary films were made in her honor. Numerous exhibitions were held around the world and she was also the subject of visual artists, including Huda Lutfi (1948–) who created a collage titled *The Goddess* (1994). French choreographer Maurice Béjart created a ballet titled *Pyramide* that was performed in Cairo on May 25, 1990, by Béjart Ballet Lausanne. The Oum Kalthoum Tower was built on the lot where her home had stood and the Kawkab al-Sharq Museum (Star of the Orient Museum) opened in Cairo on December 28, 2001, in her honor. In 2006, Sélim Nassib wrote the novel, *I Loved You for Your Voice*. Even the village where she was born and spent her childhood changed its name to "the village of Umm Kalthoum," and a monument was erected in her name in Cairo. This Egyptian superstar played an important role not only for Egyptians and the Arabic world, but in the lives of millions around the world.

Barbara Bonous-Smit

See also: Ahmad, Fadzil; Arab Classical Music; Fairuz

Further Reading

Al-Youm, Al-Masry. 2014. "This Day in History: Omm Kalthoum Passed Away." *Egypt Independent*, February 3. https://egyptindependent.com/day-history-omm-kalthoum-passed-away.

Ben Mahmoud, Feriel, and Nicolas Daniel, dirs. 2009. *Oum Kalthoum: l'astre de l'Orient* [DVD]. Performed by Oum Kalthoum. Sony Pictures Home Entertainment.

Danielson, Virginia. 1991. "Shaping Tradition in Arabic Song: The Career and Repertory of Umm Kulthum." PhD diss., University of Illinois.

Danielson, Virginia. 1996. "Listening to Umm Kulthūm." *Middle East Studies Association Bulletin* 30(2) (December), 170–173. http://www.jstor.org/stable/23061883.

Danielson, Virginia. 1997. *The Voice of Egypt: Umm Kulthum, Arabic Song, and Egyptian Society in the Twentieth Century*. Chicago: University of Chicago Press.

Danielson, Virginia. n.d. "Umm Kulthum: An Outline of Her Life." Umm Kulthum: The Star of the East, the Diva of Arabic Song. http://almashriq.hiof.no/egypt/700/780/umKoulthoum/biography.html.

Danielson, Virginia. n.d. "Umm Kulthum: The Singer and Her Music." Umm Kulthum: The Star of the East, the Diva of Arabic Song. http://almashriq.hiof.no/egypt/700/780/umKoulthoum/music.html.

De Groot, Rokus. 2005. "Perspectives of Polyphony in Edward Said's Writings." *Alif: Journal of Comparative Poetics* 25, 219–240. http://www.jstor.org/stable/4047458.

"Egyptians Throng Funeral of Um Kalthoum, the Arabs' Acclaimed Singer." 1975. *New York Times*, February 6. https://www.nytimes.com/1975/02/06/archives/egyptians-throng-funeral-of-um-kalthoum-the-arabs-acclaimed-singer.html.

Goldman, Michael, and Virginia Danielson. 1996/2006. *Umm Kulthum, a Voice Like Egypt* [DVD]. Directed and produced by Michael Goldman. Arab Film Distribution.

Marcus, Scott Lloyd. 2007. "Art Music of the Mid-Twentieth Century: Umm Kulthum and the Long-Song Tradition." In *Music in Egypt: Experiencing Music, Expressing Culture*, 117–138. New York: Oxford University Press, 2007.

Massad, Joseph. 2003. "Liberating Songs: Palestine Put to Music." *Journal of Palestine Studies* 32(3) (Spring), 21–38. doi:10.1525/jps.2003.32.3.21.

Nassib, Sélim. 2006. *I Loved You for Your Voice*, trans. Alison Anderson. New York: Europa Editions.

Salloum, Habeeb. 1995. "Umm Kalthum—Legendary Songstress of the Arabs." Umm Kulthum: The Star of the East, the Diva of Arabic Song. http://almashriq.hiof.no/egypt/700/780/umKoulthoum/aljadid-uk.html.

"Um Kalthoum, Egyptian Singer, a Favorite of Millions, Is Dead." 1975. *New York Times*, February 4. https://www.nytimes.com/1975/02/04/archives/um-kalthoum-egyptian-singer-a-favorite-of-millions-is-dead.html.

Kamancheh

Translating from the Persian as "little bow," the *kamancheh* is a bowed, four-stringed, spike fiddle native to Iranian art and folk music. It is also used in Armenia, Azerbaijan, Georgia, Uzbekistan, and Turkmenistan, with some slight variations in design and structure. The first documented description of the kamancheh dates to the 10th century. It is considered a descendant of the *rebab*, an Arab spike fiddle dating back to the eighth century, and a relative of the *lira*, an ancestor of the European violin. The kamancheh is also closely related to the *chagane*, a four-stringed instrument of similar construction, that was in common use in Azerbaijan and Iran until the late 19th century. The kamancheh has a rich cultural history, as it has been frequently referenced in Persian poetry by poets such as Masoud-e Sa'd (1046–1121), and is often depicted in Persian miniatures from the 13th to 16th centuries as being played by angels. The classical version of the instrument dates from the 15th century or earlier. It was often an important element of *motrebi*, or light music, and is the only bowed instrument used in Iranian classical music.

Generally, the kamancheh is spherical, but can be cone-shaped and open at the back. The bowl-shaped resonating chamber is traditionally carved out of walnut wood or a spherical gourd, and often displays intricate inlays and ornately carved mother-of-pearl, ivory, brass, wood, and/or bone decorations, in the tradition known as *khatam-kari*. The bridge and the sound table are constructed of animal membrane or fish skin. The kamancheh's body is connected to a long, rounded, or conical neck fixed to a metal spike (65–90 cm long) which supports the instrument when played (hence the English name, "spiked fiddle").

Over the course of the kamancheh's history, it has been documented to have had anywhere from two to six strings. Very early kamanchehs had two strings, and gradually moved to three strings by the Qajar period (1785–1925). In the early 20th century, after the introduction of the Western violin to Iran, the kamancheh's popularity diminished. Some well-known kamancheh players, such as Reza Mahjubi and Ebrahim Mansouri, turned to the violin during this time and became violin instructors. Also during this time, a fourth string was added to the kamancheh, in order to compete with the violin.

Originally, the kamancheh's strings were made of silk or gut. The modern kamancheh has strings made of gut, steel, or synthetic materials combined with metal, attached to four wooden pegs. In some cases, violin or viola strings are used as well. The kamancheh's strings were originally tuned in fourths, but are now tuned in fourths and fifths: a-e′-a′-e″. This tuning was standardized by Armenian virtuoso Sasha Oganezashvili (1889–1932) in the early 20th century. It is common practice for strings to be replaced when the desired timbre or tone is lost from overuse.

In performance, the kamancheh player usually sits on the floor, holding the instrument by the neck as the metal spike grounds the kamancheh. Alternatively, the instrument can be rested upright with the endpin on the knee, as the player is seated on a chair. In either case, the kamancheh is turned to meet the bow, rather than the bow gliding across the strings as in the case of the violin. As the bow meets the strings, the bow hair is manually tightened with the fingers to vary the sound. Overall, the kamancheh has a soft, warm, melodic timbre, often compared to the timbre of the human voice, which makes it conducive to solo, virtuoso playing as well as small ensemble performance.

In the late 1920s, the kamancheh family of instruments (soprano, alto, bass, and double bass), was created by Armenian master musician Vardan Buni. There are also variations of the kamancheh that exist in neighboring countries and regions. For example, in Iraq, the four-string spike fiddle called *joza* is a kind of kamancheh made from a hollowed-out coconut, with one end covered by a membrane and the other open. Like the kamancheh, it has a long, wooden neck with four pegs and a metal spike. The joza's steel strings are tuned in perfect fourths, and often its pitch is chosen based on the voice it accompanies. In performance, the instrument sits at an angle on the knee, and the neck is held in left hand and swiveled back and forth while playing, as with the Iranian kamancheh. The joza is primarily used as an accompanying instrument in ensembles.

In Armenia and Turkey, the *kemence* is a close relative of the kamancheh, and is often used in folk music. It is a short-necked fiddle with rounded ends, a wooden sound table, and a pear-shaped pegbox. Instead of the kamancheh's four strings, the kemence has only three, tuned in fourths, and made of gut or metal. The kemence is played with a short horsehair bow, with the player either sitting or standing, and can be used as a solo or accompanying instrument.

Since the 1979 Iranian Revolution and the consequent restrictions on Western and popular music, there has been a resurgence in Iranian classical music which has in turn, encouraged the use of traditional instruments, including the kamancheh. Today, the violin is still sometimes used in the performance of modern Iranian classical music in lieu of the kamancheh, because of its equivalent range and tuning. However, the two instruments differ in timbres; thus, for more traditional performance, the kamancheh is preferred by many Iranian musicians.

Pioneers of kamancheh playing include the pre-Qajar-era musicians Mirza Mohammad Kamancheh'I and Malek Mahmoud, as well as 19th-century Qajar musicians Esmail Khan and Bagher Rameshgar. Famous contemporary musicians include Ali-Asghar Bahari (1905–1995), Kayhan Kalhor (1963–), Ardeshir

Kamkar (1962–), and Saeed Farajpouri (1961–). Renowned kamancheh makers include Ebrahim Ghanbari Mehr (1928–) and Bayaz Amirataii (1955–).

Theresa Steward

See also: Dastgah; Iranian Classical Music; Rebab; Sufism, Music of

Further Reading

Farhat, Hormoz. 1973. *The Traditional Art Music of Iran.* Tehran: Ministry of Culture and Arts Press.

Farhat, Hormoz. 1991. "Western Musical Influences in Persia." *Musicological Annual* 27, 76–96.

Zonis, Ella. 1973. *Classical Persian Music: An Introduction.* Cambridge, MA: Harvard University Press.

Karnatic Music

Karnatic music is a style of classical music most closely associated with the southern peninsula of India. Its practice is largely confined to the modern Indian states of Karnataka, Andhra Pradesh, Kerala, and Tamil Nadu and their diasporic communities abroad. It stands in contrast to the North Indian tradition of classical music, often called Hindustani, which developed along a distinct trajectory due to Islamic and Persian influences that failed to obtain such a strong foothold in the southern kingdoms during India's medieval period.

Karnatic music is most commonly performed by small ensembles consisting of a vocalist or lead instrumentalist, an accompanying violinist, a percussionist (almost always a *mridangam* player), and a tambura player who provides śruti, or drone accompaniment. Instruments other than the voice that might lead an ensemble include the bamboo flute, sometimes called the *venu*; a large, seven-stringed lute with two resonating chambers, called a *veena*; and the violin. More recently, Western instruments such as the alto saxophone and the mandolin have also become popular. Additional percussion accompaniment might be provided by the *ghatam*, a clay pot drum; *kanjira*, a small frame drum; *morsing*, or mouth-harp; or even a system of verbal rhythmic accompaniment, called *konnakol*. Improvisation is built

---

Indian Drum Heads (India)

Iconic black dots marking the right-face drum head of the South Indian *mridangam* (called the *valanthalai*) and the smaller *daya* drum of the North Indian tabla drum set are key to the unique sound of the instruments. Both instrument's drum heads are created in a similar fashion, using a black paste called *soru* or *saatham*. The soru is made of a powder consisting of iron oxide, manganese oxide, and rice paste and applied in thin layers. The buildup of these layers forms the domed convex surface of the soru and allows the player to isolate certain musical harmonics via intricate finger strokes. The process of applying the soru (which can involve the application of more than 100 layers of paste) and making the drums themselves is closely guarded proprietary information among Indian drum makers and is often passed only between master and apprentice builder.

into the very nature of Karnatic music, but performance centers around compositions into which opportunities for various kinds of improvisation are built. Song texts are frequently written in Telugu, though Tamil, Kannada, and Sanskrit lyrics are also common. Texts in Malayalam can also be found.

Though the Karnatic tradition remains separate from the Hindustani, both share four common elements: *śruti*, *swara*, *rāga*, and *tāla*. These four concepts are intimately connected to the identity of Indian classical music styles, and starkly contrast with the familiar system of Western harmony, but it can be useful to compare them respectively to the fundamental or tonic, individual notes, scale or mode, and rhythm.

FUNDAMENTAL ELEMENTS OF KARNATIC MUSIC

All Karnatic music is based around the concept of śruti, the fundamental sound from which all other notes are derived. In many ways, śruti can be thought of like the tonic of a Western scale, except that in Karnatic music all notes of a given performance will be derived from it. A lead performer sets the śruti prior to a performance to suit his or her voice or instrument, and once set it will be established within the concert venue by the unceasing *tambura*, an unfretted, long-necked, four-string lute sounding only four pitches: the "tonic," or fundamental tone for that performance, which is called *shadja*; its fifth interval (the dominant), called *panchama*; and the octave, to which two of the tambura's four strings are tuned.

Swaras, or musical pitches, arise in a fundamental relationship to śruti. According to long-standing tradition, South Indian theorists have defined 22 distinct pitches discernible by the human ear, but there are seven fundamental swaras upon which south India's modal system is built. They are *shadja* (sa), *rishabha* (ri), *gandhara* (ga), *madhyama* (ma), *panchama* (pa), *dhaivata* (dha), and *nishada* (ni), which can be superficially compared to Western solfeggio (do re mi fa sol la ti). As the basis for śruti, shadja and panchama remain fixed throughout a performance. The other swaras are defined in variable relationship to these rather than through the kind of pure, mathematical calculation that defines the Western tempered scale.

Excepting sa and pa, every note has higher and lower variants. Ma, the subdominant, can sound an interval of a fourth or an augmented fourth in relationship to sa. The other notes—ri, ga, dha, and ni—all have three variants: low (1), middle (2), and high (3). In any given scale, or rāga, typically only one variant of each swara is used. Common exceptions are the so-called "light" ragas, in which the ascending scale (*arohana*) and descending scale (*avarohana*) may differ, much like the Western melodic minor scale.

Rāgas arise from swaras, though a rāga is defined by more than just the swaras that comprise it. They are more than just scales, but less than full melodies. Equally important to the identity of a rāga are its characteristic phrases and motifs, which notes can be sung with ornamentation (*gamaka*) and which must be sung without, and even the kinds of phrasing that must be limited or avoided altogether.

Rāgas in the Karnatic tradition are classified according to the *Mēlakarta* scheme. The mēlakarta was devised in the 17th century by the theorist Venkatamakhi as a means to systematically categorize rāgas according to their swaras. There are 72 mēlakarta rāgas, divided into two groups of 36 based on whether the relationship between the shadja and madhyama swaras is a perfect (*shudda*, or low) or augmented (*prati*, or raised) fourth. Each group of 36 is further divided into 6 *chakras* of 6 rāgas. Within a given chakra, the swaras sa, ri, ga, and pa are all fixed; only dha and ni can be changed. Mēlakarta rāgas are all *sampūrna* rāgas, or seven-note rāgas. They are also called *janaka*, or parent, rāgas, as all other rāgas can be derived from the rāgas classified within the mēlakarta. It must be noted that rāgas so "derived" might actually pre-date Venkatamakhi's systematization and were later classified to fit within the mēlakarta system. There are songs in Bhairavi rāga, for example, that were written 10 centuries before Venkatamakhi devised the mēlakarta scheme, yet they can be classified as *janya* rāga of the 20th janaka rāga, *Natabhairavi*.

A rāga defines the relationship between individual swaras rather than all pitches themselves being fixed first (e.g., in the tempered scale, the tuning pitch 'A' has a fixed frequency of 440 Hz). In other words, the swaras of a rāga derive from their relationship to śruti (the drone of shadja and panchama), which is set to best suit the voice or instrument of the lead performer. Rāgas can be notated using an alphanumeric system that identifies the swara by its first letter—S R G M P D N—and its degree (low, middle, high) by the numerals 1, 2, 3. Shadja has a single degree, S. Madhyama, the subdominant, has two: a perfect fourth, M1, and an augmented fourth, M2. The octave of any note is indicated with a superscript (for example, S' is one octave above S).

For the student of Western music, it can be instructive to compare mélakarta rāgas to corresponding Western scales. *Dheerasankarabaranam*, the 29th mélakarta rāga, corresponds in rough terms to the major scale: S R2 G3 M1 P D2 N3 S'. Natabhairavi, the 20th, sounds like the natural minor scale in which the third, sixth, and seventh intervals are lowered: S R2 G2 M1 P D1 N2 S'. Rāga Mechakalyani, the 65th mélakarta rāga, can be compared to an augmented scale: S R2 G3 M2 P D2 N3 S'.

In practice, the mélakarta is more descriptive than prescriptive. While compositions exist using all of the *sampurna* rāgas, some—particularly those mela containing close sequences of semitone intervals followed by wide leaps—are often considered less pleasing and thus are infrequently used. Some composers have written what are essentially rāga medleys in which all 72 rāgas are combined in sequence. The composition or performance of a pleasing *mélakarta rāga malika* ("garland of melakarta ragas") is considered by some to represent a genuine test of one's musical skill.

Rhythm in Karnatic music is defined by the *tāla*. A tāla consists of several parts, called *anga*, to which are assigned a fixed number of beats depending on anga and its *jati*. A singer will often keep tala through a system of hand gestures that mark the position within a given rhythmic cycle. The three main gestures are the clap, called a *thattu*; a wave, in which the clapping hand is turned palm up, called a *vechu*; and a finger count. These gestures are combined to form the three primary anga: the *laghu,* the *dhrutham,* and the *anudhrutham*. Each of these, in turn, has a symbol with which it can be notated.

The laghu is shown by a thattu (clap) followed by a finger count, beginning with the fourth (pinkie) finger and counting inward. The number of counts is determined by the jati, of which there are five—*tisra, chatusra, khanda, misra,* and *sankirna*—indicating three, four, five, seven, and nine beats respectively. The laghu is indicated by a vertical line, |. The jati is indicated by a numeral. Thus, |4 indicates a laghu of four beats.

The dhrutham is shown using a thattu followed by a vechu, a clap and a wave, and always indicates two beats. The dhrutham is notated using a circle, O. The anudhrutham is shown by a thattu and always indicates a single beat. Anudhrutham is notated with the symbol U. The *sapta tālas*, or seven basic tāla cycles, are all made using the laghu, dhrutham, and anudhrutham in combination.

Although the tāla cycle of a composition is fixed, the total number of beats (*aksharas*) for a single cycle of any of these tāla will depend upon its jati. Thirty-five talas of differing lengths can be defined in this way (seven tāla cycles multiplied by five jati). The aksharas of a given tāla are further defined by their *nadai*: the number of *mātras*, or subdivisions, within one akshara. The mātras are given the same names as the jatis. Unless otherwise specified, the nadai is chatusra, effectively a 16th-note subdivision, though tisra jati—a triplet subdivision—is also common. Skilled musicians can change nadai during the improvisational sections of a composition (discussed later) to highlight their creativity and command of tāla.

The tāla most commonly performed is undoubtedly *chatusra jati triputa tāla*, commonly called "Adi" tāla, an eight-beat cycle notated |4 O O. Perhaps the second most commonly performed tāla, *chatusra jati rupaka tala*, usually simply called "Rupaka tāla," is a six-beat cycle notated O |4. Because of its ubiquity, the gesture for rupaka tāla is often shown simply as two thattu followed by a vechu (clap clap wave).

A number of other talas are made possible using additional anga such as the *guru* (8), *plutam* (|8), and *kākāpādam* (+), representing eight, 12, and 16 beats respectively, but these are no longer commonly used. Tradition holds that there are 108 classical tālas that can be represented using the these six angas and five jatis in various combinations, though in reality there are a few more.

Two other common tālas are the "mixed" tālas *khanda* and *misra chapu*, which are five- and seven-beat tālas that do not quite fit into the sapta tāla scheme. Khanda chapu is accented on the first, third, and fourth beats; misra chapu is accented on the first, fourth, and sixth beats.

KARNATIC MUSIC IN PRACTICE

Karnatic music was traditionally learned orally within the *gurukula* system. A young student would go to live with his or her *guru*, or teacher, and when not receiving instruction would often perform chores and other tasks for the guru. Instruction often followed a call-and-response model, where the guru would sing or play a phrase which the student would then repeat until it was correctly learned. After learning basic melodic exercises and *alankaras* (rhythmic exercises based on the sapta tālas), a student would be taught simple compositions called *gītam* written to highlight the qualities of a specific rāga. *Swarajati* would then be introduced. These songs are typically be lighter fare with strong, pleasing melodies and catchy rhythms written on themes of devotion (*bhakti*), love, or courage but with more complex song forms. Both forms are sometimes performed early in a concert as light, unchallenging songs meant to warm up both the performers and the audience or at the end to bring a concert to a close. Other common short compositional forms include the *javali*, *padam*, and *thillana*. More strictly devotional forms also continue to be popular. Two of the most popular are *tevaram*, hymns in praise of Siva written between the seventh and ninth centuries CE, and *divya prabandha*, hymns composed by the Alvar saints in praise of Vishnu during the middle of the first millennium CE, though probably slightly earlier than the tevaram.

Unquestionably, the two most significant forms in Karnatic music are the *varnam* and the *kriti*. Both kriti and varnam usually consist of a *pallavi*, *anupallavi*, and *charanam*. The pallavi is a poetic couplet that acts as the thematic refrain, or what might be considered the identifying melody. It is often repeated multiple times with increasingly complex ornamental variations. The first line of Muthuswamy Dikshitar's kriti "*Vatapi Ganapathim*," for example, has eight composed variations of its first line. The anupallavi is a second couplet that acts as a contrast or thematic response to the pallavi. It also may have several composed variations, but never so many as the pallavi. The charanam (literally, the "foot") is a longer, sometimes much longer, stanza of poetic text that is sung through without variations. There may be multiple charanams, in which case they can be understood as the first verse, second verse, and so on.

Varnams are composed to highlight everything characteristic about a particular rāga: its scale and shape (some rāgas do not ascend or descend directly, like a Western scale, but weave slowly up or down), which swaras are stressed and which are avoided, how certain notes are to be approached and ornamented, common and special phrases, and so on. They are often used as the first piece in a concert.

Varnam structure can be rather complex, but because they are define the essence of a rāga and are played at multiple speeds they are ideal both as practice pieces and to build excitement in a listening audience. A varnam usually consists of the following sections: *pallavi*, *anupallavi*, *muktāyi swaras*, *charanam*, and *chittai swaras*. During performance the pallavi, anupallavi, and muktāyi swaras will be followed by the pallavi being repeated at double speed. Often this entire sequence is then repeated a second time with the final pallavi being repeated at triple speed. The charanam(s) can then be sung with a chittai swara being sung between each new stanza or refrain. Both the muktāyi and chittai swara sections are written without lyrics as such; rather, they are sung using the swara syllables sa ri ga ma pa dha ni, like singing in solfeggio syllables. Because they consist of many different sections sung at multiple tempos, and because they include multiple sections of through-composed swaras, varnams are used by musicians to develop their improvisational skills, or *manodharma*, particularly *swarakalpanas* and *niraval*.

For all of the varnam's importance, it is the kriti that has come to dominate performances, especially vocal concerts. Like the varnam, kriti usually consist of pallavi, anupallavi, and charanam. Unlike the varnam, in a kriti the performer is given considerable space for improvisation. A musician will often perform several kriti during a concert, and though kritis can be performed "straight"—that is, without including improvisation—a kriti with long improvisational sections is often the central piece in concert. In such cases, the kriti is usually introduced with an unmensurated improvisation called an *alapana*. The alapana is played or sung without the benefit of rhythmic accompaniment, but only the constant drone of the tambura or śruti box. It can be rather short, lasting only a minute or two, or quite long. When singing alapana, a singer will not vocalize swara syllables but instead use open, nonsense syllables.

To perform alapana, the musician slowly outlines the rāga, usually beginning on shadja (the "tonic"), gradually expanding the scope of the rāga through the introduction of additional swaras and key phrases. If the lead performer is accompanied by a violinist, each musician takes turns exploring larger and larger sections of the rāga. After the range of expression within the rāga has been explored, the performer comes to rest on shadja before commencing the pallavi.

As already noted, the pallavi consists of a couplet sung to multiple variations. After the pallavi and anupallavi, a performer may choose to perform a second type of improvisation called *chittaswara*, a rhythmic improvisation sung using only the swaras: sa ri ga ma pa dha ni. Instrumental performers can also perform improvisation after the anupallavi in the form of chittaswaras, though obviously the swaras themselves would not be vocalized. The charanam follows, often borrowing melodic material from the anupallavi. The last line of the charanam usually includes a *mudra*, or a reference to the composer himself, that acts as a kind of signature to the piece. The charanam is also used to stage one of the most complex forms of manodharma in Karnatic music, called *niraval*, in which a single line of text from the charanam serves as the springboard for increasingly ornate improvisation. Soloists will trade increasingly complex lines of swaras that, when performed correctly, will lead directly back into the line of text chosen to ornament with niraval. When there are multiple performers, lines or improvisation will be traded back and forth in a kind of sparring match. At its height, the performers trade shorter and shorter lines, increasing the intensity and excitement until both are again playing the composed text in unison.

Purandara Dasa (ca. 1480–1564) is considered by most to be the father of modern Karnatic music. It was he who composed the alankaras and many of the gitam learned by students. He is also credited with introducing the rāga "*Mayamalavagowla*" as a simple rāga for beginners. Three of the most revered composers in the Karnatic tradition are the so-called Trinity: Tyagaraja (ca. 1759–1847), Syama Sastri (1762–1827), and Muthuswamy Dikshitar (1776–1827).

Aaron Mulvany

See also: Mridangam

Further Reading
Sambamoorthy, P. 1973. *South Indian Music.* Madras: Indian Music Publishing House.
Viswanathan, T., and Matthew Harp Allen. 2003. *Music in South India: Experiencing Music, Expressing Culture.* New York: Oxford University Press.
Weidman, Amanda. 2006. *Singing the Classical, Voicing the Modern: The Postcolonial Politics of Music in South India.* Durham, NC: Duke University Press.

Kayokyoku

Kayokyoku is an umbrella term for Japanese popular music genres. Although the term originally meant "Western art songs" in the Meiji era, it started to refer to *ryukoka* (popular or fashionable songs) in the early Showa era (the late 1920s) when the public radio station NHK adopted the term. The production of kayokyoku involves a singer, lyricist, composer, arranger, and musicians. Kayokyoku developed in close relation to the recording industry. Established in the late 1920s, foreign-invested record companies played a major role in distributing kayokyoku. Although kayokyoku is largely based on Western popular music, it also incorporated elements from Japanese traditional folk music genres such as *kouta* (simple song often sung by geisha), *min'yo* (folk song), and *dodoitsu* (a form of poetry). Kayokyoku first flourished in the late 1930s before World War II (1939–1945), and incorporated elements of jazz and blues from the United States. Most notably, Awaya Noriko and her blues-influenced songs became popular. During the war, however, American music was banned and the music industry went dormant.

After a few years of recovery from the war, kayokyoku developed quickly, producing many hit songs toward the end of the 1940s under the U.S. occupation from 1945 to 1952. The record companies, from their early years, adopted the exclusive contract system, in which each company hired a team of singer, lyricist, arranger, and orchestra to produce recordings. A number of female singers emerged during this period, such as Namiki Michiko, whose "*Ringo no Uta*" (Song of the apple) (1946), became the first hit song after the war. These women often sang a wide variety of songs influenced by foreign genres such as blues, boogie-woogie, tango, rhumba, waltz, bolero, and Hawaiian music. Though these songs often included a genre name in their titles, they did not truthfully imitate these styles, but rather incorporated nuances of foreign styles. Some singers covered foreign songs, such as "Besame Mucho" and "Begin the Beguine," with Japanese lyrics. Because of restrictions during the war years, both musicians and audiences were hungry for foreign-influenced songs. Radio and movies were crucial in distributing and popularizing these songs.

This trend of "exotic" kayokyoku continued for several years after the end of the occupation. Jazz, which was extremely popular in the early 1950s, inspired jazz-influenced kayokyoku and jazz cover songs. Most first-class jazz musicians belonged to both a jazz band and a record-company-owned orchestra at the same time. Hawaiian music and Western (country and western) were also popular in the 1950s. These two genres introduced falsetto singing and a small ensemble including steel guitar and ukulele as an accompaniment to kayokyoku. Though it had only a short period of fame, chanson became popular and some kayokyoku songs incorporated it. In addition to these foreign-influenced songs, kayokyoku singers also sang songs whose themes were both hometown and Tokyo, reflecting the migration from rural areas to Tokyo during the late 1950s. Another trend around this time was rokabilii (rockabilly), which also influenced kayokyoku singers who both covered American rockabilly songs and sang originals.

Rockabilly-influenced songs, both cover versions and originals, continued to be popular into the 1960s. While a few production companies managed singers and were also involved with producing records, the record companies were in control of the scene, from manufacturing to distributing. These companies often produced radio and television programs that promoted their artists. *Enka* was a large part of the kayokyoku scene from the late 1950s to the 1960s. During this time, kayokyoku in general was gradually transforming itself into *wasei poppusu* (Japanese-made pop/pop-oriented kayokyoku), and the *GS bumu* (GS boom) played a crucial role in this process. GS is an abbreviation for group sounds, and this GS craze was greatly influenced by the Beatles. Numerous bands imitating the Beatles emerged in the late 1960s, including the Blue Jeans, the Tigers, and the Spiders. They sang their original versions of Beatles-type songs, which in turn influenced kayokyoku. Pop-oriented kayokyoku and enka were two major subgenres of kayokyoku.

A new trend, *nyu-myujikku* (new music) appeared and fully developed during the 1970s, which is considered to be the peak period of kayokyoku. Performed by singer-songwriters, nyu-myujikku was largely inspired by American and British rock and folk music, which in turn influenced kayokyoku. Freelance songwriters, including nyu-myujikku artists, became prominent as the record companies' exclusive contract system declined, which resulted in more diversity in kayokyoku. Record companies, now teamed up with production companies, were expanding their markets at full force. Another subgenre of kayokyoku, *aidoru* (idol) *kayo*—pop-oriented kayokyoku sung by young, good-looking girls and boys—emerged in the early 1970s. These idols mainly appealed to youths of the opposite sex. The mainstream kayokyoku that belonged to neither aidoru kayo nor enka were also pop-oriented. There were numerous hit songs in these three subgenres during the 1970s.

As kayokyoku was becoming more and more diverse during the 1980s, one of the trends that started in the late 1970s and continued into the 1980s was the incorporation of English words into the Japanese lyrics. These English words sounded fresh and innovative to the listeners of the time. This drastically changed the way people listened to kayokyoku: the sound created by the combination of words and more beat-oriented music was as important as what the lyrics meant. Aidoru kayo by both female and male singers was still very popular. One of these teen idols, Matsuda Seiko (1962–), was exceptionally successful in the early 1980s. Her success was partly due to her popularity among young girls who desired to look like her. Subsequently, an all-girl group named *Onyanko Kurabu* (Club) came out of a TV variety show in 1985. Consisting of 11 teenage girls, the group sang upbeat songs with choreography, which became a model for numerous girl groups in the later years. Rock- and Euro-beat-influenced kayokyoku appeared in the mid 1980s. Enka, inspired by a variety of genres in the 1980s, also became diverse and is still popular.

Pop-influenced kayokyoku and nyu-myujikku were gradually replaced by the term "J-pop" during the 1990s. As a result, the term "kayokyoku" has been rarely used in recent years. Therefore, it can be said that kayokyoku is closely associated with the Showa era (1926–1989).

Yoko Suzuki

See also: Enka Music; J-Pop; Min'yô

Further Reading

Aoyagi, Hiroshi. 2005. *Island of Eight Million Smiles: Idol Performance and Symbolic Production in Contemporary Japan.* Cambridge, MA: Harvard University Press.

Kelts, Roland. 2006. *Japanamerica: How Japanese Pop Culture Has Invaded the U.S.* New York: St. Marten's/Griffith.

Kitanaka, Masakazu. 1995. *Nihon no uta: Sengo kayokyoku-shi* [Japanese songs: Postwar popular tunes]. Tokyo: Shincho-sha.

Ko, Mamoru. 2011. *Kayokyoku: Jidai o irodotta uta tachi* [Kayokyoku: Songs that highlighted the time]. Tokyo: Iwanami Shoten.

Stanlaw, James. 2000. "Open Your File, Open Your Mind: Women, English, and the Changing Roles and Voices of Japanese Pop Music." In Timothy J. Craig (ed.), *Japan Pop! Inside the World of Japanese Popular Culture*, 75–100. New York: Taylor & Francis.

Stevens, Carolyn. 2007. *Japanese Popular Music: Culture, Authenticity and Power.* New York: Routledge.

Kebyar

Kebyar, or *gamelan gong kebyar*, is a type of large *gamelan* orchestra from Bali, Indonesia, primarily comprised of metallophones, gongs, drums, and cymbals. The word "kebyar" may refer to the ensemble itself, the repertoire of the ensemble, or a virtuosic passage played by the ensemble as a whole. The majority of modern Balinese gamelan compositions are for kebyar; the genre, its dances, and the associated *kreasi baru* (new creation) are an iconic representation of 20th-century Balinese musical development.

In Bali, there are approximately 40 extant types of gamelan, all of which have different histories, instrumentation, playing styles, and cultural contexts. Gamelan gong kebyar is a relatively recent innovation; the genre emerged in 1915, the period just following the completion of the Dutch colonization of Bali. Prior to colonization, Balinese gamelan were largely associated with the royal courts; following the sharp decline of the courts during the colonial period, the gamelans were transferred to the villages, and older, courtly ensembles and playing styles declined. A new genre and compositional style emerged: kebyar. Kebyar, derived from the word *byar* (flare), had its musical and compositional origins in courtly gamelan styles, particularly *gamelan gong gede*. However, changes in instrumentation, playing style, dynamics, and musical function marked it as a distinctive genre, one that marked the tension and excitement of the era and the new focus on villages and villagers as the center of society.

Kebyar ensembles require between 25 and 30 musicians to achieve full instrumentation. The majority of the instruments in the ensemble are bronze-keyed metallophones—instruments with metal keys hanging above bamboo resonating tubes which are encased in wooden cases—or gongs, both ones that hang and others that are horizontally mounted. Of the keyed metallophones, the highest in pitch are called *gangsa*. Each ensemble contains four *gangsa kantilan*, which contain 10 keys and are the highest-pitched instruments in the ensemble; and four *gangsa pemadé*, which are one octave lower than the gangsa kantilan in pitch. The *ugal*, a 10-keyed metallophone whose range extends five pitches below the lowest pitch of the gangsa pemadé, is also considered a part of the gangsa family and may be found singly or in pairs in an ensemble. Other important keyed metallophones include the two *calung* (a five-keyed metallophone whose range falls within the upper end of the ugal's range, sometimes also called the *jublag*) and the two *jegogan*, the largest and lowest of the keyed metallophones, which contains five keys and whose range extends one pitch below that of the ugal. Other keyed instruments, called *penyacah*, are sometimes found within the ensemble; the two penyacah contain seven keys and are pitched an octave higher than the calung. Each of the keyed metallophones is played by striking a key in the middle with a mallet (*pangul*) held in the right hand and subsequently damping the sound of notes struck with the left hand.

A number of different types of gongs are found within the kebyar ensemble. The largest of the gongs are called *gong agung*; each kebyar ensemble generally contains two, which hang from stands. One slightly smaller gong, the *kempur*, often hangs from a similar type of stand. Each of these types of gongs is played by striking the large raised boss in the center of the gong with a large padded mallet. A much smaller gong, called *klentong* or *kemong*, generally hangs from a much smaller carved wooden stand. The *kempli* is a single gong that is either mounted on a horizontal stand or placed on a player's lap. Two large gong-chimes, or horizontally mounted sets of smaller kettle gongs, are commonly found in kebyar ensembles. The *reyong* contains 12 kettles that are played by four musician; the *trompong*, an instrument not always present in kebyar music, contains 10 kettles and is played by a single musician. These gongs are all generally played on the boss with string-wound sticks, except the reyong, which is sometimes struck on its edge. Other gongs—such as the kempur-like *bebendé*, the kempli-sized *kajar*, and the small *kelenang*, may also appear.

Other important instruments include pairs of double-headed wooden drums with skin heads that are played either with hands or with a stick in the right hand (*kendang*); end-blown bamboo flutes (*suling*); a bowed spiked fiddle (*rebab*); and cymbals, which can be smaller and mounted (*cengceng kecek*) or larger and handheld (*cengceng kopyak*).

One distinctive aspect of the sound of Balinese gamelans in general, including gamelan gong kebyar, is that the instruments are tuned in pairs, with one at a slightly higher pitch than the other. The shimmering sound that the paired tunings create is called *ombak*, or waves. The overall kebyar tuning is to a five-pitch mode, *saih selesir* (pitches 1 2 3 5 6), within the seven-tone *pelog* tuning system that is one of two tuning systems commonly employed in both Balinese and Javanese gamelan music.

The music of gamelan gong kebyar is stratified into different layers, with each instrument class serving a distinct function within the overall ensemble. As in older gamelan styles, many portions of gong kebyar music are cyclical (*gongan*). The beat is kept by the kempli; the cycles are marked at their beginning and end by the gong agung and further punctuated by the kempur and the klentang. A core melody, or *pokok*, is played on the calung and is expanded upon by the jegogan, which links the pokok to the gongan. The gangsas and the reyong elaborate upon the pokok through rhythmically faster interlocking parts. The softer-sounding rebab and suling further elaborate on the pokok. The ugal or trompong may double the pokok, play solos, and cue the elaborating instruments. The two kendang players are the leaders of the ensemble who provide the overall cues, set the tempo, and guide the ensemble; in dance genres, they are also responsible for communicating musically between the musicians and the dancers.

Although kebyar style was originally based upon adaptations of older styles and works, the characteristic kebyar style is particularly distinctive. Unlike older Balinese gamelan genres, kebyar is often played more quickly—up to 200 beats per minute—and more loudly, with sharp dynamic contrasts. The *gongan* cycle is also regularly interrupted. Kebyar compositions often begin either with a *gineman* (quick, free-tempo solo by one or more instrumental sections) or *kebyar* (quick, free-tempo passage played by the whole group), and abrupt shifts between tempi and types of gong cycles are common. Special effects, such as striking the reyong percussively on the sides rather on the boss (*ocek-ocekan*), are also a hallmark of this style.

Virtuosic dance styles associated with the genre, collectively called *tari lepas* (free dance), were piloted in conjunction with the genre by the artist Maria beginning in the early 1920s, and helped crystallize the structure, form, and nontheatrical dance associations with the genre. A five-part compositional scheme with other short transitional passages, called *kreasi baru* (new creation), became a standard compositional form for kebyar in the mid-20th century for both instrumental and dance pieces.

While gamelan gong kebyar, like all Balinese gamelan genres, is traditionally performed entirely by men, all-female kebyar groups have emerged in Bali since the 1980s. Children's groups have also become increasingly popular since the late 20th century as well. Additionally, dozens of active kebyar ensembles exist outside the island, played by foreign and expatriate musicians alike. Despite continuing contemporary interest in reviving older Balinese gamelan styles and developing new genres and styles, kebyar remains a favorite ensemble for performances at Balinese Hindu temple ceremonies, secular concerts or competitions, and performances for tourists.

Elizabeth A. Clendinning

See also: Gamelan Orchestra (Balinese); Gamelan Orchestra (Javanese); Kendang

Further Reading

Gold, Lisa. 2005. *Music in Bali: Experiencing Music, Expressing Culture*. New York: Oxford University Press.

McPhee, Colin. 1966. *Music in Bali: A Study in Form and Instrumental Music in Bali*. New Haven, CT: Yale University Press.

Tenzer, Michael. 2000. *Gamelan Gong Kebyar: The Art of Twentieth-Century Balinese Music*. Chicago: The University of Chicago Press.

Tenzer, Michael. 2011. *Balinese Gamelan Music*. North Clarendon, VT: Tuttle.

Kecak

Kecak is a dance-drama performance genre from Bali, Indonesia, developed in the 1930s. It traditionally depicts an episode from the Hindu Ramayana epic. The dancers who enact the drama are surrounded by a chorus of men who imitate the sounds of a monkey army through imitative, interlocking vocal rhythms. The genre received its name from the primary vocalized sound, "cak," and may also be used

Kecak performance in Bali, Indonesia. Kecak is a music and dance style developed in the 1930s, based on a story from the Hindu epic the Ramayana. (Marka/Universal Images Group via Getty Images)

to describe other musical performances that make use of the distinctive interlocking vocal rhythms, such as *janger*, or modern performance genres. It is also known as *cak* or *gamelan suara* (vocal gamelan).

The vocal rhythms of kecak originated from sacred *sanghyang* dance genres in which vocal accompaniment was used to accompany entranced dancers. These sanghyang rituals can still be found in scattered villages across Bali. Today, secular kecak is better known, and its modern form was originally developed with foreign audiences in mind. In the early 1930s, expatriate German artist Walter Spies worked with local dancers, most notably Wayan Limbak, to unite the musical content with the Ramayana story. Spies's promotion of the dance-drama through kecak troupes that performed the genre both in Bali and abroad have popularized kecak internationally, making it one of the most iconic of the Balinese performing arts around the world. In Bali, nightly performances for tourists are offered at many locations, including in Ubud and at the Uluwatu temple.

The story most commonly associated with kecak is the Abduction of Sita from the Hindu epic the Ramayana. There are many versions of this story; the following is an amalgamation of Balinese versions. The godly prince Rama, heir to the throne of Ayodya, and Sita, his wife, had been banished from the kingdom by Rama's father, King Dasarata, due to the trickery of the king's wife. One day they were walking in the forest of Dandanka with Rama's brother, Laksmana, when Sita spies a beautiful golden deer and requests that Rama bring the deer to her. Rama leaves Sita under the care of his brother, Laksmana, to pursue the golden deer.

However, the golden deer is in actuality Marica, a demon-like *rakshasa* and shape shifter; he has agreed to help the Rahwana, the 10-headed rakshasa King of Alengka, capture the princess Sita. When Rama shoots the golden deer with an arrow, the deer transforms back into Marica and Rama realizes he has been tricked. Thinking she hears Rama cry out for help, Sita insists that Laksmana go to him. The reluctant Laksmana draws a magical circle around Sita, stating that no harm will come to her if she does not leave the circle.

After Laksmana leaves, Rahwana approaches Sita, disguised as a begging holy man, and asks for her help. She acquiesces; Rahwana returns to his regular form and carries her away to his palace. In some versions, the vulture-king Jatayu fights Rahwana and attempts to prevent the abduction, but Rahwana injures Jatayu greatly, and he flies away to inform Rama of what has happened.

Sita remains in Alengka for a year, trying to ward off Rahwana's advances with the help of Trijata, Rahwana's sympathetic niece. She is discovered there by the white *vanara* (monkey-like humanoid) Hanuman, who takes a token of hers back to Rama to show she is alive. Rama's allies arrive in Alengka and a battle between the forces of Rama and those of Rahwana follows. With the help of Hanuman, Sugriwa (king of the monkeys) and his monkey army, Rama is able to rescue Sita. This victory is generally the ending point of the kecak dance-drama.

Although performances may include a narrator (*dalang*), the story is primarily conveyed through the performers. Dancers portray the major characters; all are unmasked except Hanuman and Sugriwa, who wear masks on the lower halves of their faces. The performing style of the dancers derives primarily from *wayang wong*, a theatrical dance genre with semi-codified character movements for characters that are refined (*alus*), coarse (*kasar*), or comedic, among others. The dancers are surrounded by the kecak chorus, which may consist of up to 100 men, who are usually bare-chested. Members of the chorus sometimes physically help portray the story through sitting, standing, or lying down; their arm gestures; and occasionally, becoming elements of the set. Most important, however, is the music that they create.

No musical instruments are used except the voice. The vocal patterns for kecak are called *gamelan suara* (vocal gamelan) and are based on the rhythmic patterns found in other forms of Balinese gamelan. One person simulates the sound of the *kajar*, a timekeeping instrument, by chanting the syllable "pung," which keeps the beat. Other groups of men chant interlocking parts that may divide evenly into threes, fives, or sevens, or a combination of these rhythmic divisions. Yet other musicians imitate the sound of gongs, which punctuate a two-, four-, or eight-beat gong cycle (*gongan*) using syllables such as "sirr," "ting," and "mong." Other parts may be included and sung either by the cak chorus or the dancers.

The musicians may employ some or all of these musical parts at any time to tell the story, which becomes sonically most intense during the battle scene between the forces of Rama and the forces of Rahwana. Here, the chorus generally is divided along the two sides, both of which stand and chant loudly in frenetic call-and-response patterns to imitate the battling forces.

The Ramayana dance-drama described here is still the most popular performance context for the genre, but originally the performances were more impressionistic, conveying a selection of excerpts from the Ramayana and often omitting even key characters. More recently, some kecak troupes have used the medium to portray other mythological stories, or used the musical rudiments in other settings with no story at all. Most kecak choruses have been composed entirely of men, with a few of the dance roles reserved for women; however, the 1990s and 2000s saw several notable performances by female kecak troupes, none of which have persisted.

Although kecak is most widely associated with the Ramayana dance-drama, it also plays a central role in the Balinese social dance genre *janger*. This genre, also developed in the 1930s, features groups of about 10 young women and 10 young men who sing and dance together, traditionally depicting farmers at leisure. While the women primarily sing, the men provide a kecak chorus. Janger reached the height of its popularity in the 1960s with lavish performances sponsored by political parties, most notably *Partai Kommunis Indonesia (PKI)*, the communist party of Indonesia. When the PKI was ousted, many party supporters were killed, including musicians and dancers, and the genre dropped from favor. It has been revived in recent years through primary school education and governmental campaigns.

On an international scale, kecak has been incorporated into body percussion and other experimental performance styles, both collaboratively and by non-Balinese artists, such as Keith Terry. Over the past 50 years, kecak—both audiovisual recordings from a performance or isolated portions of the distinctive vocalization style—have been incorporated into popular film, including Federico's Fellini's *Satyricon* (1969), the Cohen Brother's *Blood Simple* (1984), Ron Fricke's *Baraka* (1992), and *Ice Age 2* (2006).

Elizabeth A. Clendinning

See also: Gamelan Orchestra (Balinese); Gamelan Orchestra (Javanese); Kebyar; McPhee, Colin

Further Reading

Bakan, Michael. 2013. "Italian Cinema and the Balinese Sound of Greek Tragedy: Kecak Contortions and Postmodern Schizophonic Mimesis in Pasolini and Fellini." In Kendra Stepputat (ed.), *Performing Arts in Bali: Changing Interpretations, Founding Traditions*, 363–387. Grazer Beiträge zur Ethnomusikologie/Graz Studies in Ethnomusicology, vol. 24. Graz, Germany: Institute of Ethnomusicology, University of Music and Performing Arts, Graz.

Belo, Jane. 1960. *Trance in Bali*. New York: Columbia University Press.

Dibia, I Wayan. 1996. *Kecak: The Vocal Chant of Bali*. Denpasar: Hartanto Art Books.

Dibia, I Wayan, and Rucina Ballinger. 2004. *Balinese Dance, Drama and Music: A Guide to the Performing Arts of Bali*. Singapore: Periplus.

McPhee, Colin. 1966. *Music in Bali: A Study in Form and Instrumental Music in Bali*. New Haven, CT: Yale University Press.

Tenzer, Michael. 2011. *Balinese Gamelan Music*. North Clarendon, VT: Tuttle.

Kendang

Kendang (also spelled *gendang* or *kendhang*) is a double-headed barrel drum found in the Maritime regions of Southeast Asia, including Indonesia, Malaysia, Brunei,

Singapore, and the Philippines. The instrument is used in traditional music ensembles, such as Balinese and Javanese Indonesian *gamelan*, often functioning as the leader of the group. Kendang are found in many gong-chime instrumental ensembles unique to Southeast Asia. Similar instruments exist in mainland Southeast Asia, such as in Thailand, Cambodia, Burma (Myanmar), Laos, mainland Malaysia, and Vietnam.

The kendang is believed to originate from the earlier *mridangam* of Southern India. The mridangam, bearing structural qualities similar to that of the contemporary kendang found in Maritime Southeast Asia, possibly travelled there with Hinduism and Indian mythology during the Chola Dynasty (ninth to 13th century CE)—when the dynasty was said to have maritime trade relations with the Srivijaya Empire in the Malay archipelago (Kulke and Rothermund, 2004, pp. 122–127). The kendang also shares qualities similar to those of the Indian *tavil* and *pakhavaj*, and the Sri Lankan *gata bera* (Miller and Williams, 2008, p. 38).

The kendang is a double-headed wooden drum, typically made from a single hollowed piece of wood from a jackfruit, coconut, or teak tree. The instrument is elongated in shape, and has two circular heads on either end. Assorted animal skins may comprise the two heads, although buffalo and goat are commonly used. Throughout Southeast Asia, one drumhead is tuned higher in pitch than the other. In particular regions of Southeast Asia, the kendang has two heads of differing sizes: in Java and Malaysia, the kendang has a larger right-side drum head, whereas in Bali, Brunei, and the Philippines, the heads are of equal size.

The kendang is often used in pairs throughout Southeast Asia. The pair consists of one higher-pitched and one lower-pitched drum. Throughout Southeast Asia, the lower-pitched kendang is considered "female," whereas the higher-pitched kendang is considered "male." The drum achieves its pitch either because it is physically larger or smaller in size, is tuned lower or higher using tension straps, or is internally tuned (through wood carving and hollowing techniques) so that the drum produces a fundamentally lower or higher pitch. In Malaysia, the kendang comes in two sizes: large (*ibu* [mother]) and small (*anak* [child]) (Matusky and Sooi Beng, 2004, p. 22). In Thailand, the *klong khaek* (the Thai equivalent of the kendang) does not come in two sizes, although one drum is tuned higher than the other: the higher pitch is male ([*klong*] *tua puu* [grandfather]) and the lower pitch is female ([*klong*] *tua mia* [mother]). In Indonesia, *wadon* translates to "female," and *lanang* translates to "male" (Downing, 2008, p. 259). Rattan, a palm-leaf material, is used as tension straps to stretch and tighten the heads; leather (dried cowhide) is also common (Tenzer, 2000, p. 48). In Malaysia, nylon rope is occasionally used, given its cost-effectiveness and durability (Matusky and Sooi Beng, 2004, p. 22).

Kendang varies in shape and size according to the region, style, and genre of music performed. In Bali, two principal sizes of kendang are used in gamelan music; the large *kendang wadon* and small *kendang lanang* (Tenzer, 2000, pp. 47–48). In Java, there are four dominant variations of kendang. *Kendang ketipung* is often played with the *kendang gendhing*, as a mixed pair in pieces with a faster tempo. Kendang gendhing is also used alone in stately, solemn pieces, as it is deepest in pitch and evokes feelings of magnificence. *Kendang wayangan* derives its name from *wayang*, or shadow-puppet theater. *Kendang ciblon* derives its name from the Javanese word for "water-play," a type of performance where people smack pools of water with different hand shapes to create different sounds and rhythms. Kendang ciblon is said to imitate the techniques used in water play (Lindsay, 1992, p. 22). The kendang functions as the leader of a gamelan ensemble in Indonesia, where its most essential role is to maintain and make clear to the other musicians any variations in tempi or temporal density (*irama* and *laya*, respectively). Metric shifts (from a quarter-note pulse to a half-note pulse), and temporal shifts (such as a *rallentando* or *accelerando*) are determined by the kendang. In performances with dancers, the drummer internalizes any musical cues from the dancers, and translates them to the rest of the ensemble.

Performers of the kendang in Malaysia use mnemonic devices (syllables) to differentiate between different strokes upon the four different striking surfaces. The large drum, ibu, has the terms "pak" and "duh" for its two heads; the small drum, anak, uses the terms "cak" and "ting," respectively (Matusky and Sooi Beng, 2004, p. 22). In Malaysia, the kendang is used in several ensembles, including the *kendang silat* ensemble that accompanies the Malay martial art *silat*. The instrument additionally accompanies the martial art/sport known as *tomoi*, a cognate of the Thai sport *muay Thai*. The sport was banned from northern, Islamic Malaysia, due to its prefight ritual dance with animist elements. The kendang drum patterns used in the Malay martial arts feature interlocking, hocket-like pattern similar to those in *wayang kulit*, *makyung*, and gamelan performances (Matusky and Sooi Beng, 2004, p. 11).

The *wayang kulit*, literally "puppet theater," is derived from similar shadow-puppet plays of Indonesia. *Wayang kulit jawa* ("jawa" is a cognate for Java) is a form of shadow puppetry with Javanese "ancient" origins. *Wayang kulit gedek* is performed in Northern Malaysia, and is closely related to the Thai shadow puppet theater known as *nang talung*. The kendang in this performance are in fact Thai *klong khaek* (literally, foreigner drum, the name allegorical for its Javanese or Indian origins). This genre of wayang kulit was also performed in what is today Southern Thailand, as this region was formerly the Malay Pattani Sultanate (1516–1902). *Makyung*, a dance-drama based upon Malay folk tales, features the kendang in an ensemble with *tetawak* gongs and a *rebab*, a three-stringed spike fiddle found throughout Southeast Asia (Matusky and Sooi Beng, 2004, pp. 39–41).

John Forrestal

See also: Colometry/Colometric; Gamelan Orchestra (Balinese); Gamelan Orchestra (Javanese); Gender Wayang; Malay Music; McPhee, Colin; Mridangam; Piphat

Further Reading

Downing, Sonja Lynn. 2008. "Arjuna's Angels: Girls Learning Gamelan Music in Bali." PhD diss., University of California, Santa Barbara.

Gold, Lisa. 2005. *Music in Bali*. New York: Oxford University Press.

Kulke, Hermann, and Dietmar Rothermund. 2004. *A History of India*. London: Routledge.

Lindsay, Jennifer. 1992. *Javanese Gamelan*. New York: Oxford University Press.

Matusky, Patricia, and Tan Sooi Beng. 2004. *The Music of Malaysia: The Classical, Folk, and Syncretic Traditions*. Burlington, VT: Ashgate.

Miller, Terry E., and Sean Williams, eds. 1998. *The Garland Encyclopedia of World Music; Vol. 4: Southeast Asia.* New York: Garland.

Miller, Terry E., and Sean Williams, eds. 2008. *The Garland Handbook of Southeast Asian Music.* New York: Garland.

Tenzer, Michael. 2000. *Gamelan Gong Kebyar: The Art of Twentieth-Century Balinese Music.* Chicago: The University of Chicago Press.

Tenzer, Michael. 2011. *Balinese Gamelan Music,* 3rd ed. Singapore: Tuttle.

Khaled, Cheb (1960–)

Algerian singer Cheb Khaled is universally acknowledged as the "King of Rai," a title bestowed on him at age 25 during Algeria's first rai festival in 1985. Cheb Khaled represents the "second stage" of rai, with its emphasis on youth culture, social dissent, and eclectic musical influences. Cheb Khaled's meteoric career in Algeria and France encompasses a prolific creative output: from his first cassette recording of "Trigue Lycée" in 1977 (produced at a cost of $13) to his 2012 global hit, "C'est la Vie," with the album of the same name exceeding 4.6 million sales worldwide.

Cheb Khaled was born Khaled Hadj Ibrahim (or Brahim) on February 29, 1960, in Oran, (Wahran), an ethnically diverse port city in northwestern Algeria. Oran is the cultural birthplace of the musical genre known as *rai,* or *raï,* generally translated as "opinion." Bezza Mazouzi demarcates the stages of rai into its development in the 1950s to 1970s (with rai banned from Algerian media in the early 1970s) and culmination in the early 1980s. This second stage is termed *chāb* (or *cheb*) rai, the "rai of the young," with many of its musicians born around the time of Algerian independence in 1962. Hence, "Cheb" Khaled and his cohort would bear this signifier of youth: Cheba Fadéla, her husband Cheb Sahraoui, Cheb Mami, and Cheba Zahouania, among many others.

Cheb Khaled's entrée into what Hana Noor Al-Deen (2005) calls the "pop-style era" of rai was *"Ana Mahlali Noum* (Sleep does not suit me)," first sung by Cheba Fadéla in 1979. Cheb Khaled performed two songs on the breakthrough 1988 album *Rai Rebels,* produced by Rachid Baba Ahmed: *"Ya Loualid* (Oh my child)," with Cheba Zahouania; and Sidi Boumedienne. The album cover depicts what would remain Cheb Khaled's trademark visage: a dazzling smile and a mustache. In the same year, his song *"El Harba Wayn?* (To flee but where?)" exemplified the politicized lyrics of the rai genre and served as the "anthem" of protestors in the October uprising. It was after migrating to France (in advance of the exodus of rai artists following the ban on vulgarity by the Islamic Salvation Front after the December 1991 elections) that Cheb Khaled recorded his first solo album and launched a series of iconic hit songs: "Didi," "Aicha," and "C'est la Vie." "Cheb" was dropped for his 1992 album, *Khaled,* a commercial effort orchestrated by Polygram that went gold in France, selling more than 100,000 copies. *N'ssi N'ssi* was released the following year, with *Sahra* in 1996. Tony Langlois observes the impact on the genre: "The success of Cheb Khaled abroad moved the cultural centre of gravity for Rai. . . . No longer was Rai's authenticity the sole property of one or two cities in

Algerian singer Khaled performing in 1992. Khaled is best known in the musical genre known as *rai*—an Algerian folk style. (Frans Schellekens/Redferns)

North Africa" (Langlois, 1996, pp. 264–265). Indeed, Cheb Khaled's artistic life in the diaspora has brought attention to the plight of often-marginalized Algerian immigrants.

Cheb Khaled's superstar status has engendered trans-Atlantic crossovers between genres and artistic personae. Marc Schade-Poulsen cites a 1985 article from Actuel which asserts that "Raï is at one and the same time Algeria's punk, blues, reggae, and funk. . . . Oran is the Kingston of this underground, secret, lyrical explosion. Cheb Khaled is the Bob Marley" (Schade-Poulsen, 1999, p. 29). This analogy is rooted in a variety of phenomena, including youth culture, social dissent, and the expanding reach of media linking previously unconnected domains of East and West.

Hicham Chami

See also: Rai

Further Reading

Gross, Joan, David McMurray, and Ted Swedenburg. 1992. "Rai, Rap, and Ramadan Nights: Franco-Maghribi Cultural Identities." *Middle East Report* 178, 11–24.

Langlois, Tony. 1996. "The Local and Global in North African Popular Music." *Popular Music* 15, 259–273.

Mazouzi, Bezza. 2002. "Rai." In Virginia Danielson, Dwight Reynolds, and Scott Marcus (eds.), *Garland Encyclopedia of World Music; Vol. 6: The Middle East*, 269–272. New York: Routledge.

Noor Al-Deen, Hana. 2005. "The Evolution of Rai Music." *Journal of Black Studies* 35, 597–611.

Schade-Poulsen, Marc. 1999. *Men and Popular Music in Algeria: The Social Significance of Raï*. Austin: University of Texas Press.

Khan, Nusrat Fateh Ali (1948–1997)

Nusrat Fateh Ali Khan was one of the greatest *qawwali* singers, dubbed the "*Shahenshah Qawwali*," which means "The King of Kings of Qawwali." His work earned him a plethora of international awards and honorary titles. He was a revered artist who brought Sufi music to the playback singers of Bollywood and to the silver screen in Hollywood.

Born October 13, 1948, in Fasalabad, Pakistan, to Ustad Fateh Ali Khan, Nusrat was born into a long-established family of qawwali singers which included his uncles Ustad Mubarik Ali Khan and Ustad Salamat Ali Khan. Nusrat was one of six children, with four older sisters and one younger brother, Farrukh. His father wanted Nusrat to become a doctor, but the music within the household proved to be infectious and Nusrat soon began to play the tabla and sing. Much to his father's surprise, he realized Nusrat possessed special singing ability and began giving him voice training.

It wasn't until 1964 that Nusrat performed for the very first time—but it was at the graveside of his father. This was a pivotal moment in Nusrat's life, when he decided to become a full-time qawwali singer. He continued vocal training under the direction of his uncle Ustad Mubarik, while his brother Farrukh went on to become a maestro on the harmonium. They performed locally until 1971, when his uncle Ustad Mubarik passed away. Nusrat took over leadership of the family group, and in the same year he gave his first local radio performance and later introduced the hit song "*Haq Ali Ali* (God is truth)" to the people of Pakistan.

In 1971, he married Naheed Khan and together they had one child, a daughter named Nida. In 1976, Nusrat chose his three-year-old nephew Rahat Fateh Ali Khan to start voice training, and by age 10 Rahat officially sang with the qawwali party. In the 1980s, Nusrat signed a contract with the Oriental Star Agency in Birmingham, UK, which produced more than 100 of his albums and promoted his music. In 1988, Nusrat performed at the World of Music Arts and Dance (WOMAD) founded by Peter Gabriel who later signed Nusrat to his label, Real Word Records. Nusrat toured throughout Europe and performed charitable concerts. In particular, he assisted former cricketer Imran Khan to build a cancer treatment hospital in Pakistan.

In the 1990s, Gabriel brought Canadian guitarist Michael Brook and Nusrat together to write songs. This spurred a brand new genre of music, called "qawwali fusion." The album, *Mustt Mustt* (1990) featured Western tracks and a very popular club remix of the song "Mustt Mustt" by the British music band, Massive Attack. By 1992, the University of Washington offered Nusrat a six-month residency in its ethnomusicology program, from September 1992 to March 1993. This would have meant that his qawwali party of 100 or so members would be unemployed; Nusrat sought a flexible timetable that allowed weekend concerts so his qawwali group could survive. After his stint at the University of Washington, requests for performances poured in from all over the world. Nusrat often overextended himself with these commitments, and also wrote his first-ever music score (for the Indian movie *Bandit Queen*). He went on to contribute music to *The Last Temptation of Christ* (1988) and *Natural Born Killers* (1994), and in 1995, he collaborated with Eddie Vedder on the song "The Face of Love" for the soundtrack of *Dead Man Walking* (1995).

In March 1996, Nusrat performed at the VH1 Honors Show in Los Angeles, accompanied by Peter Gabriel. He then began work on a new album called *The Prayer Cycle* while a remix of his older songs for the album *Star Rise* was also being produced. To his delight, in February 1997 his album *Intoxicated Spirit* was nominated for a Grammy Award for Best Traditional Folk Album. But tragedy struck in London, on August 16, 1997, when Nusrat succumbed to a cardiac arrest. The news shocked the world, and homage was paid to him at a huge public funeral in his hometown in Pakistan.

Even though Nusrat passed away in 1997, his voice lives on, and qawwali is now recognized on the world stage. He continues to receive posthumous awards, honorary titles, and tributes. In 2001, his name entered the *Guinness Book of World Records* for being the only qawwali artist to record 125 albums. His album *Star Rise* is regarded as a memorial to him, and his final album, *The Prayer Cycle*, was completed by Alanis Morrissette. His songs live on and have been featured in films such as *Bend It Like Beckham* (2002) and *Eat, Pray, Love* (2010).

Nadia Ali

See also: Bollywood Music; Vocables

Further Reading

Baud, Pierre-Alain. 2008. *Nusrat Fateh Ali Khan: The Messenger of Qawwali*. Paris, France: Demi-Lune.

Ellingham, Mark. 2000. *World Music: Latin and North America, India, Caribbean, Asia and Pacific*. London: Rough Guides.

Potter, John. 2000. *The Cambridge Companion to Singing*. Cambridge: Cambridge University Press.

Ruby, Ahmed Aquil. 1998. *Nusrat Fateh Ali Khan: A Living Legend*. Hoffman Estates, IL: Words of Wisdom.

Khayal

Khayal is a popular and pre-eminent genre of modern North Indian or Hindustani classical vocal music known for its improvisational flexibility. The word *khayal* means an idea, fancy, or imagination and as such it promises freedom from rigidity and infinite creative possibilities for the performing musician. Highly improvisational in nature, khayal is an abstract presentation of a raga—a mode or melodic framework. Khayal generally has two major movements: *vilambit* or *bada lhayal* with a slow tempo and *drut* or *chota khayal* with a fast tempo. A typical khayal performance includes a solo singer accompanied by a stringed drone called *tanpura*, a set of drums or tabla, and an accompanying reed instrument called a harmonium.

A characteristic khayal composition is a song in a raga and tala, typically known as a *ciz*, and usually in two sections known as *sthayi* and *antara*. The ciz is a short composition that effectively presents all the musical materials—including the *raga*, *tala*, and musical embellishments—for an improvised khayal performance. The ciz, the textual composition, is an essential component of a khayal that is then expanded through melodic embellishments within the basic framework of the chosen raga. Thus, in each khayal presentation, there are two *bandishes* or meaningful text of the song: first, the sthayi bandish is sung and then it is enhanced with slow improvisation in the forms of *alap, bol alap,* or *ragalap* (i.e., the structure for manifesting the melodic mode); this is followed by the antara and finally a faster improvisation on the sthayi with *bol tan* and *tan*. A highly imaginative genre, khayal allows six types of improvisations: alap or bol alap, *nom-tom, bolbant*, tan (*akar* and *boltan*), and *sargam*. The purpose of these improvisations is the gradual but systematic revelation of the raga by establishing its moods and traits. The typical characteristics of khayal performance are thus the choice and complex combination of the particular musical materials—the raga, the tala, and the composition itself (the ciz or bandish in khayal), as well as the types of acceptable improvisations chosen to embellish the song—that lead to the final creation of an aesthetically pleasing, formally balanced recital.

Believed to have originated in the Moghul courts, specifically patronized by the emperor Muhammad Shah (1719–1748 CE), the khayal dates back several hundred years. Romantic, soft, and delicate, khayal, as a modern style of light classical music, developed as a song of love in the women's quarters (*zenana*), outside the large reverberating halls of the *durbar* and its masculine singing voices. Khayal, in its inception as a unique genre, was sung predominantly by women who could explore the full range of the song from slow to fast and with intricate and nuanced improvisations. Like the *thumri*, khayal songs are typically composed in Vraj Bhasha, a dialect of Hindi, and are primarily romantic or devotional, bringing together both the Hindu and the Muslim poetic traditions. Unlike Thumri, the primary importance in a lhayal performance is given to the abstract ornamental nuances, the intricate musical embellishments, the improvised melodic patterns, and the vocal virtuosity of the soloist while enunciating or intoning the embellishments in her rendering of the raga, and not to the lyrical content of the bandish.

Significantly, the khayal is not performed from a written score or authoritative notations; traditionally, the genre is orally transmitted and retained in memory. There is no single rigid or authoritative formal model for a khayal performance. Instead, the artist, guided by certain basic principles, constructs her own performance by accommodating various specific techniques or predefined, yet flexible, processes, thereby creating an unlimited number of performances that are all valid renderings of the chosen raga. There are six main *gharanas* or styles of performance for a khayal: Gwalior, Delhi, Patiala, Agra, Kirana, and Jaipur, of which the Gwalior musical lineage is believed to be the oldest. Bade Ghulam Ali Khan, Bhimsen Joshi, Kishori Amonkar, Veena Sahasrabuddhe, Rashid Khan, and Ajay Chakravorty are a few of the renowned exponents of the lhayal genre.

Sutapa Chaudhuri

See also: Harmonium; Tabla; Tagore, Rabindranath; Thumri

Further Reading

Broughton, Simon, and Mark Ellingham, eds. 2000. *The Rough Guide to World Music; Vol. 2: Latin and North America, Caribbean, India, Asia and Pacific.* London: Rough Guides.

Kumar, Raj, ed. 2003. *Essays on Indian Music.* New Delhi: Discovery Publishing House.

Nettl, Bruno, and Alison Arnold, eds. 2000. *The Garland Encyclopedia of World Music: South Asia: The Indian Subcontinent.* Milton Park, UK: Taylor & Francis.

Wade, Bonnie C. 1984. *Khyāl: Creativity within North India's Classical Music Tradition.* New Delhi: Munshiram Manoharlal Publishers.

Khene

The *khene* is a South Asian free-reed mouth organ, consisting of two parallel rows of bamboo pipes. It is the predominant melodic instrument in rural Laos, and schools in northeastern Thailand sponsor khene ensembles (*khaen wong*) to play classical songs. The 16-pipe version (*khene paet* [khene eight]) is more common in Thailand, and the 14-pipe (*khene chet* or *jet* [khene seven]) was usual in Laos until the late 20th century. Variants are used by specific groups such as the Kumhu, who use an instrument with 12 pipes and an extended tail on the windchest; and the Phuan people in Xiengkhuang, whose version has one mute and 13 sounding pipes. The *khene hok* (khene six) is a child's toy with six pipes. Alternative spellings of the instrument's name include *khaen*, *kaen*, *khen*, and *khèn* (Vietnamese).

Bamboo for the pipes is harvested after one year of growth and dried for several weeks. One fingerhole is burnt into each pipe, and pipes are inserted (from longest to shortest) into a carved hardwood windchest called *tao* (gourd). Copper-silver alloy reeds are mounted in the pipe walls inside the tao. The openings in the windchest are caulked with *khisut*, a kind of insect waste. Pipes range in length from 250 cm to 3 meters. Khene making is concentrated in Roi Et province of northern Thailand. The instrument evolved from the Chinese *sheng*, and was first depicted in a European source in 1636 (Marin Mersenne's *Harmonie Universelle*).

The instrument is properly held tilted, with the hands cupped over the windchest, by a seated player; it may be played as a solo instrument, but usually provides accompaniment for solo narrative genres (*lam ploen* and *lam leuang*) and for regional styles of song (*lam* and *khap*). Since the 1940s, a central Thai theater genre called *li-ke* began crossing the Mekong, using khene and lam. In the Stung Treng province of Cambodia, the khene is played by ethnic Laotians and featured in dance drama (*lakhon ken*). Adding a khene to an ensemble (which generally gives it a more Laotian flavor), raises the question of tuning, as they produce a diatonic minor scale (not influenced by Western classical tuning). Players choose one of two pentatonic modes: *thang sun* (short way), which may be played in three *lai* (keys, including D-E-G-A-B, G-A-C-D-E, and C-D-F-G-A, considered to be the oldest), or *thang yao* (long way) in two lai (A-C-D-E-G and D-F-G-A-C).

The National School of Folkloric Music and Dance in Vientaine, Laos, has employed multiple khene teachers since the early 1990s. Expert players include Sombat Simla (Thai), Khamseung Syhanone (Laotian), and Jonny Olsen

(Californian). Khene has been featured in compositions by contemporary Western musicians such as Aerosmith, The Cranberries, Yes, and Jaron Lanier. Related Asian free-reeds include the Thai Dam *pi luang* and *pi hap*, the Bangladeshi *plung*, the Vietnamese *m'buot*, the Hmong *qeej* (which is considered to "speak" to the spirit world, rather than to "play" music), and the Chinese *sheng* and *fang sheng*.

Laura Stanfield Prichard

See also: Kendang; Malay Music

Further Reading

Lilly, Joseph. 1999. "An Introduction to the Khaen of Laos." *The Free-Reed Journal.* http://www.ksanti.net/free-reed/essays/khaenlaos.html.

Miller, Terry. 1985. *Traditional Music of the Lao: Playing and Mawlum Singing in Northeast Thailand.* Westport, CT: Greenwood.

Picken, L. E. R., C. J. Adkins, and T. F. Page. 1984. "The Making of a Khaen: The Free Reed Mouth Organ of North East Thailand." *Musica Asiatica* 4, 117–154.

Kidjo, Angelique (1960–)

Angelique Kidjo, born Angelique Kpasseloko Hinto Hounsinou Kandjo Manta Zogbin Kidjo, is an internationally acclaimed musician from Ouidah, Benin. Kidjo has written and performed in a broad range of musical styles extending from African folk to Western jazz, funk, and pop. As a United Nations Children's Fund (UNICEF) Goodwill Ambassador, she has always preserved a strong nationalistic pride that calls the world to look at the beauty of Africa. One of her missions as an artist has been to encourage other artists to join her in the struggle of exposing human rights injustices occurring in developing countries. Through her music, Kidjo presents strong political and humanitarian attitudes to a wide variety of listeners. The recipient of three Grammy Awards, Kidjo has become one of the most influential and popular musicians ever to come from Africa.

Kidjo's mother, Yvonne Kidjo, served as the director of Benin's first theater and dance ensemble and exerted a strong influence on Kidjo's dancing and music. Due to the installation of President Mathieu Kérékou in Benin, whose regime attempted to use Kidjo's music to further its Marxist-Leninist agenda, Kidjo moved to Paris in 1983 to study human rights law. She also continued her musical studies, first during a largely unsuccessful two-year stint studying classical voice and later as a student at the CIMS jazz school, where she was exposed to much of the jazz music that would shape her sound during the 1980s (Kidjo, 2006). Kidjo played with several jazz groups before beginning a nearly five-year partnership with the Dutch jazz pianist, Jasper Van't Hoff (1947–) and his ensemble Pili-Pili. Following a split from Pili-Pili to focus on a solo career, Kidjo recorded her first international solo album, *Parakou* (1989), which featured lyrics in Fon, her mother tongue. Following the success of this album, Chris Blackwell (1937–) signed Kidjo to a contract with Mango Records, with which she released her sophomore album, *Logozo* (1991). Produced by Joseph Galdo of the Miami Sound Machine, the album further explored the duty of musicians to expose the injustices they witnessed; it was also Kidjo's first album to include lyrics in Yoruba (Kidjo, 2006). Her work in the 1990s caused Kidjo to move away from layering of tracks in favor of a more collaborative approach, with each track being recorded at the same time and in the same studio. Kidjo's recorded output also features the work of French bassist Jean Hebrail, whom she married in 1987.

As a recording artist, Kidjo has been an avid and eclectic collaborator, working with such artists as Josh Groban, the Kronos Quartet, Carlos Santana, Alicia Keyes, Ziggy Marley, Branford Marsalis, Ezra Koenig from Vampire Weekend, and Philip Glass, among others. However, at the core of Kidjo's collaboration is her band, since 2002 comprised of guitarists Lionel Loueke and Dominic James. Her work with the Orchestre Philharmonique du Luxembourg has gained particular acclaim, including a Grammy Award for *Angelique Kidjo: SINGS with The Orchestre Philharmonique du Luxembourg* (2015) and her 2007 release, *DJIN DJIN*.

As a human rights activist, Kidjo, has been involved in several international efforts to raise both awareness and support for her home continent. She worked tirelessly as a UNICEF Goodwill Ambassador and founder of The Batonga Foundation, which champions the education of young African women. She has also been a participant in the Global Meeting for Sustainable Measles Mortality Reduction and Immunization System Strengthening. Additionally, Kidjo worked with the Bring Back Our Girls Movement, which raised awareness of the terrorist group Boko Haram's insurgent attacks on Nigerian schools since 2011.

Throughout the mid-1990s, Kidjo explored new musical possibilities and styles with such albums as *Aye* (1994), *Fifa* (1996), and *Oremi* (1998). Following the success of *Aye*, Kidjo and husband Jean Hebrail traversed her home country to record indigenous music for a new album. This venture resulted in *Fifa*, which is unique not only for its use of around 200 musicians (including Carlos Santana) but also for including several songs written in English. The 1998 album *Oremi*, released on the Island label, is characterized by a fusion of traditional music from Benin and music of black Americans. It was on this album that Kidjo chose to cover "Voodoo Child," first written and performed by Jimi Hendrix, to elaborate on the ways in which the two cultures were linked.

Among the large discography of Angelique Kidjo, releases such as her African Diaspora trilogy, and *Eve* (2014), have played a large role in advancing Kidjo's career. The African Diaspora trilogy is comprised of three albums: *Oremi, Black Ivory Soul*, and *Oyaya!*. The trilogy project, which began in 1998, aimed to provide links between Africa and the West by way of this African diaspora. The trilogy is characterized by a blending of musical styles which represent the slave-trade diffusion of African music as it headed into the Western hemisphere. This musical diaspora is evidenced also by collaborations with numerous Caribbean and Latin musicians. Kidjo's *Eve* (2014), named after both her mother and the biblical mother of the human race, is a testament to the women of Africa. Of that album, Kidjo remarked, "On this recording, I am letting the voices of the women show their beauty to the world" (Kidjo, 2014). By utilizing a variety of Beninese dialects (such as Yoruba, Fon, Goun, and Mina), along with a collaboration including her mother on the track "Bana," Kidjo presents her distinct ability to incorporate her roots into her music. One of her latest tracks, "Awalole" (We own it), featured on *Eve* has shown the necessity for the African people to take control of the leadership of their countries.

Phillip Alexander Ducreay

See also: Adé, "King" Sunny; Afrobeat (Afropop); Afro-Cuban Jazz; Jazz

Further Reading

Kidjo, Angelique. 2014. "Ode to African Women." http://www.kidjo.com/discography-source/2017/2/7/eve.

Kidjo, Angelique. 2016. "Career Highlights." http://www.kidjo.com/career.html.

UNICEF. 2015. "Angelique Kidjo Activity Highlights." https://www.unicef.org/people/people_47856.html.

Klezmer

The Yiddish term *klezmer* has acquired polyvalence over the centuries. It is derived from the Hebrew words *kle* and *zemer*: literally, "vessel of song." From the 16th through the early 20th centuries, it referred to Ashkenazi Jewish itinerant musicians from a hereditary class who performed for Jewish and non-Jewish weddings and functions. Following the late 20th-century klezmer revival, klezmer came primarily to connote a genre of instrumental music and song of Ashkenazi Jewish expressive culture. Klezmer music and musicians have influenced Western classical music, the cantorate, Yiddish theater music, and American popular music.

The sources of klezmer music history consist of Jewish and non-Jewish community records, ethnographic research, field recordings, and literary and artistic imagery. The ethnographic research of S. An-ski (Shloyme-Zanvl Rappoport, 1863–1920) and Joel Engel (Yuli Dimitriyevich, 1868–1927) in Podolia and Volhynia (1912–1914); Moshe Beregovski (1892–1961) in eastern Ukraine (1930s); and Joachim Stuchewsky (1891–1982) comprises the lion's share of what is now known about klezmer. Beregovski's research and tune collection are the most extensive of these sources. Beregovski (1892–1961), a Jewish Soviet ethnomusicologist, headed the Department of Musical Folklore in the Kiev Institute for Jewish Culture

---

Klezmatics

With a modern take on traditional klezmer music, the Klezmatics have led a revival in klezmer music for the past 30 years. The band unabashedly performs a hybrid style of klezmer, rooted in tradition but adaptive to and adoptive of other musical and cultural influences. The Klezmatics have worked with a variety of non-klezmer artists, such as poet Allen Ginsberg, classical violinist Itzhak Perlman, jazz musicians Herbie Hancock and Chick Corea, and playwright Tony Kushner. Formed by Jewish Americans in New York, the Klezmatics are particularly known for attempting to preserve and promote Jewish culture and fading languages by writing songs in Yiddish, Aramaic, and Bavarian. Despite their decidedly klezmer sounds (featuring clarinet and klezmer harmonic content), the Klezmatics continue to push the boundaries of traditional klezmer music, including their 2006 album of Woody Guthrie songs called *Wonder Wheel*.

beginning in 1929. He wrote extensively on genre, mode, performance practice, transmission, and the social world of the klezmer, and he collected around 1,500 instrumental tunes.

Representations of the klezmer pervade Yiddish and Central and East European literary and artistic sources from the 19th and the early 20th centuries. Stereotypes portrayed the klezmer as licentious and threatening. The two overarching images of Jewish musicians are of the fiddler and the cimbalom player. The Yiddish writers Sholem Aleichem (Shalom Rabinovitsh, 1859–1916), Mendele Moykher-Sforim (1835–1917), and Isaac Bashevis Singer (1904–1991), among others, depicted *klezmorim* in their work. Sholem Aleichem wrote about "Avrom the Klezmer" in his autobiographical novel *Funem yarid* (From the fair). He based his 1889 novel, *Stempenyu*, on real-life fiddlers from the latter half of the 19th century. The Polish poet Adam Mickiewicz's character Jankiel crystallized the image of the Jewish cimbalom player as an old, revered, Polish nationalist in his epic poem, *Pan Tadeusz*. Works by the artist Jean-Pierre Norblin de la Gourdine (1745–1830) and drawings of Michal Jozef Guzikov predate Mickiewicz's creation of the Jankiel character.

HISTORY

The Middle Ages gave rise to the professional Jewish musician in Europe and the Middle East. *Klezmorim* (plural of klezmer) served most European cities that had sizable Jewish populations. Much of what we know of the social practice of professional Jewish musicians from the Middle Ages through the Early Modern period is based on the restrictions imposed on them, either by local non-Jewish authorities or by internal Jewish community leaders. In 15th-century Germany, Jews relocated the site of a wedding in cases where a ruling family had provisionally restricted instrumental performance. In 16th-century Germany, Jews were required to pay taxes and to obtain performance authorization from local governing bodies. Regional authorities prohibited Jewish musicians from performing on certain days of the week, hours of the day, and during periods of mourning.

Jewish community leaders also regulated the activities of klezmorim. A Cracow Jewish community document from 1595 denounces klezmorim and prohibits them from performing on the street at night. A Frankfurt Jewish community charter from 1716 limited ensembles to four musicians and the performance hours to not past midnight. Minsk Jewish community records from 1797–1805 indicate that individual musicians were allowed to reside in the city and play for weddings, but forbidden to perform door-to-door on Hanukkah.

From the late 16th through the late 19th centuries, Jewish musicians formed guilds to protect their interests. In Prague, Jews were excluded from the municipal musicians' guild and not permitted to perform for non-Jewish functions. In 1641, however, the Jewish guild secured entitlement to perform for non-Jewish engagements.

In some areas, competition between Jewish and non-Jewish musicians gave rise to special decrees. In 1549, a Polish royal decree stipulated that Jews were forbidden to perform for non-Jews, and vice versa. Jewish and non-Jewish guilds occasionally reached their own agreements. In 1629 in Lvov, the Jewish and non-Jewish guilds came to a reciprocal understanding: the Jewish guild was allowed to play for Christian engagements; in turn, the Christian guild was allowed to perform for Jewish functions on the Sabbath and Jewish holidays.

From the mid-19th century onward, klezmorim and their descendants increasingly entered other professional musical worlds, such as Western concert music, the cantorate, the Yiddish theater, and jazz and other American popular musics. The European klezmer repertoire served as creative material for Jewish composers affiliated with the Saint Petersburg Conservatory (e.g., Joseph Achron, Aleksandr Krein, and Mikhail Gnesin). Jacob Hoffman (1895–1972), a virtuoso klezmer xylophonist, played percussion for the Philadelphia Orchestra and the Ballets Russes.

The great waves of immigration of East European Jews from 1880 to 1924 brought many klezmorim to American urban centers. Jewish American bandleaders of the early to mid-20th century included Abe Schwartz, I. J. Hochman, Abraham Elenkrieg, and Harry Kandel, among others. In Europe, repertoire was frequently localized and particular to a given *kapelye* (band); in America, cities developed their own distinct Jewish repertoires.

Between 1880 and 1950, American klezmer synthesized European klezmer and American musical styles; meanwhile, the clarinet superseded the violin as the primary melodic instrument, with European-born clarinet virtuosi Naftule Brandwein (1889–1963) and Dave Tarras (1897–1989) as leading proponents of the style. During the 1910s, the Oriental foxtrot emerged as a genre that fused Eastern European melodies with New Orleans jazz; "Yiddishe Blues" (1918) is considered the first recording of this style. In the 1930s, the performance of traditional klezmer repertoire dwindled just as a Jewish jazz craze took hold, as evidenced by the enormously popular recordings "Bay Mir Bistu Sheyn," "Di Greene Kuzine," and "And the Angels Sing."

Assimilation and the waning of traditional wedding rituals led to the decline of klezmer in America. The ritual function and repertoire attenuated as Jewish weddings moved from the outdoors of Europe to the catering halls of American cities. The professional Jewish musicians who performed Jewish dance repertoire in America stopped calling themselves klezmorim, largely due to its Old World connotations. Although some first-generation klezmorim found work performing at weddings and other social functions, others took on new vocations as factory workers or shopkeepers. By the second generation, New York klezmorim had adapted their skills to work in popular, classical, or club-date musics, if they had not already left the music profession altogether. Musicians who performed Jewish jobs frequently did so for the Yiddish radio, hotels in the Catskills, Hasidic weddings, or Jewish club dates.

The near-complete destruction of European Jewry in the Holocaust, Stalinist anti-Semitic campaigns, postwar Zionist hegemony, Israeli hegemony, and assimilation in America led to the near invisibility of klezmorim and the art of the klezmer in the postwar era. Then, in the mid-1970s, a handful of young American Jews began learning and performing East European Jewish roots music. They relied on a canon of recorded and print materials, and older, master musicians. This efflorescent interest came to be known as the klezmer revival, renaissance, or

The New Orleans Klezmer All Stars performing in 2017. Klezmer is a Jewish, instrumental style of music. (Douglas Mason/WireImage)

revitalization. The meaning of "klezmer" shifted from the performer of the music to the newly emergent scene and genre of music it represented. Yiddish folk song, not historically a part of klezmer, became incorporated into klezmer in the context of the revival.

Some of the early revival bands, such as the Klezmorim, the Klezmer Conservatory Band, Kapelye, and Walter Zev Feldman and Andy Statman, significantly affected the preservation, study, and transmission of this music. In the 1980s and 1990s, the bands Brave Old World and the Klezmatics took klezmer music in new artistic directions. The revival spread beyond North America, with sizeable scenes arising in Germany, Poland, and Russia. The Israeli clarinetist Giora Feidman, some of whose work predated the American revival, was especially important in shaping the klezmer revival in Europe. Musics denoted as klezmer throughout the revival have ranged from historically informed performances to creative explorations.

SOCIAL PRACTICE

Klezmorim had relatively low social status within the Jewish community, which may be attributed to the liminal position of instrumental music performance (since its prohibition in the synagogue service following the destruction of the Temple in 70 CE), and to their fraternization and performance with non-Jews and professional Roma musicians. The dismissive Yiddish saying, *"er hot a vert azoy vi der poyker bay di klezmer* (He's worth as much as the drummer in a klezmer band)" demonstrates the klezmer's inferior social standing. Nevertheless, klezmorim held their profession in comparatively high regard. This point is illustrated in *klezmer-loshn* (klezmer slang), which terms an ordinary Jew a *yold* (ordinary person or nonmusician).

The term "klezmer" first referred to the musician, rather than the musical instrument, in a Jewish community document from Cracow dated 1595. The klezmer was a part of a professional, hereditary class of musician. Klezmer dynasties were exclusively male until the early 20th century, when some klezmorim trained their daughters in the art. Klezmorim worked primarily as part of a family-based *kapelye* or *kompanye* (band). The kapelye served as a Jewish institution, paying fees to ill musicians or to widows of deceased members. Given territories often were monopolized by a primary klezmer family. In early 20th-century Galicia, for example, the Schwider klezmer family kapelye dominated Jewish music work in Lviv.

As the klezmorim were never guaranteed work, kapelyes frequently competed with one another, particularly when vying for a job for a wealthy family, or when more than one ensemble resided in an area. Scholars have discovered the competitive nature of the profession from prohibitions: for example, in Bohemia in 1641 and 1651, non-Jewish musicians appealed to local authorities to proscribe Jewish musicians from performing at non-Jewish celebrations.

Klezmer families frequently intermarried with other klezmer families; less frequently, they intermarried with *badkhonim* (plural of *badkhn*, wedding jester, or master of ceremonies) families. The renowned klezmer clarinetist Dave Tarras came from a family of badkhonim. Like other Jewish practices of onomastics, klezmorim sometimes took occupation-specific surnames, among them Klezmer, Musiker, Musikant, Bas(s), Fi(e)dler, Geiger, Zimbalist, Zimbler, Pauker, Baraban, and Secunda.

The first violinist, upon whose skillset the greater artistic merit of the ensemble often was assessed, most frequently led kapelyes. Klezmorim performed for both Jews and non-Jews (e.g., local nobility and peasants) for weddings or celebratory events. At weddings, they earned a sum from the bridal family, and the rest from guests who requested tunes. Musicians were paid hierarchically, with the first violinist paid the most and the drummer the least. Kapelyes occasionally took a badkhn or a professional dancer with them to an engagement. To make ends meet, klezmorim often worked a second occupation as barbers or craftspersons, such as watchmakers, glaziers, tailors, upholsterers, hatters, or braid makers. Another means of earning income came from music lessons.

Klezmorim had their own argot (professional slang), *klezmer-loshn*. Its most obvious function was concealment. Klezmer-loshn had its most sizable lexicon for numeric and monetary terms, followed by those for food, professions, and body parts. It shared vocabulary with *ganovim-loshn* (the Yiddish argot of criminals). However, by the time Yiddish philologists began to study klezmer-loshn in the late 19th century, it was already in decline.

Klezmorim learned their art through a variety of methods. Dynastic klezmorim observed a patrilineal passage of their knowledge and skills by rote and on-the-job training, usually from an early age. In certain instances, klezmorim took formal lessons with expert musicians, learning music fundamentals such as scales and etudes. Music literacy among klezmorim varied. Klezmorim sometimes notated their compositions and repertoire, or played European dance tunes and Western classical solo and chamber repertoire from sheet music.

MUSIC

The klezmer repertoire contained both dance and nondance music, frequently tailored to the requirements and affinities of patrons. Klezmorim accompanied the bridal party on the street to the wedding with *gas-nigunim* (street tunes). Gas-nigunim, mostly in triple meter, likely were adapted from the Moldovan or Romanian *zhok*. The genres *mazltov* (congratulations), *dobranotsh* (good night), *dobridyen* (good day), and *zay gezunt* (good-bye) functioned as greeting and farewell tunes.

Popular Jewish dance genres included the *freylekhs* (also known as *hopke, redl, karahod, dreydl, kaylekhiks, rikudl*), *sher, skotchne,* and *khosidl*, all of which are in duple meter. These dances were musically similar, but varied choreographically. The form of the freylekhs is most often binary or ternary. The sher is a group figure dance for sets of four couples. Though musically comparable to the freylekhs, kapelyes usually played specific select tunes for a sher. Skotchnes were more technically detailed than freylekhs. Klezmorim also performed a cosmopolitan, pan-European dance repertoire, such as the polka, quadrille, lancier, rondo, and waltz, as well as local repertoire, such as the Polish mazurka and Ruthenian kolomeyka. The klezmer *bulgarish* (later *bulgar*), which originated from the Bessarabian *bulgărească*, came to dominate the American klezmer repertoire in the 20th century. In America, the older klezmer repertoire came to be known simply as "the bulgars." Standard cadential formulas typically indicated the end of a tune to dancers.

Nondance music genres were performed as ritual or to listen to. The *kale-bazetsn(s)* (variants: *kale-bazingen, kale-baveynen, bazetsn di kale, bazingen di kale,* and *baveynen di kale*) accompanied the ritual seating of the bride. It consisted of interchanges of free rhythmic extemporizations usually between solo violin and badkhn. Sometimes, the ensemble punctuated the badkhn's couplets and the violinist's improvisations on the cadences. Klezmorim performed the *taksim* and *doina* for listening during the wedding banquet. These semi-improvisatory, nonmetric genres were adorned with melisma, trills, and other ornaments. Doinas and taksims were generally followed by lively, metric tunes.

Klezmorim typically varied the melodic line and imbued it with affects, such as the *krekht* (groan) or *kneytsh* (catch), as well as ornaments of pan-European musics, such as grace notes, mordents, trills, and glissandos. The contra violin player or the cellist usually extemporized an accompaniment part. Some violin pieces called for alternate tunings. *Shpiln oyf di tsvey strunes* (playing on two strings) was one such tuning (A-D′-F′-F″): a notch was cut into the nut of the violin; the top two strings (tuned in octaves) were positioned closer together; and the same finger depressed both strings.

Klezmer employs the Western major and minor scales, as well as several Jewish modes. The Jewish modes *freygish* and *mi sheberakh* (Beregovski refers to these Jewish modes as "altered Phrygian" and "altered Dorian," respectively) are characterized by their augmented second interval, signature motifs, and cadential phrases. In freygish, the augmented second interval occurs between the second and third scale degrees (e.g., G-A$^\flat$-B-C-D-E$^\flat$-F-G-F-E$^\flat$-D-C-B-A$^\flat$-G-F- E$^\flat$ -F-G); in mi sheberakh, it occurs between the third and fourth scale degrees (e.g., G-A-B$^\flat$-C$^\sharp$-D-E-F-G-F-E-D-C$^\sharp$-B$^\flat$-A-G-F$^\sharp$-G). The tonic triad in freygish is major; the tonic triad in mi sheberakh is minor. Beregovski observed that klezmorim sometimes rendered the second and fifth scale degrees slightly lower in natural minor than in other scales and modes.

Klezmorim performed solo, or as ensembles that ranged from two to 15 musicians. The ensemble size frequently was governed more by economic expediency and local mandates than by aesthetics. In 19th-century Europe, an average ensemble numbered three to six musicians. Klezmer instruments included the violin, contra violin (*sekund*), viola, lute, harp, zither, portable cimbalom (*tsimbl*), flute, clarinet, trumpet, cornet, trombone, tuba, cello, bass, bass drum, tenor drum, snare drum, tambourine, and cymbals. The harp and zither, primarily solo instruments, were defunct by the end of the 17th century. Jewish itinerant musicians favored the cimbalom from the late 17th through the early 20th centuries. A typical ensemble in late 19th-century Europe consisted of two violins, and cimbalom and/or bass, sometimes with flute. A common duo ensemble consisted of violin and cimbalom, or (less frequently) flute and cimbalom. Klezmorim were frequently multi-instrumentalists. The bandleader Nune Vaynshteyn of Kiev province, for example, "[was] an excellent fiddler who . . . was able to play all the klezmer instruments." In early and mid–20th-century America, klezmer ensembles often mirrored the instrumentation of American vaudeville or concert bands. The banjo, piano, and drum set were American additions to klezmer instrumentation.

Not unlike Roma *lăutari* (professional class of musicians), many klezmorim were virtuosic performers. Some garnered wide recognition in the European concert music world. Michal Jozef Guzikov (1806–1837) was born in the town of Shklov (in present-day Belarus) into a klezmer family. His father taught him and his brother to play Jewish and local ethnic repertoire on the violin and the flute. As a teenager Guzikov fashioned a new, folk instrument after the cimbalom, the *shtroyfidl* (straw fiddle). At age 20 he switched to this instrument full-time due to a respiratory illness. The family kapelye traveled and developed a far-reaching reputation, performing in salons and concert halls throughout Europe. Felix Mendelssohn (1809–1847), whose family had converted from Judaism to Christianity, extolled Guzikov's musical greatness in a letter to his mother dated 1836. Other exceptional klezmer artists included Stempenyu ("Yosele") Druker of Berdichev (1822–1879), Arn-Moyshe Kholodenko ("Pedotser," 1828–1902), Yekhiel Goyzman ("Alter from Chudnov," 1846–1912), Avram-Yitskhok Berezovskii ("Mitsi" or "Mitsya," 1844–1888), Nune and Rakhmiel Vaynshteyn, and Volf Tsherniavskii (1841–1930), among many others.

Amanda L. Scherbenske

See also: Ashkenazi Jews, Music of; Fiddle; Romani Music

Further Reading

Beregovski, Moshe, and Mark Slobin. 1982/2000. *Old Jewish Folk Music: The Collections and Writings of Moshe Beregovski*. Syracuse, NY: Syracuse University Press.

Feldman, Walter Zev. 2003. "Remembrance of Things Past: Klezmer Musicians of Galicia, 1870–1940." *Polin* 16, 29–57.
Slobin, Mark, ed. 2002. *American Klezmer: Its Roots and Offshoots*. Berkeley: University of California Press.
Slobin, Mark, Robert A. Rothstein, and Michael Alpert, eds. 2001. *Jewish Instrumental Folk Music: The Collections and Writings of Moshe Beregovski*. Syracuse, NY: Syracuse University Press.

Kodály, Zoltán (1882–1967)

Along with Béla Bartók (1881–1945), the Hungarian composer, ethnomusicologist, and educator Zoltán Kodály was one of the creators of a new style of Hungarian art music based on folk sources. He fostered the development of a broad-based and musically literate culture that challenged musical conservatism and promoted his signature characteristic juxtaposition of the traditional with experimental modernity. Bartók described Kodály's music as "the most perfect embodiment of the Hungarian spirit."

Coming from a musically inclined family in the rural area of Kecskemét, Kodály studied both folk and classical music as a child. His mother played the piano; his father played the violin. His elementary school training in Galánta exposed Kodály to folk songs sung by his fellow students. While studying at the Archiepiscopal Grammar School in Nagyszombat, Kodály studied the piano, violin, viola, and cello. Of his early works Kodály's *Overture in D minor* was premiered in February 1898 and his *Trio in E Major* for two violins and viola in February 1899.

Kodály matriculated at Budapest University in 1900, where he studied Hungarian and German; he also began studies at the Academy of Music, learning composition from Hans von Koessler (1853–1926). Kodály earned diplomas in composition (1904) and teaching (1905); in April 1906 he received his PhD with a dissertation titled *A Magyar népdal strófaszerkezete* (The stanzaic structure of Hungarian folksong). This research set Kodály on the course of his own fieldwork, commencing in 1905 when his collaboration with Bartók began, and continued for many decades, reflecting his interdisciplinary scholarship in music and language. Their collaboration eclipsed the assembly of folk song collections in the field and evolved into a lifelong friendship. Their initial collaboration yielded the publication of *Magyar népdalok* (Hungarian folksongs) in 1906.

The October 22, 1906, premiere of Kodály's composition *"Nyári este* (Summer evening)" enabled him to study in Berlin and Paris during the next six months, where he was exposed to the works of Claude Debussy. Upon returning to Hungary and completing another round of fieldwork collecting folk songs, Kodály was appointed professor at the Academy of Music, where he lectured in music theory and composition. A number of Kodály's pupils became internationally recognized, including Antal Dorati, Eugene Ormandy, Lajos Bárdos, and Jenő Ádám.

Kodály is one of the few artists in the 20th century to have achieved work of lasting value in a variety of fields: composition, ethnomusicology, and music education. Kodály's compositional career spans seven decades, beginning with his first surviving manuscripts (1897) to his last finished work (1966). By his own account,

Kodály began to improvise songs at the age of four and fragments in his estate indicate that he continued composing until his last days. Kodály's music highlights both a classical and a folk heritage, with a focus on melodic line reminiscent of Mozart and Haydn. Other influences include Gregorian chant, Palestrina, and Bach keyboard works. It is the Hungarian folk intonation throughout his career, however, that kept his musical style fresh and inviting. As a result, Kodály has been described as both a traditionalist and modernist, even though his music heavily relies on peasant culture.

The first public performances of Kodály's works occurred in March 1910, when Bartók and the Waldbauer-Kerpely Quartet played his opp. 2, 3, and 4. Several of his piano pieces were performed in Paris to an enthusiastic audience, and in Zürich the Willem de Boer Quartet played the *First Quartet* on May 29, 1910. On August 3, 1910, Kodály married Emma Sándor (a/k/a Schlesinger), also a talented composer, pianist, poet, and translator.

In 1911, Kodály, Bartók and others formed the New Hungarian Music Society to ensure the accurate performance of contemporary works; the enterprise was short-lived due to public indifference and official resistance. Committed to preserving his country's folk music, Kodály drafted "*Az új egyetemes népdalgyűjtemény tervezete* (A project for a new universal collection of folksongs)" in 1913, which he and Bartók submitted to the Kisfaludy Society. The proposal was declined, but the two continued work until World War I temporarily halted fieldwork excursions. Kodály then focused on composition and the scientific classification of folk material. From November 1917 to April 1919 he turned to music criticism, publishing nearly 50 reviews in the literary magazine *Nyugat* and later in the liberal daily paper *Pesti napló*. Noteworthy are his articles on the importance of folk music and his analyses of Bartók's music.

Following World War I, Universal Edition offered Kodály a publishing contract (in 1921), and his *Psalmus hungaricus*, a large-scale oratorio for tenor, chorus, and orchestra written in less than two months, premiered in 1923 to celebrate the 50th anniversary of the union of Pest, Buda, and Óbuda into Budapest. The work's Zurich premier in 1926 signaled a turning point in the international recognition of Kodály's art. Building upon the success of *Psalmus hungaricus*, Kodály resurrected his career and increased his standing with the premiere of the singspiel *Háry János* (1926) and of the six-movement suite drawn from it in 1927. These works established Kodály's international stature: Toscanini, Mengelberg, Ansermet, and Furtwängler were among the first to champion his musical works.

Between 1924 and 1932, Kodály published arrangements for voice and piano of 57 folk songs and ballads in 11 books, collectively entitled *Magyar népzene* (Hungarian folk music) and several large-scale compositions were commissioned, including the *Galántai táncok* (Dances of Galánta) celebrating the 80th anniversary of the Budapest Philharmonic Society (1933); the orchestral variations on *Felszállott a páva* (The peacock) lauding the 50th anniversary of the Concertgebouw (1939); and the "Concerto for Orchestra" for that of the Chicago Symphony Orchestra (1940). Kodály's most popular orchestral compositions include the *Dances of Galánta*, a rondo-form symphonic poem noteworthy for its orchestration and the use of 18th-century *verbunkos* music at its core; and the singspiel *Háry János* (1926), about a fictional Transdanubian character who takes part in the Napoleonic wars, which demonstrates Kodály's gift for the comedic parody. His last major compositions—including *Zrinyi szózata* (Hymn of Zrinyi) for baritone and chorus (1954), the Symphony (1961), *Mohács* for chorus (1965), and the *Laudes organi* for chorus and organ (1966)—demonstrate his mature artistic creativity.

Kodály's research is summarized in *A magyar népzene* (1937); the 1982 English edition includes new musical examples and numerous addenda selected and drafted by Kodály. The study details the importance and taxonomy of folk songs and investigates the origins and performance of both traditional and 19th-century Hungarian folk song. The classification and editing of an extensive collection was led by Kodály as head of the folk music research group at the Academy of Sciences, a task he pursued until his death. Kodály received high government decorations (1947, 1952, 1962) and three Kossuth Prizes (1948, 1952, 1957) for his work, and the Academy of Sciences published monographs marking his 70th, 75th, and 80th birthdays. Kodály served as president of the International Folk Music Council (1961) and honorary president of the International Society of Music Education (1964). He received the Herder Prize in 1965 in recognition of his work in furthering East–West cultural relations.

Equally interested in music education, Kodály wrote singing exercises and choruses for young people, which served the dual purposes of both teaching and reviving the Hungarian choral tradition. Kodály's educational concept, including relative solmization, hand signs, rhythmic syllables, and a system of musical shorthand known as "stick" notation, has had a global impact upon music education. Its use in combination with specific folk song and art music examples makes the "Kodály method" extremely important in the teaching of music. Kodály institutes span the globe: from Tokyo to Boston, Sydney, and Kecskemét, international Kodály symposia have been held biennially from 1973; the International Kodály Society was founded in 1975. His former apartment was converted into the Zoltán Kodály Memorial Museum and Archives, and serves as a center for Kodály research.

Eldonna L. May

See also: Bartók, Béla; Hornbostel, Eric Moritz von

Further Reading

Chosky, Lois. 1981. *The Kodály Context: Creating an Environment for Music Learning.* Englewood Cliffs, NJ: Prentice Hall.

Chosky, Lois. 1999. *The Kodály Method,* 3rd ed. Englewood Cliffs, NJ: Prentice Hall.

Houlahan, Michael, and Philip Tacka. 1998. *Zoltán Kodály: A Guide to Research.* New York: Routledge.

Young, Percy M. 1964. *Zoltán Kodály: A Hungarian Musician.* London: Ernest Benn.

Kora

The *kora* is a West African plucked-string instrument of the harp variety. Thus, it is classified as a chordophone. It normally has 21 strings, although the number of strings is not completely standardized (some specimens have up to 25 strings). The kora is unusual for the harp family because it also includes two bridges (or one

> ### Banjo and Kora
>
> In addition to his work with the Virginia Minstrels, blackface musician and songwriter Dan Emmett was an accomplished player of the banjo. Emmett learned the instrument from an African American slave in the 1840s; the instrument was popular among both free and enslaved African Americans during the 19th century in the United States. The popularity of the banjo was due in no small part to the instrument's connection to African and Caribbean culture. The banjo is a remade instrument based on the West African *kora*—a stringed instrument with gourd body—which was recreated in the Caribbean and later in the American South. During the antebellum period, the proximity and isolation of plantation society brought the banjo in close contact with rural whites who, along with slaves, came to favor the instrument. Many slaves are credited with teaching their masters how to play the instrument; Dan Emmett's skill on the banjo was, therefore, not lost on white audiences of the time period.

bridge with strings on either side), which (in the manner of a cello) increase the tension of the strings. The bridge supports two courses of strings, so that each hand plucks a given set of pitches. It is also unique among plucked instruments in that the resonating cavity (formed by halving a calabash gourd) faces the performer during performance. The back of the gourd faces the audience. In this way, the sound production is somewhat similar to that of the Brazilian *berimbao*.

The kora is a traditional instrument of the Mande people, whose origins go back several centuries and whose ancestral homeland is now within the borders of present-day Guinea, Senegal, Gambia, Guinea-Bissau, and Mali. Traditionally, only a certain class of musicians played the instrument. This *jali* class of Mande people are descended from only a handful of families. The kora players were responsible for praise songs (to a local ruler, for example), storytelling, and oral history and genealogy of a village. Many jali would sing and play at the same time; others simply accompanied another singer. The kora is sometimes played with other traditional instruments, but it certainly has enough color and interest to stand on its own.

The 21 strings are tuned in four different ways, although each player may use an individual tuning style. Because the instrument is not fingered (on a fingerboard, such as a lute or guitar), the tuning of the instrument is extremely important, and represents the character of the player. One standard tuning, the *tomora* tuning style, is similar to the Western world's "just" intonation. In this tuning system, the third and seventh scale degrees are slightly lower than the standard equal-tempered tuning.

The two courses of strings for each hand generally alternate pitches from low to high, but the shortest strings (giving the higher pitches) are in fact *lower* on the instrument from the perspective of the player. Thus, the lowest strings (in pitch) are actually the closest to the player's face. The player plucks these low strings with the two thumbs, while the index fingers are used to play the higher pitches. In traditional playing and teaching of the kora, the teacher will use "lower" to mean a higher pitch, and a run that goes "down" does so on the instrument itself, even though the pitches are ascending.

Much of the repertoire for the kora is of a polyrhythmic variety, with the two hands creating a fascinating, shimmering sound. This patterned type of music is termed *kumbengo*, whereas fast and virtuosic runs are called *birimintingo*. The kumbengo was used as the accompaniment to sung or spoken text. In modern kora playing, it has a purpose similar to that of "comping" in jazz: a background field of notes upon which a soloist can improvise. Occasionally the performer may strike the hard calabash shell body, or stop a previously struck string with their other fingers. Like a Western harp, the kora has a relatively long sustain, especially on the lower pitches.

Although the kora is an ancient and traditional instrument, it has seen a renaissance in the 20th and 21st centuries. Rather than using the old metallic secondary resonator attached to the bridge to amplify the delicate sound of the instrument, players now use an electronic coil pickup or contact microphone to allow the sound to be heard in concert settings. This technology is a large part of the resurgence of interest in the instrument. Professional contemporary players, such as Toumani Diabaté, regularly play alongside leading jazz and rock musicians on recordings and stages around the world. Other influential kora masters are Foday Musa Suso, Mory Kanté, Jali Nyama Suso, and Jelimadi Sissoko. The instrument has been taken up in recent years by European and American players, many of whom have been students of West African teachers.

Christopher Gable

See also: Banjo; Berimbau; Djembe; Mande Music

Further Reading

Charry, Eric. 2000. *Mande Music: Traditional and Modern Music of the Maninka and Mandinka of Western Africa.* Chicago: University of Chicago Press.

Ellingham, Mark, et al., eds. 1999. *World Music: The Rough Guide; Vol. 1: Africa, Europe, and the Middle East.* London: Rough Guides.

Koto

The *koto* is a traditional Japanese long zither. The instrument was transmitted to Japan from China by at least the early eighth century and was part of the court music orchestra (*gagaku*), a context which continues to this day. Since that time, the instrument has been disseminated throughout Japan and established in various genres and locations. By the 17th century, one koto performance tradition was especially associated with blind male professional performers, who were strictly controlled within an intensely hierarchical and male-dominated organization known as *Tōdō-za*. After major political reforms toward the end of the 19th century, which included the disestablishment of the Tōdō-za, the koto was especially popularized in a new cultural milieu, with many more players taking up the instrument.

The koto is also known by several other names, including *sō* and *sō no koto*. Three broad types of koto have been classified according to their context of performance, and include some slight differences in construction and performance practice: *gakusō*, *chikusō*, and *zokusō*. The *gakusō* is the instrument of court music (as noted earlier); *chikusō* is the name of the koto used in the performance tradition called *Tsukushigoto*, which dates from the 16th century and had a Buddhist context (the tradition continues only in reconstructed performances); and *zokusō* is a term given to the everyday koto that emerged in the 17th century with the influential player Yatsuhashi Kengyō (1614–1685). The type of koto that is particularly prevalent today is known as *Yamadagoto*, which has its roots in the performance traditional known as Yamada-ryū.

From the 20th century on, a number of innovative koto were devised. Although smaller instruments had been used before this time, primarily for use when travelling, by the 1920s a number of new designs were being made. One influential performer, Miyagi Michio (1894–1956), was pivotal in making several new instruments that were directly related to the koto. Miyagi's *tangoto* (short koto), *jūshichigen* (17-string koto) and *hachijūgen* (80-string koto) are several such examples. Of these, the jūshichigen has survived in several slightly different forms; it offers a lower register during ensemble music, but has also developed its own solo repertoire. Miyagi's hachijūgen was an experimental instrument and only one public performance is known to have taken place, when Miyagi played an original piece of his and an arrangement of a J. S. Bach prelude. In the 21st century, many more innovative instruments have appeared. Some of these have been produced for use in school education, where the koto has enjoyed a renaissance as a result of the government requiring students to have experience with "traditional" Japanese musical instruments. Such instruments are often smaller and cheaper than standard koto. In addition to these instruments, there are also bass koto, koto with 20 to 25 strings, and 30-string koto.

The koto, which measures about 72 inches long, is made from a carved-out soundboard with a backboard added to it. The wood for both of these parts is usually paulownia. The inside of the soundboard often has abstract carvings that are thought to improve the sound of the instrument. Two sound holes are carved into the backboard, one toward each end. The koto's parts are named after a dragon's body, with such parts as a dragon's back head and tail. The front end of the soundboard is made in the shape of a dragon's mouth, which even has a dragon's tongue and lips. This tongue is often used as a plaque on which pictorial decoration is applied, often depicting auspicious natural objects.

The koto has 13 strings that are stretched over two fixed bridges (one toward each end of the soundboard), and 13 movable bridges that are positioned on the surface of the soundboard. The strings are secured at the head of the instrument, with the remainder wound into two circular bundles and secured at the tail end. The fixed bridges are made of a hard wood, the movable bridges from ivory or plastic, and the strings from silk or a synthetic material.

The player wears a plectrum on each of the thumb, index finger, and middle fingers. The plectra are made in various shapes and sizes, with materials sometimes also differing (ivory, plastic, or bamboo). For example, in the Ikuta performance tradition the plectra have a rectangular shape, whereas in the Yamada performance tradition they have an oval shape. In these performance traditions, players kneel toward one long side of the instrument, either at a slight angle toward the tail as in the Ikuta school, or straight on as in the Yamada school. Koto players in gagaku sit cross-legged when playing the instrument.

The koto has a number of performance traditions. Two of the main everyday performance traditions in the present day are the Ikuta and Yamada schools. The former dates to Ikuta Kengyō (1656–1715), and the latter to Yamada Kengyō (1757–1817). At first, these traditions were located in the Kansai and Kantō regions respectively, although nowadays they have been disseminated widely throughout Japan. After the disestablishment of the Tōdō-za, many newer performance traditions developed as a result of the demise of restrictions on who was allowed to play the instrument. Within the Tōdō-za, several titles could be awarded to great players, such as the title *Kengyō*. As koto traditions developed, they sometimes divided into branches or different lineages. This process of establishing new schools sometimes resulted from changing performance practices based on the activities of an influential player.

One characteristic of many performance traditions is the awarding of diplomas and performing names. Various levels of diploma exist within different schools, and some award a performing name that is typically related to the name of the head of the school.

Various tunings are used for the koto. One main tuning is called *hirajōshi*, which is a five-note scale: C-D♭-F-G-A♭. Koto performance often includes ornamental techniques that are played by either the left or the right hand. The three plectra are worn on the right hand and the main playing stroke is by the thumb, with the index and ring fingers used for certain ornamentation or playing techniques. The left hand is used to push down on strings behind the movable bridges in order to raise the pitch of a string (usually a half or whole tone), and sometimes to add embellishments after a string has been plucked. There are also some techniques that add scratching and buzzing sounds to add a different tone color to the notes.

A number of different notations are used in specific koto performance traditions. The notations are usually tablatures that show the string to pluck rather than the pitch. A string number is depicted in the notation, with the tuning and pitch of the instrument being predetermined. Some schools, such as the Ikuta school, use a notation with the string numbers shown in columns; others, such as the Yamada school, use a horizontal notation. Some experimental forms of notation have used systems that have the tablature read from right to left, and another type used 13 horizontal lines to represent each of the instrument's 13 strings. In this latter type of notation, the notes were represented with symbols from Western notation, although the pitches were opposite: low pitches at the top of the staff, and high pitches at the bottom.

The koto appears in many different performance contexts and styles of music. Of several genres of traditional music, three are particularly representative. *Danmono* defines a genre of purely instrumental pieces. Each piece consists of a number of sections (*dan*), such as three of six. One well-known piece, "*Rokudan no Shirabe* (Investigation in six sections)," is thought to be by Yatsuhashi Kengyō and is representative of the repertory. The piece opens very slowly and gradually increases in speed throughout the six sections until the last one, where it slows down considerably before ending. A genre of koto music that dates from the 17th century is *kumiuta*, which are song cycles with koto accompaniment. These pieces are extremely slow-moving and the koto player is also the singer. A later development in koto music is the genre called *tegotomono*, which is a form of music that alternates the voice with instrumental sections, some of which are very long. This genre is well known in the *sankyoku* ensemble that comprises koto, *shamisen* (lute), and either *kokyū* (fiddle) or *shakuhachi* (flute). There are many other music genres for the koto, both old and new. From the mid-19th century, after substantial political change, many new styles of koto music emerged. Some of these genres imitated ideas from Western music, including harmony and music form. More recently, some koto players have used the instrument in pop music.

Henry Johnson

See also: Shakuhachi; Shamisen

Further Reading

de Ferranti, Hugh. 2000. *Japanese Musical Instruments*. New York: Oxford University Press.

Johnson, Henry. 2004. *The Koto: A Traditional Instrument in Contemporary Japan*. Amsterdam: Hotei.

Malm, William P. 1959/2000. *Traditional Japanese Music and Musical Instruments*. New ed. Tokyo: Kodansha International.

Wade, Bonnie C. 2005. *Music in Japan: Experiencing Music, Expressing Culture*. Oxford: Oxford University Press.

K-Pop (Korean Pop)

A type of modern, youth-based pop music that emerged in South Korea in the late 1990s and garnered regional media attention in the early 2000s, K-pop has become a global phenomenon, with fandom growing significantly across Asia, Europe, Australia, and the Americas. The term is an abbreviation for "Korean pop music," and can thus arguably be used broadly to encompass all types of Korean pop music from different historical periods; however, this hyphenated phrase is more commonly used to denote a certain type of pop music that gained popularity in this era, and is the output of a particular production system. As a highly publicized cultural export, K-pop is now one of South Korea's most popular cultural attractions, with the country embracing the musical genre as part of its contemporary cultural identity on international platforms.

HISTORY

The 1990s was a time of increasing openness in South Korean society. After a succession of military governments, the first civilian president was elected in 1992, and the nation during this era saw a loosening of restrictions in the cultural sphere as well as heightened exposure to outside cultures facilitated in part by increased travel to and from the country. This was also a time of economic growth bolstered by a rising middle class that had both more leisure time and more spending power. One of the most significant cultural developments amid this backdrop was the *sinsedae* (literally "new generation"), an urban youth population that benefited from these changes and was seen as a consumer group in its own right. The cultural

> ### K-Pop
>
> K-pop has been a tremendously popular musical style in Asia for many decades, but it did not reach the cultural consciousness of many in Europe and the United States until 2012, when K-pop artist PSY's hit "Gangnam Style" became a YouTube phenomenon (it has now amassed more than 3.3 billion plays on YouTube and is ubiquitous on radio stations across the globe). Beyond PSY's success, K-pop has adopted the American popular music tradition of image; the current K-pop leaders are a group called BTS (a/k/a Beyond the Scene), a seven-member boy band formed in 2013. Their music aside, BTS is particularly known for unique styles of dress and appearance. In fact, each band member has a well-maintained hair style which drives their social media presence. BTS were the most retweeted celebrities in the world (regardless of country of origin) in both 2017 and 2018, showing the important connectivity among image, music, and social media for modern popular music artists throughout the world.

identity of the sinsedae was not moored in tradition; instead, this generation identified more freely with overseas (predominantly American) brand names, fashion, fast food, and consumer products.

Pop music underwent consequential changes during this period, most notably at the hands of artist Seo Taiji, who was considered a poster child of the sinsedae. Born Jeong Hyeoncheol in 1972, Seo Taiji was often referred to as the "President of Culture" during and after his time. Seo started off as a guitarist in a rock band and experimented with a variety of musical styles over the course of his career, including heavy metal and gangsta rap. However, his most important contribution was the popularization of hip-hop, having successfully localized the genre for a Korean audience. Aside from rapping in Korean, he also dislodged this version of hip-hop from some of the genre's typical extramusical associations (street culture, gangs, violence). His first hit, *"Nan Arayo* (I know)," which he debuted in 1992 with two others under the group name Seo Taiji wa Aideul (Seo Taiji and Boys), was about the departure of a lover, an occasion he relays with both regret and resolve. Musically, Seo incorporated a melodic chorus following verses that were rapped, which gave the song a familiar balance; this was crucial, considering the newness of rap to Korean audiences.

Seo was not the first Korean musician to experiment with rap, but he was the one who brought it to mainstream Korean youth. Another notable element in Seo's songs was dance, which he highlighted in his performances. Here again, Seo was not the first contemporary pop musician to include dance moves in performance, but he effectively brought it to the fore, replete with hip-hop gestures, attitude, and style. This points to an integral aspect of his music, namely visual presentation. It is worth mentioning that television was a significant medium for pop music, with artists performing and debuting on television (as opposed to radio), and Seo Taiji's music was as much watched as it was listened to. This presaged, if not set the stage for, what was to come. Seo Taiji was revolutionary in other ways as well, composing, arranging, producing, and even managing himself at a time when these aspects of a pop music career were normally taken care of for a singer; he even had his own backup dancers in the Boys.

Although some may consider Seo Taiji and his music "early K-pop" or "classic K-pop," it is perhaps more useful to consider him a precursor to the K-pop era. After all, Seo's music at the time was still referred to as *gayo*, a generic Korean term for popular song. Seo Taiji captured the imagination of a generation, but his was essentially a domestic audience, with perhaps the exception of young diasporic Koreans. Indeed, Korean pop music before the arrival of K-pop was mostly a domestic affair. It wasn't until the appearance of another group, H.O.T., in 1996 that the term "K-pop" began to emerge, mostly among overseas audiences.

Created by Lee Suman (also spelled Lee Soo Man), five-member boy band H.O.T. was one of Korea's first-generation idol groups that not only amassed a significant domestic following, but also played to receptive audiences abroad, most significantly in China. With experience as a musician, producer, and radio host, and also having studied in the United States, Lee had a good handle on different musical styles and was able to formulate a model that appealed to youth in the Asian region at a time when South Korea was globalizing. His music company, which grew to become SM Entertainment, would go on to be responsible for developing many of South Korea's most successful K-pop groups.

There are parallels to be drawn between Seo Taiji and the idol groups that followed, including the multimember group concept and a focus on choreography, but there are also notable differences that have developed into pronounced distinctions today, including a difference in production system, distribution and marketing, and means of consumption. K-pop has from the time of H.O.T. looked to external audiences and markets. Indeed, the term "K-pop" is commonly understood to have been coined outside Korea, although since its inception, it has been appropriated and touted by domestic Korean media, and speaks to a conscious awareness of the music's international outlook.

STYLE AND CHARACTERISTICS

K-pop borrows from a range of global Euro-American pop styles, including hip-hop, R & B, and a variety of pop genres, from electropop and technopop to bubblegum pop. The spectrum of styles is wide enough that using the term as an all-encompassing category can be somewhat misleading. There are, however, elements that can be said to unify most of what is known as K-pop. On the surface, much of the music is very visual in nature and comes with choreography that is usually an integral part of the song. Having peaked with the rise of the Internet, K-pop has significantly gained audiences through online media platforms such as YouTube, and fans frequently consume songs in repeat watchings through which they also learn a song's signature dance moves. Although there are solo artists, K-pop is more widely known for its multimember groups, which are organized by gender. There have been mixed-gender groups, but the most successful have been boy groups and girl groups. Dance moves often highlight a group effect with synchronized choreography; solo artists typically perform with a group of backup dancers. K-pop songs characteristically contain catchy hooks and small musical figures or motives that lend themselves to easy repetition. In both choreography and music, K-pop is manageable enough that audiences can join in, and the most popular songs have been known to spur flash mobs and cover versions; this participatory nature can be seen as a significant part of K-pop's appeal.

In contrast to the Western notion that a star is "born" or "discovered," K-pop stars are "made" through a rigorous system that is well known to fans. This is not to say that talent is unimportant; but hard work, sacrifice, and discipline are the prerequisites that are usually at the core of a K-pop career. An "idol" in Korean pop culture generally refers to a young celebrity who has been trained and groomed for several years by a management agency before debuting, usually as a singer. A K-pop idol's training may include dance and vocal coaching, lessons in a foreign language, and preparation on how to talk to and interact with the media. These are critical components of a successful K-pop career, and idol trainees consequently dedicate large amounts of time at their respective management agencies practicing these aspects. Composing, writing, arranging, producing, and marketing also fall within the purview of management agencies. Thus, these agencies are a key part of the K-pop culture, as their grooming and planning intimately inform the musical character and concept of an idol group. SM Entertainment, YG Entertainment, and JYP Entertainment are among the leading K-pop management agencies and have created some of the most popular idol groups in the first decade of the 2000s.

THE KOREAN WAVE

The rise and visibility of Korean pop culture in the Asian region toward the end of the 1990s gave rise to a new term that was used increasingly by regional media: *hallyu*, or the "Korean Wave." The Korean Wave initially denoted the popularity of Korean pop culture in neighboring countries. K-pop was an important agent of this cultural phenomenon (the other being Korean TV dramas, or "K-dramas"), and by the middle of the first decade of the 21st century, South Korea had established a reputation as provider of pop culture chic. This was significant because the country had until that time not been recognized as an exporter of quality pop culture or creator of pop culture trends.

With hallyu, South Korea began to participate in an international pop culture network, joining the ranks of Japan and Hong Kong in pop culture production in the region. The Korean Wave was not a consciously engineered cultural project of South Korea; rather, it is perhaps best understood as a result of good timing. There is a constellation of things that can be seen as having contributed to the Korean Wave, from the relaxing of domestic censorship laws to the warming of relations in the region and growth in the Asian media market, to the rising production value of K-pop and Korean TV dramas and the relatively lower cost of these TV dramas at the time. Increasingly, K-pop stars are also acting in Korean TV dramas or singing on drama soundtracks, creating a synergy between these two streams.

K-pop idol groups have gained a vibrant following outside Asia, and a growth in overseas recognition and fan groups has proceeded hand in hand with more international concerts. But the biggest publicity boost came in 2012 with singer-rapper PSY's global hit, "Gangnam Style." The song's upbeat and comic video was the first in YouTube history to surpass 1 billion views and remains the most watched of all time, at well over 2 billion. PSY is somewhat of an anomaly in K-pop because he was not a product of idol management training; he also did not fit the age bracket or possess the physique of a typical K-pop idol. Yet his song and its signature "horse dance" seeped into the mainstream American pop lexicon when it debuted, and created enough attention to introduce K-pop into a global pop consciousness.

K-POP TODAY

With fan groups growing internationally, organized K-pop events have also grown in number. KCON is a large-scale music festival and pop culture convention centered on K-pop that began in Los Angeles in 2012. The yearly affair has expanded and in subsequent years the convention has also taken place in the New York area, Paris, Japan, and Abu Dhabi. K-pop idols are high-profile stars who are the pride of the South Korean pop culture industry; they are employed as brand models domestically and abroad, and often take on a de facto role as cultural ambassadors, introducing Korea to foreign audiences when they go abroad. More and more, youngsters in South Korea aspire to become K-pop stars, and with a growing number of visibly supportive parents, this musical path may be well situated to supplant the longtime popularity of traditional music lessons in classical piano or violin.

K-pop's international perspective can been seen in lyrics that increasingly contain English words, phrases, and sentences. In addition, more idols are now conversant,

K-pop group U-Know Yunho performing in 2018. K-pop is a generic term frequently used for the popular music of South Korea, but can also refer to a specific style that emerged in the 1990s. (Visual China Group via Getty Images)

if not fluent, in English as a principal second language; many idols are trained in Mandarin or Japanese as well. There is also a growing number of K-pop idols that are overseas Korean (e.g., Korean American), non-Korean Asian, or multiracial Korean. Notable current and former artists in the K-pop arena include Big Bang, Girls' Generation, Super Junior, SHINee, 2NE1, f(x), Infinite, Exo, BTS, BoA, TVXQ, Infinite, Rain, Wonder Girls, KARA, 2PM, T-ara, Sistar, Miss A, Teen Top, Got7, AOA, I.O.I., and Red Velvet, with new groups debuting consistently year to year.

The development of K-pop has also come with a real growth in other popular music genres, including "homegrown" Korean hip-hop and Korean indie music. As these genres develop in earnest, musical boundaries become more pronounced, posing challenges to the use of "K-pop" as a blanket musical category even as it remains at the forefront in the advance of Korean pop culture abroad.

Hae Joo Kim

See also: Cantopop; Chinese Pop; Indonesian Pop Music; J-Pop; North Korea, Music of

Further Reading

Chace, Zoe. 2012. "Why K-Pop Is Taking Over The World." *NPR Planet Money*, October 16. https://www.npr.org/sections/money/2012/10/16/163039109/episode-410-why-k-pop-is-taking-over-the-world.

Cho, Hae-Joang. 2005. "Reading the 'Korean Wave' as a Sign of Global Shift." *Korea Journal* 45(4), 147–182.

Howard, Keith. 2002. "Exploding Ballads: The Transformation of Korean Pop Music." In Timothy J. Craig and Richard King (eds.), *Global Goes Local: Popular Culture in Asia*, 80–95. Honolulu: University of Hawaii Press.

Kim, Chang Nam. 2012. *K-Pop: Roots and Blossoming of Korean Popular Music*. Seoul: Hollym.

Russell, Mark. 2008. *Pop Goes Korea: Behind the Revolution in Movies, Music and the Internet Culture*. Berkeley, CA: Stone Bridge Press.

Shin, Hyunjoon. 2009. "Have You Ever Seen the *Rain*? And Who'll Stop the *Rain*? The Globalizing Project of Korean Pop (K-Pop)." *Inter-Asia Cultural Studies* 10(4), 507–523.

Kulintang

Kulintang is an indigenous musical tradition from the southern Philippines that refers to a melodic instrument of horizontally laid gong-chimes, the ensemble of suspended gongs and a drum that includes the kulintang, and the music genre itself. Kulintang is significant to Philippine cultural heritage because it predates the arrival of Islam and survived 300 years of Spanish rule and nearly 50 years of American colonization. The kulintang, as a main melodic instrument, features several gong-chimes that have a raised center or "boss" to focus the pitch. The instrument is found among a number of different cultural-linguistic groups living on the coasts of the southern region of the Philippines and thus has different spellings and pronunciations, such as *kolintang* by the Maranao people or *kulintangan* by the Tausug and Sama-Bajau. The number of gong-chimes on the instrument ranges from five to nine, as does the number of larger suspended bossed gongs in the ensemble, depending mainly on the community. Other coastal and seafaring peoples of island Southeast Asia have related traditions, such as those found in parts of Indonesia and Malaysia, particularly on the island of Borneo.

The most internationally known styles of Philippine kulintang come from the Maguindanao and Maranao peoples, due to the work of two native-born scholars who immigrated to the United States in the late 1970s and received their degrees in ethnomusicology at the University of Washington: Mr. Danongan S. Kalanduyan (a Magindanao) and Dr. Usopay H. Cadar (a Maranao). Kalanduyan received the National Endowment for the Arts Heritage Fellowship Award in 1995. Both ethnomusicologists trained American and Filipino American students who have gone on to form their own groups over the past few decades, most notably Eleanor Academia of the World Kulintang Institute and Bernard Ellorin of the Pakaraguian Kulintang Ensemble.

Both Maranao kolintang and Magindanano kulintang feature a row of eight gong-chimes that ascend in pitch from left to right, though they vary in scale, tuning, and repertoire. Kulintang gong-chimes are laid in a wooden frame resting on taut strings that allow each gong some movement to ring. The frame may either rest on the ground or be elevated on legs, the latter allowing the player to sit in a chair. The beaters are made of soft wood, providing a soft but firm sound when striking the boss or raised center of each gong.

Tuning and scales of the gong-chimes of the kulintang instrument vary widely among Philippine indigenous communities and even from village to village, depending on the availability of gongs and the preference of individual players. The scales may be organized in a variety of pitch patterns, but generally are mostly pentatonic in character, including equidistant whole steps, half steps, and thirds spanning about an octave. One tuning made by the late kulintang maker Zacaria Akman Ambao in Cotabato City is $C-D^\flat-F-G^\flat-G-B-C^\sharp-E$. The technology and knowledge to forge bronze gongs is no longer available in the Philippines, but kulintang makers will make kulintang out of brass, melting down old bullet casings and padlocks, and using the lost-wax process for casting. Occasionally cheaper instruments are hammered out of sheet metal; these have a bright, loud sound.

Other instruments in the kulintang ensemble are *agung*, a large hanging bossed gong with a wide rim; *gandingan*, a set of four large hanging bossed gongs with narrow rims; *babandil* or small "time-keeper"; and a single-headed goblet-shaped drum of stretched animal skin called *dabakan*. The agung is considered an older instrument than the kulintang because it is found widely among various ethnolinguistic groups in the southern Philippines on the coasts and interior and among both Islamic and *lumad* (tribal) people. The agung's low reverberating sounds may be dampened with one hand as the other strikes the boss of the gong with a rubber-tipped mallet. Occasionally two instrumentalists (for example, among the Maranao) play a pair of agung to form an interlocking layer, the lower one being struck on the beat of a rhythmic mode and the higher in syncopation and variation. Among the Magindanao, competitions are held for agung players who exhibit their virtuosity in speed and inventiveness in improvisation using one, two, or even three gongs at a time.

The Magindanao have a unique instrument called gandingan, which is a set of four large hanging bossed gongs with narrow rims played by one player. Children or young people assist in steadying the gongs so that they do not reverberate excessively and also learn the music this way. The pitches of the gandingan ascend from lower to higher, left to right, with two gongs facing each other, and usually correspond in pitch to the lower four gongs on the kulintang. The gandingan player plays a set pattern that includes some syncopation, or may also improvise in response to the kulintang player's variations. In competitions or exhibitions, a Magindanoan gandingan player will demonstrate virtuosity in speed and improvisation, typically on three rather than four gongs. A musical language that is understood by the older generation can be communicated on gandingan in a style called *kapagapad*.

The rhythmic section of the ensemble consists of the babandil or "time-keeper" gong and the dabakan or conical-shaped drum. When no babandil is available, a player may tap the rim of the agung or gandingan to play the rhythmic mode around which other members of the group add the appropriate rhythmic pattern and melodic mode. When no dabakan is available, a player may use a chair, overturned trash can, or plastic jug to play the beat with two long flat bamboo sticks.

The structure of kulintang music is focused on improvisation on conventional melodic sets, interlocking supporting parts, and a rhythmic mode or structure that organizes the music. The melody is improvised upon by the kulintang player, traditionally a woman but nowadays either gender. The quality of performers' musicianship is based on their ability to improvise and show off their virtuosity and skill rather than executing a pre-composed piece. Magindanaon audiences are highly critical of a musician's proficiency even if they do not play the music themselves. Musicians who grow up with the tradition and play from a young age internalize basic melodies and rhythmic patterns, and this fluency allows them to demonstrate their virtuosity in performance as well as to interact closely with the improvisatory playing of the other ensemble members.

In the Magindanaon kulintang ensemble, two hands are used that play melodic, four-note patterns using rhythmic and syncopated double beats. Five types of pieces with recognizable rhythmic modes are called *binalig*, *duyog*, *sinulog*, *tidtu*, and *tagonngo*. The first four are played either in *kamamatuan* (old) style, which is slow and stately, or in *kangungudan* (new) style, which is faster and more rhythmic. Each village may have its own recognizable manner of playing these pieces, and configure the ensemble to suit the availability of instruments or players. Tagonggo is played for the *sagayan* dance or as part of a ritual for healing called *pagipat*. The babandil starts the piece first by playing a repeating pattern signaling the rhythmic mode. *Sinulog a kamamatuan* (sinulog in the old style) has a four-beat meter with a repeating pattern of quarter-eighth-eighth-quarter-quarter or long short-short long-long. The dabakan then enters with a pattern appropriate to the rhythmic mode established by the babandil. Typically two agung play an interlocking pattern of four to eight beats that adds syncopation to the rhythmic mode. The gandingan enters using a four- to eight-beat pattern that adds rhythmic and melodic variety to the rhythmic mode. Expert gandingan players such as Kalanduyan can create a dynamic and complex countermelody to the kulintang's melody. The kulintang usually enters last and is the main focus of the music. Each melodic phrase or pattern is repeated at the discretion of the kulintang player before transitioning to another pattern in the melody. The entire melody typically moves from the lower half of the kulintang to the higher register and back down. However, expert kulintang players such as the late Amal Lemuntod innovated within this tradition, and occasionally started on the higher register and moved down. The late prominent ethnomusicologist José Maceda wrote that "[t]he musical interest lies in the permutation of the cells, the performer deciding on the combination of gongs, the length of time [s]he will repeat it, when to add some and to suppress others, and when to transfer to another register or to a cell above or below" (Maceda, 2008). The typical progression of pieces starts duyog, sinulog, and binalig played in kamamatuan and then kangungudan style. There are variations on this order according to the preference of the ensemble.

Maranao kulintang tradition includes several kinds of pieces linked to different meanings and symbolism (Cadar, 1996, p. 99). For example, *kasulampid* represents a relationship of social conflict, so the kulintang player's sticks cross each other. Generally, however, the left hand of the kolintang player, exemplified by the piece *kapagonor*, keeps a steady repeating beat that functions like a drone and is played on the flat part of gong rather than on the boss. The right hand plays melodic patterns in units of two and repeats or slightly varies before moving on to another pattern. Like Magindanoan pieces, the variation, repetition, ornamentation, and extension of patterns creates unique and dynamic pieces formed out of shorter recognizable parts. Cadar writes that a drummer in a kolintang ensemble may play in an interactive way to "lure the [female] kolintang player into a variety of exchanges [by] shift[ing] his rhythmic accents [to] . . . introduce a dramatic kind of staccato to alter the mood" (Cadar, 1996, p. 96). There are two agung players in the Maranao ensemble, playing one gong each to form an interlocking part, compared to the Magindanao in which one player plays both agung. Maranao women will incorporate impressive twirling of the sticks without missing a beat.

Indigenous music in the Philippines as practiced among its original communities is fast disappearing while academics strive to preserve and research it. In some areas kulintang music is still a part of village and community life, played during weddings and celebrations or to welcome family members home from travels to Mecca or work abroad. It is still played for entertainment and sometimes for competition, and in festivals such as the annual Sharif Kabunsuwan festival in Cotabato City, Mindanao.

Mary Talusan Lacanlale

See also: Philippines, Music of the

Further Reading

Cadar, Usopay H. 1996. "The Role of the Kolintang Music in Maranao Society." *Asian Music* 27(2), 81–103.

Gaerlan, Barbara. 1999. "In the Court of the Sultan: Orientalism Nationalism, and Modernity in Philippine and Filipino American Dance." *Journal of Asian American Studies* 2(3), 251–287.

Kalanduyan, Danongan Sibay. 1996. "Maguindanaon Kulintang Music: Instruments, Repertoire, Performance Contexts, and Social Functions." *Asian Music* 27(2), 3–18.

Maceda, José. 1998. *Gongs and Bamboo*. Diliman: University of the Philippines Press.

Talusan, Mary. 2014. "Muslim Filipino Traditions in Filipino American Popular Music." In Iraj Omidvar and Anne R. Richards (eds.), *Muslims and American Popular Culture*, 387–404. Santa Barbara, CA: Praeger.

Kuti, Fela (1938–1997)

One of the most influential popular musicians of the 20th century, and a leading figure of the postcolonial African counterculture, Fela Kuti was first and foremost a cultural and political iconoclast, pioneering the Afrobeat genre of music in the 1970s and acting as a thorn in the side of a series of dictatorships in his native country of Nigeria. Through his legendary bands Afrika '70 and Egypt '80, Fela's music drew upon nearly all of the major musical styles of the African diaspora, from jazz and highlife to funk, Afro-Caribbean music and indigenous African rhythms. Meanwhile, the strident and biting political satire contained in his most famous songs earned the outspoken singer and multi-instrumentalist many powerful enemies, leading to sustained political repression and censorship that would follow him throughout his tumultuous career.

Born Olufela Olusegun Oludotun Ransome-Kuti on October 15, 1938, in Abeokuta, Nigeria, Fela was the fourth of five children of an eminent and wealthy Yoruba family. His father, the Reverend Israel Oludotun Ransome-Kuti, was an Anglican pastor and university-educated labor union activist; his mother, Funmilayo Ransome-Kuti, was a prominent women's rights leader and founder of the Nigerian Women's Union. While embracing many Western cultural values, Fela's parents also were at the forefront of the movement for Nigeria's national independence and an end to British colonial rule, which would not come until 1960, five years after the Reverend Ransome-Kuti's death.

Resisting pressure from his parents to enter a career in law or medicine, the young Fela gravitated toward the burgeoning highlife music scene in 1950s Lagos, where his parents sent him to secondary school. Performing poorly in his coursework, Fela dreamed of becoming a professional musician, and in 1958 convinced his mother to send him to the prestigious Trinity College of Music in London. Upon his arrival at Trinity, Fela took up the trumpet, and along with other African and West Indian students, formed a highlife band called Koola Lobitos. But although he performed popular African dance music for audiences, his ears became increasingly attuned to the work of such modern jazz legends as Miles Davis, Clifford Brown, and Lee Morgan.

After graduating from Trinity in 1963, Fela returned to Nigeria to pursue a career playing a fusion of highlife and jazz. While struggling to find a sound that connected with Nigerian audiences, in 1965 Fela formed a musical partnership that would play a decisive role in his future success, when he teamed up with the percussionist Tony Allen, who, like Fela, had been influenced by American jazz. Reforming the Koola Lobitos with Allen as his lead drummer, Fela enjoyed his first sustained success when he took his band on a 1967 tour of Ghana. However, when he returned to Nigeria at the conclusion of his trip, he found his home country breaking apart due to ethnic and religious animosities, and his music was ignored and overshadowed by newly emergent styles such as Congolese rhumba and African American soul. In part to escape the growing violence of the Biafran War (1967–1970) that would kill a million of his fellow countrymen, and in part to cultivate an international audience for his music, in 1969 Fela took the Koola Lobitos on a tour of the United States.

As it turned out, Fela's year in America would have a decisive impact on his evolving political and musical consciousness, as his time in the United States exposed him to the growing black nationalist and black power movements and the propulsive grooves of James Brown. Yet despite his high regard for Brown and other American musicians such as John Coltrane and Jimi Hendrix, Fela returned to Nigeria in 1970 determined to create a kind of music that would be authentically African, and not just an imitation of Western styles. As he later argued, "Africans should be taught to be able to contribute their own mind, their own culture, their own philosophy. Coming back from America in 1970, I then knew that I should not try to impress foreigners. I should impress my own people first" (Veal, 2000, p. 75).

It was through this philosophy that Fela would create Afrobeat in the early 1970s. Reforming his band as Nigeria '70 (later Afrika '70), Fela, now primarily playing the saxophone, began to develop a music that was rhythmically complex, relying upon both a Western drum set and numerous drums indigenous to the Yoruba people, such as the *akuba* conga. Melodically, Afrobeat was characterized by long, sinuous grooves punctuated by blistering instrumental solos, call-and-response patterns, and vocal chants performed by Fela and the many female backup singers he employed. Lyrically, Fela performed his songs in a kind of pidgin English that would be more easily decipherable to audiences around the African continent, ensuring that the messages contained in his music would travel far and wide.

It was through this formula that Afrobeat first emerged as a recognizable genre of music in the string of commercial hits Fela released in the early 1970s, including such songs as "Black Man's Cry," "Buy Africa," and "Why Black Man Dey Suffer." Such songs heralded Fela's identification with his African roots, but increasingly during the 1970s his music also targeted the political elite in Nigeria. Since the conclusion of the Biafran War in 1970, Nigeria had been ruled by a series of military dictatorships,

Nigerian musician and Afrobeat pioneer Fela Kuti performing in 1981. (Michael Putland/Getty Images)

as the country's political elite manipulated ethnic tensions and religious animosities between the nation's large Muslim and Christian communities, all the while profiting from Nigeria's oil and natural gas supplies while the vast majority of their countrymen lived in extreme poverty. As the son of political activists who had fought for Nigeria's independence, Fela used his music to broadcast his anger over the country's corrupt political system, through such songs as "Alagbon Close," which criticized police brutality and civil rights abuses. In response to Fela's provocations in this and other songs, the Nigerian government had Fela arrested literally hundreds of times, mainly on minor charges of drug possession and disturbing the peace.

Seeking refuge from government repression, Fela transformed his popular nightclub in Lagos into The Shrine, a sacred space where the singer could worship traditional Yoruba deities, pay homage to heroes of the struggle for black liberation, and openly denounce the Nigerian government and organized religion, particularly Christianity and Islam. Renaming the living quarters that surrounded his club the Kalakuta Republic, Fela announced his independence from Nigeria, offering his club as a space in which the repressive laws of the Nigerian dictatorship did not apply. In many ways connected to the broader global counterculture of the late 1960s and 1970s, Fela advocated the use of mind-altering drugs and principles of free love. In fact, in 1978 Fela would marry 27 women, most of them dancers who performed with him on stage, in a single day.

Such behavior made Fela a divisive figure in Nigerian society: beloved by the many urban youth who bought his records and attended his concerts at the Shrine, but reviled by the nation's elders, who saw in Fela a symbol of the decadence and debauchery that they blamed for the country's disorder and disunity. In February 1977, after Fela released the song "Zombie," which ridiculed military soldiers who served the interests of the country's dictatorship, General Olusegun Obasanjo, then head of the federal military government, ordered a raid of the Kalakuta Republic. On February 18, 1977, Nigerian soldiers entered the compound, brutalizing and torturing its inhabitants, burning down the buildings, arresting Fela, and throwing his 77-year-old mother out of a window. Passing into a coma, Funmilayo Ransome-Kuti would die one year later. In response, Fela had his mother's coffin delivered to the front door of Obasanjo, a gesture that he later memorialized in his song "Coffin for Head of State."

After the attack on the Kalakuta Republic, Fela stepped up his efforts to change Nigeria's political system, forming a party called Movement of the People and attempting to run for president of Nigeria in the 1979 elections that marked Nigeria's first democratic vote in more than a decade. (His candidacy was ultimately disallowed.) Continuing to direct his ire at political corruption, Fela remained a target of the Nigerian government well into the 1980s. In 1984, Nigeria's then-military ruler Muhammadu Buhari had Kuti arrested on charges of currency smuggling. Described as a political prisoner by many international human rights organizations, Kuti was released from jail after 20 months. In the face of ongoing government repression and censorship, during the latter half of the 1980s, Fela increasingly relied upon international audiences in order to play his music in public. Touring Europe and the United States, Fela remained an outspoken critic of political corruption in his home country, as well as Western support for apartheid South Africa, subjects covered at length in his 1989 album *Beasts of No Nation*.

Fela's musical output slowed significantly in the 1990s, as the singer grew increasingly weary of political strife and controversy. Like millions of other Africans during this time period, Fela contracted HIV/AIDS, yet refused treatment, claiming that AIDS was a "white man's disease." He died of complications from his illness on August 2, 1997, at the age of 58. Mourned throughout Nigeria and around the world, Fela's musical legacy would be carried forward by the many musicians who continued to play Afrobeat; through a popular musical that debuted on Broadway in 2009; and in the music of his eldest son, Femi Kuti, and his youngest son, Seun Kuti, both of whom became world-renowned musicians in their own right in the wake of their legendary father's passing.

David Crawford Jones

See also: Adé, "King" Sunny; Afrobeat (Afropop); Funk; Highlife; Jazz; Soul

Further Reading

Moore, Carlos. 2009. *Fela: This Bitch of a Life*. Chicago, IL: Chicago Review Press.

Olaniyan, Tejumola. 2004. *Arrest the Music!: Fela and His Rebel Art and Politics*. Bloomington: Indiana University Press.

Schoonmaker, Trevor. 2003. *Black President: The Art and Legacy of Fela Anikulapo-Kuti*. New York: New Museum of Contemporary Art.

Tenaille, Frank. 2002. *Music Is the Weapon of the Future: Fifty Years of African Popular Music*. Chicago, IL: Lawrence Hill Books.

Veal, Michael. 2000. *Fela: The Life and Times of an African Musical Icon*. Philadelphia, PA: Temple University Press.

Ladysmith Black Mambazo

Founded by Joseph Shabalala (1941–2020) in 1960 in the eastern South African town of Ladysmith, the male vocal ensemble Ladysmith Black Mambazo has established itself as one of the foremost a capella choral groups in the world, bringing forth the music of migrants, urban workers, and street musicians. The tradition began when Zulu workers from the city of Durban and surrounding small towns formed amateur male choirs modeled after church and school ensembles in the post-World War II (1939–1945) years. Shabalala's first group, The Blacks, performed Christmas concerts at farms in the small towns west of Durban. The music blended ragtime, call-and-response patterns, and indigenous part-singing first known as *ingoma ebusuku* (night music). It also incorporated step dancing (*isicathamiya*), later known as *cothoza 'mfana* (sneak up, boy). These choirs held all-night competitions in the workers' hostels; performers wore matching costumes, and executed intricate dance movements with their arms, torsos, and feet. Ladysmith Black Mambazo is known for some of the most intricate choreography in the genre, which became the standard for the music and dance of such workers' choirs.

The group took its name from Ladysmith, the town where Shabalala grew up; "black" to represent the color of oxen, the strongest beasts of burden in the town; and "mambaza," the Zulu word for a chopping axe, which represented the group's ability to vanquish its competitors. Like other ensembles, the group's early performances were in *shebeens*, workers' hostels, and community halls, for local feasts and weddings. The singing incorporates three principal sounds, according to Shabalala: a high, keening ululation; a grunting, puffing sound made with foot stomping; and a certain swaying lyricism in singing the melody line. While these sounds appear singly or in tandem in others, Ladysmith Black Mambazo was the first to combine all three in one song, creating a new polyphonic stream that became known as *mbube* (lion in Zulu). One of the group's lasting achievements is the preservation of mbube as a male Zulu choral style.

Ladysmith Black Mambazo was discovered by West Knosi, an influential producer for Mavuthela, the black subsidiary of Gallo Records—South Africa's largest recording company—which had made hits since the 1960s by combining traditional South African music with pop. Nkosi produced Ladysmith Black Mambazo and established isicathamiya, the ensemble's "stalking style," with the incorporation of terraced dynamics. Together Nkosi and Ladysmith Black Mambazo produced 22 albums, creating a unique style that merged Zulu traditional styles with gospel. Every album that the group released was designated "gold" in South Africa, selling 25,000 copies, and some have sold in excess of 200,000 copies.

While achieving a certain level of fame in South Africa, the group did not rise to prominence until it was featured on Paul Simon's *Graceland* album in 1986. As

> **Ladysmith Black Mambazo and Apartheid**
>
> Despite its artistic and commercial success, Ladysmith Black Mambazo's collaboration with singer/songwriter Paul Simon on his 1986 *Graceland* album was not without controversy. Ladysmith Black Mambazo's work on that album catapulted them and South African *isicathamiya* singing into a global audience's consciousness, and the group has since gone on to a decades-long performing career, selling millions of albums as an internationally acclaimed touring act. However, in choosing to record with the South African group, Paul Simon knowingly broke a UN-backed cultural boycott of South Africa in response to the country's policy of apartheid. Simon paid the South African musicians scale rates and treated them fairly, though the creation of *Graceland* was further complicated by the fact that two tracks from the album ("Homeless" and "Diamonds on the Soles of Her Shoes") feature vocal arrangements made by Ladysmith Black Mambazo's leader Joseph Shabalala—who was not initially given songwriting credits on the album. By breaking the boycott, Simon was able to bring visibility and notoriety to an otherwise unknown (to the West) style of music and the plight of the musicians, criticisms notwithstanding.

a result of international exposure, the group has released more than 50 albums. A short-lived contract with Warner Bros. in 1988 produced the *Journey of Dreams* (1988) and *Two Worlds One Heart* (1990) albums. Compilation albums were released by the Shanachie label in the early 1990s; then Ladysmith Black Mambazo re-signed with Gallo in the mid-1990s. Another short-term contract with Wrasse produced the *In Harmony* album. Ladysmith Black Mambazo sang at Nelson Mandela's Nobel Peace Prize ceremony at Oslo City Hall on December 10, 1993, and at Mandela's presidential inauguration in 1994. Within hours of Mandela's death on December 5, 2013, the ensemble wrote a compelling tribute to the former president.

Eldonna L. May and Morgen Chawawa

See also: Afrobeat (Afropop)

Further Reading

Erlmann, Veit. 2000. "Communities of Style: Musical Figures of Black Diasporic Identity." In Ingrid Monson, ed., *The African Diaspora: A Musical Perspective*, 83–101. New York: Garland Publishing:.

Kivnick, Helen Q. 1990. *Where Is the Way: Song and Struggle in South Africa*. New York: Penguin Studio.

Ladysmith Black Mambazo. 2019. http://www.mambazo.com/index.

Muller, Carol Ann. 2008. *Focus: Music of South Africa*. New York: Routledge.

Rhoades, Rebecca. 2000. "Ladysmith Black Mambazo: Song of South Africa." *Sing Out! The Folk Song Magazine* 44(3) (Spring), 34–45.

Shabalala, Joseph. 2005. "Ladysmith Black Mambazo." In Hand Bordouitz (ed.), *Noise of the World: Non-Western Musicians in Their Own Words*, 213–220. Berkeley, CA: Soft Skull Press.

Ländler

Ländler is an umbrella term for a type of folk dance in a quiet 3/4 time and a two-part form, typically each with eight bars. In many regions of the Alps (mainly southern German-language areas in West Switzerland, the south of Germany, Austria, and the north of Italy), ländler dances, including their regional variants, were the most important dancing forms until the 1930s. They have characteristic arm movements and include singing (or yodeling), hand-clapping, and pounding.

The first edition of a ländler, published in 1702, was written for violin. In Vienna around 1760, the *Deutsche* (German), as the ländler was then named, was en vogue and conquered the dance halls. Originally a rural dance, at the end of the 18th century the ländler merged with the menuet, which was the most popular dance form in urban-courtly areas. At the beginning of the 19th century, the ländler was partly absorbed by the *Wiener Walzer* (Vienna waltz), but is still in use today.

Around 1800, the string trio (two violins and a double bass) became the most frequent instrumentation for the ländler. Since the early 19th century, the dulcimer (in Tyrol also the harp), trumpet, and clarinet have been added. In the last third of the 19th century, the button accordion was added to the violins—or replaced them. The music, which is in a major key, is diatonic; the melody often runs in arpeggios, and the harmony only uses the two main chords (tonic and dominant).

There are three main subspecies of the ländler, with individual regional dispersion: 1) *Steirer* or *Steirischer* (the term derives from the Steiermark, an area southeast of Austria) *wickler* (a term derived from the movement; *wickeln* = to wrap), which a single couple dances with much individual freedom; 2) *landler* (the term derives from the heartland in upper Austria; *Land* = land), a group dance for representation, which is rich on figures and uses simultaneous movement of all couples; and 3) *schuhplattler* (the term derives from *schuh* = shoe, and *platteln* = *schlagen* = to beat), a courting dance with rhythmic beats on thighs, shoes, and soles of feet, often danced by young men.

The ländler has influenced classical composers, mainly from Austria, beginning with its first appearance in *12 Ländlerische Tänze* (1787) by Johann Baptist Vanhal, and the six *Ländlerische* (1791) by Wolfgang Amadeus Mozart. Franz Schubert composed 118 ländler for one or two violins or piano; Gustav Mahler used the ländler type in the "trios" of his Symphonies No. 1, 2, 4, and 9; Alban Berg embedded a ländler in his opera *Wozzeck* (1921) and in his violin concerto (1935); and Wolfgang Rihm composed *Ländler* (first version for piano, second version for 13 string instruments) in 1979.

Jörg Jewanski

See also: Austro-German Dances; Schrammelmusik

Further Reading

Carner, Mosco (editorial reviser). 2001. "Ländler." In Stanley Sadie (ed.), *The New Grove Dictionary of Music and Musicians,* vol. 14, 222–223. London: MacMillan.

Haid, Gerlinde, and Mielke-Gerdes, Dorothea. 1996. "Ländler." In Ludwig Finscher (ed.), *Die Musik in Geschichte und Gegenwart, zweite, neubearbeitete Ausgabe, Sachteil; Vol. 5,* 911–916. Kassel, Germany: Bärenreiter.

Suppan, Wolfgang. 1977. "Research on Folk Music in Austria since 1800." *Yearbook of the International Folk Music Council* 8 (1977), 117–129.

Witzmann, Reingard. 1976. *Der Ländler in Wien. Ein Beitrag zur Entwicklungsgeschichte des Wiener Walzers bis in die Zeit der Wiener Kongresse* [The Ländler in Vienna. The history and development of the Viennese waltz up to the time of the Vienna Congress]. Wien: Arbeitsstelle für den Volkskundeatlas in Österreich.

Launeddas

The *launeddas*, or triple clarinet, is the most popular Sardinian folk instrument. Made of three pipes different in size, it is a polyphonic reed woodwind instrument played through the method of circular breathing.

The bass pipe (*basciu* or *tumbu*) is the longest and has no holes. It can produce a single note only (drone) according to the intonation of the instrument. The second pipe (*mancosa manna*) is five-holed. It plays the accompaniment notes and is fastened at the bottom to the bass pipe. The last and smallest pipe (*mancosedda*) is five-holed like the mancosa manna, but is independent. It performs the melody. The three pipes are tuned using beeswax.

The launeddas can be traced back to prehistory thanks to a famous bronze statuette discovered in Ittiri which displays a launeddas player. Similar instruments are still played in northern Africa and the Middle East. Launeddas are used for both secular and religious occasions. They have been involved in magical rituals as well, as in the case of the Argia rituals, which share some characteristics with the southern Italian phenomenon of tarantism. The contemporary tradition requires the players to stand in the middle and dancers to dance in a circle around them (*su Ballu Tundu*). The dance typically follows an obsessive and hypnotic scheme. The performance lasts, on average, between twenty and thirty minutes, but may take up to an hour. Further uses—other than accompanying dances—are associated with chants, processions, feasts, and weddings.

Among the main launeddas traditions, an important role is played by the School of Sinis, with the village of Cabras as its epicentre. Its dances, such as the *passu 'e duus, passu 'e tres, su ballu crabarissu, sa pastorella (processionale), sa missa sarda, su passu 'e cantai,* have been acknowledged to be remarkably antique.

Origins of the name "launeddas" have been traced back either to the Latin *ligulella* (small tongue), or to the Etruscan *ligūn* (a sort of flute). The first studies were conducted by the Sardinian Jesuit Matteo Madao (1723–1800), who collected songs and dances, and mentioned the launeddas. In the 1960s, the Danish ethnomusicologist Andreas Fridolin Weis Bentzon (1936–1971) recorded several sonatas which he catalogued and transcribed in modern notation. Other relevant ethnomusicological studies have been conducted by Paolo Mercurio. Some of the best-known launeddas performers are Efisio Melis, Antonio Lara, and Dionigi Burranca. Luigi Lai is considered one of the most important living "heirs" of this instrument. In 1997, he performed in the song *Il poeta di corte* (The courtly poet), written by the Italian songwriter Angelo Branduardi and featured on the CD *La pulce d'acqua* (The water flea).

Jacopo Mazzeo

See also: Italian Folk Music; Nyckelharpa

Further Reading

Lallai, Giampaolo Selis Nico. 1997. *Launeddas: L'anima di un Popolo.* Cagliari; Nuoro: AM&D; ISRE.

Melis, Franco. 2002. *Launeddas la musica della tradizione Sarda registrata nei luoghi di origine.* Cagliari, Sardinia: Iscandula.

Music of Sardinia. 2005. East Grinstead, West Sussex, Great Britain: ARC Music.

Sonus de Canna Cultural Association. *Launeddas: The Ancient Musical Instrument of Sardinia.* http://www.sardinia.net/sonus/.

Lead Belly (ca. 1888–1949)

One of the most best-known African American musicians of the 20th century, Huddie (pronounced "Hugh-dee") Ledbetter, better known by his nickname "Lead Belly," has influenced some of the biggest names in rock and roll, including the Beatles, the Rolling Stones, and Eric Clapton (Leadbelly, 2014; Rockhall, 2014). Ledbetter's catalogue, which amounts to more than 500 songs, covers a number of genres, including field songs, ballads, prison songs, folk songs, gospel, blues, square dance songs, and children's songs (Leadbelly, 2014). Many of the original recordings of these songs can be found in the Library of Congress archives; some of the most famous are "Goodnight Irene," "The Midnight Special," "Black Betty," "Cotton Fields," and "Rock Island Line" (Leadbelly, 2014). Ledbetter's songs have been covered by numerous artists, including Lonnie Donegan, The Beach Boys, Elvis Presley, Abba, Pete Seeger, Frank Sinatra, Ram Jam, Johnny Cash, Tom Petty, Ry Cooder, and Van Morrison.

Ledbetter was the most famous of John and Alan Lomax's discoveries (Seeger and Unterburger, 2000, p. 533), and became known by his self-proclaimed title "King of the Twelve-String Guitar," which refers to his mastery of that instrument (Leadbelly, 2014; Szwed, 2010, p. 44). Although he was most celebrated as a 12-string guitarist, he also played piano, mandolin, harmonica, violin, and accordion (which he sometimes used to accompany his singing on recordings). He was a powerful presence (described as seeming to "give off light when he sang"), and felt that his music and talent were a gift from God (Leadbelly, 2014; Szwed, 2010, pp. 44–45).

Ledbetter lived much of his life in poverty, with long stretches in prison, but became known to the wider public following his death when his song, "Goodnight Irene," was catapulted to No. 1 on the U.S. charts by the American folk band The Weavers. His nickname, Lead Belly, is reflective of the tough life he led and refers, among other things, to his "strength, badness, and a bullet in his stomach" (Szwed, 2010, p. 44).

Huddie Ledbetter was born on January 23, 1888, on a family farm near Mooringsport, in Northwest Louisiana, as the only child of Wesley and Sally Ledbetter. He started playing music at the age of two and learned a number of instruments as a child. As a youth, his uncle Terrel Ledbetter introduced him to the guitar, which he is said to have been electrified by, and settled on the 12-string guitar because of its volume and its buzzing sound, which were thought to appeal to women. His unusually large 12-string Stella guitar, affectionately known as "Stella," became his "ticket to life and his freedom" (Leadbelly, 2014; The Lead Belly Foundation, n.d.).

Leaving school after the eighth grade, Ledbetter started making a name for himself as a singer and musician in Shreveport, Louisiana, where he performed in the saloons, brothels, and dance halls of Fannin Street in St. Paul's Bottoms, a notorious red-light district. He was exposed to a number of musical influences during this time and these aided the development of his own musical style. By the age of 16, Ledbetter left home and traveled across the Deep South, playing guitar and taking on additional work as a laborer, working in the cotton fields and on the railroads. During this time he absorbed a large repertoire of songs and styles, including primordial blues, spirituals, reels, cowboy songs, folk ballads, and field hollers. In 1917, he spent time performing on the streets of Dallas alongside the blues guitarist Blind Lemon Jefferson, from whom he learned new songs and slide-guitar technique.

African American folksinger Lead Belly plays his guitar, 1937. (Bernard Hoffman/The LIFE Picture Collection via Getty Images)

Ledbetter was known for his temper and immense strength. He was first arrested in 1915 on an assault charge in Marshall, Texas. His father had to mortgage the family farm to pay a defense lawyer, but Ledbetter was sentenced to one month on a chain gang. He escaped after three days, changed his name to Walter Boyd, and settled in DeKalb, Texas, with his wife, Althea "Lethe" Henderson. In 1917, he fought and killed one of his relatives, Will Stafford, in Dallas and was sentenced to 7–30 years' imprisonment at Imperial Farm (now Central Unit) in Sugar Land, Texas. While in prison, he became a lead singer on the work crews and would entertain guards and prisoners with his music. The Texas governor, Pat Neff, heard Ledbetter's singing, became a fan of his music, and regularly brought guests to the prison to hear him. In 1925, Ledbetter literally sang his way to freedom with his performance of a song asking Neff to release him. Although Neff had promised at his election never to pardon a prisoner, Ledbetter's sentence was commuted soon thereafter.

Back on the road, Ledbetter became popular with audiences throughout the South, singing many of the songs which he had written or heard during his time in prison. In 1930, however, he was arrested again and charged with attempted murder. He received a six- to ten-year sentence at Louisiana's Angola Prison Farm. Three years later, he was discovered there by folklorists John and Alan Lomax, who at the time were recording prison songs for the Library of Congress.

John and Alan Lomax came across Ledbetter just at the end of their visit to the plantation, and recorded many of his songs, including "Goodnight Irene" and

"Angola Blues." They returned the following year with better equipment and recorded more of Ledbetter's repertoire. By this time, Ledbetter had written a new song appealing to Governor O. K. Allen to pardon him. John and Alan Lomax left a recording of this with the governor's secretary, and the following month, on August 1, 1934, Ledbetter was granted a pardon. Upon his release, he was hired by John Lomax for two months to be his driver and field assistant. The pair visited numerous prisons in Arkansas, Texas, Louisiana, and Alabama, and Ledbetter, because of his reputation and knowledge of songs, was an inspiration to the prisoners they met.

However, the relationship between the two men became increasingly strained, and while their professional association continued for a couple of years (Ledbetter often gave performances at universities alongside Lomax's lectures), they parted company in March 1935. John Lomax gave money to Ledbetter and his new wife, Martha Promise, to return to Louisiana by bus, and sent Ledbetter's earnings to Martha in installments. From Louisiana, Ledbetter successfully sued Lomax for the full amount owed and for release from his management contract.

For the last 15 years of his life, Ledbetter sang to appreciative audiences in the leftist folk community and performed alongside singers such as Pete Seeger and Woodie Guthrie. Whereas his early life had been spent singing and working in the fields and prison farms of the rural Southern states, his later life was spent as a recording artist, folksinger, and performer in and around New York City, where he had relocated. He defined himself in the context of Southern black culture and he became known for his high-pitched vocals and powerful and percussive guitar style. He recorded for a variety of labels, including Folkways and Columbia Records, and regularly made radio appearances. He performed up until his death in 1949, recording his last session, *A Definitive Document of the Life and Music of the King of the Twelve-String Guitar*, in 1948.

Ledbetter fell ill while on tour in Europe in 1949, and was diagnosed with amyotrophic lateral sclerosis (Lou Gehrig's disease). His final performance took place at the University of Texas in a tribute concert for John Lomax, and he died on December 6, 1949, in New York City.

Ledbetter's playing style became popularized by Pete Seeger, who adopted the 12-string guitar in the 1950s and released an instructional LP on Folkways Records in 1962 with detailed explanations of both the instrument and Ledbetter's songs. In 1988, the year Ledbetter was inducted into the Rock and Roll Hall of Fame, Pete Seeger said of him, "It's a pure tragedy he didn't live another six months, because all his dreams as a performer would have come true" (Rockhall, 2014).

Francis Wilkins

See also: Blues; Field Hollers; Gospel Music; Rock and Roll; Seeger, Peter

Further Reading

Epstein, Lawrence J. 2010. *Political Folk Music in America from Its Origins to Bob Dylan.* Jefferson, NC: Mcfarland.

Leadbelly. 2014. "Huddie 'Lead Belly' Ledbetter." http://leadbelly.org/index.html.

The Lead Belly Foundation. n.d. http://www.leadbelly.org/leadbelly.html.

Perkinson, Robert. 2010. *Texas Tough: The Rise of America's Prison Empire.* New York: Metropolitan Books.

Rockhall. 2014. "Lead Belly Biography." https://www.rockhall.com/inductees/lead-belly/bio.
Seeger, Pete. 1962. *The Twelve-String Guitar as Played by Lead Belly* [LP]. Folkways Records FI 8371.
Seeger, Tony, and Richie Unterburger. 2000. "Archives: Filling the Map with Music." In Simon Broughton and Mark Ellingham (eds.), *Rough Guide to World Music,* vol. 2, 531–532. London: Rough Guides.
Snyder, Jared. 1994. "Leadbelly and His Windjammer: Examining the African American Button Accordion Tradition." *American Music* 12(2), 148–166.
Szwed, John. 2010. *The Man Who Recorded the World.* London: William Heinemann.
Wolfe, Charles K., and Kip Lornell. 1999. *The Life and Legend of Leadbelly.* Boston: Da Capo Press.

Lenya, Lotte (1898–1981)

Born Karoline Wilhelmine Charlotte Blamauer in 1898 to a poor, working-class family in Vienna, Lotte Lenya became known as the main interpreter of the songs composed by her husband, Kurt Weill (1900–1950). Famous for her unique looks and voice, Lenya later became a star in her own right and the main champion of Weill's music. She recorded most of Weill's German and American songs over a period of about 30 years, some more than once.

Lenya first heard of Kurt Weill in 1922 when she auditioned as a dancer for one of his ballets, but only heard him playing piano from the pit. She properly met him two years later when he came to work with a librettist with whom she was staying. Weill remembered her from the ballet, and they were married in 1926. In Berlin, Lenya and Weill met the poet-playwright Bertolt Brecht (1898–1956), who partnered with Weill and Lenya on some of their most successful projects. The *Mahagonny Songspiel* (1927), *The Seven Deadly Sins* (1933), and *Die Dreigroschenoper* (The threepenny opera) (1928), were shows where Lenya performed roles written or adapted for her by her husband.

Before playing the music for *Die Dreigroschenoper* the first time for Brecht, Weill announced, "I would like my wife to play Jenny, one of the prostitutes." This would not only be Lenya's first singing role, but would also become the character

---

Lotte Lenya

Despite her extensive and accomplished career as an actor and singer (Tony Award winner and Academy Award–nominated), and her extensive work with Kurt Weill and several other important musicians, composers, and visual artists, Lenya is perhaps best known to the greater cultural mainstream for her role as cantankerous Rosa Klebb in the classic James Bond film *From Russia with Love* (1963). In the film, the role sees Klebb, a former Russian intelligence officer, double-cross a Bond associate in an attempt to steal the Lektor (a decoding device) and kill James Bond in the process. It is strongly implied in the novel and the film that Klebb's character is a lesbian, and Lenya's portrayal of the complex nature of the role won her plaudits for its nuance and artistic achievement.

she performed most often. In the original form of the opera, Spelunken-Jenny (Jenny Diver) had a very minor role with only one song, but by the time the German-language film version was made in 1931, her role had been expanded. Lenya's early portrayal of this character led to steady work in German theater and the expanded film role, which included more singing, led to Lenya's association with "Jenny" and the song "Pirate Jenny."

In 1933, after fleeing Germany for London, Lenya divorced Weill but continued to work with him, singing the role of Anna I (which Weill revised for her) in *Die sieben Todsünden* (The seven deadly sins) (1933), a ballet with German songs. She reprised her role in the English-language version, *Anna-Anna*. By the time Lenya and Weill moved to America in 1935, they had reconciled, and remarried in 1937.

Lenya began her recording career in Germany around 1930, and though she performed and recorded songs in both German and English, her troubles learning to speak English were notable. This was part of the reason her career in America did not immediately match her fame in Europe. Her first role in New York was as Moses' sister Miriam in Weill's *The Eternal Road* (1937), described as an opera-oratorio with spoken dialogue. She sang briefly in the nightclub Le Ruban Bleu, and toured in a production of *A Candle in the Wind* (1942), singing a part written especially for her. In May of 1944, Lenya became an American citizen, nine years after emigrating.

Her career slowed again in 1945 when she appeared as the Duchess in Weill and Ira Gershwin's *The Firebrand of Florence* (1945). Critics felt she was miscast in the role, and her confidence was so shaken that she did not perform again until 1951. Weill's death from a heart attack in 1950 was the catalyst that put Lenya back on stage. After renewing her friendship with George Davis, a writer and editor whom she married in 1951, she began to promote and protect Weill's works. Lenya organized and sang in a series of concerts at New York's Town Hall in 1951, which sparked a revival of Weill's German music. After Davis's death in 1957, Lenya married painter Russell Detwiler in 1962. He died in 1969, and Lenya quietly married Richard Siemanowoski, a film maker, in 1971. She divorced him in 1973.

Lenya continued to perform the role of Jenny in concerts and staged productions of *The Threepenny Opera*, as well as performing in new musicals such as *Cabaret* (1966), singing Weill's music in concert, and appearing in films. She received an Academy Award nomination for her supporting role in *The Roman Spring of Mrs. Stone* (1961), and appeared as a Russian officer in the Bond film *From Russia with Love* (1964). Her final performance was in a concert of Kander and Ebb's music in 1978 at Avery Fisher Hall; she died of cancer in 1981 at the age of 83. Lenya is buried next to Weill in the Mount Repose Cemetery in Haverstraw, New York.

Melissa Cummins

See also: Ländler; Opera; Race Records; Schrammelmusik; Singspiel

Further Reading

Kurt Weill Foundation. 2015. "The Threepenny Opera." http://www.threepennyopera.org.

Sanders, Ronald. 1991. *The Days Grow Short: The Life and Music of Kurt Weill*. Hollywood, CA: Silman-James Press.

Symonette, Lys, and Kim H. Kowalke, ed. and trans. 1996. *Speak Low (When You Speak Love): The Letters of Kurt Weill and Lotte Lenya*. Los Angeles: University of California Press.

Lithuanian Music

Lithuania has rich traditions in both ethnic and Western classical music. Lithuanian ethnic music is an ancient and unique part of European folklore. The folk songs carry the archaic worldview of a settled, agriculture-based society, evoking parallels between the human and natural worlds. The tradition of classical music started in the courts and churches and was composed and performed by foreign musicians (Italian, Polish) until the nationalist movement in professional music developed in the second half of the 19th century. The popularity of music in Lithuania is reflected in grand song and dance festivals, which attract thousands of singers, dancers, and folk musicians from Lithuania and the Lithuanian diaspora around the world.

The origins of Lithuanian ethnic music are not specifically known: the corpus consists of centuries-old traditional vocal (monophonic and polyphonic) and instrumental music passed down from generation to generation. The oldest musical instruments are woodwinds such as *ragas* (horn), *daudyte* (trumpet), *birbyne* (whirrer), *skuduciai* (reed-pipes), *ozragis* (buckhorn); wooden percussion instruments such as *skrabalai* (cracklers), *tabalas* (pendent), and the 5- to 12-stringed instrument *kankles* (psaltery), which is popular to this day. International instruments—violins, clarinets, harmonicas, accordions, cymbals—became common in Lithuania in the beginning of the 20th century. Dances such as *suktinis* (the twirler) and *klumpakojis* (clog dance), round dances, games, marches (wedding or funeral), and medleys of popular song tunes are the common genres of instrumental music. *Suktinis* is a fast dance, danced in pairs using polka steps, and has lyrics that are sung. *Suktinis* is the best-known and most popular version of polka in Lithuania.

The uniqueness of the Lithuanian ethnic music is most evident in vocal music. Its main genre is a lyrical song (*daina*), rich in textual symbols and epithets, which convey an elevated, positive emotion. The types of daina include mythological, work, calendar, wedding, war-historical, ballads, children's, city romance, and humoristic-satirical songs. The most used form of songs is A A B A, A B A C, A B C A.

Sutartines, ancient polyphonic songs which combine elements of music, dance, poetry, and acting (mimic, gestures), are a unique type of Lithuanian music. They are performed by female singers in pairs or sometimes three or four voices or voice groups. The singers sing the same verse in a round style, with second and third voices using alternate tones (a second higher or lower) of the same melody, developing a constant sequence of seconds. In three- to four-voice songs, the singers enter in canon. More rare are instrumental versions, performed by men on skuduciai, maintaining the harmonies of vocal sutartines.

Sutartines as a genre flourished in the 16th to 19th centuries. The first sutartine was written down in 1582; they were collected, studied, and classified by Sabaliauskas and Slaviūnas (1958–1959). By the 20th century, sutartines had almost disappeared. In the Soviet times, in order to maintain the uniqueness of ethnic sound, Lithuanian composers heavily used seconds in harmonies in professional music. Thematic material featured melodic quotations of sutartines (e.g., composers Vainiunas, Raciunas, Balsys). Today sutartines in their original form are performed by ethnographic folklore ensembles. Folk-rock musicians such as Zalvarinis brought sutartines and that style of traditional polyphonic singing to new life in 20th-century popular music. In 2010, sutartines were inscribed on the UN's Representative List of the Intangible Cultural Heritage of Humanity.

A mass expression of Lithuanian music is the song festival (later song *and* dance festival) of the entire country. A grand event organized every four years, it lasts three days, with separate days dedicated to folklore ensemble performances, songs (choirs and choral performances), and dances. Festival participation has steadily increased: 3,000 singers representing 77 choirs participated in the first Lithuanian song festival in 1924 in Kaunas, and the song and dance festival in 2014 had 35,000 participants with 400 choirs.

Song and dance festivals are also held every five years in two other Baltic states, Latvia and Estonia. Since 1956, similar song and dance festivals have also been held in North American by the Lithuanian community in the United States and Canada, though less regularly. On November 7, 2003, the tradition and symbolism of Baltic song and dance festivals was proclaimed a Masterpiece of Intangible Cultural Heritage of Humanity, and in 2008 they were inscribed on the Representative List.

The introduction of Christianity into Lithuania in 1387 CE marked the beginning of the Western musical tradition in Lithuania. Gregorian chants were performed in churches, and musical instruments of the Renaissance (lute, viol, clavichord) were introduced. In the 15th century, professional musicians from Poland, Prussia, Hungary, and Italy started vocal-instrumental ensembles on the estates of Lithuanian rulers and gentry. In 1547, the first printed Lithuanian book, *Catechismusa Prasti Szadei* (The simple words of catechism) by Mazvydas, contained both notes and words for 10 Lithuanian hymns. Music was taught at Vilnius University, founded in 1579. In 1667, Professor Liauksminas published the first music textbook, *Ars et praxis musica* (in Latin).

The first stage production of opera in Lithuania was *Il ratto di Helena* by Italian composer M. Scacchi, performed in Vilnius on September 4, 1636. The first public theater opened its doors in 1785, and local or touring troupes regularly performed operas and ballets by Paisiello, Anfossi, Duni, Salieri, and later Cherubini, Mozart, and Rossini, among others. In 1795 Lithuania became a province of the Russian Empire, which brought Russian-Polish cultural influences. Polish composer Moniuszko lived in Vilnius where he wrote and staged the national Polish opera Halka (1848). The first Lithuanian professional composers appeared after the 1863 uprising against the Russian Empire: Naujalis; Sasnauskas; and composer and painter Ciurlionis, who wrote the first Lithuanian symphonic poems ("In the Forest," "The Sea") and works for piano, organ, and choirs. In 1906, the first Lithuanian opera, *Birute*, by M. Petrauskas, was staged in Vilnius. Training courses for organists and choir conductors were started in Kaunas, a music journal and records of Lithuanian music were published, and the music societies *Daina* (the song) and *Vilniaus kankles* (Vilnius psaltery) were established.

After the restoration of Lithuanian independence in 1918, Kaunas became the center of musical life. In 1922, the State Theatre was established. National operas (*Grazina* by Karnavicius, 1933) and ballets (*Jurate ir Kastytis* by Gruodis, 1933) were produced. Lithuanian singers (K. Petrauskas, A. Kutkus, V. Jonusaite, A. Dambrauskaite) were famous both in Lithuania and abroad, and pianists (e.g., Vainiunas) successfully performed at international competitions. The archives of musicology and folklore were established during the period 1929–1935, the journals *Muzikos barai* (Bars of music, 1931–1940) and *Vargonininkas* (The organist, 1933–1934) were published, and various music societies were founded. After the Soviet occupation in 1940, music largely became a tool of communist propaganda, although it did maintain a national spirit and uniqueness.

After World War II, a song and dance festival was organized in Vilnius in 1946. In 1956, an historical opera, *Pilenai*, by Klova was produced. Other performances and works for orchestras and choirs by composers Kutavicius, Dvarionas, and Bajoras promoted national identity. Many new music schools for children opened across the country, offering training in mostly classical vocals and instruments. Amateur and professional choirs, orchestras, string quartets, and folklore ensembles were established. Competitions for instrumentalists were organized. The Lithuanian Chamber Orchestra (conducted by Sondeckis) successfully performed abroad.

After the restoration of independence in 1990, many Lithuanian musicians studied abroad, and a new generation of composers (Martinaitis, Bartulis), conductors (Pitrenas, Rinkevicius), singers (Urmana, Montvidas), and instrumentalists become famous both within the country and abroad. Connections with the Lithuanian diaspora become stronger. In 1991, the Chicago Lithuanian Opera produced *Lithuanians* by Ponchielli in Vilnius, and singers of the Vilnius Opera Theatre participated in Chicago productions. In 1989, the first diaspora composer festival *Sugrizimas* (comeback) took place in Vilnius.

Bronius Ambraziejus and Jurgita Antoine

See also: Opera; Polka; Psaltery

Further Reading

Ambrazas, Algirdas, and Dana Palionytė-Banevičienė, eds. 2002. *Lietuvos muzikos istorija. Kn. 1. Tautinio atgimimo metai, 1883–1918* [History of Lithuanian music vol. 1. The year of national revival, 1883–1918]. Vilnius: Lietuvos Muzikos Akademija.

Antanavičius, Juozas, and Algirdas Ambrazas, eds. 2009. *Lietuvos muzikos istorija. Kn. 2. Nepriklausomybės metai, 1918–1940* [History of Lithuanian music vol. 2. The year of independence, 1918–1940]. Vilnius: Lietuvos Muzikos Akademija.

Balys, Jonas. 1954. *Lithuanian Narrative Folksongs.* Washington, DC: Draugus Press.

Čiurlionytė, Jadvyga. 1938. *Lietuvių liaudies melodijos. Tautosakos darbai* [Lithuanian folk tunes and folklore works], vol. 5. Vilnius: Lietuvių tautosakos archyvas.

Folstrom, Roger. 1998. "Music Standards in Lithuania." *Music Educators Journal* 85(1) (July), 32–34.

Gaudrimas, Juozas. 1958–1967. *Iš lietuvių muzikinės kultūros istorijos* [The history of Lithuanian musical culture], vols. 1–3. Vilnius: Valstybinė politinės ir mokslinės literatūros leidykla.

Slaviūnas, Zenonas. 1958–1959. *Sutartinės: daugiabalsės lietuvių liaudies dainos* [Polyphonic Lithuanian folk songs], vols. 1–3. Vilnius: Valstybinė grožinės literatūros leidykla.

Tauragis, Adeodatas. 1971. *Lithuanian Music: Past and Present*, trans. M. Ginsburgas and N. Kameneckaite. Vilnius: Gintaras.

Lomax, Alan and John

John Avery Lomax (1867–1948) and his son, Alan Lomax (1915–2002), were hugely influential in the world of American folklore and folksong collecting during the 20th century. Their legacies continue to be of great significance in ethnomusicology and folklore today. John Lomax is considered a pioneer in terms of preservation of American folk songs, and Alan Lomax went on to become one of the greatest American field collectors of the 20th century, whose career as a folklorist, ethnomusicologist, oral historian, archivist, writer, record producer, radio presenter, concert promoter, and filmmaker, spanned 70 years. Their work was important to the success of the American and British folk revivals of the 1940s–1960s, and their work hugely influenced folksingers such as Pete Seeger, Woody Guthrie, and Bob Dylan. Both John and Alan Lomax substantially affected the history of popular music in the United States and the United Kingdom, through their work in collecting and promoting. It was through their work that many performers, including Huddie Ledbetter ("Lead Belly"), Muddy Waters, and Jelly Roll Morton, became known to the general public; this in turn influenced musicians in the United Kingdom, including the Beatles and the Rolling Stones. The recordings of Alan Lomax can still be heard today in popular music and film, including on the soundtrack of *O Brother, Where Art Thou?* (2000) and on Moby's 1999 album *Play*.

Born in Goodman, Mississippi, in 1867, and raised in Texas, John Lomax grew up in the midst of rural farming life, his father raising horses and cattle and growing cotton and corn. John heard many cowboy songs as a child and at the age of nine formed a friendship with a former slave and farmhand, Nat Blythe. Blythe was hugely influential to Lomax, and taught him songs and dance steps. These early

---

Portable Recording Equipment

When early folklorists and anthropologists such as Frances Densmore and John and Alan Lomax traveled the globe, they often took along with their own "portable" recording equipment. *Portable*, however, did not mean as pocket-worthy as an iPhone: many of these record-cutting machines took up the space of the entire trunk of a car. Shunning the phonograph of the late 19th century (which cut songs directly onto wax cylinders), by the 1930s people were bringing the 300-pound disc recorders into the field to collect songs. The disc recorders etched the recordings directly onto metal discs, and the quality was preferred over wax cylinders—but that quality was not without a cost. The heavy recorders were cumbersome, to say the least, and fieldworkers often converted trucks, cars, and other vehicles such as hearses and ambulances to accommodate and transport the machines.

life experiences had a great effect on Lomax's later work in folklore and particular in collecting and researching cowboy songs, a subject which was to form the backbone of his career.

In 1887, Lomax initially trained as a teacher, and in 1895 he started work on a bachelor's degree in English at the University of Texas-Austin. He excelled at university and while there became editor in chief of the *Texas University Magazine*. He completed his degree in two, rather than four, years, and later became professor of English at Texas A&M University. In 1904, he married Bess Baumann Brown, and two years later he was given the opportunity to attend Harvard as a graduate student in English. He was greatly influenced by George Lyman Kittredge, successor to Francis J. Child as the professor in English literature. It was Kittredge who encouraged Lomax to go out into rural areas and collect folksong material from real-life singers.

Alan Lomax was the third of John and Bess Lomax's four children, born in Austin, Texas, in 1915. He suffered ill health as a child and was put under great pressure by his father to achieve academically. At 16 years old he was awarded a scholarship to study philosophy and physics at Harvard, but due to poor health took a break from studying after one year. It was at this time that he gained his first experience with field collecting, joining his father on a trip to the American South.

In June 1932, John Lomax had convinced the editor at MacMillan to give him an advance to edit an anthology titled *American Ballads and Folksongs*, and by obtaining funding from organizations such as the American Council of Learned Societies, made arrangements to record material under the auspices of the Library of Congress. In the summer of 1933, John and Alan Lomax travelled in a Model A Ford throughout the Southern states, across Texas and then to Louisiana, Mississippi, Tennessee, and Kentucky, recording folk songs on a wind-up Ediphone by day and camping out at night. The singers they met were mostly African American, and it was at this time that Alan Lomax experienced his first epiphany. While listening to the singing of a washerwoman, and from witnessing her intensity and seriousness, he "became convinced that folk song collecting was important, something that he had to do" (Szwed, 2010, p. 36).

Prisons held particular fascination for the collectors, and they visited a number of penitentiaries, including the Central Convict Sugar Plantation, more commonly known as "Angola." It was there that they had their first major discovery. As they were leaving, they came across Lead Belly, the self-proclaimed "king of the twelve-string guitar." The Lomaxes were so impressed by his singing that they recorded 11 record sides with him, including the first recorded versions of the song "Goodnight Irene." At the end of the trip, John Lomax was appointed "Honorary Conservator of Our Archive of American Folk-Song" by the Library of Congress. The father-and-son pair continued their collecting in 1934, traveling to southwest Texas and returning to Angola to revisit Lead Belly, who was released soon thereafter. Upon release, Lead Belly became John Lomax's driver, accompanying him on collecting expeditions and lecture/performance tours. It was this relationship which, although short-lived, provided the impetus for Lead Belly's subsequent musical fame.

John and Alan Lomax recorded thousands of songs and interviews for the Library of Congress. They were among the first collectors to recognize the immense cultural value of African American music, and they helped develop the Archive of American Folk Song (AAFS) as a national resource. In 1936, Alan Lomax travelled to Haiti, where he made more than 1,500 recordings and shot 350 feet of 8-mm color motion picture. He was later joined by Elizabeth Howard Goodman, whom he married in February 1937. In the same year, Alan Lomax became the first "assistant in charge" of the AAFS, and continued to make field trips and supply recordings to the archive until 1942. His daughter later wrote of him that "Alan was proudest of his driving—his thousands of miles and days down nameless roads seeking out the jewels of the human spirit" (Lomax Wood, 2013). Today, the entire body of Lomax material encompasses more than 100 collections, and includes 700 linear feet of manuscript, 10,000 sound recordings, 6,000 graphic images, and 6,000 moving images. The material covers the "creative expression of nearly 1000 cultural groups from around the world" (American Folklife Center, 2015).

Alan Lomax continued to work prolifically as a folksong collector throughout his life, both at home and abroad. He started producing commercial albums of folk music on Decca and Columbia Records, became involved in radio, wrote articles and book on folk music, and became recognized as a musician in his own right. He was invited to play banjo at the White House in a concert for the king and queen of England (George VI and Elizabeth) and later made a huge impression as a singer and musician on his collecting tours. In spring 1942, Alan started to be suspected as a communist threat by the Federal Bureau of Investigation, which investigated him thoroughly. They concluded that he was too independent and undisciplined to be any serious threat, but nonetheless they quietly trailed him for most of the next two decades.

In September 1950, Alan set sail by steamer for a collecting tour in Europe, leaving his wife and daughter Anne behind in New York. He collected throughout Britain and Ireland, Spain, and Italy in the 1950s, and then based himself in London, where he edited the 18-volume *Columbia World Library of Folk and Primitive Music*. During seven months in Spain, he recorded 3,000 items, and in 1953–1954 he conducted a survey of Italian folk music. For the Scottish, English, and Irish volumes, he worked with the BBC and folklorists Peter Kennedy, Hamish Henderson, and Séamus Ennis. He continued his work in radio, hosting a folk music show on the BBC home service, organized a skiffle group, and produced a Ballad opera. He was also credited as an inspiration to the founding of the School of Scottish Studies in 1951. He returned to the United States in 1959.

Alan Lomax advocated for a public role for folklore throughout his career. During the latter part of his life he coined the term "cultural equity": the idea that "the expressive traditions of all local and ethnic cultures should be equally valued as representative of the multiple forms of human adaptation on earth" (Lomax Wood, 2013). In 1983 he founded the Association for Cultural Equity (ACE), housed in the Fine Arts Campus of Hunter College, New York City, also the location of the Alan Lomax Archive. His idea was to put cultural equity on a theoretical foundation with the method of Cantometrics (song measurements), which he developed with a team of researchers as a way of relating elements of the world's traditional vocal music to features of social organization. This work culminated in the "Global Jukebox," a Cantometrics-based education program, in the early 1990s. In 1993, his book, *The Land Where the Blues Began*, linking the origins of the blues to slave labor in the American South, was published. During his later life he received a number of awards, including the Library of Congress Living Legend Award in 2000 and an honorary doctorate in philosophy from Tulane University in 2001. He died in 2002 at the age of 87.

Frances Wilkins

See also: Blues; Field Hollers; Lead Belly

Further Reading

American Folklife Center. 2015. "Lomax Family at the American Folklife Center." http://www.loc.gov/folklife/lomax.

Lomax, Alan. 1993. *The Land Where the Blues Began*. New York: Pantheon Books.

Lomax Wood, Anna. 2013. "Thinking about My Father." Association for Cultural Equity. http://www.culturalequity.org/alan-lomax/remembrance/alw.

Szwed, John. 2010. *The Man Who Recorded the World*. London: William Heinemann.

M

Madrigal

The term "madrigal" can refer either to a song for two or three unaccompanied voices, developed in Italy in the late 13th and early 14th centuries, or to a polyphonic song using vernacular text generally set for four to six voices. This second genre has no direct connections with the medieval madrigal. It was developed in Italy in the 16th century and was popular in England in the 16th and early 17th centuries. It played a central role in the development of Western music. The origin of the name can be ascribed to either *materialis* (tangible), meaning a song subjected to specific formal rules; or *matricalis*, a song in the mother tongue.

FOURTEENTH CENTURY

Comparing the early madrigal from the 14th century to contemporary genres of the Ars Nova, it is clear that it was less descriptive of *caccia* and metrically different from the *ballade*. The madrigal was strophic and had two main musical sections: stanza and *ritornello*. Its size standardized around the 1340s: two or three two-lined stanzas or tercets, with seven- or 11-syllable lines. A single or double 11-syllable *ritornello* closed each stanza. The text could be set for two or three voices, with the upper one melodically richer. The voices mostly followed a homorhythmic style (uniformity of rhythm in all voices), with frequent melismas in a characteristic improvisational style.

Some of the most significant composers of 14th-century madrigals were the Italians Gherardello da Firenze (ca. 1320–ca. 1362), Giovanni da Cascia (1340–1350), and Jacopo da Bologna (1340–1386). Although Gherardello da Firenze is remembered mostly for his liturgical compositions, his madrigals' sharp division between syllabic and melismatic sections represents a peculiar trait of his style. In some songs a remnant of the caccia is still identifiable in the presence of canonic passages. Giovanni da Cascia played a crucial role in the stabilization of the genre. He enclosed each line with melismas, while the central sections presented an unadorned syllabic style.

Jacopo da Bologna was the first composer to write three-voice madrigals, and his style was renowned for its gentleness and melodic linearity. His most famous work within this genre is certainly *Fenice fu'* (I used to be a phoenix, ca. 1360). A further remarkable madrigal is *Non al suo amante* (Not more pleasing to her lover, ca. 1350), the only known coeval composition which sets to music a poem by the Italian Francesco Petrarca. From the second half of the 14th century, the *ballata* surmounted the madrigal as the main secular genre, and the Ars Nova madrigal disappeared around the second decade of the 15th century.

16TH CENTURY AND BEYOND

The Renaissance madrigal was a through-composed vocal composition based on counterpoint. It originated in popular forms such as *frottola*, *strambotto*, and *villotta*. From those it borrowed some characteristic traits, such as the well-marked rhythm, the juxtaposition of polyphony and homophony, and the prevalence of the upper voice among the other parts. Initially it was designed for only three or four voices, but in the second half of the 16th century it became mostly five-voiced. A further crucial characteristic was the continual seeking of a progressively closer relationship between words and music, the latter of which tended to depict meanings of the text through the use of chromaticism, counterpoint, and timbre. Singers were often not professionals, but rather amateurs performing for a private audience. The topic was frequently amorous, but also could be moral or devotional. It was characterized by its pastoral setting.

The set of compositions *Madrigali de diversi musici: libro primo de la Serena* (Rome, 1530) was the first work to carry the title "madrigal" and featured songs mainly by Jacob Arcadelt (ca. 1507–1568) and Costanzo Festa (ca. 1485–1545). Published a few years later (1533), the book of madrigals in two volumes by Philippe Verdelot (ca. 1480–1530) soon became a masterwork of the early 16th century, and Verdelot and Arcadelt were considered the two main representative figures of the genre. The most famous madrigal by Arcadelt was *Il bianco e dolce cigno* (The white and gentle swan), a four-voice song set to a poem by Marquis Alfonso d'Avalos. Arcadelt was indeed considered the master of four-voice madrigals. His madrigals combine straightforward tunes and repeated introductory melodic fragments in a new fashion. In contrast, one of Verdelot's most famous compositions—*Ahimè dov'è 'l bel viso* (Alas, where is my beautiful face)—clearly denotes the transition from the typical homophonic style of the frottola to the imitational motet-like texture.

The following generation of madrigalists, of which the main figures were Adrian Willaert (ca. 1490–1562) and Cyprien (Cipriano) de Rore (ca. 1515–1565), standardized the five-part madrigal. The former was the first to make considerable use of chromaticism; the latter's madrigals mirror Willaert's style itself, with the use of clear diction, thick and continuous counterpoint, and pervasive imitation. Compared to the previous generation of madrigalists, Willaert's compositional mood is more grave, reflecting the mostly serious subjects he chose for his works. Orlando di Lasso's (ca. 1530–1594) cosmopolitan touch gave him the chance to compose secular songs in several vernacular languages such as Italian, French, and German; he was renowned for his frank and brief style.

Toward the end of the 16th century, the principal madrigalists were native Italians. Luca Marenzio (ca. 1553–1599) brought the madrigal to its highest peak of creative and technical development. He can be considered the leading and most influential composer of his time, publishing 17 books of madrigals. Most of those madrigals were five-voiced, although a considerable number were for four voices. He approached each individual text in a different manner, so it is hard to define any typical or even wide-ranging style for all his madrigals. One of his most celebrated madrigals is "*O voi che sospirate a miglior note* (O ye who sigh for better music)," in which he modulates through the entire cycle of fifths. In his songs he describes the mood of a specific word through the use of a distinctive musical solution, thus emphasizing sentiments and passions expressed in the lyrics.

His style was both imitative and homorhythmic, and it became progressively more serious as he neared old age, when his extensive experimentation with chromaticism can be compared to Carlo Gesualdo's (ca. 1561–1613) bravura. In his ninth book of madrigals (1599), the long semibreves in the upper voice of the song "*Solo e pensoso i più deserti campi* (Lonely and melancholic, the most desert lands)" present a progression of the whole chromatic scale, mirroring the meaning of the text *a passi tardi et lenti* (with delayed and slow steps).

In the late 16th century, the madrigal started to be appreciated in England. The anthology of Italian madrigals translated into English, *Musica transalpina*, was printed as late as 1588, but these works were circulated earlier in unpublished versions. Thomas Morley (ca. 1577–1602) and Thomas Weelkes (1576–1623) are considered the leading figures of the trend. The former published his first book of madrigals in 1601: *The Triumphs of Oriana*, a collection of songs in honor of Anne of Denmark, later Queen of England as wife of James I of England. His second book, published in 1609, features songs such as "Draw on, sweet night" and "Sweet honey-sucking bees."

Carlo Gesualdo, Prince of Venosa, differs from any other composer of his time due to his extreme use of chromaticism, although his earlier works can still be considered within the boundaries of the accepted dissonances. His sixth book (1611) features some of his most typical works. In *Moro, lasso, al mio duolo* (I am dying, wretched, in my grief), we find an interesting study of chromatic third relations. In the same book, the song *Beltà, poi che t'assenti* (Beauty, since you depart) shows the use of accumulated consecutive or even simultaneous dissonances. *Deh, coprite il bel seno* (Please, cover your nice bosom) from the fifth book (1611) shows how Gesualdo treatment of rhythm is subject to frequent variations.

Claudio Monteverdi (1567–1643) can be considered the latest main composer of madrigals; his works have been crucial for the development of later forms such as melodrama. Between 1587 and 1651 he published nine books of madrigals which prompted severe criticism from coeval theorists, due to his audacious development of the style. In particular, the theorist Giovanni Artusi, in his book *L'Artusi ovvero delle imperfettioni della moderna musica* (The artusi, or imperfections of modern music) (1600), attacked the song *Cruda amarilli* (Cruel Amaryllis) for its use of dissonances. Monteverdi replied by coining the neologism *Seconda prattica* (second practice) to be distinguished from the previous approach to music, which he called *Prima prattica* (early style). His freer use of dissonances clearly contravened the rigid rules of the Prima prattica, which tended to limit rather than encourage them.

In the preface to his fifth book (1605), he introduced these new ideas; in the Seconda prattica a new hierarchy subjugates the music to the text and more importance is given to soprano and bass lines, thus creating a brand new vocal hierarchy. The stylistic features of the fifth book, together with the progressively more common use of *basso continuo* for many of the madrigals, clearly show the dawn of an early baroque style. The eighth book of madrigals (*Madrigali guerrieri, et amorosi con alcuni opuscoli in genere rappresentativo, che saranno per brevi episodi fra i canti senza gesto* (Warrior madrigals in which the topic of love is generally representative and will be discussed for brief episodes), 1638) seems to restate the revolutionary ideas of the fifth volume and the seconda prattica. It is divided into two sections, the former dedicated to war topics, and the second to love. In the former the composer exploits war as an allegory of love itself; in the latter he depicts the pain of love, including themes such as infidelity and anguish.

Jacopo Mazzeo

See also: Classical Music, European; Medieval Secular Song; Opera

Further Reading

Bizzarini, Marco. 2003. *Luca Marenzio: The Career of a Musician Between the Renaissance and the Counter-Reformation.* Burlington, VT: Ashgate.

Calcagno, Mauro P. 2012. *From Madrigal to Opera: Monteverdi's Staging of the Self.* Berkeley: University of California Press.

Carter, Tim. 2000. *Monteverdi and His Contemporaries.* Burlington, VT: Ashgate.

Fellowes, Edmund Horace, Frederick W. Sternfeld, and David Greer. 1967. *English Madrigal Verse, 1588–1632.* Oxford: Clarendon Press.

Fenlon, Iain. 2013. *The Italian Madrigal in the Early Sixteenth Century: Sources and Interpretation.* Cambridge: Cambridge University Press.

Kerman, Joseph. 1962. *The Elizabethan Madrigal: A Comparative Study.* New York: American Musicological Society (Galaxy Music Corp.).

Kidger, David. 2005. *Adrian Willaert: A Guide to Research.* Routledge Music Bibliographies. New York: Routledge.

Lewis Hammond, Susan. 2011. *The Madrigal: A Research and Information Guide.* New York: Routledge.

Lincoln, Harry B. 1988. *The Italian Madrigal and Related Repertories: Indexes to Printed Collections, 1500–1600.* New Haven, CT: Yale University Press.

McClary, Susan. 2004. *Modal Subjectivities: Self-Fashioning in the Italian Madrigal.* Berkeley: University of California Press.

McKinney, Timothy R. 2010. *Adrian Willaert and the Theory of Interval Affect: The Musica Nova Madrigals and the Novel Theories of Zarlino and Vicentino.* Burlington, VT: Ashgate Gower.

Watkins, Glenn. 2010. *The Gesualdo Hex: Music, Myth, and Memory.* New York: W. W. Norton.

Whenham, John Wistreich Richard. 2007. *The Cambridge Companion to Monteverdi.* Cambridge: Cambridge University Press.

Makam

Makam is a modal system practiced in the traditional music of the eastern Mediterranean, Anatolia, the Caucasus, the Arabian Gulf, the Levant, and North Africa. In Turkey, Greece, and Armenia, it is known as *makam*; in Azerbaijan it is called *mugham*; and in Arab countries, *maqam*. It is closely related to the modal system in Iran known as *dastgah*. The spelling "makam" is the one used in Turkey, and since the founding of the Turkish Republic in 1923, it has been associated with modal practice and pedagogy in that country. Makam is used in a variety of sacred and secular contexts, including Orthodox Christian, Jewish, and Islamic ceremonies; historical interpretations of classical elite court music; modern semiclassical nightclub music; village and folk music; and contemporary popular, film, radio, and television music.

The repertoire of music composed and performed in makam has for centuries been transmitted within an oral tradition at the Ottoman court, only being notated using specially designed systems for theoretical treatises and official recordkeeping. In the 17th century, Ali Ufki (1610–1675) and Dmitri Kantemir (1673–1723) contributed to the preservation of the Ottoman repertoire through notations in their respective treatises on makam. In performance, however, there has been an emphasis on learning by rote from masters—a pedagogical method known in Turkish as *meşk*—which cultivates musicians who memorize songs and instrumental compositions and can improvise within the makam system. Today, a musician's value is determined by her or his ability to interpret modal melodies with correct intonation and tasteful ornamentation, as well as *taksim*, a structured form of improvisation that introduces the mode to be performed in ensuing instrumental or vocal compositions. In the 1930s, the makam system was adapted for staff notation by Turkish musicologists Suphi Ezgi (1869–1962) and Hüseyin Sadettin Arel (1880–1955). Currently, repertoire in conservatories focusing on makam is learned by reading from the staff notation they devised. However, purists agree that proper interpretation of the repertoire and ability to improvise still depend on intimate knowledge of the modes as passed from master to student within the meşk system (Signell, 1977; Aydemir, 2010). This situation has been facilitated with the advent of recording technology in the 20th century, the mass availability of performances by masters available on the internet, and the ability of students to record their teachers with portable devices.

The intervals of the makam system have been described as microtonal, and attempts have been made at precisely measuring them by using a combination of cents and Pythagorean commas. One hundred cents equals one half-step in the equal-tempered Western tonal system, and a single comma is roughly 23 cents. In the makam system, there are five different kinds of intervals: the small half-step (*bakiye*) is 4 commas, or 90 cents; the large half-step (*küçük mücennep*) is 5 commas, or 114 cents; the small whole step (*büyük mücennep*) is 8 commas, or 180 cents; the large whole step (*tanini*) is 9 commas, or 204 cents; and the augmented second (*artık ikili*) is 12 commas, or 271 cents (Signell, 1977).

In Arab makam theory, microtonality has been normalized to equally tempered quarter-tones that measure 50 cents, falling exactly between the half-steps of the Western tonal system. In practice, however, the intervals played by Arab musicians do not correspond to the measurements given by their theory (Marcus, 1993). Whether using Turkish or Arab measurements, however, these intervals cannot be pinpointed exactly, due to the way in which they shift according to musical context; intervals will be either raised or lowered depending on the direction of the melody.

The range of pitches of the makam system is best described using the traditional Persian and Arabic names, although Western *solfége* has commonly been used in modern conservatory training. By using the pitches from within this ambitus, modal melodies are constructed out of pentachords, tetrachords, and trichords—small scales of five, four, or three notes—known in Turkish as *çeşniler*, or "flavors." Each pentachordal, tetrachordal, or trichordal flavor is considered to have its own unique personality and identity, and therefore must be performed in such a way as to successfully bring out its individual characteristics. A makam arises out of the artistically ordered presentation of these flavors in a *seyir*, or melodic progression. The melodic progression is marked by certain goal notes: the tonic, or *durak*; the dominant, or *güçlü*; the upper tonic, or *tiz durak*, which is located an octave higher than the tonic; and other moments of suspended cadence, known as *asma kararlar*, that are characteristic of the makam. Depending on the makam, the melodic progression can begin by emphasizing either the tonic, dominant, or upper tonic as a goal note by using a particular flavor. The dominant is situated between the tonic and the upper tonic, but can be variously located on the fifth, fourth, or third note above the tonic (Signell, 1977). The makam *rast*, for example, typically begins by emphasizing the tonic pitch, rast (G in staff notation), using a melody that gives the rast flavor. In the melodic progression, there is typically a half cadence on the dominant pitch, neva (D), followed by suspended cadences on the pitches *segah* (B 1 comma flat) and *dügah* (A) (Aydemir, 2010, pp. 33–34). The pitch segah will be performed slightly higher or lower depending on whether the melody is rising to neva or descending to dügah or rast.

Adem Merter Birson

See also: Arab Classical Music; Dastgah; Ottoman Classical Music; Sufism, Music of; Taqsīm

Further Reading

Aydemir, Murat. 2010. *Turkish Makam Guide*, ed. and trans. Erman Dirikcan. Istanbul: Pan Yayıncılık.

Feldman, Walter. 1996. *Music of the Ottoman Court: Makam, Composition and the Early Ottoman Instrumental Repertoire*. Berlin: Verlag für Wissenschaft und Bildung.

Marcus, Scott. 1993. "The Interface Between Theory and Practice: The Case of Intonation in Arab Music." *Asian Music* 1993(2), 39–58.

Signell, Karl. 1977. *Makam: Modal Practice in Turkish Art Music*. Seattle, WA: Asian Music Publications.

Makeba, Miriam (1932–2008)

Miriam Makeba was the most prominent South African singer of her generation, and of the 20th century. Her international appeal as a performer and recording artist was, for portions of her career, a platform for her activism in support of causes such as civil rights, the Black Power movement, and the anti-apartheid movement. Makeba had a long and varied career, which included singing in vocal groups in her native country, acting in films, singing in stage musicals, duetting with other famous singers, and collaborating with jazz musicians. She sang in multiple languages, and at the time of her death (on stage during a performance in Italy), she was revered as one of the greatest voices of the century.

Makeba was born and raised in a township near Johannesburg, South Africa. She spent the first six months of her life in prison with her mother, who had been arrested for brewing and selling homemade beer. Makeba came from a large family, with five siblings, who mostly had to fend for themselves while their mother was away working. Their father died when Miriam was seven. She was exposed to American jazz LP records by her brothers, and her mother played several traditional instruments in the household.

Her first professional job was as the featured vocalist in the already established Manhattan Brothers, a male vocal quartet that performed music that was similar to the close harmonies of The Inkspots and The Mills Brothers. Makeba's first successful group was an all-female singing group, The Skylarks, who had a recording contract with Gallotone Records. Her first solo single was "Lovely Lies" from 1956, which was the first South African record to appear on American charts.

Because of her national success, she was chosen to be the female lead in the musical *King Kong* in 1959, which opened in that year to great acclaim. This musical was the first integrated production in South African history; even though the cast was all black, the production staff was mixed. The show played to mixed audiences also, and thus was only allowed to be presented on university campuses, in order to get around apartheid laws. *King Kong* was composed by Todd Matshikiza, and was based on the real-life story of a township boxer (Ezekiel Dlamini, nicknamed "King Kong") who found success in the ring as his personal life fell apart. Dlamini stabbed and killed his girlfriend, pled guilty and asked for the death sentence, but then committed suicide during his 15-year prison sentence. *King Kong*, against all odds, was later presented in 1961 on the West End in London, although by that time, Makeba had moved to New York and was not involved in the production or the soundtrack album.

The second major event of Makeba's life that year (1959) was her brief appearance in a film called *Come Back, Africa*. This was an anti-apartheid, American-produced movie that was part fiction and part nonfiction. Makeba only sang two songs for the film, but the exposure brought her international attention, including that of American singer Harry Belafonte. Belafonte took Makeba under his wing, and she subsequently recorded several songs produced by him (including "Pata Pata," which would not become a hit until almost 10 years later). Makeba then made the move to New York City, and appeared on national television on *The Steve*

South African singer and anti-apartheid activist Miriam Makeba performs in 1967. (Barry Philp/Toronto Star via Getty Images)

Allen Show. She became a regular in New York jazz clubs, singing in multiple languages and making a strong impression on the jazz world.

In addition to recording the multilingual "Pata Pata" with Belafonte, Makeba also released an updated version of an old Skylarks number, "The Click Song." It was released under this title in English because of the Xhosa "click" that is a unique consonant of that language. Even though Makeba considered herself first and foremost a jazz singer, her initial success on the pop charts actually laid the groundwork for the burgeoning style that became known as Afropop. This style is marked by its harmonic simplicity, infectious grooves, and generally happy lyrical content.

In 1960, after learning that her grandmother had died, Makeba attempted to return to South Africa to attend the funeral. She was denied entry, and found that her passport had simply been cancelled. This slap in the face to the budding international star was likely the result of increasing tensions between the South African government and resistance organizations such as the African National Congress. In March of that year, 69 unarmed civilians were killed by police in the Sharpeville massacre. This event escalated the conflict between whites and blacks in South Africa and in neighboring countries, and prompted Makeba to become much more vocal in her opposition to apartheid and her support of the civil rights movement in America. She addressed the United Nations in 1962 and 1964 on the subject of apartheid, and thus her music was officially banned by the South African government in retribution.

She was musically successful all throughout the 1960s, releasing several albums and even singing for President Kennedy's birthday concert in 1962. Makeba and Belafonte won a Grammy Award in 1966 for their live album *An Evening with Belafonte/Makeba*. "Pata Pata" was finally released the year after that, and became a worldwide hit.

Because of her involvement in African and African American social causes, she befriended several activists in the Student Nonviolent Coordinating Committee and the Black Panther Party. Belafonte introduced Makeba to activist Stokely Carmichael after a concert. Makeba and Carmichael were married in 1968, and shortly thereafter moved to Guinea in West Africa to escape the FBI and CIA's near-constant surveillance. Carmichael, while he still lived in the United States, was the de facto leader of the Black Panther Party, and the group's militant views on black power worried several agencies and government officials. This suspicion extended to Makeba as well, and the couple was denied reentry into the United States after visiting the Bahamas. Her popularity in the United States took a huge hit because of her association with the radical left-wing politics of the 1960s.

Upon arriving in Guinea, the newlyweds became close to President Touré, and Makeba was named an official UN delegate of the country. Although her marriage to Carmichael only lasted around five years, she remained in Guinea for 15 years of her life.

In the 1980s, after her only daughter died in childbirth and left her two grandchildren to raise, Makeba decided to leave Guinea and settle in Belgium. Another former husband of hers, trumpeter Hugh Masekela, introduced her to American singer-songwriter Paul Simon, who was then involved in recording his *Graceland* album. This album was a huge international hit, and served to resurrect Simon's solo career; in effect it rehabilitated Makeba to Western audiences as well. Makeba performed with Simon on the *Graceland* album and worldwide tour, which also included several exiled South African musicians such as Masekela and guitarist Ray Phiri.

As a result of the success of *Graceland*, Makeba was offered a new recording contract with Warner Brothers. She released several albums in this final stage of her career, and she even returned to South Africa after apartheid was dismantled in 1990.

Christopher Gable

See also: Kuti, Fela; Ladysmith Black Mambazo

Further Reading

Ellingham, Mark, et al., eds. 1999. *World Music: The Rough Guides; Vol. 1: Africa, Europe, and the Middle East*. London: Rough Guides.

Makeba, Miriam. 1971. *The World of African Song.* Chicago: Quadrangle Books.

Makeba, Miriam, and James Hall. 1988. *Makeba: My Story*. New York: New American Library.

Malay Music

Music has always been an integral part of everyday life for the Malays. During the fin de siècle, music could be heard at open-air theatrical shows known as the *wayang bangsawan*. Later, during the mid-20th century, music was used in countless films screened on makeshift cinema screens dotted along the peninsula. Coeval with the folk songs (*lagu rakyat*) and the contemporary rock-and-roll ditties (*pop yeh yeh*), film used both diegetic and nondiegetic music and has become a significant cultural artifact of the Malay people.

Historically, there is no singular group of people who identify or has been identified as "the Malays," nor an indigenous concept of "music" that exists independently among Malay arts and culture. The Malay people whom we know today are a mixture of indigenous and immigrant peoples who more or less adhere to four distinctive phenotypes considered by anthropologists and postcolonial scholars: the Malays speak *bahasa*, the Malay language; abide by Islamic doctrines; practice Malay customs known as *adat*; and originated mostly from a congregated region in the southeastern parts of Asia. Today, this area includes mainly the eastern side of Sumatra, the Malay peninsula, and numerous offshore islands. Even though the Malay culture may share similar musical characteristics with those on the Indonesian islands of Borneo and Java, arts from these locales are covered elsewhere. That said, a contentious point remains that anyone can *masuk Melayu*—"become Malay"—by assimilating into the culture, which continues to evolve. It is therefore not uncommon to detect some Arabic, Indian, and even Filipino influences in the arts and culture of this particular ethno-regional category.

Malay music is nearly always coupled with theater, rituals, and dance. Until recently, music with or without words has always served a function, which could be sacred or secular. Songs and poems (*pantuns*) are created to chronicle personal or mythical narratives, whereas chants and drumming accompany ceremonial events and deity worship. What Anglophone scholarship has termed "absolute music" can be considered a fairly new introduction into the Malay culture. This may include piano or orchestral music incorporating Malay melodies or the composition of new music using indigenous instruments, such as the various gongs or the bamboo rattles (*angklung*).

The most prevalent music that Malays, both young and old, enjoy is the Malay pop song. From classics to hits, these songs are listened to on the radio or one's personal digital devices on a daily basis. Singers are also hired to perform at weddings or other festive gatherings. Also, friends and colleagues may patronize karaoke joints or visit each others' houses for crooning sessions. Similar to American and British pop songs, the music composed by eminent Malay singer-songwriters have contrasting themes and styles that range from sentimental love songs to jazzy R & B tunes. Local adaptations of the standardized musical style have also garnered popularity. Other than the use of the Malay language, this music has distinct harmonies and ornamented melodies derived mainly from Arabic influences. These transcultural creations include the *balada nusantara* (archipelago ballad), the *irama malaysia* (Malaysian rhythm), and the *mat rock* (Malay rock).

Better-skilled and more charismatic singers attain near-instant celebrity status, as indicated by the high record sales and large turnouts at their performances at home and overseas. Some of the singers who have gained a substantial following include P Ramlee (1929–1973), Sudirman Arshad (1954–1992), M Nasir (1957–), and Zainalabidin Mohamed (1959–), among the male singers; and Anita Sarawak (1952–), Sheila Majid (1965–), Ning Baizura (1975–), and Siti Nurhaliza (1979–) among the female singers. All of these have received millions of views on YouTube.

Equally popular, on the personal level as well as within the public arena, are the religious boy bands and streetwise male choirs. Their narrative styles are differentiated by what is known as the *nasyid* and the *dikir barat*, respectively. The nasyid recitatives are either based on Arabic verses from the Quran or fashioned after praise-songs to Allah in the vernacular languages. Those who listen to nasyid groups (such as Raihan from Malaysia and Nur Irsyad from Singapore) are mostly Muslim devotees wanting to achieve a higher level of religiosity through hymnody. The quality of the musical form has been improving so much that there are now several nasyid charts (*Carta Nasyid*) for fans to nominate their favorite artists.

Whereas nasyid can be heard within the mosques, and on compact discs or other digital media platforms, dikir barat shows are usually organized for festive occasions or communal competitions. The performance consists of the melismatic call of a leader alternating with choreographed responses from a chorus that punctuates the song by repetitive hand claps and frame-drumming. The chanting can be so deafening that everyone within the vicinity is totally absorbed into the music's social content.

Other than the chant forms, some of the more indigenous aspects of Malay culture also involve instrumental accompaniments to traditional dances and martial arts. The common set-up includes the violin, the accordion, the gambus or guitar, and various Malay drums. Because the visual presentation is less spectacular than the dikir barat, the music becomes an acoustic background as the dances or martial showcase take center stage. Eventually, these chamber groups, such as *Sri Warisan* and *Sri Mahligai*, started to expand by incorporating instruments from the European orchestra. Once transformed into full-size ensembles known locally as the *Orkes Melayu* (Malay orchestra), they would stage both classical and popular concerts at community centers or performance halls across the region.

Rap and hip hop have emerged as genres that supply social commentary on everyday life. Since the turn of the 20th century, the Malay-language community has witnessed the rise of rappers and disc jockeys, such as the foursome Ahli Fiqir and duo Sleeq (debuting in 2004 and 2005, respectively). The former specializes in rap songs that deal mostly about the underclass, as represented in their hit song *Samseng* (Gangster), while the latter prefer to portray themselves as prim and proper youngsters singing about piety and fidelity. Sleeq has received support and attention from veteran actor Aaron Aziz and rapper Sheikh Haikal, and with these credentials and endorsements their popularity has increased to cover a larger portion of the regional market.

Another means of talent dissemination is via the medium of television. The most popular format in the promotion of musical talents and new songs has been the singing competition. Several programs followed one after another, such as *Anugerah*, *Malaysian Idol*, *One in a Million*, and *The Voice*. A handful of winners from these competitions have managed to carve out successful careers within the music industry: Shila Amzah, Taufik Batisah, Daniel Lee, Hady Mirza, and Jaclyn Victor. All in all, the fervent enthusiasm of the musicians and listeners has sustained the vibrancy of both the traditional and popular Malay music scenes within the region and beyond.

Jun Zubillaga-Pow

See also: Indonesian Pop Music; Kebyar; Kecak; Wayang Kulit

Further Reading

Kahn, Joel S. 2006. *Other Malays: Nationalism and Cosmopolitanism in the Modern Malay World*. Singapore: Singapore University Press.

Matusky, Patricia. 1993. *Malaysian Shadow Play and Music: Continuity of an Oral Tradition*. Oxford: Oxford University Press.

Matusky, Patricia, and Tan Sooi Beng. 2004. *The Music of Malaysia: The Classical, Folk, and Syncretic Traditions*. Aldershot, UK: Ashgate.

Maznah, Mohamad, and Syed Muhd Khairudin Aljunied, eds. 2011. *Melayu: The Politics, Poetics and Paradoxes of Malayness*. Singapore: NUS Press.

Milner, Anthony. 2008. *The Malays*. Oxford: Blackwell.

Tan Sooi Beng. 1993. *Bangsawan: A Social and Cultural History of Popular Malay Opera*. Singapore: Oxford University Press.

Zubillaga-Pow, Jun. 2014. "The Dialectics of Capitalist Reclamation, or Traditional Malay Music in Fin De Siècle Singapore." *South East Asia Research* 22(1), 123–140.

Zubillaga-Pow, Jun, and Ho Chee Kong, eds. 2014. *Singapore Soundscape: Musical Renaissance of the Global City*. Singapore: National Library Board.

Malhūn

Malhūn (also spelled *melhūn* or *milhūn*) is a poetically based musical genre considered part of the high music repertoire in Morocco, along with Andalusian music. Their privileged status allows these genres to be heard on the radio on solemn occasions, such as the period following the death of King Hassan II in 1999, after several days of Qur'anic recitation had been broadcast. These genres experienced a renaissance on the radio waves in the years following Moroccan independence in 1956, symbolic of a restored national unity and rejection of colonial cultural influence.

Antonio Baldassarre identifies the postindependence sea change that replaced protectorate-era musical programming with indigenous genres and artists. Within five years, Radio Nationale Marocaine had recorded and circulated the complete malhūn repertoire. However, new competition now existed due to the cultural industry of Egypt and the Near East, which flooded the Arab world with recordings and threatened local traditions with the specter of inferiority. The surge in *cha'abī*, a genre particular to Marrakech, partially countered the Levantine influx. Amina 'Alaoui and Touria Hadraoui would later overturn the male tradition of singing malhūn and *gharnati*, an Andalusian genre with origins in Granada.

Said Ennahid explains the etymology of the word "malhūn" as a combination of the Arabic word *lahn* (melody) and the concept of "speaking ungrammatical (or dialectal) Arabic" (Ennahid, 2007, p. 71). In fact Ennahid asserts that the majority of malhūn poets had no knowledge of classical Arabic because they were illiterate. Philip Schuyler (n.d.) describes malhūn as "closely associated" with Andalusian music, although it did not itself originate in al-Andalus, the tri-cultural region of Iberia governed by Muslim rule from 711–1492 CE. Schuyler traces the geographical roots of malhūn to the Tafilalet, a chain of oases south of the Atlas Mountains in east-central Morocco, where early poets had minimal contact with Andalusian refugees. Ennahid notes that the genre spread to Fes, Meknès, Marrakech, and Salé.

The two genres are both similar and different: Carolyn Landau comments on the stylistic characteristics that malhūn shares with the Andalus repertoire, yet makes a sharp distinction between the audience for each: the latter, an educated elite, whereas malhūn is "performed and enjoyed by a wider proportion of Moroccan society" (Landau, 2011, p. 53). Carl Davila concurs, deeming malhūn a "colloquial" genre suitable primarily for wedding celebrations (Davila, 2013). Schuyler observes that the poets and performers of malhūn have traditionally come from the artisanal classes. Although malhūn was added to the Andalusi-dominated conservatory curriculum in the mid-20th century, no theoretical or notational systems for the genre exist, and instructors are practicing performers rather than academicians.

The texts for malhūn lyrics are based on the classical *qasīdah*, a lengthy poetic form both monorhymed and monometered. Typical subjects include pleas to Allah, praise of the Prophet, elegies, descriptions of nature, and love/erotica. Schuyler points out that the influence of the *muwashshah*, an Andalusian genre, is evident in the malhūn's strophic form (four- to 10-line stanzas) and greater complexity in rhyme scheme. The anatomy of a malhūn poem consists of a*l-sarrāba*, a prelude which establishes the rhythm (*iqā'*); *al-qasīdah*, the poem itself; and *al-dardīka*, an accelerated finale. Percussive accompaniment to the poetry is provided by *deff* or *bendīr*, although Schuyler reports that the 'Aissawa Sufi order additionally incorporates *naqqāra*, double-reed pipes (*ghaita*), and six-foot-long trumpets. Urban ensembles use violins and violas, *'ud, suisin, derbuka, tar,* and *t'arija*.

Hicham Chami

See also: Andalusian Music

Further Reading

Baldassare, Antonio. 2004. "Moroccan World Beat through the Media." In Goffredo Plastino (ed.), *Mediterranean Mosaic: Popular Music and Global Sounds*, 79–100. New York: Routledge.

Davila, Carl. 2013. *The Andalusian Music of Morocco: Al-Āla: History, Society and Text*. Wiesbaden, Germany: Reichert Verlag.

Ennahid, Said. 2007. "The Archaeology of Space in Moroccan Oral Tradition: The Case of 'Malhūn' Poetry." *Quademi di Studi Arabi* 2, 71–84.

Landau, Carolyn. 2011. "'My Own Little Morocco at Home': A Biographical Account of Migration, Mediation and Music Consumption." In Jason Toynbee and Byron Dueck (eds.), *Migrating Music*, 38–54. New York: Routledge.

Schuyler, Philip. n.d. "Morocco." *Grove Music Online*. https://www.oxfordmusiconline.com.

Schuyler, Philip D. 2002. "Malhūn: Colloquial Song in Morocco." In Virginia Danielson, Dwight Reynolds, and Scott Marcus (eds.), *Garland Encyclopedia of World Music; Vol. 6: The Middle East*, 495–500. New York: Routledge.

Malouf

Malouf or *maluf* is the form of classical music associated with Tunisia and the Husseinid court of Muhammad Rashid Bey (ruled 1757–1759), the third ruler of the Husseinid dynasty. Muhammad Rashid Bey was an avid musician and played both the *'ud* (or *oud*) and the violin and he decided to revise and arrange the Andalusian form called *Gharnati* into a more organized corpus using the *nawbat* (drum) already well known. Thirteen *maqamat* (system of melodic modes) were used in Gharnati Andalusian music (Aydoun, 2001, p. 41). Muhammad Rashid Bey introduced new instrumental pieces as well as new instruments to the Andalusian nawbat that made them sound more like Ottoman music than original Gharnati. Andalusian music generated sounds that would remind the listener of a garden setting, where the vocals would sound like the twittering and chirping of birds and the music would sound like the bubbling of water fountains and the burbling of flowing water in marble channels. Muhammad Rashid Bey was influenced by the developments in Istanbul, where the poet/musician Buhurizade Mustafa Itri (1640–1711) had left his strong influence on Ottoman court music. The end of Itri's life coincided with the late flowering of Ottoman culture called the Tulip Age which influenced Tunisia. Muhammad Rashid abdicated the throne of Tunisia so that he could pursue his interest in music full time (Zghonda, 1993, p. 12).

Muhammad Rashid composed a number of instrumental pieces that were based on Ottoman forms called *peshrev* or *bashraf* in Arabic, and these were added to

Andalusian music. These are the *istiftah* or opening/introduction to the *maqam*, and the *msaddar* that already existed in the Andalusian *nawbah*, but he changed the arrangement and also composed the instrumental interludes called *tushiyah* and *farighah* (Zghonda, 1993, p. 12). He also reorganized the form of the nawbah into nine parts divided between Part One and Part Two. Part One consists of the istifatah, which serves as an instrumental introduction to the mode of the piece exploring the range and characteristics of the maqam; the *msaddar* or instrumental overture; the *abyat* (singular *bayt*) or the verses that are sung; the *btayhi*, which are verses sung to the same beat as the name of the section; the *tushiyyah*, ornamentation that is used to introduce the next maqam in the evening of musical suites; and the *barawil* (singular *barwal*), which is verses sung to a fast beat. The second part begins with an instrumental *farighah*, followed by a *draj* (plural *adraj*) or a slow song, then another farighah followed by the *khafif* or another slow song, then the finale or the *khatm* of one or two songs that end in a much more rapid tempo (Zghonda, 1993, pp. 12–13).

The verses are sung in classical Arabic, with certain ones in dialect. In both Andalusian and Maluf music, the verses in the abyat sections are in classical Arabic. The themes are of "love, nature, wine" and social issues, whereas the khatm often deal with religious topics or seeking the mercy of God (Zghonda, 1993, p. 13). The orchestra and choir are today large, with the number of instruments at around 15 and the chorus numbering close to 10 (Zghonda, 1993, p. 13). This is a fairly recent development that first occurred in the late French protectorate. In the past the numbers were small: two 'ud players, one on the larger *'ud sharqi* and one on the smaller *'ud tunisi*. Other instruments included the two-(gut)stringed bowed *rabab*, the reed flute or *ney*, and the 26-triple-stringed *qānūn*. For the drums, there is the *riqq* or tambourine; the *naqqarah* or small set of kettle drums (used by the Mevlevi Sufis); the *tar* or large, single-headed drum; and finally the single-headed hourglass-shaped baked clay drum, the *darbukah*. Today, the orchestras also include various sizes of the violin family. The cultural heritage of maluf is sustained by young people who see it as the true Tunisian art.

John A. Shoup

See also: Andalusian Music; Arab Classical Music; Darbuka; Ney; Ottoman Classical Music; Oud; Riq; Tar

Further Reading

Aydoun, Ahmed. 2001. *Musiques du Maroc*. Paris: EDDIF/Autres Temps.

Zghonda, Fethi. 1993. "Booklet notes." *Muntakhabat al-Maluf al-Tunisi* [CD]. Paris: la Maison des Cultures du Monde.

Mambo

Derived from *contradanza*, mambo is a popular music form and dance style that developed in Cuba during the 1930s, which became fashionable in the Americas and internationally throughout the 1950s.

A large migratory population of French and Haitians with French customs arrived in Cuba at the end of the 1700s, importing the *contredanse*, a European social dance, with them. In Cuba, the contredanse was transformed by the introduction of percussive instruments taken from Afro-Cuban music and the addition of a syncopation, taking the name of "contradanza," and outside Cuba also known as the *habanera*. The earliest contradanza were played by two musical groups: the *charanga* (a Cuban popular music orchestra consisting of flutes, *pailas*, *tumbadoras* or conga drums, claves, *güiro*, strings, and later a piano) and the *orquestra típica* (folkloric orchestra), a smaller brass group. The development of these orchestras supported the rise of new musical genres such as the *danzón*, the *danzonete*, the mambo, and the cha-cha-cha. One peculiarity of the danzón was the last section, called *comparsa*, a mostly improvised coda.

At the end of the 1920s, Aniceto Díaz from Matanzas, in his popular *Rompiendo la rutina* (Breaking the routine), mixed elements of the *son* into the danzón, added a vocal part, and created the *danzonete*. Then, in the late 1930s, Antonio Arcano's charanga, a group called "Arcaño y sus Maravillas," sang a refrain: "*vamos a mambear* (let's mambo)" (Sublette, 2004, p. 508). After a while, Arcano's pianist and multi-instrumentalist Orestes "Macho" López (1908–1991) wrote the first piece titled *Mambo* (1938), and later his brother Israel "Cachao" López (1918–2008), a double bassist and composer, recorded the first one, *Rarezas*, in 1940. Even if the structure was still that of a danzón, a syncopated rhythm named "mambo" appeared in the last section. Arcano's group, which played until the end of the 1950s, was the first to experiment with an early danzón-mambo style or *danzón de nuevo ritmo* (danzón with the new rhythm) (Waxer, 1994, p. 152).

Soon new ways of playing and dancing not only the danzón but also the son developed. During the 1940s, Arsenio Rodríguez (1911–1970) began to add new characteristics to son, such as clave rhythm, then he enlarged the ensemble *conjunto* with new instruments. He invented a type of son called "*montuno*" (García, 2006a, pp. 32–63), which also used a rhythm similar to the mambo. Later he claimed to be the father of the genre, even though the majority of scholars disagree (Cano, 2009, pp. 214–215).

Actually, only the addition of new instruments to typical charangas and the growing influence of jazz styles in Cuba led, in the late 1940s, to the internationally renowned mambo of Dámaso Pérez Prado (1916–1989) and in the 1950s to Enrique Jorrin's (1926–1987) cha-cha-cha.

Mambo is based on short (two-bar) and syncopated rhythmic patterns. In the first part the saxophone usually sets the rhythm and then the brass carries on the melody. The last section, like the comparsa in the danzón, is the most vivacious. Mambo is danced by couples, either entirely or slightly apart. The mambo dance, sometimes described as a variation of the rumba but with forward and backward steps, was later codified in the United States, not in Cuba (García, 2006b, pp. 509–510). The main difference between the early version of danzón-mambo style and the new mambo is not the use of the new rhythm, but the fusion of Cuban music with compositional ideas derived from big-band jazz, as done by musicians such as René Hernández, Bebo Valdés, and Pérez Prado.

Among these, Prado gained the widest popularity, to the point that he titled himself the "King of Mambo." In 1948, Prado relocated to Mexico City to form his own band, which he conducted while dancing and singing, using peculiar energetic grunts. There he invented the structure of the mambo using a horn-based big-band format, and with the RCA label he released his major hit *Mambo No. 5* in 1950 (Cano, 2009, pp. 215–216), following it with *Que rico el mambo*. As a consequence of this success, Prado started a U.S. tour. Another hit was *Patricia* in 1958, which was first heard in the film *Al Son del Mambo* in 1950; he added an organ to the brass section in *Guaglione* (1958). Prado's music and dance styles were popularized in Latin America by his appearance together with his big band in numerous Mexican films, especially during the first half of the 1950s.

When this music acquired popularity throughout the Americas, diversified styles of mambo developed locally. The most notable one emerged in New York, thanks to Machito and His Afro-Cubans, Tito Puente, and Tito Rodríguez. Mambo entered the mainstream through songs like *Papa Loves Mambo*, published in 1954, sung by Perry Como and later covered by Nat King Cole and Bing Crosby.

Even if the mambo's popularity seemed generally to decline after the rise of the cha-cha-cha, this did not happen everywhere. Much more than a syncopated rhythm and a new way of dancing, the mambo became a massive cultural phenomenon, which had a strong impact on the general popular culture. The mambo was particularly successful at the cinema: the soundtrack of Dino Risi's film *Pane, amore e . . .* (1955), starring Sophia Loren and Vittorio De Sica, used the *Mambo Italiano*, written by Bob Merrill in 1954, first recorded by Rosemary Clooney and then by many other artists worldwide. Also, *Patricia* became enormously popular in Europe, thanks to Federico Fellini's 1960 film *La Dolce Vita*. A mambo appears in the first act of Leonard Bernstein's *West Side Story* (1957) and later in the orchestral suite *Symphonic Dances* (1961) drawn from the same musical. More recently, Pink Martini's song *No Hay Problema* (*Sympathique*, 1997) was influenced by this rhythm, and Lou Bega's cover of *Mambo No. 5* (1999) ignited a pop revival of mambo.

Benedetta Saglietti

See also: Claves and Clave Rhythm; Conjunto; Puente, Tito

Further Reading

Cano, Rubén López. 2009. "*Apuntes para una prehistoria del mambo* [Notes for a prehistory of the mambo]." *Latin American Music Review/Revista de Música Latinoamericana* 30(2) (Fall-Winter), 213–242.

García, David F. 2004. "Contesting That Damned Mambo: Arsenio Rodríguez, Authenticity, and the Puerto Rican and Cuban Music Cultures of El Barrio and the Bronx, 1950s." *CENTRO Journal* 16(1) (Spring), 154–175.

García, David F. 2006a. *Arsenio Rodríguez and the Transnational Flows of Latin Popular Music*. Philadelphia: Temple University Press.

García, David F. 2006b. "Going Primitive to the Movements and Sounds of Mambo." *The Musical Quarterly* 89(4), 505–523.

García, David F. 2008. "Embodying Music/Othering Dance: The Mambo Body in Havana and New York City." In Julie M. Malnig (ed.), *Ballroom, Boogie, Shimmy Sham, Shake. The Social and Popular Dance Reader*, 165–181. Urbana: University of Illinois Press.

Giro, Radamés, ed. 1993. *El Mambo*. La Habana, Cuba: Editorial Letras Cubanas.

Gray, John. 2013. *Baila! A Bibliographic Guide to Afro-Latin Dance Musics, from Mambo to Salsa*. Nyack, NY: African Diaspora Press.

Sublette, Ned. 2004. *Cuba and Its Music: From the First Drums to the Mambo*. Chicago: Chicago Review Press.

Waxer, Lise. 1994. "Of Mambo Kings and Songs of Love: Dance Music in Havana and New York from the 1930s to the 1950s." *Latin American Music Review/Revista de Música Latinoamericana* 15(2) (Autumn-Winter), 139–176.

Mande Music

Mande music refers to the professional music-making of a variety of ethnic groups in West Africa who trace their heritage to the Mali Empire (13th to 17th centuries CE). As Mande peoples dispersed during the 19th century, they both assimilated local cultures and spread their own culture. Today their descendants in Mali and Guinea are referred to as *Maninka*, and in Senegal, the Gambia, and Guinea-Bissau as *Mandinka* (Charry, 2000, p. 1). Mande ethnic groups have four distinct spheres of professional music-making, which remain largely independent of one another: music of hunters' societies; music of the *jelis* (also known by the French term *griot*); drumming and dancing associated with life-cycle events, work, and entertainment; and modern urban electric groups (Charry, 2000, p. 1). Each musical sphere is distinct in terms of who performs that music, the instruments they use, and the repertoires they perform, although there are some interconnections.

The term "Mande" has two senses. In linguistics, it refers to one subgroup of the Niger-Congo family of languages. In this sense, it does not refer to a single language or ethnic identity, but includes many languages spoken by a variety of ethnic groups. In the local context, "Mande" has a very specific meaning, referring to a homeland situated between the upper Niger River and its tributary in the Sankarani River, near the Mali-Guinea border. Defining ethnic belonging by language use is complicated in Africa, due to the highly context-dependent use of names and the inaccuracies perpetuated by colonial naming practices that appear throughout older scholarly sources. In this entry, based on the work of Eric Charry, the term "Mande music" refers to the music of Northern Mande speakers.

The area where Mande music developed and flourishes today is centered in southwest Mali and northeast Guinea, and includes parts of Senegal, Guinea-Bissau, the Gambia, Burkina Faso, and Cote d'Ivoire. It stretches across parts of the *sahel* (shores of the desert), savanna, and woodlands of West Africa. Between approximately 800 and 1500 CE, this area was the site of a succession of great empires (Ghana, Mali, and Songhai) built on wealth from the trade of gold for salt. These trans-Saharan trade routes facilitated the arrival of Islam in western Africa, starting around 800 CE. The boundaries of the present-day countries of Ghana and Mali differ from the historical empires of the same names. Mande societies are organized around a distinction between free-born people and those born into hereditary classes of professional artisans. Among the castes of artisans are the musical-verbal artists, known as jelis.

FOUR SPHERES OF MANDE MUSIC

Hunter's Music

Hunter's music is largely unknown outside of Africa, according to Charry, and has had little role or influence in the modern nations of Mali and Guinea. Nevertheless, it has been an important source of inspiration for creative artists (including jelis), and appears to be connected to the ancient history of the region and its broader cultural patterns. Hunter's music consists of praising, chanting, and singing, accompanied by calabash harp, a metal scraper, and vocal interjections.

Hunters have traditionally had a special place in Mande society because they command knowledge and power and are linked with the founding of the Mali Empire (Charry, 2000). Today there are restrictions on open game hunting, but in earlier times the hunters' role was key to survival. Hunters were also associated with warriors because great warriors started out as hunters. In some ways, the hunter's musician or *sora* functions more like a priest, ensuring protection from the powerful forces released in the process of killing an animal. The sora also maintains the repository of the traditions, historic chants, and myths of the hunters.

The hunter's main musical instrument is a calabash harp, an instrument that is common in the savanna lands of western Africa (Charry, 2000, p. 69). There are three Mande calabash harps, two of which are used for hunter's music. The *simbi* is a seven-stringed harp played for hunters. The *bolon* is a three- or four-stringed calabash harp played for warriors. The third harp is the *kora* belonging to the jelis (discussed in the following section).

The harps are plucked with both thumbs and both index fingers. The characteristic style consists of a short melody played over and over with slight variation. Usually, one person plays and one person sings, although there may be another player who interjects vocal responses. The tradition does not emphasize solo or virtuosic playing. Melodic contours tend to be descending lines. The rhythmic feel has a subtle shift from triple to duple beat divisions or vice versa. This aspect of timing is an important aspect of Mande aesthetics.

Jeliya

"Jelis" are members of a hereditary caste of professional musical-verbal artists; their art is referred to as *jeliya*. It includes three domains of specialization: speech, which communicates historical narratives, stories, genealogies, and proverbs; song, which includes melodies, lyrics, and techniques for expanding them; and instrument playing. The knowledge and skills required to perform are handed down through a limited number of family lineages and require a lifetime of training (Charry, 2000). Jeli families are supported by the patronage of warriors, traders, and other important people. The relationship between patrons and jelis is informed more by social obligation, and a sense of historical ties, than by strict economic motivation. The origins of the jeliya are linked with Bala Faseke Kouyate, who was the jeli of Sunjata Keita, the warrior-king who founded the Mali Empire. Because jeli music is meant to inspire a patron to act, jelis have power despite their relatively low social status. Although jeli music is associated with elite patrons, it is still widely appreciated throughout Mande society.

Although jeliya is accessible and heard widely, it is restricted in practical ways. For example, only jelis have the right to play the musical instruments associated with their tradition and to sing about certain aspects of Mande social and political life (Charry, 2000, p. 90). The jeli instruments include the kora (a 21-stringed harp), *bala* (a xylophone, also called *balafon*), *koni* (a plucked lute), and in some areas, *dundun* (a large double-headed, cylindrical drum) and *tama* (an hourglass-shaped squeeze drum). Although many jelis are familiar with all aspects of the tradition, it is typical to specialize in one of the three areas. Women are almost always singers. The institution of the jeli is not unique to Mande peoples; it has analogues in Wolof (*gewel*), Fulbe (*gaulo*), Moorish (*iggio*), and Soninke (*jaare*) populations (Charry, 2000, p. 91).

The deepest expressions of jeliya are the collections of praise songs (*fasa*), which concern someone's deeds and are often epic in proportion (Charry, 2000). Jeli music has four basic elements: two styles of vocalization and two styles of instrumental accompaniment. Vocalizations are either melodic singing (*donkilo*) or improvised declamatory recitation (*sataro*). Instrumental styles are either a melodic ostinato that accompanies singing (*kumbengo*) or improvised interludes before or between sections of singing (*birimintingo*).

Drumming

Mande drumming is divided into two major culture areas: Senegambian Mandinka drumming and dancing in the west and Malian/Guinean Maninka drumming and dancing in the east. Mandinka ensembles use a three-drum format (*kutirindingo, kutiriba,* and *sabaro*). Maninka drumming uses a two-drum format with a lead drum and an accompaniment drum; Maninka ensembles include *jembes, dunduns,* and sometimes *tamas*. Traditionally, Maninka drums have different uses and repertoires, but in the modern era have been combined. Drumming and dancing are used for entertainment, agricultural work, life-cycle events (mainly circumcision, excision, and marriage), and other social and religious functions. Performances often use a circular formation with the drummers at the head of the circle. Dancers emerge singly, or by twos or threes, interact intensively with the drummers, then fall back into the circle. Those in the circle support by clapping.

Guitar and the Modern Urban Electric Groups

So-called modern music in Guinea and Mali has origins in the jeli tradition and in small orchestras, which emerged in the 1920s, playing European and Latin American popular styles (Charry, 2000, p. 242). By the 1990s, modern music groups in these countries definitively abandoned foreign influences. Becoming inward-focused on Mande traditions, musicians reached into older types of music for new combinations of instruments (Charry, 2000, p. 242). The guitar, which was brought to Guinea in the 1910s or 1920s, became an important link between the jeliya and modern electric bands. After independence, electric guitars came into use.

Elizabeth Kimzey Batiuk

See also: Djembe; Kora

Further Reading

Charry, Eric. 2000. *Mande Music: Traditional and Modern Music of the Maninka and Mandinka of Western Africa*. Chicago: University of Chicago Press.

Hale, Thomas A. 1998. *Griots and Griottes: Masters of Words and Music*. Bloomington: Indiana University Press.

Hoffman, Barbara G. 2000. *Griots at War: Conflict, Conciliation and Caste in Mande*. Bloomington: Indiana University Press.

Katz, Jonathan. 2015. "Mande jaliyaa." In Michael Church (ed.), *The Other Classical Musics: Fifteen Great Traditions*, 160–177. Woodbridge, UK: Boydell Press.

Knight, Roderic. 1984. "Music in Africa: The Manding Contexts." In Gerard Béhague (ed.), *Performance Practice: Ethnomusicological Perspectives*, 53–90. Westport, CT: Greenwood Press.

Knight, Roderic. 1992. *Music of the Mande, Parts I and II* [videotape]. New York: Tivoli.

Kouyaté, Dani. 1995. *Keita!: Heritage of the Griot*. AFIX Productions. San Francisco: California Newsreel.

Manu Chao (1961–)

José-Manuel Thomas Arthur Chao Ortega, better known as Manu Chao (and also by the stage name Oscar Tramor), is a French-born musical artist of Spanish heritage. Chao sings in a wide variety of languages, including French, Spanish, English, Italian, Arabic, Galician, and Portuguese; and combines a diverse assortment of musical styles, including punk, rock, salsa, reggae, ska, Algerian raï, and more. Chao draws influence from immigrant populations in France, his Iberian roots, and his experiences traveling extensively throughout South America. His music is popular worldwide, but more prominently in Europe and Latin America than in the United States.

During the mid-1980s, Chao formed a Spanish/English rockabilly band called Hot Pants with a group of other musicians in Paris. In 1986, Chao formed another band, Los Carayos, with his brother Antoine Chao and other friends interested in combing the punk/rockabilly sound of Hot Pants with the growing popularity of the alternative music scene in Paris at the time. In 1987, Chao, his brother Antoine, and their cousin Santiago Casariego formed yet another group, called Mano Negra (named after a Spanish anarchist group), which achieved a hit with their 1988 recording of "Mala Vida," a former Hot Pants song. Following a series of successful albums and multiple world tours, disagreements among the members and legal problems caused the group to disband in 1995.

After moving to Madrid, Spain, Chao formed a new group called Radio Bemba Sound System. After spending several years traveling through South and Central America to learn—and record—the sounds of street music and bar music in a variety of cultures, Chao released *Clandestino* in 1998 under his own name, to critical success. In 2001, Chao released his second solo album (with Radio Bemba Sound System), called *Próxima Estación: Esperanza* (Next stop: hope). This second album quickly achieved widespread popular success, leading to a subsequent tour and live recording, called *Radio Bemba Sound System*, in 2002. After a French-only album entitled *Sibérie m'était contée* (If [the story of] Siberia was told to me) was released in 2004, Chao's international release of *La Radiolina* (The small radio) in 2007 gained further popular attention worldwide. Another live album, *Baionarena*, followed in 2009.

In 2003, Chao approached Mali musicians Amadou & Mariam (Amadou Bagayoko and Mariam Doumbia), a blind duo whose recordings (since the late 1990s) have mixed the traditional Mali sound with a diverse variety of world instruments and musical elements to create a form of "Afro-blues," to collaborate vocally. He ultimately produced the duo's 2004 album, called *Dimanche à Bamako* (Sunday in Bamako). In 2009, Chao recorded an album with psychiatric patients in Buenos Aires, and produced an album for the Mali band SMOD, with Amadou & Mariam's son, Sam, in 2010.

Chao's songs typically carry a distinct left-wing message (aligning with his own political inclinations). His music mixes any number of styles and languages, but is generally influenced by British punk rock bands such as The Clash, among others. His lyrics also convey a punk-inspired sensibility, with common topics of immigration, drugs, and the working-class struggles of daily life around the world. Bits of music or lyrics in Chao's recordings are sometimes reused, such as the inclusion of "Bongo Bong" from *Clandestino* and "La Primavera" from *Próxima Estación: Esperanza* in other songs on the same recording or on later albums. Throughout Chao's musical pursuits, the artist makes a point to support, promote, and cater to marginalized populations. For example, while still recording with Mano Negra, the musician was notably reluctant to tour within the "regimented music business" in the United States, preferring instead to play the "strip joints of Paris" and the "deprived multi-ethnic suburbs" (Culshaw, 2015). Chao has reportedly turned down large advertising sponsorship contracts and only plays where and when he wants to play, often preferring to make plans to travel and perform only a relatively short time in advance. However, the artist is also a study in contradictions—anti-globalization when his own heritage and the music he offers are themselves a product of globalization; anti-big business and commercialization when his albums have brought him substantial wealth—thus lending another layer of complexity to this often-controversial global musician.

Erin E. Bauer

See also: Reggae; Rock and Roll; Salsa

Further Reading

Büyükbay, Can. 2009. "Manu Chao and Criticism of Economic Globalization." *İzinsiz Gösteri* 191 (December-January). http://www.izinsizgosteri.net/new/?writer=89.

Culshaw, Peter. 2007. "World Beater: Musical Revolutionary and Man of the People—If Only Everyone Could Be Like Manu Chao." *The Guardian,* July 14. https://www.theguardian.com/music/2007/jul/15/worldmusic.

Culshaw, Peter. 2013. *Clandestino: In Search of Manu Chao*. London: Serpent's Tail.

Culshaw, Peter. 2015. "Manu Chao Is Music's Last True Radical." *Vice Media*, January 27. https://www.vice.com/en_us/article/rq4pxm/in-search-of-manu-chao.

Reyes, Oscar. 2008. "Manu Chao, the Neighbourhood Singer." *Red Pepper*, August. https://www.redpepper.org.uk/manu-chao-the-neighbourhood-singer.

Mariachi

Mariachi is the pre-eminent musical style of Mexico. It began as an indigenous form of music among peasant farmers in Mexico's central region. Beginning in the late 19th century, it spread to more urban areas, where was promoted by the Mexican government as a cultural touchstone. While there is debate about the origin of the word "mariachi" itself, it can indicate either the type of music, the band that plays it, or an individual musician. Mariachi has a distinctive sound in its predominance of trumpets and violins as well as having a unique look in the costumes of the players. Today its influence has spread around the world and can be found in all forms of popular music as well as religious rites.

The word "mariachi" is commonly (though mistakenly) defined as a derivative of the French word *mariage* (marriage). The French Intervention in Mexico in the mid-1860s under Napoleon III of France brought influences of the French culture to the Mexican people. It was thought that local musicians were hired to play music at weddings, giving rise to the term "mariachi."

However, the word "mariachi" was found in a letter written by a Mexican priest in 1852, a full decade before the arrival of the French. It is not surprising that the word did not appear in writing before 1852, as the music evolved among rural peasant farmers, many of whom could not read or write.

Some scholars believe the word derives from music played at festivals honoring a revered local image of the Virgin Mary which was referred to as "Maria H," pronounced in Spanish as (roughly) "Maria-Achay." Some say that it comes from a local pronunciation of a popular song, "María Ce Son." Still others believe it came from the language of an indigenous Indian tribe, referring to the wood from a tree used to make guitars or the platform on which mariachis performed.

Whatever the true origins of the word, experts agree that the music developed in the rural regions of central Mexico, particularly the state of Jalisco, which extends from the center of the country to the Pacific Ocean in the west. Its centrally located capital city is Guadalajara, though the resort town of Puerto Vallarta on Jalisco's west coast is also well known. Though mariachi music has traditionally been played in many parts of Mexico, it is still strongly associated with Jalisco.

Mariachi began as folk music which evolved as part of the oral tradition in isolated illiterate communities in the central and western regions of Mexico, coming to be known as *son jaliscience*. This "son" (sound in Spanish), referred to Jalisco where it was played on string instruments by musicians dressed in the traditional clothing of local peasant farmers. The town of Cocula, Jalisco, is especially associated with the origin of modern mariachi.

As farmers abandoned rural life in the late 19th and early 20th centuries to try their luck in the city, many migrated to Guadalajara, where the music spread beyond the narrow confines of individual villages. The music became enriched as

Mexican mariachi musicians performing with traditional instruments such as the *guitarrón* (left), a large bass guitar. (Elena Zarubina/Dreamstime.com)

musicians met and learned from each other in the city. Guadalajara became especially noted for this type of music, boosting it by holding an annual mariachi festival.

When the music reached Mexico City through further migrations of peasants from the countryside into the city, the Mexican government promoted it as a source of indigenous cultural pride for the nation, especially following various political changes as the incoming administration sought to identify itself with "the real Mexico." Son music was heavily promoted both inside and outside Mexico, with the name "mariachi" becoming associated with what was considered a more urban style.

Son music also absorbed elements of traditional music from Spain both before and after urbanization. Prior to the Spanish conquest of Mexico in the 16th century, indigenous tribes played music as part of religious celebrations, using handmade flutes, drums, small percussive instruments such as rattles or maracas, and horns made of conch shells. After the Spaniards arrived, European instruments were introduced, primarily to be used during the Catholic Mass. Spanish guitars, violins, harps, brass horns, and woodwind instruments appeared. They were adopted by the local populace into festivals which might be either sacred or secular. The instruments were also modified in shape and tuning as they began to be crafted by local artisans.

During the colonial period, the Spaniards also imported the concept of a musical group containing guitars, violins, and a harp. This sound, leaning heavily on string instruments, was adapted into regional varieties depending on the preferences of the local populace. Different styles were played in different areas, but one of the most popular continued to be the son jalisciense of the state of Jalisco.

Wealthy landowners paid local musicians to play their string instruments for celebrations held at the large *haciendas*, or estates. At events among the wealthy, son jalisciense was the preferred style. Musicians who could play the son jalisciense that evolved into mariachi soon found that they could find work more readily at the haciendas, and were paid at a higher rate than those who could not. With this as an incentive, son jalisciense spurred the growth of modern mariachi music.

Part of the entertainers' appeal was the colorful costuming of the musicians, which enhanced the performance. At first the players wore their own typical peasant attire of white cotton pants and shirts with the leather sandals known as *huaraches*. Families of wealthy colonial landowners emulated the fashions of Spain. Women of the haciendas sported the brocaded, heavily embellished dresses worn at the Spanish royal court. Because local women could not afford those fashions, they made their own versions in cotton instead of silk, using brightly colored ribbons in place of expensive lace. With their full "peasant skirts" and kaleidoscopic colors, this type of fashion was perfect for swirling to mariachi music in exhibitions of rural Mexican folk dances.

Among the male musicians, some continued to dress in peasant-type attire. However, another type of mariachi fashion for men evolved in response to sociopolitical changes. The *charro* was roughly the Mexican equivalent of the cowboy in the United States. The charro was as much a fixture at the large haciendas in Jalisco as the cowboy was on big Texas ranches. However, following the Mexican Revolution, large haciendas were broken up, leaving little employment for the charros. At this same time, regular jobs for musicians on the haciendas became scarce, and they were forced to play in public places, hoping to attract attention to set them apart from others.

Much as cowboys were glorified in the United States after the heyday of the Wild West, the charros became a symbol of Mexican pride and masculinity. The *charreada* was adopted as a national sport in Mexico, with rings constructed for the competitive shows of professional charro associations, much like rodeos in the United States. To add to the spectacle, their costumes were embellished beyond the typical attire of a working ranch hand.

Mariachi musicians adopted the same type of glamorous apparel to add to their showmanship and pay tribute to Mexican pride. The costuming usually consisted of a waist-length jacket with tight pants open slightly at the ankle to fit over short riding boots. They were often ornamented with silver buttons, embroidery, spangles, or intricately cut leather, and topped by a wide-brimmed sombrero hat.

The 20th century brought several important changes to mariachi. The musicians were exposed to outside musical styles such as polkas, waltzes, and even opera, which they promptly incorporated into their compositions. Trumpets were readily available in urban centers, with an engaging brass resonance that added significantly to the mariachi sound. Mariachi was heard on the radio beginning in the 1920s, necessitating an important modification: Most mariachi tunes were longer than the standard three minutes for recordings, so the musicians were forced to arrange shorter songs. Also, to appeal to the widest possible listening audience, some elements of jazz and Cuban music were incorporated, including an even more prominent use of the trumpet to enhance the distinctive mariachi sound.

A major boon to mariachi was the 20th-century movie industry. Like Westerns in the United States, charro movies date from the infancy of Mexican film studios. Mariachi was featured in the 1936 film, *Allá en el Rancho Grande* (Out on the great ranch). Mariachi films expanded the music's popularity not only in Mexico, but also among Mexican-Americans, becoming a symbol of ethnic pride.

A significant factor in the growth of mariachi was Mariachi Vargas de Tecalitlán. This group left Jalisco for Mexico City where, in 1934, they were invited to play at the inauguration of Mexican President Lázaro Cárdenas, who was committed to showcasing the country's proud native culture as a unified national identity. Mariachi Vargas shot to stardom, and enhanced their standing with the hiring of a trained musician, Rubín Fuentes, as musical director. With the requirement that all of the group's musicians be able to read music, the tunes were able to be standardized and the musicians no longer had to pick up their songs through "playing by ear." Mariachi Vargas became the model for other groups. With two trumpets, a classical guitar, and several violins, the standard was set. It is said that the arrangements of Mariachi Vargas have become the definitive statements of what mariachi should be. Thereafter, mariachi was played at presidential inaugurations as a point of Mexican identity and pride. Mariachi musicians were also in demand at the parties of the aristocracy who imitated the ruling politicians. During the 20th century, drawn by the hope of industrial employment, more farm workers moved to urban centers like Mexico City. Many from Jalisco settled around that city's Plaza Garibaldi. Mariachi musicians performed in the plaza hoping to be hired for social events or restaurants. However, they could also be hired to play individual serenades, a practice which continues today at Garibaldi Square. It is known for being the center of mariachi music, with as many as 4,000 musicians circulating at peak times. The Mexican government has added a museum dedicated to mariachi, enhancing the square as a huge tourist attraction. Though mariachis can be hired by telephone or on the internet, people generally prefer to come to the plaza to experience the musicians.

A departure in mariachi from other musical forms is in not generally having a designated lead singer. Often certain musicians sing specific songs based on the particular vocal quality required. Most songs are about love, though themes of death, politics, betrayal, historical heroes, and the cult of machismo might be incorporated. In homage to its rural origins, country life and animals might also be spotlighted in mariachi. Probably the most famous of these is "La Cucaracha" (The cockroach). Another well-known mariachi song is the "Tapatío" of Guadalajara, familiarly known as the "Mexican Hat Dance."

Although mariachi has traditionally been dominated by male musicians, some women have broken through. An early female mariachi performer, Lola Beltrán, was spotlighted as a teenager when Mariachi Vargas invited her on stage with the group. Her rendition of "Cucurrucucu Paloma" is today considered a classic. Contemporary female mariachi groups include Mariachi Divas and Mariachi Mujer 2000.

The mariachi festival that began years ago in Guadalajara is currently the annual International Mariachi Festival, a 10-day event which attracts more than 500 mariachis who perform in venues from concert halls to the streets of the city.

Mariachi music has been incorporated into the Mass of the Roman Catholic Church in a number of cities. *Misa Panamericana* is a mariachi folk mass that is sung in Spanish and uses traditional instruments to interpret customary elements of the service.

In 2011, UNESCO honored mariachi by unanimously naming it an Intangible Cultural Heritage element.

Nancy Hendricks

See also: Guitarrón Mexicano; Mexican Regional Music

Further Reading

Greathouse, Patricia. 2009. *Mariachi.* Layton, UT: Gibbs Smith.

Lornell, Kip. 2012. *Exploring American Folk Music: Ethnic, Grassroots, and Regional Traditions in the United States.* Oxford: University Press of Mississippi.

Nevin, Jeff. 2001. *Virtuoso Mariachi.* Lanham, MD: University Press of America.

Sheehy, Daniel. 2006. *Mariachi Music in America: Experiencing Music, Expressing Culture.* New York: Oxford University Press.

Marimba (American, Guatemalan, Marimba de Arco)

The *marimba* is a wooden idiophone with bars/slats arranged from large (low pitch) to small (high pitch) and struck with mallets. Resonators, in box or tube shape, are hung underneath each key to amplify the sound of the bars. In the Americas, the marimba is found in three general forms: (1) an industrially manufactured version, used in Western art music and conservatories throughout the hemisphere; (2) a Central American version, which has spread from southern Mexico to Costa Rica; and (3) a South American version, found in the coastal regions of southwestern Colombia and northern Ecuador.

The conservatory version was developed from earlier European xylophones and designed by John C. Deagan, Ulysses G. Leedy, and Clair O. Musser in the first half of the 20th century. The origins of the other two types have been debated over

---

Marimba

The modern conservatory version of the marimba has now become an integral part of the orchestra and wind ensemble in Western classical music. The instrument is an increasingly sought-after solo, chamber, and ensemble instrument. The contemporary marimba's construction, however, is still very similar to its Guatemalan origins, and the instrument's keys are made of several varieties of rainforest hardwoods. The most sought-after of these is Honduran rosewood, which is an increasingly scarce rainforest wood recently added to international watch lists for overforesting. Honduran rosewood must dry for several years, in some cases decades, before it is used for marimba making. Its superb acoustic qualities mellow and fluctuate in various temperatures and humidity levels.

the years due to various political ideologies and the presence of the instrument among different cultures. The Central American marimba is found within indigenous and mestizo populations, whereas the South American type is performed by Afro-Colombians and Afro-Ecuadorans. Especially in Guatemala, an undercurrent of nationalism and lack of colonial records from the slave trade led to an active debate about the origins of the marimba (whether African or indigenous American) throughout the 20th century. Nonetheless, scholars have demonstrated the Latin American marimba's origin in Africa via linguistic, historical, and technological studies.

In Guatemala, the marimba is claimed as both the national instrument (1978) and national symbol (1999), having been the subject of several studies of "national" music. There are three different types of Guatemalan marimba. The *marimba de tecomates* is the closest to African predecessors, consisting of a single row of 21 to 28 keys amplified by hollowed calabash gourds attached underneath the frame. An arced branch extends toward the performer from one end to the other, which braces the marimba away from the standing performer's stomach (a cloth strap suspends the instrument from the player's shoulders). The instrument can also be played with the performer seated on the arced branch and the marimba balanced upright with sticks. A key feature of the marimba de tecomates and all other Central American marimbas is the *tela* (dried pig intestine) that is placed over a hole at the bottom of each resonator and attached with beeswax to achieve the characteristic *charleo* (buzz) sound. The *marimba sencilla*, developed in the 18th century, is more technologically complex, featuring a manufactured frame, legs, resonator boxes in place of gourds, and an expansion of the single-row keyboard to incorporate up to four performers on the same instrument. The *marimba doble*, a chromatic (double-row) marimba resembling the keys of a piano and designed to perform European music, was developed in the late 19th century and has its own controversy over its place of origin between Chiapas, Mexico and Quetzaltenango, Guatemala.

In the early 20th century, the marimba doble ensemble expanded to include two marimbas, the *marimba grande* (four performers) and *marimba tenor* (three performers, also referred to as *marimba cuache*). The standardized marimba doble is used in several overlapping performance styles, including *marimba pura* (pure marimba, a nostalgic reference to early 20th-century popular music, such as foxtrots, polkas, and the like), *marimba folklórica* (folkloric marimba, based on the Guatemalan *son*), *marimba de concierto* (formal concertized marimba, like that used in the Western conservatory tradition), *marimba orquesta* (a contemporary popular dance style combining the marimba with wind instruments and electronic drums, bass, and synthesizers), and *marimba de la Iglesia Católica* (marimba combined with chorus in Catholic church services).

Similar to the marimba de tecomates, the *marimba de arco* of Nicaragua features an arced branch connecting each end and is performed by a single musician, placing the melody in the right hand and a repeated bass pattern in the left. The marimba de arco also shares with the Guatemalan marimba sencilla the technological advancement of manufactured resonators in the shape of long tubes. Found largely in southern Nicaragua, the marimba de arco is typically performed in a trio, accompanied by a guitar to the left side of the marimba and a *guitarilla* (small, four-stringed guitar) to the right. Both string instruments are strummed, providing harmonic and rhythmic background to the melody on the marimba. Marimba de arco trios are central in the celebration of different Catholic saint's days, performing in street processions and private homes and providing the music for a series of dances collectively known as the *baile de la marimba* (dance of the marimba).

Jack W. Forbes

See also: Gyil; Salsa

Further Reading

Chenoweth, Vida. 1964. *The Marimbas of Guatemala.* Lexington: University of Kentucky Press.

Garfias, Robert. 1983. "The Marimbas of Mexico and Central America." *Latin American Music Review* 4(2), 203–228.

Kaptain, Laurence. 1992. *The Wood That Sings: The Marimba in Chiapas, Mexico.* Everett, PA: Honey Rock.

O'Brien-Rothe, Linda Lee. 1982. "Marimbas of Guatemala: The African Connection." *The World of Music* 24(2), 99–103.

Scruggs, T. M. 1998. "Cultural Capital, Appropriate Transformations, and Transfer by Appropriation in Western Nicaragua: El Baile de la Marimba." *Latin American Music Review* 19(1), 1–30.

Scruggs, T. M. 1999. "Central America: Marimba and Other Musics of Guatemala and Nicaragua." In John M. Schechter (ed.), *Music in Latin American Culture: Regional Traditions*, 80–125. New York: Schirmer Books.

Marley, Bob (1945–1981)

Bob Marley is the central figure in the development and widespread popularization of reggae music. Although his career as a recording artist and live performer was tragically cut short, he has become of the best-known and best-loved musicians in recent history. Marley's music is enjoyed by diverse audiences, from the Americas to Europe, from Africa to Asia. Even in countries where English is not widely spoken or understood, Marley's message of peace, love, and unity continues to inspire numerous people worldwide.

Robert Nesta Marley was born in 1945 to Cedella Booker, the 18-year-old daughter of Afro-Jamaican farmers; and "Captain" Norval Marley, a 60-year-old European-Jamaican who worked as an agricultural agent in St. Ann Parish. Bob saw little of his father during his childhood: when his father passed away at age 70, Cedella moved with her son to Kingston to find better job opportunities. In the urban slum of Trenchtown, Bob Marley began his musical explorations through collaboration with his stepbrother Neville "Bunny" Livingston (1947–) and other youths in his neighborhood. Marley left school at age 14 to take on an apprenticeship as a welder and to pursue his musical aspirations. With the encouragement of two other teenage musicians, Desmond Dekker (1941–2006) and Jimmy Cliff (1948–), Marley auditioned for record producer Leslie Kong. At age 17, Marley recorded five songs for Kong's Federal Studios, but was not successful in reaching an audience with them.

> **Marley Children**
>
> Since his untimely death in 1981, the legend and influence of Jamaican reggae musician Bob Marley have grown tremendously. Marley's music and political messaging are ubiquitous in Afro-Caribbean culture, and t-shirts, posters, and online postings with his likeness are commonplace. Bob Marley's legacy, however, is equally furthered by several of his children, each with distinct musical careers. Stephen Marley is a popular reggae artist and has won five Grammy Awards for his work in the genre. Stephen, Ziggy, and daughters Cedella and Sharon formed Ziggy Marley & the Melody Makers in 1979 and performed for more than two decades until 2002. Damian Marley is the youngest child of Bob Marley; in addition to performing as a reggae artist since the age of 13, he is also a successful record producer.

During this time, vocal harmony groups such as the Platters, the Drifters, and the Teenagers were popular with Jamaican audiences. Jamaican vocal duos and trios quickly began harmonizing, accompanied by the distinctive *ska* rhythm and horn section. With this in mind, Marley put together a vocal harmony group with Bunny Livingston and Peter Tosh (1944–1987). The group was coached by singer Joe Higgs, who also encouraged their choice of the name the Wailers due to the "wailing" nature of their impoverished Trenchtown neighborhood. After two years of performing at various events in Trenchtown and around Kingston, the Wailers landed a contract with Coxone Dodd's Studio One label. They recorded their first single, "Simmer Down," in 1964, and it was an immediate hit. In addition to recording originals, it was common for groups such as the Wailers to record "do-overs" (now known as *covers*) of American pop songs: one example by the Wailers is their version of "Teenager in Love," recorded in 1965. During these early years, Marley quickly emerged as the leader of the Wailers, and became responsible for most of their creative decisions.

In 1965, Marley met Rita Anderson (1946–), the lead singer of a vocal trio called the Soulettes, later known as the I-Threes. Coxone Dodd had signed the Soulettes to Studio One, appointing Marley as their manager and vocal coach. Marley quickly developed feelings for Rita, and the two were married in 1966. Bob adopted Rita's daughter, Sharon, and their own children Cedella, Ziggy (David), and Stephen were born in 1967, 1968, and 1972, respectively.

Despite recording a number of successful singles for Studio One, the Wailers had never received proper royalties for their work. Marley was determined to start his own label to maintain creative and financial control over his work. Shortly after his marriage to Rita, he left for Delaware, to live with his mother and work as much as possible to earn the necessary funds; upon his return he and the Wailers launched Wailin' Soul Records. By this time, the Marleys had become followers of Rasta preacher Mortimer Planno. The visit of Emperor Haile Selassie in 1966 further inspired the Marleys, as well as Peter Tosh and Bunny Wailer, to adopt Rasta beliefs and its attendant Ital lifestyle of traditional dress, dreadlocks, natural foods, and spiritual use of cannabis. Marley's spiritual beliefs also affected his creative output: one of the first releases on Wailin' Soul Records was "Selassie Is the Chapel," a testament to his new faith set to the tune of "Crying in the Chapel," which had been a hit for Elvis Presley in 1965.

Wailin' Soul Records was short lived, and in 1969, the band turned to producer Lee "Scratch" Perry (1936–), who had recently opened his Upsetter recording studio in Kingston. With Perry's house band, also called the Upsetters, Bob Marley and the Wailers created a distinctive sound, driven by the rhythm section of bass player Aston "Family Man" Barrett (1946–) and his brother, drummer Carleton "Carly" Barrett (1950–1987). These sessions included classics such as "Small Axe," "Don't Rock My Boat," "Kaya," "Keep on Moving," and "Trench Town Rock." The success of "Trench Town Rock," which chronicled the troubled Jamaican political climate, increased demand for the Wailers to produce more studio recordings and make live appearances. By 1971, they were the top band in Jamaica, and were also making appearances in the UK and Europe.

Pioneering Jamaican reggae musician Bob Marley performing in New York in 1976. (Allan Tannenbaum/Getty Images)

While performing in London in 1971 as the supporting act for Johnny Nash (1940–), Marley went to the offices of Island Records, a successful independent label founded by Jamaican Chris Blackwell (1937–). This meeting earned Marley an advance of 8,000 pounds, which enabled him to return to Jamaica and record the sessions that would become his band's first full-length album, *Catch a Fire*. Marley had recruited the Barrett brothers to be permanent members of his band, along with Rita's vocal trio the I-Threes, which included singers Judy Mowatt (1952–) and Marcia Griffiths (1949–). Blackwell wanted to market the album to a larger rock audience, and so he convinced Marley to include numerous keyboard and percussion overdubs to enhance the band's sound. In essence, *Catch a Fire* was a rock and reggae hybrid: its collection of songs, which included "Concrete Jungle" and "Stir It Up," was warmly received by the music press upon its release in January 1973. The Wailers toured the UK and then the United States, which raised the band's profile and created demand for a follow-up album. This would be *Burnin'*, released in October of 1973: Marley's hard-hitting songs for this album, such as

"Get Up, Stand Up," "I Shot the Sheriff," "Small Axe," and "Duppy Conqueror," ensured the album's critical and commercial success.

At this point, both Bunny Wailer and Peter Tosh felt that they were being overshadowed by Marley's leadership role in the band. Bunny in particular did not like touring, and Tosh wanted greater exposure for his original songs. By early 1974, both had quit the band, leaving Marley the challenge of recording new material without two founding members of his band. He spent most of 1974 recording his first album as Bob Marley and the Wailers, *Natty Dread*, with the Barrett Brothers' signature rhythm section, The I-Threes providing harmony vocals, and several session musicians providing guitar, keyboard, and horn parts. This album further emphasized Marley's involvement with Jamaica's political climate, with songs such as "Lively Up Yourself" and "Rebel Music," but also included poignant love songs such as "No Woman, No Cry." The new Bob Marley and the Wailers released *Natty Dread* in February 1975, and spent the summer and fall playing to sold-out venues in the United States, Canada, and the UK. This album was quickly followed by *Live!* (a recording of Bob Marley at the Lyceum in London) and *Rastaman Vibration*. By 1976, when *Rolling Stone* named Bob Marley and the Wailers "Band of the Year," Bob Marley could be considered Jamaica's first international superstar.

Meanwhile, Marley had become influential in the political climate of Jamaica. He and his wife were supporters of the People's National Party (PNP), which had defeated its primary rival the Jamaican Labour Party in 1972 to become the majority party, with its leader Michael Manley as prime minister. Marley scheduled a concert with the theme "Smile Jamaica" for December 1976, which was to be followed by the general election later in the month; thus, it became widely perceived that Marley's concert was a political rally in support of the PNP. Two days before the concert, an assassination attempt occurred that left Marley, his wife Rita, and several of his entourage injured. Marley carried on with the concert, and was successful in bringing both Manley and his rival Edward Seaga to the stage to shake hands and send a message of national unity to the 80,000 Jamaicans in attendance.

The years 1977 and 1978 were hectic for Bob Marley. The first part of 1977 was spent in London at Island Records studios, where 20 tracks were recorded that would become the albums *Exodus* and *Kaya*. During the tour in support of *Exodus*, Marley's doctors realized that a persistent foot injury was in fact melanoma, and part of the U.S. summer tour was canceled to allow for Marley's surgery and recovery. Despite this, *Exodus* became both a critical and commercial success in the United States. During his recuperation, Marley supervised the mixing of his next album, *Kaya*, and made plans for his upcoming world tour and a second Peace Concert in Jamaica in 1978. The 1978 tour resulted in the band's second live album, *Babylon by Bus*, and took Bob Marley to Japan, where he was delighted to find hundreds of young Japanese fans enthusiastically singing along with his songs.

In early 1979, Marley returned to Jamaica to begin work on *Survival*. Inspired by a recent trip to Ethiopia, Marley addressed topics specific to the liberation of African people on the continent and in the African diaspora, in songs such as "Zimbabwe," "Survival," and "Africa Unite." The album sold well in various African countries, and "Zimbabwe" became an anthem for that nation as it struggled to achieve independence from Great Britain and end white minority rule. Bob

Marley and the Wailers once again had a very successful North American tour, including four nights at the Apollo Theatre in Harlem, which finally helped Marley connect with the African American audience that had thus far eluded him. In 1980, Marley returned to the recording studio for the sessions that would become his final two albums, *Uprising* and *Confrontation*. That year, Marley was invited to play his first shows in Africa, which included the independence celebrations for the newly established nation of Zimbabwe on April 17, 1980. Bob Marley and the Wailers spent the summer touring 12 European countries, often playing six shows a week.

Bob Marley and the Wailers had just begun the U.S. leg of their 1980 tour, playing two sold-out nights at Madison Square Garden, when Marley collapsed during a jog in Central Park. Tests revealed that Marley had a large brain tumor, likely a return of the cancer that had been treated in 1977, but he insisted on continuing with the tour. Bob Marley and the Wailers played their last show on September 23, 1980, at Pittsburgh's Stanley Theatre: the rest of the tour was canceled as it was apparent that Marley was too ill to continue. Marley's family sought medical treatment from various doctors, but the cancer was too advanced to allow successful treatment. On May 11, 1981, Bob Marley passed away, surrounded by his mother, his wife Rita, and their children.

Bob Marley's legacy lives on through his children, most notably his sons with Rita Marley, who are Ziggy Marley and Stephen Marley; and his son Damien Marley, whose mother is the jazz musician and former model Cindy Breakspeare. The popularity of Bob Marley's music has continued to grow since his death in 1981, and today he is one of the most recognizable musical figures worldwide.

Hope Munro Smith

See also: Dancehall; Mento; Reggae; Ska

Further Reading
Davis, Stephen. 1988. *Bob Marley*. Rochester, VT: Schenkman Books.
Moskowitz, David. 2007. *The Words and Music of Bob Marley*. Westport, CT: Praeger.
Steckles, Garry. 2009. *Bob Marley: A Life*. Northampton, MA: Interlink Books.

Marshall Islands, Music of

The Republic of the Marshall Islands (RMI), a Pacific island nation that lies just north of the equator, is home to diverse musical traditions and practices that display influences from across the world. The country consists of 29 low-lying coral atolls and five individual islands, which lie in parallel chains, the Ratak (Sunrise) and Ralik (Sunset), that stretch northeast to southwest and are spread across 750,000 million square miles of ocean. Throughout the 19th century, European whalers made contact, and in 1857, American Protestant missionaries arrived. Thereafter, Germany (1886–1914) and Japan (1914–1944) politically administered the Micronesian archipelago. Since 1986, the country has been an autonomous republic in free association with the United States, which administered the Marshall Islands under the United Nations' Trust Territory of the Pacific Islands (1947–1986). The 2014 Marshallese population is around 70,000 people. About two-thirds of the population lives in the urban centers in the RMI—Majuro Atoll (capital atoll) and Ebeye Island (Kwajalein Atoll, across from the U.S. military base). Slightly less than one-third of the population lives in various places in the United States, such as Hawai'i, Oregon, and Arkansas. Today, Marshallese music exhibits distinctive traits of indigenous practices and cultural contacts, and, as part of a rich oral tradition, it maintains cultural cohesion through intergenerational communication and dispersal of information across these vast geographical divides.

Marshallese music is primarily vocal and text-oriented, and dance movements usually accompany live performances. "The observance of Christmas (*Kurijmoj*) . . . [is perhaps] the most prominent occasion" for musical performance (Burke and Smith, 1998, p. 748). Christmas preparations often begin in October, with *jepta* (choirs—Marshallese for "chapter") rehearsals taking place throughout the night into the early hours of the morning. In addition to Protestant hymns, which are sung together in multipart harmony without instrumental accompaniment and dance movements, the jepta groups compete through vibrant displays of musical acuity and cultural knowledge. *Piit* (line dancing) is one of the main components of jepta performance. Upbeat songs with electric Yamaha keyboard accompaniment detail important skills, such as how to tie a proper canoe knot or harvest copra. A leader directs the complementary line dancers, who act out the lyrical instructions and engage in call and response, with whistle-blown cues.

Other musical celebrations occur on holidays such as Constitution Day, Gospel Day (commemoration of the arrival of the Protestant missionaries in 1857), Liberation Day (different for each atoll, marks the liberation of the islands from Japan), and Nuclear Victims and Survivors Remembrance Day (commemoration of those affected by the U.S. nuclear weapons testing program, 1946–1958). Women's organizations, school groups, and church groups will often participate in these events. Welcoming feasts (*kamolo*, Marshallese parties), special occasions for building a house or launching a canoe, and life-cycle events, such as birthdays especially first birthdays (*keemems*), are replete with singing and dancing. Majuro-based Youth to Youth in Health has an entire repertoire of songs on health issues, from eating habits to cancer prevention. Religious music, such as 19th-century Protestant hymns, are sung at regular church services. Although these performance occasions usually showcase contemporary songs, some special events include extant traditional music and dance.

Contemporary songs are classified by lyrical content and function, and a distinction is made between precontact chant (*roro*) and songs (*al*). Genres include *al in bwebwenato* (historical songs), *al in jar* (church songs), *al in kamolo* (Marshallese-style party songs), *al in karwaunene* (welcoming songs), *al in maina* (contemporary love songs), *al in kaubowe* (cowboy songs), *al in ememej* (remembrance song), *al in tarinae* (battle songs), *al in kelok* (departure songs, songs of soul loss over a departed lover), and *al in moj* (song for a dead person). Musical styles include multipart harmonies introduced through 19th-century American Protestant hymns, American country music, rock and roll, reggae, pop, and hip-hop. The identity of a song is based on its lyrics and melody, although two different songs may share the same melody. A song may be performed in a variety of musical styles, from *a cappella* church choir to a string band with lead vocalist and guitars and ukuleles.

Although the string-band instruments were the most popular though the 1990s, today the electric Yamaha keyboard is the accompaniment instrument of choice.

Early musical instruments included sticks and drums made from indigenous plants and parts of animals. Both held practical and ceremonial uses. *Jiṃōkṃōk* are conical, wooden sticks with rounded edges, beaten together in pairs during women's sitting dances. The *aje* drum is a single-headed hourglass-shaped drum, which may have been introduced through neighboring Ponphei given its structural resemblance to the *aip*. The body is crafted from the wood of a breadfruit tree, which is light and malleable. The head is made from the inner lining of the stomach or bladder of a shark. Held on the lap or under the left arm of the performer, the drum is played on either the center or the rim and with either finger or hand strokes. Traditionally, the aje was played almost exclusively by women to accompany chanting (roro) or singing, as a signal, and to encourage men during war. Conch shells were used to signal the beginning of war. Roro accompanied many life's activities, such as navigation, battle, tattooing, and healing practices to help increase spiritual and physical strength. Some indigenous musical performance included dances, a number of which are obsolete. The *jiku*, a stick dance performed by women, and the most culturally important stick dance, the *jobwa*, are performed on special occasions. The jobwa, revealed by a spirit (*noniep*) to a man in a deep sleep on Ujae Atoll, is only allowed to be performed after receiving permission from high chiefs.

Beyond extant traditional performances, early documentation—specifically by the German ethnologist Otto von Kotzebue, who surveyed indigenous practices during four separate visits from 1817 to 1825—details the expressive range of pre-contact song and dance. In addition to use in educational, spiritual, and domestic activities, music was a central component of entertaining for guests. "Accounts of dancing from the early 1800s through the 1880s report zealous, enthusiastic, animated performance, marked by bodily contortions, especially of the upper body and arms, and convulsive grimacing and rolling of eyes" (Burke and Smith, 1998, p. 752). American Protestant missionaries banned indigenous practices, including these songs and dances. They introduced hymns, circle dancing, and written notation. The hymn book continues to be used in church services today.

Other colonial encounters contributed to the rapidly changing Marshallese musical landscape. In the 19th century, the archipelago was frequented by European whalers, who introduced melodic sea shanties to the island population; and, beginning in the 1860s, increasingly by German traders, who introduced the accordion, which has since fallen out of fashion, and a style of marching music and dance known as *maaj*, which continues to be performed across the Pacific.

With the beginning of World War I (1914–1918), Japan was granted administrative power over Micronesia by the League of Nations. Many Marshallese learned Japanese school songs (*shōka*), which were composed of simple Western melodies and used natural imagery to convey nationalistic ideologies. During World War II (1939–1945), Japan militarized the islands and Japanese battle songs (*gunka*) were heard. The Japanese began to mistreat the Marshallese, forcing them to give up all their food and beheading some who did not exactly follow orders. They also prohibited the Marshallese from speaking for fear that they would plot against their overseers. The Marshallese used songs to communicate messages about hidden food reserves. The Japanese musical presence remains in the memories of some elders who recall love songs in Japanese.

The United States, nearing the end of World War II, eventually took control of the Marshall Islands and forcibly removed the Japanese. A Kwajalein man wrote the famous song *"Bok mejam* (Take a look)" in celebration of the war's end. The song uses double entendre to caution the United States Army against mistreating the land and people as the Japanese did. However, the United States' military programs in Marshall Islands, which included the detonation of 67 nuclear weapons, Star Wars missile testing, and continued missile defense testing, posed many serious problems for the indigenous population. As American musical styles, from doo-wop to country to cowboy songs (*al in kaubowe*), were introduced on the Armed Forces radio station and in schools, the Marshallese responded with a repertoire of songs about military damages—from songs about radiation exposure to the repeat use of "Bok Mejam" at sail-in protests at Kwajalein from during the 1970s and 1980s.

Outmigration, urbanization, and the increased availability of communication technologies have shifted musical trends and modes of circulation. In the RMI's urban centers, nightclubs host live bands and karaoke nights, and are equipped with sound systems and an archive of Marshallese and American popular music that draws young adults to dance in a Westernized fashion. Keeping ties to their communities, popular Marshallese musicians—such as hip-hop musicians F.O.B., Flavah C, and Yastaman, and transgender performer Li-Cassy—will perform in clubs and festivals across the United States. String band music (now considered traditional folk music) by artists such as Ronald Jorkin and Chaninway, Jabubu, Deep Blue Sea, and Mbolen is also popular. Listeners from abroad tune into Marshallese radio stations such as VR7AB over the internet or follow Marshallese musicians over various platforms, including YouTube and Facebook.

Jessica A. Schwartz

See also: Hawaii, Music of; Philippines, Music of the; Polynesia, Music of

Further Reading

Burke, Mary E. Lawson, and Barbara Smith. 1998. "The Music and Dance of East Micronesia." In Adrienne L. Kaeppler and J. W. Love (eds.), *The Garland Encyclopedia of World Music, Australia and the Pacific Islands,* 748–766. Washington, DC: Library of Congress.

Diettrich, Brian, Jane Freeman Moulin, and Michael Webb. 2011. *Music in Pacific Island Cultures.* New York: Oxford University Press.

Tobin, Jack A. 2002. *Stories from the Marshall Islands.* Honolulu: University of Hawaii Press.

Masekela, Hugh (1939–)

One of the most internationally famous and influential African musicians of all time, the trumpeter and vocalist Hugh Masekela came of age during the height of South African apartheid. After escaping the land of his birth, he used his music to bring the struggles of black South Africans to international audiences and was active in the anti-apartheid movement of the 1970s and 1980s, particularly the campaign to free Nelson Mandela from prison. By combining the music of South Africa's townships, known as *mbaqanga*, with pop, jazz, and R & B, Masekela became a leading voice in the emerging world music genre, working with such renowned artists as Paul Simon, The Byrds, and Harry Belafonte. He was also once married to the legendary South African singer Miriam Makeba, and frequently shared the stage with her in concert venues all around the world.

Hugh Ramopolo Masekela was born on April 4, 1939, in Kwa-Guqa Township in Witbank, a coal mining town located in what is today called the Mpumalanga province of northeastern South Africa. Masekela would later vividly recall the desperate circumstances of life in Witbank, where "African miners drank themselves stuperous to blot out memory of the blackness of the mines and the families and lands they'd left behind, often never to see again" (Masekela and Cheers, 2004, p. 3). These circumstances left a lasting impression on Masekela, who years later would memorialize the horrific conditions for black South African miners in his song "Stimela." Likewise, the hard-living ways of the miners influenced the young Masekela, who began drinking alcohol at the age of 14 and struggled with substance addiction throughout his life.

Sent to St. Peter's boarding school in Johannesburg, Masekela's life took a major turn in September 1953 when he saw the Hollywood film *Young Man with a Horn*, in which Kirk Douglas played a brilliant but troubled trumpet player. Within a few months Masekela had secured his own secondhand trumpet, and soon formed a band with his schoolmates. The Huddleston Jazz Band, named after Trevor Huddleston, the Anglican priest who ran St. Peter's and who had helped Masekela and his friends buy their instruments, soon began playing local dances. A precocious musician possessed with a strong tone and confident swagger on the bandstand, Masekela became a hot commodity in the local mbaqanga scene, performing regularly with a popular band known as The Merry Makers. In April 1956, still just 17 years old, he received a trumpet that had once belonged to the legendary Louis Armstrong, who at the suggestion of Huddleston had decided to donate some of his old instruments to South African musicians. To Masekela, the gift was a sign that he had found his path in life.

That direction led him not only toward a prolific career as a musician, but also out of South Africa. In 1959, along with pianist Abdullah Ibrahim (Dollar Brand) and saxophonist Kippie Moeketsi, Masekela helped form one of the most acclaimed jazz bands in South African history, The Jazz Epistles—but the increasing repressiveness of white minority rule in South Africa ensured that the group's rise to prominence would be short-lived. Following the election of the National Party in 1948, the system of apartheid had gradually yet ruthlessly entrenched itself in South African life: results included requiring all blacks to carry passes and live in specially designated areas of the country, segregating all public facilities, denying black people the opportunity to receive a quality education, and violently suppressing any dissent against the government's policies. As a young man of talent and ambition, Masekela searched for a way out. He found it in 1960 when first he was accepted into London's Guildhall School of Music, then received a scholarship to the Manhattan School of Music in New York City. It would be another 30 years before he would return to South Africa.

While studying classical trumpet at the Manhattan School, Masekela absorbed the city's thriving jazz scene, and with the support of Miriam Makeba, as well as singer and political activist Harry Belafonte, secured his first recording contract with Mercury Records. His first album, *Trumpet Africaine* (1962), was, by his own estimation, a disaster. He soon realized that in order to find his musical voice, he would have to drop his obsession with American jazz and culture and return to his South African roots. With the encouragement of Belafonte as well as the legendary trumpeter Miles Davis, in 1965 his music took a new direction with the release of *The Americanization of Ooga Booga*, an album that skillfully interwove American bebop with bouncy South African mbaqanga melodies and Zulu lyrics sung by Masekela himself. Though record executives were skeptical that such unfamiliar music could connect with American audiences, the album ended up launching Masekela's recording career, and provides one of the 20th century's most compelling examples of the compatibility of African and African American musical idioms.

After moving out to California in 1966, Masekela signed with UNI Records and appeared at the legendary 1967 Monterey Pop Festival, to great popular and critical acclaim. On the West Coast, Masekela's music became more mainstream, featuring rich orchestrations of popular pop tunes such as Fifth Dimension's "Up, Up and Away," which became Masekela's first hit on American radio stations. In 1968, he enjoyed the biggest commercial success of his career with the release of "Grazing in the Grass," Masekela's recording of a Philemon Hou composition that was itself inspired by the bouncy township grooves that Masekela had recorded earlier in his career. Featuring his brilliant lead trumpet performance, "Grazing" rocketed to the top of the charts, transforming Masekela into an international star and providing the new soundtrack for cosmopolitan West Coast cool.

Nevertheless, by the early 1970s Masekela longed to return to his African roots. After playing at cultural festivals in Guinea and Zaire, Masekela joined the Ghanaian funk group Hedzoleh Soundz. The combination of Masekela's South African grooves with Hedzoleh's modern highlife provided an early example of the kind of world fusion music that would grow in popularity in the coming years; their 1974 album *I Am Not Afraid* also featured the first recorded version of "Stimela," Masekela's song about the struggles of South African miners.

In the wake of the Soweto uprising of June 1976, when the South African government killed dozens of students who were protesting apartheid's system of education, a new sense of political urgency entered Masekela's music. Though unable to return to his home country, Masekela frequently joined Miriam Makeba, to whom he had been married for two years from 1964 to 1966, in using music to raise awareness about the anti-apartheid struggle. He also wrote a song, "Soweto Blues," that would be released by Makeba in 1987. During the early 1980s, Masekela spent much of his time living in Southern Africa with his third wife, Jabu, first in Botswana and later in Zimbabwe, constantly fearful that South African agents would target him for assassination, as they had many other vocal anti-apartheid figures living on the continent. Nonetheless, Masekela persevered. After receiving a letter from the imprisoned Nelson Mandela in 1985, Masekela wrote one of the decade's most important songs of political protest, "Bring Back Nelson Mandela," which became an anthem for the movement to free Mandela from prison. During this time he also worked on music for the stage production of *Sarafina*, a dramatization of the 1976 Soweto uprisings that would be remade into a Hollywood film in 1992.

Masekela's outspoken opposition to apartheid made it impossible for him to return to South Africa while the government remained committed to maintaining white minority rule. However, a few months after Nelson Mandela was finally released from prison, in February 1990, Masekela set foot on the soil of his native land for the first time in three decades. In the ensuing years, he would continue his prolific recording career, and frequently appeared in concert venues both within South Africa and around the world. Finally overcoming his addictions to alcohol and drugs after an extended stint in a rehabilitation facility in 1997 and 1998, Masekela has in recent years devoted much of his time to charitable work, including founding the Musicians and Artists Assistance Program in 2001. He also serves as a board director for the Lunchbox Fund, which provides daily meals to poor South African children growing up in the Soweto township. In 2007 he was awarded the African Music Legend award by the Ghana Music Awards, and in 2010 he received the Order of Ikhamanga, one of South Africa's highest honors, for his outstanding achievements in music.

David Crawford Jones

See also: Armstrong, Louis; Jazz; Makeba, Miriam

Further Reading

Ansell, Gwen. 2004. *Soweto Blues: Jazz, Popular Music and Politics in South Africa*. New York: Continuum.

Coplan, David B. 2008. *In Township Tonight! South Africa's Black City Music and Theater*. Chicago: The University of Chicago Press.

Masekela, Hugh, and D. Michael Cheers. 2004. *Still Grazing: The Musical Journey of Hugh Masekela*. New York: Three Rivers Press.

Mbalax

A Senegalese music genre that embraces both tradition and modern musical innovations of the West, *mbalax* (Wolof for rhythm) is a cornerstone of contemporary Senegalese and Gambian culture and plays a crucial role in those countries' nightlife more specifically (Lo, 2015). Mbalax is strongly influenced by Wolof drumming traditions and is specifically tied to their indigenous drums: *sabar, bugarabu*, and *tama*. Additionally, the high-pitched and immediately recognizable vocal style of the *gewel*—the members of the Wolof hereditary caste of musician-poets—is yet another characteristic of mbalax. Like many African musical traditions, mbalax is also closely tied to dance, in this case a traditional Wolof dance style that resembles wrestling. Mbalax is represented most frequently by the music of artists such as Yassou N'Dour (1959–) and the Super Étoile de Dakar and Thione Seck (1955–). Mbalax played a crucial role in the unification of the country and its music following the era of French rule.

Many early mbalax musicians were to be born into the gewel caste; in more contemporary times, however, non-gewel musicians have sought training in the gewel style through a Sufi *marabout-taalibe* (religious master-disciple) format (Charry, 2017). Western influences on mbalax were introduced during French colonial rule in Senegal, where France was the controlling power from about 1659 to 1960. French colonization brought a variety of Western musics, including jazz, reggae, funk, rock, and Latin styles, to Senegal, undermining the popularity of traditional Senegalese music. Afro-Cuban music in particular shaped the beginnings of mbalax in both style and instrumentation. The city of Dakar, which played host to the some of the country's first radio stations and music clubs, heavily promoted jazz and salsa throughout much of the country's time under French rule and later.

The Sahel Orchestra, a cover band from the Sahel club, and specifically their album, *Bamba*, played no small part in the popularity of Latin music in Senegal, along with Dakar's radio stations. Eventually, however, groups such as The Sahel Orchestra, The Orchestra Baobab, and The Star Band began to reclaim the African roots in this music by introducing their traditional instruments and tunes to this Afro-Cuban style. Following Senegal's postcolonial independence, however, interest in traditional culture was revived, which inspired new artists and a new music.

In postindependence Senegal, musicians such as Bira Guéye began to call for a new national style of music. Guéye led the search for this new style by promoting artists who sang in Wolof at a time when music of the West still was in fashion. However, it was not until Ibra Kassé opened his famous nightclub, Le Miami, that a new national style truly began to emerge. The resident orchestra of the nightclub, The Star Band, began to introduce traditional elements to their music, such as native dialects and traditional drums, at the urging of Kassé (Lo, 2015). The Star Band's implementation of these traditional ideas began to change their original Afro-Cuban style to a new, more African style.

The popularity of Afro-Cuban music, which had held sway in Senegal because of the slave trade, eventually began to wane. During the 1970s, new instruments such as electric guitar, flute, piano, and synthesizer became widely available to Senegalese musicians. The most important advancement in this new sound, however, was the addition of the young Youssou N'Dour to the Dakar Star Band. N'Dour incorporated folk tunes into his music, helping to bring renewed popularity to traditional music. The group Super Diamono, which claimed N'Dour as a member at the age of 15, has been credited with being one of the first groups to standardize the genre (Barz, 2017b). The group's use of Wolof percussion and lyrics inspired many artists to move away from the popular Afro-Cuban style and toward this new music.

From the 1980s on, mbalax became increasingly popular in Senegal, thanks in large part to N'Dour's efforts to create a cohesive musical genre following his split with Étoile de Dakar to form the group Super Étoile in 1979. As bandleader, N'Dour continued to promote Wolof influences while also promoting other artists (such as Mbaye Faye Dieye and Alla Seck) who specialized in the Wolof tradition of *tassou*, which closely resembles rapping (Lo, 2015). Thione Seck, another mbalax artist, became especially popular through his performances with Orchestra Baobab, which

Senegalese musician Youssou N'Dour (center) leads his band, Super Étoile, during a performance of *mbalax* music. Mbalax is a style of dance music in Senegal and the Gambia. (Jack Vartoogian/Getty Images)

began in 1977. Seck, who sought to meld mbalax with reggae influences, would eventually leave the Orchestra Baobab to form Raam Daan, a pre-eminent mbalax group (Lo, 2015).

Shortly after mbalax became a firmly established genre, artists began looking for ways to distinguish themselves from each other. A consequence of this effort was the formation of several mbalax-inspired groups who sought to develop the form through innovations in instrumentation and cross-genre exploration. Artists such as Ndjolo, Castors, Black Mbolo, and Super Cayor were leaders in this synthesis. Through these innovators, the subgenres *zouk*-mbalax, rap-mbalax, rock-mbalax, and salsa-mbalax were created. These mbalax derivatives became increasingly popular with younger generations of musicians, who were intent on developing the genre. However, as mbalax entered the 1990s, these subgenres began to fall from popularity due to a larger desire to strengthen the genre as a whole in an effort to bring international attention to it.

Phillip Alexander Ducreay

See also: Afro-Cuban Jazz

Further Reading

African Music Safari. 2011. "African Music Styles: What Is Mbalax." http://www.african-music-safari.com/mbalax.html.

Barz, Gregory F. 2017a. "Mbalax." *Grove Music Online*. http://www.oxfordmusiconline.com.

Barz, Gregory F. 2017. "N'Dour, Youssou." *Grove Music Online*. http://www.oxfordmusiconline.com.
Charry, Eric. 2017. "Senegal." *Grove Music Online*. http://www.oxfordmusiconline.com.
Dieng, Amadou Bator. 2015. "Historical Overview of Senegalese Music." February 6. http://musicinafrica.net/historical-overview-senegalese-music?language=en.
Lo, Fadel. 2015. "Mbalax in Senegal." February 9. http://musicinafrica.net/mbalax-senegal.
Polak, Rainer. 2011. "Sabar." *Grove Music Online*. http://www.oxfordmusiconline.com.
"Seck, Thione." 2006. In Colin Larkin (ed.), *Encyclopedia of Popular Music*, 4th ed. Oxford: Oxford University Press.

Mbila

Mbila (plural: *timbila*) is a wooden xylophone of the *Chopi* ethnic group, who live mainly on the coast of Inhambane province in southern Mozambique. Mbila is played in a large group that is often called a "timbila orchestra," which consists of 10 to 15 xylophones of five sizes and covers a range of four octaves. Soprano, alto, tenor, baritone, and bass xylophones are called *cilanzane* or *malanzane*, *sanje* or *sange*, *dohle* or *mbingwi*, *dibhinda*, and *chikhulu* respectively (Lutero, 1980, p. 41). The bass xylophone has four notes and provides a heavy bass tone.

The keys (slats) of the mbila are made of wood from the *mwenje* (sneezewood) tree, and they are fixed to the instrument's framework. Mwenje is a highly resonant wood found primarily in the Zavala district of the Inhambane province. (Some regions use other types of wood for making mbila.) Under each wooden key, resonators are attached with beeswax. The resonators are made of *bassala* or *masala* (*Lanrocerasus caroriniana*). Bassala is a kind of gourd. Various gourd sizes are used depending on the keys. Each of the resonators has a little hole covered by tissue from the bowels of such animals as cow or pig. It gives typical vibration to the sound. Mbila are played with drumsticks capped with rubber.

Mbila are tuned within an equiheptatonic scale. The tuning system of mbila is based on the *hombe* (or *dikokoma dawumbila*), a key note of the Chopi musical system (Hogan, 2006, p. 5). The hombe is almost an absolute pitch, although there are some differences by village. Some scholars argue that mbila originated in Indonesia, because many common characteristics, such as the equiheptatonic scale, are seen in both mbila and Indonesian xylophone (Jones, 1964). However, no clear relation between Indonesian and mbila xylophones has yet been revealed.

Traditionally, the Chopi people play mbila as part of *Ngodo* (plural: *Migodo*) dance dramas. Ngodo dance drama consists of choreographed dance, music of the mbila orchestra, and lyrics. Normally, the whole Ngodo lasts about 45 minutes. Each Ngodo consists of between nine and 11 sections. Some sections are orchestral pieces, and others are dances with mbila music. When dancers sing, the musicians play softly. The song topics are often social problem or concerns. A new Ngodo is composed every two years or so. The music leader, called *Musiki waTimbila*, directs the performance (Hogan, 2006, p. 4). The leader indicates the beginning of movement with a solo phrase played by the mbila. In front of a line of timbila, the dancers and the audience stand facing the instruments. The dancers each have a shield, spear, or machete. Drum strokes accent the dance movements. The sound of the mbila ensemble is dense and complex because each player plays a different rhythm. In addition, one player's left hand often keeps a different rhythm from that in the right hand. Mbila is accompanied by a single-headed drum and small idiophones.

Traditionally, boys were taught to play the mbila by their fathers or grandfathers, and learn lots of lyrics through oral transmission of skills and seeing their elders' performances (Tracey, 1948, p. 108). Before Mozambique gained independence in 1975, transmission of mbila skills to the next generation had been threatened because of the reduction of the male Chopi population due to the migrant labor and changes in the traditional chief's role caused by colonial rule. Traditionally, chiefs of the community used to organize timbila orchestras. However, the power of the chiefs was diminished under colonial rule, and that decreased opportunities to play mbila. Moreover, Mozambique's civil war (1977—1992) heavily damaged Chopi society, and many timbila masters migrated to the capital, Maputo.

Some timbila orchestras turned to government agencies for sponsorship (Hogan, 2006, p. 6), but the revival of the timbila orchestra is mainly due to Venáncio Mbande (1930–) who had migrated to South Africa to work in the mines. He is one of the famous mbila players, composers, and craftsmen who formed a timbila orchestra in a mine. After he returned to his home in Inhambane province, he started to train young musicians. Timbila orchestra was proclaimed a Masterpiece of the Oral and Intangible Heritage of Humanity by UNESCO in 2005.

Mayako Koja

See also: Chopi People, Music of the

Further Reading

Hogan, Brian. 2006. "Locating the Chopi Xylophone Ensembles of Southern Mozambique." *Pacific Review of Ethnomusicology* 11, 1–18.

Jones, A. M. 1964. *Africa and Indonesia: The Evidence of the Xylophone and Other Musical and Cultural Factors*. Leiden, Netherlands: E. J. Brill.

Lutero, Martinho. 1980. "As Timbila." In Ganbinete de Organização do Festival da Canção e Música Tradicional (ed.), *Música tradicional em Moçambique*, 39–45. Maputo, Mozambique: Tipografia Académica.

Tracey, Hugh. 1948. *Chopi Musicians: Their Music, Poetry, and Instruments*. London: International African Institute.

Mbube

Mbube refers both to the song recorded in 1939 and, more widely, to a type of choral music sung by male Zulu migrant workers in South Africa. Mbube has come to describe a long line of Western-influenced South African pop genres, with origins in Christian hymnody and blackface minstrelsy which were introduced to South Africa in the late 19th century. The song "Mbube," recorded by Solomon Linda (1909–1962) and The Evening Birds, enjoyed great popularity in South Africa throughout the 1940s, eventually selling 100,000 copies, one of which ended up in the hands of American folk singer Pete Seeger (1919–2014). Seeger's band, The Weavers, recorded their arrangement of "Mbube"—which they misheard as "Wimoweh"—in 1952, introducing the song to a Western audience and inspiring multiple cover versions. In 1961, "Wimoweh" was reworked and recorded by The Tokens as "The Lion Sleeps Tonight," and it was in this incarnation that the song gained worldwide popularity.

With the foundation for an understanding of Western musical forms laid by the hymns of Christian missionaries, South Africans proved receptive to the music of American minstrel shows in the late 1800s. Most notably, a troupe led by African American Orpheus McAdoo made multiple visits to South Africa in the 1890s, inspiring the creation of local groups even in remote rural areas. By World War I (1914–1918), local vaudeville and ragtime troupes had made this music their own, presenting an aspirational image of the modern, sophisticated "coon" (derived, problematically, from the American caricature of black urban dandy "Zip Coon") in a style known as *isikhunzi*. By the 1930s isikhunzi was being performed in Johannesburg by respectable, middle-class quartets for working-class audiences. During this period, a performance style called *ingoma* developed in rural areas, incorporating urban song and dance practices, wedding songs inspired by Western hymns, and aggressive stamping movements. This rural style influenced early urban *isicathamiya* groups such as The Crocodiles, who developed a lighter step more suited to urban performance spaces. This light-stepping style eventually came to be known as mbube thanks to the popularity of the song of the same name, and continues to be performed today by groups such as Joseph Shabalala and Ladysmith Black Mambazo, who were catapulted to international fame by their work with American pop star Paul Simon in the 1980s. Somewhat confusingly, both isicathamiya and mbube are sometimes used today more broadly to refer to the whole range of male choral performance styles described here.

Solomon Linda moved from the poor, rural Natal region to Johannesburg in 1931, and within a few years formed The Evening Birds. They started out performing at weddings, like the ingoma bands before them, but moved on to singing at choir competitions and concerts that were often held in migrant workers' hostels. In 1939 they recorded the song "Mbube," basing the melody on a wedding song from Linda's hometown, and the lyrics on his boyhood experience of protecting herds of cattle from lions. Gallo's Records paid the group a few dollars for the rights to the recording, which by 1948 had sold 100,000 copies in Africa. Having signed over the rights, Solomon Linda and The Evening Birds received no royalties for these sales, but they became very popular performers, and recorded about 40 songs in total before finally breaking up in 1954. In addition, Linda worked in the Gallo company packing plant for the rest of his life.

Through his connection with international song hunter Alan Lomax (1915–2002), Pete Seeger obtained a copy of Linda's recording, and Westernized it as "Wimoweh," simplifying the subtle rhythmic elements and bringing the melodic elements of the original to the fore. In 1952, The Weavers, an American folk group of which Seeger was a member, released their version of the song, which was essentially a novelty song with no lyrics, and a big-band instrumental introduction took up almost half of the playing time. It became a hit and spawned many cover versions by a wide variety of artists. In 1961, a new arrangement, released by The Tokens as "The Lion Sleeps Tonight," recast "Wimoweh" as a standard pop song, adding exotic percussion, kitschy lyrics, and a new instrumental bridge. In the decades that followed, this new version was covered by even more artists than "Wimoweh." The 1994 Disney movie *The Lion King* further cemented the song in the minds of successive generations of children. Linda saw very little in the way of royalties in his lifetime, but his descendants, at least, have received some compensation.

Gerry McGoldrick

See also: Ladysmith Black Mambazo

Further Reading

Erlmann, Veit. 1990. "Migration and Performance: Zulu Migrant Workers' Isicathamiya Performance in South Africa, 1890–1950." *Ethnomusicology* 34(2), 199–220.

Erlmann, Veit. 1996. *Nightsong: Performance, Power and Practice in South Africa*. Chicago: University of Chicago Press.

Erlmann, Veit. 2004. "Communities of Style: Musical Figures of Black Diasporic Identity." In Thomas Turino and James Lea (eds.), *Identity and the Arts in Diaspora Communities*, 80–91. Warren, MI: Harmonie Park Press.

McPhee, Colin (1900–1964)

Colin McPhee was an American composer, ethnomusicologist, and pioneer in cross-cultural composition and scholarship. He is best known for his documentation of Balinese gamelan music traditions, both thriving and disappearing, during the 1930s—at a time while the island was still relatively isolated from outside influences. This research culminated in several books, most notably *Music in Bali* (1966), which is still considered to be the cornerstone of Balinese music studies. He is also regarded for his compositions written for Western instruments that incorporate Balinese musical elements, namely *Tabuh-Tabuhan* (1936).

McPhee was born in Montreal on March 15, 1900. When he was 13 years old, his family moved to nearby Toronto—a swiftly growing Canadian musical hub—where McPhee studied piano and composition at the Hambourg Conservatory. At 18, McPhee enrolled at the Peabody Conservatory in Baltimore to continue his musical studies, where he worked primarily with Gustave Strube (composition) and Harold Randolph (piano). Recognized by his instructors as a brilliant but undisciplined musician, he graduated with a teacher's certificate in piano and a diploma in composition. Returning to Toronto in 1922, McPhee took the city by storm as a piano performer, primarily of works by German composer Franz Liszt (1811–1886); he also studied and taught at the Canadian Academy. In 1924, he undertook a two-year pilgrimage to Paris, where he lived on the edge of the famed Latin Quarter, the city's bustling center of musical and literary modernism.

After returning to New York City in 1926, McPhee quickly became integrated into the city's burgeoning compositional scene and was cited by contemporaries such as Aaron Copland (1900–1990) and Henry Cowell (1897–1965) as one of the new Americanists whose work blended both European and American compositional styles. Although he also worked as an accompanist and performed both solo and in ensembles, his primary pursuit was composition. Surviving works from this period show influences of contact with other contemporary composers—especially Edgard Varèse (1883–1965), who was teaching McPhee at the time—but also the beginnings of McPhee's interest in incorporating musical ideas from outside the Western classical music tradition. For example, McPhee's *Sea Shanty Suite*, first performed in 1929, was a setting of seven shanties that evokes the drone techniques of the bagpipes.

Like many young composers of the time, McPhee began to turn toward vernacular music as compositional inspiration; however, unlike many of his peers who focused on American materials, McPhee became interested instead in music from the island of Bali, Indonesia. This interest was sparked in part by a series of recordings created with the aid of expatriate German artist Walter Spies and released by the German Odèon and Beka label in 1928. His circle of friends and colleagues at the time included a number of individuals who eventually became connected to the island: novelist Carl Van Vechten, painter Miguel Covarrubias, dancer Claire Holt, and most importantly, his new wife, Jane Belo.

The couple first traveled to Bali in 1931 and then settled there in 1932, building a house in the village of Sayan in the central part of the island near Ubud. The period during the 1930s in which McPhee and Belo lived in Bali was a time of great change on the island; Balinese society was still adapting to colonial Dutch rule and beginning to face increasing attention from foreign visitors. The McPhee soon became part of a burgeoning community of Western expatriate artists and scholars to live on the island, including Covarrubias and Spies, Beryl de Zoete, Gregory Bateson, Margaret Mead, and Katharane Mershon. Although McPhee traveled to Bali originally as a composer and envisioned himself as such throughout his six years living on the island, his primary work at the time was in learning and transcribing Balinese gamelan music and documenting Balinese life. Most notable among his Balinese teachers were I Nyoman Kalér (1897–1969), with whom he worked in resurrecting a gamelan club in Kuta; and I Madé Lebah (1905?–1996), who served not only as McPhee's chauffer, but also his guide to Balinese music. During this time, McPhee transcribed hundreds of gamelan works; although he did not play any of the gamelan instruments himself, he would check the transcriptions with his teacher by playing them back from a piano at his house.

Following three years in Bali, McPhee returned to the West for a year and a half, living primarily in New York City. There, in the midst of the Great Depression, he worked on a commission from the League of Composers, hosted a series of radio broadcasts entitled "Modern American Music," and hosted nights of Balinese music and culture in which his transcriptions of Balinese music for Western instruments accompanied silent film footage he took in Bali. McPhee traveled to Mexico City at the end of 1935 to pursue work on a "rhapsody" on Balinese themes, inspired by his Mexican colleague in composition, Carlos Chávez (1899–1978), whose compositions based on Mexican themes McPhee admired. This "rhapsody" was *Tabuh-Tabuhan* (a group of percussion instruments; it was also subtitled "Toccata for Orchestra and 2 Pianos"), which combined Balinese and Western melodic, harmonic, and rhythmic idioms. Although the piece premiered in Mexico City in 1936, its first premiere in the United States would not be until 1953.

Upon his return to Bali, McPhee resumed an active role in Balinese musical life, most notably promoting a revival of the genre *gamelan semar pegulingan*, which had become nearly extinct during the years following the dismantling of the

Balinese courts in the first decade of the 20th century. He is also credited with founding the first children's gamelan groups. Following his divorce from Belo, a failed recording project, and the beginning of pre-World War II political tensions in Bali, McPhee departed the island for the last time.

Throughout the 1940s and 1950s, McPhee struggled financially and suffered from bouts of depression. He lived in Brooklyn and took a position with the Office of War Information during the Second World War. During this time he wrote prolifically, completing a recollection of his life in Bali in *A House in Bali* (1940), which was later adapted into an opera of the same name by composer Evan Ziporyn (2009), and about his work with the children's gamelan in the children's book *A Club of Small Men* (1948). McPhee continued to compose, including several commissions and numerous transcriptions of gamelan pieces.

In 1960, McPhee accepted a teaching position at the University of California Los Angeles, where he had been invited by ethnomusicologist Mantle Hood. McPhee planned to return to Bali in the early 1960s, but his increasingly frail health prevented him from making the voyage. During this time he put the final touches on *Music in Bali*, which he had been writing over the past 20 years. The book, published three years after McPhee's death in 1963, presents a nearly comprehensive account of the performing arts in Bali and the cultural contexts in the 1930s. *Music in Bali* remains one of the most comprehensive books on Balinese gamelan in any language, and has previously been adopted as a standard textbook for Balinese arts conservatory students. McPhee remains influential as a composer, an ethnomusicologist, and chiefly a preserver and creator of Balinese music, and one of the leading figures in approaching a musical juncture between East and West.

Elizabeth A. Clendinning

See also: Gamelan Orchestra (Balinese); Gamelan Orchestra (Javanese); Kebyar; Kecak

Further Reading

McPhee, Colin. 1940. *A House in Bali*. New York: John Day.

McPhee, Colin. 1966. *Music in Bali: A Study in Form and Instrumental Music in Bali*. New Haven, CT: Yale University Press.

Oja, Carol J. 2004. *Colin McPhee: Composer in Two Worlds*. Champaign: University of Illinois Press.

Medieval Secular Song

Although most of the extant medieval sources concern music cultivated in cathedrals and monasteries, the lesser-known secular musical tradition must not be undervalued. Not only did it reflect many aspects of medieval life, therefore constituting a fundamental indirect source for historians, it also played a central role in the development of instruments, which were at that time banned from any religious application. The lack of sources for secular music is due to the high level of illiteracy outside the church, often one of the few environments where writing and reading were taught. This music relied mostly on its oral tradition.

Early forms of secular music include the famous *Carmina Burana*, consisting mostly of Goliard songs in Latin, celebrating the lives of students and wandering

> ### Isorhythmic Motet
>
> Easily one of the most peculiar forms of medieval music is the isorhythmic motet. This form was popular among European clergy and musically literate from approximately the 13th to the 15th century. Isorhythmic motets were devised as part of the Ars Nova (New Art) style of music associated with composer Phillipe de Vitry and utilized repeating rhythmic patterns called *talea* in various capacities. The fascinating part of isorhythmic motets is that talea could be structured to begin in rounds in as many as 12 different voices (and therefore starting positions), making the combinatoriality of the pattern tremendously complex and nearly indistinguishable to even the trained musical ear. The social practice of performing such a work was to get closer to God who, omnipotent, could hear the cycling talea even if mortal ears could not.

clerics. This repertoire originated in the 12th century and is recorded in the manuscripts housed in Munich at the Bayerische Staatsbibliothek. The golden age of secular music is represented by the rise of the Occitan tradition, around the end of the 11th century. Minstrels called *troubadours* (probably from the Occitan *trobar*: to write poetry) were active in the southern area of today's France. Their lyrics mainly focused on the theme of "courtly love," often portraying the woman as a beautiful but unachievable goddess.

Remarkably, we now have record of several names of composers as well as a large amount of monophonic melodies in the form of *lai, ballade, rondeau*, and *virelai*. The main source for these is the so-called *chansonnier* G, housed at the Biblioteca Ambrosiana in Milan. Furthermore, some details about troubadours' lives are recorded in *vidas* (Occitan for "lives"): short biographies in a peculiar hagiographical style. Similarly, the *razos* (Occitan for "reasons") are intended to explain the circumstances of a specific composition.

The earliest troubadour was William IX, Duke of Aquitaine (1071–1126). Bernart de Ventadorn (ca. 1130/1140–ca. 1190/1200) is considered one of the finest troubadours, both poetically and musically. The melody of his song *Can vei la lauzeta mover* has been used to set several poems, in Latin, Occitan, French, and German. Further relevant troubadours were Arnaut Daniel (*fl.* ca. 1180–1195), main exponent of the *trobar clus* (Occitan for "obscure poetry") and celebrated by Dante as inventor of the *sestina*. Female troubadours (*trobairiz*) are the first known female composers of secular music. Among them, the main figure is the Comtessa Beatriz de Día (*fl.* late 12th century), and her *A chanter m'er de so qu'en no volria* is the only song composed by trobairiz surviving with melody. The disappearance of the troubadour tradition was due to the cruel Albigensian crusade which destroyed Occitan culture in the first decades of the 13th century.

In northern France, trouvéres were subjected to the troubadours' influence and carried on, to some degree, their poetical and musical style. The language used was the *lang d'oil*, the ancestor of modern French, and the first known of its musicians was Chrétien de Troyes (*fl.* ca. 1160–1190). He is mainly renowned as author of the Arthurian romances *Perceval* and *Lancelot*. Adam de la Halle (ca. 1245–ca. 1300) is one of the last trouvéres. His masterpiece is the musical play *Jeu de Robin et Marion* (ca. 1282); yet he worked in almost every coeval genre (e.g., *rondeaux, jeux-partis, chansons*), and experimented with both monody and polyphony.

Troubadour and trouvére lyrics are strophic, and the music is mostly syllabic, confined within the range of about an octave. Similarly to plainchant, troubadour and trouvére songs have been notated with no indication of rhythm.

In the 14th century, music underwent further developments, first in France and later in Italy. The new style developed by composers such as Guillaume de Machaut (ca. 1330–1377) and Francesco Landini (ca. 1325–1397) has been named *Ars Nova* (new practice), in contrast to the *Ars Antiqua* (old practice) of the previous centuries. The Ars Nova composers made sophisticated developments to their predecessors' practice, especially in terms of rhythm and harmony. Machaut's rhythm constituted a brand new style, characterized by syncopation and interaction between duple and triple meters. He followed in the footsteps of trouvére and troubadour tradition, focusing mainly on the theme of courtly love, and exploiting various musical forms such as *rondeau* (e.g., *Ma fin est mon commencemement* [My end is my beginning]), *ballade*, and *virelai*. Landini, the major exponent of Italian *Ars Nova*, wrote *ballate*, madrigals, and motets. Although blind from childhood, he was an excellent organist, composer, and poet. His name is the eponym of the so-called *Landini cadence*, a particular cadence where each note of a major sixth interval moves outward one step to form an octave. His metrical charm and his lyricism contrast with the sharper style of Machaut.

Although musical instruments were banned from any liturgical use, the 14th century also saw a growth in the importance of instrumental music, beginning with the practice of arranging earlier vocal works for string or keyboard instruments. Medieval instruments can be grouped into five families: strings, woodwinds, brass, percussion, and keyboard. However, in the Middle Ages they were also distinguished according to their use: *bas* (light) for indoor performances, and *haut* (loud) for outdoors. Notable among the winds are the recorder, the shawm (a sort of oboe), the bagpipe (mostly used for accompanying dances), the *cornett* and the trumpet. Strings could be bowed (*rebec* and *vielle*) or plucked (lute, harp, and psaltery). The *tabor*, a large cylindrical drum, was probably the most common percussion instrument, together with the *naker* (ancestor of the modern kettledrums). The organ plays a particularly significant role in the history of Western music, as for centuries it was considered the only instrument allowed into the church. The Christian patron of music, St. Cecilia, is often pictured playing a portable organ, representing the union of music and spirituality.

Jacopo Mazzeo

See also: Classical Music, European; Gregorian Chant; Madrigal

Further Reading

Aubrey, Elizabeth. 1996. *The Music of the Troubadours*. Bloomington: Indiana University Press.

Burl, Aubrey. 2008. *Courts of Love, Castles of Hate: Troubadours & Trobairitz in Southern France, 1071–1321*. Chalford, UK: History Press.

Caldwell, John. 1978. *Medieval Music*. Bloomington: Indiana University Press.

Chrétien, Comfort William Wistar. 2013. *Arthurian Romances*. Lexington, KY: Feather Trail Press.
Doss-Quinby, Eglal, Joan Tasker Grimbert, Wendy Pfeffer, and Elizabeth Aubery. 2001. *Songs of the Women Trouvères*. New Haven: Yale University Press.
Gallo, F. Alberto. 1995. *Music in the Castle: Troubadours, Books, and Orators in Italian Courts of the Thirteenth, Fourteenth, and Fifteenth Centuries [Musica nel castello: Trovatori, libri, oratori nelle corti italiane dal XIII al XV secolo]*. Chicago: University of Chicago Press.
Hoppin, Richard H. 1978. *Medieval Music*. New York: W. W. Norton.
Leach, Elizabeth Eva. 2011. *Guillaume de Machaut: Secretary, Poet, Musician*. Ithaca, NY: Cornell University Press.
Nádas, John Louis, and Michael Scott Cuthbert. 2009. *Ars Nova: French and Italian Music in the Fourteenth Century*. Farnham, UK: Ashgate.
Peraino, Judith Ann. 2011. *Giving Voice to Love: Song and Self-Expression from the Troubadours to Guillaume de Machaut*. New York: Oxford University Press.
Taruskin, Richard. 2010. *Music from the Earliest Notations to the Sixteenth Century* (vol. 1 of *The Oxford History of Western Music*). Oxford: Oxford University Press.
Yudkin, Jeremy. 1989. *Music in Medieval Europe*. Englewood Cliffs, NJ: Prentice Hall.

Mento

Mento is a stylistically broad type of indigenous Jamaican social dance music that combines both European and African performance elements, and which developed into the country's first pan-Jamaican popular music, influencing such globally prominent genres as reggae and dancehall. Emerging as a distinct musical form somewhere between the late 19th and early 20th centuries, mento was a type of community dance music rooted in local popular or gospel songs which were known to people in the immediate area and performed at important social occasions such as funerals, weddings, annual festivals, and other types of community or life-cycle events. Typically, mento would be played alone, or in more formal contexts would

---

Mento

In an area as diverse, but interconnected, as the Caribbean, indigenous song styles often begin with similar roots but evolve separately according to local tastes. This is surely the case when comparing the Trinidadian song style calypso with the Jamaican mento, and the Antiguan benna. All three song styles display similar African roots, and it is likely that the three styles descended from the same West African social music traditions featuring lyrical social criticism. However, each has unique stylistic characteristics that are not shared by the other coeval styles. Nonetheless, mento and benna were initially marketed as "Calypso" (Mento-Calypso, for example) by the recording industry in the United States in the 1950s and 1960s, which attempted to market this new music during the calypso craze of that time period. Today, mento and calypso are well-known music styles thanks to famous artists such as Harry Belafonte and Bob Marley (respectively), whereas benna has been relegated to Antiguan traditional music, little heard beyond the island's boundaries.

The Jolly Boys, a *mento* group from Jamaica, performing in 1990. Mento was especially popular during the middle of the 20th century and influenced the development of other Jamaican styles, such as reggae. (David Corio/Redferns)

be performed after participants danced the European quadrille (a popular dance of the period), when the general mood of the occasion livened up and demanded more up-tempo music. Here the "African" elements feature more prominently, such as the use of more syncopated rhythms. Over time, it was the African influences in mento music that grew to predominate over the European performance features.

Common instruments used in the early forms of rural performances included flutes, violins, a drum, a tambourine, the jawbone of a horse, a grater played with a fork or spoon, and a stirrup that was struck with a piece of metal. Other scholars suggest that instrumentation included acoustic guitar, banjo, the rumba-box thumb piano, a locally made version of a saxophone, clarinets or flutes made from bamboo, drums, and various percussion instruments such as maracas or wood blocks.

As an evolving style with no connection to a particular religious group, social class, or community, mento developed as part of Jamaica's first wave of national popular music, both in the rural communities and the rapidly expanding city of Kingston made up of rural migrants. By the time of World War II, the city of Kingston's nightclubs featured ensembles with roots in African American dance band orchestras, playing American jazz, Cuban *son* pieces, and other types of Caribbean popular styles such as calypso. Many of these groups also featured mento pieces in their repertoire to varying degrees, replacing instruments like the rumba box or bamboo flutes and clarinets with orchestral instruments such as the drum set, upright bass, piano, and European clarinets or flutes. This phenomenon led to the emergence of a more refined dance-band mento style that was popular with urban audiences. In its more "rootsy" manifestation, mento continued to flourish in the tourist spots and hotels in affluent areas of Jamaica, performed for audiences interested in a representation of music and culture that conformed their notions about island culture and rural Afro-Jamaican life.

By the 1950s, with the development of Jamaica's recording industry, mento numbers also began to be recorded and cut for 78 rotations per minute (rpm) discs. Some refer to this time as the "Golden Age" of mento, as it was a period noted for creative and stylistic innovations in the music. Rupert Lyon, a/k/a Lord Fly (1905–1967), was one of the pioneering recording artists of the period, recording with a local businessman of Spanish and Portuguese origin named Stanley Motta (1915–1993), who built the country's first recording studio in Kingston and who started a record company called MRS (Motta's Recording Studio). "Lord Fly and the Dan Williams Orchestra" went into Jamaican popular music history as the first group to commercially record mento music, thus helping to solidify the genre's place in the country's music history. Fly's music was marketed as "mento-calypsos" so as to appeal to foreign audiences for whom calypso was a recognizable term. It was very common during this period for the terms "mento" and "calypso" to be used interchangeably, just as the term "rumba" was often used to describe to Cuban son music in foreign markets.

The era of the sound system operators such as Clement "Sir Coxson" Dodd (1932–2004) and Arthur "Duke" Reid (1915–1975) led to the decline of dance-band orchestras in Kingston that performed mentos and other types of Caribbean music. Moreover, it was American R & B and the subsequent development of ska in the late 1950s by Jamaican jazz musicians that heralded the end of mento's Golden Age. As a foundational musical style, mento continued to have an impact on the development of Jamaican popular music, most notably with the development of reggae in the late 1960s: many mento musicians from the countryside were called upon to perform on early reggae recordings because producers could not afford to pay the musicians connected with ska. By the 1990s, an increased nostalgic interest in mento led to a resurgence of the form and new recording activity, most notably by one of mento's most important bands, The Jolly Boys, who teamed up with the punk rock legend and industry idol Jon Baker (1960–).

Gavin Webb

See also: Calypso; Dancehall; Jazz; Reggae; Ska

Further Reading

Neely, Daniel T. 2007. "Calling All Singers, Musicians, and Speechmakers: Mento Aesthetics and Jamaica's Early Recording Industry." *Caribbean Quarterly* 53(4) "Pioneering Icons of Jamaican Popular Music" (December), 1–15, 110.

Neely, Daniel T. 2008. "Haul and Pull Up: History, Mento and the eBay Age." *Caribbean Studies* 36(2) (July-December), 95–120.

Merengue

Merengue is a form of Dominican music and dance that dates back to the 19th century on the island. The fast and danceable rhythm, accompanied by traditional Dominican folk songs and instruments, has gained popularity in the 20th and

21st centuries worldwide as music to both listen and dance to. Whatever its popularity outside the Dominican Republic, merengue is still considered to be the national music of that country (Heritage Institute, 2014).

Widespread acceptance and love of merengue has not always been the case on the island, however. The style began as the music of the common people, played on traditional instruments such as the *marímbula* bass and the *tambora* drum, which can be traced to African and indigenous roots. Merengue was the music of the poor and the nonwhite citizens of the nation, and as such was rejected by the elite racial and economic classes.

This changed, however, when the dictator Rafael Trujillo came to power in the 1930s. Trujillo grew up poor and took great delight in forcing members of the island's upper classes to dance to merengue music. Trujillo's support of and insistence on the importance of merengue helped the genre develop into the important element of Dominican and Caribbean culture that it is today. After the dictator's death, his presidential palace was turned into a merengue dance hall (Hanley, 1991).

It is perhaps the violent Trujillo's influence that for many years limited the performers of merengue to men and the content of the lyrics to macho images of conquest and violence. The lyrics of the early 20th century, however, also often served as news for people in poor neighborhoods. Like a Mexican *corrido*, merengue lyrics often communicated the reality of what was happening, with both people and events, to people too poor to afford a newspaper or radio (Hanley, 1991).

Over the years, there have been many important merengue artists, each leading their own orchestra or band. Some of the most famous are the brothers Wilfredo and Sergio Vargas and the first woman to be successful in the male-dominated industry, Milly Quesada, leader of the pioneering group Los Vecinos, who is today known as the "Queen of Merengue" during the 1980s.

One of the most important merengue artists in the 21st century is Elvis Crespo, a Dominican artist often credited with the resurgence in popularity of the merengue worldwide in the 1990s (Cobo, 2007). In 2014, Crespo had his tenth no. 1 song on Billboard's Tropical charts with a collaboration with reggaetón artist Pit Bull, "Sopa de Caracol-Yupi" (Mendizabal, 2014).

While the Dominican Republic is the home of merengue, the island of Puerto Rico as well as the nations of Colombia and Venezuela all produce merengue artists and music, though those nations show variations from the traditional Dominican roots of merengue. Venezuelan merengue, for example, uses a different set of instruments (guitars, mandolins, and the Venezuelan four-stringed *cuatro*) and is not usually danced to in the same way as the Dominican version (Mendoza, 2013).

In the Dominican Republic, merengue music is not complete without dance. The dance that accompanies traditional merengue music is also hugely popular around the world, in part because the basic steps are so simple to learn and the rhythm is so clear and constant. The basic steps of the dance include a series of sidesteps to the male partner's left, dragging the right leg. In this way, it is as easy to merengue as to walk. The simplicity of the basic dance has led to a whole set of myths and legends about its beginnings. One popular legend is that the dance was invented by a war hero who had one wounded leg and that others dragged their legs in his honor. Another popular myth is that the dance was invented by slaves whose legs were chained together, making short sideways steps the only way that they had to move (Heritage Institute, 2014). In this way, "authentic" traditional merengue is very different from the elaborate steps of the type of merengue performed by ballroom dancers.

Elizabeth Gackstetter Nichols and Timothy R. Robbins

See also: Conjunto (Norteños); Corrido; Reggae; Reggaetón

Further Reading

Cobo, Leila. 2007. "Merengue Mélange." *Billboard* 119(22), 18.

Hanley, E. 1991. "Milly's Merengue." *Mother Jones* 16(5), 44.

Heritage Institute. 2014. "Merengue." http://www.heritageinstitute.com/danceinfo/descriptions/merengue.htm.

Mendizabal, Amaya. 2014. "Crespo Bounds to No. 1." *Billboard* 126(3), 84.

Mendoza, Emilio. 2013. "Merengue Venezolano." In David Horn and John Shepherd (eds.), *Bloomsbury Encyclopedia of Popular Music of the World*, vol. 9. London: Bloomsbury Academic.

Mestizo Music

Belize is the home of Mestizo music. Belizean music is a mixture of Kriol, Mestizo, Garifuna, and Mayan music. Each culture is known for a special genre, but the general population listens and dances to everything. Mestizo music has a unique sound. The instrument of choice for Mestizo music is the marimba, a percussion instrument that looks like a xylophone. The marimba originated in West Africa; it is believed that a form of this instrument was brought to Guatemala, Mexico, and Belize by slaves in the 1500s. Along with the marimba they also use drum sets, double bass, and sometimes other instruments.

Mestizo indicates a mixture of Europeans (Spaniards) and Indian ancestry (Amerindians). It comes from a Spanish word meaning "mixed." Mestizos from Belize are descended from the union of the indigenous Maya and the Spanish who came following Columbus's arrival in the New World. As far as history goes, many texts indicate that the Mestizo community owes its origins to Gonzalo Guerrero, a shipwrecked Spanish sailor who despite being initially enslaved by the Maya later impressed them with his military prowess and was embraced as one of them. It is said that he became a great ally to the Mayans in the struggle against the Spanish conquistadors in Belize. The Mestizo population in Belize can be found throughout the country, but are concentrated in the Corozal and Orange Walk districts. Their ethnic heritage is such that their appearance is decidedly Hispanic.

The music of the Mestizos plays a big role in their celebrations; they also serenade with the guitar. Dances performed in village fiestas are influenced by Mestizo music. Some of their fiestas include the Mestizada, the Hog-Head, Zapateados, Jarana, Cuadriz, and Paso Doble. Mestizos regard fiestas as a means of celebration and a way to promote social bonding and cultural identity. Mestizo music has also spread into Guatemala and into the southern part of Mexico.

Many aspects of this music were standardized, such as the appropriate use of particular instruments or functions of particular songs. Quechua-language dictionaries reveal certain ideals and practices for the Inca. Specific terms distinguished between correct and incorrect singing and between low and high voices. *Taki*, a term designating dance, song, or both, could be used to describe a song of lament memorializing the life of an emperor or a local chief. The Spanish reported that a *cantar historico* (historical chant) was performed during the most important celebrations and at funeral rites. Exactly how the songs were performed is unclear, but the Mestizo historian Garcilaso de la Vega mentions in his *Cometarios reales* (written within a century of conquest of the Inca) that each song text had its own unique melody.

The new musical cultures that emerged gradually during the colonial period grew from elements drawn from the cultures of Indians, Spanish or Portuguese Europeans, and sub-Saharan Africans. Various mixtures of all these created a hybrid culture made up of Europeans, mostly Spaniards (with Portuguese in Brazil), *criollos* and mestizos, Indians, and those of African descent. After the Mayan civilization collapsed, the Mestizo people created new music that combined elements of both cultures.

As Mestizo culture took shape, the particular cultural blend, the shared life experiences over time, and the isolation of local communities led to considerable cultural diversity among those of mixed heritage. Musical life was more local and regional than it was national, and this tendency was reflected in the Mestizo music that had evolved by the 1800s. At the core of most regional musical styles that emerged with the formation of Mestizo culture, particularly in central Mexico, is the music genre known as *son*. In the early 1800s, the Gran Teatro Coliseo de la Metropoli in Mexico City and theaters in the provinces were clearinghouses for various genres of songs and dance. Theatrical interludes featured Spanish and Mestizo melodies and dances that were circulating throughout New Spain. These pieces, often called *sones*, took various forms: "La Bamba," "El Perico," and "El Palomo" were all documented in the early 1800s.

The mestizo son continues to be formally diverse, but a few generalizations are possible. It is oriented toward accompanying social dance, with vigorous, marked rhythm and fast tempo. It is performed most often by ensembles in which stringed instruments predominate, with notable regional exceptions. Its formal structure features the alternation of instrumental sections and the signing of short poetic units called *coplas*. In contrast to the Amerindian son, the mestizo son is fundamentally secular, as is reflected in its textual amorousness and wit, its extroversion, and its performative settings.

Regional sones and other unifying traits make a case for a Mestizo son "supergenre," but many regional styles of son are easily recognizable by the distinctiveness of their instrumentation, instrumental techniques, and treatment of the copla, vocal nuances, repertoire, associated dances, and other factors. Other areas that also show large influences of Mestizo music exist in Peru. Peru has a fiesta called the Fiesta of the Virgen del Carmen in Paucartambo. The major ensemble type used to provide Mestizo dance music in Paucartambo, however, combines European and pre-Hispanic Andean instruments within the same band. These groups, known simply as *orquestras típicas* (typical orchestras), feature a large diatonic harp, violins, accordion, and sometimes mandolin. However, indigenous vertical end-notched flutes known as *kenas* are also included, as are drums. Along with panpipes and trumpets, kenas were one of the main wind instruments played in the Andes before the Spanish arrived.

Other music heard during the fiesta is representative of the major Mestizo genres of Peru: the *wayno*, the *marinera*, the *yaravi*, marches, and religious hymns. Not tied to specific contexts, the first three popular genres are performed in all types of social gatherings and private music-making occasions, ranging from serenades and family birthday parties to drinking bouts with friends and theater stage performances.

Modern Mestizo music, in the west and north of Belize, is mellower than the music elsewhere. It is a modern fusion of traditional Latin-American and Iberian rhythms such as rumba, cumbia, salsa, and flamenco with influences of punk rock, ska, rap, dub, reggae, dancehall, turntablism, sampling, and other electronic implements. Lyrics, which may reference global as well as specific local matters, are very often political and oppose all kinds of repression. The often multiethnic makeup of the groups and the different migration backgrounds of their members coheres with their mostly anti-racist, anti-conservative, pacifistic, and anti-globalist attitudes—but above all Mestizo music is very danceable.

Alejandra Tapia

See also: Conjunto; Marimba; Salsa

Further Reading

Gonzales, Lorenzo. 2013. "Belizian Music Is Simple, Yet Extraordinary." *Belize Adventure*. November 5. https://www.belizeadventure.ca/belizean-music.

National Institute of Culture and History. 2015. "Mestizo." October 30. https://nichbelize.org.

World Music Network. 2011. "The Music of Belize: Drum'n'flute Legacies." April 11. https://worldmusic.net/blogs/guide-to-world-music/the-music-of-belize-drumnflute-legacies.

Mexican Regional Music

Mexican music has developed into several regional styles, differentiated by instrumentation, singing style, repertoire, and use of language. *Son* is the main secular folkloric music genre; it originated from a fusion of Spanish, African, and indigenous music. The term "son" (Spanish for "tune" or "sound") usually refers to a string-dominated genre of *mestizo* music, but can also be applied to some indigenous and folk melodies.

Mestizo *son* traditions include the *son jalisciense* (from the lowlands of Jalisco and Colima), the brisk *son jarocho* (from Veracruz), the *son arribeño* (from the Sierra Gorda), the *son calentano* (from the Balsas River basin in southern Mexico), the *son de arpa grande* (from western Mexico), and the popular trio-based *son huasteco* (adapted from the Huastec people). Since the late 18th century, these styles have shared a compound meter that can be accompanied by foot-stomping *zapateado* patterns to emphasize rhythmic shifts. This music is performed by groups of three to 12 instrumentalists, many of whom sing *decimas* (verses of 10 lines) arranged in *coplas* (couplets). Indigenous Mexican traditions include the *son abajeño* (from the Purépecha people in Michoacán) and the bilingual *son istmeño* (from the Zapotecs in Oaxaca).

By 1580, African Americans played as major role in *mestizaje* (Spanish word for the cultural amalgam resulting from the mixing of races). They were active in the official musical activities of the colony; the choir of the Oaxaca Cathedral included professional African American singers throughout the 17th century, and even an African American choir director (by 1648). In spite of laws designed to limit cross-cultural interaction, syncretic religious festivals existed as early as 1669, where African Americans and indigenous peoples would play local percussion instruments such as the *huehuetl* and sing songs for dances accompanied by harps, guitars, and drums; these were precursors to later son and *jarabe* gatherings. Modern *sones jarochos* still show discernible African influence through complex polyrhythms and responsorial singing style. Harp trios in Veracruz often feature African American musicians.

The first written records of Mexican folk music have been collected in the *Ramo de Inquisición*. In 1766, an early example of son jarocho named "Chuchumbé" became the first Mexican song to be banned (it depicts soldiers and friars fighting to seduce women). The rhymed text for the *tonadilla* (folk melody) ridiculed the authorities in Veracruz; they issued an edict banning its "lascivious *sones* and obscene *coplas*." Four trials resulted in excommunications for performing or witnessing traditional song and dance. Many coplas with *doble sentido* (double meaning) have been preserved; these older song texts include archaic word usage, poetic rural imagery, and folk wisdom.

Bandas populares (civilian brass bands) were introduced to northwestern Mexico in the 1800s. Independence from Spain and the decline of ecclesiastical influence brought Mexican secular music to greater prominence. Music and dances (such as the jarabe) associated with political insurgence became a symbol of national identity, and the first professional recording of Mexican regional music was made in Chicago (1908).

As mariachi groups began to record and tour, the modern guitar soon replaced traditional plucked strings. By the 1930s, traditional repertoire featuring son jalisciense expanded to include son jarocho and son huasteco (requiring more violins and replacing the harp with the *guitarrón*, a large deep-bodied six-string bass), identifiable by nostalgic migrants. At that time, *banda* (woodwind and brass) musicians in Sinaloa played a similar repertory of regional tunes.

Many Mexican octosyllabic tunes come from 16th-century Spain, and indigenous songs incorporate, alternate, or replace Spanish texts (sones istemeños are sung in both Zapotec and Spanish). Sones abajeños are often played in alternation with *pirekaus*, a form of native love song from Michoacán.

Son is typified by a complex triple or compound meter, with a chordal string instrument (guitar or harp) playing one distinct rhythm while the bass (guitarrón or harp) emphasizes a contrasting pattern. Here is an example commonly found in the son jalisciense and the *huapango*. Son arribeño and son hausteco feature small string trios. Indigenous performers often include traditional instruments such as ocarina, *caracol*, and *flauta de tres hoyes*. Son huasteco and huapango employ falsetto singing and focus on vocal improvisation. Some areas employ percussion, such as those from Tixtla, which require a *tapeador* tapping on a board in a wooden box; the son jarocho, which employs a *quijada* (donkey jaw) and *pandero* (wood-frame tambourine); and the *son calentano Balsas*, which combines virtuosic violins, guitars, a *tamborito* (small double drum), and competitive dancing performed on a wooden *tarima* (platform).

The son jarocho shares the rhythm and high vocal timbre (but not falsetto) of the huapango; typical instruments include the percussive harp and *jarana*, a small, deep-bodied rhythm guitar. Southern Veracruz has a strong indigenous presence, and its music is slower, employing different sizes and tunings of *requinto* and jarana guitars. The son calentano from the Tepalcatepec River basin is notable for a 36-string harp struck with the palm of the hand, accompanied by two violins, a vihuela, and a guitar with two courses of strings. As mariachi groups evolved, this instrumentation was transformed: the harp was replaced with a guitarrón, the number of violins and guitars was enlarged, and trumpets were added.

Conjunto groups use a wider variety of plucked strings, including *bajo quinto* (mixteco), *bajo sexto* and double bass (norteño), *leona* (jarocho), and *huapanguera* (huasteco). Modern mariachi groups and banda groups include brass instruments, clarinets, saxophones, accordions, and even electric instruments.

Laura Stanfield Prichard

See also: Conjunto; Conjunto (Norteño); Guitarrón Mexicano; Mariachi

Further Reading

Prichard, Laura. 2013. "Mexican Son." In George Torres (ed.), *Encyclopedia of Latin American Popular Music*, 381–383. Santa Barbara, CA: Greenwood.

Sheehy, Daniel. 2000. "Mexico." In Dale A. Olsen and Daniel E. Sheehy (eds.), *The Garland Handbook of Latin American Music*, 181–208. New York: Garland.

Stanford, E. Thomas. 1984. *El Son Mexicano*. Mexico City, Mexico: Fondo de Cultura Económica.

Mikagura

Mikagura is a music genre dating back nearly one thousand years and has long been associated with the Shinto religion native to Japan. The term *kagura* comes from ancient Japanese and originally meant "place of the gods" or "seat of the gods." However, with the importation of Chinese characters into the Japanese language, the meaning shifted to "music of the gods" (Garfias, 1968, p. 149). The genre has heavily influenced the music and dance forms found in both *nô* and *gagaku*. Within the gagaku tradition, mikagura is categorized with other accompanied vocal musics and dances originating in Japan. The genre gets its name from the *mikagura no gi* rite of the Shinto religion. This rite is held annually in mid-December to summon the gods to the earth; this music is intended to entertain the gods on their arrival. Though this genre was heavily influenced by the imperial court and has been absorbed into the larger gagaku tradition, it is also very important to key Shinto shrines. Mikagura is commonly performed at the Shinto shrine called Iwasimizu Hatimangû (in Kyoto).

The style in which mikagura is practiced today is said to date back to the mid-11th century CE. Its instrumentation uses both native and non-native instruments to accompany the Heian Period (794–1185 CE) poetry used as lyrics. The *wagon* ("wa" rhyming with "spa") is a six-string zither said to have originated in Japan, which has long been associated with the mikagura tradition. The *kagurabue* (also known as the *yamatobue*), also said to be native to Japan, is used to accompany the melody. This flute has six finger holes and is made of bamboo. It is becoming rarer, as another gagaku flute called the *ryûteki* is more commonly used today. Another gagaku instrument can be used to accompany the melody in certain contexts. The *hichiriki*, which is a double reed instrument, has a loud and nasal sound; although it was imported from mainland Asia, it is well known as a Japanese instrument today. Finally, a set of wooden clappers imported from China, known as the *shakubyôshi*, are used to mark time. Most pieces are free rhythm, with very few using a strict common meter. In addition to these instruments, there are two alternating solo singers as well as a chorus for most mikagura pieces. Each instrument, including the shakubyôshi, and the singers may have extended solo periods in a performance (Harich-Schneider, 1973, p. 579).

What we know as mikagura today probably formed around the mid-16th century but was streamlined during the Edo Period (1601–1898 CE). A further remodeling occurred during the Meiji Period (1898–1912 CE). However, today the public rarely sees this music and ceremony. It is held on the imperial grounds during specially designated times of the year in a specially prepared hall and is not open to the public.

Justin R. Hunter

See also: Gagaku; Nô Theater

Further Reading

Garfias, Robert. 1968. "The Sacred Mi-Kagura of the Japanese Imperial Court." *Selected Reports* 1(2), 149–178. Institute of Ethnomusicology, University of California Los Angeles.

Harich-Schneider, Eta. 1973. *A History of Japanese Music*. London: Oxford University Press.

Nelson, Steven G. 2008. "Court and Religious Music (1): History of Gagaku and Shōmyō." In Alison McQueen Tokita and David W. Hughes (eds.), *The Ashgate Research Companion to Japanese Music*, 35–48. Surrey, UK: Ashgate.

Terauchi, Naoko. 2001. "Gagaku." In Robert Provine, Yosihiko Yokumaru, and Lawrence Witzleben (eds.), *Garland Encyclopedia of World Music; Vol. 7: China, Japan, and Korea*, 619–628. New York: Routledge.

Min'yô

Min'yô is a general term for a wide-ranging genre of Japanese folk songs that have emerged over centuries of tradition. The word "min'yô" is derived from the German word *Volkslied*, and is written with two Chinese characters that literally mean "folk song." In general, people in Japan refer to these songs in very specific terms (e.g., "rice pounding song," "fishing song," "lullaby," etc.) and often do not refer to them collectively using the term min'yô. However, prior to its academic adoption, scholars felt that some terms used to describe these regional songs were unrefined or nondescript, such as "vulgar" and "rural" (Groemer, 2001, p. 599). To understand these issues, it can be helpful to look back to established lines of division in Japanese music genres. First, there has been a long distinction between urban or popular musics (such as *geisha* music or *koto* music), and rural or folk musics (min'yô). Second, there is a distinction between min'yô and folk performing arts or theatrics, known as *minzoku geinô*. Though they are not mutually exclusive, minzoku geinô regularly includes acting, costuming, staging, instrumentation (and more) that min'yô often downplays or excludes. The majority of min'yô is thought to have been composed by unknown amateur musicians and is typically passed down through community settings, though exceptions do exist.

Depending on the context, min'yô can be sung solo, in unison, or in a call-and-response style. Because the setting for each song varies greatly, texts are quite free and can often change over time. "Voice quality varies with function, context, mood and alcohol consumption" (Hughes, 2008, p. 289), and each region has certain idiosyncratic qualities that are cherished by the locals. The music is considered to be heterophonic, meaning that each part is similar, but with varying elements of embellishment, especially from instrumental accompaniment. The most commonly used instrument is the *shamisen*, a three-stringed, long-necked lute that originated in the Ryukyu Islands (Okinawa). Many forms exist, but the thick-necked *tsugaru-jamisen* is the most widely used. Also common are varying forms of horizontal bamboo side-blown flutes known as *takebue* or *shinobue* that are often used in festival dance songs. Another bamboo flute, the end-blown notch flute *shakuhachi*, has become popular for staged min'yô performances. Several types of drums are common, from small hand-held drums to the large *taiko* of Bon dances. Small hand-gongs called *kane* are also common (Hughes, 2008, pp. 287–288).

Min'yô is held in nostalgic esteem throughout Japan and is often quite romanticized. A common saying since the 1950s states: "folk song is the heart's home town" (Hughes, 2008, p. 282). This idea comes from the highly valued Japanese concept of *furusato*, literally "the old village," or generally "one's place of origin." This link to origin is very strong in Japan; in fact, even those from urban areas will still assert a connection to rural Japan, often through min'yô. Since the late 19th century CE, min'yô has become increasingly popularized, with "professional" folk singers gaining in numbers. Despite this, many contend that to give a truly authentic performance, one must be born and raised where the song originated (Groemer, 2001, p. 601).

Justin R. Hunter

See also: Japan, Music of; Shakuhachi; Shamisen

Further Reading

Groemer, Gerald. 2001. "Japanese Folk Music." In Robert Provine, Yosihiko Yokumaru, and Lawrence Witzleben (eds.), *Garland Encyclopedia of World Music; Vol. 7: China, Japan, and Korea*, 599–606. New York: Routledge.

Hughes, David W. 2008. "Folk Music: From Local to National to Global." In Alison McQueen Tokita and David W. Hughes (eds.), *The Ashgate Research Companion to Japanese Music*, 281–302. Surrey, UK: Ashgate.

Koizumi, Fumio. 1965. "Towards a Systematization of Japanese Folk Song." *Studia Musicologica* 7, 309–313.

Moravian Music

Originating in Bohemia in Central Europe in the mid-15th century, Moravian music has spread to countries all over the world, mainly through the mission efforts of the Moravian Church. Using the life and teachings of Bohemian reformer Jan Hus, his followers formed their own religious group, the Unity of the Brethren, and broke away from the Catholic Church in 1467 CE. Throughout the rest of the 15th and all of the 16th century, the Brethren continued to sing hymns and worship in their own language wherever they went, despite persecution from Catholic authorities. Eventually, in 1727, the Brethren's descendants who settled on German Count Nicholas Ludwig von Zinzendorf's land became the Renewed Unity of the Brethren, or the Renewed Moravian Church. Under his leadership, daily hymn singing and weekly hymn services were standardized, and the revitalized Moravian Church then spread the gospel and their musical forms all over the world. With the publication of Christian Gregor's hymnbook in 1788 and his tune book in 1794, the Moravian Church had more streamlined resources for musical expression in its far-flung mission locations.

The spread and characteristics of Moravian music are intimately intertwined with the history of the Moravian Church. The Moravians consider the founder of their movement to be Jan Hus (1369–1415 CE), the Bohemian reformer. Hus protested against the perceived worldliness of the Catholic Church and, as rector of the University of Prague and as a priest at Bethlehem Chapel, advocated living a life of strict and simple piety based on New Testament teachings. He also strove for more congregational participation in worship services by involving the congregation in hymn singing, a practice which he viewed as second only to preaching the Bible in the vernacular Czech language. Moreover, he urged the laity to partake of both the bread and wine in the Mass, rather than just the bread, as the Catholic Church had prescribed. For his controversial views, he was eventually burned at the stake at the Council of Constance in 1415. Forty-two years later, in the town of Kunwald, some of Hus's followers banded together to form their own religious society within the Catholic Church called the "Unity of the Brethren" (Latin: *Unitas Fratrum*—which is still the official name of the worldwide Moravian Church). The Brethren broke away from the Catholic Church completely in 1467, thus becoming the first Protestant church 50 years before the Protestant Reformation.

Drawing from the example of Jan Hus, the Brethren of Bohemia and Moravia (both regions are a part of the modern Czech Republic) made congregational participation in music a hallmark of their religious practice. To aid in worship, they produced the first vernacular hymnbook in 1501 (Johnson, 1979, p. 4). As the Unitas Fratrum movement spread to nearby German-speaking and Polish-speaking lands, pastors translated Hus's hymns and other Czech hymns into their own languages. One notable example was former Catholic priest Michael Wiesse (1488–1539), who translated and published the German *Ein New Gesengbuchlen* (A new little hymnbook) in 1531. Although Wiesse promoted a view of the Lord's Supper contrary to Brethren teaching in his hymnbook and got into trouble for doing so, the hymnbook was the first Brethren hymnal that contained music, and it underwent several editions throughout the 16th century.

The Brethren held on to their developing musical traditions throughout the tumultuous 16th century. Protestant reformers Martin Luther (1483–1546), Ulrich Zwingli (1484–1531), and John Calvin (1509–1564) criticized the supreme authority of the Catholic Pope to decide spiritual matters for Christians and instead asserted that the Bible was the Christian's sole authority. Such criticism fractured the unity of Western Christianity that had existed since the fifth century CE. The Brethren, sympathizing with many of the Reformers' denunciations of Catholic doctrine and practice, were often persecuted by the Catholic authorities. Even in the midst of troubled times, the Brethren used "hymnody as the primary means of expressing and transmitting their faith and doctrine" to the next generation of Brethren members and to the world.

From 1609 to 1618, the Brethren enjoyed freedom of worship in Prague, but such peace was fleeting. Near the beginning of the Thirty Years' War (1618–1648), a war that began as a conflict between Protestant and Catholic provinces, the Brethren were almost obliterated in Moravia and Bohemia. Catholic authorities assumed control in 1620 and confiscated churches (1621), exiled priests (1624), and forced the Brethren to convert to Catholicism. In response, some of the Brethren found refuge in Poland, where they were led by the Brethren bishop and internationally known education reformer John Amos Comenius (1592–1670). While in exile, he helped to keep alive Brethren worship practices, most notably their rich musical tradition. Other members of the Unitas Fratrum did not escape persecution and stayed in Moravia and Bohemia during Catholic rule. This "hidden seed" maintained their faith in secret throughout much of the rest of the 17th century.

The fortunes of the Brethren changed dramatically in 1722, when the descendants of its persecuted members found asylum on the extensive land holdings of a Saxon German count named Nicholas Ludwig von Zinzendorf (1700–1760). Zinzendorf was a man sympathetic to their cause. He was raised a Lutheran, but under the influence of his grandmother, he also embraced the Pietism movement that had been growing in popularity in several different German territories during the last few decades. Pietism, a renewal movement within Lutheranism, focused on having the heartfelt experience of a personal relationship with Jesus Christ rather than merely knowing and believing key Christian doctrines. The Brethren, too, emphasized personal piety instead of rigid dogma. Zinzendorf, the Brethren, and other persecuted Christians soon formed the town of Herrnhut ("the Lord's Watch") on his property. On August 13, 1727, after partaking of the Lord's Supper, members of the Herrnhut community experienced the presence of the Holy Spirit in a new and dramatic way and resolved to be united as one religious body. On that day, the Renewed Unity of the Brethren, or the Renewed Moravian Church, was born.

Zinzendorf, even before the official reappearance of the Moravian Church, exercised his leadership over the Herrnhut settlement in several ways. First, he led the Moravians in reforming their music practices. Zinzendorf was an accomplished hymn writer who wrote almost 900 hymns by 1725 (Johnson, 1979, p. 14) and established the tradition of picking out a daily text from the Bible and a hymn relating to the meaning of the text. He urged the Moravians to meditate upon them, practice singing the hymn, and conform their lives to the principles contained in the Bible and the hymn.

Out of this daily practice evolved the concept of the *singstunde* (singing hour), Zinzendorf's second major innovation. Once a week, the Herrnhut congregation gathered together and sang a string of songs that all had a related biblical theme. The pastor selected which hymns to sing, and everyone sang the songs from memory. Additionally, the organists and other orchestra members had to play each song from memory. The Moravians believed that using hymnbooks during the singstunde would ruin the heartfelt flow of music during the time of worship. Members of the congregation became proficient singers and players through such frequent practice. Drawing upon the old Brethren custom of congregational singing, Zinzendorf gave the custom more structure and incorporated more stringed, brass, and woodwind instruments than the old Brethren had used. Using daily texts and the singstunde remain important practices in the Moravian Church today.

Zinzendorf organized Herrnhut as an international mission hub for the rapidly expanding Moravian Church. Beginning in the late 1720s and throughout the 18th century, the Moravians started mission communities in St. Thomas in the Caribbean, Salem in colonial North Carolina, Bethlehem in colonial Pennsylvania, England, Russia, and Persia, among other locales. Zinzendorf helped these far-flung communities stay in contact with Herrnhut and one another through administering an extensive letter-writing network and by conducting personal visits to some of the locations. By maintaining worldwide organizational unity, hymnbooks and other musical practices could be effectively transmitted from one culture to another.

Another major figure in Moravian music history is Christian Gregor (1723–1801), whom many Moravian music historians consider to be the "Father of Moravian Church Music." During his almost 60 years of involvement in the Moravian Church, he was a supervisor of a Moravian boys' school, a pastor, the Church's financial administrator, and eventually bishop over the entire Church, as well as an expert musician. Under Zinzendorf's leadership, the Moravian Church eventually compiled more than 3,000 text-only hymns by 1754 (Asti, 1984, p. 23). This massive two-volume work had to be streamlined, so the Synod of 1775 commissioned Gregor for the task. He responded with publication of the *Gesangbuch* (hymnbook) of 1778, a one-volume work with only 1,750 hymns (Asti, 1984, p. 23). He followed this monumental undertaking with an accompanying tune book called the *Choral-Buch* (chorale book) in 1784. Since then, Moravian musicians all over the world have used Gregor's works as a base for their own hymnbooks and other musical works.

Jacob Hicks

See also: Austro-German Dances; Dulcimer; Kodály, Zoltán; Polish National Dances

Further Reading

Asti, Martha. 1984. *Introduction to Choral-Buch: A Facsimile of the First Edition of 1784*, ed. James Boeringer, trans. Karl Kroeger. Winston-Salem, NC: Moravian Music Foundation Press.

Fries, Adelaide L. 1962. *Customs and Practices of the Moravian Church.* Winston-Salem, NC: Board of Christian Education and Evangelism.

Hamilton, J. Taylor, and Kenneth G. Hamilton. 1967. *History of the Moravian Church: The Renewed Unitas Fratrum, 1722–1957.* Bethlehem, PA: Interprovincial Board of Christian Education, Moravian Church in America.

Johnson, John H. 1979. "Moravian Hymnody." *The Papers of the Hymn Society of America* 32, 3–24.

Knouse, Nola Reed. 2008. "The Moravians and Their Music." In Nola Reed Knouse (ed.), *The Music of the Moravian Church in America*, 1–28. Rochester, NY: University of Rochester Press.

The Moravian Music Foundation. n.d. http://moravianmusic.org.

Morin Khuur

The Mongolian *morin khuur* is a two-stringed spike fiddle used to accompany vocal music, known for its carved, horsehead-shaped headstock. Similar to other central and east Asian fiddles, the instrument became an icon of Mongolian history and identity after the Democratic Revolution in 1990 (Marsh, 2008, p. 2). Present-day Mongolia is a land-locked country to the south of Russia, and north of the Republic of China. Today, the morin khuur is recognized as a symbol of pan-Mongolian heritage.

The morin khuur's body is trapezoidal in shape, growing wider toward the bottom, and is seamlessly joined with the instrument's long neck (Pegg, 2001, p. 68). The morin khuur was found mostly in Central and Eastern prerevolutionary Mongolian groups; Western Mongolian groups had a box fiddle, the *ikil*, that did not feature a horse headstock.

Soviet standardization of Mongolian instruments took place in the 1960s and 1970s, as a way to "stabilize" instrumental traditions that were not destroyed (Pegg, 2001, pp. 256–273). These changes were an influence of Western musical pedagogy during the Mongolian People's Republic, a satellite state of the Soviet Union (1921–1992). In an effort to promote the morin khuur as a symbol of national identity across the nation, Soviet organologists attempted to standardize the instrument's size,

A Mongolian teenager in traditional dress performing on the *morin khuur*, a two-stringed horsehead fiddle played with a bow. (Wolfgang Kaehler/LightRocket via Getty Images)

use wooden soundboards (originally animal skin), and raise the morin khuur's base-level pitch range to match the open-string pitches of a European violoncello (Pegg, 2001, p. 257).

Tales regarding the origin of the morin khuur invoke sentiments of magic or spirituality (Haslund-Christensen, 1943, pp. 35–37). In one example, a magical prince from the heavens descended to Earth with his horse. He fell in love with a shepherdess who clipped the wings off of his horse at night, preventing it from flying back to the heavens. Upon taking flight, the horse plummeted to Earth and died. The tears of the prince transformed the horse into the first morin khuur: its body became the fiddle, and its hair became the strings (Pegg, 2001, p. 101, citing Haslund-Christensen, 1943). The practice of carving the horse's head into the headstock is a subject of debate for Mongolian scholars: Pegg argues that some believe it stems from an ancient shamanic practice, whereas others argue it is a contemporary phenomenon meant to replace earlier symbols such as the "moon, sun, Garuda [hinting at the 17th-century arrival of Hinduism and Tibetan Buddhism in Mongolia], [or] sea serpent" (Pegg, 2001, p. 69).

John Forrestal

See also: Erhu; Huqin; Shamanic Music in Mongolia and Inner Asia; Tuvan Popular Bands; Tuvan Throat Singing

Further Reading

Haslund-Christensen, Henning. 1943. *The Music of the Mongols, Part 1. Eastern Mongolia.* New York: Da Capo Press.

Marsh, Peter K. 2008. *The Horse-head Fiddle and the Cosmopolitan Reimagination of Tradition in Mongolia.* New York: Routledge.

Pegg, Carole. 2001. *Mongolian Music, Dance, and Oral Narrative.* Seattle: University of Washington Press.

UNESCO. 2005. "Urtiin Duu—Mongolian Traditional Folk Long Song." http://www.unesco.org/culture/intangible-heritage/25apa_uk.htm.

Mridangam

The *mridangam* is a wooden, double-faced barrel drum common in southern India. It is the primary percussion instrument played in the South Indian classical, or *Karnatic*, tradition. Its outward appearance is similar to the ceramic *khol* of eastern India or the *maddale* that accompanies *Yakshagana* in Karnataka, but its structure, acoustics, and playing techniques are markedly different.

The body of the mridangam is traditionally made out a piece of wood taken from the jackfruit tree and hollowed out until the barrel walls are approximately one inch thick. The two apertures are of differing diameters and are faced with skins made of layered animal hide; the combination of these two characteristics makes possible the peculiar acoustic properties of the drum. The drum faces are attached to the drum by lacing leather straps between the two faces across the outer body (*koddu*) of the drum. More recently, some players have begun to replace the leather straps with nylon strapping.

The right face, which produces the drum's treble sounds and is called the *valanthalai*, is made of three layers of goat and cowhide. The innermost layer of hide is a ring of goatskin that rests directly on the wood of the barrel. This is covered by a full disk of goat hide that entirely covers the aperture, which in turn is topped with a final ring made of cowhide, leaving a circular depression in the center of the drum face. This depression is filled with a black paste called *soru* or *saatham*, which is made by mixing a fine powder consisting of iron oxide and manganese oxide with rice paste. The soru must be cured for several days in the dark in order to ensure the proper consistency. After curing, small pieces of either straw or "gravel" (usually manganese granules) are placed between the outmost and middle layers of hide to enhance the tone of the drum.

The left-hand face, which produces the bass tones and is called the *idanthalai* or the *thoppi*, is also made of three layers of skin. The first layer, also called the thoppi, is a disk of goat skin that entirely covers the aperture. The thoppi is topped with two buffalo-hide rings and, like the valanthalai, all three layers are bound together with woven leather straps, called the *mootu*. During performances, the thoppi is topped with a nonpermanent paste called *rava*, made of semolina (coarsely ground durum wheat flour) and mixed with water to a thick but not sticky consistency. Some modern players have replaced this paste with a semipermanent application of silicone caulk.

Before playing, the valanthalai is tuned using a stone and wooden peg to adjust the tension in the leather straps running between the left and right faces across the body of the drum. The mridangam is placed upright, resting on the thoppi, and the musician rotates the drum while sounding a vibrating, harmonic stroke called *dhin* (discussed later). The tone must be uniform around the entire circumference of the valanthalai in order for the drum to resonate correctly during performance.

The mridangam is played while sitting cross-legged on the floor, with the body of the drum resting on and more or less perpendicular to the ground. The drummer's right leg rests slightly extended from the body and the right side of the drum is rested on the right foot and ankle.

The mridangam has four fundamental strokes—*Tha, Dhi, Thom, Nam*—which cover the basic bass and treble sounds of the instrument. To these are added a variety of other strokes that vary, to some extent, on the tradition within which the player has been trained. Two primary strokes are played on the idanthalai, or left face: (1) Tha, for which the four fingers of the left hand slap across the face of the drum, producing a sharp, flat, bass sound; and (2) Thom, for which the tips of four fingers of the left hand contact the midpoint of the thoppi, producing a resonant tone. The primary strokes on the valanthalai, or the right face, are: (1) Thi, for which the second, third, and fourth (pinky) fingers of the right hand slap across the soru, producing a sharp, flat, treble sound; and (2) Nam, for which the ring finger rests on the edge of the saatham, acting as a pivot, and the index finger snaps down across the outer ring of the drum face, producing a clear, ringing tone.

Other common strokes include, on the right face:

- Ta/Da: the pad of the index finger sharply contacts the center of the saatham.
- *Dhin*: like the nam, the ring finger acts as a pivot while resting at the edge of the saatham, but the pad of the index finger sharply contacts and rebounds from the edge of the saatham, producing a vibrating tone.
- *Chāpu*: this tone has multiple variations based on the position of the right hand. In the basic chāpu stroke, the fourth finger is kept apart from the first three.

The tip of the fourth finger strikes the edge of the saatham between the 9 and 12 o'clock positions. In the *araichāpu*, or half-chāpu stroke, the fingers are held in the same position, but the fourth finger strikes the drum face at the midpoint of the saatham.

Additionally, there is a bass stroke called *gumukki*, which is rendered by contacting the center of the left face with the fingers and then pushing the heel of the hand across the face, producing a sound most similar to the *bayan*, or left drum, of the *tabla*.

Teaching of the mridangam was traditionally conducted within the *gurukula* system, in which a student would live with his teacher, or guru, almost as a member of the teacher's family. Along with instruction, the student would be expected to complete whatever household tasks or chores the guru might assign. This relationship would commonly last years before the student was deemed accomplished enough to leave his guru. Even today, lessons are conveyed orally using *solkattu*, or spoken rhythmic syllables. The teacher will speak a series of syllables which the student both repeats orally and reproduces on the drum. Because each stroke is given a syllabic name, syllables spoken using solkattu translate directly into rhythmic patterns on the mridangam.

For example, the first full lesson usually given to beginner students is "Tha Thi Thom Nam," which covers the four basic strokes. Rhythmic patterns quickly become more complicated and are suited to fit into the wide variety of rhythmic signatures used in South Indian classical music. Because of this diversity, and to facilitate recitation, most strokes have multiple names. Thi is also called "ki," "ka," "da," and even "nu." These syllables are highly contextual, as some of these secondary names are shared between primary strokes. For example, the solkattu phrase spoken as "Ki | da" is played "Thom | Thi"; "Tha Ri Ki Da" is played "Thi Ta Thom Thi"; and "Tha Ka Jo Nu" is played "Nam Thom Thom Thi" or "Thi Thom Thom Thi." While this can initially be confusing, ultimately it allows for the recitation of lengthy, complicated rhythmic passages that can be immediately reproduced on the drum.

As a pedagogical tool, solkattu syllables can be reproduced on any drum used in Karnatic music, varying the strokes to fit the percussion instrument at hand: for example, the *kanjira*, a small frame drum covered in lizard skin and including two or three metal discs in the frame that jingle when played; the *ghatam* (clay pot); or the *morsing*, or mouth harp. Solkattu is a fully developed art in itself that can also be showcased during performances. When a musician presents solkattu during a percussion solo or as part of a percussion ensemble, it is called *konnakol*.

Aaron Mulvany

See also: Karnatic Music

Further Reading

Nelson, David P. 2008. *Solkattu Manual: An Introduction to the Rhythmic Language of South Indian Music.* Middletown, CT: Wesleyan University Press.

Sambamoorthy, P. 1973. *South Indian Music.* Madras: Indian Music Publishing House.

Sankaran, Trichy. 1994. *The Rhythmic Principles and Practice of South Indian Drumming.* Toronto: Lalith Publishers.

Musafir

Musafir is a folkloric fusion group, with origins in Rajasthan (Indian state), created by Hameed Khan Kawa in the late 1980s. It presents a strongly romanticized notion of (Indian) gypsy culture to mainly European audiences.

A celebrated tabla player, Hameed Khan Kawa was born in a village close to Jaipur (the capital of Rajasthan) and belongs to the *Kawa* community of musicians. As a young musician, he was invited to travel to Paris, together with the famous Rajasthani dancer Gulabi Sapera, where he met people with great affinity for gypsy music, such as Erik Marchand, Thierry Titi Robin, and Chico Bouchiki (founder of the Gypsy Kings).

In the late 1980s, the "India Connection theory" became popular in the West. This theory, which is supported by academic linguistic research, states that the origin of the gypsies lies in India. India Connection theory has been widely popularized and romanticized by tour managers and bookers the world over, claiming an artistic connection of various gypsy dance and music styles. It is in this context that Hameed Khan founded the group *Gitans du Rajasthan* (Gypsies from Rajasthan), which was later (1995) renamed *Musafir*, an Indo-Persian word meaning "traveler" and referring to a peripatetic lifestyle: thus, gypsies.

The idea of Musafir was to create a "folkloric cabaret," a fusion ensemble of different Rajasthani communities (e.g., *Kālbeliyā, Langā, Māngaṇiyār* and *Ḍholī*), mixing traditional folk tunes with more popular genres (such as *qawwali*, popular Indian music and Westernized sounds) and acrobatic dancing. Musafir consists of musicians playing percussion instruments such as *tabla, dholak* (popular two-headed hand drum), *manjeera* (small hand cymbals) and *kartal* (a wooden castanet-like hand percussion instrument); string instruments such as the bowed fiddles *sarangi* and *kamancha* and the variable-tension stringed instrument *bhapang*; harmonium (pump organ); wind instruments such as *pungi* (snake charmer's reed pipe) and *algooza* (double flute); and singers. Besides musicians, one young Kālbeliyā girl dances and one man plays the *faqīr*, a character who dances, blows fire, and performs all kinds of acrobatic tricks such as walking on broken glass. With this new concept, Musafir has dazzled international audiences all over the world and has been in great demand, especially in Europe and to a large extent in the United States, but also in Japan, Korea, and the Middle East.

In the 1990s, the international world music booker Arnaud Azzouz managed Musafir, reinforcing and augmenting the group's success. But at the end of the 1990s, dissension arose between Hameed and Arnaud, which lead to the splitting of Musafir. However, both men aimed to continue working with this accomplished group, so Hameed continued his project, while Arnaud hired Rajasthani musicians to continue under his management, both under the name of Musafir. This conflict was taken to court and in the end, Hameed Khan won the rights to the name Musafir, which still exists today under the management of his French wife, Marie-Noëlle Jaffré. Arnaud Azzouz continued his project under the name of the *Mahārājās* (the Kings), which was successful but no longer exists.

Three albums have been produced under the name of Musafir. The first was *Gypsies of Rajasthan* (1997)—a collaboration between Hameed Khan and Arnaud

Azzouz, and produced by Blue Flame World Music/Warner Chappell Music/GEMA. The second album, *Dhola Maru* (1999), is the work of Arnaud Azzouz during the period the two Musafirs coexisted. The third CD, *Barsaat* (2002, Blue Flame Publishing/Warner/Chappell), was an attempt by Hameed and his wife to revive Musafir following the fallout from the court case. However, Musafir was never restored to its past glory. Hameed and Marie-Noëlle have opened the Kawa Cultural Centre (Jaipur) instead, to act as a "platform for performing arts," where they produce and manage various Rajasthani-inspired groups, such as Kawa Brass Band and Kawa Circus.

Dhoad Gypsies from Rajasthan, a relatively new group (2002) led by Rais Bharti (cousin of Hameed Khan), has continued the concept of Musafir and is now the most popular Rajasthani group touring in Europe. In addition, there are other smaller Rajasthani gypsy troupes, many of which were founded by family members of Hameed and (ex-)members of Musafir. Nowadays several other managers (also nonmusicians) have mounted fusion Rajasthani folklore projects, such as "Rhythms of Rajasthan," "Music of Rajasthan," and the like, and are touring all over the world. Although Musafir has been replaced by other similar groups, it has been influential as the pioneer of Rajasthani folklorism or "gypsy fusion" in Europe and beyond.

Ayla Joncheere and Jacoba Kint

See also: Bollywood Music; Dhol; Tabla

Further Reading
Artways. 2014. "Musafir Gypsies of Rajasthan." http://www.blueflame.com/artist/musafir-gypsies-of-rajasthan.
Kawa Music. 2014. "Kawa Music." May 13. http://indiavarazsa.blogspot.com/2010/08/kawa-musical-circus.
Musafir. 1997. *Gypsies of Rajasthan.* BF 39850062 [CD].
Musafir. 1999. *Dhola Maru.* B00001IVAS [CD].
Musafir. 2005. *Barsaat.* BF 39850542 [CD].
Neuman, D., S. Chaudhuri, and K. Kothari. 2006. *Bards, Ballads and Boundaries: An Ethnographic Atlas of Music Traditions in West Rajasthan.* New York: Seagull Books.

Musicals

A popular form of 20th-century Western theater, musicals combine dramatic narratives with song and dance. They are simultaneously artistic and commercial (for-profit) ventures, primarily developed in New York City's Broadway and London's West End theaters. They rely on the collaboration of multiple individuals: composers, playwrights, directors, producers, investors, managers, technicians, costumers, choreographers, singing and dancing actors, and musicians. Musicals trace their roots to several late 19th-century theatrical genres such as variety/vaudeville shows, minstrel shows, Viennese operetta, burlesques, and spectacles. Elements of these sources constantly pop up in current musicals, whether relating to production, story, staging, and/or larger sociocultural issues like race, gender, and sexuality. Subjects of musicals run the gamut from romantic comedies to biographies of key historical figures to incendiary, political events. To this day, the genre maintains a close relationship with popular narratives and music genres.

Producers used a variety of terms to describe early musical theater pieces. These included "musical comedy," "musical play," "musical romance," and "musical farce"; these distinctions fell away in the 1940s and 1950s as people begin to refer to these works simply as "musicals." Early works interpolated popular songs with light-hearted plots, but the songs and dances did little to further the story. As the form developed in the midcentury, musicals became increasingly "integrated," meaning that all the parts—dialogue, song, and dance—worked together to tell and develop the story.

Many musical theater scholars disagree with application of the term "integration" to the history of musicals, because it implies evolutionary development or the idea that more recent works are "better" than those that came before them. Though contested, one finds the term throughout popular and academic writings on musicals. For our purposes, it is enough to know that the term is debatable; it simply serves as a historical benchmark. As with many artistic genres, it is not the most fruitful task to try to name "the first musical." However, it is helpful to point out a few of the genre's notable forebears.

Some scholars, especially those with an interest in British musical theater, point to London theater manager Georges Edwardes (1852–1915) as a founding father. He produced several successful musical comedies in London and crossed the Atlantic with a few of them. *A Gaiety Girl* (1893) and *The Geisha* (1896) were enormously successful in New York City. His shows combined burlesque and variety shows with the romantic plots of Viennese operetta, thereby establishing early musicals as a mix of low and high theater arts. Other theater managers in London and New York were more than happy to copy Edwardes's formula, as his shows brought in both audiences and money.

For American musical theater scholars, one of the most important figures was George M. Cohan (1878–1942). Cohan grew up in show business and became a talented singer-songwriter, actor, dancer, producer, composer, and playwright. His first theatrical success was *Little Johnny Jones* (known today for its songs "Give My Regards to Broadway" and "Yankee Doodle Boy") in 1904. His success lay in his ability to combine the dramatic stage with vaudeville and the exciting harmonies and syncopations of ragtime music. He went on to pen more than 500 songs, as well as produce and star in dozens of other shows.

Cohan is commemorated today by a statue in New York City's Times Square. In addition, the Paramount Building plays "Give My Regards to Broadway" from its tower every Tuesday through Sunday evening, at 7:45 p.m., as a reminder to theatergoers that their shows start soon.

Cohan greatly influenced composers and playwrights of the 1920s and 1930s, such as Jerome Kern (1885–1945), George and Ira Gershwin (1898–1937 and 1896–1983, respectively), Irving Berlin (1888–1989), and Cole Porter (1891–1964). Some shows of this period hinted at the integrated works to come, such as Kern's *Showboat* (1927). Kern collaborated with lyricist Oscar Hammerstein II (of later Rodgers and Hammerstein fame) for *Showboat*. That show ran for 575 performances (an enormous success at the time), featured one of the first racially integrated casts, and had hit songs (including "Can't Help Lovin' Dat Man" and "Ol' Man River") which also helped further the story and craft the story's tone. However, most early musicals were better known for their Tin Pan Alley hits than their plots. For example, the Gershwins' *Girl Crazy* (1930) is better known for the songs "I Got Rhythm" and "Embraceable You" than for its book, just as Porter's *Anything Goes* (1934) is best known for the songs "Anything Goes," "It's De-lovely," and "I Get a Kick Out of You." These musicals also served as launching pads for the careers of stars such as Fred and Adele Astaire, Eddie Cantor, Gertrude Lawrence, Ethel Merman, and Ginger Rogers.

The 1930s and early 1940s were dominated by composer Richard Rodgers (1902–1979) and his first creative partner and lyricist, Lorenz Hart (1895–1943). Their hits included *On Your Toes* (1936), *Babes in Arms* (1937), *The Boys from Syracuse* (1938), and *Pal Joey* (1940). Rodgers and Hart collaborated with notable directors and choreographers, including George Abbott and George Balanchine. Other notable musicals from this time include Kern's *The Cat and the Fiddle* (1931), Marc Blitzstein's *The Cradle Will Rock* (1938), the Gershwins' *Strike Up the Band!* (1930), and *Porgy and Bess* (1935, book and some lyrics by Dubose Heyward), as well as Kurt Weill's *Lady in the Dark* (1941). Rodgers and Hart parted ways in 1942, whereupon Rodgers joined forces with Oscar Hammerstein II (1895–1960) for a new project called *Oklahoma!* (1943).

Today, the team name of Rodgers and Hammerstein is virtually synonymous with the "Golden Age" or fully integrated musical. Many early musical theater scholars point to *Oklahoma!* as being the first integrated musical. However, this labeling is being challenged currently; recent scholarship points out that *Oklahoma!* represents the musicals of its period rather than being revolutionary. Regardless of the debate, *Oklahoma!* is remembered for weaving together story, song, and dance. Particularly important moments include the love duet "People Will Say We're in Love" (a psychologically revealing song) and Laurie's dream ballet (a plot-furthering dance). This musical is also important because it featured choreography by Agnes de Mille.

The "Golden Age of Musicals" roughly spans 1943 to 1964 (from *Oklahoma!* to the opening of Bock and Harnick's *Fiddler on the Roof*, though this too is much debated). The musicals from this time period form a significant portion of the musical theater repertory and feature the full orchestral (and often jazzy) sound that is often associated with "Broadway." One incredibly important work from this time period is *West Side Story* (1957). Its score by Leonard Bernstein (1918–1990) successfully bridges the divide between modernist and popular music. It is the first major stage work by Stephen Sondheim (1930–), who started his professional career as a lyricist. In addition, Jerome Robbins's (1918–1998) direction and choreography remain an iconic part of the show. Other important Golden Age musicals include Rodgers and Hammerstein's *Carousel* (1945), *South Pacific* (1949), *The King and I* (1951), and *The Sound of Music* (1959). Also important are Irving Berlin's *Annie Get Your Gun* (1946), Cole Porter's *Kiss Me, Kate* (1948), Frank Loesser's *Guys and Dolls* (1950) and *How to Succeed in Business Without Really Trying* (1961), Jule Styne's *Gypsy* (1959), and Alan Jay Lerner and Frederick Loewe's *Brigadoon*

(1947) and *My Fair Lady* (1956). Many of these shows featured songs that became jazz standards as well.

The 1960s marked a change in the history of musicals. Musicals shifted from being a source of popular music to trying to incorporate it for audience approval and/or commercial profit. Prior to the 1960s, particularly catchy songs from musicals became popular music hits via Tin Pan Alley. The entrance of rock and roll marked the death knell for these songwriters. A few attempts were made to mix musicals with rock and roll, such as Charles Strouse's *Bye Bye Birdie* (1960), but the attitude toward the new popular music genre was tongue-in-cheek and mocking. *Hair*, the 1968 "tribal love rock musical" with music by Galt MacDermot and book/lyrics by James Rado and Gerome Ragni, earned the title of "first rock musical" because of its unconventional staging, its serious incorporation of rock music, and its relevance to the current counterculture generation. Apart from the musical's new and tenuous relationship with popular music, the 1960s produced several notable shows, such as Jerry Herman's *Hello, Dolly!* (1964), Styne's *Funny Girl* (1964), Cy Coleman and Neil Simon's *Sweet Charity* (1966), and John Kander and Fred Ebb's *Cabaret* (1966).

Performers Jan Clayton and John Raitt in Rodgers and Hammerstein's musical *Carousel*. The compositions of Rodgers and Hammerstein were key in the development of musical theater during the 20th century. (Eileen Darby/The LIFE Images Collection via Getty Images)

In the 1970s a new subgenre called the "concept" or "fragmented" musical (another contested term in scholarship) flourished. Unlike the integrated musical, the concept musical focused less on story, but used song, dance, and dialogue to emphasize an overarching theme. Notable concept musicals included Stephen Sondheim's *Company* (1970) and Marvin Hamlisch's *A Chorus Line* (1975). *Company* was the first in a long line of critical (though not often commercial) successes for Sondheim. Though he wrote the lyrics for both *West Side Story* and *Gypsy* in the 1950s and composed his first musical *A Funny Thing Happened on the Way to the Forum* in 1962, his career as a composer-lyricist did not really take off until the 1970s. Important works of his from this decade include *Follies* (1971), *A Little Night Music* (1973), *Pacific Overtures* (1976), and *Sweeney Todd* (1979). Also important were productions led by director-choreographers Bob Fosse (1927–1987) and

Michael Bennet (1943–1987); Fosse directed and choreographed Stephen Schwartz's *Pippin* (1972) and Kander and Ebb's *Chicago* (1975), while Bennet helmed *Company, Follies*, and *A Chorus Line*.

The 1980s heralded the "British Invasion" and the age of the megamusical. Referring to the lavish, spectacle-driven productions of Andrew Lloyd Webber (1948–) and the team of Alain Boublil (1941–) and Claude-Michel Schönberg (1944–), megamusicals changed the musical theater landscape. Lloyd Webber stormed Broadway via London's West End with *Cats* (1981) and *The Phantom of the Opera* (1986), which brimmed with tuneful songs and an audience-pleasing mix of rock-pop and orchestral textures. Though not British, Boublil and Schönberg and their epic sung-through musical *Les Misérables* also came to Broadway through the West End. Many critics scorned these musicals for their over-the-top productions, sneering that audiences left "humming the scenery." Perhaps to the critics' chagrin, these musicals became some of the most commercially successful in the theater industry. The musicals of this period also marked a change in production with their increasing dependence on creative producers such as Cameron Mackintosh (1946–).

The megamusicals contrast greatly with the cerebral and complex musicals of Sondheim, such as *Sunday in the Park with George* (1984) and *Into the Woods* (1987). Though Sondheim's musicals have not achieve the same level of commercial success as the megamusicals, they have had a vibrant and enduring life on the regional theater scene and remain highly esteemed by musical theater aficionados and scholars alike.

Disney arrived on Broadway in 1994 with *Beauty and the Beast*. Prior to that, the Broadway theater district was run down, populated mainly with sex shops and gentlemen's clubs. Disney's business dealings with Mayor Guiliani and new zoning restrictions helped transform Times Square into the spectacular tourist destination that it is today. Disney's *The Lion King* (1997) set the record for most expensive production, which was only recently surpassed by *Spiderman: Turn Off the Dark* (2011).

The current musical scene is a mix of long-standing brands and new productions. Lloyd Webber's *The Phantom of the Opera*, having recently celebrated its 25th consecutive year on Broadway, holds the title of "Longest Running Musical." Other productions, such as *The Lion King* and Stephen Schwartz's *Wicked* (2003) continue to sell tickets steadily. Many film studios (besides Disney) are turning their sights to Broadway through the adaptation of their popular films into new musicals, and every year a few celebrated musicals are revived through new productions. Although musicals no longer act as a source of popular music, they offer a variety of musical styles from symphonic to jazz to rock. Even hip-hop and salsa make occasional appearances, notably through the musicals of up-and-coming composer-lyricist Lin-Manuel Miranda (1980–). With such a diverse array of music and stories (both new and old), musicals hold a special place in the commercial art world.

Aya Esther Hayashi

See also: Cohan, George M.; Jazz; Rap/Hip-Hop; Rock and Roll; Salsa; Tin Pan Alley; Vaudeville

Further Reading

Everett, William A., and Paul R. Laird, eds. 2008. *The Cambridge Companion to the Musical*, 2nd ed. New York: Cambridge University Press.

Knapp, Raymond. 2006. *The American Musical and the Performance of Personal Identity*. Princeton, NJ: Princeton University Press.

Knapp, Raymond, Mitchell Morris, and Stacy Ellen Wolf, eds. 2011. *The Oxford Handbook to the American Musical*. New York: Oxford University Press.

Sternfeld, Jessica. 2006. *The Megamusical*. Bloomington: Indiana University Press.

Wollman, Elizabeth L. 2006. *The Theatre Will Rock: A History of the Rock Musical: From HAIR to Hedwig*. Ann Arbor: University of Michigan Press.

N

Native American Church Music

Indigenous religions have been practiced in North and South America since before recorded history, with unison singing of vocables, chanted texts, and rhythmic percussion forming the heart of ceremonial music. Legally, the enacting of spiritual ceremonies and the maintaining of sacred ceremonial grounds is called the Native American Church, when practiced outside the boundaries of federally recognized Indian reservations.

The religious movement called Native American Church (NAC), also called Peyotism and Peyote Religion, originated in Oklahoma in the 1880s after the psychedelic entheogen peyote was introduced from Mexico and southern Texas. Entheogens are chemical substances used in shamanic or spiritual contexts for transcendence and revelation; peyote is derived from a small, spineless cactus with psychoactive alkaloids (particularly mescaline), and its name comes from the Nahuatl word *peyōtl*, meaning "glistening." Today NAC is the most widespread indigenous religion in North America, combining traditional and Christian beliefs; it was formally incorporated in Oklahoma in 1918 and has been continually regulated by the United States Congress (laws regarding peyote use were amended for clarification in 1994).

Musical instruments used in NAC peyote ceremonies include the peyote gourd rattle (a vegetable gourd symbolizing the world, filled with pebbles symbolizing prayers, mounted on a wooden stick and decorated with horsehair), the water drum (a half-filled iron kettle covered with animal hide), and drum stick. Singers accompany themselves on the rattle, and drummers maintain a fast, steady beat that may either support or be independent of the melodic pulse.

Peyote songs are unique and highly significant to the peyotist; they are considered powerful in their own right and are expected to be revered and sung appropriately. David McAllester, in his definitive study *Peyote Music* (1949), traced the origins of the song style to southwestern songs accompanied by pot drum and gourd rattle, Ghost Dance songs with limited ranges, and rhythmic patterns from Protestant hymnody. Willard Rhodes's work studying the diffusion of peyote ceremonial music throughout the Great Plains in the 1950s emphasizes that songs easily moved from one group to another and that the songs "figured importantly" in the spread of the whole ritual complex among tribes. Peyote songs contain numerous vocables made up of the following consonants combined with certain vowels: y, w, h, c, k, t, x, and n. These syllables are then grouped into compound "peyote words" such as *heyoeicinayo*, and can be combined with recognizable words to create a narrative effect.

Peyote songs share harmonic and cadential characteristics with Ute, Navajo, and especially Apache singing. Melodies feature only two durational values and are dominated by intervallic relationships of thirds and fifths. Pueblo music also shares structural elements with peyote songs; these include incomplete repetitions, isorhythmic tendencies, and distinctive melodic contours. Some peyote songs tell stories, whereas others refer to the dawn, to birds or animals, to peyote, to Jesus, to water, or to the participants themselves, urging them to repentance or prayer. Singers "pray with songs" because the songs come as a direct revelation from the spiritual realm, the gifts of Peyote. Notable composers of peyote songs include Ed Tiende Yeahquo (mentioned by Bruno Nettl in *Music of Primitive Culture* [1972] as composing more than 120 songs), Jim Pepper, and the Grammy-winning duo of Verdell Primaeux (Dakota Yancton/Ponca) and Johnny Mike (Diné/Navajo), who have recorded more than 40 NAC albums.

Full peyote rituals include prayer, the eating of peyote, the singing of peyote songs, water rituals, and contemplation. Longer rituals begin on Saturday and continue through the night, ending with a breakfast Sunday morning; this process allows connection with a holy deity or spirits, and may give healing (physical or emotional), guidance, authority, and power. A peyote staff (representing a holy presence) is passed around with the water drum and peyote rattle. The "half moon" style of peyote ceremony comes from the Lipan Apache and Comecrudo: it uses tobacco throughout the ceremony and rarely evokes Biblical scripture. The "cross fire" or "big moon" ceremony derives from Christian practices among the Caddo and Kiowa, and the Bible is used throughout the ceremony. The National Museum of the American (the newest addition to the Smithsonian Institution in Washington, D.C.) houses the largest collection of contemporary Native American artifacts and sound recordings.

Laura Stanfield Prichard

See also: Eastern Woodland Native American Music; Native American Flute; Native American Music; Native American Popular Music

Further Reading

Maroukis, Thomas Constantine. 2012. *The Peyote Road: Religious Freedom and the Native American Church*. Norman: University of Oklahoma Press.

Smith, Huston, and Reuben Snake. 1996. *One Nation Under God: The Triumph of the Native American Church*. Santa Fe, NM: Clear Light.

Snake, Reuben. 1993. *Peyote Road: Ancient Religion in Contemporary Crisis*. San Francisco, CA: Kifaru.

White, Philip M. 2000. *Peyotism and the Native American Church: An Annotated Bibliography*. Westport, CT: Greenwood.

Native American Flute

Similar to its counterparts in Europe and Asia, the Native American flute is in a class of aerophone instrument "that is shaped like a thin pipe and that is played by blowing across a hole near one end" (*Merriam-Webster*). Native American flutes encompass a wide range of variants within the woodwind class and indigenous peoples from across the Americas use the instruments for a variety of sacred and secular rites and purposes. Similar to the "drum" of Africa, the Native American flute has many names throughout indigenous cultures and just as many variants in material construction. Many Native American flute variants are played vertically, but others can also be held transversally (horizontally); because they are not keyed, they are therefore referred to as "simple-system" instruments.

One of the most iconic images of Native American flutes is that of the flute player Kokopelli, in which the character is typically illustrated with three strands or feathers coming out of his head and as being in a dance mode and playing a vertically held flute. His role in Native American mythology varies depending on the storyteller; in some stories he is helpful, in some a bother. He is, though, often credited with crucial assistance such as in bringing rain and food. Other stories describe the sound of his flute serving as a guide to lead the tribe out of danger or to woo a target of affection. His prominence in current Native American imagery is a testament to the important role that the flute plays in the culture.

The Native American flute is an important component in Native American religious and secular life practices, which often overlap, as opposed to the separations between the two that are more common to Western European and American cultures. There is no formal notation in Native American music, as traditional performance practice is for the musician to improvise only. This results in highly personal music that is spontaneous and original. The technique of playing the instrument is, as with any musical instrument, the result of disciplined practice, but the improvisations are intended to be fully expressive of the player's own emotions rather than rehearsed melodies. Today, there is a tendency to try to capture traditional music on paper, but doing so would create an inauthentic representation of the music. In other words, one really cannot buy a book of music for Native American flute and hope for it to be "the real thing."

Major components of Native American melodies include sliding between pitches, a quick movement from the last note of a phrase to a brief end-note that sounds almost like a hiccup, and a variety in the vibrato. The Western notation system has no means of recording these integral sounds on paper, so they would either have to be left out, as they were in past efforts to notate this music, leaving an incomplete and oversimplified representation of the music, or included and described in an explanatory introduction to the music. Although the latter would seem satisfactory (and is often done), these special sounds are important parts of the personal expression of the individual performer; thus, requiring their application in parts of an improvised melody would seem to codify something spontaneous.

A number of different materials are used to make Native American flutes: wood, bone, and clay. Most often the choice of materials depends on where a particular tribe lives and what their natural environment has available. Wood is the material most often used to construct Native American flutes today, as many are modeled on the flutes of the Plains tribes. The wood is cut in a variety of lengths to create flutes of higher and lower ranges and pitches. The quality of the wood and the craftsmanship of the maker in boring out the wood and the holes that the fingers cover have a direct impact on the quality of the tone. The flutes are decorated, often with elaborate carvings or embedded turquoise, although none of the decoration has an impact on the quality of the tone of the instrument. It does, however, demonstrate a relationship between the instrument and its builder.

Each flute has strapped to it a figure of an animal referred to as the "bird." While it often is in fact a bird, there are examples of bears and wolves as well. In those cases, the figure is still called a bird, as the flute sound is reflective of that of a bird. In "flute origin stories," the flute/bird is credited with leading a tribe from danger or guiding an individual's behavior. The bird is also a reminder of the role of the natural world in the sound of the flute, as well as of the outdoors as a common setting for the playing of this instrument.

Traditionally, the Native American flute has five holes, although more modern versions have six. The sixth hole allows a greater variety of tonalities to be played, including those of Western music, and thus such flutes may be more appealing to those who do not come from the Native American traditions or have not been schooled in them. For this reason, flutes often have a leather strap around the third hole so that the player can choose whether or not to utilize it.

The music played on the Native American flute is quite subtle. Listeners should pay attention to the movement from one note to another, as there are often numerous pitches in between as well as changes in the tone color. As with other flutes, the Native American flute is a monophonic instrument that plays only one note at a time. Often played solo, the lack of harmony gives the flute an organic, meditative quality that has broad appeal.

Carol L. Shansky

See also: Native American Church Music; Native American Music; Native American Popular Music

Further Reading

Borg, Odell. 2004. *"How to Play" Native American Flute.* Patagonia, AZ: High Spirits Music.

Perea, John-Carlos. 2014. *Intertribal Native American Music in the United States.* New York: Oxford University Press.

Native American Music

Native Americans are the oldest indigenous inhabitants in America, but the culture and music of American Indians are perhaps the least familiar. The reasons for this are twofold. Firstly, Native American music is very different from Western styles in both sound and function, as it is almost totally bound to and determined by wider ceremonial or social contexts. Secondly, Native American music belongs to a group of people who were for hundreds of years regarded as inferior, having little or nothing of worth to offer European settlers. It is because of this attitude that much Native American culture was destroyed during the centuries in which white European settlers sought to conquer Native Americans during the colonizing and westward expansion of the United States. In more recent years, changing attitudes have sparked a newfound appreciation and recognition of the cultural significance of Native Americans and their music.

At the time of the first European explorations of the Americas in the early 1500s, it is estimated that around 1 to 2 million people lived in North America. The population consisted of thousands of different tribes, each with its own language and each with its own set of cultural—and therefore musical—characteristics. These cultural differences have been grouped into distinct "cultural areas," with each area sharing similar cultural and musical traits. There are six main areas:

1. The Eastern Woodlands—covering the area from the Atlantic Ocean to the Mississippi River and from New Brunswick to the Gulf of Mexico.
2. The Plains—covering the area from the Mississippi River to the Rocky Mountains and from south-central Canada to Texas.
3. The Great Basin—covering the Eastern slope of the Rocky Mountains to the Sierra Nevada and from the Fraser River to the Colorado River basin.
4. The Southwest—an area that includes New Mexico, Arizona, and southern California.
5. The Northwest coast—the area from Alaska to northern California.
6. The Arctic—covering most of Alaska (apart from coastal areas) to Greenland and much of Canada.

The musical characteristics of these six cultural areas vary greatly, but they also share many similarities when judged on a broader scale.

Music plays a vital role within Native American societies. Native Americans placed a considerable amount of importance on their music, often believing it to be directly related to, and having direct consequences for, their everyday lives. Music was particularly significant because it presented a means of communication with the supernatural world. Singing was used in the treatment of the sick, in ensuring victory at war or when hunting, and in every other undertaking in which individuals felt that the outcome was beyond their own power as individuals. It is this connection between the real world and the spiritual world which makes Native American music unique and complex.

Generally speaking, Native American music is predominantly vocal, with instrumental accompaniments and very little purely instrumental music. The heavy use of vocables (simple, nonlexical, vocal sounds) highlights the uniqueness of indigenous American music. Vocables may be used together with actual words or may replace the use of words entirely. However they are used, these sounds are not improvised: each one holds some form of ritual and cultural significance. Singing in harmony is rare, and when two or more singers do perform at one time, they usually sing in unison or octaves. Singing is usually accompanied by drums or rattles. Drums may range in size from small hand-held ones to large drums that rest on the ground to be played or are suspended between posts in the ground, and may be played by several people at once. Drums may be made in a variety of ways with a variety of materials, ranging from baskets or kettles covered in animal skin to wooden boxes.

The use of drums and rattles without singing is incredibly rare in Native American music, providing a distinct contrast to the music of African and Caribbean traditions in which drumming often dominates the music. When dancers are present, they may wear shaker-like instruments, usually made from shells, to produce a rhythmic rattling during the dance. Whistles and flutes, made from wood or clay, are also common. The flute, which is often associated with love songs, is one of the only instruments used to perform melodic solos.

The tuning systems of Native American music are only slightly related to the tuning systems understood through European ideas of tonality, and microtones, as Western music would define them, are used frequently. *Portamento* (the practice of sliding between notes) is common, particularly at the end of phrases, where a descending slide is used. In general, the scales used are similar to Western diatonic scales but, in addition, pentatonic scales and scales with four or six degrees are regularly used. There is rarely a sense of tempo that stays constant throughout a piece of music; drum parts often play at a different tempo than vocal parts, and there may be frequent changes in tempo throughout a song. Longer songs are often divided into different sections which are marked primarily by changes in tempo.

There are subtle differences between Native American musics from different areas. Each cultural area, though sharing many qualities with others, employs a characteristic specific to that region.

EASTERN WOODLANDS

Eastern Woodland tribes can be divided into three musical subregions: Northeast, Southeast, and Western Great Lakes. Eastern Woodland singers generally use a relaxed and open vocal style, making use of the mid to low vocal range. Articulated attacks and releases, as well as vocal portamento, are common. Most songs use antiphonal (call-and-response) textures, though there are some documented solos and duets. This use of antiphony is unique to the Eastern Woodlands Indians. Women will sometimes double men in octaves. Changes of meter in songs are frequent, and syncopation and sforzandos are used to add rhythmic interest. There is a tendency to use scales with four, five, or six pitches.

PLAINS

Unlike the relaxed vocal tone used by most Native Americans, Plains Indian singing is characterized by a tense and nasal quality with heavy pulsations on sustained notes, especially at the ends of phrases. Songs may be decorated with portamentos and shouts or cries. Songs are usually monophonic and in strophic form, and melodies make use of four- or five-note scales. A drum supports the pulse in a steady duple time, but the tempo of the drumbeat is often different from that of the vocal line of the song. Drummers alternate the strongly accented beats with weak beats in different sections of the song. The single-headed frame drum is the most common Plains instrument. It resembles a large tambour and is played with a padded stick.

GREAT BASIN

Great Basin singers have an open and relaxed vocal quality when using the middle of their vocal range. Singers frequently ornament vocal lines through articulated breathing techniques. Songs to accompany dance in the Great Basin are monophonic and unaccompanied by instrumental parts. This is rare among Native Americans generally and unlike other regions, Great Basin music is largely vocal, with very few instruments used. The melodies of the Great Basin Indians are generally short and use a narrow range of pitches, based on scales with three, four, or five notes. Structurally, songs are phrased in pairs (e.g., AA BB CC AA BB CC, etc.).

SOUTHWEST

Southwest singers have an open and relaxed tone similar to that of Eastern Woodlands and Great Basin Indians, but their vocal range is focused on the lower end. Ceremonial songs are frequently performed by large groups all singing in unison. Large-scale songs may have up to five main sections, usually with an AABBA structure. The Southwest region is known for its vast assortment of instruments; perhaps the most common and most used is the Apache fiddle, an instrument unique to this area. This fiddle, which is often used as a solo instrument, has only one or two strings and is made using a two-foot-long, hollow century-plant stalk. The fiddle and bow strings are made of horsehair.

NORTHWEST COAST

Northwest Coast singers are known for their dramatic and emotional performances. Their songs tend to rise in pitch as the performance progresses but, in general, a lower vocal register is employed along with a relaxed and open style. Vocal lines are often decorated with ornaments such as turns and grace notes, and most songs have a monophonic texture. Songs are usually associated with stories and so have strophic forms with long and complex phrases. Most songs will require a range of about an octave, and conjunct (stepwise) melodies are based around scales of four, five, or six pitches. The meter changes frequently throughout the duration of a song, and the tempo and/or meter of the drums is often different from that of the vocal-line singers. The Northwest Coast region is well known for its beautifully carved and painted instruments. Rattles are often carved to represent birds, in particular the raven—the raven is symbolic of one of the most significant cultural heroes in Northwest Coast mythology, known as Raven.

ARCTIC

Similarly to Plains Indians, Arctic singers demonstrate a tense and nasal vocal style. Group songs are usually monophonic, with the women singing an octave higher than the men. Arctic song texts contain a mixture of vocables and Arctic language phrases, and singers make much use of vocal ornaments and decorations to add melodic and rhythmic interest. Arctic songs are short and use only a narrow range, with melodies based on four- or five-degree scales. The meter changes often and rhythmic devices such as syncopation, ties, and cross-rhythms are used.

As the white population of North America became increasingly dominant following the Civil War (1861–1865), the western areas of Indian territory became home to many northern and central Indians who had become displaced through the appropriation of formerly Indian lands. Native Americans from tribes all over the United States were forced to live in closer proximity than ever before, and the differences among their cultures diminished somewhat, with musical characteristics becoming amalgamated into one. This gave birth to the idea of pan-Indianism: a method of adopting and adapting the cultural traits of nearby tribes in order to retain some essence of Native American culture. This took the form of songs or cultural rituals and practices which became widespread across reservations throughout America.

One famous example of pan-Indianism is the Ghost Dance. The Ghost Dance, which originated around 1889, was a communal ceremony in which people sang in unison without instrumental accompaniment while dancing in circles. The Ghost Dance inspired hope of a return to a traditional way of life for Native Americans at a time when the United States government was exercising an ever-increasing degree of control over American Indians. Despite the government banning the Ghost Dance in 1890, Plains and Great Basin Indians continued to perform the ceremony privately well into the 20th century, and many sound recordings of the ritual are now available.

As well as being somewhat forced to adopt the cultural and musical traits of other Native tribes, over time Indian music began to take on characteristics of non-Indian cultures. As early as the 16th century, Jesuit missionaries began teaching Native American tribes Catholic sacred music, and during the 17th century Christian hymns were introduced to Natives by Protestant priests who translated them into Indian languages. Native Americans have also adapted European-American fiddle music, and began to employ the Western concept of performance primarily for entertainment. It has also been documented that, since at least 1920, Native Americans have inserted English words into some songs; furthermore, many Native American composers and performers have adopted contemporary popular music genres such as jazz, rock and roll, country, gospel, reggae, rap, and hip-hop. Native composers have also used Western sacred and art music idioms and have used European notation since the 19th century.

Native Americans have a long and difficult history of attempting to keep their music and culture alive, but it is not only Native Americans who have striven to protect the culture of the Native peoples. During the mid-19th century, with the publication of the writings of Henry Wadsworth Longfellow (1807–1882), public interest in the Native Americans grew, and this group of people came to be of crucial importance to Anglo-American culture. Longfellow's epic poem *The Song of Hiawatha* (1855) proved to be internationally popular, becoming a source of inspiration for many writers and composers in the second half of the 19th century. At a time when American Indians were becoming an endangered people, *Hiawatha* mythologized the American West and helped to restore public interest in the Native tribes. In 1882, the musicologist Theodore Baker (1851–1934) published his doctoral dissertation *Über die Musik der Nordamerikanischen Wilden* (About the music of the North American savages), which became the first major work on the music of American Indians. Despite Baker's interest in Indian music being something of an exception at the time, his work became a benchmark for similar studies.

In 1893, the ethnologist Alice Fletcher (1838–1923) published her *Study of Omaha Indian Music*. Fletcher went on to publish two more studies on Native American music and, following her example, the ethnomusicologist Frances Densmore (1867–1957) began to lecture on Native American music in 1895. During her research on Native American music, Fletcher lived among the peoples of the Omaha reservation while retaining academic ties with Harvard's Peabody Museum, and over the years she amassed a collection of more than 300 Native American songs and melodies.

Thanks to the work of Baker, Fletcher, and other ethnologists, specific interest in the Native American as artistic subject matter developed, and beginning around 1890 a so-called "Indianist" movement emerged in American art music. This involved composers making use of typical Native American music features and characteristics in their Western-tradition art music. Indianist music frequently employed melodies harmonized on parallel fourths and fifths, modal or pentatonic accompaniments, and cross-rhythms to evoke an American Indian sound. Composers Louis Moreau Gottschalk (1829–1869), Edward MacDowell (1860–1908), and Amy Beach (1867–1944) are some of the most acclaimed American musicians who used American Indian melodies and ideas in their work. Perhaps the most famous use of Native American musical ideas in Western art music was that by the Czech composer Antonín Dvořák (1841–1904) in 1893. Dvořák's ninth symphony, titled "From the New World," together with a string quartet and cello concerto were all written during a three-year-long stay in the United States that began in 1892. There he discovered the wonders of both Native American and African American vernacular music, and sought to create a kind of American Nationalist music by drawing upon and adapting these folk genres into his Western-tradition instrumental works. In his "New World" symphony, whose narrative is said to be based upon Longfellow's *Hiawatha* story, Dvořák used Indianist techniques, such as pentatonic melodies and cross-rhythms, to evoke a sense of the Native American through music. Dvořák's symphony helped demonstrate the serious and culturally significant nature of both Native and African American music, and his ideas influenced many American art music composers in the 20th century.

Modern technology has ended the isolation of life on reservations and, since the end of World War II, Native Americans have moved further toward urban centers, thereby increasing the contact that Indians and Americans from a variety of other ethnic backgrounds (European, Latino, Afro-Caribbean, Asian) have with each other. Though much of the oldest Native American music is now lost, American Indian culture is not extinct, and their music is now a revitalized art form that consciously strives to preserve tradition.

C. M. Gregory-Thomas

See also: Eastern Woodland Native American Music; Native American Church Music; Native American Flute; Native American Popular Music; Navajo, Music of; Vocables; Yuman Music

Further Reading
Hamm, C. E. 1983. *Music in the New World*. New York: Norton.
Kingman, D. 1990. *American Music: A Panorama*. New York: Schirmer Books.

Nicholls, D., ed. 1998. *The Cambridge History of American Music.* Cambridge: Cambridge University Press.

Pisani, M. V. 2005. *Imagining Native America in Music* [e-book]. New Haven: Yale University Press.

Native American Popular Music

American popular music includes a long history of Native American artists as successful musicians and innovators across genres. In the past and the present, some artists focus on indigenous identities, while others do not. Musicians who have influenced American popular music in general span genres from jazz bassist Oscar Pettiford (Cherokee/Choctaw); folk singer, songwriter, and guitarist Peter LaFarge (Naragansett); country band Apache Spirit (Apache); rock guitarist Jesse Ed Davis (Kiowa/Comanche); reggae singer Casper Loma-da-wa Lomayesva (Hopi); punk group Blackfire (Diné); hip-hop artist Litefoot (Cherokee); indie singer and guitarist Nick Sherman (Ojibway); to saxophonist and poet Joy Harjo (Muskogee) and cellist Cris Derksen (Cree), whose music defies genre categorization.

In the United States and Canada, indigenous children were involuntarily sent to residential schools from the mid-19th to late 20th centuries. Young people were removed from their homes and deprived of their language, music, and spiritual practice as part of government efforts to assimilate indigenous culture. At the same time, children's creativity with music in these settings is a testament to indigenous resilience. Survivors such as cornet player Luther Standing Bear (Sioux) reflected on the loss that communities experienced through residential schooling.

Members of jazz bands like the Nez Perceans brought their own ideas and expressive talent to the music they played. After leaving institutional school, jazz trombonist Russell Moore (Tohono O'odham) went on to play with the Louis Armstrong Big Band in the 1940s, while vocalist and saxophonist Jim Pepper (Creek/Kaw) recorded the song "Witchitai-To," which incorporated peyote music, in 1971. Other jazz greats, such as singer Mildred Bailey (Coeur d'Alene), who released important jazz recordings throughout the 1930s, did not attend the state-run boarding schools.

Musicians organized and performed as part of the American Indian Movement in the 1960s and 1970s. Country musician Floyd Red Crow Westerman (Dakota) survived residential school, where he played guitar. As an adult, he released political songs such as "Missionaries" and "B.I.A.," the latter of which incorporates singing on vocables as it criticizes the Bureau of Indian Affairs. Tom Bee (Dakota) and the rock band XIT released albums with intertribal messaging, notably *Plight of the Redman* in 1972 and *Silent Warrior* in 1973. That same year, rock band Redbone, including members Lolly Vegas and Pat Vegas (Yaqui/Shoshone) and Tony Bellamy (Yaqui), released the song "We Were All Wounded at Wounded Knee," which recalled the 1890 massacre at a moment of political importance. Singer, guitarist, and composer Buffy Sainte Marie (Cree) has released politically engaged songs since the 1960s. Her 2015 album *Power in the Blood* includes compositions that recall earlier activist songs such as her 1964 "Now That the Buffalo's Gone" and 1992 "Bury My Heart at Wounded Knee," which connect colonialism to social ills. Sainte Marie performed songs from her forward-looking album *Carry It On* at the 2015 Closing Ceremonies for the Truth and Reconciliation Commission Report, which aimed to bridge gaps between indigenous and nonindigenous peoples.

Hip-hop musicians carry forward this legacy of creativity and resistance. Rapper Eekwol (Cree) has used her music as part of antiviolence efforts. Using lyrics samples, and other aspects of their music, JB the First Lady (Nuxalk/Cayuga), Drezus (Cree/Saulteaux), Frank Waln (Lakota), and Leonard Sumner (Anishinaabe) added their voices to the Idle No More movement. This grassroots movement for environmental activism and indigenous rights began in Canada in 2012 and then expanded to the United States and across the globe. Hip-hop and R & B musicians, such as singer Inez (Stó:lō) and producer DJ Boogey the Beat (Anishinaabe), are part of a growing movement speaking out for missing and murdered indigenous women.

Though some Native American popular music addresses many serious topics, humor also shines through. Singer, guitarist, and flutist Keith Secola (Anishinaabe) wrote "NDN Kars," a comical rock song that makes fun of the stereotypical reservation vehicle. This very popular song was featured on the soundtrack of the film *Dance Me Outside* and is often covered.

Native American popular music may be performed in English, French or Spanish, as well as in First People's languages. Singer and multi-instrumentalist Sewepagaham (Cree/Dene) incorporates lyrics in Cree into songs such as "Tipiskaw Pisim." Other albums in folk, country, and rock that showcase Native languages include *Nunaga* by Jaaji (Inuit/Mohawk), *Sedzé* by Leela Gilday (Dene/Diné), *Spirit Flies* by Leonard Adam (Dene/Diné), and the self-titled album by duo Kashtin (Innu).

Other Native American popular musicians have used traditional singing or instruments and developed new styles of performance. Tanya Tagaq (Inuk) performs a unique style of throat singing on both solo music and collaborations. Her genre-defying album *Animism* won her the 2014 Polaris Prize. An innovator in Hawaiian guitar music beginning in the 1930s, Phillip Kunia "Gabby" Pahinui (Native Hawaiian) played, composed, and arranged music for steel guitar and slack-key (*kī hōʻalu*) guitar. His 1946 "*Hiʻilawe*" inspired future generations of guitarists. Pahinui's son Cyril Pahinui, renowned for his distinctive slack-key guitar style, was honored in 2014 with the Na Hoku Hanohano Lifetime Achievement Award.

Some artists' choices to speak publicly about their Native American heritage demonstrate the messiness of the broad category called Native American popular music. There are ongoing conversations and controversies around what exactly it means to assert that a particular kind of popular music is "Native." Some indigenous artists, including those who do and do not use specific references to Native music in their performances, have spoken about a fear that they will be pigeonholed as only appealing to a Native audience. Other musicians, such as legendary guitarist Jimi Hendrix (Cherokee), have won recognition among mainstream audiences. The DJ trio A Tribe Called Red, who created a type of electronic music called "powwow step," won a 2014 JUNO Award in a mainstream category, Breakthrough Group of the Year. Other artists have sparked controversy when discussing their

The Canadian group A Tribe Called Red blends electronic music with First Nations music for a unique sound. (Isaiah Trickey/FilmMagic)

heritage as it relates to their status as popular musicians. Though neither was raised with strong connections to a Cherokee community, both rapper Yelawolf and singer Miley Cyrus have talked about having Cherokee heritage. Taken together, these examples show the complexities of identification within the realm of Native American popular music.

Liz Przybylski

See also: Eastern Woodland Native American Music; Native American Flute; Navajo, Music of; Rap/Hip-Hop; Vocables

Further Reading

Browner, Tara. 2009. *Music of the First Nations: Tradition and Innovation in Native North America*. Champaign: University of Illinois Press.

Deloria, Philip. 2004. *Indians in Unexpected Places*. Lawrence: University Press of Kansas.

Diamond, Beverly. 2002. "Native American Contemporary Music: The Women." *The World of Music* 44(1), 11–39.

Dueck, Byron. 2013. *Musical Intimacies & Indigenous Imaginaries*. New York: Oxford University Press.

Geiogamah, Hanay, and Jaye T. Darby, eds. 2010. *American Indian Performing Arts: Critical Directions*. Los Angeles: UCLA American Indian Studies Center.

Hoffman, Elizabeth. 2012. *American Indians and Popular Culture*. Santa Barbara, CA: Praeger.

Perea, John-Carlos. 2014. *Intertribal Native American Music in the United States*. New York: Oxford University Press.

Samuels, David. 2004. *Putting a Song on Top of It: Expression and Identity on the San Carlos Apache Reservation*. Tucson: University of Arizona Press.
Standing Bear, Luther. 2006. *Land of the Spotted Eagle*. Lincoln: University of Nebraska Press.
Troutman, John William. 2009. *Indian Blues: American Indians and the Politics of Music, 1879–1934*. Norman: University of Oklahoma Press.

Navajo, Music of

The Navajo are a Native American people descended from Athapaskan-speaking hunters, gatherers, and raiders who entered the American Southwest from Canada between 900–1200 CE. Navajo creation stories and songs locate the people between four sacred mountains: Sierra Blanca Peak (Dawn or White Shell Mountain) on the east, Mount Taylor (Blue Bead or Turquoise Mountain) on the south, the San Francisco Peaks (Abalone Shell Mountain or Yellow Mountain) on the west, and La Planta Mountain (Obsidian Mountain or Black Mountain) on the north.

Seventeenth-century Spaniards such as the Franciscan friar Benavides called the Navajo *Apaches de Nabajó* (large planted fields) and the nearby Tewa-speaking peoples used the word *navahu* to mean either "large cultivated lands," or "to take from the fields." The neighboring Zuñi and Hopi called them the *Tasuvah* (head pounders), and the Navajo call themselves the *Diné* (the People). The Diné were more fortunate than many Native peoples: after their incarceration at Fort Sumner from 1864 to 1868, they were allowed to return to part of their traditional homeland. Washington Matthews, an army surgeon stationed in Navajo country in the 1880s and 1890s, was the first to publish detailed reports on Navajo arts, music, philosophy, and cosmology.

The modern Navajo Nation is situated on 24,000 square miles of southern Utah, northern Arizona, and a "checkerboard" region in northwestern New Mexico. The local economy depends to a small extent on farming and raising livestock, and to a larger extent on mining and timber harvesting. Traditional arts such as turquoise work, silversmithing, weaving, and song contests now drive tourism. Music featured in public cultural performances tends to emphasize the shorter, but more spectacular, curing chantways, with their prayer sticks, sand paintings, and body paint.

The Diné genius for adapting new elements to their traditional cultural forms is evident in much of their daily life and music, which is almost entirely vocal. The strongest neighboring influences have come from the Pueblo, from whom the Diné developed a sedentary lifestyle. Pueblo ceremonies and rituals form the basis of many sacred songs.

Traditional music is based on more than two dozen ceremonies, called "chants," which are performed to restore harmony between the universe and an ill person. A Navajo might, for example, be treated for a respiratory infection, and then conduct a Windway ceremony to resolve the disharmony with the Wind People that led to the illness. David McAllester emphasizes: "Motion is a key to sacred power in Navajo thought. Speech, song, and prayer are wind in motion shaped by the added power of human articulation" (McAllester, 1954, p. 31).

Ceremonies re-enact the creation story in a complex web of thousands of lines of poetry, recited in prayers and sung in cycles of interrelated episodes. Verses tend to alternate male and female deities; they reflect the duality that shapes much of this matrilineal culture. Many recordings exist of the buoyantly melodic popular songs for the Skip (or Round) Dance and the Yeibichai Dance; the texts consist of vocables. Large collections are held by Wesleyan University, Indiana University, the University of New Mexico, and the Library of Congress. The scholarly Navajo Studies Conference was established in 1986, and a new museum/library building at Diné College was dedicated in 1997.

Like other Southwestern vocal styles, Navajo songs are performed in unison, often to the accompaniment of rattles or a basket drum. Modern singers also employ a "pueblo-style" drum with a resonating chamber made of a series of stapled wooden strips with two deerskin membranes. Only one ceremony uses a pottery drum: the Enemyway accompaniment requires an earthenware vessel, half-filled with water, with a buckskin membrane. This three-day ceremony presents ways to cope with dangers from outside Navajo culture and is based on myths about the warrior Enemy Slayer. It has become so popular that a spinoff has developed from it: the Navajo Song and Dance Contest, both a colorful spectacle and a controversial social event.

Traditional and contemporary music are constantly juxtaposed in the Navajo world. The Navajo Song and Dance Contest focuses on a fundraising competition that features singers and dancers performing traditional Squaw Dance music such as the *Jóó Ashílá* traveling song taken from the Enemyway ceremony. The Two-step requires dancers to lift their feet upward in a sprightly manner, and the Skip features a toe-heel, heel-toe "skipping" movement. Women choose a male partner, join hands or hook elbows, and move in a clockwise circle of couples with the males on the outside. Circle dance songs have an underlying movement in sets of threes and have short texts framed by the vocables "hee nee ya." Loud singing and keeping a good percussive unison beat are the criteria for winning. Also, a variety of "Miss Navajo" contests judge traditional cultural components (singing of ceremonial songs, corn grinding, traditional food preparation, etc.). Many Diné participate in the Navajo Song and Dance Contests; however, some question whether it is acceptable for songs and dances to be excerpted from the Enemyway ceremony (a ritual performed between the first thunder of spring and the first frost of winter) and turned into a generic contest format held at any time of year.

There are now roughly 300 ceremonial singers who are expertly versed in the texts, sacred properties, procedures, and philosophy from one to six of the great curing ceremonials. In addition, most Diné know and perform shorter rituals taken from a repertory of prayer-stick cuttings, jewel and pollen offerings, and "short sings." Although much of the tradition is fixed, the possible combinations are endless, each one being carefully planned to fill a particular personal need. Diné ceremonials are individual and occasional rather than group-oriented and calendrical.

The Blessingway or *Hózhóóji* ceremony is central to Diné religion and philosophy; it is considered to be the earliest Navajo ritual. This three-part series of songs and actions honors the deity Changing Woman (the mother of Enemy Slayer) and protects the participants from dangerous powers invoked during the ritual; the songs are preventative rather than curative. The girls' puberty rite reenacts the story of Changing Woman's birth by initiating the girl into adulthood and blessing the community. The marriage ritual symbolizes Changing Woman's growth, and the House Blessing honors the maturity of the deity. The "prayer of *hózhó*" litany is the concluding formula for many Blessingway prayers ("Beauty before me, beauty behind me . . ."); *hózhó* is the Navajo word for beauty, peace, and harmony.

Athapaskan music emphasizes the tonic, third, fourth, and fifth; songs have a central section that is often performed an octave higher than the opening and closing material, and these elements have survived in current popular song forms. The choruses of songs are highly melodic, with scales based on the open triad, while the verses employ only three or four tones.

Because the Diné traditionally transmit songs by oral tradition, there is no standardized system for transcription. Although a song may begin on any pitch, the mode of the melody is maintained and varies for different types of songs. Falsetto singing is confined to Yeibichai Nightway chants. Rhythmic structures are additive, so multiple time signatures and final phrases have varying lengths. Meters of 6/8 and 9/8 are common, with drums providing a steady beat, and metrical changes add an intriguing and compelling aural complexity to the music. Song texts usually combine vocables and translatable words, and most ceremonial songs end with a cadential pattern of distinctive vocables.

The Navajo language has a large numbers of speakers, with some who use Navajo as their first language, and some of whom are monolingual. Diné are exposed to the language on a daily basis through radio programs, newspapers, language immersion programs, cultural events, and both traditional and popular songs. Navajo hymnals, published music, and the *Adahooniliggi* ("Current Events," a monthly newsletter), use the Harrington-LaFarge Navajo alphabet, established in the 1930s.

Most Navajo adults prefer that the language be spoken and sung elaborately, with picturesque and elaborate use of metaphor, simile, and personification; locations in songs are usually directional or nonspecific; and many texts begin in the fourth person, often translated as "one," or with the word *jiní* ("it was said") to emphasize the autonomy of the singer.

Laura Stanfield Prichard

See also: Densmore, Frances; Native American Music; Native American Popular Music; Yuman Music

Further Reading

Frisbie, Charlotte. 1967. *Kinaaldá: A Study of the Navaho Girls' Puberty Ceremony*. Middletown, CT: Wesleyan University Press.

McAllester, David. 1954. *Enemy Way Music: A Study of Social and Ethical Values as Seen in Navaho Music*. Cambridge, MA: Peabody Museum of American Archaeology and Ethnology, Harvard University.

McCullogh-Brabson, Ellen. 2001. *We'll Be in Your Mountains, We'll Be in Your Songs: A Navajo Woman Sings*. Albuquerque: University of New Mexico Press.

Mitchell, Frank. 1978. *Navajo Blessingway Singer: The Autobiography of Frank Mitchell*. Tucson: University of Arizona Press.

Ney

A *ney* or *nay* is an open-ended, obliquely held flute that is used in many Middle Eastern music types. Because of the breathy quality of its sound, it is often held in high regard by Sufi groups such as the 13th-century Mevlevis. For the Mevlevis, the ney represents human breath; being made out of a natural reed, it also represents the writing pen (made from the same type of reed) called a *qalam*. The founder of the order, Jalal al-Din Rumi, opened his poem the *Mathnawi* with a dedication to the reed flute (Marcus, 2007, p. 98). Today, the ney is occasionally made of metal such as a rifle barrel.

Different lengths of ney (between five or six) are needed to play the different pitch levels, as a single instrument does not have the needed range; however, all ney are composed of nine sections pertaining to the natural growth of a reed that "have specific, yet unarticulated, acoustic and symbolic functions" (Marcus, 2007, p. 98). A ney has six finger holes on the front and one for the thumb on the back. The player presses his lips on the lip of the end and blows down the inside of the flute to make the sound. The player can change the pitch by the amount of air blown, and if more or less wind is supplied, the octave changes up or down. In Turkey and Iran, neys have mouthpieces that look like small disks made of wood, horn, or metal, whereas in the rest of the Arab world, they are played without the aid of a mouthpiece. The mouthpiece helps players direct their wind and produces a stronger sound, yet still one that has the very breathy sound for which the instrument is famous.

In classical Arab music, as in Turkish (Ottoman) and Persian classical styles, the ney holds a special place associated with the human body's desire for unity with God, especially for Sufis. The human body is compared to the reed, pulled from its home in the marshes, empty of anything and longing to go back to its origin. This is seen to be like humankind: pulled away from God at birth, an empty vessel that must be filled and seeking final rest with God, the creator.

Lagrange notes that the ney has other names, such as the *suffarah* and the *'uffatah*, and that the *kawalah* or *kaval* in Turkey are closely related (Lagrange, 1996, p. 23). The kawalah has the same number of holes for the fingers as a ney, but is usually made of wood rather than a reed, and is a single piece of carving. Both are played the same way, even being held at an oblique angle, and they both are end-blown flutes. The ney, however, is used in urban, classical music and is the only wind instrument used in Arab classical orchestras (Marcus, 2007, p. 99). The Turkish kaval is used in folk music and sometimes is included in folk-inspired modern pieces.

John A. Shoup

See also: Arab Classical Music; Iranian Classical Music; Ottoman Classical Music; Sufism, Music of

Further Reading

Glassé, Cyril. 1991. *The Concise Encyclopedia of Islam*. San Francisco, CA: Harper San Francisco.

Lagrange, Frédéric. 1996. *Musiques d'Egypt*. Paris: Cité de la Musique/Actes Sud.

Lane, Edward W. 1989. *Manners and Customs of the Modern Egyptians*. Cairo: The American University in Cairo Press.

Marcus, Scott. 2007. *Music in Egypt*. Oxford: Oxford University Press.

Racy, Ali J. 2003. *Making Music in the Arab World: The Culture and Artistry of Tarab*. Cambridge: Cambridge University Press.

Shannon, Jonathan Holt. 2006. *Among the Jasmine Tree: Music and Modernity in Contemporary Syria*. Middletown, CT: Wesleyan University Press.

Nisiotika

Nisiotika is a distinct genre of Greek music, song, and dance that consists of a corpus of light, upbeat pieces generally dealing with the sea, love, drinking, warfare, exile, and jollification. Nisiotika music originated in the Greek islands (*nisiá*) of the Archipelago, primarily from the Sporades and the Cyclades groups of islands but also from the Dodecanese and the Northeast Aegean islands. It derives from older local traditional music, such as folk melodies, popular rhythms, shared poetic structures, and regional dances, all influenced by the music cultures of the various conquerors of this area (Ottomans, Arabs, and Venetians), as well as by the music of Asia Minor Greeks.

Most researchers draw a major differentiation between traditional Greek music of the islands and music from the mainland. The distinction between these two genres consists mainly of the following features:

1. As a rule, the island dances are in simple meters, usually of two or four beats, whereas in mainland Greece one can also find asymmetric rhythms, such as the *kalamatianós* dance in 7/8 (3 + 2+2/8).
2. Unlike music of the Greek islands, music of the mainland is performed primarily on anhemitonic modes, which are musical scales without semitones.
3. The usage of rhyme and melodic improvisation characterizes island music, whereas in the mainland these elements are rarely observed.
4. The typical combination of musical instruments in Greek mainland music was initially the duo *davul* and *zurna* (later davul and clarinet), whereas in the islands it was the pair *toubi* and lyre (or lute and violin).

Although there is a common basis in a characteristic "island sound" that extends all through the insular zone of Greece, the apparent seclusion of its islands has led to an independent shaping of particular music cultures. The majority of the nisiotika are played on lyre, clarinet, bagpipe, violin, guitar, mandolin, lute, and dulcimer. Modern versions of nisiotika employ other popular, nontraditional instruments such as the synthesizer, the electric and acoustic guitars, the bouzouki, and sometimes the drums or extra percussion. Nisiotika songs incorporate the common poetic form of rhyming couplets with extemporaneous verses, which is frequently encountered in Mediterranean insular cultures as a cultural practice of improvised musical and lyrical dialogue.

The most familiar occasion for performing nisiotika music is the *panigýri*, an annual religious feast that takes place outdoors, usually in large open-air plazas at the side of the church. These festivities—full of music, dance, food, and drink—bring together local inhabitants and operate like symbolic venues that reinforce social and cultural coherence. Other major instances of nisiotika performances are wedding and baptism ceremonies, carnival fiestas, the Clean Monday and Easter Sunday celebrations, as well as name-day or birthday parties and family gatherings.

The music of the Aegean islands is a vivid and cheerful expression of local insular cultures. This attribute is clearly revealed in their dances, which are characterized by the elegance of footsteps and the pounce of the dancers' knees. Traditional nisiotika include, among others, *bálos, soústa, syrtós, tráta, karsilamás*, and *(i) kariótikos* dance. They are mostly sequence dances done in an open or closed circle or couples, dancing opposite (*karsilamás*) or paired (*bálos*).

The most representative of the Aegean islands music, the *bálos* tune is usually rapid, lyrical, and enjoyable. It accompanies a partner dance that adapts all aspects of courtship (appeal, romance, demonstration of male and female roles, negative reaction, chase, capture, and final submission). According to earlier narratives about bálos, as men could not get straightforward access to the women's area, they invented this kind of dance in order to flirt with them. The dance consists of simple, tripping hops decorated with delicate figures and variations. Both the themes and the style of bálos resemble those of soústa. *Tráta* is a traditional commemorative dance based on the song "*I tráta mas i koureloú* (Our ragged fishing boat)." It is performed by a chorus of women who hold their hands crossways, mimicking the hauling of the nets and symbolizing the everyday process of fishing.

Syrtós is a line or circle dance, during which the participants hold their hands at shoulder level or a handkerchief by its two edges and dance in a counterclockwise direction. This is a pan-Hellenic dance, but it is performed differently from one place to another. Each insular form of syrtós is named after the specific island where that version is danced: for example, *skyrianós* from Skyros, *skopelítikos* from Skopelos, and *hiótikos* from Chios. *(I)kariótikos* is one of the most recognizable Greek island dances, and it derives from Ikaria. Its performance is structured on slow-moving walking footsteps which accelerate to quicker ones. The dancers hold each other's shoulder and dance in a circle. In most instances, the piece of music that accompanies (i)kariótikos is the well-known "*I agápi mou stin Ikariá* (My love in Ikaria)" by Giórgos Konitópoulos.

During the 1970s and 1980s, there was a massive outburst of nisiotika songs and dances through the appearance of several musical groups that performed in taverns and nightclubs in Athens, as well as in specific festivals in other provincial towns of Greece. The famous Konitópoulos family (notably Mihális, Giórgos, Kóstas, Vagélis, Agéliki, Násia, Eléni, and Iríni) from the island of Naxos stimulated the wide diffusion of the genre through their huge discographic production and live concerts. Maríza Koch, a female musician, singer, and songwriter, contributed to the revival of the nisiotika through the urban art-folk musical movement called *Néo Kýma* (New Wave), mixing up traditional melodies with electronic instrumental fusions. The rebirth of nisiotika music was supported by the music folklorist Símon Karás and the renowned traditional music singer Dómna Samíou. In addition, the *éntehni* (art) band *Dynámeis tou Aigaíou* (Forces of the Aegean) seems to have played a significant role in the reorchestration of older traditional island melodies by means of a delicate new musical treatment.

The popularity of island songs was also increased by the MINOS-EMI production of the 1982 record *Ta nisiótika* (Island music), sung by Yánnis Pários, a widely admired lead singer of light popular Greek music and love ballads. Later on, the nisiotika performers (both instrumentalists and vocalists) were accused of lapsing into the subordinate, vulgar aesthetics of the Greek *laikó* (pop) and *skyládiko* (doggy) song, and castigated for the commercialization, electrification, and loss of the genre's authenticity. Nowadays, most Greeks, especially the younger listeners, have become familiar with the nisiotika songs and dances through the revivals and renewals of the traditional island music. Because a fair amount of the nisiotika music has become part of the pan-Hellenic repertoire, these pieces can be heard and danced all over the country as well as in Greek diaspora communities.

Nick Poulakis

See also: Cretan Lyra; Greek Popular Music

Further Reading

Cooper, David, and Kevin Dawe, eds. 2005. *The Mediterranean in Music: Critical Perspectives, Common Concerns, Cultural Differences.* Lanham, MD: Scarecrow Press.

Dawe, Kevin. 2007. *Music and Musicians in Crete: Performance and Ethnography in a Mediterranean Island Society.* Lanham, MD: Scarecrow Press.

Jinkinson, Roger. 2005. *Tales from a Greek Island.* London: Racing House Press.

Kallimopoulou, Eleni. 2009. *Paradosiaká: Music, Meaning and Identity in Modern Greece.* Burlington, VT: Ashgate.

Nô Theater

Nô (also commonly spelled *noh*) is a theatrical genre that has been performed since the Muromachi Period (1392–1568 CE) and is known for its stoic yet exceptionally emotional performance. *Nô*, which translates as "skill," came under the patronage of the ruling military government, the *shogunate*, in the 14th century CE and reached its height as a ceremonial art form during the Edo Period (1603–1868 CE, also known as the Tokugawa Period). If *kabuki* is theater of the people, then nô is theater of the military class. In writings on Japanese art forms, nô is often described as an isolated theater genre, but in performance practice nô is traditionally presented with interludes of small comedic pieces called *kyôgen*. Typically, kyôgen performances are inserted between nô plays, often with unrelated texts. Nô is known for its seriousness that intertwines drama, dance, and music, whereas kyôgen are short comedic skits often using pantomime and dialogue with music being downplayed (Takakuwa, 2001, p. 629). Both art forms are traditionally male-only performance practices and are preserved by independent lineages of actors or schools.

Nô and kyôgen, which have been linked together for 600 years, come out of folk theater forms known as *sarugaku* and *dengaku*. Sarugaku, like early nô and kyôgen, was performed with no fixed staging and often occurred in places ranging from dry riverbeds to shrines and temples to wealthy patrons' homes. Beginning in the early 14th century CE, the well-known actor, dancer, playwright, and producer Zeami Motokiyo (1363–1443 CE) and his father Kan'ami Kiyotsugu, members of a famous sarugaku family troupe, developed nô as a separate art form out of sarugaku. When Kan'ami died, Zeami, just 22 years old, inherited the responsibility of carrying on the traditions of the family troupe (Rimer and Yamazaki, 1984, p. xviii). Zeami used the knowledge passed down from his father to push nô to new heights, and his treatises on the art form still serve performers and researchers in Japanese studies today. During the 16th century CE, the shogunate patronage dwindled as the classes became locked in a civil war. Despite the elite status that nô derived from its patronage, folk forms of nô began to spring up. After the country was unified again under the shogunate military rule, the strong Tokugawa family came to power and reinvented nô as their court's ceremonial art form. Under the Tokugawa family's rule, nô actors were given the rank of *samurai* and only their sons were allowed to continue the traditions, now strictly produced with no deviation from its codified forms (Brandon, 1997a, p. 145). The art form developed by Zeami was once known for individual interpretation based on his notions of aesthetic, style, and production, but the nô that we see today came out of the Edo Period as a rigorously produced art form with very little variation, taught through exacting tradition.

There are three groups of performers in nô: actors, chorus, and instrumental accompanists. These groups work in concert to produce a multilayered performance practice. The actors of the nô drama come from different schools of training, some with traditions dating back to the Muromachi Period. Actors in the nô drama train throughout their entire careers in one of three role types. The first subgroup of actors plays the main roles, known as *shite* (pronounced shee-tay). They wear intricately carved masks depicting characters, ranging from women and men of varying ages to all sorts of nonhuman gods and demons. These masks can be hauntingly beautiful or grotesque depending on the role, and are key elements in the overall look of a nô performance. The second subgroup of actors plays the *waki*, a secondary character. The waki never wear masks and do not often dance. In general, the waki could be considered an onstage guide, often providing context and narration. Though he rarely interacts directly with the shite, he does work with the shite to push the story forward. The final subgroup includes actors who play the kyôgen roles, both in nô and in the separate comedic interlude pieces. In the nô setting, these actors perform either subordinate roles that sum up elements of the story or provide brief moments of comedic relief in the otherwise serious stories.

The actors in the chorus, along with the shite and waki, deliver the text of the play. Today, the chorus typically has eight members, but in the 18th century CE it could have as many as 25 members. The relationship between the main actors and the chorus has changed since Zeami's time, and today they serve in supporting roles to each other. It should be noted that the chorus is a dramatic role and not a musical one. The chorus members are not simply back-up to the shite; rather, they help to extend the sung and spoken text from the shite to create a transcendent viewpoint of the character (Fujita, 2008, p. 136).

The verbal component of nô, based on literary texts, is the most important in the art form. The music, staging, dance, and other elements all play secondary roles to the elaborate texts. The shite role and the chorus deliver these texts in a fixed number of stylized forms of melodic and rhythmic patterns. These patterns deliver incredible emotion for the characters, but the same melodic form may be used to express both sorrow and joy (Fujita, 2008, p. 135), so the uninitiated may not understand the meaning based on the melody alone. To truly understand a performance, one must understand the texts on which the performance is based.

The instrumental accompaniment of the Nô drama, known as the *hayashi*, is made up of four instruments: one flute and three drums. The *nôkan*, a horizontal side-blown flute with seven finger holes, is similar in appearance to the *ryûteki* from the *gagaku* ensemble. It is made of bamboo and wrapped with cherry bark and is typically lacquered on the inside. A unique element of the nôkan is the addition of a small tube, known as the *nodo*, between the mouthpiece and the first finger hole. This addition produces a sharp and abrupt timbre that also disrupts the natural relationship between intervals, shifting the nôkan away from absolute pitch (Takakuwa, 2001, p. 634). The nôkan provides small melodic motions either to introduce scenes or to heighten the text being delivered by the chorus and actor. Like their ryûteki counterparts in gagaku, nôkan musicians use a form of *shôga* (oral mnemonic) to memorize the melodic material of each play.

There are two hand drums and one stick drum in the hayashi. The two hand drums, generally called *tsuzumi*, are played as a pair. The larger drum accents and initiates patterns, while the smaller drum develops rhythmic texture. Both are hourglass-shaped, with two leather drum heads strung together from each side of the body. The larger drum, *ôtsuzumi*, is held on the musician's left hip and struck with his right hand. The cords that hold the heads are strung tightly and it is common practice to heat the drum heads prior to the performance. This practice allows the musician to produce two tones by striking the heated head in different ways. The smaller drum, *kotsuzumi*, is held on the musician's right shoulder with the left hand and struck with the right hand. The cords on the kotsuzumi are not strung as tightly as those on the ôtsuzumi. In this way the kotsuzumi player can control the tension being placed on the heads of the drum. This produces four distinct tones indicative of the kotsuzumi. The musician uses one to four fingers to strike the drum head, which produces different sounds and volumes. Also, the struck head can be dampened to produce a softer tone during performance.

The stick drum, called *shimedaiko* (or generally *taiko*), is barrel-shaped and raised off the ground by a wooden frame. Two leather heads are strung over the body in a fashion similar to the tsuzumi. A hide patch is added to the top head where the drum is struck by wooden sticks called *bachi*. Though common, the shimedaiko is not used in every performance. It is typically used in plays that feature gods, demons, or other nonhuman characters.

The sonic atmosphere of nô is both stark and complex. The sound of the chant is known as *utai* (sung text) instead of *ongaku* (music) and is the key feature in performance. The musical accompaniment provided by the hayashi only elevates the text being vocalized through the utai. The instruments may also add to the theatrics of the dancer's actions, accentuating and highlighting movement. Utai is characteristically tight and has an extended vibrato. It is divided into two modes: *yowagin*, a melodic mode; and *tsuyogin*, a dynamic mode. Yowagin is used in most plays and includes more variants in pitch. Tsuyogin is less common, used mainly for nonhuman characters. Though tsuyogin uses the same pitch range as yowagin, it uses far fewer variants on the main pitches, producing a somewhat monotonous yet energetic chant. Both fixed and free-form rhythm styles are used. Fixed styles use poetic phrasing divided into eight, four, and two beats (Takakuwa, 2001, p. 632).

Performers are quite adept at switching between chanting modes and rhythmic styles to create tension in certain scenes. The tempo continually fluctuates during a performance according to the actor's discretion. His delivery is based on his ability to read an audience and the atmosphere around him. Zeami considered nô to be a means for both actor and audience to reach a level of contentment and enlightenment, and it is the actor's role to guide the performance through chant and dance into this enlightened state.

The visual aspect of nô is both simple and striking. The dance component combines pantomime and stylized motions made by actors dressed in elaborate *kimono* and costumes. The masks of the shite are carved and painted with understated emotion, but the actor uses fixed hand and arm gestures to increase the emotional affect. For example, to express extreme grief, the actor slowly lifts his hands to hide his face. The hands are positioned flat with extended fingers, the palms toward the actor's face. While discussing "artistic effects," Zeami states in one of his treatises, "Even in a theatrical endeavor that seems to have no special atmosphere about it, the spectators can find this simplicity fascinating because of the special mood it creates" (Rimer and Yamazaki, 1984, p. 184). Because the chant and utai are center stage, the dance adds to this atmosphere where the stories unfold.

Nô is also known for its stylized but simple stage. The stage we know today was standardized around 1600 CE. It is a raised platform of about 19 square feet. The stage floor is polished cypress wood and a traditional temple-like roof covers the dance area. Though nô is often performed indoors, in outdoor settings the roof both aids in protection from the elements and also acts as a frame to locate the audience's attention on the stage (Brandon, 1997a, p. 178). Four pillars sit on the four corners of the main dance area. On stage left sits the chorus and upstage, behind the dance floor, the hayashi. A bridgeway, usually 20 to 40 feet long, brings the actors to the main stage area from the dressing rooms. This bridge way acts as transitional space for the actor to become a part of the story.

The repertory of nô is quite expansive. It consists of some 250 pieces, with the majority of these created five and six centuries ago (Emmert, 1997, p. 19). Though new plays have been written over the centuries, a common sentiment exists that the repertory is sufficient in number and therefore no new plays have to be added. The repertory is filled with stories based on early Japanese literature. In his treatises, Zeami encouraged playwrights to center their stories on history and legends of familiar events and characters. Common themes include Chinese legends and Japanese mythology and history—especially the famous 12th-century CE war between the Heike and Genji clans (Brandon, 1997a, p. 146). Especially today, audiences may not comprehend every word delivered through the heightened speech and elaborate singing style, but the stories are best understood by those familiar with the source materials and famous story lines.

Justin R. Hunter

See also: Bunraku; Gagaku; Kabuki

Further Reading

Brandon, James R. 1997a. *The Cambridge Guide to Asian Theatre*. Cambridge: Cambridge University Press.

Brandon, James R., ed. 1997b. *Nō and Kyōgen in the Contemporary World.* Honolulu: University of Hawai'i Press.
Emmert, Richard. 1997. "Expanding *Nō*'s Horizons: Considerations for a New *Nō* Perspective." In James R. Brandon (ed.), *Nō and Kyōgen in the Contemporary World,* 19–35. Honolulu: University of Hawai'i Press.
Fujita, Takanori. 2008. "*Nō* and *Kyōgen*: Music from the Medieval Theatre," trans. Alison Tokita. In Alison McQueen Tokita and David W. Hughes (eds.), *The Ashgate Research Companion to Japanese Music,* 127–144. Surrey, UK: Ashgate.
Malm, William P. 2000. *Traditional Japanese Music and Musical Instruments (The New Edition).* Tokyo: Kodansha International.
Okuyama, Keiko, and Reese, Heinz-Dieter. 2001. "Theatrical Genres: Overview." In Robert Provine, Yosihiko Yokumaru, and Lawrence Witzleben (eds.), *Garland Encyclopedia of World Music; Vol. 7: China, Japan, and Korea,* 653–655. New York: Routledge.
Rimer, J. Thomas, and Masakazu Yamazaki, trans. 1984. *On the Art of the Nō Drama: The Major Treatises of Zeami.* Princeton, NJ: Princeton University Press.
Takakuwa, Izumi. 2001. "Nô and Kyôgen." In Robert Provine, Yosihiko Yokumaru, and Lawrence Witzleben (eds.), *Garland Encyclopedia of World Music; Vol. 7: China, Japan, and Korea,* 629–637. New York: Routledge.

Nongak

Also referred to as *pungmul* and by many other names, *nongak* is a multifaceted percussion-band music and dance tradition in Korea that also incorporates elements of ritual and drama. The term "nongak" is a combination of two Sino-Korean characters that translate literally to "farmer's music" or "farming music." As its name suggests, it is historically a rural practice that accompanies farm labor to alleviate boredom and enliven farmers' spirits, though it is also performed in community festivals and village rituals. As a ubiquitous genre throughout the country, there exist many regional and local variations in music, costume, dance, and instrumentation. Today, nongak has become a symbol of traditional music and culture in both North and South Korea, and preservation efforts in the latter have allowed it to thrive in new ways as traditional rural practices disappear due to the country's rapid modernization. In 2014, UNESCO inscribed nongak as an Intangible Cultural Heritage of Humanity (UNESCO, 2015).

The music of nongak centers on a core set of four percussion instruments: a *jing*, a large brass gong (16 inches in diameter); a *kkwaenggari* or *swe*, a small gong (around 8 inches in diameter); a *janggo*, an hourglass-shaped, double-sided wooden drum; and a *buk*, a double-sided wooden barrel drum. Other instruments used in nongak include the *taepyeongso*, a conical double reed; the *nabal* (literally trumpet-bugle); and the *sogo*, a small handheld drum. Each instrument plays a specific role within the music and dance. There are typically two primary swe players who lead the entire ensemble by signaling rhythmic changes using visual and musical cues, and also direct dance movements and formations. Musically, the swe outlines the rhythmic cycle (*jangdan*), controls the tempo, and improvises rhythms that accentuate particular aspects of the rhythmic cycle. The janggo provides the foundation of the rhythmic cycle. The buk provides bass tones and accentuates the strong beats of the rhythmic cycle. The jing punctuates the beginning of the rhythmic cycle and other strong beats. The taepyeongso provides improvised melodic accompaniment to the percussion band, drawing musical material from local folk songs, and the nabal can be used to give signals. The sogo, however, produces very little sound, and serves mainly as a dance prop (Hesselink, 1996, pp. 143–155).

This percussive genre centers on rhythmic cycles or patterns (*jangdan* or *karak*) that are played in sequence, with up to 12 rhythmic cycles in a performance. Each rhythmic pattern is repeated at length while the drummers perform specific dances and formations that are associated with that particular rhythm. Individual performers can improvise within a narrow framework that does not distort the overall structure of the rhythmic cycle or the cohesiveness of the entire band. Rhythms in Korea are traditionally orally transmitted with the use of vocables and mnemonics called *kueum*, which signify specific playing techniques and rhythms. These vocables and mnemonics are also able to convey stresses, accents, dynamic range, and overall "groove" of the rhythmic cycle (Hesselink, 1999, pp. 8–10).

Nongak drummers at a festival in Yeongam, South Korea. Wind instruments and gongs are also used in nongak. (Jon Lusk/Redferns)

As a complex and comprehensive genre, many assert that one should not consider any one particular aspect of nongak to be more important than another, or consider them in distinctly separate terms (Hesselink, 1999, p. 6). For instance, there is continuous movement and dance concurrent with the drumming. Performers wear hats with streamers and ornate feather flowers (*sangmo*) and are able to manipulate these streamers to execute complex figures and movements. Furthermore, those performing sangmo are completely in unison with one another, all while simultaneously dancing and playing complex rhythmic patterns. The *japsaek*, or village characters, add elements of drama to nongak by representing and playing the typical village characters such as the aristocrat, hunter, monk, grandmother, and beautiful maiden.

Nongak plays an important role in village shamanic rituals (*kut*) and festivals. Rituals can include village shrine rituals, agricultural rituals, and village cleansing rituals that serve to drive away evil spirits in the village and propitiate the guardian spirits (Park, 2014, p. 2). In the Honam Chwado region, nongak is performed in Lunar New Year rituals on the first full moon to "stamp out bad energy, appease the spirits and pray for a good fortune and blessings" (Kwon, 2012, p. 72). Even as traditional village life continues to decline in the face of modern development, the genre continues to be adapted to new uses and contexts. One can find it in university clubs, elementary schools, modern stages, tourist performance venues, and on the streets leading groups of protesters. After the devastation of the Korean War, the South Korean government proactively pursued the preservation and promotion of the country's traditional heritages by creating the Cultural Properties Preservation Law in 1962. Nongak was soon designated Important Cultural Asset no. 11 in 1966. This designation has been continually amended to recognize specific regions that are representative of a distinct style of nongak, of which today there are six: Jinju Samcheonpo, Pyeontaek, Iri, Gangneung, Imsil Pilbong, and Gurye Jansu (Cultural Heritage Administration of Korea, 2015).

The term "nongak" is a recent subject of debate by scholars and practitioners. Some scholars have opposed the use of this term, arguing that ruling authorities during the Japanese occupation (1910–1945) used it in order to belittle the practice or "limit this activity to just 'music' by 'farmers' in order to disguise or erase its much broader use and meaning among the colonized" (Hesselink, 2006, p. 15). Furthermore, because the term "nongak" confines the meaning of this genre to the spheres of just "music" and "farming," it does not represent the complexity of the genre's current performance contexts and its diverse use in social functions (Hesselink, 2006, p. 16; Kwon, 2012, pp. 73–74). Hence, many scholars and practitioners prefer the term *pungmul* as a generic term for rural drumming and dance throughout South Korea. Nonetheless, many use the word "nongak" frequently; both UNESCO and the South Korean government use this term in their designations.

Tanner Jones

See also: Janggu

Further Reading

Cultural Heritage Administration of Korea. 2015. "Intangible Cultural Heritage of Humanity." https://english.cha.go.kr/cop/bbs/selectBoardArticle.do?ctgryLrcls=CTGRY2 10&nttId=58151&bbsId=BBSMSTR_1205&uniq=0&mn=EN_03_02.

Hesselink, Nathan. 1996. "Changdan Revisited: Korean Rhythmic Patterns in Theory and Contemporary Performance Practice." *Han'guk ŭmak yŏn'gu* [Studies in Korean music] 24, 143–155.

Hesselink, Nathan. 1999. "Kim Inu's 'P'ungmulgut and Communal Spirit': Edited and Translated with an Introduction and Commentary." *Asian Music* 31(1), 1–34.

Hesselink, Nathan. 2004. "Samul Nori as Traditional: Preservation and Innovation in a South Korean Contemporary Percussion Genre." *Ethnomusicology* 48(3), 405–439.

Hesselink, Nathan. 2006. *P'ungmul: South Korean Drumming and Dance*. Chicago: University of Chicago Press.

Hesselink, Nathan. 2010. "Taking Culture Seriously: Democratic Music and Its Transformative Power in South Korea." *The World of Music* 52(1/3), 670–701.

Howard, Keith. 1991. "Why Do It That Way? Rhythmic Models and Motifs in Korean Percussion Bands." *Asian Music* 23(1), 1–59.

Kwon, Donna. 2012. *Music in Korea: Experiencing Music, Expressing Culture.* New York: Oxford University Press.
Kwon, Donna Lee. 2015. "'Becoming One': Embodying Korean P'ungmul Percussion Band Music and Dance through Site-Specific Intermodal Transmission." *Ethnomusicology* 59(1), 31–60.
Lee, Katherine In-Young. 2012. "The Drumming of Dissent during South Korea's Democratization Movement." *Ethnomusicology* 56(2), 179–205.
Park, Peter. 2014. "P'ungmul Kut (Percussion Music Rituals): Integrating Korean Traditions with Modern Identities." PhD diss., University of Washington.
Pungmul-Korean Drumming. https://pungmul.wordpress.com/utdari-%EC%9B%83%EB%8B%A4%EB%A6%AC.
UNESCO. 2015. "Nongak, Community Band Music, Dance and Rituals in the Republic of Korea." http://www.unesco.org/culture/ich/en/RL/00717.

Nordic Jazz

"Nordic jazz" refers to jazz music emanating from Scandinavian countries such as Sweden, Denmark, and Norway. Over the past four decades, these countries have established vibrant, distinctive, state-supported jazz scenes.

Situated along important trade routes, Scandinavian countries were exposed to American jazz recordings early, and a thriving local jazz culture has existed there dating back to at least to the 1930s. Scandinavian jazz slowly achieved international acclaim beginning in the 1950s with the work of Swedish cool-jazz baritone saxophonist Lars Gullin (1928–1976), who won *Downbeat*'s "New Star" category in 1954, becoming the first European to win a jazz poll in the United States. In the 1960s, Swedish singer Alice Babs (1924–2014), who frequently collaborated with Duke Ellington and Danish alto saxophonist John Tchicai (1936–), emerged as a prominent figure in the free jazz movement and appeared on numerous landmark albums, including Albert Ayler's *New York Eye and Ear Control* (1965) and John Coltrane's *Ascension* (1966). The current global reputation of Nordic jazz is inseparable from the popularity of releases from Manfred Eicher's (1943–) German-based ECM Records in the 1970s, which regularly featured Scandinavian musicians, notably Norwegian bassist Arild Andersen (1945–), drummer Jon Christensen (1943–), guitarist Terje Rypdal (1947–), and saxophonist Jan Garbarek (1947–); Swedish pianist Bobo Stenson (1944–) and bassist Palle Danielsson (1946–); and Danish trumpeter Palle Mikkelborg (1941–). Often recorded at Rainbow Studios in Oslo with engineer Jan-Erik Kongshaug (1944–), these releases featured a sparse, high-reverb aesthetic that came to define Nordic jazz in the era.

Critic Stuart Nicholson famously identifies a common, so-called "Nordic tone" in the playing of some Scandinavian jazz musicians. Characterized by the use of indigenous folk material and a minimalistic impulse toward long, sustained notes, clarity, repetition, and extended periods of silence, Nicholson describes the Nordic tone as distinctively Scandinavian and interprets it as evoking the solitude and open spaces of the region. Pianist Jan Johansson's (1931–1968) influential 1964 album *Jazz på svenska* (Jazz in Swedish) established an important precedent for using Scandinavian folk melodies, and, under the guidance of American expatriates

George Russell (1923–2009) and Don Cherry (1936–1995), Garbarek and others continued this tradition. Garbarek's output, in particular, has come to be most associated with the Nordic tone, especially his early ECM albums *Afric Pepperbird* (1970), *Triptykon* (1973), and *Dis* (1977), as well as his work as part of Keith Jarrett's short-lived "European Quartet." In recent years, scholars such as Tony Whyton have criticized the "Nordic tone" concept as a cliché that unfairly stereotypes the music of Scandinavian jazz musicians.

Today, Sweden, Denmark, and Norway all subsidize jazz music, providing education, sponsoring concerts and festivals, and more. This governmental support has helped make Scandinavia the home of one of the most important contemporary jazz cultures. Nordic jazz has continued to thrive into the 21st century, embodied in the work of musicians as diverse as Swedish pianist Esbjörn Svensson (1964–2008), bassist Lars Danielsson (1958–), and saxophonist Mats Gustafsson (1964–); Norwegian pianist Tord Gustavsen (1970–), trumpeter Mathias Eick (1979–), and saxophonist Karl Seglem (1961–); and Danish pianist Søren Kjærgaard (1978–), guitarist Jakob Bro (1978–), and bassist Jonas Westergaard (1976–).

Brian F. Wright

See also: Jazz; Parker, Charlie

Further Reading

Bares, William. 2011. "Sounds of Silence: The Politics and Poetics of Norwegian Jazz." *American Music Review* 41(1), 9–15.

Heffley, Mike. 2005. *Northern Sun, Southern Moon: Europe's Reinvention of Jazz*. New Haven, CT: Yale University Press.

Hellhund, Herbert. 2012. "Roots and Collage: Contemporary European Jazz in Postmodern Times." In Luca Cerchiari, Laurent Cugny, and Franz Kerschbaumer (eds.), *Eurojazzland: Jazz and European Sources, Dynamics, and Contexts*, 431–446. Boston: Northeastern University Press.

Lake, Steve, and Paul Griffiths, eds. 2007. *Horizons Touched: The Music of ECM*. London: Granta Books.

Nicholson, Stuart. 2005. "Celebrating the Glocal: The Nordic Tone in Jazz." In *Is Jazz Dead? (Or Has It Moved to a New Address)*, 195–222. New York: Routledge.

Nicholson, Stuart. 2014. "The Globalization of Jazz." In *Jazz and Culture in a Global Age*, 89–154. Lebanon, NH: Northeastern University Press.

Whyton, Tony. 2012. "Europe and the New Jazz Studies." In Luca Cerchiari, Laurent Cugny, and Franz Kerschbaumer (eds.), *Eurojazzland: Jazz and European Sources, Dynamics, and Contexts*, 366–380. Boston: Northeastern University Press.

North Korea, Music of

The music of the Democratic People's Republic of Korea (the formal name of North Korea, abbreviated DPRK) is characterized by Korean identity and musical traditions, as employed in service of the state ideology. As such, an understanding of the ideological pillars of the DPRK is crucial to understanding its musical culture. The DPRK was declared in 1948 under the leadership of Kim Il Sung (1912–1994), a military leader against Imperial Japan in the World War II, under the patronage of communist regimes of the Soviet Union and, later, China. Despite those alliances, the fundamental ideology of the DPRK is the *Juche* idea. Juche aims to ensure sovereignty through national self-reliance expressed in several key areas: the development of a Korean-style socialist state, and an oft-repeated "single-hearted unity" of ideology whose source and summit is absolute devotion to Kim Il-sung—lauded with the titles of Great Leader, and Eternal President—and his successors, his son Kim Jong-il (1941–2011), and grandson, Kim Jong-un (born 1982 or 1983).

Closely connected to Juche is the *Songun*, or "military first" principle, for two reasons: the belief that survival and the right of self-determination cannot be ensured by reliance on outsiders for defense, and the fact that the DPRK's territorial aspirations do not end at the 38th parallel. The Korean War ended in an armistice, leaving the DPRK technically at war with the United States and the Western-backed government of the Republic of Korea (South Korea), and the DPRK continues to present itself as the salvation of the entire Korean peninsula from imperialism and other affronts. As armed struggle threw off Japanese domination, the Songun principle intends to accomplish the same against other adversaries of the DPRK.

Therefore, all forms of art in the DPRK exist to further the goals of the state, which is said to act in the name of the people. All three leaders have enjoyed close national press coverage of their "field guidance" on an unlimited array of subjects, from the arts to agriculture, military strategy, architecture, and economics. In that context, both Kim Il-sung and Kim Jong-il are credited with extensive commentaries on the role of the visual and performing arts in society, beginning with Kim Il-sung's "On Some Questions Arising in our Literature and Art" (1951) in which scholar Keith Howard notes the influence of Mao Zedong's Yan'an speeches, and of Soviet-style socialist realism.

It is arguable that Kim Jong-il's commentaries may carry the most influence, due to his close interest in the arts in general, and his role in elaborating on and enforcing his father's teachings, with his career culminating in succeeding his father as supreme leader. By the time of Kim Jong-il's commentaries, the national hagiography of Kim Il-sung was firmly codified: The "Great Leader" was lauded as the origin and embodiment of the DPRK's national ideology.

Musical guidelines from the leaders range from the general to the very specific. General guidance includes standard exhortations that "[t]he form of literary and artistic works must also be good, but their ideological content is more important" (Kim, 1992a, p. 196) to "make an active contribution to establishing the Party's monolithic ideological system among Party members and other working people" (Kim, 1992b, p. 391) and "promoting socialist construction in the northern half of the country and making full preparations for the great revolutionary event of national reunification" (Kim, 1992b, p. 392).

More abstractly, the middle Kim urged composers to strike a balance between "restorationism" with folk material that might trigger nostalgia for pre-revolutionary times and conditions, and an adaptation of national aesthetic traits for the revolutionary era, while not pursuing novelty for novelty's sake, or falling into "flunkeyism" through the excessive imitation of foreign music (Kim, 1992b, p. 391). He also urged that composers of North Korea should create their own style of opera and not copy European forms, which he called "outdated" (Kim, 1992a, p. 202).

In concrete terms, Kim Jong-il presented guidelines for composition, performance, and instrumentation, stressing that "[s]ongs that are too jumpy with melodies that rise and fall too sharply are both difficult to sing and unsuited to the sentiments of Koreans" (Kim, 1992b, p. 390). In addition, he specified that "lyrics should be written in verse form," and that "[w]e must categorically reject singing in a harsh voice" (Kim, 1992b, pp. 391, 394). Echoing a preference of Kim Il-sung, he declared that "even when one and the same song is sung, it is better to hear women sing it than men" (Kim, 1992b, p. 394).

For instrumentalists, Kim Jong-il urged close attention to the ideal key for performing a given work, and prescribed the following formula for instrumental breaks: "You should direct the emotional content properly by bringing it to a crescendo before the next stanza is started" (Kim, 1992b, p. 394).

In order to avoid "flunkeyism" and blind allegiance to non-Korean aesthetics, Kim also discouraged the use of Western woodwind instruments, saying in 1968 that, "from now on, woodwind instruments should be used as little as possible in instrumental music." He added that "the use of the piano should also be reviewed," and that the collective effort of ensemble accompaniment was preferable to that of a single pianist. Above all, he urged the development of "an orchestra of our national instruments," while allowing the incorporation of Western instruments such as the electronic organ so long as they were assimilated in the creation of culturally and ideologically appropriate music (Kim, 1992b, p. 395).

While Kim Jong-un has liberalized some elements of the performing arts, the preceding principles are easily found in actions regarding present-day music of the DPRK. Orchestral ensembles favor stringed instruments, woodwinds are often adaptations that bear less of a likeness to Western instruments, and pianos are not as ubiquitous as they are in the West. Vocal performances heavily favor female soloists, and thematic material focuses on the leaders, the land, national construction and defense, and other ideological subjects.

Exemplars of North Korean music include the Mansudae Art Troupe (which is the successor of both the Central Art Troupe and the Pyongyang Art Troupe), the Pochonbo Electronic Ensemble, the Unhasu Orchestra, the all-female Moranbong Band, and the Wanjaesan Light Music Band. Military choruses and ensembles abound, as music remains a crucial element of ideological formation and morale. The DPRK also sponsors a state symphony orchestra.

According to the *International Directory of Music and Music Education Institutions*, each province in the DPRK has a state-sponsored college of arts. However, the Pyongyang University of Music and Dance is the flagship national institution.

Maristella J. Feustle

See also: K-Pop; Nongak

Further Reading

Howard, Keith. 2003. "The People United: Music for North Korea's 'Great Leader' and 'Dear Leader.'" http://freemuse.org/graphics/Publications/PDF/howard05022003.pdf.

Kim Jong-il. 1992a. "Let Us Compose More Music Which Will Contribute to Education in the Party's Monolithic Ideology: A Speech to Officials in the Field of Literature and Art and Composers, June 7, 1967." In *Selected Works*, 195–207. Pyongyang: Foreign Languages Publishing House.

Kim Jong-il. 1992b. "On the Direction Which Musical Creation Should Take: A Talk to Creators, October 25, 1968." In *Selected Works*, 390–397. Pyongyang: Foreign Languages Publishing House.

"North Korea." International Directory of Music and Music Education Institutions. https://idmmei.org/?country=NORTH+KOREA&type=&keyword=&searchSubmit=SEARCH.

Norwegian Folk Music

The folk music of Norway is the product of a long and complex series of traditions. From its pre-Christian roots to its modern cosmopolitan identity, folk music has played a central role in the history of Norwegian people and their shared heritage with their Scandinavian neighbors, especially Denmark and Sweden. Norwegian folk music is, therefore, a reflection of the diversity of its people. With rural traditions that have remained isolated for centuries and an eclectic urban population, which has grown steadily since the mid-19th century, Norway's folk music remains a dynamic resource of cultural synthesis, historic preservation, and modern identity.

The earliest folk traditions extend back to Norway's aboriginal roots. The Sami people—an indigenous group of northern arctic dwellers—have occupied Norway and parts of Scandinavia and Russia as far back as the first century CE. However, relatively little is known about their traditions before the late medieval period. As hunters, fishers, and herders, their lifestyle was dominated by a harsh but resilient existence in one of Europe's most forbidding climates. Oral traditions and the absence of extensive written records have left little evidence from which to construct a complete picture of the degree to which early Sami populations participated in a musical culture. Nevertheless, one practice passed down to more recent generations is the tradition of singing *joiks* (*yoiks*). Joiks are songs that are frequently performed a cappella (without musical accompaniment), though in some cases it is probable that simple reed instruments (known as the *fadno*) and drums were used to accompany singers. These chants are personal and improvisatory in nature, and their style can vary widely from one performer to another. Like other medieval chants from across Europe, joiks are expressive of distinctive musical affects. Some joiks celebrate the spirituality of nature, whereas others are used to express a particular emotion, thus echoing the Samis' close connection to the land. As with much of Norwegian folk music, a sense of collective identity can be found alongside the individual stamp of the performer.

One of the most important elements to flow from early Norwegian cultures is not their musical practice, however, but the many legends that surrounded their pre-Christian roots. Stories of the Norwegian landscape, especially the description of magical trolls who lived among the country's many picturesque *fjords* (narrow cuts in the land made by the movement of glaciers), have served as important themes in songs, ballads, and folk dances. This early history would become an indispensable wellspring of Norwegian identity in the national awakening of the 19th century.

In the later medieval period, Norway's union with Denmark in 1380—a relationship it would share for more than four centuries, until 1814—laid the foundation for an extensive tradition of music-making. This political shift marked more than a change of monarchy; it led to the cross-fertilization of neighboring cultures that often made strictly Norwegian practices inseparable from authentically Danish traditions. In addition, the rise of Lutheranism in the wake of the 16th-century Reformation gave birth to new streams of Christian pietism. The influence of German clergy throughout much of Scandinavia was strong, but Southern Norway was particularly susceptible to these Protestant influences.

As a result of these political, religious, and cultural transformations, Norwegian vocal traditions were augmented to include the singing of hymns, which remain an iconic symbol of Norwegian spirituality and identity to this day. These hymns, often set to text in the local vernacular, quickly became a central feature of Norwegian music-making throughout the 17th century. In addition, the tradition of singing the *stev*, or folk song, persisted after the Reformation, as did the singing of longer ballads (epic folk tunes). Ballads were extremely important to the preservation of Norwegian tales and bear witness to the power of the oral tradition of the Norwegian people. Other vocal forms that became more widespread in practice over the 16th and 17 centuries include the *lokk*. The lokk belongs to a popular category of herding songs known as *kulning*. These unique songs contained a combination of spoken words, singing, and shouting, and were used widely by rural communities which employed them in a domestic setting (usually to call their animals home).

Another considerable tradition that gained momentum in the generations after the Reformation is the playing of the Norwegian fiddle, or Hardanger fiddle (*hardingfele*). This string instrument derives its name from the Hardanger region of Norway, which is located along its western coast. Although the fiddle resembles the violin in its construction, it is distinguishable from its modern family member by its larger body and a unique set of sympathetic strings. These special strings are placed underneath the set that is played (with a bow or the finger), and create a unique resonating effect (often called "drones"). Some of the earliest surviving Hardanger fiddles can be dated back to the mid-17th century. However, their use spread quickly and became more widely known over the course of the 18th century. As with many folk traditions, performance practices vary widely by region, as do the ornate carvings that commonly adorn the instrument casing.

The Hardanger fiddle served to popularize another branch of folk music, which developed alongside Norway's vocal traditions: folk dances. Dance music—one of the largest and most pervasive folk traditions in Norway—constitutes a large repertoire that was used extensively by peasant classes. Folk dances were played in the home and in communal settings, and could exemplify a wide range of themes, from a celebration of the seasons to nature and pastoral life. Different dance traditions can be found throughout Norway and are often named according to their region of origin (such as Telemark, Hallingdal, and Valdres). This category of instrumental dance music is often referred to as *slåtter*, and includes many different types, such as the *springar* (a couple's dance in 3/4 time), *halling* (a lively dance in duple meter), and the *gangar* (a walking dance often in duple meter). In addition to changes in meter, contrasts in tempo, mood, and rhythmic accents all differentiate the many styles. In this respect, Norway shares many similarities with Denmark and Sweden, which also popularized fiddle music throughout the 18th century.

The music of folk dances, like vocal music, survived through written manuscripts and—more commonly—a carefully preserved performance (oral) tradition. This feature also accounts for the Hardanger fiddle's improvised performance practices. The popularity of fiddle dances waned only in the latter 18th century when the spread of German Lutheran practices decried the performance on Hardanger fiddles for recreational purposes.

Other traditional instruments that were commonly used prior to the 19th century include wind instruments, such as the *bukkehorn* (goat horn), *lur*, *tungehorn*, and *seljefløyte* (willow flute); and plucked instruments, such as the *harpeleik* (chorded zither), *langeleik* (box dulcimer), and *munnharpe*. These instruments were used to perform folk tunes or to accompany the performance of folk songs and dances.

Despite these changes, all of these elements present a case of unity within diversity amid Norway's cultural traditions. From early joik and religious hymns to the emergence of a dynamic body of folk songs, peasant traditions from across Norway have coexisted while maintaining their unique regional characteristics. At the same, this eclectic body of locally based music constitutes both larger Norwegian and Scandinavian identities. For centuries, there was relatively little tension between definitions of "Norwegian," "Danish," and "Scandinavian" music. These classifications overlapped and embodied the syncretic nature of the many subcultures that inhabited the Scandinavian peninsula. For this reason, it is more accurate to refer to this body of repertoire as Norwegian "musics," for no particular cultural trend constitutes or exhibits a singular Norwegian identity prior to the 19th century.

Only during the first half of the 1800s did the cultural climate undergo a large shift that would dramatically alter that way in which "authentic" folk music would be redefined. At the height of the Napoleonic wars, Norway ended its centuries-long political union with Denmark in 1814, established a separate state, and ironically began a new union with Sweden. Many people throughout Norway were unsettled by these occurrences and, as a result, began a crusade for national independence. This new movement called for freedom—both politically and culturally—from Norway's Scandinavian neighbors.

Although complete sovereignty would not be achieved until 1905, the 19th century remained a period of cultural awakening in Norwegian folk art, characterized by debates over authenticity. In the musical domain, these events helped spark a wave of national romanticism. For musicians, as with written/spoken language, this meant a new consciousness of Norway's history, epic legends, and folk music, which became tools to distinguish Norway from its Scandinavian counterparts and instill pride in its people. As with many 19th-century European countries, this national program encompassed three main endeavors: (1) collecting and publishing folk music; (2) developing a new body of repertoire that blurred the definitions between folk and "high art"; and (3) finding new ways of disseminating folk music throughout Norway and, indeed, to the rest of the world.

Folk musicians and historians from England to Russia began collecting folk tunes in earnest over the course of the 19th century, with the serious goal of arousing national pride and belonging. In this respect, Norway was no different from the rest of Europe. One of the most prominent early collectors of folk music was Ludvig Mathias Lindeman (1812–1887). Lindeman was an organist but spent a significant portion of his career collecting, cataloging, arranging, and preserving folk music. He published his first collection of more than 1,000 folk tunes in 1840 and followed that eight years later with perhaps his most popular volume: *Ældre og nyere norske Fjeldmelodier* (Old and new Norwegian mountain melodies). Many of his examples present simple, four-part settings of folk tunes, which made this rich body of repertoire available to new audiences as never before (Lange, 1958).

The new accessibility of tunes, combined with the circulating currents of nationalism, led to dramatic transformations in the realm of composition. Figures such as Halfdan Kjerulf (1815–1868) and Rikard Nordraak (1842–1866) forged a new style, which blended characteristics of folk and high art as they pursued their collective goal of making folk music accessible to a new generation of nationalists (Gelbart, 2007). This aim was one they shared with their literary colleagues, who simultaneously adopted the task of preserving and creating Norwegian literature for a population in Norway that was slowly waking to idea of cultural independence. The close connections between musicians and writers is especially evident in the case of Nordraak, who set the text of the Norwegian poet Bjørnstjerne Bjørnson (1832–1910) to music that would later become the national anthem: *"Ja, vi elsker dette landet* (Yes, we love this country)."

The next generation of composers helped to create an even broader appeal of folk music. This era was dominated by the celebrated life and works of Edvard Grieg (1843–1907), whose music became a staple of households throughout Norway while serving as a beacon of nationalism to people throughout Europe. Grieg's work was prolific, and included works for orchestra, solo piano, voice, and strings. From his folk song settings for piano to his more than 150 songs that incorporated a variety of different Norwegian dialects, Grieg's oeuvre stands as testament to the lasting value of folk music amidst changing values in musical style and syntax.

As these 19th-century composers embodied the spirit of folk music with new zeal, so too did many performers also take up the national torch. Ole Bull (1810–1880) was a noted violinist, whose extreme virtuosity captivated audiences throughout his life. Frequent concert tours throughout Norway, Europe, and even America took Norwegian folk music (and the sounds of the Hardanger fiddle) well beyond its geographic origins. In addition, Agathe Backer-Grøndahl (1847–1907) was a well-known contemporary whose compositions and piano performances became powerful examples of the new malleability of folk music through varied song settings and musical arrangements.

Ryan R. Weber

See also: Fiddle; Icelandic Ballads; Joik; Nordic Jazz; Nyckelharpa

Further Reading

Cai, Camilla, and Einar Haugen. 1992. *Ole Bull: Norway's Romantic Musician and Cosmopolitan Patriot*. Madison: University of Wisconsin Press.

Falnes, Oscar J. 1993. *National Romanticism in Norway*. New York: AMS Press.

Gelbart, Matthew. 2007. *The Invention of "Folk Music" and "Art Music": Emerging Categories from Ossian to Wagner*. Cambridge: Cambridge University Press.

Goertzen, Chris. 1997. *Fiddling for Norway: Revival and Identity.* Chicago: The University of Chicago Press.
Grimley, Daniel. 2006. *Edvard Grieg: Music, Landscape, and Norwegian Identity.* Woodbridge, UK: The Boydell Press.
Hardanger Fiddle Association of America. 2011. "What Is a Hardanger fiddle?" http://www.hfaa.org/Home/about-the-hardanger-fiddle.
Herresthal, Harald. 1993. "From Grieg to Lasse Thoresen: An Essay on Norwegian Musical Identity." *Nordic Sounds* 2, 3–9.
Hopkins, Pandora. 1986. *Aural Thinking in Norway: Performance and Communication with the Hardingfele.* New York: Human Sciences Press.
Horton, John. 1963. *Scandinavian Music: A Brief History.* New York: W. W. Norton.
Jorgenson, Theodore. 1993. *History of Norwegian Literature.* New York: Macmillan.
Lange, Kristian. 1958. *Norwegian Music: A Brief History.* London: Dennis Dobson Ltd.
Yoell, John H. 1974. *The Nordic Sound: Explorations into the Music of Denmark, Norway, and Sweden.* Boston: Crescendo.

Nueva Canción

A number of demographic, sociocultural, and political developments contributed to the rise of a the movement of socially conscious music known as Latin American New Song (*nueva canción*) during the second half of the 20th century. New Song represents a grouping of local manifestations that emerged in various Latin American countries in the wake of massive rural-to-urban migration and took shape during a period of dramatic political upheaval in the region. Broadly speaking, New Song musicians adapted rural traditional musical genres for performance among urban, middle-class audiences. In some locales, artists expressed antipathy for the Anglo-American popular music that had come to dominate the mainstream media in their cities, but elements of European and American rock and folk were important influences for many composers of New Song. The involvement of classically trained musicians and collaborations with artists in theater, visual arts, and poetry served to further transform the aesthetics of the traditional sources upon which New Song was based.

Most New Song artists and their followers had leftist political inclinations, and many had ties to communist or socialist political parties, organizations, or governments. Although a great number of songs did address social and political issues, in general writers sought to craft meaningful and poetic texts that marked a departure from folk music in its traditional form on the one hand, and from commercially oriented popular musics on the other. From the outset, a philosophy of Latin American solidarity was common in song texts and in writings about the significance of New Song movements. This pan-Latin outlook was enacted musically, as many groups incorporated folkloric genres and instruments from across the continent, and it was also lived out on the stages of international New Song festivals, where the top representatives from different nations came together frequently from the 1970s through the 1990s. Though New Song's popularity was strongest during this period, the movement has left a profound legacy for Latin American culture: Latin Americans of different ages and class backgrounds continue to sing and listen to the music, and contemporary high-profile musicians cite New Song artists among their major influences.

In the "Southern Cone" of South America (Argentina, Uruguay, and Chile), large-scale migration from rural areas to urban centers starting in the 1920s led to the growth of folk music in the region's major cities toward mid-century. Ensembles from Argentina's pastoral northwestern region, such as Los Chalchaleros and Los Fronterizos, had a big impact in that nation's capital, Buenos Aires, during the folklore boom of the 1950s. The seed for a socially conscious current in the Argentine folk scene was sown by the singer-songwriter and guitarist Atahualpa Yupanqui (1908–1992). Yupanqui traveled extensively throughout Argentina researching the music genres and poetic forms of the countryside, both of which he incorporated into his own compositions. He set texts evoking the hardships of indigenous mountain-dwellers and peasants in the Argentine highland northwest to songs in that region's *zamba* and *vidala* styles. In *"El arriero* (The herder)" (1944), Yupanqui depicts the rugged environment in which this archetypal figure labors, alluding in the refrain to the unequal status between herders and the owners of the cattle they guide. Inspired by Yupanqui's work, a group of musicians and intellectuals launched a movement they called the *nuevo cancionero argentino* at a concert in the city of Mendoza in 1963. The artists who came together under this banner, which translates literally as the "new Argentine songbook," advocated for a renewal of the country's national popular music. Although the manifesto that poet Armando Tejada Gómez (1929–1992) wrote for the movement was not overtly political, it outlined several key values that were shared by supporters of New Song throughout Latin America: a desire that expressive forms from all regions and groups be represented; a negative view of the dominance of foreign music (i.e., European and North American); contempt for commercial interests in art; and a wish to exchange ideas with similar movements elsewhere in the continent.

The major musical voice of the nuevo cancionero argentino was undoubtedly the singer Mercedes Sosa (1935–2009), who became the leading interpreter of works by politically committed Argentine composers. Among other classics, she sang and recorded Tejada Gómez and César Isella's *"Canción con todos* (Song with everyone)" (1969), an anthem of Latin American unity, and rocker León Gieco's *"Sólo le pido a dios* (I only ask God)" (1978), an appeal for peace. Like other artists with leftist stances, Sosa was forced into exile from 1979 to 1984 by an increasingly repressive military regime.

The Argentine folk revival also affected the participants of the Uruguayan branch of New Song. Singer-composer Daniel Viglietti (1939–) was influenced by Argentine folk music when he started performing his songs in the early 1960s, but he was also a fan of the Beatles and brought his training as a classical guitarist to his music as well. Viglietti was a militantly political artist and open supporter of leftist guerrillas seeking to foment revolution in Uruguay. His song *"A Desalambrar* (Let's take down the fences)" (1968), which addresses inequitable land distribution, was prohibited from play on government-sponsored media in 1969, and Viglietti was sent into exile in 1972 by a regime that was heading toward authoritarianism. The music of another important figure, Alfredo Zitarrosa (1936–1989), made extensive use of Uruguay's traditional *milonga* and *candomble* styles. Despite his membership in the Communist Party, Zitarrosa evaded government persecution for a time, thanks to his widespread popularity. Nevertheless, after a dictatorship was installed in 1973, he too was forced to live outside the country.

The term *nueva canción* itself is most closely associated with Chile, where the First Festival of Chilean New Song was held in 1969. The socially conscious musicians who shaped this movement over the course of the 1960s were reacting in part against the commercialized urban folkloric music scene that had arisen starting in the 1930s under the label of *música típica* (typical music). Criticism of música típica focused on the fact that it was based almost entirely on the *tonada* and *cueca* genres of Chile's central zone, to the exclusion of other regional forms. Progressives further felt that música típica's song-lyrics projected an overly romanticized image of the countryside that glossed over the difficult conditions faced by the people who actually worked the land. Nevertheless, nueva canción artists owed a significant debt to folklorists who helped expose urban Chileans to a wider range of traditional practices over the preceding decades. In fact, the folklorist-performer Violeta Parra (1917–1967) is considered to be one of the artistic pioneers of Latin American New Song, along with Argentina's Yupanqui. In the 1950s, Parra collected songs from traditional performers in various regions of the country and performed them on stage, radio, and recordings for urban audiences. Later, toward the 1960s, Parra's original compositions began to address political topics, although the love-themed "*Gracias a la vida* (Thanks to life)" (1966) became her best-known song after Mercedes Sosa made it the centerpiece of her repertoire. Parra's original version was based on the *sirilla* rhythm of southern Chile.

In the musical output of the generation that consolidated nueva canción in the mid-1960s, the lyrical focus turned to Latin America's marginalized peoples. Singer-songwriter Víctor Jara's (1932–1973) catalog is indicative of the breadth of topics covered, from the exhausted peasant laborer profiled in "*El arado* (The plow)" (1965) to outrage at a massacre of squatter families in "*Preguntas por Puerto Montt* (Questions about Puerto Montt)" (1969). The ensembles Quilapayún and Inti-Illimani, formed by university students in the Chilean capital, Santiago, sought to evoke the perseverance of South America's indigenous communities by choosing names in native languages and by adopting musical elements from the music cultures of the Andes—this region had been united under the Inca Empire before the arrival of Spanish conquistadores. Quilapayún, Inti-Illimani, and others worked in a musical format that prominently featured the Andean panpipes, *kena* flute, *charango* (small guitar), and *bombo* drum. Performances of nueva canción thrived in intimate coffeehouse-like spaces called *peñas*, such as the Peña de los Parra, run by Violeta Parra's children Angel and Isabel.

Most of the artists identified with Chilean nueva canción actively supported the campaign that brought the socialist Popular Unity coalition led by Salvador Allende to power in 1970. During Allende's time as president, many of these musicians received official support from the government. The military coup of September 11, 1973, drastically altered the movement's trajectory. Nueva canción music was effectively banned and several groups and individuals were forced into exile. Víctor Jara, who had become a figurehead for nueva canción, was tortured and then murdered by soldiers in the days following Allende's overthrow.

One of the most influential political developments for leftists in Latin America during the 1960s was the triumph of the Cuban Revolution in 1959. Many of the musicians discussed earlier have spoken about that revolution's great impact on their political outlooks or have written songs about it. The prominence that Cuba occupied in the political consciousness of progressive musicians was reinforced, firstly, by events that brought many of these individuals to the island, and secondly, by the flowering of a vigorous song movement in Cuba known as *nueva trova* (which also translates loosely as "new song"). In 1967, the Casa de las Américas (Americas House) in Cuba's capital, Havana, hosted the International Meeting of Protest Song, which was attended by Daniel Viglietti and the Parra siblings, among others. Cuba's representative to the event was Carlos Puebla (1917–1989), a singer in the *guajira* folk genre who had written several pieces celebrating the revolution in its earliest days. Puebla's song "*Hasta Siempre* (Until forever)" (1965), which is dedicated to the revolutionary hero Che Guevara, became a classic of the New Song repertoire. The 1967 Meeting served as the impetus for the foundation of the short-lived Protest Song Centre, which provided a group of young, rebellious Cuban singers with platforms for dissemination of their music. These musicians faced interference for a time from bureaucrats who questioned their commitment to the revolution's ideals. However, by the end of 1972 most were on the state payroll under the auspices of the Nueva Trova Movement, which had been established as a government-supported, country-wide institution.

Nueva trova derived its name from an earlier *trova* tradition that had been practiced by turn-of-the-20th-century tradesmen, who had an affinity for playing music in a variety of styles, including *guajira* and *bolero*. These *trovadores* (singers of trova) sang about Cuban scenery, women, and patriotism in two-part harmony while accompanying themselves on acoustic guitar. The singers of nueva trova adopted this performance model centered on the singer-songwriter-guitarist, although they also experimented with different types of groupings. Some nueva trova composers, such as Pablo Milanés (1943–), further linked themselves to "old" trova by incorporating musical elements from traditional Cuban genres. However, American and British rock and folk music also had a strong influence on many young musicians, and the songs of different writers thus varied stylistically. A diverse range of themes could similarly be found in song texts. Numerous works tackled political themes, and lyrics expressing solidarity with anti-authoritarian, anti-imperialist, and revolutionary causes were common, as in Silvio Rodríguez's (1946–) "*Canción urgente para Nicaragua* (Urgent song for Nicaragua)" (1980). Sara González's (1951–2012) "¿Qué dice Usted? (What are you saying?)" (1977) exemplifies the re-imagining of gender relations that characterized much songwriting in nueva trova. Nevertheless, it was songs of a romantic ilk, such as Milanés's "Yolanda" (ca. 1969) and Rodríguez's "*Ojalá* (I hope)" (1969), which made these two singers household names throughout Latin America.

Though New Song from the Southern Cone and Cuba had the highest profile internationally, related movements sprang up throughout Latin America during the 1970s. The emergence of nueva canción in Puerto Rico coincided with the height of the independence struggle in that U.S. territory; notable performers included the ensembles Taoné and Haciendo Punto en Otro Son, along with the singer-songwriter

Roy Brown. In the Dominican Republic, the research and performance group Convite sought to revalorize traditional Afro-Dominican music that had long been overlooked by elites. Like so many other seminal figures of New Song, Nicaragua's Carlos Mejía Godoy (1943–) set his socially conscious lyrics over a musical framework rooted in local folk styles. Carlos and his musician brother Luis Enrique performed at the historic Concert for Peace held in the Nicaraguan capital, Managua, in 1983, which brought together many New Song greats from all over Latin America. This concert was one of many similar international festivals held over the decades that helped establish the pan-Latin scope of the New Song movement. Ecuador has been host to a series of such festivals, including the Third Festival of Latin American New Song in 1984 and three occurrences of the All of Our Voices festival (named after a lyric from the refrain of "Canción con todos") in 1996, 2003, and 2012. Before his death, singer-songwriter Alí Primera (1942–1985) was Venezuela's most prominent representative at these events. Although the wave of protest music that swept Portuguese-speaking Brazil during the 1960s remained somewhat separate from New Song, distinguished personalities from the Brazilian movement, such as Chico Buarque and Caetano Veloso, collaborated with the likes of Mercedes Sosa and occasionally made appearances at New Song festivals.

Joshua Katz-Rosene

See also: Andean Region, Music of the; Bolivia, Music of; Cumbia

Further Reading

Carrasco Pirard, Eduardo. 1982. "The Nueva Canción in Latin America." *International Social Science Journal* 94(4), 599–623.

Jara, Joan. 1984. *An Unfinished Song: The Life of Victor Jara.* New York: Ticknor & Fields.

Milstein, Denise. 2006. "The Interactions of Musicians, Mass Media and the State in the Context of Brazilian and Uruguayan Authoritarianism." *Estudios interdisciplinarios de América latina y el Caribe* 17(1), 83–104.

Moore, Robin. 2006. *Music and Revolution: Cultural Change in Socialist Cuba.* Berkeley: University of California Press.

Pacini Hernández, Deborah. 1991. "'La Lucha Sonora': Dominican Popular Music in the Post-Trujillo Era." *Latin American Music Review* 12(2), 105–123.

Rios, Fernando. 2008. "La Flûte Indienne: The Early History of Andean Folkloric-Popular Music in France and Its Impact on Nueva Canción." *Latin American Music Review* 29(2), 145–189.

Schechter, John M. 1999. "Beyond Region: Transnational and Transcultural Traditions." In John Schechter (ed.), *Music in Latin American Culture: Regional Traditions*, 424–457. New York: Schirmer Books.

Scruggs, Thomas M. 2002. "Socially Conscious Music Forming the Social Conscience: Nicaraguan *música testimonial* and the Creation of a Revolutionary Moment." In Walter Aaron Clark (ed.), *From Tejano to Tango: Latin American Popular Music*, 41–69. New York: Routledge.

Nyckelharpa

Sometimes called *knaverharpa*, the *nyckelharpa* ("keyed fiddle" or literally, "key harp") is a traditional Swedish string instrument that has been used in folk music since the Middle Ages. Its strings are shortened by pins on ivories (keys or pegs) in a playing mechanism (*nyckellåda*, the key box) in the instrument's neck. The keys press against the strings, functioning as tone dividers, and the strings are stroked with a bow. It is for this reason that the nyckelharpa is often categorized as a chordophone or stroked keyboard instrument.

The nyckelharpa is usually played with a strap around the neck, angled horizontally in front of the musician, in a fashion comparable to a key instrument or guitar. The nyckelharpa has undergone changes throughout its history: earlier types of the instrument had a flat board and a drone string. The flat board made it possible to reach both the melody string and the drone with the bow.

The nyckelharpa has been central to dances and musical ceremonies in parts of Sweden since the early 17th century. The instrument is believed to have originated in northern Germany, but the nyckelharpa has been used widely in many places in Sweden and parts of Denmark. However, its popular use is clearly centered in eastern parts of Sweden, particularly the area of northern Uppland. Here, the nyckelharpa's history has been documented throughout the centuries—from Middle Ages murals of nyckelharpa-playing angels until today—and its repertoire has continued to be developed throughout the 20th century.

Scholars differentiates between five models of the nyckelharpa: The *enkelharpa* ("simple fiddle") developed around the early 17th century; the *kontrabasharpa* ("contra-drone fiddle") in the late 17th century; the *silverbasharpa* ("silver-bass fiddle") around 1830; the *kontrabasharpa med dubbellek* ("contra-drone fiddle with two rows of keys") around 1860; and finally the *komatisk nyckelharpa* (the modern "chromatic keyed fiddle"), which developed around the 1920s. In the wake of a renewed interest in the instrument and its tradition in the 1960s and early 1970s, a four-row nyckelharpa was developed, but never became as popular as its chromatic predecessor.

The different stages of the instrument's development represent changing conceptions of

A street musician plays the *nyckelharpa*, a traditional Swedish instrument with frets that is played with a bow. (Matthew De Lange/Dreamstime.com)

"sound" and playing techniques. In earlier instruments, keys had up to four pins and shortened several strings simultaneously, which facilitates the playing of melodies, but makes it impossible to play more than two strings. The later komatisk nyckelharpa, with an added bass bar and a less arched top, has 16 strings: three melody (keyed) strings (G-C-A), one drone string (C), and 12 resonance strings. Its less arched top is designed to make it sound more "pleasant."

Central to the preservation of its tradition and further development of the nyckelharpa repertoire was Eric Sahlström (1912–1986). Originally from Tobo in the northern Uppland region, Sahlström was a highly respected player of the nyckelharpa, and with his commitment to teach courses on constructing and playing the instrument, he contributed significantly to its renaissance from the 1960s onward and effectively rescued the tradition from extinction. Particularly in the 1970s, the nyckelharpa underwent an exponential explosion of interest during the so-called *spelmanrörelsen* (folk musician movement) and the numbers of nyckelharpa players in Sweden likely peaked in the mid-1980s.

The nyckelharpa is still built and played all over Sweden today, and it occupies an exceptional position in modern folk music. An estimated 10,000 nyckelharpa players are active in Sweden, and the instrument has been well established in music education in the context of a new wave of folk music in the 20th century. The instrument has also spread beyond the confines of Sweden: today musicians all over Europe, North America, and Japan play the nyckelharpa. The instrument is also occasionally used in popular music and art music.

Melanie Schiller

See also: Fiddle; Norwegian Folk Music; Yodeling

Further Reading

Ling, J. 1979. *Nyckelharpan: Studier i ett Folkligt Musikinstrument; with an abbreviated version in English "The Keyed Fiddle,"* trans. Patrick Hort. Stockholm, Sweden: Prisma.

Ling, J., G. Ahlbäck, and G. Fredelius. 1991. *Nyckelharpan Nu och Då: The Nyckelharpa: Present and Past*, trans. Skans Viktoria Airey. Stockholm, Sweden: Svea fonogram.

Lundberg, D., K. Malm, and O. Ronström. "The Nyckelharpa People." In *Music Media Multiculture. Changing Musicscapes*, 228–245, trans. Kristina Radford and Andrew Coultard. Stockholm, Sweden: Svenskt visarkiv.

Lundberg, D., and G. Ternhag. 2005. *Folkmusik I Sverige*. Örlinge, Sweden: Gidlunds Förlag.

Ralyea, J. 1980. *Shepherd's Delight: Guide to Repertoire for Hurdy-Gurdy, Musette (Bagpipes), Organized Hurdy-Gurdy, Wheel-Fiddle, Keyed Fiddle (Nyckelharpa), and Marine Trumpet*. Chicago: Hurdy-Gurdy Press.

Olatunji, Babatunde (1927–2003)

Babatunde Olatunji, the celebrated Nigerian drummer, musician, composer, bandleader, teacher, and humanitarian, was born in the coastal village of Ajido, Nigeria, on April 7, 1927. His mother was a potter and his father, Zannu Lofinda Olatunji, was a very popular and beloved leader and fisherman in the village who died suddenly two months before Olatunji's birth. Life in this small Yoruba farming and fishing village was rich in the cultural arts. Olatunji was surrounded by Yoruba art, dance, and music, including traditional singing and storytelling. Drumming played an important role in the lives of the villagers and Olatunji was drawn to the percussion instruments, especially the drums. Beginning at the age of three, he developed a strong passion for drumming and spent many hours following and listening to the master drummers of his village and nearby villages, some of whom provided him with lessons. His mother made his first *apesi* drum, an hourglass-shaped instrument that was made of clay and wrapped with woven cane. In fact, Olatunji became quite a virtuoso at a young age on the drums. In his youth, Olatunji was exposed to American jazz, blues, and gospel music via BBC radio broadcasts in Nigeria, and he was drawn to the music of Dizzy Gillespie, Count Basie, Duke Ellington, and others.

Known as "Baba," his name *Babatunde* means father, "the great man who died has come back in your person." *Olatunji* signifies "honor and wealth have been revived in the family." By tradition, chiefs were often chosen from the father's side of a family and favored the first-born male. Since his father died before he became a chief of the village, Olatunji was groomed for that prominent and powerful position since birth. This included knowledge of all of the rituals, traditions, and rules of the village and being surrounded by the love of the villagers. The intense pressure that this placed on Olatunji made him realize at about age 12 or 13 that he did not care for this position.

Because Olatunji was being prepared to become the village chief, he was homeschooled and later received special schooling in the village. Located in the church, the village school was taught by high school graduates. By age 12 he exhibited strong scholastic ability, and thus was sent to the Baptist Academy in Lagos, where the academic standards were exceptionally high. His aunt, Adisatu Vaughan, who lived in Lagos, became his second mother and her husband, Joseph Adeyemi Vaughan, an administrator at the Government Printing Press, was like a stepfather. Adisatu and Joseph Vaughn worshiped in the African Methodist church where Joseph was a deacon, and Olatunji became a devout Christian. He was later baptized in this church, taking the Christian name of Michael Gabriel. In Lagos, Olatunji was encouraged to sing in the African Methodist church choir where drumming and chanting were allowed.

> ### Drums of Passion (Olatunji)
>
> The 1960 release *Drums of Passion* by famed Nigerian percussionist Babatunde Olatunji is widely credited with popularizing West African music in America and Europe. Released by Columbia Records, *Drums of Passion* capitalized on the West's interest in exotic music and benefited from the meteoric rise and fall of the American cultural mainstream fascination called the "Calypso Craze." The album features a variety of West African musical styles from Nigeria and elsewhere led by master drummer Olatunji. *Drums of Passion* was recorded in high-fidelity analog sound and was a favorite of audiophiles of the time period to test the quality of their in-home audio/stereo systems. *Drums of Passion* has sold more than 5 million copies since its release in 1960, and Babatunde Olatunji became a household name among musicians and fans the world over.

Instead of pursuing higher education in England, as would have been customary, Olatunji dreamed of coming to America to further his education. Olatunji earned a four-year scholarship in 1950 from the Rotary International Foundation to study at Morehouse College in Atlanta, Georgia. He set sail for America on March 27, 1950, commencing a trip that took 27 days to reach St. Louis. Olatunji's first day in America at a YMCA in St. Louis was not the most welcoming: there he experienced his first taste of racial discrimination, in the form of Jim Crow laws. This was totally new and quite a shock for him. The following day he made his way to Atlanta via a segregated train where blacks had to stay in one section and whites in another. More experience with segregation and discrimination in Atlanta would have a profound effect on Olatunji.

With a career goal of becoming a diplomat, Olatunji majored in political science at Morehouse College. He joined the Morehouse jazz band and also formed a small African ensemble. He regularly performed music of his homeland at various social events in Atlanta, at both black and white churches. Among his classmates were Rev. Martin Luther King, Jr. and Maynard Jackson. Olatunji also became involved with the civil rights movement, performing concerts and attending some rallies.

Following graduation in 1954, Olatunji enrolled in New York University's (NYU) Graduate School of Public Administration and International Relations. Without a scholarship, Olatunji supported himself by forming a small African troupe that performed various gigs in New York City.

At NYU, Olatunji met Amy Bush, an African American librarian. She came from a family of professionals (doctors, dentists, educators) from Tuscaloosa, Alabama. Her undergraduate work was at Talladega College, a black institution. She wanted to continue graduate studies at the University of Alabama, but was refused admission, as blacks were not allowed to study there. Instead, she studied at Syracuse University on a scholarship. In 1957, Olatunji married Amy Bush in Tuscaloosa, Alabama. Struggling to pay his bills while at NYU, Olatunji was unable to find a grant or a means to support his research for his dissertation, so he worked as a clerk at the Institute of International Education. However, the pressures of work and school soon became difficult. Many invitations were coming in for him and his African troupe to play and he gladly accepted gigs to perform in numerous concerts and events for the civil rights movement. (His troupe eventually became known as Drums of Passion.) Music played such a prominent role in Olatunji's life that he gave up his scholastic career goals and focused more on a profession as a drummer.

Between September 18, 1958, and November 21, 1958, Olatunji was the featured artist with the Radio City Symphony Orchestra, where he did four performances every day. Reviews in the major New York newspapers were enthusiastic and these helped promote his career. He soon got an agent and appeared on numerous radio shows and live performances. Olatunji was soon heard on the *Ed Sullivan Show*, the *Today Show*, *To Tell the Truth*, and other television programs. Olatunji performed for seven weeks at Radio City Music Hall with the Radio City Symphony. One work he performed, *African Fantasy*, caught the attention of record producers for Columbia Records, who were so impressed with what he heard that they immediately signed Olatunji to record *Drums of Passion*. This album not only opened the doors for Olatunji, establishing him as a major artist, but also exposed millions of Americans to the art of African drumming. Pop, rock, and jazz artists; dance companies and studios; college and high school students; and the general public were all captivated and influenced by the work. The impact of *Drums of Passion* was strongly felt, and the album sold more than 50 million copies.

Olatunji's career peaked in 1962, though the huge success of the *Drums of Passion* album resulted in the release of more recordings on the Columbia label: *Afro-Percussion, Zungo!* (1961); *Flaming Drums!* (1962); *High Life!* (1963); and *More Drums of Passion* (1966). His contract ended in 1965, but this did not stop him from performing and recording. He recorded *Soul Makossa* for Paramount (1973) and *Jingo* for Arista (1978). He later signed with Rykodisc, for which he recorded *Drums of Passion: The Invocation* (1988), *Drums of Passion: The Beat* (1989), and *Drums of Passion: Celebrate Freedom, Justice, and Peace* (1993).

In 1967, Olatunji and John Coltrane founded the Olatunji Center of African Culture in Harlem. There students were afforded dance and music lessons. Teachers also received training in these arts. Drummers, dancers, and singers all flocked to this center and he was kept busy teaching. Coltrane donated monthly funds to the Center, as did the Rockefellers and the National Endowment for the Arts. Coltrane's last performance was at the Center, which closed in 1984.

During the 1980s and 1990s, Olatunji continued to offer workshops on African drumming. He collaborated and performed with many notable artists, including Count Basie, Art Blakey, John Coltrane, Marilyn Crispell, Duke Ellington, Mickey Hart, the Grateful Dead, Stan Getz, Freddie Hubbard, Quincy Jones, Yusef Lateef, Max Roach, Sonny Rollins, Carlos Santana, Pete Seeger, Billy Taylor, and McCoy Tyner. *Drums of Passion: The Beat* was released in 1986 with Olatunji and Carlos Santana. In 1991, the ensemble Planet Drum was formed by Olatunji and Mickey Hart. They toured together and teamed up with the Grateful Dead on the album *Planet Drum*, which won a Grammy Award in 1991. On the Chesky label, Olatunji recorded *Love Drum Talk* (1997). It received a Grammy nomination in 1998 for the Best World Music Album. In 1993, he published the *Drums of Passion Songbook* and ventured into educational videotape with *African Drumming*.

As an educator, Olatunji was a faculty member at several colleges and universities in the United States, including the Omega Institute in Rhinebeck, New York; Kent State University (1970s); and the Elma Lewis School of Fine Arts in Boston (1968–1982). He was a faculty member at the Esalen Institute in California from the 1970s until his death in 2003. He also conducted special workshops and seminars, including Kodo Drum of Japan, *Universita Degli Studi di Napoli* (Naples, Italy), University of Ghana International Center for African Performing Arts, and Virginia Museum of Fine Arts (Richmond).

During his final years, Olatunji was plagued by complications from diabetes and required hospitalization in 2001. He died on April 6, 2003, at Salinas Valley Memorial Hospital from the effects of diabetes. Many special tributes were made in honor of him and on April 21, 2007, the National Conference of Artists (NCA) held a special tribute honoring Olatunji and the 48th anniversary of his first album, *Drums of Passion*.

Barbara Bonous-Smit

See also: Highlife; Kuti, Fela

Further Reading

Olatunji, Babatunde. 1988/2011. *Drums of Passion: The Invocation.* Smithsonian Folkways HRT 15000.

Olatunji, Babatunde, and Robert Atkinson. 2005. *The Beat of My Drum: An Autobiography.* Philadelphia: Temple University Press.

Olatunji, Babatunde, and Betty Warner Deitz. 1965. *Musical Instruments of Africa: Their Nature, Use and Place in the Life of a Deeply Musical People.* New York: John Day.

Olatunji, Babatunde, Anthony "Sanga" Francis, and Sikiru Adepoju. 1993/2004. *African Drumming* [DVD]. Directed by Cecilia Mastrorilli. Warner Bros.

Palmer, Robert. 1981. "Olatunji Bids Farewell." *New York Times*, January 19.

Stewart, Gary. 1992. "The Beat Goes On: Olatunji." In *Breakout: Profiles in African Rhythm*, 87–96. Chicago: University of Chicago Press.

Opera

Opera (from the Latin, plural of *opus* [work]) is a musical genre that encompasses singers, instrumentalists, theatrical elements, and sometimes dance. Opera as a Western European classical work began in Italy in the late 16th century. As a genre, opera is vast and there are numerous types of opera and opera singing classifications. Opera is still viewed as a higher art form due to its social elements, beginnings, and its great expense to produce. The genre continues to reach new audiences internationally as economies grow.

Most operas include the following components: libretto (the text); operatic singing via arias (solo songs), duets, trios, and choruses; recitative (sung text meant to imitate speech); acting; instrumental accompaniment; scenery; staging; lighting; and costumes. Sometimes the composer of the music works with a librettist; less commonly, the composer is also the librettist of an opera. An example of the latter is the 19th-century German composer Richard Wagner (1813–1883).

> **Mozart: *The Magic Flute***
>
> Although it was not the most successful commission of his lifetime, Mozart's *Die Zauberflöte* (the magic flute) is likely Mozart's most successful *singspiel*, and paved the way for future composers of the genre and foreshadowed musical theater in the United States nearly a century later. Written in 1791, *The Magic Flute* is an opera in two acts that combines singing with spoken dialogue; unlike typical opera of the time period, the plot and songs in a singspiel can be unrelated. *The Magic Flute* is particularly known for Mozart's combination of exotic folk and vernacular music and instruments into the classical genre of the time. Today, *The Magic Flute*—yet another genre-defining work of Mozart—is one of the most widely performed operas of any composer across the world.

Italian Renaissance composers Emilio de' Cavalieri (1550–1602), Giulio Caccini (1551–1618), and Jacopo Peri (1561–1633), who were a part of the Florentine intellectual society, developed the genre *dramma per musica* (drama through music) that would later become known as opera. The first opera, Peri's *Dafne* (1598), was meant to revive the classical Greek drama of the same name.

There are various types of opera, including the French *comédies-ballet*, a spoken play with musical interludes and dance, which was popular between 1664 and 1670. French playwright Molière (1622–1673) and Italian-born French composer Jean-Baptiste Lully (1632–1687) collaborated on this subgenre with their *Le Bourgeois gentilhomme* (The bourgeois gentleman) (1670). The opéra-ballet of the late 17th through the late 18th centuries, a popular genre at the French court, featured music (solos, recitatives, and chorus numbers), dance, and drama. This genre employed a prologue and three or four acts which had different storylines but shared a theme, and the plot related to mythical and pastoral subject matter. An example is *Les Indes galantes* (The amorous Indies) (1735) by Jean-Philippe Rameau (1683–1764). *Ballet-héroïque* and its subgenre, *pastorale-héroïque*, were forms of opéra-ballet. Another type was *opéra féerie*, which dealt with magical elements or fairy tales.

The *tragédie lyrique*, created by Lully and librettist Philippe Quinault (1635–1688), dealt with mythological or epic subject matter. In this form, which would last until the early 19th century, the action had to be natural, so the music was based on recitative, not arias. This musical entertainment for the court of Louis XIV, which consisted of a good amount of ballet and a grand French overture, was sometimes viewed as rigid. Lully's tragédies lyriques included *Alceste* (1674) and *Armide* (1686).

The French masque, which was quite popular at the English court in the 16th and 17th centuries, involved mythological and allegorical subjects. A masque consisted of dancing, singing, instrumental music, poetry, and costumes. English playwright Ben Jonson (1572–1637) created a masque called *Lovers Made Men* (1617). The English Restoration (1660–ca. 1700) saw the rise of the semi-opera, a spoken play with numerous musical interludes, including some in the masque form. The protagonists rarely participated in the musical parts. For the semi-operatic *King Arthur* (1691), Henry Purcell (1659–1695) wrote the music to a libretto by John Dryden (1631–1700).

Opera seria (serious opera) was a type of 18th- and 19th-century stage work based on tragic or heroic characters. The libretti of Pietro Metastasio (1698–1782) were used for many of the opera seria, and the singing was primarily *secco* recitative ("dry" recitative with sparse instrumental accompaniment) and long *da capo* arias (a song in three sections, with the last repeating the first). The hero was typically cast for a castrato voice. Antonio Vivaldi (1678–1741) and Alessandro Scarlatti (1660–1725) composed in this form. English composer Thomas Arne (1710–1778) created *Artaxerxes* (1762), the first opera seria in English. German-born British baroque composer George Frideric Handel (1685–1759) and Austrian classical composer Wolfgang Amadeus Mozart (1756–1791) also contributed to this genre (for example, Mozart's *La clemenza di Tito* (The clemency of Titus) from 1791).

The *intermezzo* (sometimes referred to as a *burletta*, meaning "little joke" in Italian) was an Italian comic genre that was typically added as a later scene at the end of an opera seria's act and during intermissions. *La serva padrona* (The servant turned mistress) (1733) by Giovanni Battista Pergolesi (1710–1736) was originally an intermezzo between acts of the composer's opera seria *Il prigionier superbo* (The proud prisoner) before it was transformed into an *opera buffa*. The opera buffa, popular in 18th-century Italy, was influenced by the intermezzo. It was sung throughout with alternating recitatives and arias usually in da capo form. A subtype of opera buffa, *dramma giocoso* (drama with jokes) was a genre label often applied to Italian comic operas of the 18th century, specifically works by librettists Carlo Goldoni and Lorenzo Da Ponte. An example is Mozart's *Don Giovanni* (1787). These dramas employed major choral finales to emphasize the ending of an act. The *farsa* (farce), a one-act Italian comic opera, was popular in the late 18th and early 19th centuries. It was usually performed back-to-back with another farsa as well as two ballets. This work made no use of choruses, stage effects, or scene changes. The *pasticcio* (pastry) was a type of comedic stage work of the late 17th through the 18th centuries. Multiple sources that featured arias from pre-existing works provided the framework for this genre. Handel's *Elpidia* (1725) is a farsa.

The mid-18th-century French *opéra comique* consisted of spoken dialogue, arias, and a carefree subject matter, but it was not completely comic in nature. During the French Revolution (1789–1799), some composers gave the genre a more serious edge by using politically focused storylines, such as *Léonore* (1798) by French tenor and composer Pierre Gaveaux (1761–1825). Like the opera buffa, the finales of the opéra comique had a sped-up, comical quality. The opéra comique thrived in the 19th century with works like *Le Comte Ory* (The Count Ory) (1828) by Gioachino Rossini (1792–1868) and *La Fille du Régiment* (The daughter of the regiment) (1840) by Gaetano Donizetti (1797–1848). The *drame lyrique* was a type of opéra comique of the late 18th and early 19th centuries that had a more serious plot based on mythological or classical history but using modern-day settings.

The Spanish *zarzuela* (from *zarza*, meaning "bramble bush") was comprised of music interspersed with spoken dialogue. The zarzuela was introduced at the Spanish court in the 17th century. An example is *Acis y Galatea* (1708) by Antonio Literes (1673–1747). This genre experienced a revival in the 19th century due to the nationalistic sentiment of the time. Zarzuela composers included Francisco Barbieri (1823–1894) and Joaquín Gaztambide (1822–1870). The form lasted into the 20th century, during which jazz and operetta elements were added.

The ballad opera, which originated in early 18-century England, was a parody stage work. Meant to make fun of Italian opera, ballad opera was comprised of tunes of known ballads and spoken dialogue. This genre was also produced in neighboring Scotland and Ireland, as well as the United States. *The Beggar's Opera* (1728) by English poet and dramatist John Gay (1685–1732) is the most popular example.

In Germany, the *singspiel* (song-play) of the 18th century utilized spoken German dialogue and folk-like singing with a lighthearted, magical, or moralistic plot line. Mozart's *Die Entführung aus dem Serail* (The abduction from the seraglio) (1782) is a prime example. The *zauberoper* (magic opera), a *singspiel* of the 18th and early 19th centuries, featured stage machinery and spectacle as well as magical themes. Mozart's *Die Zauberflöte* (The magic flute) (1791) is a zauberoper. The 19th-century *spieloper* (opera play), a German comic opera, is closely related to the *singspiel*. *Die lustigen Weiber von Windsor* (The merry wives of Windsor) (1849) by German composer Otto Nicolai (1810–1849) is a spieloper.

The French *opéra bouffe* of the middle to late 19th century consisted of spoken dialogue and carefree music. The genre was meant for entertainment and satire, as in *Orphée aux enfers* (Orpheus in the underworld) (1858) and *La vie parisienne* (Parisian life) (1866) by German-born French composer Jacques Offenbach (1819–1880). In contrast, the *grand opéra* is a grandiose work in five acts, of which *Les Huguenots* (1836) by German composer Giacomo Meyerbeer (1791–1864) is an example that has had staying power. Meyerbeer's orchestral accompaniment of the chorus and soloists tends to be on the heavy side. *Aida* (1871) by Giuseppe Verdi (1813–1901) is an *opera ballo* (opera dance), an Italian version of the grand opéra.

The Italian *semiseria* (half-serious) opera of the early 19th century—a work that combined a mixture of comedy and tragedy—usually had a happy ending. Rossini's *La gazza ladra* (The thieving magpie) (1817) and Donizetti's *Linda di Chamounix* (1842) are semiseria operas.

The German *liederspiel* (song-play) of the early 19th century includes songs that use pre-existing words set to new music. Johann Friedrich Reichardt (1752–1814) composed the first liederspiel, *Lieb' und Treue* (Love and loyalty), in 1800. The *märchenoper* (fairytale opera), sometimes called *feenmärchen*, *märchenspiel*, *volksmärchen*, or *féerie*, was a popular 19th-century German operatic genre for composers such as Engelbert Humperdinck (1854–1921) with his *Hänsel und Gretel* (1893).

The operetta of the mid-19th through the mid-20th centuries was a light opera with spoken dialogue, dance, and melodic songs. Austrian Johann Strauss II (1825–1899) wrote *Die Fledermaus* (The bat) in 1874, and the English duo Gilbert and Sullivan (dramatist William Schwenck Gilbert (1836–1911) and composer Arthur Sullivan (1842–1900)) created operettas with a satirical emphasis, such as *The Pirates of Penzance* (1879).

After *Lohengrin* (1850), Wagner labeled his operas "music dramas." The music drama provided a total fusion of all arts with all of the arts on equal footing. The subject matter was usually grounded in Arthurian or Germanic folklore. The orchestra was grand in size and sound, and played an integral role in the storyline by performing repeated themes associated with a character, place, or idea called a *leitmotif* (leading motive). The music was intentionally dissonant, and, especially in later music dramas such as *Tristan und Isolde* (1865), Wagner made the transition between aria and recitative seamless, as if to provide a never-ending melody.

The *verismo* (realism) literary movement affected late 19th-century Italian opera. The verismo opera, a melodrama, is represented most clearly in *Pagliacci* (Clowns) (1892) by Ruggero Leoncavallo (1857–1919) and *Cavalleria rusticana* (Rustic chivalry) (1890) by Pietro Mascagni (1863–1945). These works portray the reality of rural and poor society in a musical, dramatic, and visual way, and their texts were based on novels.

Nationalist opera in Eastern Europe developed out of a musical movement in which composers sought to create music that utilized their native language, folk songs, dances, or subject matter based on their national identity and history. Russian composer Mikhail Glinka (1804–1857) composed a nationalist opera, *A Life for the Tsar* (1836), and other Russians followed suit, including Modest Mussorgsky (1839–1881) with his *Boris Godunov* (1872). Hungarian Ferenc Erkel (1810–1893) composed operas with historical storylines, such as *Hunyadi László* (1844). *Bluebeard's Castle* (1911) by Béla Bartók (1881–1945) is the best-known Hungarian opera. Czech nationalist opera included *The Bartered Bride* (1865) by Bedřich Smetana (1824–1884), *Rusalka* (1900) by Antonín Dvořák (1841–1904), and, in the 20th century, *Jenůfa* (1903) by Leoš Janáček (1854–1928). Semen Hulak-Artemovsky (1813–1873), the first Ukrainian opera composer, wrote his *Zaporozhets za Dunayem* (A cossack beyond the Danube) in 1863. In Poland, Stanisław Moniuszko (1819–1872) composed a four-act opera, *The Haunted Manor* (1864). Nationalist tendencies continued into the 20th century with Azerbaijani composer Uzeyir Hajibeyov (1885–1948) and his opera *Leyli and Majnun* (1908), considered to be the Muslim world's first opera, and *Absalom and Eteri* (1919) by Georgian composer Zakaria Paliashvili (1871–1933).

French symbolism, a literary movement of the late 19th and early 20th centuries, affected opera. Symbolist opera related the music to the words, an object, a person, or emotion. *Pelléas et Mélisande* (1902) by Claude Debussy (1862–1918) is set to playwright Maurice Maeterlinck's symbolist play of the same name (1893) and features music that symbolizes objects such as doves and fountains via a motif (a recurring musical fragment).

Expressionist opera took its cue from the earlier German movement in poetry and painting in which the creator presented an artwork from a subjective perspective. Distortion and deep emotional exploration are key traits, as are violence and volatile behavior. The monodrama (single play) that involved one main character was a type of expressionist opera created by Austrian Arnold Schoenberg (1874–1951). His *Erwartung* (Expectation) (1909) is an example, as is *La Voix humaine* (The human voice) (1959) by French composer Francis Poulenc (1899–1963). *Wozzeck* (1922) by Austrian Alban Berg (1885–1935) and *Il prigioniero* (The prisoner) (1948) by Luigi Dallapiccola (1904–1975) are expressionist operas. The *zeitoper* (opera of the times) of the 1920s and 1930s usually dealt with relevant socio-political issues. *Jonny spielt auf* (Jonny plays) (1927) by Austrian Ernst Krenek (1900–1991), the satire *Neues vom Tage* (News of the day) (1929) by Paul Hindemith (1895–1963), and *Die Bürgschaft* (The pledge) (1932) by Kurt Weill (1900–1950) are of the zeitoper genre.

Chinese classical opera of the 20th century was influenced by Western operatic styles but made use of the Chinese language. An example is *The White Haired Girl* (1945) by Yan Jinxuan (1924–). This is not to be confused with *Jīngjù* (Peking opera), which is a much older and nationalistic theatrical form that utilizes song, dance, speech, and combat.

A 20th-century opera that used a smaller orchestra in a reduced setting was called *chamber opera*. Some examples are *The Rake's Progress* (1951) by Russian composer Igor Stravinsky (1882–1971) and *The Turn of the Screw* (1954) by British composer Benjamin Britten (1913–1976). Politically focused operas appeared throughout the 20th century, such as *Intolleranza 1960* (1961) by Italian Luigi Nono (1924–1990), *Nixon in China* (1987) by American John Adams (1947–), and *The Doctor of Myddfai* (1996) by English composer Peter Maxwell Davies (1934–).

Because opera began during a time when microphones did not exist, singers had to project their voices loudly enough to be heard over the orchestra. Operatic singing requires formal training with a strong emphasis on breath control and beautiful tone. Singers are classified into a number of *Fachs* (voice types) based on their agility, power, timbre (quality of the sound), and *tessitura* (vocal range at which the voice sounds the strongest). Female voice types include the contralto, mezzo-soprano, and soprano (with subtypes coloratura, soubrette, lyric, spinto, and dramatic soprano). Some of the male voice types are the bass, bass-baritone, baritone, tenor, German heldentenor (heroic tenor), and countertenor. There is also the castrato (a male singer who was neutered early in his life in order to retain a higher singing voice), made famous by the 18th-century Italian castrato singer Farinelli (1705–1782).

Before the Classical period (1750–1820), male castratos or any female vocal type sang the role of the female protagonist. The role of the male protagonist was also sometimes cast for the castrato singer. The French preferred an *haute-contre* (high tenor voice) to that of the castrato for their male roles. After the mid-18th century, roles were usually cast as follows: female sopranos as the female protagonist, mezzo-sopranos as other main characters, contraltos as pants or trouser roles (dressed as a man), tenors as the male protagonist, and baritones and basses as comic or supporting roles.

The early operas of the late 16th and 17th centuries were meant for private audiences at court; however, during the Baroque period (1600–1750), the general public viewed opera in theaters and opera houses. As the technological industry boomed in the 20th century, famous opera singers were able to reach a larger audience segment via radio, recordings, and (later) television performances. Singers such as Enrico Caruso, Maria Callas, Franco Corelli, Jussi Björling, and later Leontyne Price, Joan Sutherland, José Carreras, Luciano Pavarotti, Jessye Norman, and Plácido Domingo rose to operatic fame.

It was common practice for opera houses to present translated productions so the regional audience members could understand the language. However, by the 1950s, scholarly preferences shifted in terms of the importance of authenticity and use of the original language and libretto. Filmed and televised productions covered this concern by displaying subtitles on the screen. Beginning in the 1980s, surtitles or supertitles were used at opera houses, sometimes on a screen above the stage or on a small screen in front of each seat.

In order to appeal to a broader audience, opera companies have presented their works outside of the opera house, sometimes in an outdoor arena. Other modern tactics include making a company's website more vibrant and appealing, and offering low ticket prices for students. Beginning in 2006, a fairly successful measure has been the *Live in HD* series for The Metropolitan Opera (The Met), in which some of the opera season's live performances are broadcast to local movie theaters. This effort has provided more people with a type of live performance experience without having to attend and pay for tickets to one of the expensive productions at The Met. This series has reached an international audience because hundreds of movie theaters offer this program. Some companies have offered online download or live viewing of their opera productions. For example, as of 2015, The Opera Platform, a three-year online project, has offered free, live viewing of productions given by 15 European companies from 12 countries, and it provides subtitles in six languages.

The expense of opera production and performance is such that some European opera houses rely on public subsidies from taxpayers. Other donations for opera houses internationally come from corporations, individuals, grants, foundations, and government agencies. Contemporary operas are generally not as long-lasting or accepted by the general public, so opera companies strive to support new commissions while recognizing that the older operas of the 18th and 19th centuries have the most staying power and moneymaking potential. Because opera is currently more affordable and understandable, opera companies have fewer barriers in the way of gaining relationships with new audience members while preserving their current ones.

Emily A. Bell

See also: Bartók, Béla; Classical Music, European; Icelandic Ballads; Jingju; Singspiel; Taiwanese Opera

Further Reading

Bokina, John. 1997. *Opera and Politics: From Monteverdi to Henze.* New Haven, CT: Yale University Press.

Donington, Robert. 1990. *Opera and Its Symbols: The Unity of Words, Music and the Myth.* New Haven, CT: Yale University Press.

Groos, Arthur, and Roger Parker, eds. 2014. *Reading Opera.* Princeton, NJ: Princeton University Press.

Hamm, Charles. 1966. *Opera.* Boston: Allyn and Bacon.

Kerman, Joseph. 1952. *Opera as Drama.* New York: Random House.

Lindenberger, Herbert. 1998. *Opera in History from Monteverdi to Cage.* Stanford, CA: Stanford University Press.

Original Dixieland Jazz Band

The Original Dixieland Jazz (or Jass) Band was a group of white musicians from New Orleans who helped to popularize the term "New Orleans jazz" and "Dixieland" in the late 1910s. *Dixieland* is a style of early jazz that developed at the start of the 20th century in New Orleans and was later spread, by bands such as the Original Dixieland Jazz Band, to Chicago and New York. In 1917, the Original Dixieland Jazz Band provided the first-ever recordings of jazz music, which triggered the propagation of jazz throughout the United States. The band's contribution to the history of jazz music is significant but, while the band's name is well known, people generally know little about the individuals who played in it or their music.

In 1916, five musicians from New Orleans, led by trumpeter Nick LaRocca (1889–1961), came together to form the Original Dixieland Jazz Band. In addition to LaRocca, the band consisted of clarinetist Larry Shields, trombonist Eddie Edwards, pianist Harry Ragas, and drummer Tony Sbarbaro. These musicians, who were largely self-taught, experimented with style and technique to develop a playing style that differed significantly from their ragtime origins. Jazz, instead of demanding that performers play straight notes as written, allowed players to improvise arrangements that distinguish one performer or performance from another through the anticipation of beats, swinging, grace notes, an enriched harmony, and the development of brief motivic units into a more continuous line. LaRocca characterized himself as "an ignorant scholar of music" who was fortunate enough to have been exposed to opera and classical music during his youth. Through opera he experienced how different melodies could be played against one another, and he discussed the Original Dixieland Jazz Band's music in relation to this idea, noting that "what we had was nothing but a conversation of instruments. You take the *Livery Stable Blues*, for instance . . . they're three distinct melodies working together."

In 1916, LaRocca took the band to Chicago and on to New York in 1917, where they began making recordings. The Original Dixieland Jazz Band initially recorded two sides in early 1917 for Columbia Records, but the label failed to release the

---

New Orleans and Dixieland

The birthplace of jazz, New Orleans lays an important claim to several genres of American popular music. This is due to the city's importance as an industrial port during the latter half of the 19th century and the early 20th century. Around 1900, New Orleans was one of the busiest ports in the United States (second only to New York City) and was the gateway to the major commerce shipping routes in the Caribbean. The city thus became a confluence of cultures and peoples, and it was this intermingling that led to music of various cultures—including French, Acadian, Spanish, Caribbean Creole, English, African American, and Native American—cross-pollinating to create genres such as Dixieland and early jazz. Perhaps the most iconic of these meeting places was Congo Square, where, despite Jim Crow laws throughout the American South, one could hear a white string band, African drumming group, jazz group, and Dixieland group sharing the park on any given Sunday.

The Original Dixieland Jazz Band, pictured in 1920, made the first jazz band recordings in 1917. (GAB Archive/Redferns)

albums. The Victor Record company later recorded *Livery Stable Blues* and *Dixie Jass Band One-Step*, which triggered the great Jazz Age. These first recordings sold more than 1 million copies and the band became nationally famous within a few months. The Original Dixieland Jazz Band began touring military bases and by 1919 had found their way to London, taking the jazz craze with them.

The Original Dixieland Jazz Band's music was revolutionary: their unique sound was inimitable and their mass of admirers helped them become the most highly paid dance orchestra in the world in the late 1910s. Despite the obvious African American origins of both ragtime and the new jazz style, LaRocca's attitude toward these origins was incredibly dismissive—an attitude typical of early Dixieland musicians which was central to their perception of their music and culture. Supporting this attitude, it is a fact that until the 1920s, white musicians often had far greater access to performance opportunities than black bands did, and a white band playing jazz would inevitably be much more popular with white audiences than any black musicians would, at a time when racial tension was high and racist attitudes were common.

The recording of jazz was an important move for popularizing the genre, and allowed jazz to spread and evolve more quickly than any previous new style of music. It also proved significant to the popularity of the phonograph: sales rose from $27.1 million in 1914 to $158.7 million in 1919. Records stimulated the search for artistic examples and models of jazz, and recordings soon became the principal educational tool for young jazz musicians across America. LaRocca was the first Dixieland musician to make a conscious effort to record music and to obtain copyrights and, despite the band's attitude to the African American origins of jazz, the Original Dixieland Jazz Band proved vital in the history of jazz in that the style, in part, owes its mass popularity to them through their readily accessible recordings and performances.

C. M. Gregory-Thomas

See also: Dixieland; Jazz; Joplin, Scott; Ragtime

Further Reading

Brunn, H. O. 1960. *The Story of the Original Dixieland Jazz Band*. Baton Rouge: Louisiana State University Press.

Peretti, B. W. 1992. *The Creation of Jazz: Music, Race, and Culture in Urban America*. Urbana: University of Illinois Press.

Suhor, C. 2001. *Jazz in New Orleans: The Postwar Years through 1970*. London: Scarecrow Press.

Ottoman Classical Music

Ottoman classical music is called *Klasik Türk Müzigi* or *Türk Sanat Müzigi* in Turkish, and those terms refer to music that was produced by Sufi groups (in particular, the *Mevlevi* or *Mawlawi*), as well as in the Ottoman court (Bates, 2011, p. 31). The term *sanat* is often translated as "art," but it is originally *sana'ah* in Arabic, which means "craft" more than art. Like the other classical music of the Middle East, Ottoman music is based on a system of modal scales called *maqamat* (*maqam* in singular). Turkish classical music not only includes the maqam system that originated in Byzantium, Iran, and Arabia, but also includes influences from Central Asian minstrel traditions called *'ashiq* in Turkish. *'Ashiq* is Turkish (and Arabic) for a lover and in this instance means a lover of God. Most *'ashiq* poetry is about humanity's love for God, and is often associated with Sufi music, which has been for centuries the music of the Turkish minstrels who sing both the works of others and their own. It provides the Turkish people with the oldest sung poetry that is now part of sanat music. It connects classical music of the city to the rural *türkü* (popular folk-inspired) songs.

Ottoman music began as Saljuq music (the Saljuqs of Rum ruled from 1077–1308 CE) based in Konya with the compositions of the mystics, Jalal al-Din Rumi (1207–1273) and Yunus Emre (1238–1320). Rumi, founder of the Mevlevi order of Sufis, lived and died in Konya; he emphasized the reed flute called *ney* or *nay* in that it represented the breathing of a human with its sound and was used as the writing tool or *qalam* for the Qur'an. Emre did not belong to any one order, but joined *dhikr* (remembering God) of Turkish Sufi groups including the Mevlevi and the Bektashi of Haji Bektashi Vali (1209–1271). Yunus composed poems in Turkish, whereas during his time, other mystics wrote poems in Arabic or Persian; therefore, he was more like the Turkish Anatolian bards or *'ashiq*. He was followed by other Turkish mystics such as Pir Sultan Abdal (1480–1550), who is among the most important figures of the 'Alevi, a heterodox Shi'ite group. The Ottomans, originally a Beylik (principality) of the Saljuqs, ruled their vast empire from 1299 until 1922 and inherited the vast musical heritage of the Arabs, Persians, and Turks as well as of the Byzantines who fell to the Ottomans in 1453.

During the Ottoman period, several major centers of music developed, in Istanbul, Aleppo, Baghdad, Damascus, Cairo, and Tunis. As noted by the musician Julien Weiss, musicians used "a learned synthesis of Byzantine, Persian, Arab, and Turkish influences" that resulted an "incomparable degree of richness and eclecticism" (Weiss, 2006, p. 20). Arabs were often brought or were sent to Istanbul to perform for various Sultans. In the 19th century, the Ottoman governor (*Khedive*) paid for the Cairo school, which closely collaborated with Istanbul. The Egyptian singer Yusuf al-Manyalawi (1847–1911) sang for both the Khedive Isma'il Pasha (who ruled from 1863–1879) and the Sultan 'Abd al-Hamid II (who ruled from 1876–1909).

Generally, in Middle Eastern modal music, modes are divided between principal and secondary modes that are further divided into branches (Farmer, 2001, pp. 203–204). In Arabic music, there are 24 main modes, but in Turkish music the number is much larger, with up to 962 modes and more than 52 pitches (Sadak, 2006, p. 22). Arab (Syrian in particular) and Turkish classical music are very closely related, and it is hard to distinguish the two; in fact, this corpus is frequently called Arab-Turkish court music (Weiss, 2006, p. 17).

Composers invented modes as time went on: the Ottoman Sultan Salim III (ruled 1789–1807), a major composer of his day, invented 15 new modes (Ayangil, 2008, p. 11). Modes were named for the note that was the prominent/dominant (*güclü perdesi* in Turkish) or final note (*durak nagmesi* in Turkish) of a tetrachord or pentachord that serve as a "tonal anchor" (Feldman, 2001, p. 22; Racy, 2003, p. 97). In Ottoman music, a piece is made up of a suite (*fasil*) that is composed of an instrumental prelude called a *peshrev*; a short four-line classical poem in either Turkish or Persian, and in some cases in Arabic, called a *beste*; and then an instrumental conclusion called a *saz sema'i*. The poetry is called *rubi'at*, of which the most famous are those of 'Umar Khayyam (1048–1131), who lived under the Saljuq Sultan Malik Shah (ruled 1072–1092), and other vocal pieces, often of Sufi origin, are called *sema'i*. The various parts are joined by improvisation called a *taqsīm* that features specific instruments. During the 19th and early 20th centuries, other vocal pieces were incorporated into the fasil, such as *sharqi* (light art songs) and *gazel*, love songs that were popular at the *gazino* or nightclubs (Feldman, 2001, p. 31).

The instruments used have changed greatly since early Ottoman times; this was noted by the Moldovan prince Dimitrie Cantemir (1673–1723) (*Kantemiroglu* in Turkish). He produced one of the most extensive collections of early Ottoman music, called *Kitabü Ilmü'l-Musiki 'ala Vechi'l-Hurûfât* and known as the *Kantermiroglu Edvari* (the Cantermir essays), which "preserves over 350 instrumental pieces of the 16th and 17th centuries" (Feldman, 2004, p. 16). He noted that the instruments depicted in Turkish/Persian miniatures, mainly of Persian and Central Asian origin, had largely been replaced by European types such as the violin. These older instruments were the *çeng*, a harp with 24 bronze strings; the *kopuz*, a short-necked lute with four double strings; the *sherud*, a deep-sounding *'ud* that was tuned an octave lower than the regular 'ud; the *kemançe*, a spiked fiddle with three horsehair strings; the *santur*, a hammered zither; and the *miskal*, a panflute of 22 reed pipes. In addition, the *qānūn* strings changed from bronze to animal gut, thereby greatly changing the sound. Of the original instruments, the ney (an end-blown reed flute), the *daire* (a frame drum), and the *nakkare* (a small kettle drum) remained unchanged. These are the main instruments used in Mevlevi music.

Around the same time, 'Ali Ufki Bey (1610–1675), born in Poland as Vojciech Bobowski, converted from Judaism to Islam and wrote an encyclopedia of Turkish music and instruments called *Mecmua-i Saz ü Sôz* (Encyclopedia of instruments and songs). This writing was different in that it used Western notation; it is the oldest surviving documentation of Ottoman music with notation (Karakaya, 2004, p. 18). Bey and Cantemir were in Istanbul just before or during of the great flowering of Ottoman culture called the Tulip Age (1718–1730). The Tulip Age coincided with the rule of Sultan Ahmad III (ruled 1703–1730) and the life of the great Ottoman composer Buhuri-zade Mustafa Efendi, called Itri (1640?–1712). He was the first Ottoman composer to take a more Turkish approach to music. Before him, Persian had been the main influence on Ottoman music, but, as Ra'uf Yetka Bey wrote, "Itri was able to eliminate this influence completely and has the honor of creating a pure Turkish style" (Öncel, 2008, p. 10). Itri was among the most famous composers of his time; in addition, he was named music teacher to the women of the palace, music teacher to the famous Palace School, and chief soloist to the Sultan's palace choir. His works number between 1,000 and 2,000 and include such masterpieces as *Neva Kar*, which was written on poetry by the Persian poet Hafiz of Shiraz (1315–1390).

Itri was followed by one of the composer Sultans, Salim III (ruled 1789–1807), who wrote around 103 pieces that can be verified (Öncel, 2008, p. 34). His interest in music included Western forms, and in 1797 he had the first European performance in Istanbul that included the performance of an opera (Öncel, 2008, p. 30). Under the pen name of Ilhami, he composed poetry of various types in what is called "simple Turkish," understandable to all social classes. He encouraged known musicians to codify music and solidify the maqamat into more understandable forms; as a result, he developed 15 new ones (Öncel, 2008, p. 31). He also made changes in military music, introducing Western military bands and bugle calls to replace the *mehter* bands of the Janissaries as part of his reforms called *nizam-i cedid* (new order). Ottoman music became even more heavily influenced by Western styles in the 19th century as the Sultans themselves became interested in Western music. In 1828, Giuseppe Donizetti was invited to Istanbul and establish an opera school there (Bates, 2011, p. 33).

Nonetheless, Ottoman music remained important not only in Turkey, but also in the Arab provinces of the empire, long after the European powers France and Britain took control of them. Within Turkey, Ottoman music survived the Atatürk period, both after the replacement of Arabic script with Latin script in 1928 and the linguistic "cleansing" of Arabic and Persian words from Turkish in 1932. Performers such as Haci Arif Bey (1831–1885) and Tanburi Cemil Bey (1873–1916) had students such as Münir Nurettin Selçuk (1900–1981), who in turn taught the likes of Zeki Müren (1931–1996), Müzeyyen Senar (1918–2015), and Bulent Ersoy

(1952–present), who have preserved and maintained classical styles for today. Atatürk liked the voices of Müzeyyen Senar and Safiye Ayla, both trained in classical Turkish music, and in recent decades a CD of his favorite songs was released as part of the *Archive Series of Legendary Voices*. Recently, in Turkey, there has been a revival of interest in Ottoman music by the younger generations who seek to connect themselves to their past.

John A. Shoup

See also: Arab Classical Music; Iranian Classical Music; Malouf; Ney; Oud; Qānūn; Sufism, Music of

Further Reading

Ayangil, Ruhi. 2008. Booklet notes. *Bestekâr III. Selim Hân* [CD]. Istanbul: Istanbul Büyükshehir Belediyesi.

Bates, Eliot. 2011. *Music in Turkey*. Oxford: Oxford University Press.

Emre, Yunus. 2015. *Turkish Classical Music* [CD]. Washington, DC: Smithsonian Folkways Archives, UNESCO Collection.

Farmer, Henry George. 2001. *A History of Arabian Music*. New Delhi: Goodword Books.

Feldman, Walter. 2001. Booklet notes. *Volume IV, Ottoman Suite: Lazlar—Music of the Sultans, Sufis and Seraglio* [CD]. New York: Traditional Crossroads.

Feldman, Walter. 2004. Booklet notes. *Bezmârâ Mecmua dan Saz ve Söz* [CD]. Istanbul: Kalan Müzik Yapim.

Karakaya, Fikret. 2004. Booklet notes. *Bezmârâ Mecmua dan Saz ve Söz* [CD]. Istanbul: Kalan Müzik Yapim.

Öncel, Misra, ed. 2008. *Ottoman Sounds: Magnificent Ottoman Composers*. Istanbul: Boyut Publishing Group.

Racy, A. J. 2003. *Making Music in the Arab World*. Cambridge: Cambridge University Press.

Sadak, Sami. 2006. Booklet notes. *Al Kindi: Parfums Ottomans: Musiques de Cour Arabo-Ottoman* [CD]. Montreuil, France: Chant du Monde.

Sultan Bestekârlar: Turkish Classical Music Composed by Ottoman Sultans [CD]. 1999. Istanbul: Kalan Müzik Yapim.

Weiss, Julien Jalal al-Din. 2006. Booklet notes. *Al Kindi: Parfums Ottomans: Musiques de Cour Arabo-Ottoman* [CD]. Montreuil, France: Chant du Monde.

Oud

The *oud* is a short-necked, fretless lute common in certain musical cultures of the Middle East, the Levant, North Africa, and the Mediterranean. It assumes a central role especially in Arab music, where it is considered the king of musical instruments. It also occupies a prominent place in the traditional music of countries such as Turkey, Greece, Armenia, Azerbaijan, and Iran. The Arabic name *al-'ud* means "wood," and was most likely given to describe its construction entirely of wooden components. The wooden soundboard distinguishes the oud from other plucked lutes that have a soundboard made of stretched animal skin. Another key feature of the oud is its short, fretless neck, which allows for the flexible intonation necessary for the ideal execution of the traditional modal system known as *maqam* (*makam*, in Turkish). The short length of the neck also differentiates it from other wooden, long-necked, and fretted lutes such as the *tanbur, bağlama, buzuq,* and *setar*. Its presence at the Andalusian courts beginning in the ninth century is believed to have led to its gradual dissemination into Europe in the form of the lute; the name al-ʻud eventually came to be pronounced "lauta," "luthe," and "lute."

Historically, the oud has gone through stages of development with respect to its number of strings and their tuning. The most common variety in use today has 11 strings, with five double-coursed unison notes and one single-coursed note. The single-coursed note is the lowest-sounding pitch on the instrument. The strings are arranged mainly in fourths, with two tuning systems currently in general use, Arab and Turkish. Arab tuning is most commonly C-F-A-d-g-c, whereas Turkish tuning is a whole step higher and is arranged in all fourths: C#-F#-B-e-a-d. Although variations on these tunings exist, these two are commonly accepted as the defaults on which the others are based. Through its history, the material used for the strings has changed from horsehair, to gut in later times, to the quality nylon and silver-wound silk strings in use today. The plectrum, called *mızrap* in Turkish and Persian and *risha* in Arabic, was in the medieval period made from an eagle feather. Later on, performers used different materials such as cherry bark, hard leather, cow horn, and tortoise shell. Recently, picks made of quality plastics have also begun to be used.

The bowl is constructed of 17 to 22 wooden ribs curved over a pear-shaped mold and separated from one another by thin wooden strips. The ribs are made of a variety of woods, the most common being maple, walnut, mahogany, yew, and rosewood. The highest quality instruments use wood that has been aged for at least several months. Recently, more exotic woods have been introduced from locations such as South America, Africa, and India, such as Brazilian snakewood, African padouk, and Indian palisander. The ribs are arranged either all of a single type or a combination of two different, contrasting types of wood alternated for visual effect. This ribbed construction, first developed by oud-making luthiers, has since been incorporated in other instruments, including the bağlama, buzuq, European lute, and tanbur (Bates, 2011, p. 35). In addition to their visual impact, the choice of wood type for the bowl has an impact on the tone of the instrument: harder woods give a more brittle sound and softer woods give a more mellow tone.

The soundboard is made of two thinly-cut spruce planes glued together in the center. One main sound hole is cut into the center of the soundboard, with two smaller sound holes on either side of it. The sound holes are decorated with elaborate, hand-carved rosettes made of cow horn, ivory, or bone. The rosette designs are usually intricate geometric patterns that use floral motifs or calligraphy. On the inside of the soundboard are bracing patterns that are critical to the projection and resonance of the instrument. There is also a small pick guard made of tortoise shell to protect the soundboard from being damaged by the plectrum. The neck is attached at the joint between the bowl and the soundboard, and its fingerboard is made of ebony. The pegbox is attached to the end of the fingerboard and bent back at approximately a 45-degree angle. With its curved bowl, wooden soundboard, carved rosettes, fretless neck, and bent-back pegbox, the oud is prized for its visual beauty as much as its distinctive, plucked wooden tone. For this reason, luthiery (the art of lute-making) is considered alongside performance as being among the highest of art forms.

Concomitant with the tuning differences, there are distinctions in the construction of the Arab and Turkish-style ouds: the Arab is somewhat larger than the Turkish and uses a different bracing pattern on the soundboard. Additionally, within Arab construction, there are two main styles, the Iraqi and the Syrian/Egyptian. The Iraqi oud has an oblong soundboard and bowl construction, and the sound holes are in the shape of ovals without rosettes.

The craft of luthiery is central to the culture of oud performance practice and music. Traditionally, the luthier's shop has been an important location not only for the making, repair, and sale of instruments, but also for the dissemination of musical knowledge within an oral tradition. This holds true for both the making of instruments and performance practice. Would-be luthiers are trained as apprentices to the master, learning the craft in close proximity to the master until they develop the ability to establish their own practice. The shop also serves as a gathering place for performers, and at any one time a mix of musicians from early beginners to experienced amateur and professional musicians may come to test instruments and disseminate knowledge (Bates, 2011, pp. 36–37).

Manolis Venios (1845–1915), also known as Manol, was born into a Greek family living in Istanbul. During the Ottoman period, Istanbul (then known as Constantinople), was a cosmopolitan area, with communities of Turks, Greeks, Armenians, and Jews living together. Manol's original profession was varnisher, but he later gained a reputation as a builder of ouds of exceptional quality. He took on a number of apprentices, many of whom went on to become famous luthiers in their own right. Manol's ouds today rank among the most highly prized of all Turkish instruments. Nahat ouds were made by at least two generations of a family of craftsmen in Damascus, Syria. Abdo Nahat (1860–1941) followed his father, George Yousef Nahat, into the oud-making business. Abdo and his brother Roufan first began building ouds in 1880 in the family workshop, and their ouds bear the mark "Ikhwan Nahat" (Nahat Brothers). In 1938, Abdo immigrated to Brazil, where he continued to build instruments until his death three years later. Abdo Nahat's ouds are generally regarded as the finest Arab ouds ever made.

Performers of the oud are recognized for their mastery of modal improvisation, or *taqsīm* (*taksim*), and their ability to embellish a song or instrumental composition with idiomatic ornamentation. In the early 20th century, distinctive national playing styles emerged, centered primarily in Cairo and Istanbul. Toward the middle of the century, a third, Iraqi school centered in Baghdad became prominent. These schools, however, provide only rough models for playing styles, and there is considerable influence among them.

The Egyptian school is associated with virtuosi such as Muhammad el-Qasabji (1892–1966), Riyad el-Sunbati (1906–1981), and Farid el-Atrache (ca. 1915–1974). Each of these performers were considered masters in the art of taqsīm and ornamentation, and they were also important in the composition of the "long song," a genre that reached its peak in the radio performances of Umm Kulthumm in the 1950s, as well as in music for movies in Egyptian cinema of the early 20th century.

Of these three, Farid el-Atrache was perhaps most popular, due to his exceptional singing voice and his ability as an actor in films featuring his own compositions. Born in Syria, his family emigrated to Egypt in the immediate aftermath of World War I. He studied music at a conservatory and oud privately as an apprentice under el-Sunbati. In the 1930s, he began his career as an oud player at the Egyptian national radio. His taqsīm playing incited musical ecstasy, known in Arabic as *tarab*, in his audiences due to his fast and powerful plucking technique and exciting cadences, or *qaflat*; recordings of his improvisations often feature large crowds cheering for their favorite parts. In his films, he nearly always took the role of the romantic lead who would attract love interests with music. Some of his films include *Intisar al-Shabab* (1941) and *Lahn al-Kholoud* (1952). Today, the Palestinian-American virtuoso Simon Shaheen (1955–) is a major proponent of this performance style and repertoire.

The Turkish school actually is comprised of a combination of ethnic Greeks, Armenians, and Turks, many of whom lived and performed together in nightclubs in Istanbul, known as *gazino*, as well as for the Turkish national radio. The style was developed during the first half of the 20th century by performers such as Yorgo Bacanos (1900–1977), "Udi" Hrant Kenkulian (ca. 1900–1978), and Kadri Şençalar (1912–1989), among others. The playing styles of these virtuosi are associated with what has become known as *Türk Sanat Müziği* (Turkish art music). In such a genre, there would be an extended suite of songs, modal improvisations, and instrumental compositions known in Turkish as *fasıl*, and the oud playing is characterized by technical virtuosity, extensive ornamentation, and a rapid plucking style with quick runs and fills-in between vocal phrases of songs.

A later category of Turkish oud performance developed in the second half of the 20th century and is exemplified by Cinuçen Tanrıkorur (1938–2000), who established a unique style based on the Turkish tanbur. Other great mid–20th-century virtuosi who developed the instrument in an artistic and soloistic direction include Şerif Muhittin Targan (1892–1967) and Mutlu Torun (1942–). Targan was born in Istanbul into a wealthy family that traces its lineage back to the Prophet Muhammad. He aimed to elevate the oud to respectability such that it could be seen as a virtuosic solo instrument. He served as the dean of the Baghdad conservatory from 1936 to 1937, and married Turkish singer Safiye Ayla (1907–1998) in 1950.

In the middle of the 20th century, Munir Bashir (1930–1997) helped to develop the Iraqi school of oud playing. He took lessons from Şerif Muhittin Targan and was influenced by him to further develop the instrument as a solo instrument. During the 1970s, he began to perform concerts of only solo improvisation, thus inventing the genre of the solo oud recital (Poché, 2002). In the other traditional styles, the oud played a role primarily as an accompaniment to song or as part of an ensemble for an instrumental composition. It would only play solo during the modal improvisations. Bashir expanded on this solo improvisation, making it the focal point of the recital, which would consist of several taqsīm linked together to form a larger composition or suite. The most prominent musician to continue in this tradition today is Naseer Shamma (1963–). Shamma's concerts, like those of Bashir, consist of a string of improvisations that are performed in front of a respectfully silent and contemplative audience, thus contrasting with the earlier 20th-century Egyptian and Turkish styles.

The oud has enjoyed a prominent reputation in history as an instrument of legendary character and medieval scientific significance. It is said that in the seventh century, Barbat, master musician to Husrev Perviz, the last shah of the Iranian Sasanid dynasty, played the instrument that bore his name, "BARBAT," for the shah while he was seated in his garden and was immediately taken into royal service. After the barbat passed to the Arabs in the seventh century, it took the name *al-oud*, which means "wood" in Arabic. Later Arab and Persian authors attributed the invention of the oud to Pythagoras or Plato and claim that Plato was a brilliant performer who was able to affect his audience so strongly that he could first calm them, then put them to sleep, and finally awaken them with his music (Grame, 1972). The ninth-century Islamic philosopher, Hisham ibn al-Kalbi (d. 819 CE), mentioned that the oud was invented by a son of Abel, called Lamech. After a long life, Lamech finally had a son who died when he was five years old, and Lamech grieved sorely for him. He took the boy's body and hung him on a tree and said: "His form will not depart from my eyes until he falls in pieces, or I die. Then his flesh began to fall from his bones till (only) the thigh remained, with the leg, foot, and toes. So he took a piece of wood, split it, made it thin, and began to arrange one piece on another. Then he made a chest to represent the thigh, a neck to represent the leg, a peg-box the same size as the foot, and pegs like the toes; and to it strings like sinews. Then he began to play on it and weep and lament, until he became blind: and he was the first who sang a lament. What was made was called an oud because it was made from a piece of wood" (Grame, 1972, p. 27).

The oud takes on special significance in other ninth and 10th-century Islamic writings. In these sources, it is a more theoretical instrument rooted in Pythagorean tradition connecting the musical harmony in the proportional division of a string with the harmony that exists in the creation of the universe. Al-Kindi (801–873 CE), in his *al-Musawwitat al-watariyyah*, postulates connections between the strings of the oud, the natural elements, and the humors (Shehadi, 1995, p. 22). Al-Farabi (872–950 CE) also includes an important diagram of the oud in his *Kitab al-Musica al-Kabir*. Both Kindi and Farabi were oud players as well as music theorists.

Adem Merter Birson

See also: Arab Classical Music; Bashir Brothers (Munir and Jamil); Ottoman Classical Music; Taqsīm

Further Reading

Bates, Eliot. 2011. *Music in Turkey*. Oxford: Oxford University Press.

Grame, Theodore. 1972. "The Symbolism of the 'Ūd." *Asian Music* 3(1), 25–34.

Marcus, Scott. 2002. "Music in Performance: *Oud* Lessons with George Michel." In Virginia Danielson, Dwight Reynolds, and Scott Marcus (eds.), *Garland Encyclopedia of World Music; Vol. 6: The Middle East*, 45–46. New York: Routledge.

Poché, Christian. 2002. "Snapshot: Munir Bashir." In Virginia Danielson, Dwight Reynolds, and Scott Marcus (eds.), *Garland Encyclopedia of World Music; Vol. 6: The Middle East*, 622–624. New York: Routledge.

Shehadi, Fadlou. 1995. *Philosophies of Music in Medieval Islam*. Leiden, The Netherlands: Brill.

Owiyo, Suzanna (1975–)

Suzanna Owiyo has become an important artist in African popular music since her debut in 2002. Her influence as a singer, songwriter, guitarist, *nyatiti* player, and activist has made her a household name in Kenya, and a key figure in world music. Her music is inspired by her country, heritage, and commitment to social change. Owiyo has often been compared to American popular music legends Tracy Chapman (1964–) and Nina Simone (1933–2003) due to the social and political messages found in many of her songs. Owiyo sings most of her songs in *dholuo*, her native language. Her music often features the nyatiti, an eight-stringed, plucked lyre with a large resonating chamber that is typically associated with male performers. The nyatiti became a staple of the Benga music movement in Kenya in the 1960s. Owiyo was inspired to learn the nyatiti from her grandfather, and by the world's first female nyatiti player, Eriko Mukoyama (Anyango; 1981–). Owiyo's role as an activist for projects in Africa and around the world has given her the opportunity to meet world leaders such as Nelson Mandela (1918–2013) and President Barack Obama (1961–).

Born on May 10, 1975, in Kasaye village, Nyakach, Kenyan popular music artist Suzanna Owiyo has become an Afro-fusion artist of international fame. *Afro-fusion* is the term given to commercialized Kenyan music that combines elements associated with international pop music and Kenyan traditional music. Owiyo began her career in 1998 as a backup singer for singer-songwriter Sali Oyugi. In 2000, she continued singing back-up for the group Bora Bora Sound, based in Kisumu. After studying at the Kenya Conservatoire of Music, Owiyo began her solo career. Her debut album, *Kisumu 100*, was released in 2002, and earned her a nomination for Most Promising Female Artist at the Kora Music Awards. The following year she won in the same category at the Kisima Awards. The album was released internationally in 2004, retitled *Mama Africa*. That same year, Owiyo performed at the Nobel Peace Prize Concert alongside Andrea Bocelli, Patti LaBelle, and Tony Bennett. In 2007 she released her second album, *Yamu Kudho*. On June 27, 2008, Owiyo joined actors, recording artists, and world leaders at the Nelson Mandela Concert in Hyde Park, London, celebrating the 90th birthday of the South African activist and political figure, as well as his 46664 charity for HIV/AIDS awareness.

Suzanna Owiyo's music reflects the traditions of her Luo heritage, along with the social injustices of her generation. Although many of her compositions have been written with the intention to spark conversations about various world issues, others are meant to honor her homeland. The song that launched her career, "Kisumu 100," is one example. This piece was written for the centennial celebration of the city, and meant as a tribute to Kisumu. The lyrics describe the narrator's desire to return to Kisumu. The song's syncopated rhythms and fingerpicked guitar are representative of Owiyo's style. African musicians adopted Western instruments such as the guitar shortly after the turn of the century, making it a particularly significant addition to Owiyo's music. Owiyo's alto range is frequently stretched no more than an octave in her songs. An example of this is found in the song "Anyango Pod Itin" from her third album, *My Roots*. This piece again features highly syncopated rhythms, as well as the instrument with which Owiyo is most

Kenyan singer-songwriter Suzanna Owiyo performing in 2011. (Samuel Dietz/Getty Images)

associated, the nyatiti. On stage, Owiyo has gained recognition for her high-energy and charismatic performances. Other works by Owiyo include the songs "*Idhe wa kamande*," "Minwa Mary," and the album *Yamo Kudho* (2007).

Along with her music career, Suzanna Owiyo is also involved in many social and political movements. In 2010, Owiyo launched her third album, *My Roots*. The album covered many social issues, such as corrupt politicians, violence against women, and addiction. In February of 2013, Owiyo was named a Goodwill Ambassador for the United Nations Environment Programme. Her song "Be Counted" was written for that organization. As a Goodwill Ambassador, Owiyo has worked on the global initiative to reduce food waste. Owiyo has also been involved with HIV/AIDS prevention, as well as the girl's empowerment campaign "Because I am a girl." The project is run through Plan International, an organization founded in 1937. Owiyo collaborated with a group of African musicians to produce a song for the project. The song, also entitled "Because I am a Girl," was written in an effort to bring awareness to the campaign, which works to end gender-based violence and discrimination in Africa.

Jessica Freyermuth

See also: Afrobeat (Afropop)

Further Reading

Byrne, Jennifer. 2004. "Suzanna Owiyo: Mama Africa." *Sing Out!* 48(3), 112.

Elliott, David J., Stephen J. Messenger, Marissa Silverman, and Kari K. Veblen, eds. 2013. *Community Music Today*. New York: Rowman & Littlefield.

Kalumba, Robert. 2008. "The Night Suzanna Owiyo Performed." *Africa News Service*, October 11. *General OneFile*. http://go.galegroup.com/ps/i.do?id=GALE%7CA1 86805173&v=2.1&u=ksstate_ukans&it=r&p=ITOF&sw=w&asid=6cacc8899312a e5caaee84288c7bb09e.

Kerongo, Grace. 2011. "Suzanna Owiyo's 'My Roots' Launch Attracts Nairobi's Finest!" *Africa News Service*, May 24, 2011. *General OneFile*. http://go.galegroup.com/ps/i .do?id=GALE%7CA257082103&v=2.1&u=ksstate_ukans&it=r&p=ITOF&sw =w&asid=50a9910fb01eb0309ba9477feb3da434.

Maina, Christine Wambui. 2012. "The Repertoire of Kayamba Africa: Contemporary Reworking of Traditional Musics in Nairobi." Master's diss., University of Cape Town.

Mukei, Catherine. 2011. "Suzanna Owiyo Dedicates New Album to Girls." *Africa News Service*, May 13, 2011. *General OneFile*. http://go.galegroup.com/ps/i.do?id=GALE%7CA256237803&v=2.1&u=ksstate_ukans&it=r&p=ITOF&sw=w&asid=05814c4c91f30dca3ee9cc8c1d5a72c2.

Musila, Grace A. 2005. "Age, Power and Sex in Modern Kenya: A Tale of Two Marriages." *Social Identities* 11(2), 113–129.

Owiyo, Suzanna. 2004. *Mama Africa* [CD]. ARC Music Productions B002D63EUW.

Owiyo, Suzanna. 2010. *My Roots* [CD]. Kirkelig Kulturverksted B0042NFBRS.

"UNEP Appoints Singing Sensations Eric Wainaina and Suzanna Owiyo as Kenyan Goodwill Ambassadors" [press release]. 2013. *Africa News Service*, February 21. *General OneFile*. http://go.galegroup.com/ps/i.do?id=GALE%7CA319704577&v=2.1&u=ksstate_ukans&it=r&p=ITOF&sw=w&asid=6308f864a13e99d9c472be8c811f709e.

Pakistan, Music of

Pakistan has long been a crossroads of Asian cultures, and the music of Pakistan reflects its diverse and multi-ethnic history. Music in Pakistan can be broadly classified as classical, regional, or popular, though the line dividing the last two categories is sometimes extremely permeable. Classical, regional, and popular traditions have all been shaped by Persian, Turkish, Arabic, Central and South Asian, and even more Western influences as they have swept across the subcontinent.

Musical practice in Pakistan is part of the larger Indo-Muslim tradition that spans the northern subcontinent. As in India, musicians were traditionally brought up within a *gharana*, a musical school or lineage that defines a characteristic style of performance. Gharanas have been founded around particular genres—such as *ghazal, qawwali, khayal, dhrupad, thummri*—or instruments, but the most famous have historically been centered around a royal court (e.g., Delhi, Gwalior, Patiala, etc.). Within Pakistan, the Patiala gharana especially dominates singing style. A gharana develops around the *ustad-shagird* relationship, also called the *gurukula* system in India, in which a student may live with a teacher for years in order to receive intensive training.

The classical music tradition in Pakistan shares close links with the Hindustani tradition of northern India. As practiced today, it is largely vocal. Two of the most common genres of performance are *dhrupad* and *khayal*. Dhrupad is a rigorous song form famously patronized by the Mughal courts, particularly the court of Akbar in the last half of the 16th century. Though there are many earlier references to a style called "dhrupad," much of the theory and musical material that make up the modern repertoire were developed in the royal courts of Gwalior at the beginning of the 16th century. The dhrupad verse form consists of four lines of text of no fixed length. It is usually performed by a solo vocalist, sometimes a duo, accompanied by the *pakhawaj* drum and a drone usually supplied by two *tamburas* (an unfretted, long-necked lute sounding only the first, fifth, and octave of the performance scale). The performance of the song proper is typically preceded by a long, unmetered improvisation called an *alāp*, during which the singer explores the expressive possibilities of the *raga* to which the text has been set. Traditionally these improvisations could last more than an hour, but with the advent of recording technology at the beginning of the 20th century and the changing tastes of the modern listener, such long alaps are rare in contemporary performance. Dhrupad's popularity as a vocal style waned with the coming of khayal in the 18th century.

Khayal came to prominence in the first half of the 18th century under the patronage of the Mughal emperor Muhammad Shah, whose court musician, Naimat Khan, is generally credited with making the style popular. Khayal is a musical style rather than a song type. Its repertoire is made up of short poems called *bandish*, which consist of two to eight lines usually written in Urdu. Each bandish is associated with a raga rather than with a specific melody, and singers are given the freedom to render the bandish however they choose, so long as the text and raga remain unchanged. Great khayal singers are known for their marvelous flights of improvisation within these relatively loose constraints. A typical performance will include a *barā khayal*, or great khayal, set in a slow tempo and often lasting 30 minutes or longer; and a *chhota khayal*, a shorter khayal set in the same raga but to a quicker tempo.

Instrumental classical music no longer thrives in Pakistan, though it is still practiced in parts of the country, particularly in Karachi and Lahore. Formerly the *sarod* and *sarangi* were quite popular, along with the more famous *sitar*. Less common instruments included a hammered dulcimer descended from the Persian *santur* and the *jalatarang*, a set of clay cups filled with water to pitch and struck with wooden sticks.

Spanning the division between classical and popular traditions is qawwali, a style made internationally famous by the late Nusrat Fateh Ali Khan. Qawwali's roots lie in Persian Sufism, which was brought east to what is now Pakistan and India at the end of the 12th century by Afghan and Turkic invaders. By the end of the 13th century, a member of the Sufi Chisti order, Amir Khusro Dehlavi, had fused Persian musical elements with Indian, shaping what it now known as qawwali.

A qawwali singer, called a *qawwal*, is one who sings an utterance of the Prophet Muhammad (*qaul* in Arabic)—and indeed, the qawwali repertoire consists largely of devotional songs of praise. A group of qawwalis called a *humnawa*, or a qawwali party, and most often is composed of a lead singer, one or two supporting singers, two drummers (a tabla player and a dholak player), and a chorus. The chorus consists of four to five men who highlight key parts of the song text by repeating phrases and verses. They also support the rhythm with unison clapping. The harmonium, a small reed organ pumped by the player's hand, provides additional melodic support and is usually played by the lead singer and/or his supporting singer.

Qawwali is largely sung in Urdu, Punjabi and its dialect Saraiki, and Persian, though many pieces created during the qawwali's classical Mughal period written in Awadhi or Braj Bhasha ("Eastern" and "Western" Hindi) are still popular today. Qawwali is a spiritual music full of religious feeling, but it is much more a style of performance than it is a fixed corpus of genre-specific songs and texts. The lyrics of a particular qawwali song may come from one of any of a number of poetic forms, and the text that is sung as a qawwali may have an independent life as another devotional form. *Hamd* (poetry in praise of Allah), *naat* (poetry in praise of the Prophet Muhammad), and *manqabat* (poetry in praise of Sufi saints or the Imam Ali) can all be included in the qawwali repertoire, but are also frequently performed in other contexts. A fourth genre, *marsiya*, is written both to praise and lament those who fell in support of Imam Hussein against the Ummayad caliph, Yazid I, at the Battle of Karbala (680 CE), but these would be performed exclusively for Shi'a audiences.

An important secular genre sung during qawwalis but also enjoying a broad popularity in its own right is the *ghazal*. Ghazals originated in Persia as love poetry and were already popular by the time they were brought to Pakistan by Muslim invaders in the 12th century. By the 18th century, ghazals had been fully incorporated into regional traditions and were being composed widely in Urdu. Many of the most famous ghazals are by Mirza Ghalib (1797–1869), who composed in both Urdu and Persian in the courts of the last Mughal emperors. Ghazals are composed according to strict rules, including alternating rhyming couplets and the introduction of the theme in the first line. Every couplet of the ghazal must contribute to the whole meaning of the poem in totality, but each must also be able to stand alone by representing a single idea. Though the performance of ghazals was once the purview of the regal elite, today they are enjoyed across Pakistan, a fact due in no small part to its early adoption by the record industry in the early 20th century, because a ghazal performance could be more easily made to fit within the constraints of the medium.

In addition to styles of music that enjoy a level of general popularity, Pakistan can also be characterized by its regional forms of music and dance. Today there are four provinces in Pakistan—Sindh, Punjab, Balochistan, and Khyber-Pakhtunkhwa—as well as the Federally Administered Tribal Areas (FATA), Azad Kashmir, and Gilgit-Baltistan, each populated by different ethnic groups with different languages, traditions, and musical cultures.

In Sindh, the southeasternmost province abutting India, the most popular vocal genre is *kafi*, which has much in common with qawwali. It, too, has strong ties to Sufism and was traditionally performed at *dargahs*, shrines built to Sufi saints. It has strong ties to oral traditions and to specific poets, especially Shah Abdullah Latif Bhitai and the Punjabi Sufi saint Adbullah Shah Qadri, known more commonly as Bulle Shah. Far more than qawwali, however, kafi is associated with mendicant orders; as such, it is usually set much more simply than qawwali. Kafi might be performed by a single singer, who often doubles as the harmonium player, and a dholak drummer. Mendicant singers might accompany themselves on an *ektara* (Sindhi, *yaktaro*), a percussive one-stringed instrument with a limited melodic range made from a large gourd. Kafi is also found in the neighboring regions of Balochistan and Punjab, where it is also quite popular.

Punjab is the home of the Patiala gharana, which dominates so much of the character of classical music in Pakistan. However, it is the *Mīrāsī* who form the heart of musical culture in Punjab. The Mīrāsī are a hereditary caste of professional musicians and genealogists patronized by clients across the social spectrum for festivals, weddings, and other joyous occasions. Similarly, arising out of the Sikh tradition come the *dhadi*, singers of ballads accompanied by the *dhadd*—a small, hand-held tension drum comparable in construction to the Nigerian "talking drum." Cords connect the drum's two faces across its hourglass-shaped wooden body, and the drummer can change the drum's pitch by squeezing or releasing the tension on these cords across the drum's thin waist. Originally dhadi sang only heroic ballads meant to inspire valor on the field of battle, but their repertoire has since expanded to include historical and romantic ballads. Along with the drum from which they take their name, dhadi singing is frequently accompanied by the sarangi, a bowed fiddle common across the northern subcontinent and believed to most closely mimic the human voice.

The performance of *qissa* used to be a popular pastime in Punjab. Qissa are tragic romantic ballads inspired by local folktales and often, but not always, performed to musical accompaniment. The most popular qissa is undoubtedly the story of Heer and her lover, Ranjha, the most famous version of which was composed by Waris Shah in the mid-18th century. While the performance of qissa, like other popular oral-tradition entertainments, is less common today than it once was, the story of Heer continues to be one of the most loved stories in both Pakistani and Indian Punjab.

Punjab's most internationally recognized contribution to music and dance is undoubtedly *bhangra*, a term which has been used to denote several related dance styles. Today bhangra is an extremely energetic dance style practiced by both men and women. It is characterized by its rhythms, which are closely associated with the *dhol* drum, and its costume. Men typically wear brightly colored *dhoti* (also called *chaadra*)—a length of cloth wrapped around their legs—a long *kurta* (shirt), and a vest. On their heads they will also wear a turban, called a *pagri*, which today is often topped with a fan. Women's dress is typically a brightly colored *salwar kameez* and *dupatta* (a long, light scarf). Bhangra has made a considerable impact internationally since the late 1980s, influencing both club music and contemporary choreography.

In Balochistan, folk music has been heavily influenced by neighboring Iran to its west, Afhganistan to its north, and Pakistani Sindh to its east. This influence can be seen in both its instruments and its dance. Lutes with origins in Afghanistan and Persia—*rebab, tar,* and *saz*—are common. Wind instruments include the *surnay*, a brash double reed; and the *doneli*, a pair of flutes played together by a single musician. The *suroz*, particular to Balochistan, is a kind of bowed fiddle comparable to the sarangi. It has three to four melody strings and up to eight sympathetic strings that are tuned to the raga being played and vibrate sympathetically to the harmonics of the bowed strings. Another instrument found throughout Pakistan, but most popular in Balochistan, is the *benju* or *bulbul tarang*, a kind of plucked dulcimer. Up to a meter in length, its strings run over a fret board in two courses, melody and drone. Connected to the fret board are keys fashioned after a typewriter or, less commonly, a piano. Depressing a key shortens the struck string, raising the pitch. The instrument can be made out of whatever materials are at hand, but the strings are typically steel, giving the benju a bright, metallic sound.

Oral tradition has always been important in Balochistan. Its traditions were so highly esteemed that formerly, upon the birth of a son, heroic epics would be recited instead of the *azan*, the Islamic proclamation of faith that traditionally greets the birth of a son across the Muslim world (Badalkhan, 2003, p. 229). Two of the most important kinds of singing in Balochistan are *zahīrok* and *sheyr*. Zahīrok, coming from the word *zahīr* (longing), is a body of folk tunes often sung as work or travel songs. It takes the form of couplets sung to a fixed number of melodies, occasionally with a third line acting as a refrain. The total number of zahīrok melodies is uncertain, but by most counts there are fewer than 40 (Badalkhan, 2009, p. 235).

Sheyr, in contrast, is a genre of narrative verse composed in regular meter but irregular rhyme, and sheyr verses are sometimes sung to zahīrok melodies. When performed by professional musicians, sheyr is usually accompanied by suroz and *dambūrag*, a plucked two-string lute played by the singer himself. Most Balochi know at least a few lines of sheyr, and those who can recite sheyr are highly esteemed.

Popular dances in Balochistan include the *do-chapi* and *lewa*. Of Persian origin, do-chapi is a mid-tempo circle dance performed by men. It is nearly always accompanied by the *surna* and dhol, but can also include a bowed fiddle (suroz or sarangi) or one of the long-necked lutes common to the region. Lewa is also of foreign origin, but belonging to the ethnic Siddhis. The Siddhi are descended from east Africans, mostly Bantu, who were brought to the region as slaves from about the eighth century CE or came later as traders. Lewa is superficially similar to do-chapi—a circle dance, performed by a group of men, accompanied by surna and dhol—but its African influences are evident both in its movements and in its music.

Pashtuns—who live in the FATA areas bordering Afghanistan but also have a large refugee community in Karachi—have a long oral folk music tradition. Like other groups in Pakistan, there is a rich traditional of epic balladry in Pashto called *badala*. Although badala can be sung by just about anyone in a private setting, the tradition is maintained by a community of professional musicians who normally perform it accompanied by the rebab—a short-necked plucked lute with origins in Central Asia and Afghanistan—the harmonium, and the tabla. Badala are composed of couplets of irregular length, though 12 syllables is common, and either a consistent final rhyme (AA, BA, CA . . .) or a rhymed hemistich pattern (AA, BB, CC). They are normally sung through without repetition. Other forms of narrative poetry frequently set to music include the *tappa*, believed to be one of the oldest forms of written poetry in Pashto, and the *charbaita*. Songs set as dialogue or sung in duet, like the charbaita, are common among Pashtuns. *Loba*, for example, are written as romantic dialogue between lovers, but because of the rigidly gender-segregated nature of Pashtun culture men and women rarely sing them together. As with the rest of Pakistan, ghazals are extremely popular among the Pashtun, but often reflect more Persian, Arabic, and Turkish influence than ghazals in Sindh and Punjab.

Pashtun dance is often martial in character and is practiced in both Pakistan and Afghanistan. The most common style is *Attan*, which is danced in groups to the accompaniment of drums. Attan begins slowly but gradually builds in tempo and momentum over the course of the dance, which can last several hours. *Khattak* (not to be confused with *Kathak* dance, one of the classical forms of Indian dance) is said to have its roots in the Greco-Bactrian kingdom that came to dominate the region that spans from what is now northern Afghanistan to large parts of Pakistan by the second century BCE. Traditionally danced with swords as a show of skill and dexterity, today khattak is often danced by large groups of men with empty hands at weddings and other celebratory events.

Sadly, the performance of regional and folk music in Pakistan has diminished greatly in recent years. Increased religious radicalization and the growing influence of the Taliban in tribal and rural areas and in cities such as Quetta and

Karachi have curtailed the public performance of music and dance, not just at large public festivals but also at weddings, births, and other traditional events. Also, while music programs remain a staple on regional language stations, the explosive growth of the television medium over the past decade has had an undeniable impact on the performance of longer narrative traditions such as badala, qissa, and sheyr.

Aaron Mulvany

See also: Karnatic Music; Mridangam; Tabla

Further Reading
Arnold, A., ed. 2000. *The Garland Encyclopedia of World Music; Vol. 5: South Asia, the Indian Subcontinent.* New York: Garland.
Badalkhan, S. 2003. "Balochi Oral Tradition." *Oral Tradition* 18(2), 229–235.
Badalkhan, S. 2009. "Zahīrok: The Musical Base of Baloch Minstrelsy." In Richard K Wolf (ed.), *Theorizing the Local: Music, Practice, and Experience in South Asia and Beyond*, 305–336. New York: Oxford University Press.
Qureshi, R. 2006. *Sufi Music of India and Pakistan: Sound, Context and Meaning in Qawwali.* Karachi, Pakistan: Oxford University Press.
Schreffler, G., ed. 2011. *Journal of Punjab Studies, Special Issue: Music and Musicians of Punjab* 19(1–2).
Yusuf, Z., ed. 1988. *Rhythms of the Lower Indus: Perspectives on the Music of Sind.* Karachi, Pakistan: Department of Culture and Tourism, Government of Sindh.

Pansori (P'ansori)

A uniquely Korean dramatic vocal folk genre, *Pansori* was originally developed by lower-class entertainers during the mid- to late Joseon Dynasty (1392–1910), specifically in the early 18th century. Accompanied by a barrel-shaped drum (*puk*), a single professional folk musician (*kwangdae*) performs a folk tale through speech, songs, and acting. The singer wears a traditional Korean costume (*hanbok*) and holds a folding fan as well as a handkerchief, both of which are used as props. The drummer, also wearing a traditional Korean costume, uses sets of rhythmic cycles (*changdan*) to support and advance the plot as well as to accompany the melodies, which are in several melodic and stylistic modes (*cho*); the drummer performs with a bare left hand and with a mallet in the right hand. The drummer also narrates calls of encouragement (*chuimsae*) at the end of phrases, such as "nice" or "right on." The melodic modes help create certain melodic qualities, aesthetic effects, and feelings. Melodic modes and rhythmic cycles change depending on the character and the mood of the story.

Through the end of the 19th century, the genre today known as Pansori was referred to by various terms, such as *sori, jabga, chang,* or *taryeong*. The term "Pansori," coined by Nosik Jeong (1940), is derived from *pan*, a gathering place, and *sori*, which means "sound," and refers to the various songs performed by the vocalist. Besides the stylized songs, written in verse, Pansori also comprises dialogue or prosaic narration (*aniri*) as well as dramatic action (*pallim*), such as movement and dance, and gestures (*norumsae*). Interactions between the singer and the audience, such as audience exclamations, responses, or questions, are a vibrant part of Pansori performances, which last between three and eight hours. Pansori reclaimed wide recognition with the movie *Sopyonje* (1993), which depicts the struggles of three Pansori singers during the 1950s, emphasizing the clashes of traditional Korean culture with Japanese and Western influences.

A poem by Song Man-jae (1788–1851), *Kwanuhui*, mentions 12 Pansori repertoires. Though originally an oral genre, Shin Chae-hyo (1812–1884) wrote down six of the 12 Pansori with revisions to reflect upper-class values: Song of Chunhyang (*Chunhyangga*), Song of Shim Chong (*Shimchongga*), Song of the Underwater Palace (*Sugungga*), Song of Hungbu (*Hungbuga*), Song of the Red Cliff (*Chokpyokka*), and Song of Pyongangsoe (*Pyongangsoega*). All but the last one were notated and have thus been transmitted to the present time; these five Pansori are commonly referred to as *madang*. To satisfy the specific interests of the audiences, songs created by the kwangdae musicians, which were derived from folk tales, proverbs, and stories and expressions of the people, were often inserted into the established Pansori. Audiences were comprised of people from a broad range of social strata, from commoners to aristocrats. Bang-song Song also notes that Shin Chae-hyo contributed to the genre Pansori by composing short epic songs (*tanga*) that are sung before the main part of the Pansori (Song, 2000, p. 30). Such introductory songs are structurally simpler and help the vocalist to warm up.

During the early stages of Pansori development, performances were frequently part of shamanistic rituals. Melody and rhythm of early Pansori were therefore influenced by shamanistic music. Later, Pansori was performed on a variety of occasions. Among other events, Pansori was performed at three-day celebrations for the passing of the state examination by a public official. Such success was celebrated with a festival called *hongpae kosa*, during which a variety of music, acrobatics, and other forms of entertainment was performed in addition to Pansori. Generally, the themes in Pansori mirror Korean Confucianism, specifically in regard to loyalty to the king, respect for parents, fidelity to the husband, brotherhood, and sincerity to friends (Um, 2001, p. 900).

Pansori reflects everyday life, especially tales of sorrow and woe. Therefore, Pansori must express grief. Even though some Pansori narratives have a positive outcome, "the process of suffering itself seems more important to the audience than the happy outcome" (Pihl, 1994, p. 5), which enables the audience to experience a catharsis. Because the single vocalist performs all roles (storyteller, narrator, and all characters), performing Pansori requires a high number of vocal timbres and vocal qualities from the vocalist. Especially characteristic are forced, rough, and raspy vocalizations. To obtain the necessary vocal strength and vocal qualities, Pansori performers train for many years and ideally experience pain and suffering in order to express the hardship of life and *han*. "Han" may refer to feelings such as grief, sorrow, longing, distress, suffering, regret, unsatisfied desire, bitter feeling, or spite (Willoughby, 2000). The often harsh vocalization supports the interpretation of the text. Among other techniques, singers make use of "voice breaking," vibrato, and microtonal melodic embellishments.

Pansori was an important source for the development of *sanjo*, an instrumental solo performance genre, and for the development of Kayagum Pyongchang, a dramatic vocal genre in which one or more vocalists accompany themselves on a 12-stringed Korean zither (*kayagum*). During the 20th century, several Pansori singers created a dramatic version (*changguk*, translated as "sung drama") with several singers, similar to the Western operatic genre.

Nico Schüler

See also: Janggu; North Korea, Music of; Sanjo

Further Reading

Choe, Tong-Hyon. 2010. *Pansori Tongpyonje Wa Sopyonje* [Pansori Eastern-style singing and Western-style singing]. Seoul, Korea: Minsogwon.

Jang, Yeonok. 2014. *Korean P'ansori Singing Tradition: Development, Authenticity, and Performance History.* Lanham, MD: Scarecrow Press.

Jeong, Nosik. 1940. *Joseon changgeuksa* [History of Joseon's vernacular song]. Seoul: Joseon ilbosa.

Pihl, Marshall R. 1994. *The Korean Singer of Tales.* Cambridge, MA: Council on East Asian Studies/Harvard University Press.

Song, Bang-song. 2000. *Korean Music: Historical and Other Aspects.* Seoul, Korea: Jimwoondang.

Um, Hae Kyung. 2001. "P'ansori and Kayagŭm Pyŏngch'ang." In Robert C. Provine, Yoshihiko Tokumaru, and J. Lawrence Witzleben (eds.), *Garland Encyclopedia of World Music; Vol. 7: East Asia: China, Japan, and Korea,* 897–908. London: Routledge.

Um, Hae Kyung. 2013. *Korean Musical Drama: P'ansori and the Making of Tradition in Modernity.* Farnham, UK: Ashgate.

Willoughby, Heather. 2000. "The Sound of Han: P'ansori, Timbre and a Korean Ethos of Pain and Suffering." *Yearbook for Traditional Music,* 17–30.

Parker, Charlie (1920–1955)

Charlie Parker was one of the most influential jazz musicians of his time, playing a crucial role in the development of bebop. Pieces such as "Koko," "Donna Lee," and "Embraceable You" demonstrate Parker's unique ability to create a melody out of anything. He once claimed that "an improviser should be able to use any note against any chord—it was simply a matter of placing it in the right context" (Gioia, 2011, p. 188). Parker's music was heavily driven by altered tones; he is credited as being among the first to construct improvised melodies over the higher intervals of the chords, such as the ninths, 11ths, and 13ths. Wanting to move away from the swing tradition, Parker was conservative in his use of pronounced rhythmic syncopation and instead would incorporate heavy accents and a mixture of legato and detached notes to construct his phrases. Parker's stylistic developments shaped an entire generation of musicians and revolutionized jazz music in the 20th century.

Growing up at a pivotal turning point in African American history, Parker witnessed a period in which jazz music flourished, and helped to usher in an era of musical innovation. Exhausted with the swing repertoire, Parker worked diligently to create a new sound for the next generation, soon to be known as "boppers." Born in Kansas City, Kansas, to Addie and Charles Parker Sr., Charles "Yardbird"

> **Charlie Parker**
>
> Well known to jazz fans the world, over from casual to aficionado, Charlie Parker's influence on jazz history is great. Beyond his priceless catalog of audio recordings, Parker's influence on jazz at large lives on in transcriptions of his work. Chief among these is the *Charlie Parker Omnibook*, which is a collection of 60 Parker solos sampled across the scope of his career. The solos were first transcribed and annotated by jazz pedagogues Jamey Aebersold and Ken Slone in 1978. Since that first edition, the *Omnibook* has become a widely used source of material in jazz education across the globe; jazz artists of nearly every instrument and genre study Parker's work via these transcriptions in order to learn the harmonic foundations and musical language of the style.

Parker Jr. started playing alto horn in fifth grade and was given his member's card (dubbing him a professional musician) by the time he was 15. Practicing upward of 15 hours a day, Parker jammed all around Kansas City, finding most of his gigs along the infamous 18th and Vine area. Although Parker was constantly playing, the musicians around him did not think he had the chops to make it as a professional musician. Band leader Oliver Todd (1916–2001) said, "If you had told me that he [Parker] would be famous, I wouldn't have believed it" (Haddix, 2013, p. 16). Parker studied and admired musicians such as Lester Young (1909–1959) and Buster Smith (1904–1991), the latter becoming a musical "father" to Parker.

In the summer of 1937, Parker traveled to the Lake of the Ozarks, a reservoir in central Missouri, where he could entertain resort patrons while perfecting his craft. When the summer ended, Parker returned to Kansas City a new player. Parker found steady work with the Tommy Douglas Band and continued to gig around Kansas City until drug addiction cost Parker his place in Harlan Leonard's band, the Kansas City Rockets. In the spring of 1939, he took a train to New York City to further pursue his musical career. While in New York, Parker participated in late-night jam sessions at Minton's Playhouse and Monroe's Uptown House. Both locations allowed Parker the freedom to develop his musical approach and lay the groundwork for bebop. Experts believe these sessions also contributed to Parker's addiction, who frequently mixed coffee and Benzedrine so he could stay up all night playing.

Parker's stylistic breakthrough came while he was playing the song "Cherokee" one night at Dan Wall's Chili House in Harlem. During the piece, Parker discovered that he could make the higher intervals of the chords into a melody, thereby completely changing his sound. Parker brought his new style back to Kansas City and quickly joined the Jay McShann Orchestra. Parker's place in McShann's group proved fruitful, and he contributed virtuosic solos on a number of the band's recordings, including "Honeysuckle Rose" and "Ornithology."

Dizzy Gillespie (1917–1993) was another important influence in Parker's life. A contemporary of Parker's, the young trumpet player was also searching for a new sound in an era of swing music. "Charlie Parker and I were moving in practically the same direction too, but neither of us knew it" (Gillespie and Fraser, 1979, pp. 116–117). In 1945, Gillespie and Parker took their new style to a six-week

Jazz saxophonist Charlie Parker performing in New York, ca. 1947. Parker was key in the development of bebop. (William P. Gottlieb/Ira and Leonore S. Gershwin Fund Collection, Music Division, Library of Congress)

engagement in Los Angeles. At the end of the contract, Parker's addictive problems resurfaced and Gillespie was forced to leave him behind. Parker continued to work in LA throughout 1946, but a nervous breakdown, coupled with alcoholism and heroin addiction, eventually led to an extended stay at the Camarillo State Hospital. He later wrote "Relaxin' at Camarillo" as a tribute to his time there.

In April of 1947, Parker returned to work and formed a quintet with which he recorded some of his most famous pieces. The quintet included Miles Davis on trumpet, drummer Max Roach, bassist Tommy Potter, and pianist Bud Powell. The years 1949 to 1951 were creatively prolific for Parker both on tour and in the studio. Parker's final years were mostly spent gigging sporadically, especially during the two-year suspension of his New York cabaret license. By 1954, Parker's health was in serious decline, and on March 12, 1955, he succumbed to pneumonia.

Jessica Freyermuth

See also: Bebop; Jazz

Further Reading
Crouch, Stanley. 2013. *Kansas City Lightning: The Rise and Times of Charlie Parker*. New York: HarperCollins.
Gillespie, Dizzy, and Al Fraser. 1979. *To Be or Not . . . to Bop*. New York: Doubleday.

Gioia, Ted. 2011. *The History of Jazz*, 2nd ed. London: Oxford University Press.
Haddix, Chuck. 2013. *Bird: The Life and Music of Charlie Parker*. Chicago: University of Illinois Press.
Russell, Ross. 1996. *Bird Lives!: The High Life and Hard Times of Charlie (Yardbird) Parker*. Cambridge: Da Capo Press.
Woideck, Carl. 1996. *Charlie Parker: His Music and Life*. Ann Arbor: The University of Michigan Press.

Pashto Music

Pashto music is the indigenous music of the Pashtun people, the largest single Afghan ethnic group, who are found throughout Afghanistan. In particular, they are located around and between the cities of Kandahar and Kabul, and in the Northwest Frontier Province (NWFP) and neighboring regions of western Pakistan. There is also a sizable Pashtun diaspora, with the largest numbers found in the United States, Canada, and the United Kingdom, which has its own version of the Pashto musical tradition. Because Afghanistan is located at the crossroads of historical trade and invasion routes, the musical traditions of the entire country have been influenced by a number of foreign cultures, including Arab, Chinese, Indian, Mongolian, and Persian. Pashto music is no exception: it has been particularly influenced by Indian instruments and music, which have been combined with traditional Pashto sounds.

GENRES

Pashto music is traditionally divided into seven genres: Tappa, Charbeta, Neemakai, Loba, Shaan, Badala, and Rubayi.

Tappa

Tappa, a form of Pashto poetry with lines of two unequal meters, is the most popular form of traditional musical expression. Tappa is notable in that it is sung both in times of grief and in times of happiness by all classes, genders, and ages. Children, adults, and the elderly, laborers and peasants, men and women all sing tappa. It is generally accompanied by the stringed *rubab* and the *mangay*—a vessel for storing water that sees life as an instrument when empty. Tappa has also been accompanied by full orchestra.

Charbeta

Charbeta is an epic poem set to song, the performance of which normally follows a tappa. Charbeta often recounts the heroic exploits of legendary figures and at times includes expressions of romance. This song style is often sung by two singers and has a rapid tempo in which the singers alternate lines, which are themselves either sung or recited.

Neemakai

Neemakai are songs about love or daily life and are generally composed and performed by women. Often consisting of only one or two lines, which are repeated, they are often combined with tappa that relate to the subject of the neemakai.

Loba

Loba are a very popular form of folk duets that normally tell love stories. Thus, the two (or occasionally more), singers represent the lover and the beloved (a man and a woman) and sing back and forth to each other, replying in poetic form.

Shaan

Performed either in private religious ceremonies or at social gatherings, *shaan* are used to indicate and celebrate times of happiness, including births and weddings.

Badala

Badala, another form of traditional Pashto folk music, most often consists of a ballad or an epic poem. It is accompanied by the rubab, the mangay, the *baja* or harmonium (a type of organ on which the keys are played with one hand, while the other is used to pump air into it), and the *tabla* (a percussion instrument similar to the bongos). The latter two instruments, which have their origins in India, reveal one influence India has had on traditional Pashto music.

Rubayi

Rubayi Indian music heavily influences the last of the seven traditional Pashto genres as well, as rubayi is the Pashto form of the Indian *ghazal*. Generally sung before the start of a badala and often representing the loss of or separation from love, this song type most clearly represents the crossroads of cultures for which Afghanistan is known, as it has been influenced over the ages by poetry from Turkish, Persian, and Arabic cultures.

TRADITIONAL INSTRUMENTS

There are a number of traditional Pashto and Afghan musical instruments in addition to those mentioned earlier. Among the most common are the Chatralay *sitar*, a stringed instrument originating in the Afghanistan-Pakistan border region; the *shpelai*, a bamboo flute; a banjo, which is plucked and keyed, rather than just strummed; and a *dhol*, a two-sided percussion instrument. European and Asian instruments are also commonly used to play or accompany Pashto music.

Popular music developed slowly and only after the 1950s, when radio ownership became widespread throughout Afghanistan; thereafter it developed a large following. This music combined Afghan, Indian, and European instruments and was heavily influenced by Indian and Pakistani film culture. Other influences spread from Iran and the Arab world. Popular music was performed in Pashto as well as other Afghan languages, including Dari, a Persian dialect.

Pashto music, like other types of Afghan music, survived numerous changes of government through the end of the 1970s. Despite their strong musical heritage, during the Soviet invasion (1979–1989) and the Afghan Civil War (1989–1996), music took a back seat to fighting off first invading forces and then each other. During Taliban rule (1996–2001), though they were primarily Pashtun themselves, instrumental music, public performances of music, and all other forms of artistic expression were banned; therefore, within Afghanistan music was limited to the underground until the fall of the Taliban regime. The Pashto diaspora in Pakistan was instrumental in keeping their musical traditions alive during these years.

Today, in the Pashto diaspora there exist hip-hop and rap artists, including DJ Besho, Awesome Qasim, and Soosan Firooz, who sing in a combination of Pashto, Dari/Farsi, and English. Traditional music also remains popular in the diaspora population, in particular the music of Ubaidullah Jan Kandaharai, who died in 1980, but was regarded as the leading musical figure in the south of Afghanistan. Within Afghanistan, music as a whole has re-emerged from the shadows, with groups such as the Kaboul Ensemble gaining worldwide fame. Traditional Pashto music has also reappeared, particularly in the south of the country.

Jonathan Z. Ludwig

See also: Rebab

Further Reading

Sakata, Hiromi Lorraine. 2002. *Music in the Mind: The Concepts of Music and Musician in Afghanistan.* Washington, DC: Smithsonian Institution Scholarly Press.

Sakata, Hiromi Lorraine. 2013. *Afghanistan Encounters with Music and Friends* (Bibliotheca Iranica Performing Arts). Costa Mesa, CA: Mazda Publishers.

Sarmast, Ahmd. 2009. *A Survey of the History of Music in Afghanistan: Special Reference to Art Music from c. 1000 AD.* Saarbrücken, Germany: VDM Verlag.

Philippines, Music of the

Philippine music encompasses a large range of material, from centuries-old genres to modern-day popular songs, that reflects its diverse influences: from Southeast Asian neighbors to the colonial legacies of Spain (1565–1896) and the United States (1898–1946). The Philippines' contemporary national identity is embodied by Original Pilipino Music (OPM), including artists of international acclaim such as Lea Salonga, Charice Pempengco, Apl.de.Ap of the Blackeyed Peas, and Arnel Pineda of Journey. Music of the Philippines may be grouped into broad categories consisting of indigenous, folk, and contemporary forms, but variations exist within and between each category depending on the specific cultural-linguistic group, region, and time period. In global circulation, Philippine music is performed wherever Filipino communities are found, especially in cultural shows displaying costumes, music, and dance.

The Philippines is an island nation of some 7,000 islands, predominately Christian in religion because of Spanish colonization from 1565 to 1898, and English-fluent in official contexts such as government, education, and commerce due to its history as a colony of the United States from 1898 to 1946. In addition to ethnic, cultural, and linguistic diversity, rural and urban lifeways coexist along with lifestyles of wealth and extreme poverty. The three main regions of the Philippines are the northern region of the largest island, Luzon; the central region of the Visayas, including the island of Palawan to the west; and the southern region of Mindanao. Luzon includes the national capital Manila, and is home to both lowland Christianized Filipinos and small pockets of indigenous people in the mountain highlands of the Cordillera. Christianized Filipinos also dominate the central region of the Visayas, but speak languages and dialects different from those of the groups in Luzon. The second largest island, Mindanao, has historically been the stronghold of Muslim Filipinos who thwarted the Spanish colonization, and has thus preserved musical traditions connected to the rest of Southeast Asia, most notably bronze gong-chime ensembles (see the entry for "Kulintang"). From the mid-20th century on, vast migrations sent large numbers of Christian Filipinos to Mindanao, displacing the Muslim groups. Muslim Filipino communities headed north and established themselves in Manila, and missionaries converted indigenous people to Christianity. Seafaring groups such as the Sama-Bajau live between the Philippines and Malaysia, often adapting to the laws and influences of both countries. The current total population of the Philippines is 101 million, including 2.2 million Filipino citizens who work abroad in Saudi Arabia, the United Arab Emirates, and Singapore as overseas contract workers and whose remittances are vital to the national economy. The number of Americans reporting Filipino heritage exceeds 2.6 million, making them the second largest Asian American group in the United States after the Chinese.

Eight major languages with dozens of different dialects are spoken in the Philippines. The national language Pilipino (Anglicized as "Filipino") is based on the Tagalog language and incorporates Spanish and English words and phrases. Many of the educated elite, including government officials, academics, radio and television news personnel, military and business people, speak Pilipino, English, and sometimes their home dialect. In the Visayas, people frequently use Cebuano, the main language of Cebu, rather than Tagalog or Pilipino as the lingua franca.

Christian Filipinos (including Catholics) account for 90% of the population, Muslim Filipinos constitute about 5%, and the rest is made up of diverse indigenous groups called *lumads* ("tribal" people) and people of mixed heritage such as Chinese, Spanish, or European. People of South Asian descent have long resided in the Philippines, even before Spanish colonization, and continue to migrate there. Many Vietnamese refugees arrived after the Vietnam War before immigrating to the United States during the late 1970s. Over the past few decades, immigrants from South Korea have arrived, formed communities, and established thriving businesses in the Philippines. Tourism from other Asian countries, Australia, Europe, and the United States are an important part of the Philippine national economy. Culture and music in the Philippines continue to develop and grow with the influx of diverse peoples and influences in modern times.

Musical examples from three broad categories of indigenous, folk, and modern musics are described here, with the caveat that there are countless more genres, songs, instruments, and cultural groups to learn about. These three broad categories of Philippine music are typically performed in Filipino cultural shows around the world.

INDIGENOUS MUSIC

Indigenous music of the Philippines is characterized by a great variety of bamboo and gong instruments and ensembles as well as vocal music (Maceda, 1998). Indigenous music predominates among lumad (tribal) peoples in pockets of communities found from the highlands of Luzon to the southern island of Mindanao, and also Islamized groups traditionally from the southern region. Although these lumad and Muslim groups differ culturally and religiously, both similarly resisted Spanish colonialism and Christianization, and thus preserved a precolonial musical heritage like that of other indigenous peoples in Southeast Asia.

The Cordillera mountain range on the large island of Luzon spans a total area of 7,100 square miles and is home to the Bontok, Ibaloy, Ifugao, Isneg, Kalinga, Kankana-eys, and Tingguan/Itneg groups. Once collectively called *Igorots* by outsiders, this pejorative term is deployed today to indicate pride in their cultural identity. Each lumad subgroup has a separate dialect and is culturally distinct from, though closely related to, their neighbors. These distinctions are found in different types of ensembles, names of instruments, and repertoire. Singing for entertainment or ritual is performed solo or in a small ensemble. Group songs are used to accompany work such as plowing and planting the fields or pounding rice. Rituals and feasts, including wedding ceremonies, peace pacts, and honoring deities and ancestors, foster a sense of social cohesion. Cordillera groups employ the use of flat gongs called *gangsa gansa*, or *gangha*, in contrast to the bossed gongs of lumads in Mindanao, although the number, pitch, and way of playing vary among these groups. The flat gongs may be struck with a mallet or the hand using damping and ringing techniques for different timbral effects.

Among the Kalinga, six people, traditionally male, hold one *gangsa* each of graduated sizes and arranged in pitch from low to high. Each player employs two playing styles called *topayya* and *pattong*. Topayya is played using the hands, with the performer kneeling and resting the gangsa on his thighs. The four biggest and lowest gongs of the six play the same rhythm, but stagger their entries so that they create a texture of overlapping beats. The left hand taps a steady beat while the right hand uses a sliding motion to dampen every other beat. A hocket is created by each ringing tone that contributes one pitch to the overall melody of sequential tones. The fifth gangsa plays a faster ostinato or repeating pattern, and the sixth gangsa player improvises more freely. This music often accompanies a dance called *salidsid* in which a woman and man act out a courtship resembling a rooster chasing a hen. In the pattong playing style, the gangsa is hung on a string and held with one hand as the other hand strikes it with a soft mallet, alternately dampening and letting it ring. The players in this style may dance in a line or a big circle while coordinating a hocket melody.

There are many types of bamboo instruments among the Cordillera groups, including percussive buzzers and tubes, jaw harps, and flutes. Bamboo stamping tubes are pounded vertically on the ground with one hand as the other hand alternately dampens and uncovers the opening at the top of the tube to change the timbre. Each of the six tubes in the ensemble contributes one pitch in a sequential hocketing melody similar to the method for playing the gangsa. An ensemble of bamboo buzzers of various sizes, which are struck on the palm of the player's hand, are also played in a similar way. A notched flute ensemble produces hocketing melodies with one player contributing one pitch to the composite melody. The bamboo jaw harp, called *kubing* among the Kalinga, is played solo and uses the mouth as a resonator to vary the timbre of its sounds and even produce words. The kubing is often used to communicate intimately in courtship. Solo aerophones that produce exquisite, complex melodies include end-blown flutes and a traverse flute called the *tongali* that uses nose-blown air. The nose flute has a long stem with a very narrow bore and is sometimes covered with intricate etchings; it is also used in courtship. A bamboo polychordal zither called *kolitong* by the Bontok and Kalinga is played solo; it consists of thin strips of bamboo wound around a tube that are plucked with the fingers, producing a musical texture similar to the other bamboo ensembles.

Characteristic of the indigenous or precolonial music of the southern Philippines are bronze gongs, which are similar to those in neighboring cultures on the island of Borneo, and in Malaysia and Indonesia. Bonze gongs are found among both non-Muslim lumad groups and Muslim groups. In contrast to the flat gongs of Cordilleran groups, bronze gongs in the southern Philippines have a raised center called a *boss* or *knob* and exist in various sizes from small to large, and high to low pitch. These instruments are highly prized possessions and very few families in a village are wealthy enough to own them. The large heavy knobbed gong, generally referred to as *agung*, is found among the Bagobo, Manobo, T'boli, Subanun, Mansaka, Tagukaolu, and Bukidnon (Maceda, 1998, p. 25). These gongs, which have turned-in rims, vary in size but are always played hanging. The T'boli, concentrated around Lake Sebu, typically use four large gongs. The lowest agung provides a steady beat, acting as a drone, and smaller hanging gongs provide the higher-pitched melody (Maceda, 1998, p. 26). Music accompanies dances used for entertainment or in rituals. Among the Muslim groups, the melodic instrument called kulintang or *kolintang* is distinguished from instruments of the lumad groups by being laid horizontally on a wooden frame rather than on a hanging frame. (See "Kulintang" for more on this instrument.)

FOLK MUSIC

Philippine "folk music" generally refers to music influenced by 333 years of Spanish colonization and religious conversion, which includes song forms and genres, vocal music, and a string ensemble called a *rondalla*. The rondalla is a string orchestra typically composed of several sizes of stringed instruments, played with a plectrum in tremolo style, that provide melodic and harmonic parts. These include the instruments *bandurria, laud, octavina,* and Western guitar and double bass. Sometimes a drum set is included. The bandurria is similar in construction to a mandolin and has six pitches. The lowest, G, is a single string; D and A have two courses; and the higher strings, E, B, and F#, have three courses. The laud, a middle-range instrument, uses the pitches F#-B-E-A-D-G and similarly has one single course, two double courses, and three triple courses (i.e., 14 strings). The octavina's strings are tuned G-D-A-E-B-F#, following a similar pattern of courses. Although these instruments have names and shapes similar to those found in Cuba, Mexico, and Spain, their tuning, materials, and style of playing and repertoire are distinctly Filipino. Traditional repertoire dates back to the Spanish period and includes *harana* (Spanish for serenade) and *kundiman* (Tagalog for love song) compositions that are used in courtship, wherein a group of men or boys serenade a young woman. The syncopated *habanera* rhythm in 2/4 and transitioning from a minor key to a major key are typical musical features.

Folk music is important to Filipino national identity. Between Spanish and American rule, Filipinos declared a brief but significant independence from Spain in June 1898. During this time, the Spanish-American war was already under way, and rather than surrender to their former subjects, the Spanish colonial government ceded the Philippines to the United States in December 1898. The Philippine national anthem "*Lupang Hinirang*" (Tagalog for "chosen land") was written during this period in Spanish by José Palma and later translated into Tagalog in the 1940s. Julian Felipe wrote the music, taking some inspiration from *Aida*'s "Grand March" (Verdi) and the French national anthem "La Marseillaise." The well-known patriotic song "Bayan Ko" exemplifies the classic kundiman composition and was written during this time period by José Alejandrino, a general in the Philippine revolutionary army.

MODERN-DAY MUSIC

Colonization of the Philippines by the United States (1898–1946) coincided with the rise of American popular music and influenced Philippine musical culture, beginning with military brass bands playing American patriotic marches and continuing to ragtime, jazz, and other forms. After World War II, the Philippines was granted independence by the United States in 1946. During these years, popular styles such as vaudeville, American folk and patriotic songs learned through American-controlled school systems, American films, and later jazz and rock and roll flourished in Philippine culture and created new styles.

Today, various American popular musics, including R & B, Asian pop, and Original Filipino Music, dominate the radio airwaves, the club scene, and international video programs such as MTV Asia. Since the 20th century, Filipino musicians playing Western-style music have been popular and influential throughout Asia. Contemporary art music and popular music mix with and cross-influence each other in dynamic reconfigurations and creative responses to economic and political pressures, social and cultural changes such as migration, and the music industries of the Philippines, Asia, and the world. For example, the art music compositions of Antonio Molina, Francisco Santiago, Lucrecia Kasilag, José Maceda, Ramon

Santos, and Francisco Feliciano incorporate melodies, techniques, and elements from a variety of Philippine music with modern and avant-garde musical language and forms. Popular and rock musicians such as Freddy Aguilar, Joey Ayala, and Grace Nono incorporate Philippine music into their songs. Filipino Americans such as Eleanor Academia of World Music Institute, Susie Ibarra, and Ron Quesada of Kulintronica, along with master musician Danongan Kalanduyan, rework kulintang music into their own styles of rock, world, and electronic music. Sama-Bajau and Magindanao native musicians are creating new genres of indigenous Southeast Asian pop.

Mary Talusan Lacanlale

See also: Kulintang; Malay Music; Marshall Islands, Music of

Further Reading

Brandeis, Hans, and Johann Stockinger. 1995. *Music and Dance of the Bukidnon-s of Mindanao: A Short Introduction.* Vienna, Austria: Universität Wien.

Buenconsejo, José S. 2002. *Songs and Gifts at the Frontier: Person and Exchange in the Agusan Manobo Possession Ritual, Philippines.* New York: Routledge.

Cadar, Usopay H. 1996. "The Role of the Kolintang Music in Maranao Society." *Asian Music* 27(2), 81–103.

Castro, Christi-Anne. 2011. *Musical Renderings of the Philippine Nation.* New York: Oxford University Press.

Cultural Center of the Philippines. 1994. *CCP Encyclopedia of Philippine Art,* vol. 6. Manila: Cultural Center of the Philippines.

Ellorin, Bernard B. 2008. "Variants of Kulintangan Performance as a Major Influence of Musical Identity among the Sama in Tawitawi, Philippines." Master's thesis, University of Hawaii at Manoa.

Eugenio, Damiana L., ed. 1996. *Philippine Folk Literature Series; Vol. 7: The Folk Songs.* Manila, Philippines: De La Salle University Press.

Gaerlan, Barbara S. 1999. "In the Court of the Sultan: Orientalism, Nationalism, and Modernity in Philippine and Filipino American Dance." *Journal of Asian American Studies* 2(3), 251–287.

Gonzalves, Theodore S. 2010. *The Day the Dancers Stayed: Performing in the Filipino/American Diaspora.* Philadelphia: Temple University Press.

Irving, D. R. M. 2010. *Colonial Counterpoint: Music in Early Modern Manila.* Oxford: Oxford University Press.

Maceda, José M. 1998. *Gongs and Bamboo.* Diliman: University of the Philippines Press.

Mirano, Elena Rivera. 1992. *Musika: An Essay on the Spanish Influence on Philippine Music.* Manila: Sentrong Pangkultura ng Pilipinas.

Mora, Manolete. 1990. *Interpreting Utom: An Ethnographic Account of the Musical Instrumental Practice of the T'boli of Mindanao, Philippines.* Clayton, Canada: Monash University.

Ng, Stephanie. 2005. "Performing the 'Filipino' at The Crossroads: Filipino Bands in Five-Star Hotels Throughout Asia." *Modern Drama Journal* 42(2), 272–296.

Pfeiffer, William. 1976. *Indigenous, Folk, and Modern Filipino Music.* Dumaguete City, Philippines: Silliman Music Foundation.

Reyes, Michiyo Yoneno. 2002. "Under Attack: Mass Media Technology and Indigenous Musical Practices in the Philippines." In Timothy J. Craig and Richard King (eds.),

Global Goes Local: Popular Culture in Asia, 40–57. Hong Kong: Hong Kong University Press.

Santos, Ramon Pagayon. 1994. *Musika: An Essay on the American Colonial and Contemporary Traditions in Philippine Music.* Manila: Sentrong Pangkultura ng Pilipinas.

Talusan, Mary. 2014. "Muslim Filipino Traditions in Filipino American Popular Music." In Iraj Omidvar and Anne R. Richards (eds.), *Muslims and American Popular Culture*. Santa Barbara, CA: Praeger.

Trimillos, Ricardo. 1986. "Music and Ethnic Identity: Strategies among Overseas Filipino Youth." *Yearbook for Traditional Music* (18), 9–20.

Piazzolla, Astor (1921–1992)

The bandoneón player and composer Astor Piazzolla developed the traditional Argentinean tango from music for dancing to music for listening by adding elements from classical music and jazz. There were other musicians in the same field of *tango nuevo*, such as Alfredo Gobbi (1912–1965), but Piazzolla became the most important. With him, the bandoneón—mainly used by European emigrants in the bordellos in the suburbs of Buenos Aires and Montevideo, and associated with sex and low society—became an established instrument.

Born in Argentina, Piazzolla was raised in New York, where he learned to play bandoneón (his father was a tango aficionado) and was exposed to jazz and classical music. The latter was the kind of music he first played on the bandoneón, not tango music. In 1937, he moved to Buenos Aires, and two years later joined Aníbal Troilo's *Orquesta típica* as a bandoneón player, also writing arrangements until 1944. In 1941, he started to study with Alberto Ginastera and in 1946, he broke with tango and devoted himself entirely to classical music. After winning a composition prize, he had the opportunity to study in Paris with Nadia Boulanger in 1954–1955, who helped him return to his Argentinean roots: the tango.

Home again, he founded the *Octeto Buenos Aires* (active until 1958), his first ensemble with two bandoneóns, electric guitar, piano, two violins, cello, and double bass, with which he broke with traditional tango and created the *tango nuevo*. From then on, he performed his own compositions (and, bit by bit, less music by other tango composers) with a variety of ensembles in which he was the band leader. Always included was (at least) one bandoneón, which was played by Piazzolla himself.

In 1960, he founded the *Quinteto Nuevo Tango* (active until 1970): bandoneón, electric guitar, piano, violin, and double bass, which became the standard for modern tango ensembles. The orchestration of the *Quinteto Nuevo Tango* differed from the traditional tango ensembles quartet (bandoneón, guitar, violin and flute) or sextet (*sexteto típico*: two violins, two bandoneóns, piano, and double bass). During the 1920s and 1930s, there were two camps, the traditionalists and the renovators, each different in the size of the ensembles and the use of rhythm, melody, and harmony. Whereas the traditionalists enlarged the ensemble, often to 10 or more musicians (including four bandoneóns and four violins), the modernists used the sextet. When the bands became bigger, they needed professional arrangers. This is why Piazzolla worked with Troilo during the 1940s.

Astor Piazzolla

As a close cousin of the German accordion, the bandoneón has significant competition for attention within the various variants of the bellows-driven reed instrument family. The bandoneón, developed around 1850 by the German Heinrich Band, is a further development of the concertina and was used as a substitute for an organ to play church music. It reached its highest popularity in Argentina at the turn of the 20th century, where it became a typical tango instrument because of its somber sound. Despite its importance in Latin America, the instrument is mostly utilized in Argentinian tango music. Its relevance outside of this region is due in large part to composer Astor Piazzolla—himself a virtuosic performer on the instrument. After a long career as a tango musician and composer, Piazzolla shelved his bandoneón and travelled to Paris to study with French composition teacher Nadia Boulanger, convinced that his vernacular-music past was not lacking in artistic importance. At the encouragement of Boulanger, Piazzolla combined his knowledge of tango, jazz, and Western classical music to create a new style later known as tango nuevo. It was his compositions and bandoneón playing in tango nuevo that brought Piazzolla's compositions to greater Western cultural consciousness and enshrined them in the annals of Western art music history.

In 1968, Piazzolla composed an opera, which he called a "tango operita," *María de Buenos Aires*, which combined elements of opera, cantata, and oratorio, on a libretto by the Uruguayan poet Horacio Ferrer. Its story is narrowly connected with the history of tango. It was the first "tango opera" ever, receiving its first performance in Buenos Aires in 1968; since then, it has been performed many times around the world and recorded several times, (e.g., by Gidon Kremer and his *Kremerata Musica* in 1998). Piazzolla's collaboration with Ferrer led to a new kind of tango nuevo song, most famously his song "*Balada para un loco* (Ballad for a crazy man)" (1969). In 1971, he enlarged his quintet to a nonet (Conjunto 9, active until 1972), adding a quartet with a second violin, viola, cello, and percussion. Its style was more complex and the rhythm more open. With his *Octeto Eletrónico* (1975–1977), with bandoneón, violin, electric guitar, electric bass, piano, electric organ, synthesizer, and percussion, his style integrated more rock influences. In 1978, he reshuffled his quintet and toured internationally; their last album was *La Camorra* (1988). In 1989, he founded a sextet with two bandoneóns, electric guitar, piano, cello, and double bass; replacing the violin with a cello gave the ensemble a darker sound. In August 1990, he was stricken by a cerebral hemorrhage in Paris and died two years later in Buenos Aires.

His tango nuevo was a natural way of developing the traditional tango, which was a pair dance in 2/4 meter, or a tango-canción with a simple musical structure: a melody with changing syncopated and regular rhythms, accompanied with syncopations of the habanera and proceeding bass lines as well as basic key harmonies. There was almost no change of musical structure until the 1950s. Piazzolla enriched the tango with contemporary sounds. He used elements of classical music such as fugue, counterpoint, ostinato, polyphony, atonality, polyrhythm, and time change, influenced by Johann Sebastian Bach, Igor Stravinsky, and Béla Bartók. Piazzolla added new instruments such as electric guitar (in 1955) and percussion (in 1963). He even used an electronic instrument, a synthesizer, in his Octeto Eletrónico. Also, he enriched his music with elements of jazz, such as extended harmony, syncopation, improvisation, and the use of the vibraphone (in *María de Buenos Aires*). For these pieces, he invited jazz musicians to join his ensembles. In addition, Piazzolla used new playing techniques for tango musicians, such as strikes with the violin bow, string accents in high position, staccati as well as glissandi, percussive effects of every instrument, and virtuoso runs of the bandoneón.

He composed on the piano rather than on his instrument, the bandoneón. Like classical music, his tango music is all written out, including space for improvisation. The basic rhythm is 3 + 3 + 2 (in contrast to the very square rhythm of the traditional tango), a heritage of the tango in the milonga (compare the second set *Milonga* of his *Concerto for bandoneon, guitar and string orchestra*, 1985). Fast and strongly syncopated parts of the composition alternate with slow and sad segments, where (often) the bandoneón plays a romantic melody with long sounding notes. Piazzolla's music, which has a distinctive style, is recognizable after a few seconds, having an emotional depth and energy that are rare in 20th-century classical music. But his music cannot be categorized as classical music, jazz, or world music; it is in between.

Until the 1980s in Argentina, his tango nuevo was refused by traditionalists. But in European jazz festivals—Piazzolla played and recorded with Gerry Mulligan (saxophone) and Gary Burton (vibraphone)—and as a composer for symphony orchestra and for film music (e.g., *Henry IV* [dir. Marco Bellocchio, 1984] and *Sur* [dir. Fernando Solanas, 1988]), Piazzolla became more and more popular; sometimes he played more than 200 concerts a year. Piazzolla also composed many classical pieces. The classical piece composed before his lessons with Boulanger show his departure from tango, whereas the ones after 1955 are tango nuevos: e.g., *Concerto for bandoneón and orchestra* (1979), *Cinco piezas* for guitar (1980), *Le grand tango* for cello and piano (1982), *Tango suite* for two guitars (1984), *Concerto for bandoneón, guitar, and string orchestra* (1985), *Four for tango* for string quartet (1989), and *Five tango sensations* for string quartet (1989). In his *Histoire du tango* for flute and guitar (1986), each of the four pieces evokes an epoque in tango history: a bordello (1900), a café (1930), a nightclub (1960), and a modern-day concert (1980s).

The second half of the 1990s—several years after Piazzolla's death—was the height of his popularity. Worldwide leading classical instrumentalists recorded tango-nuevo CDs, such as Daniel Barenboim (piano), Roberto Aussel (guitar), Yo-Yo Ma (violoncello), Gidon Kremer (violin), and The Kronos Quartet (string quartet). Today, Piazzolla, next to Mauricio Kagel and Alberto Ginastera, is regarded as one of most popular and important Argentinean composers, and has become a national hero. Carlos Gardel (1890–1935, tango-canción), Aníbal Troilo (1914–1975, tango for dancing) and Astor Piazzolla are the most important tango musicians, representing different styles.

Jörg Jewanski

See also: Andalusian Music; Tango

Further Reading

Azzi, María Susana, and Collier, Simon. 2000. *Le Grand Tango. The Life and Music of Astor Piazzolla.* Oxford: Oxford University Press.

Bach, Caleb. 1991. "A New-Age Score for the Tango." *Américas* 43(5–6), 14–21.

Brunelli, Omar García, ed. 2008. *Estudios sobre la obra de Astor Piazzolla* [Studies on the work of Astor Piazzolla]. Buenos Aires, Argentina: Gourmet Musical Ediciones.

Cannata, David Butler. 2005. "Making It There: Piazzolla's New York Concerts." *Latin American Music Review/Revista de Músico Latinoamericana* 27(1) (Spring/Summer), 57–87.

Gorin, Natalio. 2001. *Astor Piazzolla: A Memoir.* Portland, OR: Amadeus Press [trans. and expanded version by Fernando Gonzalez of *Astor Piazzolla. A Manera de Memorias* (1990, Buenos Aires: Atlantida)].

López, Sonia Alejandra. 2003. *'María de Buenos Aires'. Eine Monographie der Tango-Operita von Astor Piazzolla und Horacio Ferrer* ["María de Buenos Aires." A monograph on the tango-operetta by Astor Piazzolla and Horacio Ferrer]. Tutzing, Germany: Schneider.

Astor Piazzolla in Portrait. 2004. BBC/Opusarte [featuring the films *Tango maestro* (2004, dir. Mike Dibb), and *Tango nuevo* (1989, dir. Tony Staveacre)].

Pimba

Pimba is a genre of contemporary Portuguese pop music, characterized by lyrics that emphasize obvious sexual innuendo and clichés sung over simple and catchy instrumental music. Developed in the 1990s, the genre continues to be popular among rural and immigrant audiences, but it falters against folk music traditions that utilize similarly straightforward musical and textual content but wish to be considered more artistic and poetic. Among Portuguese cultural communities, pimba has come to represent Portuguese working-class culture, and the term often signifies music or cultural productions that are considered tacky or artistically unrefined, despite the genre's widespread popularity.

Pimba resembles other Portuguese pop and folk genres in its characteristic instrumental accompaniment, which features a predominant accordion sound. Beyond accordion, pimba typically utilizes a variety of instrumental sounds (guitars, percussion, synthesizer), most of which are produced digitally. In live settings, pimba performances typically include only the singer, an accordionist, and a keyboardist (electronic keyboard), and often singers will perform alone to a prerecorded backtrack. Musically, pimba is difficult to characterize, as it lacks many musically distinctive qualities aside from its accordion-heavy sound, but it bears a resemblance to other folk and pop music traditions, which feature short, catchy melodies, basic harmonic structures, and cheap, mass-produced quality—not unlike much of the music produced in the global pop music industry.

Many of pimba's defining elements derive from its textual content, which is characterized by frequent use of sexual metaphor and wordplay—often quite vulgar—and clichéd romantic themes. Though, musically, pop music in the style of pimba was prevalent in Portugal throughout the late 20th century, the genre designation developed after several Portuguese pop songs in the mid-1990s utilized the term "pimba" (a word that previously signified, more simply and without innuendo, a sudden and unforeseen event) as a euphemism for a sex act. The first such song was Portuguese pop rock band Ex-Voto's 1993 hit single "Subtilezas Porno Populares" (Popular porn subtleties), though the musical style of the song bears a stronger resemblance to rock than to later iterations of pimba.

Following the popularity of Ex-Voto's single, several other artists began using the term "pimba" in a similarly sexualized manner, leading to increasing use of the term as a specific genre designation. Many consider the 1995 hit song "Pimba Pimba" by the Portuguese singer known simply as Emanuel (Américo Pinto da Silva Monteiro, 1957–) the first song to popularize the new genre. "Pimba Pimba" makes more overt and frequent use of the sexualized term "pimba": whereas in Ex-Voto's single, for instance, the term made only a single appearance, Emanuel's song utilizes the repeated refrain *"Nós pimba, nós pimba"* (We "pimba," we "pimba"), which aptly summarizes the sexual suggestions laced throughout the song's text. Moreover, Emanuel's "Pimba Pimba" also standardized the typical musical sound of the pimba genre, with an upbeat pop setting that features cheap-sounding accordion, winds, and vocal backing.

Though largely popularized in the mid-1990s following the success of Emanuel, similar musical styles and themes were already prevalent in Portuguese pop music from the 1980s, and some artists such as Quim Barreiros (1947–) are considered part of the pimba genre, though their musical productions existed before the term and genre were popularized. Barreiro's song "Bacalhau à Portuguesa," for instance, utilizes the popular Portuguese cuisine *bacalhau* (a type of dried salt cod used in many traditional Portuguese dishes) in overt double entendre.

The often vulgar and cheap quality of both the music and text has made pimba a subject of controversy among Portuguese folk musicians. Pimba betrays roots in Portuguese folk music styles, many of which also come from and remain popular in rural communities and utilize accordion-based instrumental accompaniment and vocal performance. Furthermore, pimba songs often borrow musical and rhythmic content from existing Portuguese folk songs. Barreiro's "Bacalhau à Portuguesa," for instance, utilizes the syncopated rhythms and instrumental sound of Portuguese folk dance and song. In general, however, Portuguese popular musicians who produce music in more traditional folk styles, such as Tony Carreiras (António Manuel Mateus Antunes, 1963–), boast a more artistic and subtle poetic content, if still sometimes sexual and romantically clichéd, and higher-quality productions. Though largely despised by Portuguese elite culture, the genre remains popular, and pimba songs are commonly performed at celebrations, such as religious festivals and weddings, across Portugal, as well as in Portuguese-American communities along the U.S. East Coast.

Danielle M. Kuntz

Further Reading

Brucher, Katherine. 2009. "*Viva* Rhode Island, *Viva* Portugal! Performance and Tourism in Portuguese-American Bands." In Kimberly DeCosta Holton and A. Klimt (eds.), *Fashioning Ethnic Culture: Portuguese-American Communities along the Eastern Seaboard*, 201–224. Dartmouth: University of Massachusetts Press.

DeCosta, Kimberly. 2005. *Performing Folklore: Ranchos Folclóricos from Lisbon to Newark*. Bloomington: University of Indiana Press.
Hispanic Division, Library of Congress. 1999. "The Portuguese in the United States." http://www.loc.gov/rr/hispanic/portam.

Pipa

Pipa, also called Chinese lute, is a four-string plucked instrument, which is popular in China, Japan (*biwa*), and Korea (*bipa*). It has a short neck and a pear-shaped wooden body with 19 to 30 frets; it is often found in the hands of heavenly maidens depicted in paintings, such as the famous Flying Apsaras in the caves in Dunhuang, China. In the Eastern Han dynasty, the name described the plectrum's plucking strokes—"pi" means to pluck forward and "pa" to pluck backward—and pipa was played on horseback. The strings are usually tuned to A-d-e-a, from the lowest to the highest (a is the one below middle C), but there are various ways of tuning. During the 20th century, softer twisted-silk strings have been substituted for nylon-wound steel strings, which are too strong for human fingernails to pluck, and false nails, which are constructed of plastic or tortoise shell, are attached to the fingertips with elastic tape to play.

Before the Tang dynasty, "pipa" was a generic term that included all the pear-shaped and plucked instruments. The history of the pipa can be traced back to the Qin dynasty (221–206 BCE). Originally it had a straight neck and round-shaped body, instead of pear-shaped, and was played horizontally with a plectrum, like a guitar. It soon became one of the most popular instruments in China, and it bears the name *Qin-pipa* or *Qinhanzi* today.

During the Wei, Jin, North-South dynasties (220–589 CE), according to Wang Sengqian's (425–485) writing *Collection of Music*, the Queen Wei Wende played pipa, which shows that pipa had been accepted and played by royals and the elite in their societies. The most famous pipa player during this period was Ruan Xin (fl. third century), one of the Seven Sages of the Bamboo Grove. His name became a synonym of the Qin-pipa, which was developed into another Chinese instrument

---

Pipa

The pipa has a long and storied history as a traditional Chinese musical instrument. However, the instrument can be integrated with Western musical instruments, and modern performers of the pipa are taking the instrument in many new directions and venues, including contemporary art music, rock, and American popular music. Several art-music composers—most notably Philip Glass, Terry Riley, Minoru Miki, and Lou Harrison—have written compositions featuring the pipa. Rock bands such as Incubus (on the 2001 song "Aqueous Transmission") and Björk ("I See Who You Are" from her 2007 album *Volta*) feature the pipa prominently. Other artists and engineers are experimenting with adding electric pick-ups to the pipa to allow the instrument to be played with electronic amplification and effects processing, thus further expanding the role and repertoire of this traditional Chinese instrument.

named *ruanxin*, or simply *ruan*. Meanwhile, the pear-shaped pipa had been introduced to China through the Silk Road from Central Asia/Gandhara, during the Wei, Jin, North-South dynasties. Because it was imported from foreign countries and had a bent neck, it was called *Hu-pipa* or *quxiang-pipa*. Apart from the four-stringed pipa, there were also *wuxian pipa* (literally means "five-string pipa"; also known as *Kuchean pipa*), which was a five-string, straight-necked pipa; and a six-string pipa, as well as the two-string *hulei*. All of them were considered to belong to the pipa family.

From the Wei, Jin, North-South dynasties onward, through the Sui and Tang dynasties, the popularity of the pear-shaped pipa increased, reaching its height during the Tang Dynasty (618–907 CE). It became a principal musical instrument in the imperial court, and many Persian and Kuchan performers and teachers were very active in Chang'an, the capital of the Tang dynasty. Pipa was played as a virtuoso solo instrument as well as a part of the orchestra for *daqu* (grand suites), a form of an elaborate music and dance performance. Several poets wrote poems about pipa during the Tang Dynasty. Bai Juyi (772–846) wrote a legendary *Xinyuefu* entitled "The Song of the Pipa Player" (*Pipa Xing*) which told a sad story about an old female pipa player whom he met at on the Xunyang River at Jiujiang, China. Yuan Zhen (779–831) composed "A Song of Pipa" (*Pipa Ge*), which was also a Xinyuefu.

Wu Man plays the *pipa*, a four-stringed plucked instrument from China, during a performance by the Silk Road Ensemble on June 9, 2009. (Hiroyuki Ito/Getty Images)

Pipa fell out of favor in the court during the Song dynasty (960–1276), but continued to be popular as a folk instrument. Gao Ming (ca. 1305–1359) wrote a play for *nanxi* (southern-style Chinese play) named "Tale of the Pipa" (*Pipa ji*), a story about Zhao Wuniang, an abandoned wife, who set out to find her husband and played pipa to make a living during the journey.

During the Ming dynasty, fingernails replaced the plectrum, and the horizontal playing position had changed to the vertical position by the Qing Dynasty. The early version of the pipa had four frets on the neck, but during the early Ming Dynasty extra bamboo frets were attached to the soundboard, increasing the range of the instrument. The number of frets gradually increased to 10, 14, or 16 during the Qing Dynasty, then to 19, 24, 29, and 30 in the 20th century.

The construction of the pipa symbolizes ancient Chinese belief. Its body, by traditional Chinese measurement, is three feet five inches long, which represents the three powers (heaven, the earth, and humanity) and the five elements (metal, wood, water, fire, and earth). Similarly, the four strings represent the four seasons.

Pipa is strongly connected to the image of Wang Zhaojun, a lady who was sent by the Emperor Yuan (ruled 49–33 BCE) of the Western Han dynasty (206 BCE-9 CE) to marry the Chanyu Huhanye of Xiongnu in order to establish friendly relations between the two countries through marriage. It is believed that when Wang Zhaojun left her hometown, she was extremely sad and reluctant to marry Chanyu Huhanye. As she sat on the saddle, she began to play sorrowful melodies on pipa to express her emotions. In most of the paintings of Wang Zhaojun, she is always on horseback, holding her pipa and showing a sorrowful face. There are a couple of famous piece for pipa that depict this story, such as "Lamentations of Lady Zhaojun" (*Zhao Jun Yuan*), which has also been arranged for other Chinese instruments; and "Zhaojun's Exile to the Barbarians" (*Zhao Jun Zhu Sai*).

The repertoire for pipa can be categorized as *wenqu* (lyrical music) or *wuqu* (martial music), and *da* (large or suite) or *xiao* (small). Wenqu pieces usually describe love, sorrow, and scenes of nature, such as "The Lofty Moon" (*Yue'er Gao*), "High Mountains Flowing Water" (*Gaoshan Liushui*), "White Snow in Spring Sunlight" (*Yangchun Baixue*), and "Flowery Moonlit River in Spring" (*Chunjiang Hua Yueye*). Wuqu are relatively faster and more rhythmic, and often depict scenes of battles. Famous wuqu pieces include "The Warlord Takes off His Armor" (*Bawabg Xie Jia*) and "Ambush from Ten Sides" (*Shi Mian Maifu*).

Chloe Hsun Lin

See also: Jingju

Further Reading

Bang-song, Song. 1973. "The Korean *Pip'a* and Its Notation." *Ethnomusicology* 17(3), 460–493.

Chunfang Fei, Faye. 2002. *Chinese Theories of Theater and Performance from Confucius to the Present*. Ann Arbor: University of Michigan Press.

Myers, John. 2002. *The Way of the Pipa: Structure and Imagery in Chinese Lute Music*. Kent, OH: Kent State University Press.

Piphat

Thai *wong piphat* is a genre or style of ensemble, typically consisting of woodwind and percussion instruments. Prior to standardization efforts initiated by the Thai Department of Fine Arts in the 1930s, ensembles varied by region or performance. The Department of Fine Arts classified, standardized, and created a "Classical tradition," thereby standardizing each ensemble's instrumentation. The term *wong* refers to a band. *Piphat* refers to *pii*, the reed instrument used in the ensemble, and *phat* means "to perform music" (Morton, 1976, p. 104). Wong piphat is considered a high-art form in Thailand today, and notwithstanding the decline of the ensemble's role in the homes of the elite, such ensembles have found a new home within academic circles both in Thailand and in academic communities around the world.

Wong piphat music is pentatonic. Thai music utilizes five tones of a seven-tone system, omitting the *mon* style of music, which uses the two discarded pitches as passing tones (Morton, 1965, pp. xiv–xv). Thai music features "polyphonic stratification": each instrument plays a variation of a core melody, with each variation featuring idiomatic characteristics of that instrument. In the case of wong piphat music, the *pii* and *ranat ek* (a boat-shaped xylophone played with two mallets) play the same melody with characteristics idiomatic to themselves.

Initially, the wong piphat ensemble accompanied shadow plays: *khon* (masked dramas performing episodes from the Ramakien), and *lakhon* (unmasked). Today, six variations of the wong piphat ensemble exist (for instrumentation, see Morton, 1976, pp. 105–111). *Khruang ha* (small piphat) has been used since the Ayutthaya period (1351–1767 CE). The *piphat khruang yaay* is considered the high development of the piphat, with the addition of metallophones and *ranat ek* during the reign of King Rama IV (1808–1868). The piphat khruang yaay accompanies both khon and lakhon today. The *wong piphat khruang khuu*, or double piphat, refers to the pair of ranat ek leading the group.

The *piphat hang nong* ensemble accompanies Buddhist cremation ceremonies. This ensemble features the *klong khaek* and *pii chawaa*, both of which are believed to have Javanese origins (Morton, 1976, p. 103). The pii chawaa (a cognate of "Java") replaces the *pii nai*, presumably because of its clamorous, wailing qualities. The *piphat mon* ensemble did not gain popularity until the cremation of Queen Thepsirin (1834–1862), who was of *mon* descent (ethnically Burmese). The ensemble features the *khong mon wong yaay* and *wong lek*—semicircular sets of suspended gong-kettle drums similar to the Burmese *kyi waing*, or the *mon Bat Kine* half-moon-shaped gong-kettle instrument. The piphat mon has substantially replaced the piphat hang nong for cremation ceremonies, especially in central Thailand (Wong, 1998). *Piphat deukdamban* was created in 1898 by Prince Narisara Nuwattiwong (1863–1947). The ensemble consists of quieter instruments, and features the *saw uu*, a two-stringed bowed lute. Replacing the pii are the *khlui phiang aw* and *khlui uu*, large- and medium-sized bamboo flutes. *Lakhon deukdamban*, a hybridized genre of dance that fuses Western theatrical arts and Thai performance, developed during the reign of King Rama V (1853–1910).

John Forrestal

See also: Colometry/Colometric; Kendang; Malay Music; Mridangam

Further Reading

Miller, Terry. 1994. *A History of Siamese Music Reconstructed from Western Documents, 1505–1932*. DeKalb: Center for Southeast Asian Studies, Northern Illinois University.

Morton, David. 1965. "Traditional Instrumental Music of Thailand." PhD diss., The University of California, Los Angeles.

Morton, David. 1976. *The Traditional Music of Thailand*. Berkeley: The University of California Press.

Wong, Deborah. 1998. "Mon Music for Thai Deaths: Ethnicity and Status in Thai Urban Funerals." *Asian Folklore Studies* 57(1), 99–101. http://ccbs.ntu.edu.tw/FULLTEXT/JR-EMISC/DEBORAH.HTM.

Wong, Deborah. 2001. *Sounding the Center: History and Aesthetics in Thai Buddhist Performance*. Chicago: University of Chicago Press.

Yupho, Dhanit. 1960. *Thai Musical Instruments*. Bangkok: Siva Phorn.

Polish National Dances

Polish national dances have been symbolic of Polish national identity throughout the country's turbulent history and are representative of the nation's soul and spirit. They portray a Polish national pride and a homogenous Polish identity that was frequently on the brink of destruction under occupying foreign powers, such as during the three partitions in 1772, 1793, and 1795 when Poland was divided between Prussia, Austria, and Russia on the initiative of Frederick the Great of Prussia. Both Polish musical idiom and Polish dances were a source of strength and unity for people in these difficult times.

There are four Polish national dances from four different geographic areas, each of which has distinctive music, movements, and colorful costumes: *polonaise* (*polonez*), *mazurek*, *oberek*, and *krakowiak*. As documented by Jan from Lublin, the oldest collection of dance tunes that were recognized as folk dances and the oldest source containing rhythmic structures can be traced to the first part of the 16th century.

The polonez, with its noble and stately character, has always been associated with the most highly regarded national causes, and it was given the status of the primary national dance of Poland. In the 16th century, Polish folk dances resembling the present polonez were danced by the lower ranks of the gentry. At first they were danced to a sung accompaniment, but after they became popular among the aristocracy, instrumental musicians played them at court dances. The Polish name of the dance, "polonez," stems from the polonized form of the French term *polonaise*, which was introduced in the 17th century; it was derived from the *chodzony* (walking dance) and known as a *pieszy* (pedestrian) or *chmielowy* (hops) dance.

The Polish term "polonez" replaced the earlier name of "Polish dance" in the 18th century when it entered the dance repertoire of the nobility. Originally, the polonez, or polonaise, was a dance done by men alone (often while wearing armor), but it became a dance for couples in the 19th century. The polonaise is usually danced in costumes of the Polish nobility of the 17th century; specifically, theatrical (not everyday) costumes from the period of the Duchy of Warsaw (1811–1814) created by Napoleon before his defeat in 1815 (empire dresses, cavalry uniforms). The dance was performed in both formal and public ceremonies, particularly at weddings or as the first dance of a formal ball. The polonaise posture symbolizes the national pride of the Polish people: dancers hold their heads straight and high, while the hands' movement is slow, elegant, and gracious. The first couple dancing the polonez used to lead the dance at court balls, not only in Poland but also throughout Europe in the 18th and 19th centuries.

Polonaise also appeared in chamber music, concertos, and opera, often with the title *Polacca*. During the period of the partitions when Russia occupied one-third of Poland, Russian composers were attracted to the form of the polonaise, which acquired a meaning of "dignity" and "royalty" and was often associated with the appearance of the Tsar, or rulers in general. It also appeared in Russian operas as a symbol of the Polish gentry (e.g., Mussorgsky's *Boris Godunov*, Tchaikovsky's *Eugene Onegin*). Moreover, the polonaise of Michal Kleofas Ogiński, especially his "Farewell to the Homeland," became extremely popular in Russia and have been rescored for different instrumental settings.

As the polonaise ceased to be essentially a dance with sung accompaniment and became chiefly instrumental, it underwent stylistic and formal changes. Its melodies became more ornamental. The Germans, for whom the polonaise represented "Polish taste and Polish style," frequently included the polonaise as a movement in dance suites and sonatas (e.g., Bach, Schubert, Mozart). The most famous composer of polonaise is Frederic Chopin (Szopen) (1810–1849), the Romantic-era composer. His well-known Polish contemporaries include Michal Kleofas Oginski, Wojciech Zywny, Józef Elsner, Józef Kozlowski, and Karol Kurpinski. In the 20th and 21st centuries, the National Folk Ensembles *Mazowsze* and *Śląsk* have become known internationally for their performance of polonaise and the other Polish national dances in their beautiful and colorful costumes.

The mazurka, or in Polish *mazurek*, is another Polish national dance, and became the symbol of "Polishness" and the hope for freedom when its well-known music was adopted as the Polish national anthem. When Poland was absorbed by occupying powers in 1795 and the country was wiped from the map, many Poles emigrated to the neighboring countries; in 1797, "Mazurek Dabrowskiego," first known as "Song of the Polish Legion," was written by Jozef Wybicki near Bologna in Italy. It included lines such as "Poland will never be destroyed while we are alive." It was created for the troops of General Jan Dabrowski, who served under Napoleon during his conquest of Europe with the hope of regaining Polish independence. "Mazurek Dabrowskiego" became the symbol of hope not only for Poles but also for neighboring Czechs, Ukrainians, and Serbs in their struggle for freedom from foreign interventions.

The historical sources are unclear, so the origin of the melody of the dance called mazurka remains a mystery. There are many spellings and variations of the dance name (including *mazur*, *mazurek*, and *mazurka*, among others) due to its wide popularity and adoption by many cultures and languages. However, the dance is known around the world by Polish people. The name of the dance comes from the region of Mazovia in the eastern regions of Poland. The people of the province were called Mazurs; thus, the dance "mazurka" derives from the inhabitants of the region. Augustus II, the Elector of Saxony and King of Poland (1697–1733) introduced the mazurka dance into the courts of Germany. The dance became fashionable in higher social circles in Paris, then London, and in general in Western Europe after Poland was partitioned.

In the 1830s and 1840s, the mazurka enjoyed its greatest popularity in the high-society salons and parties. It was especially popular among the Polish exiles in Paris and their aristocratic patrons. After Russia's occupation and partition of Poland, the mazurka also became popular among the Russian aristocracy and peasantry. In the 19th century, *mazur* was danced in court to an instrumental music accompaniment. It is prominent in operas such as *The Haunted Manor (Straszny Dwor)* and *Halka* by celebrated Polish composer Stanislaw Moniuszko. Other composers of mazur include Fryderyk Szopen (Chopin), Henryk Wieniawski, Karol Szymanowski, and Alexander Zarzycki. The dance itself is highly improvisatory, having no set figures; more than 50 steps exist. The dance is full of contrast: it is lively, fast-paced, and joyful but also elegant, dignified, and bold. The tempo is fast but irregular, accentuated by the clicks of the dancers' boots. Both men and women wear fur-lined jackets or costumes from different regions of Poland. This fast-paced, energetic dance became a national symbol in several distinct ways through its music and movement patterns.

The oberek, also known as *obertas* (common in the 19th century) or *ober* (the name used less frequently), is the most vivacious and acrobatic of the four national dances. The oberek originated in the villages of Mazowsze in central Poland; it is danced by couples to instrumental music in triple meter. It has never been danced by the nobility or in the costumes of the nobility; it is truly a "folk" dance. The name "oberek" is derived from the verb *obracac sie*, meaning "to spin." The dance's main movement is rotational: the dancers spin and twirl around the room. In central Poland, dances from the family of the mazur (*kujawiak, mazur, oberek*) were often performed in a set preceded by a *chodzony* (walking dance, a folk polonaise) and organized by their increasing tempos. The set ended with an oberek. However, this 19th-century practice was abandoned early in the 20th century.

The oberek is a national dance not only because it is common all over Poland, but also because it is danced by all the social classes. Different regions, however, still retain their local style, variations, and specific tunes. Folk dance ensemble often perform the national form of the oberek in the costumes from Łowicz, Mazovia (the central part of the region). The dance is very joyful, noisy, and exuberant. The dancers use many ornamental and acrobatic figures, including jumping, kneeling, and clicking the feet. Women wear colorful striped wool skirts with scarves tied around the head; the men wear white shirts with wide sleeves, waistcoats, and loose trousers. The oberek is very often improvised on the spot, especially when danced at wedding ceremonies in villages. The National Folk Song and Dance Ensembles *Mazowsze* and *Slask* perform "most artistic, but stylized rendition[s]" of the oberek.

The oberek is danced by couples who are placed on a circle and rotate both around the whole circle and around their own axis (to the right). The dancers follow the direction "against the sun" (*pod slonce*, counterclockwise). The strongest dancer may ask for a change of direction of the whole group, which then would dance *"ze sloncem"* (with the sun, clockwise). The most difficult change of direction involves a simultaneous change of the rotation around the personal axis, performed to the left only by the best dancers. In central Poland, the music for the oberek is typically performed by a small village band, a *kapela*, dominated by the violin. The size and exact makeup of the kapela depended on the part or region of the country from which it originated.

In classical music, the name "oberek" was used by composers of stylized dances, starting with Oskar Kolberg, who collected obereks from Mazovia in four volumes of his study dedicated to the Mazowsze region and in two volumes dedicated to the Kujawy region. Other Polish composers of obereks include Henryk Wieniawski, Roman Statkowski, Karol Szymanowski, Aleksander Tansman, and Grazyna Bacewicz. The fastest mazurkas by Fryderyk Chopin (such as his Mazurka, op. 56, no. 2) are also examples of obereks;. In contrast to the mazurka, polonez, and krakowiak, the title "oberek" is very rare in the music of Western composers and, interestingly, it does not occur among the titles of Polish dances composed in 19th-century America.

Krakowiak is a Polish dance from the region of Kraków, the old capital of Poland (used by the Piast and Jagiello dynasties until the 16th century) and the center of the southern region of the country, called Malopolska. The dance dates back to the 16th and 17th centuries, when it was included in organ and lute tablatures. In the mid-19th century, the krakowiak became a popular ballroom dance in Austria and France and became a "national dance" of Poland. For Poland, this was a time of occupation and unsuccessful uprisings (1831, 1848) which sought to regain the country's independence. The krakowiak, polonaise, and mazurek were perceived in the Parisian salons as symbols of solidarity with the oppressed Polish nation. At the same time, the krakowiak became a choice of composers who transformed it into an extensive and even virtuosic form, beginning with Fryderyk Szopen's "Krakowiak" and including pieces by Zygmunt Noskowski, Ignacy Jan Paderewski, and Roman Statkowski. The krakowiak eventually lost its popularity as a functional dance (with both peasants and gentry). Instead, it became an impressive "exhibition" dance to be watched and applauded. The colorful costumes and fast tempo have contributed to the ongoing appeal of the krakowiak among the Polish people and their descendents all over the world.

The three most characteristic steps in krakowiak are: the *galop* (fast running forward), the *hołubiec* (jump with clicking the heels and stamping), and the *krzesany* (also stamping with the foot). When performed on the stage, it includes a variety of group figures, in addition to the turns, jumps, running and stamping steps. The *strój krakowski* (Kraków costume) is the favorite among the various regional costumes of Poland and has come to symbolize the traditional costume of Poland in general. The women wear white shirts with broad sleeves and collars decorated with lace, colorful waistcoats with sequins and rich embroidery, coral beads, flowery skirts with white lace aprons, and wreaths of flowers with many colored ribbons in their hair. Their high-laced red boots have heels with metal tips and they accentuate each click or jump. The men wear long, embroidered coats, white shirts, striped pants, and embroidered waistcoats. Their accessories include a special belt with decorative strings of small metal plates, and a square hat with peacock feathers.

All four of the national dances are symbolic of Polish spirit throughout the centuries; romantic and nostalgic but also rich, lively, and forever joyful.

Anna Hamling

See also: Austro-German Dances; Polka

Further Reading

Czekanowska, A. 1990. *Polish Folk Music: Slavonic Heritage—Polish Tradition—Contemporary Trends*. Cambridge: Cambridge University Press.

Stęszewski, J. 1995. "Polish National Character in Music: What Is It?" In T. Walas (ed.), *Stereotypes and Nations: Kraków: International Cultural Centre 1991*, 225–230. Kraków, Poland: International Cultural Centre.

Polka

The polka was an exceptionally popular social dance from the mid-19th century through the early 20th century. The dance is in 2/4 meter and generally includes three steps and a hop, though interpretations vary widely. Rather than a standard form, the polka might best be understood as a phenomenon. Socially, "polkamania" swept through Europe and America during the 1840s; politically, the dance became an important tool for identity-building among immigrant communities in the United States by the end of the 19th century.

Many of the earliest descriptions of the polka are in Czech, yet the polka was likely related to or inspired by Polish dancing. The word *polka* translates from the Czech as "Polish woman," but might also originate from the Czech root "*půl*" (diminutive "*půlka*" or "half," describing the dance's half-time rhythm), or "*pole*" ("field," describing the polka's possible beginnings as a peasant round dance).

The conflation of the Czech and Polish cultures in the polka allowed both nations to harness the popularity of the dance to promote their own political aims. On the one hand, the invention of Czech dances such as the polka and the use of the Czech language in codifying those dances (the language had been banned in higher social settings since 1780) were at the center of a Czech National Rebirth, which dominated Prague's middle classes by the second half of the 19th century. On the other hand, many Polish-Americans celebrated the dance as an important part of their heritage during the 20th century (even though, as some scholars argue, the polka is rarely performed among folk musicians in Poland today). In any case, the

---

Lawrence Welk and Polka

Dubbed the king of "Champagne Music"—a title given by his detractors but embraced by his supporters—bandleader Lawrence Welk was a champion of European heritage dances such as polkas, landlers, and the like, and his popular weekly television program aired more than 1,000 episodes from 1951 to 1982. At a time when the youth of America were gravitating toward Elvis, the Beatles, Van Halen, and the Cure, Welk held steadfastly to the ethnic-inspired big-band dance music of the mid-century, and it was not uncommon to see an organ, bagpipes, concertinas, accordions, and other less mainstream instruments accompanying songs. Welk himself often left the conductor's podium to dance polkas, merengues, and other period dance styles of the 1950s and 1960s with audience members during the show tapings. The show also featured several African American performers in its regularly occurring cast, and tap dancing remained a staple of show content long after the style's heyday in terms of popularity.

polka played and continues to play a key role in identity- and community-building for both Czechs and Polish-Americans.

Explanations of the polka's beginnings reflect the early stirrings of the Czech National Rebirth. The most popular origin story, first printed in the periodical *Bohemia* in 1844, names Anna Chadimová as the dance's inventor. According to the account, Chadimová performed the polka one Sunday afternoon in Kostelec nad Labem (a city just north of the Czech capital of Prague) for an audience that included the town's head musician, Josef Neruda. Neruda's transcriptions allowed the polka to travel to Prague, where it was enthusiastically received. Jaroslav Langer printed an earlier account in the *Časopis českého musea* (1835), where he explained that the polka was an adaptation of the Polish *krakowiak*. The krakowiak, he explained, had become mixed with local Czech dances and, coupled with a localized style unique to Eastern Bohemia, became the polka. In his landmark Czech-German dictionary of 1837, Josef Jungmann defined the polka simply as a Polish dance.

In contrast to those origin stories, one of the most prolific of the early polka scholars, Zdeněk Nejedlý (1878–1962), argued that the dance was actually an urban falsification that did not belong to Czech folk culture. He stressed the polka's possible foreign roots in the krakowiak and the perpetuation of the dance especially among urban (as opposed to rural peasant) communities. Nejedlý's writing illustrates the ways in which the polka became enmeshed in political works and theory through history. His situating of the polka as a bourgeois dance that threatened a true Czech culture is consistent with the policies of Czechoslovakia's communist administration, for which Nejedlý worked as the First Minister of Culture and Education from 1948 to 1962.

In more recent research, John Tyrrell has challenged Nejedlý's scholarship and argues that the polka has little in common with the krakowiak. German scholar Karl Horak has further argued that the polka was only a renamed schottische in its beginnings (Tyrrell, 1988). It is worth noting that the word "polka" appears in an English-language music collection—P. L. Duport's *Miss George Anna Reinagle: Music Book for Fancy Tunes* (1825)—before any of the Czech mentions.

Regardless of the dance's exact national origins, the polka traveled to much of Europe from Prague during the 1830s and 1840s. A Bohemian military band introduced the dance in Vienna, Austria, in 1839; the polka also reached St. Petersburg, Russia, in 1839; a dance master named Johann Raab performed the polka in Slavic costume at the Theatre Odéon in Paris in 1840; and the polka reached England by way of dance master Eugène Coulon, who presented the dance in London in 1844.

The polka's reception in Paris was especially enthusiastic. Leading choreographers and fashion trendsetters Henri Cellarius and Eugène Coralli quickly refined the dance to suit French tastes, and their newly adapted versions contributed much to the polka's rising popularity. These choreographers' ensuing rivalry also culminated in a public polka contest, from which Coralli emerged victorious, which further fuelled the polkamania that swept through Europe during the 1840s.

In London, the polka became especially linked with high fashionability (and removed from its Bohemian roots). An article for the *Illustrated London News* (May 11, 1844) provides close descriptions of the steps for a "true" polka—one learned first-hand from Eugène Coralli (who traveled to London in 1844) that was "danced at the balls of the nobility and gentry"—before concluding: "la polka is a noiseless dance; there is no stamping of heels or toes, or kicking of legs in sharp angles forward. This may do very well at the thresholds of a Bohemian *auberge*, but is inadmissible into the *salons* of London or Paris." The author's writing reveals that the polka served the elite and that its Bohemian background was to be suppressed.

The polka was received equally enthusiastically in the United States. Like the *Illustrated London News*, the popular American periodical *Godey's Lady's Book* provided a full description of the dance for readers in November of 1845, though the author noted 10 possible figures among the steps (compared to London's four). The author also emphasized the scandal associated with the polka: "What blind and tender confidence must she not have in her cavalier, to thus cast herself so dangerously into his arms! But, also, with what ardent and devoted anxiety does her partner receive her . . . What affection is required between both! It is a figure that we would . . . not recommend to have introduced into our ball rooms." Shock at the closeness of the polka (which was typical for any newly introduced couple's dance) only helped perpetuate its fashionability, which eventually inspired James K. Polk to call on the dance—and its pun—in his 1844 presidential campaigns.

The polka's fashionable nature also manifested more generally in Europe and the United States in women's clothing. Skirts were shortened to allow for the sight of ladies' feet (and to avoid damaging their dresses during the rigor of the dance), shortened polka jackets also appeared, and polka dots became a newly admired pattern in fabrics. Western art music composers such as Bedřich Smetana (1824–1884) and Johann Strauss I (1804–1849) and II (1825–1899) also included polkas in their compositions.

Part of the polka's success had to do with its ties to the middle class, and it was sometimes seen as deposing the dances of the aristocracy, especially the minuet, waltz, and gallop (galop). Refugees from this Great Emigration also inspired waves of sympathy and rallying displays of Polish culture. Nejedlý himself described the suffering Poles as "the mouthpiece of all [Czech] people" (Nejedlý, 1925, p. 112). Additionally, many refugees such as the pianist Frederic Chopin were aristocrats who settled in France, where they were welcomed enthusiastically in the wake of France's own revolution for their elite status.

Though the polka persisted throughout much of the 19th century, dances like the tango surpassed its popularity during the early 20th, except among immigrant communities in United States. An estimated 2.5 million Poles arrived in the United States at the end of the 19th and early 20th centuries, and this population harnessed the polka toward building a new sense of community and identity as Polish-Americans. A boom in the availability of music recordings, as well as the rising prominence of radio broadcasts, also contributed to the polka's continued growth.

Today, polka music in the United States is divided into five main categories: Polish, Slovenian (or "Cleveland"), Bohemian (or Czech), German (or "Dutchman"), and Mexican (or conjunto). Polish and Slovenian styles are prominent in urban centers surrounding the Great Lakes (e.g., Detroit and Cleveland). These styles embrace elements of modern popular music, particularly in their orchestration;

traditional polka scoring would include squeezeboxes (the accordion and similar instruments) and military brass, but the Polish and Slovenian styles also use electronic instruments. In contrast, the Czech and German styles occupy more rural spaces in the Midwest, such as Wisconsin and Nebraska, and are generally more conservative; their performers identify themselves not as "polka" bands, but as "old time" bands. Conjunto is prominent in areas of Texas and Arizona. It is characterized by its use of accordion and *bajo sexto* (a 12-string bass guitar).

Individual performers helped codify regional polka styles. Among many others, prominent musicians include Walter "Li'l Wally" Jagiello, who helped define the Polish style; "Polka King" Frankie Yankovic, who helped establish the Slovenian style and is well known across genres; Romy Gosz, who was celebrated for his Czech style; John Wilfahrt, whose sound came to characterize Dutchman; and Narcisco Martínez, whose playing set the foundations for conjunto.

The International Polka Association (IPA) was founded in 1968 and continues to play an important role in organizing and promoting the polka. The IPA hosts an annual Polka Convention, which travels among Chicago, Detroit, and Buffalo each year. The IPA also manages the Polka Hall of Fame and Museum in Chicago. Additional halls of fame include the National Cleveland-Style Polka Hall of Fame in Cleveland, Ohio, and the Wisconsin Polka Hall of Fame in Appleton, Wisconsin.

Kelly St. Pierre

See also: Accordion (Americas); Accordion, Types of; Polish National Dances; Schottische

Further Reading

Bukowczyk, John J. 1987. *And My Children Did Not Know Me: A History of the Polish Americans*. Bloomington: Indiana University Press.

Greene, Victor. 1992. *A Passion for Polka: Old-Time Ethnic Music in America*. Berkeley: University of California Press.

Keil, Charles, Angeliki V. Keil, and Dick Blau. 1992. *Polka Happiness*. Philadelphia: Temple University Press.

Knowles, Mark. 2009. *The Wicked Waltz and Other Scandalous Dances: Outrage of Couple Dancing in the 19th and Early 20th Centuries*. Jefferson, NC: McFarland.

Leary, James P. 1988. "Czech- and German-American 'Polka' Music." *Journal of American Folklore* 101, 339–345.

March, Richard. 1989. "Slovenian- and Polish-American 'Polka' Music." *Journal of American Folklore* 102, 81–85.

Nejedlý, Zdeněk. 1925. "Polka." *Naše řeč* 9(4), 108–114.

Tyrrell, John. 1988. *Czech Opera*. Cambridge: Cambridge University Press.

Polynesia, Music of

Early European contact with the more than 1,800 peoples of Polynesia resulted in descriptions of drumming, dancing, and vocal music, and Christian missionaries found that singing was the most effective route to the conversion of native peoples. Although indigenous Polynesian languages had no collective term for "music" (or musical instruments), it is more intrinsic to societal functions than dance. Syllabic, intoned recitation and solo melismatic chant are found in regional variants through the Pacific; multipart choral singing (sometimes over a drone) thrives in western and central Polynesia.

By the 19th century, most Polynesians had come into contact with European folk songs (through whalers and traders), and hymnals started to be published in local languages: for example, the people of Tuvalu were introduced to Christian hymns by the recently converted Samoans. Dance, a conspicuous feature of social life, has drawn comments ranging from condemnation by explorers and missionaries to enthusiastic appreciation from travelers and anthropologists. Polynesian dance (both standing and sitting) is a visual extension of sung poetry conveyed through indirectness, often in honor of chiefs or other important people, and Polynesian dancers are considered storytellers, rather than actors. Specialists compose poetry, add music and movements, and rehearse for months before a public ceremony. The most notable studies placing this important cultural form in its social context were conducted in the Cook Islands, the Marquesas Islands, New Zealand, Tahiti, Tokelau, Tonga, and Hawaii. Studies from Rotuma and Samoa focus more on the clowning and theatrical elements used in dance.

New Zealand Maori dance includes several types: *haka* (posturing and war dances ending with a violent movement and out-thrust tongue), *waita-a-ringa* (action songs with more graceful hand movements, often set to Western music), and *poi* (women rhythmically swing one to four balls attached to strings of different lengths). In Hawaiian *hula*, the performer is dancer, singer, and instrumentalist simultaneously, with important narrative and interpretative elements.

A notable hybrid style originating in Hawaii became known as Pan-Polynesian Pop (by the 1950s) and Pan-Pacific Pop (by the 1960s), after being adapted in parts of Micronesia and Melanesia. The past 25 years have witnessed a renaissance in indigenous music and dance and new popular styles. Traditional chants and dances and new works in these idioms are featured at local festivals, civic functions, international gatherings such as the Festival of Pacific Arts (featuring 2,000 artists every four years throughout Oceania), and choreographed cultural presentations by the Polynesian Cultural Center (sponsored by the Mormon Church) in Laie, Oahu, Hawaii.

Polynesian musical instruments were traditionally less valued than the voice and are associated primarily with public dance performance. Body percussion such as clapping and slapping is augmented by slit drums, rolled mats beaten with sticks (Samoa and Futuna), sounding boards beaten with sticks (Rennell and Bellona), gourds slapped with the hand and thumped on the ground (Hawaii), small vertical drums (Hawaii), and small rattles. Tall, single-headed temple drums with sharkskin membranes were the highest-status instruments in central eastern Polynesia and Hawaii and survive in major museums worldwide. Two-headed drums modelled on Western drums—the "tin" (for kerosene or crackers, beaten with sticks), and the "box" (wooden packing crates beaten with the hands)—are essential to certain evolved dance genres in western and central Polynesia. The only indigenous Polynesian chordophone was the mouth-bow, but European-style plucked strings such as the four-string ukulele (Hawaii), coconut banjo (Cook Islands and the Marquesas), and six-string guitar have contributed to modern musical styles.

Conch-shell trumpets called *pu* (both end-blown and side-blown) and slit drums were used both for signals and to announce important events. Small bamboo (side-blown) nose flutes were widespread, and panpipes were indigenous to the Samoa-Tonga area. In New Zealand, where there is no bamboo, the Maori make exceptionally fine ærophones of other materials. Brass bands are mostly connected with the government, police, military, and schools.

GEOGRAPHY

The eastern region of the Pacific Ocean comprises 18 island groups lying in a rough triangle extending over 30 million square kilometers, from Hawaii (north), Easter Island (east), to New Zealand (south, with more than 90% of the area's total land mass). The name "Polynesia" derives from the Greek words *poly* (many) and *nesos* (island). Fiji, at the western central edge of the region, is closely related to Polynesia through music, dance, and culture, but is part of Melanesia (lying closer to Australia) and Micronesia (near continental Asia).

Prehistoric settlement patterns led to movement from larger volcanic islands to smaller coral atolls, but 20th-century Polynesians have reversed this process, returning to larger population centers in search of economic opportunity and a more urban lifestyle. Migration has been focused within the same group of islands (as from Tuamotu to Tahiti) and between countries with strong historical relationships (from the Cook Islands, Samoa, and Tonga to New Zealand).

WESTERN POLYNESIA

In this area of the central Pacific, Tonga and Samoa are the dominant islands, with significant musical life on Niue, Tokelau, Tuvalu (formerly the British colonial Ellice Islands), and Wallis and Futuna. Religious music is not known to have been associated with these cultures before European contact, as traditional social organization focused on lineage and village. Three types of wooden slit drums (the smaller *pate*, from Tahiti; the *lali*, from Fiji; and the large *logo*, created by missionaries as a bell) signal modern church events. Most other kinds of percussion, flutes, and chordophones are now obsolete. Populations with American ties such as American Samoa and Hawaii have made significant contributions to the culture of the West Coast cities of the continental United States.

The nine inhabited islands of the Samoan archipelago (four forming the independent state and five comprising the territory of American Samoa), form a distinct and homogenous musical area centered around vocal music using a formal style of speech. All musical performances are considered "songs," which may heighten emotions or add dignity through group participation in ceremony. Larger villages have resident composers (usually male) who create rhyming texts lines without vocables. Several hundred *fagomo* legends with embedded *tagi* songs form a popular type of night-time entertainment, accompanied by rolled floor mats beaten with sticks and flicked with the hands. Medicinal incantations are still widely trusted to cure headaches, hiccups, skin blemishes, and choking on a fishbone.

Samoan children's group games incorporate short songs centering on two tones a perfect fourth apart; youth also sing during activities such as gathering shellfish, massaging adults, teasing pets, and losing a tooth. Around the beginning of the 20th century, war and paddling songs became dissociated from their original contexts and dance styles evolved: the large groups of singing dancers were replaced by nonsinging dancers who performed independently.

Modern Samoan group songs in traditional genres (welcome, farewell, praise, sorrow) are composed for village events; they are added to local repertoires without individual titles or marks of ownership. Village choirs strongly favor the lowest voice (*malu*), which is taught first, a whole strophe at a time, before the upper parts (*usu* and *ato*) are added. There are often two or three times as many basses as tenors in male choirs, although mixed choruses maintain a balance of voice parts. Groups perform seated, and song leaders are expected to be able to teach all parts from memory, regulate clapping during dance songs, and lead the highest vocal line. There is no written record of music associated with pre-Christian religion.

On Nukunonu, one of the three coral atolls of Tokelau (north of Samoa), traditional chanting was encouraged by the more liberal Catholic mission. *Haumate* chants are performed at modern funerals for the laying out of the body, *tuala* accompany wedding processions, and dance requires more poetically complex songs. Competitive *fatele* (action songs) are presented in dialogue between "home" and "visiting" groups at all festive occasions.

Tuvalu has experienced drastic changes in religion, social organization, music, and dance due to the systematic Christianization of the archipelago after 1861 by the London Missionary Society. Church choirs, ceremonial chants repurposed as entertainment, and radio have led to the domination of European-American traits, but Tuvalu's independence in 1978 encouraged a revival of traditional local forms such as play songs, *taanga* (genealogical songs), *onga* and *fakunau* (chanted dance songs). While most Tuvalu singing resembles Polynesian speech-song and level recitative, triadic music is also present due to influences from neighboring Melanesia. Pentatonic, melismatic responsorial dance songs emerged after the arrival of Samoan missionaries and flourished from 1890 to 1915.

Tonga was not colonized by 19th-century Western powers, so older dances such as *ula* and *faha'iula* survive alongside new dances requiring song (from both the dancers and a large group of singers standing at the rear). The *fangufangu* nose flute is still taught in schools, but the blowing of multiple conch trumpets for entertainment at cricket matches has declined. Multipart singing in three to eight parts, with the melody in the second lowest position, is integral to all choral music. Accomplished composers are called *punake*, and stereotyped melodic progressions and cadential formulæ are common to *lakalaka* and *ma'ulu'ulu* dances. Song texts are often repeated, as audiences derive great satisfaction from deciphering the historical and mythological allusions from their texts. Audience encouragement (even shouting) inspires dancers to achieve a state of inner exhilaration called *mafana* (shown by tilting the head to the side). Numerical notation was introduced to Tonga in the 19th century for the teaching of Mormon hymns, and male falsetto is employed for the highest part in *hiva kakala* songs. As in Samoa, spoken *fananga* fables are enlivened by one or more short *fakatangi* songs, and children sing hundreds of activity songs.

Tongan dance remains a functioning part of the socio-political system, and is abstractly literary in its interpretation. The most important modern type is lakalaka, danced by up to 200 people performing sideways steps in place; it can be described as a sung polyphonic choral speech with specific choreography for men (*me'etu'upaki*, a standing dance with changes of formation and twirled dance paddles) and women (*fa'fahiula*, with dancers seated in a curved row, using hand and arm movements to interpret selected words). Another contemporary group dance is ma'ulu'ulu (Samoa and Tonga), in which poetry is conveyed visually through arm movements by seated participants, usually from a school or church.

The solitary atoll of Niue maintains a tradition of men's challenge dances (*koli takalo*) and songs (*lologo takalo*). Dancers divide into two opposing warrior groups and enact alternating martial movements to loud rhythmic recitations, culminating in mimed hand-to-hand combat. Niue's unique nose flute with two or three fingerholes (originally *kofe*, or bamboo, now called *kikihoa*) shifted from wooden construction to bamboo and does not have a preferred scale.

EASTERN POLYNESIA

In eastern Polynesia, traditional social organization was highly stratified and focused on lineage and religious practices. These were centered in ceremonies on the *marae* (outdoor platform temples), and on concepts of *mana* (spiritual power or cosmic energy) and *taboo* (forbidden behaviors and objects), which governed people's lives. Chanters were specialists responsible for memorizing and reciting important texts, including long genealogical chants that validated a chief's mana.

Tahiti dominates the Society Islands and the rest of the central eastern region of Polynesia, including the Cook Islands and most of French Polynesia (the Austral, Gambier [Mangareva], Marquesas, and Tuamotu Islands). Eastern Polynesian culture extends all the way to the tiny islands of Pitcairn in the southeast. Tahitian songs such as the topical *ute* (with eight-beat couplets and male grunting) are found throughout the region. Traditional chants were collectively named *mako*, although modern usage restricts the term to long, flowing monotonic poems with occasional notes a minor third below the main tone. Interplay of vowel length and word stress with the musical structure is very complex.

Sacred and secular hymn singing forms an especially important part of the musical heritage of the Cook Islands. The atoll of Pukapuka has three villages that still perform *tila* (wrestling chants, named after the *tila*, or mast, of a canoe), which are short, triple-meter recitations underscored by hand clapping and syncopation that gradually accelerate as performers dance. Pukapukan *lalau* (fishing chants) were the principal group songs of paternal lineages (and later, the villages) to celebrate fishing contest victories, and other chants for individuals survive (laments, love chants, and boasting songs). Manihiki and Rakahanga, formerly occupied alternately for reasons of food conservation, are noted within the Cook Islands for the distinctive sound of their *ura pau* dance drumming (using the largest number of slit-drums, with higher tunings than anywhere else in Polynesia).

There are at least 40 named song types in the southern Cook Islands. In addition to the Tahitian ute and the missionary *himene*, indigenous types include the *pe'e* (historical and love songs performed as an integral part of storytelling), *amu* (unison praise songs and laments relating a life story or great deeds, performed and composed mostly by women and accompanied by wailing), and *karakia* (male incantations or invocations). One type specific to Mangagia has disappeared due to missionary activity: the night-time *tara kakai* (death talks) ceremony described by William Gill in 1875, with its crying songs, funeral games, and dirges accompanied by weapons, has been replaced by the *'eva*, men's songs honoring warriors or battles. Competitive music performances and the annual Constitution Day celebrations in Rarotonga feature sacred and secular music, including the spectacular *'ura pa'u* dance and its accompanying percussion ensemble (the *pakau tarekareka*).

An impressive Polynesian culture flourished on Easter Island (Rapanui) before the arrival of the first Europeans on Easter Sunday, 1772. Ceremonial dances performed at the *ahu* (sacred sites with the famous huge stone images) were a form of worship. Ancient stories (some still extant today) were written in script or glyphs on *kohua rongorongo* (wooden tablets) and chanted by specialists at rites of the bird-man cult and other ceremonies. Chile annexed the island in 1888 and began regular ship service in 1954, bringing popular Latin forms such as the *corrido*, tango, and waltz through performing *conjuntos*. Contemporary Tahitian music is the most popular "foreign" music on Easter Island, and there has been a recent resurgence of interest in learning and performing traditional spirit chants (*akuaku*), *riu* (laments and funeral lineages), and dance.

French Polynesia embraces five archipelagos, and a high level of intelligibility persists among the distinct languages that had emerged by the time of European exploration. Although varying histories have created musical diversity in the region, the language and performance traditions of Tahiti have dominated the whole area since 1880.

The eight volcanic Society Islands can be divided musically by southeastern and northwestern choral singing practices. Society Islands dance is known for its extremely fast hip movements; in pre-missionary times, groups of professional traveling entertainers called *Arioli* expressed social comment through danced dramas, and chiefs or priests could be satirized in an effort to improve social conditions. The *Hieva* (now the most important dance occasion in French Polynesia) and the annual revels, popularly called *Tiurai*, have included folkloric competitions of Tahitian singing since July 1881. Dance troupes from the Cook, Austral, Tuamotu, Marquesas, and Society Islands travel to Tahiti to compete and to learn from each other. The conversion of Tahiti in 1815 marked a turning point in Pacific history, and led to the development of three indigenized genres of choral singing.

The five Austral Islands to the southwest of Tahiti maintain eight- to 13-part choral singing with high-pitched soloists; these exhibit the richest and fullest textures of Tahitian-language himene. The inhabitants of the 76 coral atolls that form the Tuamoto archipelago were converted by Mormon missionaries in 1845, and there is a strong French military presence due to continued nuclear testing at the southern end of the chain. The Austral Islanders have embraced Tahitian polyphonic choral singing styles and are famed for the accompaniment style known as *ta'iri pa'umoto*, a rapid, percussive strumming method introduced by anthropologist Kenneth Emory during the Bishop Museum's 1934 expedition. Western popular songs have largely replaced archaic *fagu* chanting.

Seven thousand people inhabit six of the high volcanic Marquesas Islands (known locally as Te Fenua 'Enata) to the northeast. They share a unique, continuing musical legacy transcribed in the 1920s and systematically recorded in 1989. Ancient Marquesans used an extensive musical vocabulary: early 19th-century sources document distinct vocal registers, types of body percussion, and more than 130 genres of music and dance (many of which survive today). The term *mea kakiu* (old things) embraces traditional music sung in Marquesan as well as new compositions in those styles, such as declamatory chants, women's improvised greeting calls, genealogies, and laments. The *mahohe maha'u* (pig dance) and the *putu* (a circle dance accompanied by hand claps) are for male dancers, whereas mixed groups perform topical songs and finales. *Mea hou* (new things) include church music, pan-Pacific pop, and dance music from Tahiti. These songs exhibit language diversity, wider melodic range, functional harmony, and strophic or refrain form.

Laura Stanfield Prichard

See also: Hawaii, Music of; Marshall Islands, Music of; Polynesian Hymns

Further Reading

Kanahele, George S. 1979. *Hawaiian Music and Musicians*. Honolulu: University of Hawaii Press.

McLean, Mervyn. 1977. *Annotated Bibliography of Oceanic Music and Dance*. Warren, MI: Harmonie Park Press.

Roberts, Helen H. 1926/1977. *Ancient Hawaiian Music*. Honolulu: Peter Smith.

Polynesian Hymns

Hīmene is a pan-Polynesian term for *a cappella* choral singing. Originally applied to Christian hymn singing in Tahiti, the term now includes secular civic choral singing. Syllabic, intoned recitation and solo melismatic chant are found in regional variants through the Pacific; multipart choral singing (sometimes over a drone) thrives in western and central Polynesia.

In the 19th century, hymns and chants were introduced by Protestant and Catholic missionaries to Polynesia. Early European contact with the more than 1,800 peoples of Polynesia resulted in descriptions of drumming, dancing, and vocal music, and Christian missionaries found that singing was the most effective route to the conversion of native peoples. Some islanders adopted hīmene arrangements and singing styles directly, while others borrowed from other Polynesians: for example, the recently converted Samoans introduced Christian hymns to the people of Tuvalu.

HAWAII

Traditional Hawaiian music is predominantly vocal: the term *mele* applies to poetic texts as well as their recited presentation. These are usually composed in advance and range from sacred prayers (*mele pule*) and funeral laments (*mele kanikau*) to love songs and informal game chants. Western music was introduced to Hawaii (formerly called the Sandwich Islands) in 1778, and the first Congregational missionaries arrived in 1820 on the *Thaddeus* from Boston. By the 1820s, Hawaii was a popular destination for whaling ships, and the Congregationalists published a hymnal in 1823 (*Na hīmeni Hawaii*, enlarged from 47 to 100 hymns in 1827). Missionary Sybil Bingham noted the first "singing school" in 1824 and Hiram Bingham founded the Kawaiaha'o Church in Honolulu in 1836 (where Hawaiian kings, including Kamehameha III, worshipped and sang). The *hīmeni* (hymns), especially those of Lorenzo Lyons (1807–1886, also known as Laiana), remain in current use: they have influenced popular music song forms and can be heard in nightclubs and touristic outdoor performances. *Na Himeni Hoolea* (1837–1867) and *Ka Lira Hawaii* (1844–55) were the largest Hawaiian sacred hymn collections published in the 19th century, with 403 and 215 hymns respectively in the last editions.

WESTERN POLYNESIA

In this area of the central Pacific, traditional social organization focused on lineage and village. Religious music is not known to have been associated with these cultures before European contact; there is no written record of music associated with pre-Christian religion. Three types of wooden slit drums (the smaller *pate*, from Tahiti; the *lali*, from Fiji; and the large *logo*, created by missionaries as a bell) signal modern church events.

Tuvalu has experienced drastic changes in religion, social organization, music, and dance due to the systematic Christianization of the archipelago after 1861 by the London Missionary Society. While most Tuvalu singing resembles Polynesian speech-song and level recitative, triadic music is also present due to influences from neighboring Melanesia. Pentatonic, melismatic responsorial dance songs emerged and flourished after the arrival of Samoan missionaries from 1890–1915.

Tonga was not colonized by 19th-century Western powers, so older dances such as *ula* and *faha'iula* survive alongside new dances requiring song (from both the dancers and a large group of singers standing at the rear). Multipart singing in three to eight parts, with the melody in the second lowest position, is integral to all choral music. Numerical notation was introduced to Tonga in the 19th century for the teaching of Mormon hymns, and male falsetto is employed for the highest part in *hiva kakala* songs. Seventh-Day Adventist and Latter-day Saints (Mormon) hymnals in Tongan are widely used.

EASTERN POLYNESIA

In eastern Polynesia, traditional social organization was highly stratified and focused on lineage and religious practices. These were centered in ceremonies on the *marae* (outdoor platform temple), and on concepts of *mana* (spiritual power or cosmic energy) and *taboo* (forbidden behaviors and objects), which governed people's lives.

Sacred and secular hymn singing forms an especially important part of the musical heritage of the Cook Islands. Traditional night ceremonies such as *tara kakai* disappeared due to missionary activity, and were replaced by *'eva*, men's songs honoring warriors or battles. From 1857, native missionaries (primarily from Rarotonga) taught literacy with the Rarotongan Bible and hymnal, bypassing the vernacular *mako* chants. These *īmene tapu* (sacred hymns) could be sung in a variety of styles, including *reo metua* (earlier hymns with organum-like parallel movement in fourths/fifths and contrapuntal elements), *īmene tuki* (grunted or recited hymns), *īmene āpi'i Sāpati* (Sunday/Sabbath school hymn tunes borrowed from Sankey Island in the 20th century), and new freely composed hymns combining English and Pukapukan. This last type (the most popular) uses two structural parts and a piercing, strident tone: women's music (*tumu*) is followed by men's music (*malū*). Since the 1960s, optional decoration in the high tessitura of the soprano/tenor range results in pitch instability (this trait was brought from the remote northern Cook Islands atoll of Penrhyn/Tongareva). Full-voiced singing of high notes in the chest register is typical of Cook Islands hymn singing, and contrasts with the singing of quick *hē* vocables that render a song "sweet."

In common with other Cook Islands, Penrhyn has strong traditions of both sacred and secular *hīmene*. *Hīmene taranga* feature historical or legendary tales, and *hīmene tapu* or *tuki* interpret biblical episodes. The regular *uapou* religious discussions held in the minister's house divide the congregation in two, each group supporting its leader's speeches with one *hīmene*. *Tamau* (alto) and *marū* (bass) parts are taught and fixed in content, whereas *perepere* soloists are allowed to improvise. Individual compositions contain 1 or 2 melismatic solo parts with rapid "breaking into pieces" (*hatihati*) on the syllable *hē*.

Manihiki and Rakahanga in the Cook Islands also feature polyphonic hīmene with staccato *he* vocables known as *fatifati* (breaking up). Manihiki solo singers (perepere) uniquely emphasize rocking gently, shutting their eyes, and sometimes waving their hands and dancing slowly during hymn singing. Competitive musical performances use both sacred and secular material: uapou meetings at Cook Islands' churches began with divisions singing hīmene tapu (sacred hymns) indoors, followed by competitive outdoor singing of *hīmene tuki* (hymns featuring unison grunting from the men used as decoration). Hīmene singing was introduced into Aitutaki in 1821 by two Tahitian pastors brought to the island by missionary John Williams. New hīmene are composed regularly in all seven villages. Each village is required to contribute two new hīmene—one hīmene tuki (with up to seven named parts) and one with a hymnbook text—twice a year (for Christmas and for the New Year); these are premiered at combined services in the church in Arutanga and favorites are maintained in the repertory for more than 30 years.

The eight volcanic Society Islands can be divided musically by southeastern and northwestern choral singing practices. The evangelization led by the London Missionary Society (1797–) and the conversion of Tahiti in 1815 marked turning points in Pacific history, leading to the development of three indigenized genres of choral singing. Missions from Tahiti, using native catechists and local languages, were launched throughout the Pacific. English missionaries introduced British hymn and psalm tunes.

Tahiti and the five Austral Islands to its southwest (evangelized by native Tahitian Protestant catechists in the 1820s) maintain multipart choral singing with high-pitched soloists; these exhibit the richest and fullest textures of Tahitian-language hīmene. Because missionary-instigated censure of indigenous performance practices in the 1830s to 1840s failed to uproot local dances and singing styles, the French colonial administration began to encourage the revival of dance performances and public choral singing. The inhabitants of the 76 coral atolls that form the Tuamoto archipelago were converted by Mormon missionaries in 1845, and have a strong French military presence due to continued nuclear testing at the southern end of the chain. They have embraced Tahitian polyphonic choral singing styles. The Fête Nationale (1881–, renamed *Heiva* in 1985) was the most important stimulus to Tahitian performance traditions. The annual July revels (*Tiurai*) have included folkloric competitions of Tahitian choral singing since 1881.

Tahitians distinguish five genres of hīmeni: *hīmene puta* (translated Western hymns in homophonic, chordal arrangements), *hīmene nota* (four-part written hymns with new Tahitian texts and some antiphonal alternation), *hīmene rū'au* (old-style Protestant hymn singing in three parts dating to the 1870s), *hīmene tuki* (incorporating choral grunting in the Cook Islands manner), and *hīmene tārava* (the most complex multipart style, originating at Bible-study meetings to repeat or paraphrase texts). Hīmene tārava may have as many as 13 vocal parts and exist in three distinct regional styles; all begin with one woman, called *fa'aafaafa* (to awaken), singing a stanza. Other in the chorus join in by catching (*haru*) her melodic line and harmonizing it in two to nine parts. Rhythmic punctuation consists of male grunting (*hā'ūr*) by a group seated in the rear and virtuosic perepere are added over some stanzas. Choral singing in the southern Austral Islands of Ra'ivavae and Rapa have 11 and 13 vocal parts respectively, with the richest and fullest textures of Tahitian-language hīmene.

On Easter Island (Rapa Nui), the furthest east of the Polynesian Islands, a rich tradition of ceremonial dances and songs existed prior to the arrival of the first Europeans on Easter Sunday, 1722. Catholic missionaries from Tahiti arrived in 1864, bringing a style of monophonic, unison chant that was adopted by the islanders. The Tuamotan archipelago has embraced two types of polyphonic Tahitian choral singing (hīmene rū'au and hīmene tārava) as practiced in the Windward (Society) Islands. They are used to perform poetic chants of praise, and are also used by Catholics and Mormons with doctrinally appropriate texts. The nearby Gambier archipelago (also called Mangareva) adopted Catholicism in 1838. In contrast to Protestant efforts elsewhere, Roman Catholic priests actually encouraged the adaptation of indigenous singing styles to Catholic devotional material. *'Akamagareva* (literally, "to make Mangarevan"), sacred counterparts to secular *kapa* songs, flourished alongside Latin Gregorian chant. By the time of the Bishop Museum's Mangarevan Expedition (1934), no pre-Christian musical instruments were extant. Following the vernacular language reforms of the second Vatican Council in 1967, the archdiocese of Tahiti discontinued the use of Latin (including Gregorian chant) and adopted hymns in French and Tahitian.

The northeastern Marquesas Islands (known locally as Te Fenua 'Enata) share a unique, continuing musical legacy transcribed in the 1920s and systematically recorded in 1989. *Mea kakiu* (old things, or traditional music) contrasts with *mea hou* (new things) including church music, pan-Pacific pop, and dance music from Tahiti. These Western-influenced styles exhibit language diversity, wider melodic range, functional harmony, and strophic or refrain form.

Laura Stanfield Prichard

See also: Hawaii, Music of; Marshall Islands, Music of; Polynesia, Music of

Further Reading

Fanshawe, David. 1995. *Spirit of Polynesia* [CD]. Saydisc CD-SDL 403.

A complete listing of historical Hawaiian hymnals is available at https://amykstillman .wordpress.com/hawaiian-language-protestant-hymnals-a-checklist.

Presley, Elvis (1935–1977)

Elvis Aron Presley, popularly known as the "King of Rock and Roll," was a guitarist, singer, actor, and an iconic figure in the development of rockabilly and rock and roll music in the 1950s. Combining the influences of country and western, gospel, and rhythm and blues (R & B), he brought African American musical elements into records that were marketed primarily to white audiences. For many, his edgy musical style, cultivated sex appeal, and suggestively gyrating hips became a symbol of teenage rebellion. Though scholars debate when rock and roll definitively emerged, Presley unquestionably played an important role in establishing its sound.

Presley was born to parents Gladys and Vernon Presley in East Tupelo, Mississippi. Both parents grew up in poor sharecropping families, and at the time of Presley's birth Gladys was a factory seamstress and Vernon was working one of many odd jobs. Presley's early years were profoundly influenced by a close-knit extended family and by the First Assembly of God Church, to which his family was deeply committed. He received his first guitar as a gift for his 11th birthday; his uncle Vester and a country/hillbilly musician known as Mississippi Slim provided his first, informal guitar instruction. When he was 13, his family moved to Memphis, Tennessee, the city that Presley called home for the rest of his life. During his later

---

Elvis

Arguably the most iconic American popular music artist of the 20th century, Elvis Presley will, in the very least, occupy a seat in the pantheon of influential musicians in American music. Beyond his unique image and notorious social behavior, Elvis is known for his particularly honed voice. His voice is characterized as displaying influences of blues, country, hillbilly, crooners, jazz, classical, and seemingly every other notable genre of American popular music. However, his voice defies restriction to any one of these classifications and has become, in itself, the point of reference. Other artists sound like Elvis, he like them, in very much the same way one might describe the way a skunk smells to someone new to the scent. In this way, Elvis was able to create a sonic signature that pierced the airwaves, and in so doing paved the way for American popular artists of future generations (such as Janice Joplin and Michael Jackson) to seek out and develop unique and original vocal styles.

teenage years, Presley began sporting his iconic "greaser" hairdo and sideburns, as well as flashy clothing purchased at a store marketing to African American men.

In the summer of 1953, shortly after high school graduation, Presley made his first recording. The private vanity record cost $3.98 and featured him crooning the songs "My Happiness" and "That's When Your Heartaches Begin." Following a second vanity recording, Sun Records owner Sam Phillips (1923–2003) invited him to make commercial records. Phillips had already experienced some success recording African American R & B artists, and when he began recording Presley, Phillips was reputedly looking for a white performer who captured the black R & B sound in order to market the music to a growing white audience. Though Presley's first recording was unsuccessful, his subsequent recording of "That's All Right" (originally recorded by blues singer Arthur Crudup) became tremendously popular. Backed by electric guitarist Scotty Moore and bassist Bill Black (eventually joined by drummer D. J. Fontana), the group called themselves The Blue Moon Boys and toured regionally while their songs received favorable airplay on local radio stations. A series of singles, including "Good Rockin' Tonight"/"I Don't Care If The Sun Don't Shine," "Milk Cow Blues Boogie"/"You're a Heartbreaker," and "Baby Let's Play House"/"I'm Left, You're Right, She's Gone," continued to build their audience.

Presley's music first attracted the notice of country and western audiences in the south, and in October 1954 he signed a contract to appear regularly on *Louisiana*

American singer and actor Elvis Presley during a performance in 1955. Presley was an important figure in the popularization of rock and roll. (Bettmann/Getty Images)

Hayride, a popular country radio program whose broadcast reached large portions of the United States. At a later appearance on Hank Snow's *All Star Jubilee*, Presley met 'Colonel' Tom Parker, the former carnival hustler and savvy businessman who became Presley's visionary, if self-interested, personal adviser and manager. Thanks to Parker's negotiations, RCA Victor bought Presley's contract and all recordings made with Sun Records for $35,000.

Presley's first LP record, *Elvis Presley* (issued by RCA), was the first rock-and-roll album to top Billboard's pop charts and was also the first rock-and-roll album to break $1 million in sales.

His recordings of "Heartbreak Hotel" and the single "Hound Dog"/"Don't Be Cruel" further secured his national and international fame, the latter topping American charts for 11 weeks. The height of Presley's popularity continued throughout the 1950s and extended into film and television. He made his Hollywood debut in the 1956 film *Love Me Tender*, a Civil-War era story named after the ballad he sings in the film. His third movie, *Jailhouse Rock* (1957), was especially memorable, featuring both a strong soundtrack and innovative choreography for the title number, which spent seven weeks at the top of *Billboard* charts.

Parker and RCA managed to sustain Presley's career during the two years he spent drafted into the armed forces (1958–1960) by issuing new compilations and albums of previously unreleased material. Following his discharge, Presley devoted much of the following decade to film-making, with 27 of his 33 films dating from this period. Most of these films are often categorized as "Elvis films," a genre unto their own that may be described generally as low-budget, quickly made, highly profitable films usually featuring Presley in the role of a troublemaking, goodhearted, Southern heartthrob (Jeansonne, Luhrssen, and Sokolovic, 2011, pp. 164–165). It was during this time that he became addicted to diet pills in attempt to maintain his Hollywood figure.

In the 1970s, following the success of the 1969 singles "In the Ghetto" and "Suspicious Minds," Presley attempted to regain the height of his musical fame by leaving film to return to stage tours and issuing several live albums. He maintained a rigorous touring schedule throughout much of the decade, which placed strain on both his health and his marriage to Priscilla Beaulieu (they later divorced). To keep up with the schedule, Presley self-administered dangerous combinations of stimulants and sedatives and was forced to cancel a number of appearances due to illness. Just before leaving on another scheduled tour, he was found dead on the bathroom floor at his Graceland mansion; a preliminary report from the coroner cited the cause of death as cardiac arrhythmia (Jeansonne, Luhrssen, and Sokolovic, 2011, p. 196). At the time of his death, Presley's RCA record sales exceeded $4.5 million, and he had earned $4.3 billion as a musician (Sauers, 1984, pp. 32, 1).

Presley's music has made a lasting impression on American society. Many myths surround the singer and his legacy, and he remains one of the major pop icons of the 20th century. He has been inducted into the Rock and Roll Hall of Fame (1986), the Rockabilly Hall of Fame (1997), and the Gospel Music Hall of Fame (2001).

Christy J. Miller

See also: Blues; Country Music; Gospel Music; Rock and Roll

Further Reading

Doll, Susan M. 1998. *Understanding Elvis: Southern Roots vs. Star Image.* New York: Garland.
Jeansonne, Glen, David Luhrssen, and Dan Sokolovic. 2011. *Elvis Presley, Reluctant Rebel: His Life and Our Times.* Santa Barbara, CA: Praeger.
Jorgensen, Ernst. 1998. *Elvis Presley: A Life in Music.* New York: St. Martin's Press.
Mason, Bobbie Ann. 2003. *Elvis Presley.* New York: Viking.
Quain, Kevin, ed. 1992. *The Elvis Reader: Texts and Sources on the King of Rock and Roll.* New York: St. Martin's Press.
Sauers, Wendy, comp. 1984. *Elvis Presley: A Complete Reference.* Jefferson, NC: McFarland.

Psaltery (Bowed, Unbowed)

The psaltery has a rich and complex history that can be traced back more than two millennia, with ties to ancient civilizations in southern Europe, the Middle East, and Central Asia. It is an ancestor of the autoharp, hammered dulcimer, Finnish *kantele*, Russian *gusli*, and European zither, among others, all of which feature a set of strings (wire or gut) stretched horizontally over a flat soundboard with some manner of tuning pegs. The performing repertory of the psaltery is as diverse as its lineage, encompassing countless popular styles as well as solo sonatas, stylized dances, and other formal concert pieces. The instrument continues to find favor with early-music practitioners and amateur musicians throughout the world.

In the Hornbostel–Sachs classification system, the psaltery is a member of the zither or simple chordophone family, a broad category of stringed instruments that includes the harpsichord and modern piano. Its name derives from the ancient Greek *psaltērion* and Latin *psalterium*, terms associated with instruments akin to the harp or lyre. The history of the psaltery is closely intertwined with that of the Turkish *qānūn* (or *kanun*), although their reciprocal influences and the extent to which these and similar instruments developed independently is a subject of ongoing inquiry. It is widely believed that the psaltery first appeared in Europe around the end of the 12th century and that it flourished through the late Middle Ages. Many have linked its decline to the rise of chromaticism in the 15th century, though dividing bridges were sometimes added to expand the number of available pitches.

Early psalteries came in a variety of shapes and sizes ranging from nearly square to triangular to rounded. The trapezoid design, which had been favored in Moorish Spain, was increasingly common by the 14th century. Throughout its history, the instrument has been played by plucking the strings with the fingers or with a plectrum, such as a feather quill. The performer typically sits with the psaltery on the lap, although smaller models may be played while standing with the instrument resting on the arm or against the chest. Several methods of bowing the psaltery developed in the early to mid-20th century, coinciding with a resurgence in the instrument's popularity. Performers may use one bow or several, the latter accommodating double or triple stops. Some bowed psalteries include a second set of strings that the performer strums with one hand to accompany a bowed melody played by the other.

Joseph E. Jones

See also: Dulcimer; Guzheng; Koto; Qānūn; Zither

Further Reading
Baines, Anthony, ed. 1962. *Musical Instruments Through the Ages.* London: Pelican Books.
Marcuse, Sibyl. 1975. *A Survey of Musical Instruments.* New York: Harper & Row.
Munrow, David. 1976. *Instruments of the Middle Ages and Renaissance.* London: Oxford University Press.
Peekna, Andres, and Thomas D. Rossing. 2010. "Psalteries and Zithers." In Thomas D. Rossing (ed.), *The Science of String Instruments.* New York: Springer.
Remnant, Mary. 1978. *Musical Instruments of the West.* London: Batsford.

Puente, Tito (1923–2000)

Ernesto Antonio "Tito" Puente was one of the most renowned performers and composers of Latin music in the 20th century. A pioneer in the genre, he was often called "The King of Latin Music" as well as "King of Latin Jazz," "King of the Timbales," and simply "El Rey." During a career that lasted more than 60 years, he was best known for mambo and Latin jazz compositions that were in demand as dance music; for fusing different musical styles; and for bringing the big-band sound to traditional Latin music. His music has been featured in numerous movies, such as *The Mambo Kings* and *Calle 54*, as well as television programs including *The Cosby Show* and *The Simpsons*. One of his best-known compositions from 1963, "Oye Como Va," gained tremendous popularity when it was recorded in 1970 by the rock group Santana. The song remains a classic of Latin-flavored American music, being named by National Public Radio (NPR) in the year 2000 as one of the "NPR 100: The Most Important American Musical Works of the 20th Century."

Puente was born on April 20, 1923, in New York City, and was the eldest son born to homemaker Ercilia Puente and Ernesto Puente, a factory foreman. Both of his parents were Puerto Rican immigrants who spoke no English and lived in the Spanish Harlem section of New York City. Puente later said he was fortunate to have lived there, surrounded by the sounds of great jazz and Latin music. His mother called him "Ernestito," an affectionate term in Spanish meaning "Little Ernest," and this was later shortened simply to "Tito." At around age seven, his mother, believing he had potential musical talent, enrolled in him in piano lessons. By age 10, he switched to percussion after hearing Gene Krupa's powerful drum work on Benny Goodman's recording of "Sing, Sing, Sing."

In the 1930s, he formed a song-and-dance team with his sister Anna, but injured an ankle in a bicycle accident, which prevented his pursuing a professional career in dance. Concentrating on music from the age of 13, he played instruments including the piano, saxophone, and vibraphone as well as percussion instruments. Puente eventually became a virtuoso on the *timbales*, a pair of percussive, high-pitched drums. Puente debuted as a professional musician at age 15, both freelancing and

American musician Tito Puente, known for his Latin-tinged jazz compositions, performing in 1993. (Clayton Call/Redferns)

apprenticing with various Latin jazz groups (including the popular Machito and His Afro-Cubans) beginning in 1942. Puente made his first recordings in the early 1940s with Vincent Lopez and His Orchestra.

Puente was drafted into the Navy during World War II and served on the escort carrier *USS Santee*, where he earned a Presidential Citation for service. When he returned home at the end of the war in 1945, he discovered that he had been replaced in Machito's band. Under the GI Bill, he was able to study music at New York's Juilliard School of Music from 1945 through 1947, completing a formal education in composition, conducting, orchestration, and theory. He said that he wrote compositions that began as jazz and then he would add a Latin beat.

In 1947, Puente found work with the Copacabana Orchestra and played with other notable groups until attaining the post of musical director for the Pupi Campo Orchestra in 1947. In 1949, he formed his own band, The Piccadilly Boys, later called Tito Puente and His Mambo Boys, and finally the Tito Puente Orchestra. By the 1950s, the band was attracting large crowds and Puente became a Latin music sensation. Promoter Federico Pagani offered him a Sunday matinee spot at the prime venue which would become the Palladium Ballroom, located at New York's Broadway at 53rd Street. Billed as "The Genius and Giant of Latin Rhythms," the Puente sound burst forth, led by Puente's prominent placement in front of the band playing timbales and vibraphone.

Promoter George Goldner signed Puente to Tico Records, and Puente's first record *Abaniquito* was a favorite of disc jockey Dick "Ricardo" Sugar, who played it nightly on his WEVD radio show. The band's work at the Palladium continued bringing fame to Puente and his orchestra. Stars like Marlon Brando, Marlene Dietrich, and Frank Sinatra were seen there, at what became called the "Home of the Mambo." On one of his first Tico recordings, Puente introduced the vibraphone on "Por Tu Amor," popularizing the instrument in Latin music and gaining admirers for his fusion of jazz and Latin music. In 1950, Puente moved to RCA Victor records, releasing hit recordings such as "Ran Kan Kan," "Babarabatiri," and "El Rey del Timbal." With the addition of Cuban drummer Ramon "Mongo" Santamaria, the band's fame exploded.

Puente released what is considered his masterpiece, *Dance Mania*, in 1958. With the image of a striking flame-haired woman on its fiery red cover, the album sold more than a half million records and helped fuel the American mambo craze of the era. *Dance Mania* was added to the National Recording Registry in 2002. In the late 1950s, promoter Bobby Quintero helped Puente win the title "King of Latin Music" by beating fellow Latin musician Perez ("King of the Mambo") Prado in a contest where the public voted for their favorite band. The 1959 Cuban revolution, in which Fidel Castro took power in Cuba, brought new talent from that country to the United States. In the early 1960s, Puente was instrumental in introducing Americans to legendary Latin singers such as Celia Cruz ("Queen of Latin Music").

In 1960, when RCA Victor felt that the musical tastes of young people were changing, they dropped Puente's contract. Puente then returned to Tico Records, where in 1963 he recorded his classic "Oye Como Va." In 1968, he hosted his own TV show on Spanish-language television, called *The World of Tito Puente*. That year, in recognition of his prominence, he was chosen to be Grand Marshal of New York City's Puerto Rican Day Parade. In 1969, Puente was honored by being given the key to the City of New York in a ceremony marking his contribution to the world of music.

The year 1969 was a watershed in music, highlighted by the explosive debut of the rock group Santana at Woodstock. This new Latin rock style added Carlos Santana's electric guitar to the sound but drew its roots from Puente. When Puente's classic "Oye Como Va" was recorded by Santana in 1970, new audiences were introduced to Puente's music. Santana also covered Puente's 1956 recording of "Para Los Rumberos."

In 1991, at the age of 68, Puente released his hundredth album, *El Numero Cien*, and continued recording and touring. In addition to more than 100 albums, he has earned four Grammy Awards (and eight nominations, more than any other Latin musician before 1994).

Puente has always been active in Hispanic causes as well as nurturing new talent. He founded the Tito Puente Scholarship Foundation to benefit musically gifted children, with the foundation later forming partnerships to provide scholarships for music students across the nation. Puente made guest appearances in films, including *Radio Days, Armed and Dangerous,* and *The Mambo Kings*. He appeared at California's Monterey Jazz Festival in 1984 and on television's *The Cosby Show* as well as *The Simpsons*. He has a star on the Hollywood Walk of Fame, a U.S. Medal of the Arts, honorary doctoral degrees, lifetime achievement awards, and the adulation of millions of fans around the world.

In the year 2000, he was still performing. After a show in Puerto Rico when he was 77 years of age, he suffered a heart attack and was flown to New York City for surgery, but died during the night. In 2003, he was posthumously honored with the Grammy Lifetime Achievement Award.

Nancy Hendricks

See also: Batá Drums; Cumbia; Mambo; Salsa

Further Reading

Conzo, Joe, with David A. Perez, eds. 2012. *Mambo Diablo: My Journey with Tito Puente.* Milwaukee, WI: Backbeat Books.

Loza, Steven. 1999. *Tito Puente and the Making of Latin Music.* Champaign: University of Illinois Press.

Payne, Jim, and Tito Puente. 2006. *Tito Puente—King of Latin Music.* Briarcliff, NY: Hudson Music.

Salazar, Max. 2002. *Mambo Kingdom: Latin Music in New York.* New York: Schirmer Trade Books.